UNITED STATES ARMY IN WORLD WAR II

The War in the Pacific

THE FALL OF THE

PHILIPPINES

by

Louis Morton

MILITARY INSTRVCTION

OFFICE OF THE CHIEF OF MILITARY HISTORY

UNITED STATES ARMY

WASHINGTON. D.C., 1953

Library of Congress Catalog Card Number: 53–63678

Reprinted 1969

For sale by the Superintendent of Documents, U.S. Government Printing Office
Washington, D.C. 20402 - Price $8.50

UNITED STATES ARMY IN WORLD WAR II
Kent Roberts Greenfield, General Editor

Advisory Committee
(As of 1 January 1953)

James P. Baxter
President, Williams College

William T. Hutchinson
University of Chicago

Henry S. Commager
Columbia University

S. L. A. Marshall
Detroit News

Douglas S. Freeman
Richmond News Leader

E. Dwight Salmon
Amherst College

Pendleton Herring
Social Science Research Council

Col. Thomas D. Stamps
United States Military Academy

John D. Hicks
University of California

Charles S. Sydnor
Duke University

Charles H. Taylor
Harvard University

Office of the Chief of Military History
Maj. Gen. Orlando Ward, Chief

Chief Historian	Kent Roberts Greenfield
Chief, War Histories Division	Col. George G. O'Connor
Chief, Editorial and Publication Division	Col. B. A. Day
Chief, Editorial Branch	Joseph R. Friedman
Chief, Cartographic Branch	Wsevolod Aglaimoff
Chief, Photographic Branch	Capt. A. T. Lawry*

*Succeeded Capt. K. E. Hunter 28 April 1952.

iii

The History of

THE WAR IN THE PACIFIC

prepared under the direction of Louis Morton

This volume, one of the series UNITED STATES ARMY IN WORLD WAR II, is the fourth to be published in the subseries THE WAR IN THE PACIFIC. All the volumes will be closely related, and the series will present a comprehensive account of the activities of the Military Establishment during World War II. A tentative list of subseries is appended at the end of this volume.

. . . to Those Who Served

Foreword

The soldier reading these pages would do well to reflect on the wisdom of the statement exhibited in a Japanese shrine: "Woe unto him who has not tasted defeat." Victory too often leads to overconfidence and erases the memory of mistakes. Defeat brings into sharp focus the causes that led to failure and provides a fruitful field of study for those soldiers and laymen who seek in the past lessons for the future.

The statesman and the informed citizen reading these pages will realize that our military means as well as our estimates and plans must always be in balance with our long-range national policy. This lesson—signposted by the Battle of Manila Bay; the Treaty of Paris, signed in December 1898 when we decided to keep the Philippines; the Washington Conference of 1921–22; and the Manchurian Crisis of 1931—we ignored before Pearl Harbor. The result was defeat on the field of battle and the loss of the Philippine Islands.

The author of *The Fall of the Philippines*, Louis Morton, served overseas as a historical officer in the South Pacific area and in the Philippines during World War II. Since 1945 he has been chief of the Pacific Section, Office of the Chief of Military History, Department of the Army. He holds a Doctor of Philosophy degree from Duke University, is the author of a volume on American colonial history, and has written a number of articles dealing with military affairs.

Work on this volume was begun in early 1947. The reader may gain some idea of the size of the task of writing this history by an appraisal of The Sources.

ORLANDO WARD
Maj. Gen., U. S. A.
Chief of Military History

Washington, D. C.
26 June 1952

Preface

The author's debts for aid in preparing this volume are numerous and heavy. The largest is to those officers who survived the campaign and the ordeal of prison camp. Their memories, and the precious notes they had hidden so carefully during the bitter days of Japanese imprisonment, provided material without which the record of this campaign would have been forever lost. These officers gave freely of their time and their contribution is apparent on every page and in almost every footnote. In a sense, they are as much the authors as the writer of this preface.

Special acknowledgments must be made to Mr. Stanley L. Falk and Dr. George C. Groce who, with ingenuity and perseverance, aided the author in his search for the materials needed for this work. The search was an exciting and rewarding adventure and is described in full at the end of the book. Both men also labored long and mightily to mold the fragmentary materials thus assembled into a form which greatly eased the author's work and performed cheerfully the many other arduous and time-consuming tasks which are the lot of every author. Without Mr. Falk's special knowledge of the enemy's records and operations, reinforced by information willingly furnished by the enemy himself, this volume would have been less precise and far longer in preparation.

The author owes a large debt also to many individuals who directly and indirectly gave him much valuable assistance: to Dr. Kent Roberts Greenfield, Chief Historian and General Editor of this series, for his wise counsel and guidance, for encouragement and never-failing support; to Mr. Wsevolod Aglaimoff and his staff who spent many months at the drafting boards to provide the maps to guide the reader through the jungles and mountains of the Philippines; to Miss Margaret E. Tackley who searched diligently and in remote corners for the pictures with which to illustrate this volume; to Miss Ruth Stout, the editor, and Mr. Ronald Sher, the copy editor, who edited the manuscript and guided it through the printers; to Mr. Leonard B. Lincoln, the indexer; to Mr. Israel Wice and his aides who patiently filled the author's numerous requests for aid in securing records; and to those of his colleagues, in and out of uniform, who read this volume in manuscript and made numerous and helpful suggestions. All these and others placed their special knowledge and skill freely and generously at the disposal of the author, but he alone is responsible for any shortcomings this volume may possess.

L. M.

Washington, D. C.
26 June 1952

Contents

CONTENTS

CONTENTS

Tables

Maps

CONTENTS

Illustrations

CONTENTS

Photographs are from the Department of Defense files, except for that on page 533, the Japanese photographs on pages 143, 233, 465, 539, 548, 568, and 573, and the photograph on page 583, reproduced through the courtesy of Col. William C. Braly.

PART ONE

PREWAR PLANS AND PREPARATIONS

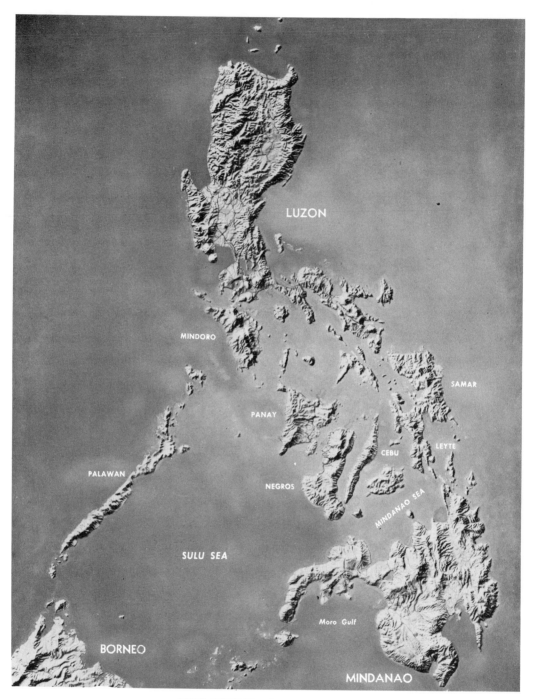

THE PHILIPPINE ISLANDS

CHAPTER I

The Philippine Islands

Since the third century, the Philippine Islands had been under foreign influence, first from Hindu-Malayan empires in Sumatra, Indochina, and Borneo, and then from the Chinese beginning with the early Ming dynasty. Shortly after 1400 Mohammedanism was introduced, and for more than one hundred years all of the islands south of Luzon, and the southern portion of that island, were subject to the Mohammedans of Borneo. During this period, the Japanese established a loose control over northern Luzon and maintained a trading post at Aparri, on the north tip of the island. (*Map 1—inside back cover*)

European interest in the Philippine Archipelago began with the visit of a Spanish expedition under Ferdinand Magellan in 1521. But it was not until 1565 that the Spaniards established a permanent settlement in the Islands, on Cebu. Five years later they conquered Manila and then gradually extended their control over many of the Islands. Late in the sixteenth century the military ruler of Japan, Hideyoshi, claimed suzerainty over the Islands. This claim was apparently neither intended nor taken seriously, but the Spanish did pay "tribute" for a short time to avoid trouble, secure trading rights in Japan, and protect the Jesuit missionaries there. Until 1898, despite unsuccessful efforts by the Portuguese and Dutch and one successful effort by the British (1762–1764) to wrest the Islands from her, Spain ruled the Philippines.

The impress of these centuries of foreign influence and control gave to the Philippines a strange mixture of Oriental and Occidental institutions. The original inhabitants were pushed back into the mountains and the Malayans became the dominant racial type. From later invasions came the Mohammedan religion and the Moslem customs prevalent in the south; from China came the impetus to trade and commerce, still largely controlled by the Chinese; and from Spain came the dominant religion, Christianity, the Roman law, and other features of Western civilization.

The United States seized the Philippine Islands from Spain in May 1898 after Admiral Dewey's victory in Manila Bay, during the Spanish-American War. Formal title to the Islands was granted the United States by the Treaty of Paris in December of that year. By the acquisition of the Philippines the United States at one step advanced its frontiers nearly 7,000 miles across the Pacific Ocean and "gave hostages to fortune in a sense which the American people have never fully realized." [1] Possession of the Islands made the United States an Asiatic power, with full responsibility for maintaining the peace and *status quo* in that area.

The government of the Islands was placed in the hands first of a Philippine commission and later of a governor general, both appointed by the President of the United

---

[1] Hector C. Bywater, *Sea Power in the Pacific* (rev. ed., Boston and New York, 1934), p. 254.

States. The Filipinos, once their opposition ended, were allowed an increasingly large measure of self-rule and elected the members of the lower house of the legislature, the Philippine Assembly. In 1913, they were granted free trade with the United States, and three years later, in the Jones Act, were permitted a limited autonomy.

A succession of able American governors established a happy relationship between the two countries, and a steadily increasing sentiment for Philippine independence found ready support in the American Congress. A bill for Philippine independence was passed by Congress, over President Hoover's veto, in January 1933, but vetoed by the Philippine legislature. It was passed again, with some changes, as the Tydings-McDuffie Act, on 24 March 1934, and this time approved by the Philippine legislature.

The Tydings-McDuffie Act provided for the recognition of Philippine independence after a ten-year transitional period. During these ten years the United States would be allowed to "maintain military and other reservations and armed forces" in the Islands, and the President of the United States would have the power "to call into the service of such armed forces all military forces organized by the Philippine Government." [2] When the transitional period was over, the United States would abandon all military installations in the Islands.

The Tydings-McDuffie Act left open the question of naval reservations, but authorized the President to negotiate with the Philippine Government for American naval bases in the Islands. The closing date for such negotiations was set at two years after the recognition of independence. Until

then "the matter of naval reservations and fueling stations," the Act provided, "shall remain in its present status." [3]

A year after the passage of the Tydings-McDuffie Act, the Filipinos adopted a liberal constitution based on the American model and established an interim government known as the Commonwealth. Elections in which Manuel Quezon was chosen as president followed soon after, and before the end of 1935 the Philippine National Assembly met to draft plans for local defense.

The Islands

Comprising almost 7,100 known islands and islets, the Philippine Archipelago lies approximately 500 miles off the Asiatic mainland and extends 1,150 miles almost due north and south from Formosa to Borneo. Strategically situated in the geographic heart of the Far East, the Islands are centrally located in relation to Japan, China, Burma, French Indochina, Thailand, Malaya, and the Netherlands Indies. They lie athwart the trade routes leading from Japan and China through the South China Sea to southeast Asia and the rich supplies of oil and minerals in the Indies. Vital areas in Japan and along the Chinese coast are within quick striking distance by sea and air of the Philippines. Over 5,000 miles from Honolulu and 7,000 miles from San Francisco, Manila, the chief city and capital of the Islands, is only 1,800 miles from Tokyo. Formosa and Hong Kong are less than 700 miles distant, Singapore 1,500 miles, and Truk in the Caroline Islands 2,100 miles.[4] The Caroline, Marianas, and the Marshall Islands, stretching across the Central Pacific, lie along the

[2] *48 U.S. Statutes at Large,* H.R. 8573, pp. 456–65, The Philippine Commonwealth and Independence Law, P.L. 127, Sec 2(a) 12, approved 24 Mar 34.

[3] *Ibid.,* Secs 10(b) and 11.
[4] All distances are in airline statute miles.

SIGNING THE CONSTITUTION OF THE PHILIPPINE COMMON-WEALTH, 23 MARCH 1935. *Seated, left to right: George H. Dern, Secretary of War; President Franklin D. Roosevelt, signing the Constitution of the Philippine Commonwealth; Manuel L. Quezon, President, Philippine Senate; standing, left to right: Brig. Gen. Creed F. Cox, Chief, Bureau of Insular Affairs, War Department; Frank Murphy, Governor General of the Philippine Islands; Cordell Hull, Secretary of State; Key Pittman, Chairman, Foreign Relations Committee, U. S. Senate; Pedro Guevara, Philippine Resident Commissioner; Miguel Cuaderno, Vice President, Philippine National Bank, Manila, P. I.; Manuel Roxas, Representative, Philippine Legislature, Delegate, Constitutional Assembly; Francisco A. Delgado, Philippine Resident Commissioner.*

United States lines of communication with the Philippines.

The land area of the archipelago totals about 115,000 square miles. Only 460 of the Islands have an area greater than one square mile, and only eleven boast an area greater than 1,000 square miles. These eleven islands account for 94 percent of the total land area in the archipelago. The largest and most important is Luzon (40,420 square miles) in the north, where Manila is located. Next in size to Luzon is Mindanao (36,527 square miles) in the south, followed by the islands in the central group, the Visayas: Samar, Negros, Panay, Leyte, Cebu, and others.[5]

The climate of the Islands is tropical, with an average yearly temperature be-

[5] Unless otherwise noted, this description of the Philippine Islands is based upon *Civil Affairs Handbook: Philippine Islands,* 12 vols., Army Service Forces (ASF) Manual M 365–1 to 12.

tween 78° and 80° F. The year may be divided generally into dry and wet seasons, which come at different times on the east and west coasts because of shifts in the seasonal winds or monsoons. From June to September, when the monsoon blows from the southwest, the weather offers little difficulty to the landing of a hostile military force on the favorable beaches along the east coasts. The period of the northeast monsoons, October through April, is the best time for landings along the western China Sea coasts. Most of Mindanao, a portion of the Visayas, and southern Luzon have no dry season and no pronounced maximum rainy season.

The people of the Philippines are mostly of Malayan stock, and in 1941 numbered 17,000,000. In that year, Cebu and central Luzon were the most heavily populated areas, and Manila, with 684,000 inhabitants, was the largest city. There were nearly 30,000 Japanese nationals in the Islands, more than two-thirds of whom were concentrated in Davao, the chief port of Mindanao. The 117,000 Chinese constituted the largest foreign group in the Islands; on Luzon there were almost 9,000 American civilians.

Over sixty-five dialects are spoken in the Islands. When the United States acquired the Islands, a small percentage of the people spoke Spanish; after forty years of American occupation about 27 percent spoke English and 3 percent Spanish. Of the many native dialects, Tagalog, the language of the wealthy and influential residents of central Luzon, was chosen as the basis for a national language in 1937, although twice as many people spoke the Visayan dialect. While the many dialects have certain similarities, it is not possible for the natives in different parts of the Islands to understand each other readily. This fact made the recruitment of Filipinos for military service on a national scale difficult, since troops recruited from one island often could not understand their American or Tagalog officers, or troops from other islands.

The Philippines are predominantly agricultural, the principal crops being rice (the chief element in the Filipino diet), copra, sugar, hemp, tobacco, and corn. The far-ranging mountain areas are a source of gold and silver, and of the more important base metals, such as iron, chrome, manganese, copper, and lead. Sixty percent of the Philippines is covered by forest, much of it hardwoods. The fishing banks off Manila Bay and the Sulu Archipelago supplement the Filipino diet and are the basis of one of the more important industries in the Islands. Even after many years of American occupation there was little manufacturing in the Philippines, most of the inhabitants being engaged in home industries or in the processing of agricultural products such as sugar, hemp, and coconuts.

With interisland and coastal shipping carrying the bulk of Philippine products, there was no great need for roads and railroads. Only on Luzon was there a road and rail net adequate to support large-scale military operations. Of the 14,270 miles of highway in the archipelago in 1940, more than half were in central and southern Luzon. There were only 50,000 motor vehicles in the Islands; the Filipinos relied on the powerful carabao, or water buffalo, for transportation as well as labor. The two railway systems in the Islands, the government-owned Manila Railway Company on Luzon and the American-owned Philippine Railway Company on Panay and Cebu, had a total of 840 miles of narrow gauge track.

Most of the principal towns and cities were linked by telephone, telegraph, or radio, and all parts of the archipelago by the government postal system. The American-owned Philippine Long Distance Telephone Company connected Manila with most important towns on Luzon, as well as the principal population centers on Panay, Negros, Cebu, and Mindanao. In addition, forty provincial governments operated their own telephone systems so that many small towns and villages had at least one telephone joining them with Manila. Cable connected Manila with Guam, Shanghai, and Hong Kong, and four transoceanic radio stations provided communication with the outside world.

The Philippine Islands are largely mountainous, with elevations as high as 10,000 feet. Narrow coastal plains can be found on most of the islands, and there are numerous short, swift-running streams. Large plain areas and navigable rivers are few. On every island are sand beaches, some of them extensive, but few open on lowlands where there is space for military maneuver.

Luzon, with one tenth of its total area a large plain, and another 5,000 square miles forming a magnificent river valley, is the one island in the Philippines whose terrain permits military operations on a large scale. In the north, closed in by mountains on the east and west, is a valley extending southward for over 120 miles and with an average width of 40 miles. Flowing north through the valley is the Cagayan River. Along the west coast is a narrow plain offering only limited opportunities for military operations. A road runs along this coast from the tip of Luzon towards Manila. Southern Luzon is a volcanic region, part plain and part mountain, with numerous deep indentations forming bays and gulfs, and with many beaches suitable for the landing of a military force.

The central portion of Luzon is composed of a plain extending north about 120 miles from Manila Bay to the Lingayen Gulf. With mountains to the east and west, the plain is well protected from invasion except at its two extremities. It is the most highly developed economic area in the Philippines and the one most suitable for mobile warfare.[6]

The three most important military highways on Luzon are Routes 1, 3 and 5—two-lane, all weather roads with concrete or asphalt surface. Each enters the capital and each has numerous access roads linking Manila with all parts of the island. Of the 704 miles of railroad on Luzon in 1941, about half were in the central plain, which, in addition, contained 250 miles of private railway lines. All of the road, with the exception of a short stretch above Manila, was single track.

From the South China Sea the southern entrance to the central plain is through Manila Bay, one of the finest natural harbors in the Far East. Opening out from a 12-mile-wide entrance between high headlands, the bay expands toward the low-lying plain to a width of thirty miles. Thirty miles from the entrance lies Manila, and to its north and south are other harbors large enough to shelter seagoing vessels. Mariveles, just inside the northern entrance, is an excellent and easily reached anchorage, and the headland of Sangley Point, where the Cavite naval base was located, has always been recognized as one of the finest ports in the bay.

---

[6] Data on the central Luzon plain comes from Terrain Study 94, Philippine Series: Central Luzon, I, prepared by the Allied Geographical Sec, GHQ Southwest Pacific Area (SWPA), 18 Oct 44.

MANILA HARBOR. *The Bataan peninsula, partly shrouded in fog and clouds, is visible twenty-five miles across Manila Bay.*

On either side of the entrance to Manila Bay are high volcanic peaks covered with luxuriant tropical foliage. North of the entrance is the Bataan peninsula; to the south is Cavite Province. From a military point of view, the more important and more easily defended of the headlands is the Bataan peninsula, a rocky extension of the Zambales Mountain range which separates the central plain of Luzon from the China Sea.

Across the entrance to Manila Bay are several small islands. The largest and most important, Corregidor, lies two miles off Bataan and, with Caballo, separates the entrance into the North and South Channels. Shaped like a tadpole with its tail to the east, Corregidor measures three and one half miles in length and one and one half miles at its widest point. One mile south of the tip of the tail is Caballo, less than one third the size of Corregidor. In the South Channel, about a mile from the southern headland, lies El Fraile, a rock about 200 by 100 yards jutting up into the entrance of Manila Bay. Just outside and to the south of the entrance is Carabao, the fourth of the small islands whose location in Manila Bay gave them a strategic importance out of all proportion to their size. In the history of American plans for the defense of the Philippines, these islands loom large.

The Philippine Army

Before the establishment of the Commonwealth Government in 1935, no effort was made to prepare the Philippines for their own defense. The United States had assumed all obligations for national defense and maintained a garrison in the Islands for that purpose. This garrison numbered about 10,000 men, half of whom were Philippine Scouts, a U.S. Army unit in which the enlisted men, with some exceptions, were native Filipinos and most of the officers American. After 1913 the Philippine garrison was called the Philippine Department, a regular U.S. Army establishment commanded by an American general officer. The Philippine Constabulary, first organized in 1901, was the national police force, but by training and organization had a military character. Thus, except for their experience with the Constabulary, the Filipinos had had no military tradition upon which to build a national army.[7]

One of the first problems of the newly established Commonwealth Government was to make provision for the defense of the archipelago. Such a task required a man with proven military and executive ability, and, since there was no likely candidate in the Philippines, the President-elect Manuel L. Quezon turned to the United States for help. In the summer of 1935, he induced his friend, Gen. Douglas MacArthur, then Chief of Staff of the U.S. Army, to become the military adviser to the new government in its effort to organize a national army.[8] President Roosevelt's consent was readily obtained and arrangements quickly concluded.

MacArthur's title in his new assignment was Military Advisor to the Commonwealth Government; his mission, to aid in the "establishment and development of a system of National Defense." The authority given him was unusually broad. He was authorized to deal directly with the Secretary of War and the Chief of Staff and, "in all cases not specifically covered," to use his own judgment. "Your mission must be accomplished—," he was told, "ways and means are largely left to you." [9] Although there was no official connection between the Philippine Department, the U.S. Army command in the Islands, and the Office of the Military Advisor, the department commander, Maj. Gen. Lucius R. Holbrook, was informed that assistance to General MacArthur was "the most important peacetime mission of your command." [10]

General MacArthur selected Majs. Dwight D. Eisenhower and James B. Ord as his principal assistants. With the aid of a special committee from the Army War College, they prepared a plan to provide the Philippine Commonwealth with a system of national security by 1946, the date the Islands would become independent. This plan called for a small regular army, a conscription system, a ten-year training program of two classes a year to build up a reserve force, a small air force, and a fleet of small motor torpedo boats to repel an enemy landing. The tactical organization of this army was to be based on divisions of approximately 7,500 men. Armament and

[7] The Philippine Army: Its Establishment, Organization, and Legal Basis, prepared by Phil Research and Info Sec, U.S. Army Forces in the Far East (USAFFE), 26 Jan 45, p. 1, copy in Office of the Chief of Military History. A large number of the sources used in the preparation of this volume are on file in that office, hereafter referred to as OCMH.

[8] Manuel L. Quezon, The Good Fight (New York, 1946), pp. 153–55.

[9] Ltr of Instructions to Gen MacArthur, signed by the Acting Adjutant General, 18 Sep 35, in War Plans Division, War Department General Staff (WDGS), file 3389-31. At the time this letter was prepared General MacArthur was still Chief of Staff, U.S. Army. This file is hereafter referred to as WPD with appropriate file number.

[10] Ltr of Instructions to CG Phil Dept, signed by Actg TAG, 18 Sep 35, WPD 3389-31.

equipment for the new army was to be of a type suitable to the economy and terrain in the Philippines.[11]

The staff of the Military Advisor was always small. In addition to the officers he took with him, General MacArthur secured the services of four other officers from the Philippine Department when he reached Manila. He also employed as a civilian assistant a retired naval officer, Sidney L. Huff, to advise in naval matters. On the death of Colonel Ord in an airplane accident in 1938, Lt. Col. Richard K. Sutherland was brought into the staff, and when Colonel Eisenhower returned to the United States the next year, Lt. Col. Richard J. Marshall was chosen to replace him. In October 1937, Capt. Hugh J. Casey joined MacArthur's staff to advise in engineer matters, and later Maj. William F. Marquat was designated antiaircraft officer. All of these men remained with General MacArthur through the war years.[12]

The first legislative measure of the Philippine National Assembly was the passage, on 21 December 1935, of the National Defense Act, which embodied the plan proposed by General MacArthur. In explaining the bill to the Assembly, President Quezon emphasized that the defense program must be carried out economically and should be "passively defensive." It would be impossible

for reasons of economy, he declared, to develop an adequate fleet in the short time allotted and with the money available.[13]

The National Defense Act provided for a regular force of 10,000 men and a reserve force which was expected to reach 400,000 by the middle of 1946. The regular establishment was also to include the Philippine Constabulary, then consisting of about 6,000 men, so that more than half of the regular army from the start consisted of partially trained men. All Filipinos between the ages of twenty-one and fifty were liable for military service. After a 5½-month training period Filipinos would become a part of the reserve force. There were to be two classes a year, each to consist of 20,000 men with the regulars serving as training cadres. For the training of junior officers a military academy patterned after West Point was to be established at Baguio on Luzon. It was expected to graduate about 100 officers each year.[14]

For military purposes the Commonwealth was divided into ten military districts with functions comparable to those of the prewar corps areas in the United States. Each district had an approximately equal population, and each was to provide initially one reserve division and ultimately three. Luzon, together with several outlying islands (Mindora, Palawan, Masbate), had five military districts; Mindanao and the Sulu Archipelago together constituted another; and the Visayas four more. In each district the military commander was responsible during peacetime for training and for

[11] Memo, Maj Gen Dwight D. Eisenhower for President Quezon, 22 Jun 42, Operations Division, WDGS, Executive Office files (hereafter cited as OPD Exec O). This memorandum with accompanying notes is included in an article by Louis Morton, "The Philippine Army 1935–1939: Eisenhower's Memorandum to Quezon," *Military Affairs*, XII (1948), 103–07.
[12] Intervs, author with Maj Gen Richard J. Marshall, ret., 7 Apr 48, and with Col LeGrande A. Diller, formerly aide to Gen MacArthur, 28 Apr 48. The author's notes on these and certain other interviews are on file in OCMH. Interviews on which no notes were taken have no file designation.

[13] Message to the First National Assembly on National Defense, 25 Nov 35, in Joseph R. Hayden, *The Philippines, A Study in National Development* (New York, 1942), p. 738.
[14] The Philippine Army: Its Establishment, Organization, and Legal Basis, pp. 4, 18. The Constabulary was separated from the Army in 1938, but again made a part of it late in 1941.

the preparation of defense plans; in time of war for the defense of his district. The provincial governor was responsible for the enforcement of the recruitment and mobilization laws.[15]

Although the district commanders were responsible for defense plans, the Office of the Military Advisor drew up the plans for all the major islands—Luzon, Cebu, Negros, Panay, Leyte, Mindanao, Bohol, Mindoro—as well as many of the smaller ones. Since these plans were to be employed by the Philippine Government after that nation had received its independence, they were based on the assumption that there would be no U.S. Army forces in the Islands and that all forces would come from the Philippine Army. The plans of the Military Advisor also called for the establishment of seacoast defenses along the seven straits which give access to the inland waters of the Philippine Islands.[16]

The defense of the coast line—longer than that of the United States—posed an extremely difficult problem. The National Defense Act made no provision for a navy but established in the army an Off Shore Patrol. This organization was to consist of fast motor torpedo boats of a British design. Contracts for thirty-six of these vessels, to be completed by 1946, were placed with British shipbuilders under specifications that called for a boat 65 feet long, with

a 13-foot beam, three 12-cylinder engines, and a speed of 41 knots. Armament would consist of two torpedo tubes, depth charges, and light antiaircraft guns.[17] "A relatively small fleet of such vessels," said General MacArthur, ". . . will have distinct effect in compelling any hostile force to approach cautiously and by small detachments."[18]

The National Defense Act also made provision for an air force, to be utilized primarily for coast defense. By 1946 the Commonwealth expected to have a fleet of approximately 100 fast bombers, supported by other tactical types. They would be used with the Off Shore Patrol to keep hostile craft away from the Philippine coast.

The basic concepts which determined the nature and organization of the Commonwealth military establishment are perhaps best explained by MacArthur himself. The underlying principle, he said in a speech in 1936, was to create a defensive force of such strength as to make an invasion so costly in lives and money that "no Chancellory in the World, if it accepts the opinions of the military and naval staffs, will ever willingly make an attempt to willfully attack the Philippines . . . ." The Islands, MacArthur pointed out, had "enormous defensive advantages" in their geographical separation from possible enemies, mountainous character, heavy forests and jungles, narrow beaches and limited communications. Luzon, the probable objective of an enemy, he reminded his listeners, had only two areas in which "a hostile army of any size could land." "Each of these," he added, "is broken by strong defensive positions, which if properly

[15] The National Defense Act, Commonwealth Act No. 1, Titles II and III, Secs 17 to 59, in The Philippine Army: Its Establishment, Organization, and Legal Basis, App. I, p. 12.

[16] Ltr, Maj. Gen William C. Dunckel, ret., to author, 11 May 48, OCMH. General Dunckel was on MacArthur's staff, and was responsible for the preparation of the plans. In all, he prepared about seventy documents including estimates of the situation, general and special staff annexes, and the like. Interv, author with Lt Gen Richard K. Sutherland, ret., formerly chief of staff to Gen MacArthur, 12 Nov 46, OCMH.

[17] Catherine Porter, "Preparedness in the Philippines," Far Eastern Survey, April 7, 1941, pp. 65–66.

[18] Philippines Herald, January 26, 1940, quoted in Hayden, The Philippines, pp. 740–41.

manned and prepared would present to any attacking force a practically impossible problem of penetration."

When the development of the Philippine Army was completed, MacArthur believed it would be strong enough to oppose successfully "any conceivable expeditionary force." It would have a great advantage also in being assigned only one mission: defense of the homeland. Each unit of the army would operate over ground it knew well and which had been "deliberately selected and organized for defense."

The absence of a battle fleet in the plan of defense, MacArthur explained, was due to the defensive mission of the military establishment. The major duty of a large navy, he pointed out, was to protect overseas possessions. For the Philippines, which had no colonies, the only naval task was that of inshore defense. This defense would be provided by "flotillas of fast torpedo boats, supported by an air force," whose task would be to deny the enemy an opportunity to bring its forces close enough to Philippine shores to debark his troops and supplies. All these preparations, he believed, would, by 1946, place the Islands "in a favorable posture of defensive security." [19]

The development of the Philippine Army was slow. The year 1936 was devoted to the building of camps, organization of cadres, and the special training of instructors, drawn largely from the Constabulary. The commander of the Philippine Department provided Philippine Scouts as instructors and detailed U.S. Army officers to assist in the inspection, instruction, and administration of the program. By the end of the year instructors had been trained and camps established.

The first group of 20,000 men was called up on 1 January 1937 and by the end of 1939 there were 4,800 officers and 104,000 men in the reserves. Infantry training was given at camps scattered throughout the Philippines; field artillery training was concentrated in the vicinity of the U.S. Army's Fort Stotsenburg near Angeles, about fifty miles north of Manila, and specialized training was given at Fort William McKinley just south of Manila. Coast artillery instruction was carried on at Fort Stotsenburg and at Grande Island in Subic Bay by personnel supplied largely by the American commander at Corregidor.[20]

One of the greatest difficulties encountered in the organization of the Philippine Army was the creation of a satisfactory officer corps. In the Constabulary were Filipino officers with excellent training and experience, but their interests lay in law enforcement rather than military training. Some of the best officers came from the Philippine Scouts; these men rapidly became senior officers in the Philippine Army. The great problem was to train junior officers to command the training camps and reserve units once these were formed. Since no graduates could be expected from the projected military academy at Baguio for four years the most promising men in each semiannual class of reservists were selected for an additional six months' training as noncommissioned officers. The best of these were chosen for officer training and

---

[19] The quotations in this and the preceding two paragraphs are from the speech delivered in 1936 and printed in *Cornejo's Commonwealth Directory of the Philippines* (1939 ed.), pp. 759–84.

[20] Notes on the Philippine Army, 1941–1942, a typescript, undated and unsigned, evidently prepared in Hq USAFFE during the war, pp. 1–3, OCMH; memo, Eisenhower for Pres Quezon, 22 Jun 42, OPD Exec O.

became 3d lieutenants upon graduation from Officer Candidate School. Senior ROTC units in colleges and universities were established to provide additional junior reserve officers.

The air program of the Philippine Army, though its development was slow, met with few serious obstacles. The first Philippine Army airfield was built just outside of Manila, and by the time the first runway was completed three trainers were available for pilot training. This course was supplemented by courses in military flying and technical training given in the United States to selected air force students. By 1940 the Philippine Army Air Corps had about forty planes and one hundred trained pilots. Practice in light bombing and gunnery had been given, and the entire instructional system, General Eisenhower observed later, was "on a very sound basis." [21]

The program for the building of a fleet of motor torpedo boats did not progress well. Only two had been delivered by the end of 1939 when the war in Europe destroyed any hope of securing additional boats from England. An effort was made to produce the torpedo boats locally by purchasing the engines and the right to build from the British design, but by October 1941 only one boat had been completed. Meanwhile, with the assistance of the U.S. Navy, the training of boatmen and mechanics continued.[22]

No military plan for the defense of an archipelago such as the Philippine Islands could have had serious prospects of success against a determined enemy with a powerful fleet without great reliance on more effective naval support than that provided by patrol boats. The Philippine Government had neither the industrial capacity nor the wealth to build and support a navy which could compete with that of a first class naval power. President Quezon had frankly admitted this in November 1935. Such naval support could come only from the United States. No provision, it is true, had been made in the Tydings-McDuffie Act for the use by the U.S. Navy of naval bases in the Islands after 1946. But such a possibility had not been specifically denied and it was undoubtedly believed that arrangements for their use would be made at a later date. Certainly, the Philippine Government did not anticipate that the United States would stand idly by if the security of the Philippines was threatened.

---

[21] Memo, Eisenhower for Pres Quezon, 22 Jun 42, OPD Exec O.

[22] Porter, "Preparedness in the Philippines," *Far Eastern Survey,* April 7, 1941, p. 66; interv, author with Gen R. J. Marshall, 7 Apr 48; ltr, MacArthur to Gen George C. Marshall, Chief of Staff, U. S. Army, 28 Oct 41, WPD 4477-2.

CHAPTER II

U.S. Army Forces, Far East

By the middle of 1941 international developments had heightened the tension between the United States and Japan and made the defense of the Philippines an urgent problem. The Nazi-Soviet pact, followed by the German Army's march into Poland in September 1939, had destroyed completely any hope for a peaceful settlement in Europe. The events of the following year made it evident that the United States might soon be involved in war with the Axis in Asia as well as Europe. Denmark and Norway had been invaded by Hitler's armies in April, Holland and Belgium were conquered in May, and on 21 June France surrendered. Not long after, Japanese troops, with the acquiescence of the Vichy Government, moved into French Indochina. In September, Germany, Italy, and Japan concluded the Tripartite pact, and the following April, Russia and Japan reached agreement and signed a neutrality pact, thus freeing the latter for extension of her empire southward.

American efforts to halt Japanese aggression in Asia had met with little success. On 26 July 1940 Japan was notified that the commercial treaty of 1911 would be abrogated. On the same day Congress granted the President authority to control exports to Japan. Immediately he put the export of oil and scrap iron under government license and banned the shipment of aviation gasoline to that country. By the early part of 1941 shipments of scrap iron, steel, gasoline, and other important war

material from the United States to Japan had practically ceased.

While the United States market was being closed to Japan, American economic support to China was increased. In November 1940 Chiang Kai-shek's government was lent $50,000,000 through the Export-Import Bank; by the end of that year loans to China had reached a total of $170,000,000. Despite these moves, perhaps because of them, Japan continued to exert pressure on the French and Dutch colonies in Southeast Asia to "co-operate" in economic matters.

The possibility of war in the Far East was too real to be ignored and a reluctant Congress began to loosen the purse strings. But the years of neglect could not be remedied quickly. The demand for planes and weapons was great and the supply was limited. The Philippines was only one of many bases that had to be protected. Hawaii, Alaska, and Panama—which formed a strategic triangle whose defense was considered essential to the safety of the continental United States—had also been neglected and their needs had to be filled first. "Adequate reinforcements for the Philippines at this time," wrote Gen. George C. Marshall, "would have left the United States in a position of great peril should there be a break in the defense of Great Britain." [1]

---

[1] *Biennial Report of the Chief of Staff of the United States Army, July 1, 1941 to June 30, 1943 to the Secretary of War* (Washington, 1943), p. 6.

What the United States needed more than anything else was time. But Japan's occupation of naval and air bases in southern Indochina on 22 July 1941 gave warning that time was short. The Philippine Islands, already almost entirely surrounded, were now further threatened and America's position in the Far East rendered precarious. Measures to strengthen the defense of the Philippines could be put off no longer.

The Recall of General MacArthur

The establishment of a new American command in the Far East and the recall of General MacArthur to active duty in the U.S. Army were already under consideration when Japan moved southward in July 1941. A month earlier Joseph Stevenot, a prominent American businessman in Manila and president of the Philippine Long Distance Telephone Company, in an interview with Secretary of War Henry L. Stimson in Washington, had urged a closer relationship between the Military Advisor and the commander of the Philippine Department. Stimson had relayed this suggestion to General Marshall at a meeting during which both men discussed MacArthur's status and agreed he was the logical man to command in the Far East in the event of an emergency.[2]

By a coincidence, on the same day that Stimson talked with Stevenot, Maj. Gen. George Grunert, the Philippine Department commander, asked permission from the War Department to include representatives of the Commonwealth Government in conferences then being held in Manila. The purpose of these meetings was to formulate plans, based on the expected use of $52,-000,000 in sugar excise funds, for improving the defenses of the Islands. The reason for Grunert's request was to permit him to work more closely and directly with General MacArthur without going through official government channels. Close contact between the department commander and the Military Advisor, he pointed out, was an obvious necessity in making defense plans. General Marshall approved Grunert's request without question, adding that "MacArthur's support will be invaluable to you in the accomplishment of the difficult task with which you are confronted." [3]

The first direct bid for the recall of General MacArthur came from the former Chief of Staff himself and was contained in a letter to General Marshall.[4] In this letter

<hr>

[2] Henry L. Stimson, Diary, entry of 21 May 41; memo, Brig Gen Leonard T. Gerow for Chief of Staff, 29 May 41, sub: Consultation with Mil Advisor . . . , WPD 3251-49; ltr, Marshall to MacArthur, 20 Jun 41, OCS 20850-15. Chief of Staff is hereafter referred to as CofS and the Office of the Chief of Staff as OCS. General Gerow was at the time acting chief of WPD. The relevant portion of Mr. Stimson's diary was made available to the author by Mr. Rudolph A. Winnacker, formerly historian of the Office of the Secretary of War and the author of a forthcoming volume in this series on the history of that office.

Frazier Hunt, in his book *MacArthur and the War Against Japan* (New York, 1944), page 12, states that MacArthur offered his services to President Roosevelt early in the spring of 1941. The author has been unable to find the documentary evidence in the files of the Department of the Army to support this assertion.

[3] Ltr, Marshall to Grunert, 29 May 41, WPD 3251-49.

[4] The author has been unable to find a copy of this letter in the files of the War Department but its contents are summarized in a memorandum written by General Gerow and addressed to the Chief of Staff on 6 June 1941 (WPD 3251-50). From internal evidence it appears that MacArthur on the same day wrote a letter covering the same subjects to the President and the Secretary of War. See also ltr, Marshall to MacArthur, 20 Jun 41, WPD 3251-50.

MacArthur stated that since the Philippine Army was to be absorbed by the U.S. Army in the near future—a step not yet contemplated by the War Department—he intended to close out the office of Military Advisor. A new American military command embracing all U.S. Army activities in the Far East, comparable to the British command in that area, should be established, he told the Chief of Staff, and he, MacArthur, be named commander.

The idea of creating a high command in the Far East had been broached before, but never by so influential a source. In January 1941 the intelligence officer of the Philippine Department had recommended to his superior in Washington that such a command be established. This proposal differed from MacArthur's in that the department commander was to be designated commander in chief of such a command, while MacArthur put forward his own nomination.[5] The Philippine Department G–2 continued to urge this move during the first six months of 1941, but there is no evidence that it was ever considered by the General Staff in Washington until June of that year, after General MacArthur's letter to the Chief of Staff.[6]

MacArthur's proposal was sent to the War Plans Division of the General Staff for study. On 6 June Brig. Gen. Leonard T. Gerow, acting chief of the division, sent his recommendations to the Chief of Staff. He agreed that the British had created such a command, but pointed out that their situation was quite different from that faced by

the Americans. The British had accepted strategic direction of naval forces in the Far East, and their troops were scattered throughout the area. U.S. Army forces were concentrated in the Philippines and had responsibility only for the defense of the Islands. Gerow therefore recommended against the establishment of a new command in the Far East. If MacArthur was called to active service, he wrote, it should be as commander of the Philippine Department.[7]

Despite the recommendations of the chief of War Plans, the official reply to MacArthur's letter expressed a sentiment entirely favorable to the proposal. This reply was contained in a letter dated 20 June from the Chief of Staff to General MacArthur. In it Marshall told the Military Advisor that the War Department's plans for the Philippine Army were not as broad as MacArthur believed, but that the decision to close out his office rested with him. All that the U.S. Army planned to do at the present time, he said, was to train about 75,000 Filipinos for a period of from three to nine months, contingent upon the appropriation by Congress of the sugar excise and currency devaluation fund.

Both the Secretary of War and I [Marshall continued] are much concerned about the situation in the Far East. During one of our discussions about three months ago it was decided that your outstanding qualifications and vast experience in the Philippines make you the logical selection for the Army Commander in the Far East should the situation approach a crisis. The Secretary has delayed recommending your appointment as he does not feel the time has arrived for such action. However, he has authorized me to tell you that, at the proper time, he will recommend to the

[5] Ltr, G–2 Phil Dept to G–2 WD, 18 Jan 41, sub: Comments on Current Events, 8–18 Jan 41, Military Intelligence Division 10641-374-50. Military Intelligence Division is hereafter referred to as MID with appropriate file number.

[6] Ibid.; see also ltrs, 13 and 26 Mar 41, MID 10641-374-58, -59.

[7] Memo, Gerow for CofS, 6 Jun 41, WPD 3251-50.

President that you be so appointed. It is my impression that the President will approve his recommendation.[8]

The appointment of General MacArthur as commander of all Army forces in the Far East was part of the larger problem of mobilization and training of the Philippine Army. By July 1941 it was clear that some decision on the use of the Philippine Army would soon have to be made. On 7 July MacArthur presented his views on the mobilization and training of the Philippine Army in a personal letter to the Chief of Staff, adding that the creation of a high command for the Far East "would result in favorable psychological and morale reactions." [9] A week later General Gerow summarized for the Chief of Staff the steps being taken for improving the defenses of the Philippine Islands, and on 17 July made the following specific recommendations:

1. That the President, by executive order, call into the service of the U.S. for the period of the emergency all organized military forces of the Commonwealth.
2. That General MacArthur be called to active duty in the grade of Major General and assigned as commander of Army Forces in the Far East.
3. That $10,000,000 of the President's Emergency Fund be allotted to cover the costs of mobilization and training of the Philippine Army for a period of three months.
4. That the training program of the Philippine Army for an additional six to nine months be financed from the sugar excise fund, or from other funds appropriated for this purpose.
5. That 425 Reserve officers be sent to the Philippines to assist in the mobilization and training of the Philippine Army.[10]

Within a week these recommendations had been approved by the Chief of Staff and the Secretary of War. The Secretary immediately requested President Franklin D. Roosevelt to issue the necessary executive order, already drafted and approved, for calling the military forces of the Commonwealth into active service of the United States. "Due to the situation in the Far East," Stimson wrote, "all practical steps should be taken to increase the defensive strength of the Philippines Islands." One of the most effective measures to accomplish this would be to call the Philippine Army into active service for a year's training. Such a program, Stimson estimated, would involve about 75,000 men and would cost about $32,000,000, which would be met by the sugar excise fund. Pending appropriation by Congress, the funds to initiate the program could be met from the President's emergency fund.[11]

Stimson's recommendations reached the President at a time when he was thoroughly aroused by Japan's occupation of air and naval bases in Indochina on 22 July. Already he had broken off negotiations with Japan for a settlement of Far Eastern problems and was considering economic reprisals in the form of a freeze on Japanese assets in the United States. On 26 July, the day after Stimson made his recommendations, the President put the freeze into effect and issued the military order which would

[8] Ltr, Marshall to MacArthur, 20 Jun 41, OCS 20850-15; see also unused draft of this letter in WPD 3251-50. The last paragraph of the copy sent stated: "This letter is also an acknowledgment of your letters to the President and to the Secretary of War. Please keep its contents confidential for the present."
[9] The writer has been unable to find a copy of this letter. A summary of its contents can be found in a memo, Gerow for CofS, 14 Jul 41, sub: Philippine Islands [P.I.], WPD 3251-52.

[10] Ibid.; memo, Gerow for CofS, sub: Emergency Mobilization and Tng of Phil Army, 17 Jul 41, WPD 3251-52.
[11] Ltr, Stimson to President, 25 Jul 41, OCS 18136-34.

bring into the service of the United States the armed forces of the Philippines.[12]

The President's military order did not mention General MacArthur by name; it was carefully worded so as to place the forces in the Philippines under a general officer of the United States Army, "to be designated by the Secretary of War from time to time." The actual induction of Philippine Army units was to be accomplished by orders issued by that general officer.

The War Department immediately followed up the President's action by establishing, that same day, a new command in the Philippines, with headquarters in Manila. This command, to be called U.S. Army Forces in the Far East (USAFFE), would consist of the Philippine Department, those military forces of the Commonwealth ordered into active service for the period of the emergency, and such other forces as might be assigned. At the same time, MacArthur was recalled to active duty, effective on 26 July, with the rank of major general, designated as the general officer referred to in the military order, and put in command of U.S. Army Forces in the Far East.[13] With the establishment of USAFFE and the simultaneous induction of the military forces of the Commonwealth Government, the two separate military establishments which had existed in the Philippine Islands since 1935 were placed for the first time under one command.

The recall of Douglas MacArthur to active duty at the age of 61 brought back into the U.S. Army one of its most able and experienced senior officers. Son of General Arthur MacArthur of Philippine fame, he had graduated from the Military Academy in 1903 as a second lieutenant of engineers. Since then his record had been one of rapid advancement and brilliant achievement. His first assignment had been in the Philippines as a construction officer and he had been aide to his father when the senior MacArthur was chief military observer with the Japanese Army in the war against Russia. In 1907 he served as aide-de-camp to President Theodore Roosevelt. After various assignments in the United States he was ordered to Washington in 1913 for duty with the Chief of Engineers. The following year he accompanied the Mexican expedition to Vera Cruz as assistant engineer officer.

In World War I Douglas MacArthur's record was outstanding. Transferring to the infantry, he served as chief of staff of the 42d Division, the Rainbow Division, and as commander of the 84th Brigade of that division. He was wounded twice, served briefly in the occupation and returned to the United States in 1919 as a brigadier general of the National Army. That year, at the age of 39, he was appointed Superintendent of the Military Academy at West Point over a number of senior generals. From West Point he went to the Philippines where he commanded in turn the District of Manila and the 23d Brigade. In January 1925 he was appointed a major general and returned to the United States the following month.

For the next three years General MacArthur commanded a corps area in the United States. In 1928 he returned to Manila as commander of the Philippine Department. Upon completion of this assignment he was brought back to the United

---

[12] The military order and other material relating to this subject are filed in WPD 3251-52.

[13] Rad, Marshall to MacArthur, 26 Jul 41, OCS 18136-35; ltr order, CofS to MacArthur, sub: Active Duty, Tab C, Incl 4, WPD 3251-52.

States where he commanded the Ninth Corps Area on the west coast for a month and on 1 November 1930 was appointed Chief of Staff, U.S. Army. He held this post five years before going to the Philippines as Military Advisor to the Philippine Commonwealth. On 31 December 1937, after thirty-eight years' service, eighteen of them as a general officer, MacArthur retired from the Army with the rank of general, to become field marshal in the Philippine Army a short time later. His return to active duty on 26 July 1941 was as a major general, his permanent rank before retirement. The next day action to promote him to the rank of temporary lieutenant general was initiated and approved two days later, effective 27 July.

The Organization of USAFFE

The immediate tasks facing General MacArthur were, first, to establish his headquarters and organize his command on an efficient basis; second, to induct and train the Philippine Army; and third, to secure the necessary supplies and reinforcements to put his forces on a war footing.

The first task was quickly accomplished. From the small group of Army officers who had been detailed to the Office of the Military Advisor and from U.S. Army organizations in the Philippines, MacArthur secured enough officers to form a nucleus for his headquarters. By mid-August he had a small and highly efficient staff in Headquarters, USAFFE, located at No. 1, Calle Victoria, in the walled city in Manila. His principal staff officers were men who had been with him for some time. For the most part they were men in the prime of their lives. The chief of staff and deputy chief of staff were 47 and 46 years old respectively at the time USAFFE was organized and had already served under MacArthur for several years. All the officers on the general staff were under 50 years of age, and of the three special staff officers who had been requested specifically by name, the youngest was 43 and the oldest 52.

For his chief of staff, General MacArthur selected the senior officer of the military mission, Lt. Col. Richard K. Sutherland. Entering the army as a private after his graduation from Yale in 1916, Sutherland rose to the rank of captain before the end of World War I. During the peace years, he attended the Infantry School, Command and Staff School, Ecole Supérieure de Guerre, and the Army War College. Conceded by most to be a brilliant, hard-working officer, he was selected for MacArthur's staff in 1938 after a tour of duty in Shanghai. Gen. George C. Kenney, who served with him for four years, remarked, "He knew so many of the answers that I could understand why General MacArthur had picked him for chief of staff." But he also noted that among Sutherland's traits were egotism and "an unfortunate bit of arrogance." [14] Promoted directly to brigadier general in August 1941, Sutherland remained MacArthur's chief of staff until 1946, rising finally to the rank of lieutenant general.

For the next important post in USAFFE, the deputy chief of staff, MacArthur chose Lt. Col. Richard J. Marshall who had occupied a similar position in the Military Advisor's office. Promoted rapidly, first to colonel and in December 1941 to brigadier general, Marshall had, in MacArthur's opinion, "no superior as a supply officer in the Army." [15]

---

[14] Gen. George C. Kenney, *General Kenney Reports* (New York, 1949), p. 26.
[15] Rad MacArthur to Marshall, No. C–62, 10 Jul 42, OPD Strategy File, III.

PHILIPPINE SCOUTS *at Fort McKinley firing a 37-mm. antitank gun in training, above; below, engineers preparing sections for a pontoon bridge.*

U.S. Army in the Philippines

When General MacArthur assumed command of U.S. Army Forces in the Far East, the Philippine Department consisted of 22,-532 men, 11,972 of whom were Philippine Scouts.[16] Of the 1,340 officers, 775 were reservists on active duty. The largest group of men—7,293—was assigned to the infantry, and the Coast Artillery Corps was next with 4,967. Almost the entire strength of the command was stationed on Luzon.

The largest single U.S. Army unit in the Philippines was the Philippine Division, commanded by Maj. Gen. Jonathan M. Wainwright. Theoretically, it was a square division, but was not equipped as such, and lacked a brigade organization and some of its organic elements. All of the enlisted men in the division, except those in the 31st Infantry and a few military police and headquarters troops, were Philippine Scouts; the 31st was the only American infantry unit in the Islands composed entirely of Americans. In addition to this regiment, the Philippine Division contained the 45th and 57th Infantry (PS).[17] Authorized strength for these Scout regiments was 2,435 officers

and men, and for the 31st, 1,729. In July 1941 the former were slightly below strength and the latter was 402 overstrength in officers and enlisted men.[18]

Field artillery components of the Philippine Division consisted of the two-battalion 24th Regiment (truck-drawn British 75-mm. guns) with 843 officers and enlisted men, and one battalion of the 23d, with 401 men and armed with 2.95-inch mountain guns (pack). Plans existed for the organization at a later date of the 26th Field Artillery and a separate battalion of 155-mm. guns for use with the division. The division also included the standard engineer, ordnance, signal, military police, medical, and quartermaster units. The total strength of the Philippine Division on 31 July was 10,-473 men, distributed as shown in Table 1.

The Philippine Division rarely functioned as a division, for its elements were scattered. Headquarters and the bulk of the division were at Fort William McKinley, just south of the city. The 31st Infantry was stationed at the Post of Manila, in the city itself, and a battalion of the 12th Quartermaster Regiment was located in the Manila port area. The 1st Battalion, less one company, of the 45th Infantry was stationed at the Post of Limay on the southeast coast of the Bataan peninsula. The rest of the division, including the artillery components, the 12th Ordnance Company, and a platoon of the quartermaster regiment, was at Fort Stotsenburg, about fifty miles north of Manila, close to Clark Field.

The major nondivisional U.S. Army ground elements in the Philippines in July

---

[16] Unless otherwise noted, this and subsequent material on the strength of American and Philippine troops is taken from Phil Dept., Machine Rcds Unit Station Strength Rpts, 31 Jul 41, Strength Accounting Branch, and from Phil Dept War Plan ORANGE, 1940 Revision (Short title HPD WPO–3). Flyleaf of Copy No. 6 has an AG strength report of 21 Jul 41 attached.

Up to January 1941 the Scouts had had a strength of 6,500; at that time the President of the United States had authorized an increase in their strength to 12,000. Telg, TAG to CG Phil Dept, No. 635, 28 Jan 41, AG 320.2 Phil Dept (1–19–41).

[17] The 43d Infantry (PS) is also listed in some reports. Actually, this unit consisted of 329 men, formerly part of the 45th Infantry, who had been detached for duty at Zamboanga in Mindanao and at Camp John Hay, near Baguio on Luzon.

[18] HPD WPO–3, G–1 Annex, Exhibit F. Strength figures in this source were computed from tables and are the estimated strengths as of Mobilization (M) Day. Those figures are close to the actual strength at the beginning of 1941 when the plan was prepared, but some of the units listed in Table 1 were not yet organized.

TABLE 1—STRENGTH OF PHILIPPINE DIVISION, 31 JULY 1941

Unit	Total	Officers	Enlisted		
			Total	American	Philippine Scouts
All Units..............................	10,473	a 516	9,957	2,036	7,921
Hq and Hq Co.............................	181	30	151	4	147
Special Troops.............................	5	5	0	0	0
31st Infantry.................................	2,100	114	1,986	1,986	0
45th Infantry.................................	2,265	117	2,148	1	2,147
57th Infantry.................................	2,279	118	2,161	0	2,161
23d FA Regt.................................	401	10	391	0	391
24th FA Regt.................................	843	39	804	0	804
12th MP Co.................................	136	5	131	5	86
12th QM Regt.................................	592	18	574	0	574
12th Med Regt.................................	421	22	399	0	399
12th Ord Co.................................	142	3	139	0	139
12th Sig Regt.................................	227	10	217	0	217
14th Engr Regt.................................	870	24	846	0	846
4th Vet Co.................................	11	1	10	0	10

a Includes 15 Philippine Scout Officers: 2 Hq, 2 Sp Trs, 3 45th Inf, 1 57th Inf, 5 24th FA Regt, 1 12th QM Regt, and 1 14th Engr.

Source: Phil Dept, Machine Rcds Unit Station Strength and Misc., Officers and Enlisted Men, Jul 41.

1941 included the Harbor Defenses of Manila and Subic Bays, a cavalry regiment, two field artillery regiments, and quartermaster, signal, and military police units. The Harbor Defenses were commanded by Maj. Gen. George F. Moore, who had his headquarters at Fort Mills on Corregidor. They included not only the defenses of Corregidor, but also those on Caballo Island (Fort Hughes), El Fraile (Fort Drum), and Carabao (Fort Frank)—all at the entrance to Manila Bay—and Fort Wint on Grande Island at the entrance to Subic Bay.

The 26th Cavalry was a Philippine Scout organization with two squadrons of three troops each. It was considerably smaller than a similar regiment in the United States and had a strength of 784 enlisted men and 54 officers. The home station of the regi-

ment, except for one troop, was at Fort Stotsenburg; Troop F was stationed at Nichols Field, south of Manila.[19] Also at Fort Stotsenburg were two Philippine Scout field artillery regiments, the 86th and 88th, the first with a strength of 388 and the second with 518 men.

Service and supply elements in the Philippine Department at the end of July 1941 totaled approximately 2,500 officers and men, exclusive of those serving with the Air Forces. The largest part of these troops were assigned to quartermaster and medical units, stationed at the various posts on Luzon, and at Pettit Barracks in Zamboanga

[19] Lt. Col. William E. Chandler, "26th Cavalry (PS) Battles to Glory," in three parts, Armored Cavalry Journal, LVI, Nos. 2–4 (March–August 1947).

(Mindanao). A military police company, the 808th, was stationed in Manila, as were the headquarters of the Philippine Department and of USAFFE. (*See Table 2.*)

On 4 August, the air forces in the Philippines were brought under the control of MacArthur's headquarters, "except for routine administration and supply," and redesignated the USAFFE Air Force. It was only a token force. Of the 210 aircraft in the Islands, only the thirty-one P–40B's could be considered modern aircraft; the others, consisting of P–26's, P–35's, B–10's, B–18's, A–29's, C–39's and observation planes, were largely obsolescent. One field alone, Clark Field near Fort Stotsenburg, could accommodate heavy bombers.[20]

Air Forces headquarters was located at Nielson Field on the outskirts of Manila; the majority of the planes were based at either Nichols, also near Manila, or Clark Field. The 4th Composite Group at Clark Field had under it a headquarters squadron, three pursuit squadrons, one bombardment squadron, and an observation squadron. The 20th Air Base Group at Nichols Field contained miscellaneous supporting units, including the 27th and 28th Materiel Squadrons, and the 19th Air Base Squadron. Total strength of the air forces was 254 officers and 2,049 men.[21]

With the establishment of USAFFE, the Philippine Department became a subordinate command. The headquarters staff was left largely intact, although General MacArthur designated some of its members to serve on his staff in addition to their regular duties, but the mission of the Department was narrowed until its principal task became the training and supply of the Philippine Army. In effect, it became a service command, "an administrative echelon," MacArthur explained, "analagous to a Corps Area." [22] Planning and the tactical control of field troops, organized into task forces, were now centered in USAFFE.

Under the circumstances, there seemed little need for the services of so senior an officer as General Grunert, and MacArthur recommended that he be relieved and another officer "who had not enjoyed such high command" be appointed to the position. Pointing out that Grunert would complete his tour of duty in less than four months, MacArthur declared, "It would be advantageous to relieve him, as I am loath, as long as he is here, to contract the functions of the Department Commander. . . ." [23] The War Department accepted this suggestion and on 23 October named MacArthur commander of the Philippine Department, relieved Grunert, and ordered him back to the United States.[24] Thus, the Philippine Department, which had been for so long the highest Army command in the Far East, became, in fact first and later in name, a service command. The headquar-

[20] USAFFE GO 4, 4 Aug 41, copy in History of Fifth Air Force (and Its Predecessors), Air Hist Off; Army Air Action in the Philippines and the Netherland East Indies, p. 11, prepared by the Asst Chief of Air Staff Intel, Hist Div, and filed in Air University Hist Off.

[21] Army Air Action in Phil and NEI, p. 11. The aircraft in the 4th Composite Group at this time were as follows: 21 P–26's, 56 P–35's, 31 P–40B's, 10 O–46's, 3 O–19E's, 10 A–9's, 1 C–39, 9 A–27's, 14 B–10Bs, and 18 B–18's.

[22] Extract of rad from CG USAFFE in memo, Maj Gen William Bryden, DCofS for ACofS G–1, 13 Oct 41, OCS 18136-78; see also memo, Bryden for WPD, 7 Oct 41, OCS 18136-71.

[23] Extract of rad from CG USAFFE in memo, Bryden for ACofS, G–1, 13 Oct 41, OCS 18136-78.

[24] Memo, Bryden for TAG, n.d., sub: Order for Gens Grunert and MacArthur, AG 210.311. Note on memo: "Action taken, October 23, 1941."

TABLE 2—STRENGTH AND COMPOSITION OF U.S. ARMY TROOPS IN PHILIPPINE ISLANDS,
31 JULY 1941

Unit	Total	Officers	Enlisted		
			Total	American	Philippine Scouts
All Units.............................	22,532	ᵃ 1,434	21,098	9,161	11,937
Hq USAFFE................................	5	5	0	0	0
Hq and Hq Det Phil Dept..................	289	125	164	163	1
Philippine Division.......................	10,473	516	9,957	2,036	7,921
26th Cavalry..............................	838	54	784	0	784
43d Infantry..............................	329	16	313	0	313
86th FA...................................	388	12	376	0	376
88th FA...................................	518	17	501	0	501
808th MP Co..............................	69	4	65	65	0
Harbor Defenses (Ft Mills).................	5,360	204	5,156	3,698	1,458
Hq and Hq Btry.......................	418	32	386	316	70
59th CA..............................	1,415	34	1,381	1,381	0
60th CA..............................	1,896	41	1,855	1,855	0
91st CA..............................	783	26	757	0	757
92d CA...............................	653	26	627	0	627
USAMP ᵇ *Harrison*.....................	47	7	40	36	4
Station Hospital......................	144	35	109	109	0
Chemical Warfare Det..................	4	3	1	1	0
Air Corps.................................	2,407	275	2,132	2,132	0
Headquarters.........................	109	18	91	91	0
4th Composite Group..................	1,393	232	1,161	1,161	0
20th Air Base Group..................	842	19	823	823	0
Tow Target Det.......................	42	1	41	41	0
Weather Det..........................	21	5	16	16	0
Service Detachments.......................	1,836	188	1,648	1,065	583
Quartermaster Corps....................	505	31	474	182	292
Medical Dept..........................	526	132	394	233	161
Ordnance Dept.........................	173	9	164	164	0
Corps of Engineers....................	196	7	189	189	0
Signal Corps..........................	348	6	342	224	118
Chemical Warfare Service..............	68	2	66	54	12
Finance Dept..........................	20	1	19	19	0
Other ᶜ...................................	20	18	2	2	0

ᵃ Includes 26 Philippine Scout Officers.
ᵇ U.S. Army Mine Planter.
ᶜ Includes officers and enlisted men for which no specific unit was indicated.

Source: Phil Dept, Machine Rcds Unit Station Strength and Misc., Officers and Enlisted Men, Jul 41.

CEREMONY AT CAMP MURPHY, RIZAL, *15 August 1941, marking the induction of the Philippine Army Air Corps. Behind Lt. Gen. Douglas MacArthur, from left to right, are Lt. Col. Richard K. Sutherland, Col. Harold H. George, Lt. Col. William F. Marquat, and Maj. LeGrande A. Diller.*

ters which had made the plans and preparations for war had no tactical control when war came.

Philippine Army: Mobilization and Training

The major task of the hurriedly assembled staff of Headquarters, USAFFE, was to work out a plan for the mobilization, training, and supply of the Philippine Army. Within a few days of his appointment, General MacArthur had selected 1 September as the day when mobilization of the Philippine Army would start. This left thirty days in which to select camp sites, enlarge and improve existing camps for the first reservists, and build new camps.

The integration of the armed forces of the Philippine Commonwealth into the service of the United States was to be gradual. Elements of the ten reserve divisions were to be called into service at regular intervals until 15 December 1941, when the mobilization would be complete. The Philippine Army Air Corps would be inducted separately. Reserve units engaged in their normal yearly training were not to be inducted unless war came. It was hoped in this way to continue the development of the Commonwealth's defense program and at the same time mobilize and train the Philippine Army. Commonwealth forces coming under United States control would retain their national integrity; they would have their own uniforms, rations, military law, scale of pay, and promotion list; would requisition through their own supply channel until 1 December; but would be paid by the U. S. Army. The Regular Army of the Philippine Comonwealth and the Constabulary were not to be inducted immediately.

A construction program was to be started immediately since there was only enough housing for about one third of the 75,000 men scheduled for induction. Camp sites would have to be selected and facilities for training built. The first units called would use existing or temporary quarters and, as camps were completed, additional units would be inducted. By 15 December, when the last units would be mobilized, the entire construction program would be completed.[25]

On 15 August, less than three weeks after he had assumed command of USAFFE, General MacArthur incorporated into the American forces the Philippine Army Air Corps of six squadrons and approximately 500 men. A few days later he issued orders calling into the service by 1 September ten infantry regiments—one from each of the

reserve divisions—and the cadres of most of the other divisional units.[26]

As housing facilities became available, USAFFE brought other elements of the Philippine Army into service. Early in November the second infantry regiment of each of the divisions was called up, to be joined before the end of the month by the division headquarters and the service elements. But time was running out. When war came not a single division had been completely mobilized and not one of the units was at full strength. None of the antitank battalions was ever organized because of the lack of equipment, and the shortage of organic artillery forced many of the divisions to go into battle without full artillery components.[27]

To each division were assigned about forty U.S. Army officers and twenty American or Philippine Scout noncommissioned officers who served as instructors. The officers were usually attached to division and regimental staffs; the enlisted men served in battalions and companies. The position of the instructor was an anomalous one. When one instructor asked for a clarification of his status he was told: "You have no command status. You have no authority. But you are directly responsible for the success or failure of the regiment."[28]

While it is not possible to state definitely the strength of the Philippine Army by mid-December 1941, an estimate of the number of Filipinos available for combat can be

---

[25] Notes on the Philippine Army, 1941–1942, p. 2; *Sixth Annual Report of the U.S. High Commissioner to the Philippine Islands, 1 July 1941–30 June 1942* (Washington, 1943), p. 16; Admin Plan for Ten Reserve Divs . . ., Hq USAFFE, 10 Aug 41, OCMH; Report of Operations of USAFFE and USFIP [U.S. Forces in the Philippines] in the Philippine Islands, 1941–1942, pp. 3 ff. This last report with its eighteen annexes constitutes the basic Army report on the various aspects of the Philippine campaign and was prepared in 1946 by a staff under General Wainwright, formerly commander of USFIP. Each of the annexes is separately titled and paginated and was prepared by officers in the relevant headquarters. The basic report is cited hereafter as USAFFE-USFIP Rpt of Opns; its annexes will be referred to by their own titles, listed in The Sources, page 588, below.

This report was prepared in five copies, one of which is on file in AG and another in OCMH. The author has used throughout this volume the copy in OCMH.

[26] USAFFE GO 6, 19 Aug 41, copy in OCMH; *Sixth Annual Report of High Commissioner*, p. 15.

[27] USAFFE-USFIP Rpt of Opns, pp. 13, 14.

[28] Col Richard C. Mallonée, senior instructor of 21st FA(PA), Bataan Diary, 2 vols., I, 23. The diary was borrowed by the author and a photostat copy is on file in OCMH. See also South Luzon Force (SLF) and II Corps Rpt of Opns, p. 4, Annex V, USAFFE-USFIP Rpt of Opns.

made. On the basis of the authorized strength of a Philippine division (7,500 men), the total divisional strength of the Philippine Army reserve would be 75,000 men. To this figure must be added the strength of the 1st Regular Division, a part of the regular establishment, and the Constabulary, plus nondivisional and provisional units formed after the start of war. A rough estimate of the number of men in the Philippine Army, therefore, would be approximately 120,000, a figure which is confirmed by later reports on the number of men surrendered and by postwar claims for back pay and pensions.[29]

Upon mobilization of the first elements of the ten reserve divisions, schools were established to provide special training for officers and selected enlisted men of the Philippine Army who in turn would train other Filipinos as the mobilization progressed. At Baguio a command and staff school was established to train a few American colonels and senior Philippine officers who were to command Philippine Army divisions, as well as certain key officers slated for the staffs of these divisions. Schools for the training of infantry cadres were established in each division mobilization district. Americans and Philippine Scouts served as instructors, and the students consisted of the cadres of the infantry elements of the divisions, regimental and battalion staffs, com-

pany commanders, platoon leaders, first sergeants, cooks, and company clerks. In addition to specialized training, each student took the basic infantry course.[30]

Coast artillery schools were established at Fort Mills (Corregidor) and Fort Wint (Grande Island), and field artillery cadres were trained at the Philippine Army training center at Camp Dau, near Fort Stotsenburg. Two engineer schools were established, with instructors from the 14th Engineer Regiment (PS), the engineer component of the Philippine Division. A signal and a medical school were organized at Fort William McKinley; a second medical school was established for the training of nondivisional cadres; and in the port area of Manila was a quartermaster motor transport school.[31]

The training of the Philippine Army was beset with numerous difficulties. In many units there was a serious language barrier, not only between the American instructors and the Filipinos but also among the Filipinos. The enlisted men of one division spoke the Bicolanian dialect, their Philippine officers usually spoke Tagalog, and the Americans spoke neither.[32] In the Visayas the problem was even more complicated since most of the officers were Tagalogs from central Luzon and the men spoke one or more of the many Visayan tongues. Transfers were made to alleviate the situation, but no real solution to the problem was ever found.[33]

[29] Memo, CofS for Secretary of War (SW), n.d., sub: Reinforcement of the Philippines, OCS 18136-124; memo, Col Joseph K. Evans, Chief, SE Asia Sec, for Maj Thomas R. Clarkin, SW Pacific Sec, OPD, 5 Aug 42, sub: US and PA Divs in Phil Campaign, OCMH; memo, Col John R. Deane for Admiral Harold R. Stark, 7 Feb 42, OCS 18136-232; intervs, author with numerous officers on the division and corps level who served in the Philippine campaign. The author had been unable to find any strength reports of the Philippine Army by USAFFE after 31 October 1941.

[30] USAFFE-USFIP Rpt of Opns, pp. 3–4; interv, author with Brig Gen Clifford Bluemel, 14 Apr 48, OCMH. General Bluemel commanded the 31st Division (PA).
[31] USAFFE-USFIP Rpt of Opns, p. 8.
[32] SLF and II Corps Rpt of Opns, p. 6.
[33] Visayan-Mindanao Force (V-MF) Rpt of Opns, p. 17, Annex XI, USAFFE-USFIP Rpt of Opns.

Discipline in Philippine Army units left much to be desired, according to U.S. Army officers. Until war was declared there were no courts-martial. Since the Philippine Army retained its national integrity after induction, Philippine Army headquarters was responsible for discipline and punishment. Many of the officers and noncommissioned officers were untrained and unqualified for their assignments. There were some first sergeants and company clerks who could neither read nor write.

Training facilities and equipment were almost nonexistent. Target ranges had been hurriedly improvised but many units went into battle without ever having fired their weapons. There was a serious shortage in almost all types of equipment. The clothing was old and much of it not fit for use; shoes were rubber soled and quickly wore out. The uniform usually consisted of the blue fatigue suit, and when that wore out, anything that could be found. There were serious shortages in personal equipment, blankets, mosquito bars, and shelter halves. The supply of Enfield and Springfield '03 rifles was adequate but that of many other weapons, entrenching tools, gas masks, and steel helmets was not. After the outbreak of war, units secured supplies wherever and whenever they could, and the amount was usually dependent upon the initiative and energy of the individual supply officers.[34]

The difficulties of mobilizing and training the Philippine Army can best be shown by following the experiences of a single division. The 31st Division (PA) was organized on 18 November at a camp near San Marcelino in Zambales Province, Luzon.[35] An American Army officer, Col. Clifford Bluemel, who had commanded the 45th Infantry (PS) and later the staff and command school at Baguio, was assigned as division commander with a staff consisting of Philippine Army and Scout officers.

When the division was organized, its camp was still under construction. The buildings were about 80 percent complete, and in the absence of a water system a few shallow wells were used. Work on sanitary installations had just begun.

One of the division's regiments, the 31st Infantry (PA), had been mobilized on 1 September and was already in camp when Colonel Bluemel arrived. The 32d Infantry had been inducted on 1 November but did not join the division until 6 December. Starting on 25 November the third infantry element of the division, the 33d Infantry, began arriving in camp. Between 18 and 30 November, the medical battalion, motor transport, service, and division headquarters companies were mobilized. The signal company was organized on 1 December when a cadre which had been in training at Fort McKinley for three months arrived at camp. The 31st Field Artillery Regiment began mobilizing on 12 December, after the outbreak of war, and was finally organized with two battalions on 26 December, after the division had already moved to Bataan.

The 31st Division, like the other Philippine Army divisions, suffered from shortages in personal and organizational equip-

[34] *Ibid.*, pp. 17–20; SLF and II Corps Rpt of Opns, pp. 6–7; USAFFE-USFIP Rpt of Opns, pp. 19–20.

[35] This account is drawn from the Report of General Bluemel on the 31st Division Philippine Army. It was borrowed from the author and a copy is on file in OCMH. Cited hereafter as Bluemel, 31st Div (PA) Rpt of Opns.

ment. Every man was equipped with a rifle, the .30-caliber Enfield rifle used by American troops in World War I. The stock was too long for the small Philippine soldier and the weak extractor often broke and could not be replaced. Of the other infantry weapons, there was one Browning automatic rifle for each infantry company and eight .30-caliber Browning water-cooled machine guns for each machine gun company. Each infantry regiment had two .50-caliber machine guns and six 3-inch trench mortars, 70 percent of the ammunition for which proved to be duds. Artillery equipment for the division consisted of eight World War I model 75-mm. guns which were delivered to the division on the evening of 7 December, without sights or fire control equipment. The 31st Field Artillery, therefore, could only organize two of the six firing batteries it was authorized.

Organic transportation was virtually nonexistent. Division headquarters and the motor transport company could muster only one sedan, one command car, one bantam car, one 1½-ton truck and one ½-ton truck. The 31st Infantry had only one command car and eight 1½-ton trucks, which was more than the other regiments had. The division was deficient also in communications and engineer supplies, office equipment, spare parts, and tools.

The personal equipment of the Philippine soldier in the 31st Division left much to be desired. His uniform consisted of shorts, short-sleeved shirt, and cheap canvas shoes with a rubber sole that wore out in about two weeks. Some of the men were fortunate enough to draw leather shoes. For warmth and protection against mosquitoes, the Filipino wore his blue fatigue uniform. There were no surplus stocks for issue or replacement. The division received no steel helmets, but did have gas masks.

Rations were purchased by the individual organizations with funds furnished the unit commanders by the Philippine Army. Zambales Province, where the 31st Division was located, did not produce enough food for its own needs, and as additional units joined the division the procurement of food became a difficult problem. The division railhead scheduled to open on 1 December did not begin operations until a week later, after the war had started, because of the inexperience of Filipino supply officers.

The training program of the division began theoretically on 1 September, when the 31st Infantry was mobilized, but it was not until 24 November that the men first fired their rifles on the target range at the Olongapo Naval Station. One battalion fired fifty rounds per man, and another twenty-five rounds. The third battalion never fired at all, for permission to use the range was withdrawn by the Navy when the 4th Marine Regiment arriving from China, was stationed at Olongapo. No other range was available for the division, and the one under construction was not completed when war came.

The men in the 31st Infantry were more fortunate than those in the other regiments, many of whom never even fired a rifle before entering combat. Nor had their previous five and a half months' training under Philippine Army supervision been of much value, according to Colonel Bluemel. Practically none of the men, he observed, had fired as many as five rounds with the rifle or the .30-caliber machine gun. None had fired the .50-caliber-machine gun or the mortar. Bluemel's judgment of the value of the early training program was borne out by the experience of other Philippine Army division commanders.[36]

The field artillery units received even less training than the infantry. As soon as the two batteries were organized, they fired two rounds per gun. Most of the men had never fired a 75-mm. gun and many had never even seen one fired. The engineer battalion had been constructing a road since its arrival in camp and received no other training. The cadre of the signal company was commanded by a Filipino who had received inadequate training at Fort McKinley.

This man, who was to be division signal officer, was unable to establish radio communication with units a mile away in the same camp.

All officers in the division, with few exceptions, were Filipinos with little or no knowledge of tactics or of the method of training troops for combat. In some cases, their understanding of English was inadequate. As the war progressed, it became necessary to replace many of the Filipino battalion commanders with American officers. The enlisted men seemed to the division commander to be proficient in only two things: "one, when an officer appeared, to yell attention in a loud voice, jump up and salute; the other, to demand 3 meals per day." [37]

---

[36] In addition to General Bluemel's report, see Col. Clyde A. Selleck, Notes on the 71st Division, pp. 2–8, and Col. Ray M. O'Day, History of the 21st Division (PA), 2 vols., I, 1–5. Colonel Selleck commanded the 71st Division (PA) and Colonel O'Day was the senior American instructor with the 21st Division (PA). Both documents were borrowed from the authors and copies are on file in OCMH.

---

[37] Bluemel, 31st Div(PA) Rpt of Opns, p. 4.

CHAPTER III

The Reinforcement of the Philippines

When General MacArthur assumed command of U.S. Army Forces in the Far East, there was no program in the War Department for any immediate large-scale reinforcement of the Islands. As a matter of fact, the War Department specifically told MacArthur that he could have "no additional forces, except approximately 400 reserve officers to assist in training the Philippine Army. . . ."[1] Within a few days, there was a complete reversal of policy in the War Department. The first sign of this change came on 31 July when General Marshall approved a proposal by the War Plans Division to reinforce the Islands' defense "in view of the possibility of an attack."[2] The next day MacArthur was informed that he would receive substantial reinforcements and Marshall told his immediate staff, "It was the policy of the United States to defend the Philippines." This statement so impressed the Chief of the War Plans Division that he entered it in his office diary.[3]

The reasons for this change of policy are nowhere explicitly stated. Undoubtedly many factors both political and military contributed to the American Government's firm stand in July and August 1941. One of these was recognition of the potentialities of air power and especially of the Army's new heavy bomber, the B–17, called the Flying Fortress. In Stimson's opinion, the success of B–17 operations in Europe was responsible for creating an optimistic view in the War Department that the Philippines could be successfully held.[4] A striking force of such heavy bombers, it was argued, would act as a deterrent to Japanese advances southward and would strengthen the United States position in the Far East.

Another cause for optimism was the recall of General MacArthur to active duty. No one knew as much as he about the Philippines and no one believed more completely that it could be held if the Japanese allowed sufficient time for reinforcement.

The possibility of establishing an effective defense against Japan in the Philippines and thereby preventing Japanese domination of the Western Pacific without altering the major lines of strategy already agreed upon "had the effect," Stimson said, "of making the War Department a strong proponent of maximum delay in bringing the

---

[1] Rad, TAG to CG USAFFE, No. 1712, 28 Jul 41, OCS 18136-39.

[2] Memo, WPD for CofS, 31 Jul 41, sub: Additional Armament for Phil, OCS 18812-61.

[3] Gen Gerow's Off Diary, entry of 31 Jul 41, OPD Exec O; rad, TAG to CG USAFFE, No. 1197, 31 Jul 41, AG 320.2 (7–28–41) Orgn and Reinf for USAFFE.

[4] Henry L. Stimson and McGeorge Bundy, On Active Service in Peace and War (New York: Harper & Brothers, 1948), p. 388.

Japanese crisis to a climax. . . . In their [Stimson's and Marshall's] eyes the Philippines suddenly acquired a wholly new importance and were given the highest priority on all kinds of military equipment." [5]

Ground Forces

The first official War Department program for a large-scale reinforcement of the Philippines during this period was proposed by War Plans on 14 August. In a memorandum for the Chief of Staff, General Gerow argued that those reasons which had limited the size of the Philippine garrison—lack of funds, personnel, and equipment, plus the inability of the Navy to support a large force—were no longer entirely valid. With its present strength, he pointed out, there was a real doubt if the Philippine garrison could resist a Japanese attack, a contingency which he considered probable in view of Japan's attitude. To strengthen the garrison and increase its chances of holding Luzon and especially Manila Bay, General Gerow recommended that the Philippines be reinforced by antiaircraft artillery, modern combat planes, and tanks. The amount that could be sent, Gerow admitted, would be limited by the number of ships available for transport duty to the Far East. "The best that can be done at the moment," therefore, would be "to adopt a definite plan of reinforcement and carry it forward as availability of shipping permits." [6]

Gerow's recommendations were approved and two days later, on 16 August, General MacArthur was notified that the following units would sail from San Francisco between 27 August and 5 September:

the 200th Coast Artillery Regiment (AA) consisting of 76 officers and 1,681 enlisted men; the 194th Tank Battalion (less Company B), with 54 tanks, 34 officers, and 390 enlisted men; and one company (155 men) of the 17th Ordnance Battalion. [7]

There had been some mention earlier of the possibility of sending a division to the Philippines, and on 5 September the Chief of Staff asked MacArthur if he wanted a National Guard division (probably the 41st). MacArthur replied that he did not need this division since he already had one U.S. Army division (the Philippine Division) and was mobilizing ten Philippine Army divisions. He asked instead for authority to reorganize the theoretically square Philippine Division into a triangular division, adding, "Equipment and supply of existing forces are the prime essential." "I am confident if these steps are taken with sufficient speed," he said, "that no further major reinforcement will be necessary for accomplishment of defense mission." [8]

The reinforcement of the Philippines now enjoyed the highest priority in the War Department. MacArthur's request for permission to reorganize the Philippine Division was approved immediately. He was promised additional aircraft as well as the funds needed for airfield construction and the antiaircraft guns and equipment to protect the fields once they were built. "I have directed," wrote General Marshall, "that United States Army Forces in the

---

[5] *Ibid.*, pp. 388–89.

[6] Memo, Gerow for CofS, 14 Aug 41, sub: Reinf of Phil, WPD 3251-55.

---

[7] Rad, TAG to CG USAFFE, No. 56, 16 Aug 41; memo, Brig Gen Harry L. Twaddle for TAG, 15 Aug 41, sub: Augmentation of Phil Dept. Both in AG 370.5 (8–1–41), Part I.

[8] Rads, Marshall to MacArthur, No. 121, 5 Sep 41 and MacArthur to Marshall, No. 277, 7 Sep 41, both in AG 320.2 (7–28–41) Orgn and Reinf for USAFFE.

Philippines be placed in highest priority for equipment including authorized defense reserves for fifty thousand men." [9]

As a result, General MacArthur's requests for men and supplies during the next few months received almost instant approval by the War Department. "I wish to express my personal appreciation for the splendid support that you and the entire War Department have given me along every line since the formation of this command," he told the Chief of Staff in a personal letter. "With such backing the development of a completely adequate defense force will be rapid." [10]

Through no fault of the War Department or a lack of desire on the part of the Chief of Staff, General MacArthur's confidence in the rapid development of an adequate defense for the Philippines was not entirely justified. The task was a heavy one and limited by many factors beyond the control of the military. The industrial capacity of the United States was only just beginning to turn to the production of war material; the needs of a rapidly expanding citizen army had to be met; Great Britain and Russia were in critical need of supplies; and shipping space was extremely limited.

The reinforcements promised MacArthur on 16 August were dispatched with the greatest speed and by 12 September General Marshall was able to report considerable progress. The antiaircraft artillery regiment, the tank battalion of 54 tanks, and reserve supplies had already been shipped from San Francisco. During the month, 50 more tanks, and 50 self-pro-

pelled mounts for 75-mm. guns were to be sent. [11]

These reinforcements reached MacArthur before the end of September. The arrival of the 200th Coast Artillery Regiment (AA) gave him 12 additional 3-inch guns, 24 37-mm. guns, and a similar number of machine guns. Armored reinforcement consisted of the 192d and 194th Tank Battalions each with 54 tanks. And he could count on 25 more 75-mm. guns on self-propelled mounts (SPM) already en route and due to arrive in Manila on 15 October. [12]

The arrival of the two tank battalions with their 108 light tanks, M–3, were a welcome addition to the Philippine garrison. On 21 November a Provisional Tank Group consisting of the 192d and 194th Tank Battalions and the 17th Ordnance Company (Armored) was established, with Col. James R. N. Weaver in command.

As Military Advisor, MacArthur had proposed a plan to protect the inland seas by emplacing heavy coastal guns at the entrance to the key straits leading into these waters. The War Department had approved this plan and sent 24 155-mm. guns (without fire control equipment) to the Philippine Commonwealth to carry out this program, scheduled for completion in April 1942. MacArthur now proposed to extend this plan to include northern Luzon and asked the War Department for 4 12-inch and 4 8-inch railway guns, 22 more 155-mm. guns, and 30 searchlights. When em-

[9] Rad, Marshall to MacArthur, No. 137, 9 Sep 41, AG 320.2 (7–28–41) Orgn and Reinf for USAFFE.

[10] Memo, CofS for President, 9 Sep 41, OCS 18136-48.

[11] Memo, Marshall for Stark, 12 Sep 41, OCS 18136-56-1/2.

[12] Memo, Gerow for SW, 2 Oct 41, sub: Personnel and Supplies for Phil, OCS 18136–70; memo, Brig Gen George F. Moore for CofS, 28 Oct 41, sub: Shipment of Tanks and SPM's, OCS 18136-65B; interv, author with Brig Gen Charles G. Sage, formerly CO 200th CA, 28 Feb 51.

placed, he argued, these guns would present an enemy advancing on Manila with "fixed position gunfire, the lightest of which will be of sufficient proportions to interfere with troop landings and the operations of lightly armored vessels."[13] The letter was received in Washington at the beginning of December, too late to result in action.[14]

General MacArthur's request for authority to reorganize the Philippine Division as a triangular division had been readily granted. To accomplish this reorganization, MacArthur said he needed an infantry regiment, a field artillery headquarters and headquarters battery, two field artillery battalions, a reconnaissance troop, and a military police platoon for the division.[15] The War Department agreed to provide these units and the staff began the detailed work necessary to select and ship them.

MacArthur's plans for the Philippine Division were explained in a letter he wrote to the Chief of Staff on 28 October. He wished, he said, to have the division at war strength and trained intensively for combat. "It would be impolitic," he thought, "to increase the number of Philippine Scouts above the authorized 12,000, for all recruits would be taken from Philippine Army reservists to serve at higher rates of pay than the Philippine Army can pay." The only way, then, to increase the strength of the division was to secure an additional infantry regiment and two battalions of artillery from the United States. With these units and the American 31st Infantry, he could form two American combat teams in the

Philippine Division. The Scouts thus released could be used to bring the 91st and 92d Coast Artillery Regiments of the Harbor Defenses up to strength, retain several small units already in existence, and provide station complements for Forts McKinley and Stotsenburg. The Philippine Division would then be free to train for combat and would be available "for instant use." "The entire plan," he told General Marshall, "will be placed in effect upon the arrival of the new regiment."[16]

MacArthur's plans included also the establishment of four major tactical commands, directly subordinate to USAFFE. On 2 October he requested authority, which was readily granted, to activate a headquarters and headquarters company for each "with average strength approximately those of Army Corps."[17] He also asked for army and corps troops to establish a balanced force, and for a field artillery brigade, a chemical company, three signal battalions, a medical supply depot, and a military police company, all at full strength and with complete organization and individual equipment. By the end of October he had requested almost 12,000 men: for the Philippine Division, 209 officers and 4,881 enlisted men; for army and corps troops, 340 officers and 6,392 enlisted men.

During the next month MacArthur continued to ask for additional units and individual specialists, and by the middle of November the War Department had approved for transfer to Manila 1,312 officers, 25 nurses, and 18,047 enlisted men belonging to units. Individual specialists totaled 200 officers and 2,968 enlisted men. The units

---

[13] Ltr, MacArthur to Marshall, 17 Nov 41, WPD 3251-69.

[14] Ltr, Marshall to MacArthur, — Dec 41 (not sent), WPD 4477-2.

[15] Rad, MacArthur to Marshall, No. 354, 17 Sep 41, AG 320.2 (7-28-41) Orgn and Reinf for USAFFE.

[16] Ltr, MacArthur to Marshall, 28 Oct 41, WPD 4477-2.

[17] Rad, MacArthur to TAG, No. 465, 2 Oct 41, AG 320.2 (7-28-41) Orgn and Reinf of USAFFE.

selected for this overseas movement, including the 34th Infantry for the Philippine Division, were scheduled for shipment, first for January 1942, but later, ironically, on 8 December 1941.[18]

These reinforcements and supplies were all intended for the regular U.S. Army establishment; requisitions for the Philippine Army were made and considered separately. His plan of induction had hardly been completed when MacArthur began to request from the War Department large amounts of supplies for his Philippine troops. During August alone he called for 84,500 Garand rifles (M1), 330 .30-caliber machine guns, 326 .50-caliber antiaircraft machine guns, 450 37-mm. guns, 217 81-mm. mortars, 288 75-mm. guns with high-speed adapters, and over 8,000 vehicles of all types for the ten Philippine Army divisions he planned to mobilize.[19] On 18 September he was told that because of lend-lease commitments and production schedules it would not be possible to send most of these items. Especially unwelcome was the news that Garand rifles were not available and that the Philippine Army divisions would have to continue to use the Enfield and '03's with which they were equipped.[20]

MacArthur nevertheless continued to request equipment for the Philippine Army, asking, on 10 September, for 125,000 steel helmets, as well as chemical, engineer, and signal equipment. A month later, the request for the helmets was approved. They would be shipped immediately and the other equipment would be shipped at a later date.[21]

Since the Philippine Army was not limited in size by law as was the U.S. Army, MacArthur was in the unique position of being able to raise as many troops as the War Department could equip. On 20 September he asked for "complete organizational equipment" for a number of army and corps units to be formed principally of Philippine Army personnel. Included were 2 155-mm. and 3 105-mm. howitzer regiments, a motorized battalion of 155-mm. guns, 3 antitank gun battalions, and service, signal, and medical units.[22] These requests were approved and a shipping schedule established.

Most disturbing was the shortage of light artillery and machine guns in the Philippine Army divisions. By the end of September the Philippine Army had only 48 75-mm. guns. At least 240 were required to equip the artillery regiments of the ten reserve divisions and another 36 for field artillery training centers. Also needed were 37-mm. guns for the antitank battalions and .50-caliber machine guns. Realizing that the supply of these guns was limited, MacArthur expressed a willingness to accept as substitutes obsolete models or smaller weapons. "Strongly recommend," he appealed to the Chief of Staff, "improvisation to the extent of providing substi-

---

[18] Ltr, MacArthur to Marshall, 28 Oct 41, WPD 4477-2; rad, MacArthur to Marshall, No. 354, 17 Sep 41, and memo, Twaddle for CofS, 4 Nov 41, sub; Reinf for Phil Dept, both in AG 320.2 (7–28–41) Orgn and Reinf for USAFFE.

[19] Rads, MacArthur to TAG, Nos. 122, 184, and 236, dated 15, 23, and 28 Aug 41, AG 400 (8–12–41) Supplies and Equip for USAFFE.

[20] Rad, TAG to CG USAFFE, No. 181, 19 Sep 41, and ltr, TAG to CG USAFFE, 23 Sep 41, sub: Supplies for Phil Army and Phil Dept, both in AG 400 (8–12–41) Supplies and Equip for USAFFE.

[21] Memo, Actg ACofS for TAG, 6 Oct 41, sub: Issue of Equip to USAFFE, G–4 27573-18.

[22] Rad, CG USAFFE to TAG, No. 378, 20 Sep 41, AG 400 (8–12–41) Supplies and Equip for USAFFE.

tute arrangement in spite of lowered efficiency for any types available in the United States." [23]

By mid-November, the War Department had taken action to ship 40 105-mm. howitzers to the Philippines. These weapons were to be given to U.S. Army units and would release to Philippine Army units a like number of 75's. In addition, 10 75-mm. pack howitzers were to be taken from the vital Canal Zone and 48 British 75-mm. guns and 123 .30-caliber machine guns from the equally important Hawaiian garrison for the Philippine Islands, an indication of the importance which the defense of the archipelago had acquired in the eyes of the War Department. From the United States itself would come 130 75-mm. guns, 35 37-mm. guns (M1916) and 14 .30-caliber machine guns. [24]

No action was taken until October to supply the thousands of vehicles MacArthur had requested. During that month a large number of jeeps, ambulances, trucks, and sedans became available and on the 15th the War Department released these vehicles for the Philippine Army, "subject to the availability of shipping." [25] A request for clothing for the Philippine Army was also approved, as was the equipment for ten 250-bed station hospitals and 180

sets of regimental infirmary equipment. [26] An early requisition for 500,000 C rations and enough 55-gallon drums to hold 1,000,000 gallons of gasoline was filled during the summer. Strangely enough, the drums arrived filled although the gasoline had not been requested. This unexpected windfall proved extremely fortunate. A large portion of the gasoline was stored on Bataan and was most welcome during the campaign. [27]

The approval of requisitions and orders for shipment did not result in any immediate increase in the supplies of the Philippine Army. Time was required to order the stocks from depots and factories, pack and ship them to the port of embarkation, find the vessels to transport them, and finally get them to the Islands. In September, the Navy began sending cruiser escorts with Army transports and merchant ships on their voyages between Hawaii and Manila. This procedure frequently meant that the transports had to stop at Honolulu, sometimes reload, and then sail west at a speed equal to that of the slowest vessel in the convoy.

The shipment of supplies was dependent upon the number of cargo vessels available to the Army. This number was never large and the Navy, for a time, threatened even this limited supply. In September the Navy announced its intention to convert three transports to escort carriers. General Marshall protested this decision vigorously,

---

[23] Rad, MacArthur to Marshall, No. 430, 27 Sep 41, AG 400 (8–12–41) Supplies and Equip for USAFFE.

[24] Rad, TAG to CG USAFFE, No. 506, 12 Nov 41; memo, WPD for CofS, 12 Nov 41, sub: Machine Guns, 37-mm. Guns and 75-mm. Guns for Ten Phil Army Div; rad, TAG to CG USAFFE, No. 541, 15 Nov 41. All in AG 400 (8–12–41) Supplies and Equip for USAFFE.

[25] Ltr, TAG to QMG, 15 Oct 41, sub: Issue of Equip to USAFFE, AG 400 (8–12–41) Supplies and Equip for USAFFE.

[26] Rad, QM USAFFE to TQMG, no number, 1 Oct 41; memo, SGO for G–4, 9 Oct 41, sub: Medical Supplies and Equip for Phil Army; ltr, TAG to SGO, 19 Nov 41, same sub. All in AGO 400 (8–12–41) Supplies and Equip for USAFFE.

[27] QM Rpt of Opns, p. 4, Annex XIII, USAFFE-USFIP Rpt of Opns.

pointing out to the Chief of Naval Operations that it would delay the delivery of much-needed reinforcements to MacArthur by over two months.[28] Despite the favorable outcome of this protest, a large backlog of troops and approximately 1,100,000 tons of equipment destined for the Philippines had piled up in U.S. ports or depots by November. A group of shipping experts, including representatives from the War Department General Staff, Office of the Quartermaster General, the Navy, and Maritime Commission, met on 10 November to discuss ways of breaking the shipping block. As a result of this meeting a shipping schedule was established which recognized the priority of the Philippines over Hawaiian defenses and advanced the troop movements scheduled for mid-January to 17 and 20 December. Altogether, nine vessels were assigned to the Manila route, to sail in November and December. They would bring to MacArthur one light and one heavy bombardment group, a pursuit group, one reconnaissance squadron, a regiment of infantry, a brigade of field artillery, two battalions of light artillery, together with ground and air service units.[29] Had these vessels, the last of which was to leave the United States on 20 December, reached the Philippines the Japanese would have faced a far stronger force when they landed on Luzon.

Air Forces

In July 1941 the air force in the Philippines was still a token force, unable to withstand "even a mildly determined and ill-equipped foe."[30] Air Corps headquarters in Washington had been urging for some time that additional planes be sent to the Philippines and the Joint Board, early in 1940, had proposed an increase in air strength for the island garrison.[31] The following July 1941 Maj. Gen. Henry H. Arnold, chief of the newly created Army Air Forces, came forward with the strongest proposal yet made for the reinforcement of the Philippines. This proposal called for the transfer to the Philippines of four heavy bombardment groups, consisting of 272 aircraft with 68 in reserve, and two pursuit groups of 130 planes each.[32] These planes, wrote Brig. Gen. Carl Spaatz, chief of the Air Staff, would not be used for an offensive mission, but to maintain "a strategical defensive in Asia.[33]

General Arnold's recommendations, approved in August, were not easily carried out.[34] To have raised that number of planes in the summer of 1941 would have meant stripping the fields in the United States as well as all other overseas bases. Moreover, many of the heavy bombers were still on the production lines. What could be scraped together was shipped immediately and by mid-August General Gerow re-

---

[28] Memo, Marshall for Stark, 25 Sep 41, sub: Conversion of Troop Transports, OCS 17396-56B.

[29] Memo, Gerow for ASW, 10 Nov 41, sub: Shipping for Phil, OCS 18136-121.

[30] Wesley F. Craven and James L. Cate, eds., *The Army Air Forces in World War II*, Vol. I, *Plans and Early Operations: January 1939 to August 1942* (Chicago, 1948), 177.

[31] Mark Skinner Watson, *The Office of the Chief of Staff: Prewar Plans and Preparations*, UNITED STATES ARMY IN WORLD WAR II (Washington, 1950) p. 416.

[32] Memo, Arnold, for CofS, 19 Jul 41, cited in Craven and Cate, *The Army Air Forces in World War II*, I, 178.

[33] Memo, Spaatz for Maj Gen George H. Brett, 26 Aug 41, cited in Army Air Action in Phil and NEI, p. 12.

[34] MacArthur on 31 July had already been told of plans to send him a squadron of B–17's. Rad, TAG to CG USAFFE, No. 1197, 31 Jul 41, AG 320.2 (7–28–41) Orgn and Reinf for USAFFE.

ported to the Chief of Staff that thirty-one modern fighters of the P–40 type were on their way. Meanwhile General Arnold made arrangements to send fifty more directly from the factory. These, too, were soon on their way and by 2 October had arrived in the Philippines.[35]

Some weeks earlier a historic flight of nine Flying Fortresses had reached Manila by air. These planes were part of the 19th Bombardment Group (H), which had been selected for transfer to the Far East. After a flight from Hamilton Field near San Francisco, the Group's 14th Squadron, under Maj. Emmett O'Donnell, Jr., left Hickam Field in Hawaii on 5 September for Clark Field via Midway, Wake, Port Moresby, and Darwin. This pioneering 10,000-mile flight, almost all of it over water, was successfully concluded a week later, establishing the fact that the Philippines could be reinforced by air.[36] But the Midway–Wake route could not be considered safe in the event of war with Japan since it passed over the mandated islands and work was begun after October to develop a South Pacific ferry route.[37]

Once the pioneering flight had been successfully concluded, all heavy bombers sent to the Philippines went by air via the Central Pacific route. On 9 September, General Marshall told MacArthur that two additional squadrons of the 19th Group— the 30th and 93d—would leave the next month. At that time the ground echelon of the two squadrons and the headquarters sailed from San Francisco. The air echelon of twenty-six B–17's followed soon after. By 22 October these planes had arrived at Hickam Field in Hawaii. After a short stopover they flew on to Clark Field where all but two reported on 4 November; the other two followed soon after.

The flight of the 30th and 93d Squadrons was one in a scheduled series which called for the shipment of 33 heavy bombers in December, 51 in January 1942, and 46 more in February. By March 1942 the War Department planned to have 165 heavy bombers in the Philippines.[38]

Scheduled for shipment after the 19th Bombardment Group was the 7th. The ground echelon reached Hawaii late in November and was held there until naval escort could be secured. The air echelon, scheduled to fly to the Philippines via the Midway route during late November and early December, had completed only the first leg of the journey before war came.[39]

In addition to heavy bombers, MacArthur was also promised a light bombardment group of three combat squadrons. Selected for shipment was the 27th Bom-

---

[35] Memo, Gerow for CofS, 14 Aug 41, sub: Reinf of Phil, WPD 3251-55; rad, TAG to CG USAFFE, No. 56, 16 Aug 41, and memo, Twaddle for TAG, 15 Aug 41, sub: Augmentation of Phil Dept, both in AG 370.5 (8–1–41), Part I; memo, CofS for Stark, 12 Sep 41, OCS 18136-56-1/2; memos, Gerow for SW, 2 Oct and 10 Nov 41, subs: Personnel and Supplies for Phil and Shipping for Phil, OCS 18136-70 and 121.

[36] The arrangements made for this flight and the details of the trip are described in Army Air Action in Phil and NEI, pp. 12–20. A readable account of the flight can be found in Walter D. Edmonds, *They Fought With What They Had* (Boston, 1951), pp. 1–13.

[37] For a full discussion of this important route, which later became the chief link between the United States and New Zealand and Australia, see Development of the South Pacific Air Route, AAF Hist Study 45, Air University Hist Off.

---

[38] Army Air Action in Phil and NEI, pp. 24, 29. Estimated production of B–17's and B–24's for the period was 220 aircraft, thus demonstrating the importance which the War Department attached to the defense of the Philippines at this time.

[39] *Ibid.*

bardment Group (L). The Air Corps experienced some difficulty in securing the 52 A–24's for this group but by early November the planes had been collected. The pilots and ground personnel reached the Philippines during November but the A–24's, loaded on a separate transport, were held at Hawaii with the ground echelon of the 7th Bombardment Group and failed to reach their destination.[40]

At the end of November General Marshall summarized for the Secretary of War the air reinforcements already shipped or scheduled for shipment to the Philippines. At that time, he noted, there were 35 B–17's already in the Islands and 52 A–24's were due there—they never arrived—on the 30th. Fifty P–40's had reached MacArthur in September, Marshall explained to Stimson, thus giving him a total of 81 modern fighters. In addition, 24 P–40's had left San Francisco on 19 October, and 40 more on 9 November. By 31 December, General Marshall estimated, the Philippines should have a total of 240 fighters of the latest type.[41]

By now the War Department was fully committed to an all-out effort to strengthen the air defense of the Philippines. General Arnold, in a letter to the commander of the Hawaiian Air Force on 1 December, expressed this view when he wrote: "We must get every B–17 available to the Philippines as soon as possible." [42] His statement was not an exaggeration. On the outbreak of war there were 913 U. S. Army aircraft scattered among the numerous overseas bases. This number of aircraft included 61 heavy, 157 medium, and 59 light bombers and 636 fighters. More than half of the total of heavy bombers and one sixth of the fighters were already in the Philippines.[43] (See Table 3.) Within a few months this number would have been raised considerably.

The arrival of the bombers and additional pursuit planes, with the promise of more to come, led to a reorganization of the air forces in the Philippines. Early in the fall of 1941 General MacArthur had asked for Maj. Gen. Lewis H. Brereton, a senior air officer, as his air commander. This request was approved and early in October Brereton was relieved of command of the Third Air Force and called to Washington. There, in a series of conferences at Army Air Force headquarters, the form of a new air organization, to be called the Far East Air Force, was drawn up.[44]

General Brereton arrived in the Philippines on 3 November. He saw MacArthur that same day, and gave him the latest views about reinforcements and developments within the War Department. By the middle of the month the reorganization of the air forces had been accomplished and a short time later MacArthur told Marshall,

---

[40] Ibid.

[41] Memo, Marshall for SW, 25 Nov 41, sub: Reinf of Phil, OCS 18136–124. A detailed account of the air reinforcements sent to the Philippines can be found in Army Air Action in Phil and NEI, Chs. I and II. A condensation of this account has been published in Craven and Cate, The Army Air Forces in World War II, I, 175–85. For training and state of readiness of the Far East Air Force, see Edmonds, They Fought With What They Had, pp. 43–56.

[42] Ltr, Arnold to Maj Gen Frederick L. Martin, 1 Dec 41, quoted in Craven and Cate, The Army Air Forces in World War II, I, 193.

[43] Craven and Cate, The Army Air Forces in World War II, I, 193; Army Air Forces in the War Against Japan, 1941–1942, (HQ AAF, 1945), pp. 2 ff.

[44] Army Air Action in Phil and NEI, p. 31.

Douglas B–18A

Martin B–10B

Republic P–35

Boeing B–17D

Curtiss P–40E

Boeing P–26A

TABLE 3—AIRCRAFT IN PHILIPPINES AND
HAWAII, 1 DECEMBER 1941

Type and Model	Philippines	Hawaii
Bombers:		
B–17C [a]	35	12
B–17D [a]		
B–18A	18	33
A–20A [a]	0	12
A–27	9	0
B–10B	12	0
Fighters:		
P–40C [a]	0	12
P–40B [a]	0	87
P–40E [b]	107	39
P–36A	0	14
P–26A	16	0
P–35A	52	0
Misc. (Incl. Obsn, Cargo, etc.)	24 34	22
TOTAL	277	231

[a] Modern combat aircraft.

[b] There is disagreement in all sources on the figure of 107 P–40's. Some writers place the figure at 90 and Walter D. Edmonds estimates that there were "only 54 first-line, combat-worthy fighter planes to throw against the Japanese on the morning of December 8." *They Fought With What They Had,* p. xii.

Sources: For the Philippines, memo, Gerow for CofS, — Nov 41, sub: Airplanes in P. I., Incl 1, 19 Nov 41, WPD 3633-20. The P–40 strength is from memo, CofS for SW, 25 Nov 41, sub: Reinf of Phil, OCS 18136-124; Craven and Cate, *The Army Air Forces in World War II,* I, 191-92.

For Hawaii, Craven and Cate, *The Army Air Forces in World War II,* I, 171.

"Brereton has taken hold in an excellent manner." [45]

The newly activated Far East Air Force, with headquarters at Nielson Field in Manila, included the V Bomber Command, the V Interceptor Command, and the Far East Service Command. The main element of the bomber command, led by Lt. Col. Eugene L. Eubank, was the 19th Bombardment Group with its thirty-five B–17's. Only two squadrons of the original group, the 30th and 93d, were in the Philippines. On 16 November, the 28th Squadron, a medium unit, was also assigned to the group and equipped with B–17's and on 2 December the 14th Squadron joined the group. In addition to heavy units, the bomber command also contained the ground echelon of the 27th Bombardment Group, whose fifty-two A–24's were delayed at Hawaii and never reached the Philippines. [46]

The V Interceptor Command, first under Brig. Gen. Henry B. Clagett and later Col. Harold H. George, consisted initially of the 24th Pursuit Group with the 3d, 17th, and 20th Squadrons. When, in November, the

[45] Lt. Gen. Lewis H. Brereton, *The Brereton Diaries, 3 October 1941–8 May 1945* (New York: William Morrow & Company, Inc., 1946), p. 18; ltr, MacArthur to Marshall, 29 Nov 41, WPD 3489-21; USAFFE GO 28, 14 Nov 41, copy in History of the Fifth Air Forces (And Its Predecessors), App II, Doc 3, Air University Hist Off.

[46] *Pearl Harbor Attack, Hearings Before the Joint Committee on the Investigation of the Pearl Harbor Attack* (Washington, 1946), Part 11, pp. 5317–39. This source will be hereafter cited as the *Pearl Harbor Attack Hearings.* The Joint Committee hearings produced altogether 39 volumes, 11 of which contain the hearings themselves and 18 the exhibits presented during the course of the hearings. A separate volume, the 40th, contains both the majority and minority reports.

21st and 34th Squadrons arrived in Manila, they were attached to the group, pending arrival of their own organization (which never arrived). The Interceptor Command was considerably modernized during the fall of 1941 and by 7 December all but one of its pursuit squadrons were equipped with P–40's.[47]

The prerequisites for an effective air force are not only modern and sufficiently numerous attack and interceptor aircraft, but adequate fields, maintenance and repair facilities, and the antiaircraft artillery and air warning service to defend these installations. The lack of fields in the Philippines was recognized early. Within eighty miles of Manila there were six fields suitable for pursuit planes and only one, Clark, for heavy bombers. Outside of Luzon were six additional Army fields, useful principally for dispersal. More were needed to base the large number of modern aircraft due to arrive before the end of the year. In August General MacArthur was allotted $2,-273,000 for airfield development and in October $7,000,000 more. The largest part of these funds was to be expended on Luzon, at Nichols and Clark Fields, with auxiliary fields at Iba, on the Zambales coast west of Clark, and various points on northern Luzon.[48]

In mid-November MacArthur decided to establish a heavy bomber base in northern Mindanao at Del Monte, which since September had had a strip capable of landing B–17's. This decision was based on the belief that heavy bombers on Luzon would be subject to attack and that they should therefore be moved south, out of reach of the enemy. His plans, MacArthur told the Chief of Staff on 29 November, called ultimately for a bomber base in the Visayas, but until such a base was completed he expected to use the field at Del Monte.[49] Work on Del Monte Field was rushed and by the beginning of December it was able to accommodate heavy bombers.[50]

Despite the arrival of reinforcements and the airfield construction program, the air defense system remained inadequate because of the shortage of antiaircraft artillery and aircraft warning equipment. MacArthur had requested warning equipment in September and had at that time presented a plan for the establishment of an air warning service. The War Department had approved the project and by mid-September three radar sets had been shipped with three more scheduled for shipment in October. In addition, $190,000 was allotted for aircraft warning construction, with an additional $200,000 to be included in the supplemental estimate for the fiscal year 1942 for the construction of three detector stations and one information center.

The one air warning service company of 200 men in the Philippines was entirely inadequate to the needs of the Far East Air Force. In November General Arnold recommended, and the Chief of Staff approved, the shipment of an aircraft warning

---

[47] Army Air Action in Phil and NEI, pp. 33, 43.
[48] Ibid., pp. 11, 22.

[49] Ltr, MacArthur to Marshall, 29 Nov 41, WPD 3489-21.
[50] Army Air Action in Phil and NEI, p. 47; Craven and Cate, The Army Air Forces in World War II, I, 188; Edmonds, They Fought With What They Had, pp. 53–56.

CLARK FIELD *looking westward. In the upper left center, abutting the foothills of the Zambales Mountains, lies Fort Stotsenburg. The rectangular, tree-lined area is the parade ground.*

service battalion to the Philippines.[51] The 557th Air Warning Battalion was organized in the United States and on 6 December 1941 arrived in San Francisco, too late for shipment to the Philippines.

When war came there were seven radar sets in the Islands, but only two had been set up and were in operation. In the absence of the necessary equipment and personnel, USAFFE had organized a makeshift air warning service. Native air watchers stationed at strategic points reported plane movements by telephone or telegraph to the interceptor command at Nielson Field, which in turn relayed the information to Clark. It was this primitive system,

augmented by the radar sets established at Iba and outside Manila, that was in operation when war came.[52]

That other prerequisite for a balanced air force, antiaircraft artillery, was also slow in reaching the Far East. In the Islands when MacArthur assumed command was the 60th Coast Artillery (AA). In anticipation of heavy reinforcements he organized in August the Philippine Coast Artillery Command with Maj. Gen. George F.

---

[51] Memo, Spaatz for CofS, 13 Nov 41, sub: Equip for Phil AWS, OCS 18136-112.

[52] Army Air Action in Phil and NEI, p. 45; Craven and Cate, *The Army Air Forces in World War II,* I, 186. On the basis of interviews and other evidence, and despite the statement of the aircraft warning officer, Walter Edmonds concludes that only one set, the one at Iba, was in operation. *They Fought With What They Had,* p. 59n.

Moore in command. Plans provided for an area defense of the four fortified islands in Manila Bay (Corregidor, El Fraile, Caballo, and Carabao) and the southern tip of Bataan. One antiaircraft gun battery with a platoon of searchlights was stationed at Fort Wint in Subic Bay. When the 200th Coast Artillery (AA) arrived in September it was ordered to Fort Stotsenburg to protect Clark Field. Both antiaircraft units were equipped with 3-inch and 37-mm. guns, .50-caliber machine guns, and 60-inch Sperry searchlights. The 3-inchers were an old model with a vertical range of 27,000 feet.[53]

The two antiaircraft units alone obviously could not defend the fields of the rapidly growing Far East Air Force, let alone meet civilian defense requirements. Of necessity, therefore, the air defenses included only the Manila Bay area and Clark Field; all other installations were left virtually without defense against air attack. General Brereton was rightly concerned about the lack of antiaircraft defense and observed, even before he left Washington, that sending heavy bombers to the Philippines without providing proper antiaircraft protection would probably be suicide. But there was little that could be done in the short time available. Maj. Gen. Joseph A. Green, Chief of Coast Artillery, suggested that elements of the Harbor Defenses be re-

assigned to antiaircraft duty, but the proposal was rejected.[54]

The War Department and the Air Forces continued to show concern over the antiaircraft defenses of the Islands, about which they did not have too clear a picture. A radio to General MacArthur for information elicited the reply on 27 November that an increase in armament was required and that detailed plans were being forwarded by mail.[55] These plans were sent on 1 December but even before then War Plans had recommended the dispatch of three antiaircraft regiments and two antiaircraft brigade headquarters to the Philippines. These units were to utilize the equipment then in the Islands, thus reducing shipping requirements. Action on this proposal was begun at the end of November, when time had almost run out. When war came, the antiaircraft defenses in the Philippines were little better than they had been three months earlier.[56]

Naval Forces

Naval forces assigned to the defense of the Philippines were organized into the U.S. Asiatic Fleet. Normally stationed in Asiatic waters, this fleet by mid-1941 was based in

---

[53] Rad, TAG to CG USAFFE, No. 1197, 31 Jul 41, AG 320.2 (7–28–41) Orgn and Reinf for USAFFE; Rpt of Phil CA Command and Harbor Defenses of Manila and Subic Bays, pp. 1–10, Annex VIII, USAFFE-USFIP Rpt of Opns.

An attempt was made after 7 December 1941 to provide the city of Manila with additional protection from air attack by splitting the 200th and forming another regiment, the 515th Coast Artillery (AA).

[54] Memos, Green for CofS, 5 and 7 Nov 41, sub: AAA Defenses in Phil, AG 320.2 (7–28–41) Orgn and Reinf for USAFFE; Army Air Action in Phil and NEI, p. 44.

[55] Rad, MacArthur to Marshall, No. 991, 27 Nov 41, AG 320.2 (7–28–41) Orgn and Reinf for USAFFE.

[56] Ltr, MacArthur to Marshall, 1 Dec 41, WPD 3489-21; ltr, Gen Moore to CG USAFFE, 29 Nov 41, sub: Modification of Armament, AG 320.2 (7–28–41) Orgn and Reinf of USAFFE; memo, Gerow for CofS, 29 Nov 41, sub: AAA Personnel for Phil, WPD 4559-8.

On 29 November permission was requested and secured to convert one battery of the 59th Coast Artillery (US) and two batteries of the 91st (PS) to antiaircraft.

Manila with headquarters in the Marsman Building. Admiral Thomas C. Hart commanded the fleet and reported directly to the Chief of Naval Operations in Washington. The 16th Naval District headquarters was at Cavite on the south shore of Manila Bay.

Hart's fleet consisted of the flagship, the heavy cruiser *Houston*; 1 light cruiser; 3 destroyer divisions with 13 overage four-stack, flush-deck destroyers of World War I vintage; and 17 submarines. The underwater craft were organized into Submarine Squadron 20, supported by tenders and 1 rescue vessel. Air elements of the fleet were under Patrol Wing 10, composed of 24 PBY's and 4 seaplane tenders. Patrol and miscellaneous craft included 7 gunboats, 1 yacht, 6 large minesweepers, 2 tankers, and 1 ocean-going tug. Also a part of the fleet but stationed in Shanghai was the U.S. Marine Corps' regiment, the 4th Marines.[57]

Obviously such a force was not capable of withstanding even momentarily the Japanese *Combined Fleet,* and Admiral Hart had authority to retire to bases in the Indian Ocean if necessary. From the small detachments of sailors in the 16th Naval District little more could be expected than assistance in protecting local naval installations. The 4th Marines could be of considerable help in the defense of the Philippines if it could be taken out of China in time.

Although Allied naval forces in the Far East were not expected to provide direct support for the Philippine Islands in case of war with Japan, they would, if Japan attacked them, fight the common enemy. The British, in May 1941, had in Far East-

ern waters 1 battleship, 1 aircraft carrier, 4 heavy and 13 light cruisers, and a few destroyers. The Dutch could contribute 3 light cruisers, 7 destroyers, and 15 submarines. By December of that year the British Fleet in the Far East had been augmented by 3 battleships and 3 destroyers.[58]

The bulk of American naval strength in the Pacific was assigned to the Pacific Fleet. Before 1940 the main body of the Pacific Fleet had been based on the west coast of the United States. In May 1940 the Navy announced that the fleet, which had sailed to Hawaiian waters for war games, would be based at Pearl Harbor indefinitely. This decision had been made by President Roosevelt in the belief that the presence of the fleet would act as a deterrent to Japan.[59] A year later the Pacific Fleet, now based at Pearl Harbor and commanded by Admiral Husband E. Kimmel, consisted of 9 battleships, 3 aircraft carriers, 12 heavy and 8 light cruisers, 50 destroyers, 33 submarines, and 100 patrol bombers. The strength of this fleet was substantially the same on 7 December 1941 when the attack on Pearl Harbor came.[60]

---

[58] *Ibid.,* Part 15, Exhibit 86, pp. 1901–06, and Exhibit 49 (The United States-British Staff Conversations report of 27 Mar 41), pp. 1485–1550. The short title of this second report is ABC–1.

[59] *Ibid.,* Part 16, Exhibit 106, pp. 2161–69; Samuel E. Morison, *History of United States Naval Operations in World War II,* Vol. III, *The Rising Sun in the Pacific, 1931–April 1942* (Boston, 1948), pp. 56–58.

[60] Navy Basic War Plan, RAINBOW 5, in *Pearl Harbor Attack Hearings,* Part 18, Exhibit 129, p. 2932. The vessels in the Southeast Pacific Force were added to those of the Pacific Fleet in these computations. These figures should be compared with those presented at the Joint Congressional Investigation and published in Part 15, Exhibit 86, pp. 1901–06. The latter figures show more light cruisers and destroyers than are listed in the RAINBOW plan.

---

[57] Navy Basic War Plan, RAINBOW 5, 26 May 41, in *Pearl Harbor Attack Hearings,* Part 18, Exhibit 129, p. 2932.

Although Admiral Hart had been told in May 1941 that he would receive no additional surface ships for his fleet, he was able to do much to put his force in readiness for action before the outbreak of war. Beginning in July, three to six PBY's maintained constant watch along the southern boundary of the archipelago and later linked with the Dutch Navy's air patrol north of Borneo. The mining of Manila and Subic Bays was pushed through to completion, in co-operation with the Army, by the end of August and provided security against all but submarines and shallow-draft surface craft. The Navy's base at Mariveles, on the southern tip of Bataan, was rapidly built up and on 22 July the drydock *Dewey* was moved there from Olongapo. By the end of the month the base at Olongapo was being used by the navy only as an auxiliary air base and as a station for Marines and some naval personnel.[61]

In the six months before war the Asiatic Fleet was reinforced strongly in underwater craft. On 8 November 8 large submarines of the Pacific Fleet arrived in Manila and on the 24th 4 more, accompanied by the tender *Holland,* joined the fleet. Together with those already assigned, Admiral Hart now had 29 submarines.[62]

The fleet was further reinforced in September by six motor torpedo boats, considered ideally suited for operation in Philippine waters. Twelve had been allocated but the remainder were never received. In addition, General MacArthur told Admiral Hart that he would mobilize the naval com-

ponent of the Philippine Army, with its two motor torpedo boats, whenever Hart desired.[63]

Early in November the Navy Department directed Hart to withdraw the marines and the gunboats from China, a move which the admiral had proposed earlier. Five of the gunboats made the trip from China to Manila successfully, leaving the *Wake,* stripped and ready for demolition—it was later seized by the Japanese—and the *Tutuila* for the Chinese. Two *President* liners were chartered and sent to Shanghai where the majority of the 4th Marines was stationed; the detachments at Pekin and Tientsin were to load at Chinwangtao. On 27 and 28 November the regiment, with attached naval personnel and civilian refugees, embarked on the two vessels for the Philippines. Arriving on 30 November and 1 December, the regiment was assigned the mission of guarding the naval stations on Luzon, particularly the new base at Mariveles. One of the vessels, the *President Harrison,* started back to Chinwangtao to embark the remaining marines but fell into Japanese hands. With its weapons and equipment, and consisting of long service men and a full complement of regular officers, the 4th Marines (strength, 750 men) formed a valuable addition to the infantry force in the Islands.[64]

[61] Admiral Thomas C. Hart, Narrative of Events, Asiatic Fleet Leading up to War and from 8 December 1941 to 15 February 1942 (hereafter cited as Hart, Narrative of Events, Asiatic Fleet), pp. 16–18.

[62] *Ibid.,* pp. 27, 31.

[63] Ltr, MacArthur to Marshall, 28 Oct 41, WPD 4477-2; William L. White, *They Were Expendable* (Cleveland, 1944), pp. 4–6.

[64] Hanson W. Baldwin, "The Fourth Marines at Corregidor," in four parts, *Marine Corps Gazette* (November 1946–February 1947), Part 1, p. 14; Hart, Narrative of Events, Asiatic Fleet, pp. 32–33; Morison, *Rising Sun in the Pacific,* p. 155; Brig Gen Samuel L. Howard, Rpt on 4th Marines, Sep 41–6 May 42, 26 Sep 45, USMC Hist Sec. This last report was written from memory and notes by Howard after his release from prison camp in 1945.

Summary

In a letter prepared on 5 December 1941 but never sent, General Marshall outlined for General MacArthur what had been and was being done to strengthen USAFFE. "Reinforcements and equipment already approved," he said, "require over 1,000,000 ship tons." Fifty-five ships had already been obtained and approximately 100,000 ship tons of supplies were en route, with twice this amount ready for immediate shipment to ports of embarkation. Requests for equipment for the Philippine Army, except those for the M1 rifle, had been approved, and uncontrolled items of supply were being shipped as rapidly as they could be assembled and loaded on ships. "Not only will you receive soon all your supporting light artillery [130 75-mm. guns]," Marshall told MacArthur, "but 48 155-mm. howitzers and 24 155-mm. guns for corps and army artillery." Except for certain types of ammunition, the defense reserve for the U.S. Army forces in the Philippines would be completed in April 1942, and for the Philippine Army by July of that year. Three semimobile antiaircraft artillery regiments were scheduled to leave the United States soon, but the 90-mm. antiaircraft gun could not be sent since it had not yet been fully tested. A sum of $269,000,000 had been requested from Congress for the support of the Philippine Army, and early passage of such legislation was expected. "I assure you," Marshall closed, "of my purpose to meit to the fullest extent possible your recommendations for personnel and equipment necessary to defend the Philippines." [65]

---

[65] Draft ltr, Marshall to MacArthur, —Dec 41 (not sent), WPD 4477-2. Memorandum attached states letter was prepared 5 December, but WPD on 11 December recommended it not be sent.

The last vessels carrying supplies to the Philippines were assembled in convoy in Hawaii and on 7 December were still on the high seas. In the convoy were the 52 dive bombers of the 27th Bombardment Group, 18 P-40's, 340 motor vehicles, 48 75-mm. guns, 3,500,000 rounds of .30- and .50-caliber ammunition, 600 tons of bombs, 9,000 drums of aviation fuel, and other heavy equipment and supplies. Also aboard were the two light field artillery battalions and the ground echelon of the 7th Bombardment Group (H).

The military force in the Islands at the beginning of December, while not as large as MacArthur soon hoped to have, was considerably larger than it had been five months earlier. The air force had been reorganized, modern bombers and fighters had been brought in, and a start made on the creation of a balanced force. The strength of air force troops on 30 November was 5,609, more than double the July strength. The Far East Air Force had more than 250 aircraft, concentrated largely on Luzon. Less than half of these planes were suitable for combat, and much of the equipment was still in ports of embarkation. There were 35 B-17's at Clark Field and 107 P-40's at various fields on Luzon. A primitive aircraft warning system was in operation, and an antiaircraft artillery regiment was stationed at Clark Field. Much remained to be done, but the Philippines could boast a stronger air complement of modern combat aircraft on 7 December than any other base, including Hawaii and Panama.

Naval forces assigned to the Asiatic Fleet had also been considerably strengthened. By 7 December this fleet consisted of 1 heavy and 2 light cruisers, 13 old destroyers, 32 PBY's, 6 gunboats, 6 motor torpedo boats, and miscellaneous vessels. Its

TABLE 4—STRENGTH AND COMPOSITION OF U.S. ARMY TROOPS IN PHILIPPINE ISLANDS, 30 NOVEMBER 1941

Unit	Total	Officers	Enlisted		
			Total	American	Philippine Scouts
All Units...	31,095	ª 2,504	28,591	16,643	11,957
Hq USAFFE..	61	61	0	0	0
Hq and Hq Co Det Phil Dept.......................	553	249	304	304	0
Hq N Luzon Force..................................	38	38	0	0	0
Hq S Luzon Force..................................	10	10	0	0	0
Hq Visayan-Mindanao Force.........................	9	9	0	0	0
Philippine Division...............................	10,233	517	9,716	1,807	7,909
26th Cavalry......................................	842	55	787	0	787
43d Infantry......................................	328	15	313	0	313
86th FA Regt......................................	395	22	373	0	373
88th FA Regt......................................	538	34	504	0	504
808th MP Co.......................................	160	5	155	155	0
192d Tank Bn......................................	588	36	552	552	0
194th Tank Bn.....................................	410	36	374	374	0
200th CA AA.......................................	1,809	77	1,732	1,732	0
Harbor Defenses...................................	5,225	335	4,890	3,318	1,572
Hq and Hq Btry................................	438	42	396	326	70
59th CA.......................................	1,303	66	1,237	1,237	0
60th CA.......................................	1,765	72	1,693	1,693	0
91st CA.......................................	837	49	788	27	761
92d CA..	672	45	627	0	627
USAMP *Harrison*..............................	46	8	38	34	4
Station Hospital..............................	160	50	110	0	110
Chemical Warfare Det..........................	4	3	1	1	0
Air Corps...	5,609	669	4,940	4,940	0
Far East Air Force	237	43	194	194	0
Headquarters..................................	147	47	100	100	0
4th Composite Group...........................	326	11	315	315	0
19th Bomb Group...............................	1,374	183	1,191	1,191	0
24th Pursuit Group............................	1,264	187	1,077	1,077	0
27th Bomb Group...............................	804	87	717	717	0
2d Obsn Sq....................................	183	42	141	141	0
20th Air Base Group...........................	584	24	560	560	0
Tow Target Det................................	49	6	43	43	0
Weather Det...................................	20	1	19	19	0
5th Air Base Group............................	204	16	188	188	0
V Bomber Command..............................	21	1	20	20	0
48th Materiel Sq..............................	216	11	205	205	0
Chemical Warfare Det..........................	180	10	170	170	0
Service Detachments...............................	4,268	317	3,951	3,452	499
Quartermaster Corps...........................	821	38	783	487	296
Medical Dept..................................	757	187	570	507	63
Ordnance Dept.................................	1,050	40	1,010	1,010	0
Corps of Engineers............................	744	29	715	715	0
Signal Corps..................................	629	16	613	488	125
Chemical Warfare Det..........................	240	5	235	224	11
Finance Dept..................................	27	2	25	21	4
Other ᵇ...	19	19	0	0	0

ª Includes 31 Philippine Scout Officers.

ᵇ Includes officers for which no specific unit was indicated.

Source: Phil Dept, Machine Rcds Unit Station Strength and Misc., Officers and Enlisted men, Nov 41.

strongest element was the submarine force of 29 underwater craft.

Ground forces in the Philippines had been considerably reinforced, too, in the few months since General MacArthur had assumed command. The ten reserve divisions of the Philippine Army had been two-thirds mobilized and although poorly equipped and trained represented a military force of some size. Wthin a week after the outbreak of war it numbered over 100,000 men. The U.S. Army garrison in the Islands had been increased by 8,563 men since 31 July. The number of Philippine Scouts, fixed by law, remained the same, approximately 12,000. The number of American enlisted men increased by 7,473 and officers by 1,070. (*See Table 4;* compare with Table 2.) The largest proportionate increase was among service troops. As of 31 July, 1,836 men were assigned to service detachments; four months later the number had increased to 4,268. During this same period, the number of Air Corps troops had increased from 2,407 to 5,609.[66] Total strength of the en-

tire U.S. Army garrison on 30 November 1941 was 31,095 officers and enlisted men.

In the four months since General MacArthur's assumption of command, the flow of men and supplies to the Phillipines had increased tremendously and all preparations for war had been pushed actively and aggressively. Time was running out rapidly, but at the end of November many still thought it would be several months before the Japanese struck. The month of April 1942 was commonly accepted as the critical date and most plans were based on that date. By 1 December MacArthur had organized his forces, but still needed much to place them on a war footing. Most of his requests had been approved by the War Department and men and supplies were already on their way or at San Francisco awaiting shipment. The record of accomplishment was a heartening one and justified the optimism which prevailed in Washington and in the Philippines over the capacity of the Philippine garrison to withstand a Japanese attack.

---

[66] This strength is from a Machine Records Unit report dated 30 November 1941. The strength of the air forces as of 7 December 1941 was 754 officers and 6,706 enlisted men. Craven and Cate, *The Army Air Forces in World War II,* I, 170.

CHAPTER IV

Prewar Plans, Japanese and American

By the summer of 1941, as the United States was beginning to strengthen the Philippines, Japan had reached "the crossroads of her fate." [1] The economic sanctions imposed by America, Great Britain, and the Netherlands had cut her off from the strategic materials necessary to support the war in China and threatened eventually to so weaken the Japanese economy as to leave Japan defenseless in a struggle with a major power. The leaders of Japan were faced with a difficult choice. They could either reach agreement with the United States by surrendering their ambitions in China and southeast Asia, or they could seize Dutch and British possessions by force.

The second course, while it would give Japan the natural resources so sorely needed, almost certainly meant war with Great Britain and the Netherlands. In the view of the Japanese planners, the United States would also oppose such a course by war, even if American territory was not immediately attacked. Such a war seemed less dangerous to Japan in the fall of 1941 than ever before and, if their calculations proved correct, the Japanese had an excellent chance of success. The British Empire was apparently doomed and the menace of Russian action had been diminished by the German invasion of that country and by the Japanese-Soviet neutrality pact.

The major obstacles to Japan's expansion in southeast Asia was the United States. But Japanese strategists were confident they could deprive the United States of its western Pacific base in the Philippines and neutralize a large part of its Pacific Fleet at the start of the war. In this way they hoped to overcome America's potential superiority and seize the southern area rapidly.

The Japanese Plan

Japanese strategy for a war with the United States, Great Britain, and the Netherlands was apparently developed in about six months by *Imperial General Headquarters.* [2] Although this strategy was never em-

[1] History of the *Army Section, Imperial General Headquarters,* 1941–45, p. 9. This volume is No. 72 in the series, Japanese Studies in World War II, of which 113 are now available in OCMH in both the original and translated versions. Although both versions have been used in the preparation of this volume, reference throughout is to the translated version unless otherwise noted. For a description of this series see below, The Sources, pp. 595–96.

[2] Statement of Lt Gen Masami Maeda, CofS *14th Army,* 7 Mar 50, Allied Translator and Interpreter Section (ATIS), Document 56234, in Interrogations of Former Japanese Officers, Philippines-Japanese Invasion, Mil Hist Div, GHQ Far East Command (FEC) and Supreme Commander Allied Powers (SCAP), 2 vols., II. Joint Statements of Col Takushiro Hattori and Capt Sadatoshi Tomioka, chiefs of the Army and Navy Operations Sections, respectively, of *Imperial GHQ,* 3 May 49, ATIS Doc 50459, and of Lt Gen Shinichi Tanaka and Col Hattori, 3 May 49, ATIS Doc 52361, both in Statements of Japanese Officials on World War II, GHQ FEC, Mil Intel Sec, 4 vols., I, 352–53, IV, 196.

bodied in one document, it can be reconstructed from separate Army and Navy plans completed by the beginning of November 1941. Thereafter it was modified only in minor respects.[3]

Strategic Concepts

The immediate objective of Japanese strategy was the capture of the rich Dutch and British possessions in southeast Asia, especially Malaya and the Netherlands Indies. (*Map 2*) To secure these areas the Japanese believed it necessary to destroy or neutralize the U.S. Pacific Fleet at Pearl Harbor, deprive the United States of its base in the Philippines, and cut America's line of communications across the Pacific by the seizure of Wake and Guam. Once the coveted area to the south had been secured, Japan would occupy strategic positions in Asia and in the Pacific and fortify them immediately with all the forces available, chief reliance being placed on mobile

---

[3] The plan of operations worked out by Imperial GHQ about the middle of November 1941 was destroyed by fire. Certificate of Yozo Miyama, Chief, Archives Sec, *1st Demobilization Bureau,* Defense Doc 2726, International Military Tribunal for the Far East (IMTFE).

The description of Japanese strategic concepts is derived from the following documents: (1) Central Agreement Between the Japanese Navy and Army, (2) The Imperial Navy's Course of Action in Operations Against U.S., Great Britain, and the Netherlands, (3) *Combined Fleet* Top Secret Operation Order 1, 5 November 1941, and (4) Comments of Former Japanese Officers regarding The Fall of the Philippines. The first two are reproduced in United States Strategic Bombing Survey (USSBS), *The Campaigns of the Pacific War* (Washington, 1946), Apps. 13 and 14, pp. 43–49; copies of the last two are in OCMH. The orders and plans of the Army General Staff can be found in Hist *Army Sec, Imperial GHQ;* History of *Southern Army* 1941–1945, Japanese Studies in World War II, No. 21; *14th Army Opns*, 2 vols., Japanese Studies in World War II, Nos. 1 and 2.

naval and air forces. These positions were to form a powerful defensive perimeter around the newly acquired southern area, the home islands, and the vital shipping lanes connecting Japan with its sources of supply.

The area marked for conquest formed a vast triangle, whose east arm stretched from the Kuril Islands on the north, through Wake, to the Marshall Islands. The base of the triangle was formed by a line connecting the Marshall Islands, the Bismarck Archipelago, Java, and Sumatra. The western arm extended from Malaya and southern Burma through Indochina, and thence along the China coast. The acquisition of this island-studded area would give to Japan control of the resources of southeast Asia and satisfy the national objectives in going to war. Perhaps later, if all went well, the area of conquest could be extended. But there is no evidence that it was the intention of the Japanese Government or of the Army and Navy to defeat the United States, and so far as is known no plan was ever drawn up for that purpose. Japan apparently planned to fight a war of limited objectives and, having gained what it wanted, expected to negotiate for a favorable peace.

Operations to secure these objectives and others would begin on the first day of war when Japanese military and naval forces would go into action simultaneously on many fronts. Navy carrier-based aircraft would attack Pearl Harbor. Immediately after, joint Army and Navy air forces would strike American air and naval forces in the Philippines, while other Japanese forces hit British Malaya. After these simultaneous attacks, advance Army units were to be landed at various points in Malaya and the Philippines to secure air bases and favor-

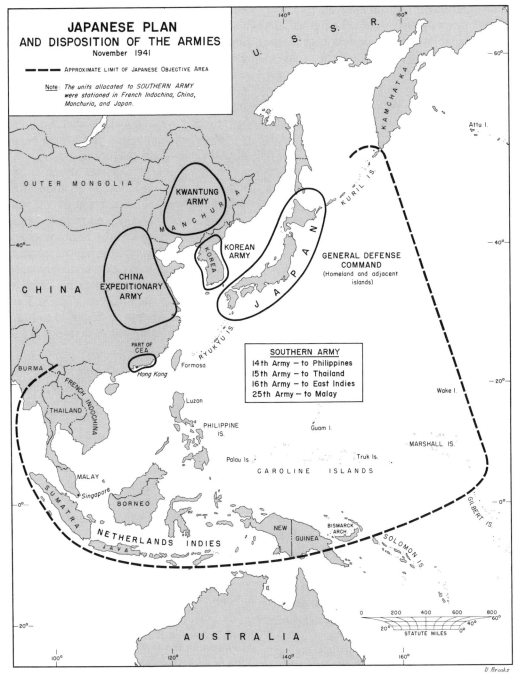

JAPANESE PLAN
AND DISPOSITION OF THE ARMIES
November 1941

▬ ▬ APPROXIMATE LIMIT OF JAPANESE OBJECTIVE AREA

Note: *The units allocated to SOUTHERN ARMY were stationed in French Indochina, China, Manchuria, and Japan.*

U. S. S. R.

KAMCHATKA

Attu I.

OUTER MONGOLIA

KWANTUNG ARMY

MANCHURIA

KOREAN ARMY

KOREA

CHINA EXPEDITIONARY ARMY

CHINA

GENERAL DEFENSE COMMAND
(Homeland and adjacent islands)

J A P A N

KURIL IS.

PART OF CEA

Hong Kong

RYUKYU IS.

Formosa

BURMA

FRENCH INDOCHINA

THAILAND

SOUTHERN ARMY
14th Army — to Philippines
15th Army — to Thailand
16th Army — to East Indies
25th Army — to Malay

Luzon

PHILIPPINE IS.

Wake I.

Guam I.

MARSHALL IS.

Palau Is.

Truk Is.

CAROLINE ISLANDS

MALAY

Singapore

BORNEO

SUMATRA

NETHERLANDS INDIES

JAVA

NEW GUINEA

BISMARCK ARCH.

SOLOMON IS.

GILBERT IS.

AUSTRALIA

0   200   400   600   800
STATUTE MILES

U. Brooks

MAP 2

able positions for further advances. The results thus obtained were to be immediately exploited by large-scale landings in the Philippines and in Malaya and the rapid occupation of those areas. At the same time Thailand was to be "stabilized," Hong Kong seized, and Wake and Guam occupied. The conquest of the Bismarck Archipelago would follow the seizure of the last two islands.

The occupation of Java and Sumatra was to begin after this initial period. While Java was being attacked from the air, Singapore was to be taken under fire from the land side by Japanese forces moving down the Malay Peninsula. Once that fortress was reduced these forces were to move on to northern Sumatra. Meanwhile, other Japanese forces moving southward through the Netherlands Indies were to join those in Sumatra in the final attack on Java.

Japanese planners anticipated that certain events might require an alteration of these plans and accordingly outlined alternative courses of action. The first possibility was that the Japanese-American negotiations then in progress would prove successful and make war unnecessary. If this unexpected success was achieved all operations were to be suspended, even if the final order to attack had been issued.[4] The second possibility was that the United States might take action before the attack on Pearl Harbor by sending elements of the Pacific Fleet to the Far East. In that event, the *Combined Fleet* would be deployed to intercept American naval forces. The attacks against the Philippines and Malaya were to proceed according to schedule.

If the Americans or British launched lo-

cal attacks, Japanese ground forces were to meet these while air forces were brought into the area to destroy the enemy. These local operations were not to interrupt the execution of the grand plan. But if the United States or Great Britain seized the initiative by opening operations first, Japanese forces were to await orders from *Imperial General Headquarters* before beginning their assigned operations.

The possibility of a Soviet attack or of a joint United States-Soviet invasion from the north was also considered by the Japanese planners. If such an attack materialized, operations against the Philippines and Malay would be carried out as planned while air units would be immediately transferred from the home islands or China to destroy Russian air forces in the Far East. Ground forces were to be deployed to Manchuria at the same time to meet Soviet forces on the ground.

The forces required to execute this ambitious plan were very carefully calculated by *Imperial General Headquarters*. At the beginning of December 1941 the total strength of the Army was 51 divisions, a cavalry group, 59 brigade-size units, and an air force of 51 air squadrons. In addition, there were ten depot divisions in Japan.[5] These forces were organized into area commands widely scattered throughout the Far East. (*See Table 5.*) The largest number of divisions was immobilized in China and large garrisons were maintained

---

[4] Hist *Army Sec, Imperial GHQ*, pp. 10, 15; *14th Army Opns*, I, 15.

[5] Data on the strength of the Japanese Army and Navy are derived from Hist *Army Sec, Imperial GHQ*, p. 30. A mixed brigade at this time consisted of three to six infantry battalions in addition to supporting and service troops. Strength varied from 3,000 to 10,000 men. An air regiment was generally composed of three squadrons and was the basic operational unit in the Japanese Army Air Force.

TABLE 5—ORGANIZATION AND DISPOSITION OF JAPANESE ARMY, 1 DECEMBER 1941

Area	Headquarters	Divisions	Brigades [a]	Air Squadrons
Homeland	Imperial GHQ General Defense Command [b]			
	Eastern District Army	52 Division	4	
		Imperial Guard, 2d, 3d, 51st, 57th Depot Divisions		
	Central District Army	53, 54th Divisions	3	
		4th, 5th, 55th Depot Divisions		
	Western District Army	6th, 56th Depot Divisions	3	
	Northern District Army	7th Division	1	
	1st Air Group			9
Manchuria	Kwantung Army	10th, 28th, 29th Divisions	1	
	3d Army	9th, 12th Divisions	4	
	4th Army	1st, 14th, 57th Divisions	5	
	5th Army	11th, 24th Divisions	4	
	6th Army	23d Division	1	
	20th Army	8th, 25th Divisions	4	
	Defense Command		5	
	Air Corps (Directly attached units)			21
	2d Air Group			35
China	China Expeditionary Army			
	North China Area Army	27th, 35th, 110th Divisions	5	
	1st Army	36th, 37th, 41st Divisions	3	
	12th Army	17th, 32d Divisions	3	
	Mongolia Garrison Army	26th Division, Cavalry Group	1	
	11th Army	3d, 6th, 13th, 34th, 39th, 40th Divisions	2	
	13th Army	15th, 22d, 116th Divisions	5	
	23d Army	38th, 51st, 104th Divisions	1	
		4th Division (at Shanghai under direct command of Imperial GHQ)		
	1st Air Brigade			16
Korea	Korea Army	19th, 20th Divisions		
Formosa	Formosa Army			
For the South	Southern Army [c]	21st Division	1	
	14th Army	16th, 48th Divisions	1	
	15th Army	33d, 55th Divisions		
	16th Army	2d Division	1	
	25th Army	Imperial Guard, 5th, 18th, 56th Divisions		
	3d Air Group			48
	5th Air Group			20
	21st Ind Air Unit			2
	South Seas Detachment (at Bonins under direct command of Imperial GHQ)		1	
Total		51	59	151

Remarks:

  [a] Brigades include all brigade size units, i. e., garrison forces in China and Manchuria, South Seas Det., etc.

  [b] Command of the General Defense Command over each district army and the 1st Air Army in the Homeland was limited to only the matters pertaining to defense of the Homeland.

  [c] Although the 21st, 33d and 56th Divisions were assigned to the Southern Army, they were still in North China, Central China and Kyushu, respectively, on 1 December 41. Their departures from the above areas were 20 January 1942 13 December 1941 and 16 February 1942, respectively. 56th Division was placed under the command of 25th Army on 27 November 1941.

Source: Compiled by the Reports and Statistical Division of the *Demobilization Bureau,* 14 January 1952.

in Manchuria, Korea, Formosa, Indochina, and the home islands. Only a small fraction of Japan's strength, therefore, was available for operations in southeast Asia and the Pacific.

In the execution of this complicated and intricate plan, the Japanese planners realized, success would depend on careful timing and on the closest co-operation between Army and Navy forces. No provision was made for unified command of the services. Instead, separate agreements were made between Army and fleet commanders for each operation. These agreements provided simply for co-operation at the time of landing and for the distribution of forces.

The Plan for the Philippines

The Japanese plan for the occupation of the Philippines was but part of the larger plan for the Greater East Asia War in which the *Southern Army* was to seize Malaya and the Netherlands Indies while the *Combined Fleet* neutralized the U.S. Pacific Fleet. The *Southern Army* was organized on 6 November 1941, with Gen. Count Hisaichi Terauchi, who had been War Minister in 1936, as commander. His orders from *Imperial General Headquarters* were to prepare for operations in the event that negotiations with the United States failed. Under his command were placed the *14th, 15th, 16th and 25th Armies,* comprising ten divisions and three mixed brigades. *Southern Army*'s mission in case of war would be to seize American, British, and Dutch possessions in the "southern area" in the shortest time possible. Operations against the Philippines and British Malaya were to begin simultane-

ously, on orders from *Imperial General Headquarters.*[6]

Southern Army immediately began to prepare plans for seizure of the southern area. To *14th Army,* consisting of the *16th* and *48th Divisions* and the *65th Brigade,* was assigned the task of taking the Philippine Islands. The campaign in the East Indies was to be under the control of *16th Army;* the *15th Army* would take Thailand. The *25th Army* was assigned the most important and difficult mission, the conquest of Malaya and Singapore, and was accordingly given four of the *Southern Army*'s ten divisions. Air support for these operations was to be provided by two air groups and an independent air unit. The *5th Air Group* was assigned to the Philippine campaign.[7]

Beginning on 10 November a number of meetings attended by the senior army and navy commanders were held in Tokyo to settle various details in the execution of the plans. The commanders of the *14th, 16th,* and *25th Armies,* in session with the Premier (who was also the War Minister), the Army Chief of Staff, and General Terauchi, were shown the *Imperial General Headquarters* operational plans, given an outline of the strategy, and told what their missions would be in the event of war. In the discussions between Army and Navy commanders that followed this meeting a few modifications were made in the general strategy and the specific operational plans

---

[6] *Southern Army* Opns, p. 6. The operations order given by the commander of the *Southern Army* was destroyed by fire. Certificate of Yozo Miyama, *1st Demob Bureau,* Defense Doc 2726, IMTFE.

[7] *Southern Army* Opns, pp. 4–6. An air group was roughly the equivalent of a U.S. numbered air force, and was the largest tactical unit in the Japanese Army Air Force at that time.

were put into final form.[8]   On the 20th *Southern Army* published its orders for the forthcoming operations, omitting only the date when hostilities would start.

Specific plans for the seizure of the Philippine Islands were first developed by the Japanese Army's General Staff in the fall of 1941.   As the plans for the southern area were developed, the Philippine plan was modified to conform to the larger strategy being developed and to release some of the forces originally assigned *14th Army* to other, more critical operations. The final plan was completed at the meetings between the *14th Army* commander, Lt. Gen. Masaharu Homma, and the commanders of the *5th Air Group* (Lt. Gen. Hideyoshi Obata), the *3d Fleet* (Vice Adm. Ibo Takahashi), and the *11th Air Fleet* (Vice Adm. Nishizo Tsukahara), held at Iwakuni in southern Honshu from the 13th to the 15th of November.

The general scheme of operations for the Philippine campaign called for simultaneous air attacks starting on X Day, the first day of war, against American aircraft and installations in the Philippines by the *5th Air Group* (Army) and the *11th Air Fleet* (Navy).   While the air attacks were in progress, advance Army and Navy units were to land on Batan Island, north of Luzon; at three places on Luzon: Aparri, Vigan, and Legaspi; and at Davao in Mindanao.   The purpose of these landings was to seize airfields.   The air force was to move to these fields as soon as possible and continue the destruction of the American air and naval forces from these close-in bases.

When the major part of American air strength had been eliminated, the main force of the *14th Army* was to land along Lingayen Gulf, north of Manila, while another force would land at Lamon Bay, southeast of the capital. These forces, with close air support, were to advance on Manila from the north and south.   It was expected that the decisive engagement of the campaign would be fought around Manila. Once the capital was taken, the islands defending the entrance to Manila Bay were to be captured and Luzon occupied.

Imperial General Headquarters and *Southern Army* expected General Homma to complete his mission in about fifty days; at the end of that time, approximately half of the *14th Army,* as well as the Army and Navy air units, were to leave the Philippines for operations in the south.[9]   The remaining elements of the *14th Army* were then to occupy the Visayas and Mindanao as rapidly as possible.   Little difficulty was expected in this phase of the operations and detailed plans were to be made at the appropriate time.   The Japanese considered it essential to the success of *Southern Army* operations to gain complete victory in the Philippines before the end of March 1942. Forces assigned to the Philippine campaign, small as they were, were required in other more vital areas.

The Japanese plan was based on a detailed knowledge of the Philippine Islands and a fairly accurate estimate of American and Philippine forces.[10]   The Japanese were aware that the bulk of the American and

---

[8] *Ibid.,* pp. 6–8; *14th Army* Opns, I, 14.   Unless otherwise specified, this account of the *14th Army*'s plan for the conquest of the Philippines is taken from the *14th Army* Opns, I and II.   The translation has been checked against the original Japanese study prepared by the *1st Demob Bureau.*

[9] Statement of Col Hattori, 2 Nov 47, ATIS Doc 49125, Statements of Japanese Officials on World War II, GHQ FEC, Mil Intel Sec, IV, 315.

[10] Japanese estimates of the strength and composition of the Philippine garrison, military installations, terrain, and weather, are discussed in *14th Army* Opns, I, 5–8, 10–14.

Philippine forces was on Luzon and that the U.S. Army garrison had been increased since July 1941 from 12,000 to 22,000. Eighty percent of the officers and 40 percent of the enlisted men were thought to be Americans and the rest, Filipinos. American troops were regarded as good soldiers, but inclined to deteriorate physically and mentally in a tropical climate. The Filipino, though inured to the tropics, had little endurance or sense of responsibility, the Japanese believed, and was markedly inferior to the American as a soldier. The American garrison was correctly supposed to be organized into one division, an air unit, and a "fortress unit" (Harbor Defenses of Manila and Subic Bays). The division was mistakenly thought to consist of two infantry brigades, a field artillery brigade, and supporting services. The Japanese knew that MacArthur also had one battalion of fifty-four tanks—which was true at that time—and believed that there was also an antitank battalion in the Islands. The harbor defenses were known to consist of four coast artillery regiments, including one antiaircraft regiment.

The Japanese estimated that the American air force in the Philippines was composed of one pursuit regiment of 108 planes, one bombardment regiment of about 38 planes, one pursuit squadron of 27 planes, and two reconnaissance squadrons of 13 planes. American aircraft were based on two major fields on Luzon, the Japanese believed. They placed the pursuit group at Nichols Field, in the suburbs of Manila, and the bombers at Clark Field. Other fields on Luzon were thought to base a total of 20 planes. The Japanese placed 52 Navy patrol and carrier-based fighter planes at Cavite and 18 PBY's at Olongapo.

The strength of the Philippine Army and the Constabulary, the Japanese estimated, was 110,000 men. This strength, they thought, would be increased to 125,000 by December. The bulk of the Philippine Army, organized into ten divisions, was known to consist mostly of infantry with only a few engineer and artillery units. This army was considered very much inferior to the U.S. Regular Army in equipment, training, and fighting qualities.

Though they had a good picture of the defending force, Japanese knowledge of American defense plans was faulty. They expected that the Philippine garrison would make its last stand around Manila and when defeated there would scatter and be easily mopped up. No preparation was made for an American withdrawal to the Bataan peninsula. In October, at a meeting of the *14th Army* staff officers in Tokyo, Homma's chief of staff, Lt. Gen. Masami Maeda, had raised the possibility of a withdrawal to Bataan. Despite his protests, the subject was quickly dropped.[11]   Staff officers of the

[11] Interrog of Gen Maeda, 10 May 47, Mil Hist Div, GHQ FEC; statement of Gen Maeda, 2 Mar 50, ATIS Doc 56234; statement of Lt Col Yoshio Nakajima, 6 Feb 50, ATIS Doc 56349; statement of Lt Col Monjiro Akiyama, 2 Mar 50, ATIS Doc 56232; statement of Lt Col Hikaru Haba, 2 Mar 50, ATIS Doc 56233; statement of Col Motoo Nakayama, 21 Mar 50, ATIS Doc 56640. Colonel Nakajima was, at the beginning of the Philippine Campaign, Intelligence Officer, *14th Army,* and subsequently its Operations Officer. When Colonel Nakajima was made Operations Officer, Colonel Haba, formerly Assistant Intelligence Officer, *14th Army,* was promoted to Intelligence Officer. Colonel Akiyama was *14th Army* Air Officer, and Colonel Nakayama, Senior Operations Officer, *14th Army.* Copies of these ATIS documents and interrogations are in Interrogations of Former Japanese Officers, Mil Hist Div, GHQ FEC, I and II.

48th Division also claimed to have discussed the question of Bataan before the division embarked at Formosa. The consensus then was that while resistance could be expected before Manila and on Corregidor, Bataan "being a simple, outlying position, would fall quickly." [12]

The Japanese originally planned to assign to the Philippine campaign six battalions for the advance landings, two full divisions for the main landings, and supporting troops. So meager were the forces available to *Southern Army* that General Homma was finally allotted for the entire operation only 2 divisions, the *16th* and *48th*. Supporting troops included 2 tank regiments, 2 regiments and 1 battalion of medium artillery, 3 engineer regiments, 5 antiaircraft battalions, and a large number of service units. Once Luzon had been secured, most of the air units and the *48th Division*, as well as other units, were to be transferred to the Indies and Malaya. At that time Homma would receive the *65th Brigade* to mop up remaining resistance and to garrison Luzon. The *16th Division* would then move south and occupy the Visayas and Mindanao.

The *14th Army* commander had also counted on having the support of a joint Army and Navy air force of 600 planes. But one of the two air brigades of the *5th Air Group* and some of the naval air units originally destined for the Philippines were transferred to other operations. The addition of the *24th Air Regiment* to the *5th Air Group* at the last moment brought the combined air and naval strength committed to the Philippine campaign to about 500 combat aircraft.

Air and Naval Plans

Air operations against the Philippines would begin on the morning of X Day when planes of the Army's *5th Air Group* and the Navy's *11th Air Fleet,* would strike American air forces on Luzon. These attacks would continue until American air strength had been destroyed. For reasons of security, there was to be no aerial or submarine reconnaissance before the attack, except for high-altitude aerial photographs of landing sites.[13]

By arrangement between the Japanese Army and Navy commanders, Army air units were to operate north of the 16th degree of latitude, a line stretching across Luzon from Lingayen on the west coast to the San Ildefonso Peninsula on the east. Naval air units were made responsible for the area south of this line, which included Clark Field, the vital Manila area, Cavite, and the harbor defenses. This line was determined by the range of Army and Navy aircraft. The Navy Zero fighters had the longer range and were therefore assigned missions in the Manila area. Carrier planes of the *4th Carrier Division*, originally based at Palau, were to provide

---

[12] Statement of Col Moriji Kawagoe, CofS *48th Div,* 9 Mar 50, ATIS Doc 56354; statement of Maj Makoto Nakahara, Opns Officer, *48th Div,* 13 Mar 50, ATIS Doc 56372, *ibid.*

[13] The material on naval plans is taken from Naval Operations in the Invasion of the Philippines, Japanese Studies in World War II, No. 13, *2d Demob Bureau,* pp. 1–6. Like other studies in this series, it is filed in OCMH and has been checked against the original. Morison, *Rising Sun in the Pacific,* pp. 161–63, is useful for the organization of Japan's naval forces. See also *Combined Fleet* Top Secret Operations Order 1, in *Pearl Harbor Attack Hearings,* Part 13, Exhibit 8, pp. 432–84.

air support for the landings at Davao and Legaspi.[14]

Once the advance units of *14th Army* had landed and secured airfields, the main force of the *5th Air Group* was to move up to the fields at Aparri, Laoag, and Vigan, while naval air units would base on the fields at Legaspi and Davao. The airfield near Aparri was mistakenly believed to be suitable for heavy bombers and the bulk of the *5th Air Group* was ordered there. It was anticipated that the forward displacement of the air forces would be completed by the sixth or seventh day of operations. During this week a naval task force from the *3d Fleet* was to provide protection for the convoys and carry out antisubmarine measures in the Formosa area and in Philippine waters.

Naval surface forces assigned to the Philippines operations were under the *3d Fleet.* This fleet, commanded by Admiral Takahashi, was primarily an amphibious force with supporting cruisers and destroyers. Its principal mission was to support the landings in the Philippines by minelaying, reconnaissance, escorting the troops during the voyage to the targets, and protecting them during landing operations. No provisions was made for surface bombardment of shore objectives, presumably in the interests of secrecy.[15]

Because of the many landings to be made at widely scattered points in the Philippine archipelago it was necessary to organize

the *3d Fleet* into numerous special task forces. For the landing on Batan Island the *Third Surprise Attack Force* of 1 destroyer, 4 torpedo boats, and other small craft was organized. The naval escort for the landing of the advance units on Luzon consisted of the *First, Second,* and *Fourth Surprise Attack Force,* each composed of 1 light cruiser, 6 or 7 destroyers, transports, and other auxiliary craft. The *Legaspi Force (Fourth Surprise Attack Force)* was to be staged at Palau, and since it could not be supported by the planes of the *11th Air Fleet* it included the *South Philippines Support Force,* comprising the *4th Carrier Division* and 2 seaplane carriers with 20 planes each. The units landing at Davao were to be covered by this same force.

To support the main landings Admiral Takahashi created the *Close Cover Force,* which he commanded directly, composed of 1 light and 2 heavy cruisers, and 2 converted seaplane tenders. Two battleships and 3 heavy cruisers from Vice Adm. Nobutake Kondo's *2d Fleet,* then operating in Malayan and East Indian waters, were also to support the landings, which would be additionally supported by 3 of the escort groups. The *Lamon Bay Attack Group,* in addition to 1 light cruiser and 6 destroyers, included 6 converted gunboats and 1 battalion of naval troops.

Concentration of Forces

Early in November the forces assigned to the Philippine campaign began to move to their designated jump-off points. The *5th Air Group* arrived in southern Formosa from Manchuria during the latter part of the month. On 23 November two of the advance detachments stationed in Formosa boarded ship at Takao and sailed to Mako in the Pescadores. Between 27

---

[14] The *11th Air Fleet* had originally planned to use carrier-based fighters to neutralize southern Luzon, but the pilots trained for this mission were transferred with their planes to the Pearl Harbor operation. During the fall of 1941 the improvement of the Zero fighters and the rapid advancement in pilot training made it possible to utilize land-based fighters on Formosa for long-distance sorties against Luzon.

[15] Morison, *Rising Sun in the Pacific,* p. 166.

November and 6 December the *48th Division* (less detachments) concentrated at Mako, Takoa, and Kirun, and made final preparations for the coming invasion. The first units of the *16th Division* sailed from Nagoya in Japan on 20 November, followed five days later by the remainder of the division. Part of this division concentrated at Palau and the main body at Amami Oshima in the Ryukyus. On 1 December, when General Homma established his command post at Takao, he received final instructions from *Southern Army*. Operations would begin on 8 December (Tokyo time).

The Plan of Defense

Plans for the defense of the Philippine Islands had been in existence for many years when General MacArthur returned to active duty. The latest revision of these plans, completed in April 1941 and called War Plan ORANGE–3 (WPO–3), was based on the joint Army-Navy ORANGE plan of 1938, one of the many "color" plans developed during the prewar years. Each color plan dealt with a different situation, ORANGE covering an emergency in which only the United States and Japan would be involved. In this sense, the plan was strategically unrealistic and completely outdated by 1941. Tactically, however, the plan was an excellent one and its provisions for defense were applicable under any local situation.[16]

[16] Unless otherwise noted, this section is based on the Philippine Department Plan ORANGE, 1940 Revision. (Short title: HPD WPO–3), AG 326. The author has also had the benefit of conversations with the Philippine Department Commander, General Grunert, with Generals Sutherland and Marshall, and with various division commanders and staff officers who participated in the planning and execution of the plan.

WPO–3

In War Plan ORANGE it was assumed that the Japanese attack would come without a declaration of war and with less than forty-eight hours' warning so that it would not be possible to provide reinforcements from the United States for some time. The defense would therefore have to be conducted entirely by the military and naval forces already in the Philippines, supported by such forces as were available locally. The last category included any organized elements of the Philippine Army which might be inducted into the service of the United States under the Tydings-McDuffie Act.

An analysis of Japanese capabilities, as of 1 July 1940, led the Philippine Department planners to believe that the enemy would send an expedition of about 100,000 men to capture Manila and its harbor defenses in order to occupy the Philippines, sever the American line of communications, and deny the United States a naval base in the Far East. It was expected that this operation would be undertaken with the greatest secrecy and that it would precede or coincide with a declaration of war. The garrison therefore could expect little or no warning. The attack would probably come during the dry season, shortly after the rice crop was harvested, in December or January. The enemy was assumed to have extensive knowledge of the terrain and of American strength and dispositions, and would probably be assisted by the 30,000 Japanese in the Islands.

Army planners in the Philippines expected the Japanese to make their major attack against the island of Luzon and to employ strong ground forces with heavy air and naval support. They would probably land in many places simultaneously in order to spread thin the defending forces and assure the success of at least one of the landings. Secondary landings or feints were also expected. It was considered possible that the Japanese might attempt in a surprise move to seize the harbor defenses with a small force at the opening of hostilities. Enemy air operations would consist of long-range reconnaissance and bombardment, probably coming without warning and coordinated with the landings. The Japanese would probably also attempt to establish air bases on Luzon very early in the campaign in order to destroy American air power and bomb military installations.

Under WPO–3 the mission of the Philippine garrison was to hold the entrance to Manila Bay and deny its use to Japanese naval forces. There was no intention that American troops should fight anywhere but in central Luzon. U.S. Army forces, constituting the Initial Protective Force, had the main task of preventing enemy landings. Failing in this, they were to defeat those forces which succeeded in landing. If, despite these attempts, the enemy proved successful, the Initial Protective Force was to engage in delaying action but not at the expense of the primary mission, the defense of Manila Bay. Every attempt was to be made to hold back the Japanese advance while withdrawing to the Bataan peninsula. Bataan was recognized as the key to the control of Manila Bay, and it was to be defended to the "last extremity."

To reinforce the Initial Protective Force, Philippine Army units were to be mobilized immediately upon the outbreak of war and would be ready to participate in the defense of Bataan. If used as anticipated in WPO–3, which was prepared before July 1941, the Philippine Army would be under the command of the Philippine Department commander and would be utilized to defend Manila Bay. The plan did not contemplate using Philippine Army units for the defense of the entire archipelago.

WPO–3 divided Luzon, the principal theater of operations, into six sectors with a mobile reserve. Detailed plans for the defense of each sector were made by the sector commanders. The commander of the Philippine Division, the only U.S. Army division in the Philippines, in addition to conducting operations in the sector or sectors assigned to him, was to organize the defenses of Bataan and to command operations there if necessary.

Air support was to be provided by the 4th Composite Group, the predecessor of the Far East Air Force. This group was to obtain information of enemy location, strength, and disposition by continuous reconnaissance, attack the Japanese whenever conditions were favorable, and support ground operations. In order to keep this air force in operation as long as possible, its planes were to be employed "conservatively" and every effort was to be made to supplement the strength of the group by taking over the Philippine Army Air Corps and commercial planes.

The navy was to set up defensive coastal areas at the entrances to Manila and Subic Bays. At the first sign of an attack a defensive area was to be set up around Manila to control all shipping and a patrol system established for Manila and Subic Bays. The Army, through the Department quartermaster, would control all shore facilities at the port of Manila.

The supply plan in WPO–3 was a complicated one. Provision had to be made to supply the six sectors during the initial phase of operations and to withdraw supplies into Bataan where a base would be established to support a prolonged defense. Supply officers estimated that they would probably require enough supplies for 31,000 men (the Bataan Defense Force)—later raised to 40,-000 men—to last 180 days. The defense reserve already on hand, except for ammunition, was considered by the planners sufficent to supply such a force for the period required in a defensive situation. The bulk of the supplies was stored in the Manila area which lacked adequate protection from attacking aircraft. In the event it became necessary to move the supplies to Corregidor and Bataan, the enemy would have to be delayed long enough to carry out this operation.

Prior to the start of operations on Bataan, supplies were to be moved rapidly to the peninsula. At the same time the Corregidor reserves, set first at a 6-month supply for 7,000 men and then for 10,000 men, were to be brought up to the authorized allotment. Philippine Department depots and installations in the Manila area were to be maintained just as long as the tactical situation permitted. Depots at Fort Stotsenburg, Fort William McKinley, Tarlac, San Fernando, Manila, and elsewhere would supply the various sectors. A Bataan Service Area was to be established, initially to assist in organizing the final defense positions and ultimately to supply the entire force after it had withdrawn to Bataan for the last stand. All stocks in the Department, except those of the Harbor Defenses of Manila and Subic Bays, would eventually be transferred to Bataan.

Plans for local procurement included the exploitation of the Manila area with its

commercial warehouses, factories, and transportation facilities. Procurement districts, coinciding roughly with the sector boundaries, would be established later.

Troops would take the field with two days of Class I supplies (rations), one emergency ration, and two days of fire. Class I and III supplies (gasoline and lubricants) would be issued automatically thereafter at rail or navigation heads; Class II, IV, and V supplies (clothing, construction and other heavy equipment, and ammunition) would be requisitioned from depots as needed. The issue of supplies to Philippine Army units would depend upon the speed with which they were mobilized and their location.

The transportation of troops and equipment, the planners realised, would be a difficult problem. There was a large number of passenger buses on Luzon, centrally organized and operated. The 4,000 trucks on the island were of varying type, size, and condition and were mainly individually owned. Passenger buses were to be requisitioned immediately by the Army for use as personnel carriers. Since it would take longer to requisition trucks, cargo requirements were to be kept to an absolute minimum. In the initial move by the mobile forces toward the threatened beaches, little difficulty was expected with motor transportation. Later, as supply requirements rose and as troops moved back toward Bataan (if the enemy could not be repelled at the beaches), motor pools were to be formed. When Philippine Army units were mobilized the drain on the motor transport services was expected to increase greatly since these units had no organic motor transportation.

Nothing was said in WPO–3 about what

was to happen after the defenses on Bataan crumbled. Presumably by that time, estimated at six months, the U.S. Pacific Fleet would have fought its way across the Pacific, won a victory over the *Combined Fleet,* and made secure the line of communications. The men and supplies collected on the west coast during that time would then begin to reach the Philippines in a steady stream. The Philippine garrison, thus reinforced, could then counterattack and drive the enemy into the sea.

Actually, no one in a position of authority at that time (April 1941) believed that anything like this would happen. Informed naval opinion estimated that it would require at least two years for the Pacific Fleet to fight its way across the Pacific. There was no plan to concentrate men and supplies on the west coast and no schedule for their movement to the Philippines. Army planners in early 1941 believed that at the end of six months, if not sooner, supplies would be exhausted and the garrison would go down in defeat. WPO–3 did not say this; instead it said nothing at all. And everyone hoped that when the time came something could be done, some plan improvised to relieve or rescue the men stranded 7,000 miles across the Pacific.[17]

The MacArthur Plan

General MacArthur had the answer to those who saw no way out of the difficulty in the Philippines. The defeatist and defensive WPO–3 was to be transformed into an aggressive plan whose object would be the defeat of any enemy that attempted the

conquest of the Philippines. An optimist by nature, with implicit faith in the Philippine people, MacArthur was able to inspire the confidence and loyalty of his associates and staff. His optimism was contagious and infected the highest officials in the War Department and the government. By the fall of 1941 there was a firm conviction in Washington and in the Philippines that, given sufficient time, a Japanese attack could be successfully resisted.

In pressing for a more aggressive plan, enlarged in scope to include the entire archipelago, MacArthur could rely on having a far stronger force than any of his predecessors. His growing air force included by the end of November 1941 thirty-five B–17's and almost 100 fighters of the latest type. Many more were on their way. The performance of the heavy bombers in early 1941 justified the hope that the South China Sea would be successfully blockaded by air and that the Islands could be made a "self-sustaining fortress." [18]

MacArthur could also count on the Philippine Army's ten reserve divisions, then being mobilized and trained, and one regular division. During his term as Military Advisor, he had worked out the general concept of his strategy as well as detailed plans for the use of this national army. As commander of U.S. Army Forces in the Far East he could plan on the use of the regular U.S. Army garrison as well as the Philippine Army. He was in an excellent position, therefore, to persuade the War Department to approve his own concepts for the defense of the Philippines.

Almost from the date of his assumption of command, MacArthur began to think about replacing WPO–3 with a new

[17] Louis Morton, "American and Allied Strategy in the Far East," *Military Review,* XXIX (December 1949), 22–40.

[18] Stimson and Bundy, *On Active Service,* p. 388.

plan.[19]   From the first, as is evident from his establishment of the Philippine Coast Artillery Command, he apparently intended to defend the inland seas and the entrances to Manila and Subic Bays. By September his plans had progressed sufficiently to enable him to inform General Wainwright of his intention to reorganize the forces in the Philippines and to give that officer his choice of commands.[20]

The opportunity to request a change in plans for the defense of the Philippines came in October, after MacArthur received a copy of the new war plan, RAINBOW 5, prepared by the Joint Board some months earlier. This plan, which was world-wide in its provisions and conformed to arrangements with the British staff, called for a defensive strategy in the Pacific and Far East and recognized Germany as the main enemy in the event of a war with the Axis. Based on the assumption that the United States would be at war with more than one nation and would be allied with Great Britain, RAINBOW accepted implicitly the loss of the Philippines, Wake, and Guam. Like ORANGE, it assigned Army and Navy forces in the Philippines the mission of defending the Philippine Coastal Frontier, defined as those land and sea areas which it would be necessary to hold in order to defend Manila and Subic Bays. Also, as in ORANGE, the defense was to be conducted entirely by Army and Navy forces already in the Philippines, augmented by

such local forces as were available.[21]   No reinforcements could be expected.

MacArthur immediately objected to those provisions of RAINBOW relating to the Philippines and called for the revision of the plan on the ground that it failed to recognize either the creation of a high command for the Far East or the mobilization of the Philippine Army. In a strong letter to the War Department on 1 October, the former Chief of Staff pointed out that he would soon have a force of approximately 200,000 men organized into eleven divisions with corresponding corps and army troops, as well as a strengthened air force. There could be no adequate defense of Manila Bay or of Luzon, he said, if an enemy was to be allowed to land and secure control of any of the southern islands. With the "wide scope of possible enemy operations, especially aviation," he thought such landings possible. He urged, therefore, that the "citadel type defense" of Manila Bay provided in the ORANGE and RAINBOW plans be changed to an active defense of all the islands in the Philippines. "The strength and composition of the defense forces projected here," General MacArthur asserted, "are believed to be sufficient to accomplish such a mission." [22]

The reply from Washington came promptly. On the 18th General Marshall informed MacArthur that a revision of the Army mission had been drafted in the War Department and was then awaiting action by the Joint Board, "with approval ex-

---

[19] Interv, author with Col Diller, 20 May 49. Wainwright mentions also that as Philippine Division commander he worked during May, June, and July 1941 to secure revisions of WPO–3. General Jonathan M. Wainwright, *General Wainwright's Story, the Account of Four Years of Humiliating Defeat, Surrender, and Captivity* (New York: Doubleday & Company, Inc., 1946), p. 10.
[20] Wainwright, *General Wainwright's Story,* p. 21.

[21] Joint Army and Navy Basic War Plan RAINBOW 5, Joint Board (JB) 325, Serial 642-5, OPD Reg Doc.
[22] Ltr, MacArthur to TAG, 1 Oct 41, sub: Opns Plan R–5, WPD 4178-18. MacArthur repeated the same request, in virtually the same language, in a personal letter to Marshall on 28 October 1951, WPD 4477-2.

GENERAL MACARTHUR *with Maj. Gen. Jonathan M. Wainwright on 10 October 1941.*

pected within the next ten days." Mac-Arthur's recommendation that the Philippine Coastal Frontier be redefined to include all the islands in the archipelago, Marshall continued, would also be presented to the Joint Board for approval. The assignment of a broader mission than that contained in RAINBOW, Marshall explained, was made possible because of the increased importance of the Philippines "as a result of the alignment of Japan with the Axis, followed by the outbreak of war between Germany and Russia." [23] General Marshall took advantage of the fact that Brereton was just then leaving for the Far East to send his reply to MacArthur by personal courier.

Brereton arrived in Manila on 3 November and was warmly greeted by his commander in chief. After reading Marshall's note, MacArthur, in Brereton's words, "acted like a small boy who had been told that he is going to get a holiday from school." He jumped up from his desk, threw his arms around Brereton and exclaimed, "Lewis, you are just as welcome as the flowers in May." Turning to his chief of staff, General Sutherland, he said, "Dick, they are going to give us everything we have asked for." [24]

With this notice that his plans would soon be approved by the Joint Board, MacArthur immediately organized his forces to execute the larger mission. On 4 November he formally established the North and South Luzon Forces, and the Visayan-Mindanao Force, all of which had actually been in existence for several months already. [25]

Approval by the Joint Board of the

RAINBOW revisions requested by MacArthur was forwarded from Washington on 21 November. In the accompanying letter, General Marshall made the significant observation that air reinforcements to the Philippines had "modified that conception [purely defensive operations] of Army action in this area to include strong air operations in the furtherance of the strategic defensive." [26] He also told MacArthur to go ahead with his plans "on the basis of your interpretation of the basic war plan."

In the revised joint RAINBOW plan, the Philippine Coastal Frontier, which had been defined as consisting of Luzon and the land and sea areas necessary to defend that island, was redefined to include "all the land and sea areas necessary for the defense of the Philippine Archipelago." [27] In effect, this gave MacArthur authority to defend all of the Philippine Islands.

The Army task originally assigned in RAINBOW was simply to defend the coastal frontier. The November revision not only enlarged the coastal frontier but gave MacArthur the following additional tasks:

1. Support the Navy in raiding Japanese sea communications and destroying Axis forces.

2. Conduct air raids against Japanese forces and installations within tactical operating radius of available bases.

3. Co-operate with the Associated Powers in the defense of the territories of these Powers in accordance with approved policies and agreements. [28]

---

[22] Memo, Marshall for MacArthur, 18 Oct 41, sub: USAFFE, WPD 4175-18.

[24] Brereton, *Diaries,* p. 19.

[25] USAFFE-USFIP Rpt of Opns, p. 15.

[26] Ltr, CofS to CG USAFFE, 21 Nov 41, sub: U.S.-British Co-operation in the Far East, WPD 4402-112. The first draft of this letter used the phrase "strong offensive air action" in the place of "strong air operations in the furtherance of the strategic defensive."

[27] *Ibid.,* incl, extract copy of Changes in Joint Army and Navy Basic War Plan, RAINBOW 5.

[28] *Ibid.*

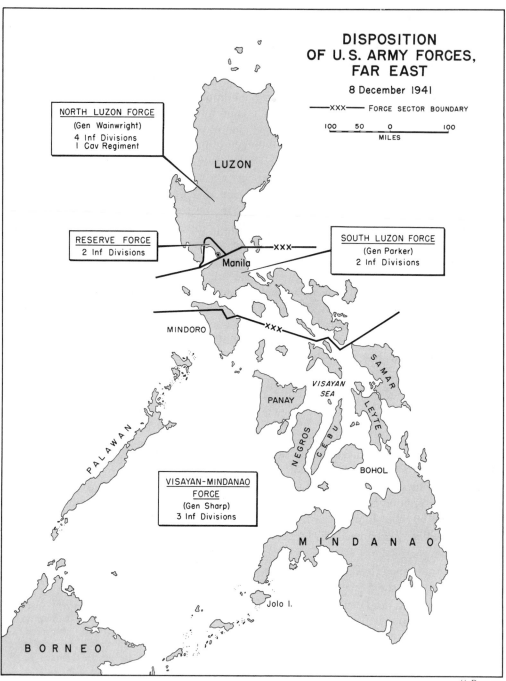

DISPOSITION
OF U.S. ARMY FORCES,
FAR EAST

8 December 1941

——×××—— FORCE SECTOR BOUNDARY

100   50   0   100
MILES

NORTH LUZON FORCE
(Gen Wainwright)
4 Inf Divisions
1 Cav Regiment

LUZON

RESERVE FORCE
2 Inf Divisions

Manila

SOUTH LUZON FORCE
(Gen Parker)
2 Inf Divisions

MINDORO

SAMAR

VISAYAN
SEA

PANAY

LEYTE

NEGROS

CEBU

BOHOL

PALAWAN

VISAYAN-MINDANAO
FORCE
(Gen Sharp)
3 Inf Divisions

M I N D A N A O

Jolo I.

B O R N E O

H. Damon

MAP 3

It also provided specifically for a defense reserve for 180 days, instead of the 90-day level originally granted to General Grunert. These additional tasks recognized the existence of an effective air force in the Philippines capable of striking at Japanese lines of communications and bases, such as Formosa, and the fact that the Philippine Army had been inducted into federal service by including it with forces available to accomplish the tasks assigned.

Once his plan to defend all of the islands had been approved, General MacArthur was able, on 3 December, to define the missions of the four major tactical commands created a month earlier. (Map 3) The North Luzon Force, which had been under the command of Brig. Gen. Edward P. King, Jr., from 3 to 28 November, now came under General Wainwright. This force had responsibility for the most critical sector in the Philippines, including part of the central plains area, Lingayen Gulf, the Zambales coast, and the Bataan peninsula. General Wainwright was instructed to protect airfields and prevent hostile landings in his area, particularly at those points opening into the central plains and the road net leading to Manila. In case of a successful landing the enemy was to be destroyed. In contrast to WPO–3, which provided for a withdrawal to Bataan, MacArthur's plan stated there was to be "no withdrawal from beach positions." The beaches were to "be held at all costs." [29]

Immediately on receipt of these instructions General Wainwright was to prepare detailed plans to execute his mission. Front-line units were to make a reconnaissance of their sectors and emplace their weapons. Positions four hours distant from the front lines were to be selected for the assembly of troops.

On 3 December, when Wainwright received his mission, his North Luzon Force consisted of three Philippine Army divisions—the 11th, 21st, and 31st—the 26th Cavalry (PS), one battalion of the 45th Infantry (PS) on Bataan, two batteries of 155-mm. guns, and one battery of 2.95-inch mountain guns. The 71st Division (PA), though assigned to North Luzon Force, could be committed only on the authority of USAFFE. Wainwright was promised additional troops when they arrived from the United States or were mobilized by the Philippine Army.

The South Luzon Force, under Brig. Gen. George M. Parker, Jr., was assigned the area generally south and east of Manila. Like the force to the north, it was to protect the airfields in its sector and prevent hostile landings. General Parker was also enjoined to hold the beaches at all costs. The South Luzon Force was much smaller than that in the north. It consisted initially of only two Philippine Army divisions, the 41st and 51st, and a battery of field artillery. Additional units were to be assigned at a later date when they became available. [30]

The Visayan-Mindanao Force under Brig. Gen. William F. Sharp was charged with the defense of the rest of the archipelago. Its primary mission was to protect the airfields to be built in the Visayas; its secondary mission was to "prevent landings of hostile raiding parties, paying particular attention to the cities and essential public utilities." Since landings in force south of

---

[29] Ltr Order, CG USAFFE to CG North Luzon Force (NLF), 3 Dec 41, sub: Defense of Phil, AG 381 (12–3–41) Phil Rcds. Brig. Gen. Maxon S. Lough assumed command of the Philippine Division when General Wainwright transferred to North Luzon Force.

[30] Ltr Order, CG USAFFE to CG SLF, 3 Dec 41, sub: Defense of Phil, AG 381 (12–3–41) Phil Rcds.

Table 6—Assignment of Forces, USAFFE, 3 December 1941

Sector	Troop Assignment	
	U.S. Army	Philippine Army
North Luzon Force	Force Hq and Hq Co (U.S.) 26th Cavalry (PS) One bn, 45th Inf (PS) Btry A, 23d FA (Pk) (PS) Btrys B and C, 86th FA (PS) 66th QM Troop (Pk) (PS)	11th Division 21st Division 31st Division 71st Division (used as directed by USAFFE)
South Luzon Force	Force Hq and Hq Co (U.S.) Hq and Hq Btry, Btry A, 86th FA (PS)	41st Division 51st Division
Visayan-Mindanao Force	Force Hq and Hq Co (PS)	61st Division 81st Division 101st Division
Reserve Force	Hq, Philippine Dept Philippine Division (less one bn) 86th FA (PS) less dets Far East Air Force	91st Division Hq, Philippine Army
Harbor Defenses	Headquarters 59th CA (U.S.) 60th CA (AA) (U.S.) 91st CA (PS) 92d CA (PS) 200th CA (U.S.), assigned to PCAC	

Source: Ltr Orders, CG USAFFE to CG NLF, SLF, V-MF, 3 Dec 41, AG 381 (12–3–41) Phil Rcds; USAFFE-USFIP Rpt of Opns, pp. 17–18.

Luzon would not have had any decisive results, no mention was made of the necessity of holding the beaches.[31]

The Visayan-Mindanao sector would also include the coastal defenses of the inland seas when these were completed and General Sharp was to provide protection for these as well. One battalion of the force was to be prepared to move to Del Monte in Mindanao with the mission of guarding the recently completed bomber base there.

[31] Ltr Order, CG USAFFE to CG V-MF, 3 Dec 41, sub: Defense of Phil, AG 381 (12–3–41) Phil Rcds.

No American or Philippine Scout troops were assigned to the Visayan-Mindanao Force, except those in headquarters. For the rest, the force consisted of the 61st, 81st, and 101st Divisions, all Philippine Army. (*See Table 6.*)

On Luzon, between the North and South Luzon Forces was the reserve area, including the city of Manila and the heavily congested area just to the north. This area was directly under the control of MacArthur's headquarters and contained the Philippine Division (less one battalion), the 91st Division (PA), the 86th Field Artillery (PS), the Far East Air Force, and the headquarters of the Philippine Department and the Philippine Army. The defense of the entrance to Manila and Subic Bays was left, as it always had been, to Gen. Moore's Harbor Defenses augmented by the Philippine Coast Artillery Command.[32]

During the last few months of 1941 the training of both U.S. Army and Philippine Army units progressed at an accelerated pace. The strength of the Scouts, an elite organization with a high *esprit de corps,* had been brought up to its authorized strength of 12,000 quickly. Membership in Scout units was considered a high honor by Filipinos and the strictest standards were followed in selection. To provide the training for the new Scout units, as well as Philippine Army units, a large number of officers was authorized for USAFFE. By the fall of 1941 they began to arrive in Manila. Training of U.S. Army units was also intensified during this period. By the beginning of December, General Wainwright later wrote, "the American and Philippine Scout organizations were fit, trained in combat principles and ready to take the field in any emergency." The omission of Philippine Army units is significant.[33]

The Last Days of Peace

Already there had been warnings of an approaching crisis. On 24 November the Pacific and Asiatic Fleet commanders had been told that the prospects for an agreement with Japan were slight and that Japanese troop movements indicated that "a surprise aggressive movement in any direction, including attack on Philippines or Guam was a possibility.[34] Three days later a stronger message, which the War Department considered a "final alert," went out to Hawaii and the Philippines. The Army commanders, MacArthur and Lt. Gen. Walter C. Short, were told:

Negotiations with Japan appear to be terminated to all practical purposes with only the barest possibility that the Japanese Government might come back and offer to continue. Japanese future action unpredictable but hostile action possible at any moment. If hostilities cannot, repeat cannot, be avoided the United States desires that Japan commit the first overt act. This policy should not, repeat not, be construed as restricting you to a course of action that might jeopardize your defense. Prior to hostile Japanese action you are directed to undertake such reconnaissance and other measures as you deem neessary. Report measures taken. Should hostilities occur you will carry out the tasks assigned in RAINBOW 5. . . .[35]

At the same time the Navy Department sent to its Pacific commanders an even stronger message, to be passed on to the Army commanders in Hawaii and the Philippines. "This dispatch," it read, "is to be considered a war warning. Negotiations with Japan . . . have ceased and an aggressive move by Japan is expected

---

[32] USAFFE-USFIP Rpt of Opns, pp. 17–18; Ltr Order, CG USAFFE to CG Phil Div, 6 Dec 41, sub: Movement Plans, AG 381 (12–3–41) Phil Rcds.

[33] USAFFE-USFIP Rpt of Opns, p. 26.

[34] Rad, OPNAV to Comdrs Pacific and Asiatic Fleets, 24005, 24 Nov 41 in *Pearl Harbor Attack Hearings,* Part 14, p. 1405. This message was given to MacArthur by Hart.

[35] Rad, Marshall to MacArthur, 27 Nov 41, OCS 18136-118; *Report of the Joint Committee on the Investigation of the Pearl Harbor Attack,* 79th Cong., 2d sess., Doc 244 (Washington, 1946), cited hereafter as *Pearl Harbor Attack Report,* pp. 199–201. The message sent to Hawaii, Panama, and the Western Defense Command included a statement that the civilian population should not be alarmed. *Pearl Harbor Attack Hearings,* Part 14, p. 1389. *Ibid.,* Part 39, p. 84, contains Mr. Stimson's account of these events; Part 3, p. 1021, includes a memo, Gerow for Marshall, 27 Nov 41, sub: Far Eastern Situation, WPD 4544-13.

within the next few days." Navy commanders were alerted against the possibility of a Japanese invasion of the Philippines, Thailand, or Malaya, and were told to take appropriate defensive measures.[36]

Immediately on receipt of the 27 November warning, MacArthur, Hart, and the Hon. Francis B. Sayre, U.S. High Commissioner to the Philippine Islands, met to discuss the measures to be taken. Sayre presented the President's view to Mr. Quezon and told him that Roosevelt was relying upon the full co-operation of the Commonwealth.[37] The next day MacArthur reported to the Chief of Staff the measures taken in the Philippines to prepare for a Japanese attack. Air reconnaisance had been extended and intensified "in conjunction with the Navy" and measures for ground security had been taken. "Within the limitations imposed by present state of development of this theater of operations," he said, "everything is in readiness for the conduct of a successful defense."[38]

The first week of December 1941 was a tense one for those in the Philippines who had been informed of the latest steps in the negotiations with Japan. American planes continued to notice heavy Japanese ship movements in the direction of Malaya, and unidentified aircraft—presumed to be Japanese—were detected over Luzon. On the 5th of December the commander of Britain's Far Eastern Fleet, Admiral Sir Tom Phillips, came to Manila to confer with Admiral Hart and General MacArthur about joint plans for defense. The next day news was received that a Japanese force had been sighted in the Gulf of Siam

heading westward. Admiral Phillips left immediately by plane for Singapore where his flagship, *Prince of Wales,* lay at anchor, next to the battle cruiser *Repulse.*[39]

On 6 December, Saturday, MacArthur's headquarters ordered North Luzon Force to be ready to move promptly to its assigned positions on beach defense, and Wainwright noted that around his headquarters at Stotsenburg "the tension could be cut with a knife."[40] In response to a warning against sabotage, MacArthur told General Arnold that a full air alert was in effect and all aircraft dispersed and placed under guard.[41]

Sunday, 7 December—it was the 6th in Washington—was a normal day, "nothing ominous in the atmosphere, no forebodings or shadows cast by coming events."[42] Men went about their work as usual. The only excitement arose from the fact that the Clipper, with its anxiously awaited mail sacks, was due. The last letters from home had reached the Islands ten days before.

That night the 27th Bombardment Group gave a party, recalled as a gala affair with "the best entertainment this side of Minsky's," at the Manila Hotel in honor of General Brereton.[43] Brereton records conversations with Rear Adm. William R. Pur-

---

[36] *Pearl Harbor Attack Hearings,* Part 14, p. 1406.

[37] *Ibid.*

[38] Rad, MacArthur to Marshall, No. 1004, 28 Nov 41, OCS 18136-118.

[39] Hart, Narrative of Events, Asiatic Fleet, p. 36; Morison, *Rising Sun in the Pacific,* pp. 156–57, 188–89. Specific instances of Japanese reconnaissance missions are noted in Edmonds, *They Fought With What They Had,* pp. 61–63.

[40] Wainwright, *General Wainwright's Story,* p. 17.

[41] Rad, MacArthur to Arnold, 6 Dec 41, quoted in Brereton, *Diaries,* pp. 36–37; Craven and Cate, *The Army Air Forces in World War II,* I, 191.

[42] Col James V. Collier, Notebooks, 4 vols., I, 42. Colonel Collier was Assistant G–3, USAFFE and later G–3, Luzon Force. He kept these notebooks for his three sons while he was in prison camp. They were loaned to the author, and a photostat copy is on file in OCMH. They will be hereafter referred to as Collier, Notebooks, with the appropriate number.

[43] Army Air Action in Phil and NEI, p. 52.

nell and Brig. Gen. Richard K. Sutherland, Hart's and MacArthur's chiefs of staff, during the course of the evening. Purnell told him that "It was only a question of days or perhaps hours until the shooting started" and that he was standing by for a call from Admiral Hart. Sutherland confirmed what Purnell had said, adding that the War and Navy Departments believed hostilities might begin at any time. Brereton then immediately instructed his chief of staff to place all air units on "combat alert" as of Monday morning, 8 December.[44]

Except for the few senior officers who had an intimate knowledge of events, men went to bed that night with no premonition that the next day would be different from the last. The Clipper had not arrived, and the last thoughts of many were of family and home, and the hope that the morrow would bring "cheerful and newsy letters." [45] Many listened to the radio before going to bed, but the news was not much different from that of previous days. Some heard American music for the last time. At Fort Stotsenburg a few officers of the 194th Tank Battalion listened to the Concerto in B Flat Minor before turning in. On the last night of peace Tschaikowsky's poignant music made an impression which was to be deep and lasting.[46]

[44] Brereton, *Diaries*, pp. 37–38.

[45] Collier, Notebooks, I, 42.
[46] Col. Ernest B. Miller, *Bataan Uncensored* (Long Prairie, Minn., 1949), p. 64.

PART TWO

THE ISOLATION OF THE PHILIPPINES AND
THE JAPANESE LANDINGS

CHAPTER V

The First Days of War

For those on the west side of the international date line, the "date which will live in infamy" came on 8 December 1941. Few responsible military or naval men had believed that the Japanese would be able to strike in more than one place. The number and diversity of their attacks took the Allies completely by surprise. During the early morning hours of the 8th, Japanese naval and air forces struck almost simultaneously at Kota Bharu in British Malaya (0140), Singora, just across the border in Thailand (0305), Singapore (0610), Guam (0805), Hong Kong (0900), Wake, and the Philippines.[1]

Landing operations began almost immediately. By dawn, Japanese forces were in possession of Shanghai. Even as the first bombs were dropping on Hong Kong, Japanese troops were on their way into the leased territory. By the end of that day they were only a few miles from Kowloon, which they took on the 13th. Hong Kong fell on Christmas Day.

Within an hour after the first bombardment of Kota Bharu, Japanese troops from Indochina began to land on the beaches against bitter opposition. The same day, when the main force of the *25th Army* arrived, the beachhead was secured. The landings at Singora were unopposed. There, the troops marched down the east coast of the Kra Isthmus, while one division crossed the Thailand–British Malay border and moved down the west coast. Thus began a two-month campaign which ended with the fall of Singapore on 15 February.

On Guam the air attacks continued for two days. Finally, at dawn on the 10th, the *South Seas Detachment* and supporting naval units landed on the island. A few hours later, the garrison there surrendered. This was the first American possession to fall into Japanese hands. At Wake Island, the Marine detachment under Maj. James P. S. Devereux was better prepared for the enemy and offered heroic resistance. The first attempt to land was beaten off and the Japanese returned to Kwajalein to lick their wounds and collect more troops for the next attempt. They were back at Wake on the 22d and the next morning landed in force. That same day the garrison surrendered.[2]

The fall of Wake and Guam cut the line of communications between Hawaii and the Philippines and left the United States with no Central Pacific base west of Mid-

---

[1] All times are Tokyo time.

[2] Lt. Col. Robert D. Heinl, Jr., *The Defense of Wake* (USMC Hist Sec, 1947); Opns of *South Seas Detachment*, 1941–42, Japanese Studies in World War II, No. 36, p. 3. For operations at Hong Kong and in Malaya, see *Japanese Landing Operations, December 8, 1941–June 8, 1942*, Military Intelligence Service (MIS) Campaign Study 3.

way, 4,500 miles from Manila. But even before this, on the first day of war, the Japanese attack on Pearl Harbor had destroyed the Battle Force of the Pacific Fleet and nullified all plans to come to the aid of the Philippines.

East of the date line, Vice Adm. C. Nagumo's *Pearl Harbor Striking Force* of six carriers reached its launching position 200 miles north of Oahu exactly on schedule, at 0600 on the morning of 7 December (0100 of the 8th, Tokyo time). Two Jakes (Zero-type reconnaissance planes), which had taken off at 0530 to reconnoiter, returned with the report that, except for the richest prize, the three carriers, the entire Pacific Fleet was in port. Pilots of the *First Air Fleet,* amidst shouts of "banzai" from their comrades, took off from the flight decks and climbed above the overcast into a magnificent sunrise. At 0750, while "Pearl Harbor was still asleep in the morning mist," [3] the Japanese planes came in over the island. Five minutes later, just an hour before Nomura presented his government's reply to Mr. Hull, they dropped their first bombs.[4]

The next two hours of that Sabbath morning in Hawaii were a nightmare. Bombs and torpedoes dropped everywhere, on the ships in the harbor, on Army installations, on depots, and other targets. Dive bombers machine-gunned planes on the ground and men on the ships. Within a half hour every battleship at Pearl Harbor had been badly damaged.

Hickam and Wheeler Fields were struck in the first attacks. The Army planes, parked in close order, wing tip to wing tip, made perfect targets. By ten o'clock the raid was over and the last Japanese planes had returned to their carriers, leaving behind them death and destruction. Tactical surprise had been as complete as strategical surprise.[5]

The Japanese pilots knew exactly what to go after. Though there were ninety-four naval vessels in the harbor they concentrated on the Battle Force, sinking 3 battleships, capsizing 1, and damaging 4 more. In addition to the battleships, 3 light cruisers, 3 destroyers, and miscellaneous vessels were badly damaged. Ninety-two naval planes were lost and 31 damaged. The Army lost a total of 96 planes, including those destroyed in depots and those later stripped for parts. Army and Navy installations were badly hit. Fortunately, the Japanese failed to destroy the repair shops at Pearl Harbor or the oil tanks, filled to capacity. The carriers, then at sea, escaped the attack altogether. American casualties for the day were 2,280 men killed and 1,109 wounded. The Japanese lost only 29 aircraft and 5 midget submarines. "The astoundingly disproportionate extent of losses," concluded the Joint Committee which investigated the attack, "marks the

---

[3] The quotation is from an account by a Japanese naval officer and is quoted in Morison, *Rising Sun in the Pacific,* p. 94.

[4] At 0800, Admiral Kimmel broadcast the message: "Air Raid on Pearl Harbor. This is no drill." Secretary Knox, when he read the message in Washington, exclaimed, "My God! This can't be true, this must mean the Philippines." *Pearl Harbor Attack Report,* p. 439.

[5] The best account of the attack on Pearl Harbor has been written by Morison, *Rising Sun in the Pacific,* Ch. V. For the Air Forces story, see Craven and Cate, *The Army Air Forces in World War II,* I, 194–201. Much personal testimony and first-hand accounts of the attack can be found scattered through the Congressional hearings on the Pearl Harbor attack. A summary of the action can be found in *Pearl Harbor Attack Report,* pp. 53–72.

greatest military and naval disaster in our Nation's history." [6]

With this smashing blow, the Japanese made obsolete the carefully prepared plans of defense in the event of war in the Pacific.[7] The RAINBOW plan called for the progressive movement of the Pacific Fleet across the Central Pacific by the capture of the Caroline and Marshall Islands and the establishment of an advanced base at Truk. The fleet would thus open the line of communications, establish superiority in the western Pacific, and come to the relief of the Philippine Islands. Along this protected line of communications would flow the supplies and men that would enable the Philippine garrison to beat back any Japanese effort to seize the Islands. By 1000 on the morning of 7 December, the force required to put RAINBOW into effect, the Battle Force of the Pacific Fleet, lay in ruins in Pearl Harbor. The Philippines were isolated, cut off from the nearest base 5,000 miles away, even before they had felt the first blow of the war. Their only hope now lay with the Far East Air Force and the Asiatic Fleet.

The Attack on Clark Field

The duty officer at Asiatic Fleet headquarters in the Marsman Building in Ma-

nila on the night of 7–8 December (Philippine time) was Lt. Col. William T. Clement, USMC. At 0230 of the 8th (0800, 7 December, Pearl Harbor time), the operator at the Navy station intercepted the startling message, "Air Raid on Pearl Harbor. This is no drill." Recognizing the technique of the sender, an old friend stationed at Pearl Harbor, the operator brought the message to Colonel Clement. Within a half hour, it was in Admiral Hart's hands. He broadcast the news to the fleet immediately, and then, with his chief of staff, hurried to his office.[8]

Shortly after 0330 General Sutherland received the news of the Pearl Harbor attack, not from the Navy but from commercial broadcasts. He passed the news on to MacArthur over the private wire to the general's penthouse apartment in the Manila Hotel, then notified all commanders that a state of war existed with Japan. Troops were ordered to battle position immediately.[9]

At Clark Field the news flash about Pearl Harbor was also picked up from commercial broadcasts. The operator immediately notified headquarters at the field and all units were alerted. "I knew," Brereton later wrote, "we could expect an attack from the Japs any time after daylight." Before leaving for MacArthur's headquarters, he ordered Colonel Eubank, the

---

[6] *Pearl Harbor Attack Report,* p. 65. The breakdown of casualties is as follows:

	Killed	Wounded
Navy and Marines	2,086	749
Army	194	360
Total	2,280	1,109

In an earlier volume of this series, Watson, *Chief of Staff,* page 517, the number of dead is placed at 2,403, including civilians. Mr. Watson's figures are from Morison, *Rising Sun in the Pacific,* page 126, and are based on 1947 estimates.

[7] Min, JB Mtg, 8 Dec 41, OPD Reg Doc.

797–257 O–66—7

[8] Hart, Narrative of Events, Asiatic Fleet, pp. 36–37; Morison, *Rising Sun in the Pacific,* pp. 168–69. Captain Morison secured additional information from Admiral Hart by interview after the war.
[9] Hunt, *MacArthur and the War Against Japan,* p. 27; Wainwright, *General Wainwright's Story,* p. 18; intervs, author with Col Diller, 24 Aug 49, Gens Sutherland and Marshall, 12 Nov 46 and 7 Apr 48, OCMH. Admiral Hart states that Colonel Clement, unable to "get response from USAFFE Headquarters," passed the news "to one of the staff duty officers at his home." Ltr, Hart to Maj Gen Orlando Ward, 19 Dec 51, OCMH.

bomber commander at Clark Field, to come down to Manila at once. At about 0500 in the morning Brereton was waiting outside MacArthur's office for orders.[10]

By breakfast, the news of the attack on Pearl Harbor had reached all ranks. The men had for so long accepted the fact that war with Japan might come that the event itself was an anticlimax. There was no cheering and no demonstration, but "a grim, thoughtful silence." [11] War with Japan was not, for the American and Philippine troops, a remote war across a wide ocean. It was close and immediate.

Prologue to Attack

On Formosa airfields, 500 miles away, Japanese Army and Navy pilots were standing by, their planes gassed and ready to take off for Luzon, when the first news of Pearl Harbor reached Manila. Around midnight of the 7th dense clouds of heavy fog had closed in on the island, blanketing airfields and preventing the scheduled take-offs at dawn.

This unforeseen development filled the Japanese commanders with nervous apprehension. The timetable for the attack was extremely close and left little leeway. As the early morning hours rolled by, anxiety increased. By this time, the Japanese believed, the American high command in the Philippines would have received news of Pearl Harbor and either sent the Far East Air Force southward or set up an effective defense against the impending raid. All hope of surprise would be lost.

Even more frightening was the possibility

that this delay would enable the heavy bombers of the Far East Air Force to attack the planes lined up on Formosa fields. Indeed, at 0800, the Japanese intercepted an American radio message which they interpreted as meaning that such an attack would come off in two hours. At 1010 a Japanese plane mistakenly reported B-17's approaching Formosa and the frightened Japanese began passing out gas masks.[12]

Japanese fears of an American attack against Formosa were not without foundation. Such plans had already been made and target data had been prepared. The objective folders were far from complete, however, and lacked calibrated bomb-target maps and bomb release lines for given speeds and altitudes. "But we had something complete enough," thought Capt. Allison Ind, a Far East Air Force intelligence officer, "to make this bombing mission a very far cry from the blind stab it would have had to be otherwise." [13]

---

[12] Interrog of Capt Takahashi Chihaya, Imperial Japanese Navy (IJN), 20 Oct 45, and of Comdr Ryosuke Nomura, Opns Officer, *23d Air Flotilla, 11th Air Fleet,* 28 Nov 45, in USSBS, *Interrogations of Japanese Officials,* 2 vols. (Washington 1946) I, 74–76; II, 531; *14th Army* Opns, I, 41.

It is difficult to understand the origin of the 0800 message. While there was discussion of such a raid at USAFFE, there was no need to send radios on the subject. It is possible that orders sending B-17's at Clark aloft to avoid being caught on the ground were in some way intercepted and misunderstood by the apprehensive Japanese. *14th Army* Opns, I, 41, refers to the report as "intelligence reports," but does not indicate its origin any further. *5th Air Gp* Opns, Japanese Studies in World War II, No. 3, p. 6.

[13] Lt. Col. Allison Ind, *Bataan, The Judgment Seat* (New York, 1944), p. 92. Material used with the permission of The Macmillan Company, publishers.

The official air force account of the attack on Clark Field is contained in Craven and Cate, *The Army Air Forces in World War II,* I, 201–14. General Brereton has a full account in his *Diaries,* pages 38–44, which must be considered as the evidence of an interested party in the dispute which

---

[10] Brereton, *Diaries,* pp. 38–39. It is evident from internal evidence that the diary for this period was put in its present form at a later date and cannot therefore be considered always a contemporaneous record.

[11] Mallonée, Bataan Diary, I, 34.

On his first visit to USAFFE headquarters about 0500, General Brereton had been unable to see MacArthur and had talked with Sutherland. At that time he had requested permission to carry out a daylight attack against Formosa. MacArthur's chief of staff had told him to go ahead with the necessary preparations, but to wait for MacArthur's authorization before starting the attack. Brereton returned to his headquarters at Nielson Field, where he talked with Colonel Eubank, who had just flown down from Clark Field. Orders were issued to get the B–17's ready. At about 0715 Brereton apparently went to MacArthur's headquarters again to request permission to attack Formosa. Again he was told by Sutherland to stand by for orders.[14]

About this time the Far East Air Force commander received a transoceanic telephone call from his air force chief, General Arnold. Brereton explained what he was trying to do, and Arnold told him what had happened at Pearl Harbor, so that, as he later explained, Brereton would not be caught in the same way and have his "entire air force destroyed." [15]

By this time, reports of enemy flights were being received at air force headquarters and planes of the Interceptor Command were sent up. Around 0800 the heavy bombers at Clark Field were ordered aloft on patrol, without bombs, to avoid being caught on the ground.

At 1000 Brereton renewed his request to take offensive action. "I personally called General Sutherland," he says, "and informed him . . . that if Clark Field was attacked successfully we would be unable to operate offensively with the bombers." [16] Again the request was denied. Ten minutes later, Colonel Eubank started back to Clark Field with instructions to dispatch a photographic reconnaissance mission immediately to southern Formosa.

---

later arose over responsibility for the disaster. Army Air Action in Phil and NEI, Chapter III, covers the Clark Field attack and is substantially the same as that given in the air force history.

Official records of the events surrounding the attack are practically nonexistent. An effort has been made by the author to supplement the existing accounts with interviews with those participants not interviewed by the air force historians. Persons interviewed were Generals Sutherland and R. J. Marshall, Colonels Diller, Collier, and Campbell, the last of whom was aircraft warning officer of USAFFE.

Mr. Walter D. Edmonds, who was commissioned by the air force to write the account of air operations in the Philippines, interviewed General Sutherland in Manila in June 1945, as well as a large number of air force officers. A copy of his notes taken on the Sutherland interview is included in Army Air Action in Phil and NEI, Appendix 9, and a portion is printed in Craven and Cate, *The Army Air Forces in World War II*, I, 205. The information Edmonds secured is directly at variance with information the present author secured in two interviews with General Sutherland. Edmond's findings are embodied in an article entitled "What Happened at Clark Field," *The Atlantic* (July 1951), pp. 20–33.

[14] Summary of Activities, Far East Air Force, entry of 8 Dec 41, in Air University Hist Off. This document is evidently a transcription from notes hastily made during December 1941. Errors in dating the year of entry are explained as the result

of "harried field conditions." Despite the imperfections of this document it remains one of the few written contemporary sources for the events of 8 December 1941. Ltr, Col Wilfred J. Paul, Air University Hist Off, to Gen Ward, 7 Dec 51, OCMH. The official air force account in Craven and Cate, *The Army Air Forces in World War II*, I, 206 note, takes cognizance of the mistakes in dating in this document. Edmonds, "What Happened at Clark Field," pages 24–26, contains an excellent account of the discussions at air force headquarters that morning.

[15] Gen. Henry H. Arnold, *Global Mission* (New York: Harper & Brothers, 1949), p. 272.

[16] Brereton, *Diaries*, p. 40. The author has also used a letter written by Brereton to the AAF Hist Off expanding the diary entries. 1st Ind, Brereton to Paul, 30 Jan 43, Air University Hist Off. See also Edmonds, "What Happened at Clark Field," p. 25.

No sooner had those orders been issued than Brereton received a telephone call from General MacArthur. He told MacArthur that since Clark Field had not yet been attacked, he would hold the bombers in readiness until he received reports from the reconnaissance mission already authorized. They agreed that if no reports were received, the bombers would attack Formosa late that afternoon. MacArthur left to Brereton "the decision for offensive action." [17]

Brereton called in his staff and told them of his conversation with MacArthur. Orders were then dispatched to Clark Field to call in the heavy bombers. Three were to be readied for the photo reconnaissance mission; the others were to be briefed for offensive missions. At 1120 Field Order No. 1 of the Far East Air Force was sent by teletype to Clark Field. It confirmed Brereton's instructions to Eubank, given at 1045, to attack southern Formosa with two heavy bombardment squadrons "at the latest daylight hour today that visibility will permit." By 1130 the bombers were back on the field, being loaded with 100- and 300-pound bombs; the fighters had also returned to base for refueling. At 1156 Brereton gave Sutherland a full report of the situation over the telephone, and informed him that he planned to attack Formosa fields late that afternoon.[18]

General Sutherland's account of the pro-

posed raid on Formosa differs from the air force story. On one occasion, Sutherland recollected that there had been some plan to bomb Formosa on 8 December but that "Brereton said he had to have the photos first." On another occasion Sutherland took the opposite and more consistent position that when Brereton asked for permission to attack Formosa, he, Sutherland, had ordered a reconnaissance first.[19]

General MacArthur's statements do not throw any light on this question. He had received word from Washington early that morning (at 0530) that hostilities with Japan had begun, and that he was to carry out the tasks assigned in RAINBOW.[20] Brereton's surmise, therefore, that he was not permitted at first to attack Formosa because MacArthur was under orders not to attack unless attacked first and that the Pearl Harbor attack "might not have been construed as an overt act against the Philippines" must be dismissed.[21] MacArthur had authority to act, and RAINBOW specifically assigned as one of his missions "air raids against Japanese forces and installations within tactical operating radius of available bases."[22]

[17] Summary of Activities, Far East Air Force, entry of 8 Dec 41. General Brereton omits entirely any mention of his conversation with General MacArthur, and states that he received the authorization to attack Formosa at 1100 from General Sutherland. In an interview with the present author in June 1951, Sutherland declared that he does not recall that Brereton spoke with MacArthur that morning. Brereton, Diaries, p. 41.
[18] Summary of Activities, Far East Air Force, entry of 8 Dec 41.

[19] The first version was given in his interview with Walter D. Edmonds in Manila in June, 1945. The second version was given in an interview with the present author in November 1946. This author interviewed Sutherland a second time in June 1951 and on being presented with both versions, Sutherland was most emphatic in asserting that it was he who had ordered the reconnaissance because Brereton did not have sufficient information to warrant an attack against Formosa. USAFFE and air force records do not contain any material relating to this incident.
[20] Rad, Marshall to MacArthur, No. 736, 7 Dec 41, WPD 4544-20.
[21] Brereton, Diaries, p. 39n; ltr, Brereton to Paul, Air University Hist Off.
[22] Ltr, CofS to CG USAFFE, 21 Nov 41, sub: U.S.-British Co-operation, incl, War Plan RAINBOW 5, WPD 4402-112.

General Brereton's surmise, however, was not entirely without foundation. It was evidently based on the 27 November warning from the War Department. That warning had stated that "if hostilities cannot be avoided the United States desires that Japan commit the first overt act." [23] The War Department had been careful, however, not to restrict MacArthur's freedom of action, and had authorized him in the same message to "undertake such reconnaissance and other measures as you deem necessary" prior to hostile Japanese action. In the event of war he was to execute the tasks assigned in RAINBOW.

In the period between the receipt of this message and the outbreak of hostilities, the B–17's had flown reconnaissance missions north of Luzon in the direction of Formosa. Their search sectors, according to General Sutherland, reached to "the southern edge of Formosa with one segment of the pie running up the east coast of the island a little way." [24] But General Brereton declares that he was instructed by MacArthur to limit reconnaissance to "two-thirds of the distance between North Luzon and Southern Formosa." [25] Later, he says, he secured permission to extend the northern limit of the search sector to the international treaty boundary between the Philippines and Formosa. [26] On the basis of Sutherland's statement, then, it was possible to conduct a partial reconnaissance of Formosa before the war; according to Brereton there was no prewar reconnaissance on MacArthur's orders.

On Brereton's proposal to bomb Formosa, General MacArthur expressed himself most clearly. When Brereton's diaries were published in 1946, MacArthur released a statement to the press recounting in full his recollection of the events of 8 December 1941. The press release, issued on 27 September 1946, read:

General Brereton never recommended an attack on Formosa to me and I know nothing of such a recommendation having been made. . . . That it must have been of a most nebulous and superficial character, as no official record exists of it at headquarters. That such a proposal, if intended seriously, should have been made to me in person by him; that he never has spoken of the matter to me either before or after the Clark Field attack. That an attack on Formosa with its heavy concentrations by his small bomber force without fighter support, which because of the great distance involved, was impossible, would have had no chance of success. [27]

On 8 December, in summarizing the results of the Japanese attack, MacArthur had told the War Department: "I am launching a heavy bombardment counterattack tomorrow morning on enemy airdromes in southern Formosa." [28] It is evident, then, that MacArthur himself planned, by the afternoon or evening of the 8th, to execute an attack against Formosa with the remaining B–17's.

Faced with these conflicting accounts, the historian can be sure only of five facts: (1) That an attack against Formosa was proposed; (2) that such an attack was deferred in favor of a photo reconnaissance mission requested either by Brereton or Sutherland; (3) that about 1100 on 8 December a strike

[23] Rad, Marshall to MacArthur, 27 Nov 41, No. 624, WPD 4544-13; see above, Ch. IV, p. 71.

[24] Interv, Edmonds with Sutherland, Jun 45, and confirmed in interv, Morton with Sutherland, 12 Nov 46.

[25] Brereton, *Diaries*, pp. 34–35.

[26] *Ibid.*

[27] *New York Times*, September 28, 1946, p. 6.

[28] Rad, MacArthur to AGWAR, No. 1133, 8 Dec 41. The raid was canceled the next day. Rad, MacArthur to AGWAR, No. 1135, 9 Dec 41. Both in AG 381 (11–27–41 Gen) Far East.

against Formosa, to take place that day, was finally authorized; (4) that the heavy bombers were back on Clark Field after 1130 on the morning of 8 December; and (5) that MacArthur planned an attack against Formosa for the morning of 9 December.

The Attack

The Japanese, fearing an air attack against Formosa, had meanwhile made haste to get their planes off the ground. The fog, which had grounded the *11th Air Fleet,* had lifted to the east at dawn, permitting twenty-five twin-engine Army bombers to take off for Luzon.[29]

Shortly before 0900 the Japanese Army bombers were reported by the aircraft warning service on Luzon to be heading south over Lingayen Gulf in the direction of Manila. It was probably this report that sent the B–17's at Clark Field aloft without bombs. The 20th Pursuit Squadron at Clark took off to intercept the strike and the 17th Pursuit Squadron rose from Nichols Field to cover Clark. But the Japanese Army planes, limited to targets north of the 16th latitude, turned east as they approached Lingayen Gulf. One group struck Tuguegarao at about 0930 while another concentrated on barracks and other installations at Baguio, the summer capital of the Commonwealth, where Quezon was staying at this time. The Japanese bombers returned to base without having sighted any American aircraft. Far East Air Force reports between 1000 and 1030 of a flight of enemy bombers, first in the Cagayan valley, and then "turned around and pro-

ceeding north," apparently referred to these Japanese Army planes.[30]

By the time the false report of approaching B–17's had been received on Formosa, the fog had lifted sufficiently to permit the naval planes of the *11th Air Fleet* to take off. At 1015, a force of 108 twin-engine bombers escorted by eighty-four Zeros set out for Clark and Iba. Only the very best and most experienced pilots had been assigned to this important mission.[31]

As the Japanese planes approached northern Luzon, the airborne American aircraft received the all-clear signal and were instructed to land. By 1130 nearly all the planes were back at their bases. The two squadrons of B–17's were on Clark Field, loading with gas and bombs for the raid against Formosa. The 20th Pursuit Squadron was also at Clark after its vain attempt to intercept the last Japanese flight. At Nichols, the 17th Pursuit Squadron, which had been covering Clark, was landing to refuel. The 3d and 34th Pursuit Squadrons were standing by at Iba and Del Carmen.[32]

Shortly before 1130, reports of an approaching enemy formation began coming in to the plotting board at Nielson.

[29] *5th Air Gp* Opns, p. 16.

[30] Summary of Activities, Far East Air Force, 8 Dec 41; Craven and Cate, *The Army Air Forces in World War II,* I, 207–08; Edmonds, "What Happened at Clark Field," p. 24; *5th Air Gp* Opns, p. 16; USSBS, *Japanese Air Power* (Washington, 1946), p. 7.

[31] Japanese Naval Opns in Phil Invasion, pp. 6–7; interrog of Capt Takahashi and Comdr Nomura, USSBS, *Interrogations of Japanese Officials,* I, 75; II, 531.

[32] The account of the attack is based, except where otherwise noted, on Craven and Cate, *The Army Air Forces in World War II,* I, 207–13; Brereton, *Diaries,* pp. 38–44; History of the Fifth Air Force (and its Predecessors); Edmonds, "What Happened at Clark Field," pp. 28–31; Japanese Naval Opns in the Phil Invasion, p. 6; *5th Air Gp* Opns, p. 12.

In addition to radar reports, almost every postmaster along the northwest coast of Luzon reported the high-flying enemy bombers to the air warning center by telephone or telegraph.[33] Colonel George, chief of staff of the Interceptor Command, was in the plotting room when the reports were coming in, and predicted "that the objective of this formidable formation was Clark Field." [34]

At about 1145, according to Col. Alexander H. Campbell, the aircraft warning officer, a warning message went out to Clark Field by teletype. If the message did not get through, as is frequently asserted, this fact was not known to the officers in the plotting room at Nielson. It is asserted also that an attempt to warn the field by radio over the Far East Air Force net was made, but with no success. The reason for this failure can only be guessed. Col. James V. Collier, a G–3 officer in USAFFE headquarters, later stated, "The radio operator had left his station to go to lunch," and another source states, "Radio reception was drowned by static which the Japanese probably caused by systematic jamming of the frequencies." [35] Apparently other available means of communication, such as the long distance telephone lines, telegraph, and the command radio net to Fort Stotsenburg, were not used or thought of. Colonel Campbell did get a telephone message through to Clark Field and talked with an unknown junior officer there. This officer intended, said Campbell, to give the base commander or the operations officer the message at the earliest opportunity.[36]

Meanwhile, Colonel George at Nielson had dispersed his fighters to meet the attack. The 34th Squadron was ordered to cover Clark Field; the 17th, the Bataan peninsula; and the 21st, the Manila area. The 3d Squadron at Iba was dispatched to intercept a reported enemy formation over the South China Sea.[37] At Clark Field, two squadrons of B–17's and the 20th Pursuit Squadron were still on the ground. Sometime shortly before 1145 the fighters were ordered aloft as soon as refueling was completed to cover their own base.[38]

The 3d Pursuit Squadron took off from Iba to intercept the enemy flight over the South China Sea. A thick haze of dust prevented the 34th at Del Carmen from taking off, and at 1215 the 20th Pursuit Squadron at Clark, whose planes had just completed refueling, made ready to take off.[39]

At that moment the first formation of Japanese bombers appeared over Clark

---

[33] Collier, Notebooks, I, 49.

[34] Ibid.

[35] Ibid., 50; Army Air Action in Phil and NEI, p. 55.

[36] Interv, author with Col Campbell, Sep 46; Collier, Notebooks, I, 50. Colonel Campbell's notebook contains the following entry: Sgt. Alfred H. Eckles, Hopkinsville, Ky., was on duty with Maj. Sam Lamb's communication detail Hqrs. F. E. A. F. Dec. 8th and carried message to Teletype operator re flight of planes heading toward Clark Field, saw it sent and acknowledged as received by them. This at about 11:45 (?) A. M., about 30–45 min. before arrival of bombers and bombing of Clark Field. I, together with Coyle, George and Sprague watched this particular flight for considerable length of time. I kept urging them to do something about it, but they insisted on waiting until they reached a certain distance from field. Sprague typed wrote out message showed it to George and myself. I asked what "Kickapoo" meant in message. Was told it meant, "Go get 'em." Sprague then took message into Teletype Room for transmission, about 15 minutes before bombing.

[37] Craven and Cate, The Army Air Forces in World War II, I, 209.

[38] Hist of Fifth Air Force, p. 16. This statement would imply that Colonel George was in communication with the pursuit squadron at Clark Field after 1145, although the Bomber Command could not be reached at this time.

[39] Hist of Fifth Air Force, p. 16.

Field.[40] All but one of the B–17's was lined up on the field and the fighters were just getting ready to take off. After the warning of the Pearl Harbor attack, and after the loss of several valuable hours because of bad weather, the Japanese pilots did not expect to find so rich a harvest waiting for them. But they did not question their good fortune. The first flight of Japanese planes consisted of twenty-seven twin-engine bombers. They came over the unprotected field in a V–formation at a height estimated at 22,000 to 25,000 feet, dropping their bombs on the aircraft and buildings below, just as the air raid warning sounded. As at Pearl Harbor, the Japanese achieved complete tactical surprise.

The first flight was followed immediately by a similar formation which remained over the field for fifteen minutes. The planes in this formation, as in the first, accomplished their mission almost entirely without molestation. American antiaircraft shells exploded from 2,000 to 4,000 feet short of the targets. After the second formation of bombers, came thirty-four Zeros—which the Americans believed were carrier based—to deliver the final blow with their low-level strafing attacks on the grounded B–17's, and on the P–40's with their full gasoline tanks. This attack lasted for more than an hour.

With the first high wail of the siren, the men on the field below streamed from the mess halls. As the bombers passed over, the Americans could see the falling bombs glistening in the sunlight. Then came the explosions, hundreds of them, so violent that they seemed to pierce the eardrums and shake the ground. Throwing aside momentary disbelief and stupefaction, the men rushed to their battle stations. The scene was one of destruction and horror, unbelievable to the men who only a few minutes before had been eating lunch or servicing the planes. Flash fires sprang up and spread rapidly to the trees and long cogon grass around the field "roaring and crackling like an evil beast." [41] Dense smoke and a heavy cloud of dust rose over the field.

Against such odds, the Americans could offer little opposition. The 200th Coast Artillery (AA) experienced considerable difficulty with its 3-inch gun ammunition, the most recent of which was manufactured in 1932. The percentage of duds was abnormally high and "most of the fuses were badly corroded." Only one of every six shells fired, says one observer, actually exploded.[42] Acts of personal heroism were commonplace. Ground and combat crews manned the guns of the grounded planes, and men dashed into flaming buildings to rescue their comrades as well as supplies and equipment. Others braved the strafing gunfire to aid the wounded. One private appropriated an abandoned truck and made seven trips with wounded men to the station hospital.

During the attack, 3 P–40's of the 20th Pursuit Squadron managed to get into the air, but 5 more were blasted by bombs as

---

[40] It is not possible to state the exact time of this attack. Like so many other matters, this question, too, is controversial. The author has selected this time, about 1220, since it is supported by the weight of evidence. Walter D. Edmonds gives the time as 1240 in his account of the attack. *They Fought With What They Had,* pp. 100, 102n.

[41] Miller, *Bataan Uncensored,* p. 67.

[42] *Ibid.;* Prov CA Brig (AA) Rpt of Opns, p. 3, Annex IX, USAFFE-USFIP Rpt of Opns; interv, author with Gen Sage, 28 Feb 51.

they taxied for the take-off.[43] A similar number was caught in the strafing attack. The 3 airborne fighters shot down 3 or 4 Japanese fighters.

The 34th Pursuit Squadron, still at Del Carmen, could see the great clouds of smoke rising from Clark. The old P–35's of the squadron finally managed to take off and were soon in action against the superior Zeros over Clark. Though outclassed and outnumbered, the squadron knocked down three enemy fighters without loss to itself. But few of its planes were without serious damage. The 17th and 21st Pursuit Squadrons, on patrol over Bataan and Manila, made no effort to attack the Japanese aircraft, presumably because the communications center at Clark had been bombed out and news of the raid did not reach the Interceptor Command in time to dispatch aid.[44]

The *11th Air Fleet*'s attack against Clark was even more successful than the worried Japanese had expected. The operation had been well planned and executed. The first flights of bombers had concentrated on the hangars, barracks, and warehouses, and left them a burning ruin. Some of the grounded planes had been damaged in these bombings but the greatest casualties were inflicted by the low-level attacks of the Zeros which followed. Casualties in men were fifty-five killed and more than one hundred wounded.

Simultaneously with the raid against Clark, other *11th Air Fleet* planes were attacking the fighter base at Iba. The 12 planes of the 3d Pursuit Squadron, which had been patrolling over the China Sea, low on gas, returned to base. As they were circling to land, Iba was struck by 54 Japanese twin-motored naval bombers escorted by 50 Zeros. Effective action by the P–40's resulted in the loss of 2 Japanese fighters (probables) and kept the Zeros from carrying out the low-level attacks which were so successful at Clark. But the losses at Iba were almost as great as at Clark. Barracks, warehouses, equipment, and the radar station were destroyed. Ground crews suffered heavy casualties and all but 2 of the 3d Squadron's P–40's were lost.

The reaction from Washington headquarters of the Air Forces was delayed but explosive, despite a radio from MacArthur stating that the losses had been "due to overwhelming superiority of enemy forces." [45] General Arnold, when he received the news of the losses in the Philippines, "could not help thinking that there must have been some mistake made somewhere in my Air Force command," and he decided "to tell Brereton so." [46] Brereton had just returned from an inspection of Clark Field when he received a transoceanic telephone call from an irate General Arnold asking "how in the hell" an experienced airman like himself could have been caught with his planes down. Apparently he felt his explanation had not satisfied General Arnold, for he immediately reported the conversation to MacArthur and asked his help in presenting the situation to the Army Air Forces chief. According to Brereton, MacArthur was furious. "He told me to go back and fight the war and not to worry,"

---

[43] This account of the operations of the 20th Pursuit Squadron is based on an interview with the squadron commander, Col. Joseph H. Moore, 12 August 1949. It varies slightly from the official air force account which places four planes in the air before the attack.

[44] It is strange that the pilots over Bataan and Manila did not see the heavy columns of smoke and dust rising from Clark, only fifty miles away.

---

[45] Rad, MacArthur to Arnold, 10 Dec 41, AG 381 (11–27–41 Gen) Far East.

[46] Arnold, *Global Mission*, p. 272.

Brereton recorded in his diary. "As I walked out of his office he asked Sutherland to get General Marshall on the phone." [47] Unfortunately, there is no record of the telephone conversation that followed.

Thus, after one day of war, with its strength cut in half, the Far East Air Force had been eliminated as an effective fighting force. Of the modern combat aircraft, only 17 of the original 35 B–17's remained. Fifty-three P–40's and 3 P–35's had been destroyed, and an additional 25 or 30 miscellaneous aircraft (B–10's, B–18's, and observation planes) were gone. In addition, many of the planes listed as operational were heavily damaged. Installations at Clark and Iba were either burned out or badly hit. Total casualties for the day were 80 killed and 150 wounded. The total cost to the Japanese was 7 fighters.[48] The conclusion of the Joint Congressional Committee which investigated the Pearl Harbor attack, that it was the greatest military disaster in American history, is equally applicable to the Philippines.

Post-Mortem

The catastrophe of Pearl Harbor overshadowed at the time and still obscures the extent of the ignominious defeat inflicted on American air forces in the Philippines on the same day. The Far East Air Force had been designed as a striking force to hit the enemy before he could reach Philippine shores. The heavy bombers were an offensive weapon, thought capable of striking the enemy's bases and cutting his lines of communication. Hopes for the active defense of the Islands rested on these aircraft. At the end of the first day of war, such hopes were dead.

The tragedy of Clark Field, where the heavy bombers were caught like so many sitting ducks, becomes even more tragic when one considers the strange sequence of events that preceded it. Even before the war, the danger of basing the B–17's on Clark Field had been recognized. General MacArthur had written to General Marshall on 29 November, "The location of potential enemy fields and types of aircraft indicate that heavy bombers should be located south of Luzon where they would be reasonably safe from attack." He intended at the time to base the bombers in the Visayas.[49] Time did not permit the construction of fields there, but before the outbreak of hostilities he did order General Brereton to move the heavy bombers from Clark Field to Mindanao.[50]

During the first week in December, Brereton had sent two squadrons of B–17's to the recently constructed field at Del Monte in Mindanao. The decision to move only two squadrons, Brereton states, was based on the expected arrival from the United States of the 7th Bombardment Group which was to be stationed at Del Monte. Had all the heavy bombers on Clark been transferred to Mindanao, there would have been no room for the 7th when it arrived.[51]

---

[47] *Ibid.;* Brereton, *Diaries,* p. 50. General Sutherland has no recollection of such a telephone call. Interv, author with Sutherland, 12 Jun 51.

[48] Japanese Naval Opns in Phil Invasion, p. 7. An additional fighter of the *4th Carrier Squadron* was lost at Davao. Craven and Cate, *The Army Air Forces in World War II,* I, 213. There is some disagreement on the number of P–40's lost, some sources placing the figure as low as 42. USSBS, *Japanese Air Power,* p. 7.

[49] Ltr, MacArthur to Marshall, 29 Nov 41, WPD 3489-21.

[50] *New York Times,* September 28, 1946, p. 6; interv, author with Sutherland, 12 Nov 46.

[51] Brereton, *Diaries,* pp. 35–36.

General Sutherland's version of the same incident differs considerably from that of the air force commander. It was at his insistence, he recollected, that even the two squadrons were sent south. "General Brereton," he says, "did not want them to go." Sutherland says he had ordered all the B–17's moved to Del Monte. On checking, he had found that only half of the planes had been sent and that General MacArthur's orders had not been obeyed.[52]

Wherever the responsibility lies for failing to move all the B–17's south, there still remains the question of why the remaining bombers were caught on the ground. Brereton argues that had he been permitted to attack Formosa when he wished, the planes would not have been on the field. Implicit is the assumption that if the raid had been successful, the Japanese could not have made their own attack. MacArthur denied knowledge of such a proposal in 1946, but in a radio sent on 8 December 1941 he stated that he intended to attack Formosa the next morning. General Sutherland, in one interview, claimed that Brereton was responsible for deferring the attack, and in another interview, that he himself deferred the attack because the Far East Air Force did not have sufficient target data for such an attack. It is clear that this project was discussed by Brereton and Sutherland, that MacArthur mentioned it in a radio that day, and that authorization to execute the attack was delayed until 1100 that morning.

Whether such an attack would have had a serious chance of success is not argued by either Sutherland or Brereton. Knowing now what the Japanese had at

Formosa, the possibility of a successful raid by the B–17's seems extremely remote. The Far East Air Force admittedly had sketchy information on the strength and disposition of the Japanese forces on Formosa. Had it been known that there were over five hundred Japanese planes waiting on Formosa, ready to take off, it is doubtful that anyone would have considered the project seriously. Moreover, the B–17's would have had to fly to Formosa, out of fighter range, unescorted. Once there, they would have been greeted by swarms of Zeros. "An attack on Formosa, with its heavy air concentrations," MacArthur later wrote, ". . . was impossible, would have had no chance of success."[53] Sutherland's request for a photo reconnaissance mission prior to an attack would appear, therefore, to have been entirely justified. The heavy bombers were indeed far too valuable to risk in so hazardous a mission.

Another unresolved question is why the warning of approaching Japanese aircraft did not reach the bomber commander at Clark Field in time to meet the attack. All forces in the Philippines had knowledge of the attack on Pearl Harbor hours before the first Japanese bombers appeared over Luzon. A dawn raid at Davao had given notice that the Japanese had no intention of bypassing the archipelago. The early morning bombings on Luzon gave even more pointed warning that an attack against the major airbase in the Islands could be expected. Colonel Campbell testifies that Clark Field had received word of the approaching Japanese aircraft before the attack. Colonel Eubank states that no such warning was ever received. Other officers speak of the breakdown of commu-

[52] Intervs, author and Edmonds with Sutherland. General Kenney was also told this story by Sutherland. *General Kenney Reports*, p. 27.

[53] *New York Times*, September 28, 1946, p. 6.

nications at this critical juncture. There is no way of resolving this conflicting testimony.

Assuming that Colonel Eubank did not receive the warning from Nielson Field, there still remains one final question. Were the aircraft on the field adequately dispersed for wartime condition? It is not possible to state definitely how the aircraft were dispersed when they came in at 1130. There surely must have been some recognition of the danger of an enemy air attack at any moment. The Japanese state that they were "surprised to find the American aircraft lined up on the field." [54] And at least one flight of four B-17's was lined neatly on the field when the Japanese came over. Captain Ind tells of finding photographs, one of which was taken by an American pilot flying over the field, showing the planes inadequately dispersed for any but high-level bombing attacks. "This entire set of photographs," he says, "was removed from my desk a few nights later. No one seemed to know what had happened to them." [55] This question, like the others, remains unanswered.

The full story of the events which preceded the Japanese air attacks against the Far East Air Force on the first day of the war will probably never be known. There was no time for reports, and if any records ever existed they have since been lost. The historian must rely on the memories of participants whose stories conflict at numerous points. General Arnold, eight years after the event, wrote that he was never able "to get the real story of what happened in the Philippines." Brereton's diary, in his opin-

ion, did not provide "a complete and accurate account," and General Sutherland's story "does not completely clear it up, by any means." [56]

Whatever the answers to the questions one may ask about the events of 8–9 December 1941 on Luzon, the significance of these events is clear. As at Pearl Harbor, the Japanese had removed in one stroke the greatest single obstacle to their advance southward. The Philippine garrison could expect little help in the near future. It was now almost entirely surrounded. The only path open lay to the south, and that, too, soon would be closed.

The Fleet Moves South

The mission of the Asiatic Fleet in the event of war was to support the defense of the Philippines "as long as that defense continues." The actual employment of local naval defense forces was entrusted to the commander of the 16th Naval District, who was responsible for the joint tactical and strategical employment of his forces in co-operation with the Army. The commander of the Asiatic Fleet, at his discretion and when the situation demanded, was authorized to "shift base to British and Dutch ports." [57]

The force assigned for this task was pitifully small and deployed over a distance of more than 1,500 miles, from northern Luzon to Borneo. In the Manila Bay area were 5 destroyers, 2 of which were under repair and 3 on patrol; 27 submarines with their 3 tenders—3 of the underwater craft

---

[54] Interrog of Comdr Nomura, 28 Nov 45, USSBS, *Interrogations of Japanese Officials*, II, 531; Japanese Naval Opns in Phil Invasion, p. 6.

[55] Ind, *Bataan, The Judgment Seat*, p. 101.

[56] Arnold, *Global Mission*, p. 272.

[57] Navy Basic War Plan RAINBOW 5 (Short Title: WPL–46), 26 May 41, Ch. III, reproduced in *Pearl Harbor Attack Hearings*, Exhibit 129, Part 18, p. 2875.

were being overhauled; 28 Catalinas (twin-engine patrol bombers or PBY's); 4 utility planes; and 1 observation plane. The planes were organized into Patrol Wing 10 under Capt. F. D. Wagner, with one full squadron operating from Sangley Point, Cavite, and the remainder from Olongapo. In addition, there were 6 gunboats, a similiar number of motor torpedo boats, 5 minesweepers, and other auxiliary craft in the area. At Mariveles was the floating dry dock *Dewey*. The installations of the 16th Naval District, commanded by Rear Adm. Francis W. Rockwell, were centered in Manila and Subic Bays—at Cavite, Corregidor, and Olongapo—with approximately 2,000 officers and men assigned. The reorganized and strengthened 4th Marines, with a strength of 1,600 and commanded by Col. Samuel L. Howard, was at Olongapo.[58]

The bulk of the surface strength of the Asiatic Fleet, organized into Task Force 5, was based south of Manila Bay. The flagship of the task force, the heavy cruiser *Houston*, was at Iloilo, in Panay. The light cruiser *Boise*, which belonged to the Pacific Fleet, was also in the Visayas, off Cebu, where she had gone after her arrival in Manila on 4 December with an Army convoy. At the Dutch Borneo port of Tarakan was the light cruiser *Marblehead* accompanied by 5 destroyers, and at Balikpapan were 4 more destroyers and a tender.[59] The remaining 2 submarines of the Asiatic Fleet were on patrol off the Luzon coast, 1 in Lingayen Gulf and another in Sorsogon Bay. Patrolling to the south and linking up with the Dutch patrols from Borneo were 2 small aircraft detachments, 1 at Davao and another on a small island south of Palawan.[60]

On the morning of 8 December, the only portion of the Asiatic Fleet to come under fire was the small aircraft detachment at Davao with the tender *Preston*. After the attack from the *Ryujo*-based dive bombers and fighters, *Preston* let pass four Japanese destroyers, and then slipped out of Davao Gulf to escape southward.

Before noon of the 8th, Rear Adm. William A. Glassford, commander of Task Force 5 and recently arrived from China, left by plane for Iloilo to hoist his flag aboard the *Houston*. He was joined there by the *Boise* from Cebu. That evening the aircraft tender *Langley*, protected by two destroyers, slipped out of Manila Bay under cover of darkness to join the cruisers at Panay. From there Glassford, on orders from Admiral Hart, led his small fleet south to Dutch Borneo to pick up oil and to assemble the rest of his force. He met no enemy ships on the way, only a long line of merchant vessels making good their escape.[61] Thus, by the end of the first day of war, the striking force of the Asiatic

---

[58] Hart, *Narrative of Events, Asiatic Fleet*, pp. 30 ff; Morison, *The Rising Sun in the Pacific*, pp. 158–60. Strength of the 16th Naval District and 4th Marines was obtained from papers lent to the author by Admiral Rockwell, and from rad, COM 16 to OPNAV, 31 Dec 41, Off of Naval Rcds.

[59] The deployment of the fleet southward had been made as a result of the war warning of 27 November which ordered a "defensive deployment."

Ltr, Hart to Ward, 19 Dec 51, OCMH. The destroyers at Balikpapan were ordered to Batavia on 6 December, and en route were redirected to Singapore. They were later recalled to Borneo to join the rest of Task Force 5. Hart, *Narrative of Events, Asiatic Fleet*, pp. 36, 41.

[60] The disposition of the fleet is also covered in *The Java Sea Campaign*, Office of Naval Intelligence (ONI) Combat Narratives, pp. 1–6.

[61] Hart, *Narrative of Events, Asiatic Fleet*, p. 37; *The Java Sea Campaign*, ONI Combat Narrative, pp. 4–6.

Fleet, Task Force 5, was steaming south, and on 10 December had left Philippine waters.

The Japanese Gain Air and Naval Supremacy

The Japanese followed up their successes of the first day of war with a series of air attacks aimed at destroying or driving American air and naval power from the Philippines. Before dawn of the 9th 7 Japanese naval bombers struck Nichols Field near Manila. The Japanese had planned a larger attack but the fog had again rolled in over Formosa during the early morning hours. The 7 bombers were enough to do the job. The loss of 2 or 3 P–40's, as well as other planes, and the destruction of ground installations completed the havoc begun at noon the previous day.[62]

On the 9th ground crews worked desperately to patch up the damaged planes, and units were reorganized. Antiaircraft defenses, especially in the Manila area, were strengthened, and one battery of the 60th Coast Artillery (AA) which had left Corregidor after dark on the 8th was in position on the morning of the 9th to furnish local protection for the port area, Nichols Field, and the oil storage and railroad yards.[63] About five hundred men of the 200th Coast Artillery (AA) from Clark Field were dispatched to Manila during the day, supplied with equipment from the Philippine Ordnance Depot, and organized into a provisional antiaircraft regiment, later designated the 515th.[64]

The air attack against Formosa which General MacArthur had promised for the 9th never materialized.[65] At 0800 one B–17 took off from Clark Field for a photo reconnaissance mission over Formosa but was forced back because of mechanical difficulty. Army fighters flew reconnaissance missions over northern Luzon and the PBY's of Patrol Wing 10 continued their patrols to the west and northwest. Numerous reports of enemy sightings were received but on investigation proved to be unfounded. Such reports, Hart noted, placed all Japanese vessels in one of two categories, "either a Transport or a Battleship!"[66] The Japanese also searched north Luzon during the day for evidence of American air activities.[67]

On the 9th, the thirteen heavy bombers on Mindanao moved forward to Luzon. Six of the Flying Fortresses landed at ill-fated Clark Field at 1430; the rest reached San Marcelino, an emergency field along the west coast of Luzon, later in the afternoon. The B–17's at Clark refueled and took off immediately after their arrival, remaining in the air until dark to avoid being caught on the ground as had the others the day before.[68]

[62] Craven and Cate, The Army Air Forces in World War II, I, 213; Japanese Naval Opns in Phil Invasion, pp. 6–7.
[63] Harbor Defenses Rpt of Opns, p. 18.
[64] Prov CA Brig Rpt of Opns, p. 1.

[65] Rad, MacArthur to AGWAR, No. 1133, 8 Dec 41, AG 381 (11–27–41 Gen) Far East.
[66] Hart, Narrative of Events, Asiatic Fleet, p. 38; Brereton, Diaries, p. 45; interv, Edmonds with Sutherland, Jun 45.
[67] 5th Air Gp Opns, p. 16.
[68] Craven and Cate, The Army Air Forces in World War II, I, 214. There seems to be some confusion as to the number of B–17's at Del Monte. The History of the Fifth Air Force states that only 12 heavy bombers were based there. Brereton states that 16 B–17's had gone to Mindanao on the 5th, and Craven and Cate, as well as Brereton, state that 13 flew up from Mindanao to Clark Field on the 9th. Brereton, Diaries, pp. 36, 44–45; Craven and Cate, The Army Air Forces in World War II, I, 214. The author has accepted these last figures.

JAPANESE AIR ATTACK ON 10 DECEMBER 1941 *left warehouses on fire at Nichols Field, above; below, at Cavite Navy Yard, small-arms shells explode (left) as the torpedo-loaded barge (center) burns.*

The weather over Formosa on the morning of 10 December was threatening, but the Japanese, anticipating a change for the better, decided to press their advantage. Naval planes took off about 1000 to strike Luzon again. This time the target was the Manila Bay area.[69] First warning of the approach of Japanese planes reached the Interceptor Command at Nielson Field at 1115, and fighters were immediately dispatched to cover Manila Bay, the port area, and Bataan. A half hour later, the enemy aircraft hit the Del Carmen Field near Clark, and the Nichols and Nielson Fields, near Manila. So severe was the attack against Nichols and so great the number of bombs dropped that the men at Nielson, nearly two miles away, thought the bombs were falling on their own field. The pattern set at Clark Field two days earlier was repeated. High-level bombers came in first and hit the barracks, offices, and warehouses. The fighters then came in at low level to strafe the grounded planes and installations. American planes returning to refuel were attacked by Zeros and destroyed. There was no antiaircraft fire and no fighter protection over the field; all the pursuits were engaged over Manila Bay.[70]

The naval base at Cavite received no less attention than Nichols Field. The Japanese force had divided north of Manila, and part had turned east toward the army installations. The rest, 54 bombers, had continued south toward Cavite on the south shore of Manila Bay. Half of these bombers attacked ships and small craft in the bay and the remainder went on toward the

naval base. With maddening deliberation, the bombers flew over Cavite, dropping their bombs from a height of 20,000 feet, above the range of the 9 3-inch antiaircraft guns protecting the base. Almost every bomb fell within the navy yard. After the first run, the first flight withdrew and the other 27 bombers, having completed their attack against ships in the bay, flew in to strike the target.[71]

The attack lasted for two hours. As at Clark and Nichols, the opposition was feeble and the damage extensive. The entire yard was set ablaze; the power plant, dispensary, repair shops, warehouses, barracks, and radio station received direct hits. Greatest damage was done by the fire which spread rapidly and was soon out of control. Admiral Rockwell estimated that five hundred men were killed or seriously wounded that day.[72] The large submarine *Sealion* received a direct hit, but *Seadragon* was pulled away in time by its tender. The most serious loss to the submarine force, however, was the destruction of well over two hundred torpedoes.[73]

Throughout the attack, Admiral Hart had watched the destruction of Cavite from atop the Marsman Building. That night, after receiving an account of the damage done, he reported to the Chief of Naval Operations in Washington that he regarded Manila untenable as a naval base since the

[69] Japanese Naval Opns in Phil Invasion, pp. 7–8.
[70] Ind, *Bataan, The Judgment Seat*, pp. 119–20; Craven and Cate, *The Army Air Forces in World War II*, I, 218; Diary of Cpl L. Arthutick, 17th Pursuit Sq, OCMH; Japanese Naval Opns in Phil Invasion, p. 7.

[71] Admiral Rockwell, Narrative of Naval Activities in Luzon Area, 1 Dec 41–19 Mar 42, p. 4, Off of Naval Rcds; Japanese Naval Opns in Phil Invasion, p. 7; Morison, *Rising Sun in the Pacific*, p. 171.
[72] Rockwell, Naval Activities in Luzon Area, p. 4.
[73] Morison, *Rising Sun in the Pacific*, p. 172; *The Java Sea Campaign*, ONI Combat Narrative, p. 6. Admiral Hart states that the submarine torpedoes had been moved to Corregidor and that the torpedoes lost were destroyer torpedoes. Ltr, Hart to Ward, 19 Dec 51, OCMH.

enemy had control of the air, but promised to "continue submarine and air operations as long as possible." [74] He then sent 2 destroyers, 3 gunboats, 2 submarine tenders, and 2 minesweepers south to join Task Force 5. "It is unfortunate," he noted in his report, "that two or three additional small ships were not sent south at this time." [75]

The naval vessels were not the only ships to move south. At the start of the war there had been about forty large merchant ships, many with valuable cargoes, in Manila Bay. The Navy had promptly closed the bay to all outbound traffic, and had extinguished the lighthouses on Corregidor and two other outlying islands.[76] Fortunately the merchant vessels had escaped attack during the first day of operations.

In the next two days, many commercial vessels sought protection in Manila Bay and were guided through the mine fields by the inshore patrol. During the attack of the 10th, the Japanese had dropped a few bombs among these ships, scoring one hit. Admiral Hart had told the shipmasters on the 11th that their vessels would be safer in Visayan ports, and that evening the commercial vessels began to steam out of Manila Bay. All but one finally escaped.[77] The Japanese had missed a golden opportunity to cripple Allied shipping.

On the morning of the 11th the fires at

Cavite were burning more fiercely than ever. Evidently there was no chance of saving the yard. When Rockwell reported to Hart in Manila that day the two men agreed to salvage as much as possible from the ruins. Remaining supplies were to be distributed among the installations at Manila, Corregidor, and Mariveles. The base at Sangley Point was to be maintained as long as possible, and when no longer tenable the radio station and fuel supply were to be moved to Corregidor.[78]

Meanwhile, the Japanese air force continued the systematic destruction of the air and naval forces remaining in the Philippines. There had been no raids on the 11th, largely because the weather over Formosa had been bad. The planes returning from the raid on the 10th had been forced to set down wherever they could, thus scattering units among the many Formosan fields. The next day was spent in reassembling the units.[79] On the 12th and 13th the Japanese again attacked in force. On these two days hundreds of Japanese Army and Navy planes struck targets on Luzon at will in a final effort to destroy the remnants of the Far East Air Force and the Asiatic Fleet.

By this time American air power was at a low ebb. There were only 22 P–40's in commission, with 6 more promised if they could be repaired in time. In addition, between 5 and 8 P–35's and a handful of the obsolete P–26's were operational. Sixteen heavy bombers were still in commission but 5 of these were suitable only for low-altitude flights and another 4 were not fit for tactical missions. With the Far East Air Force thus reduced in strength it

---

[74] Rad, CINCAF to OPNAV, 10 Dec 41, 101330, War Diary of 16th Naval Dist, Off of Naval Rcds. The Navy Department approved Hart's action and at a meeting of the Joint Board on 10 December informed the Army of Hart's decision. Min, JB Mtg, 10 Dec 41, OPD Reg Doc.

[75] Hart, Narrative of Events, Asiatic Fleet, p. 39.

[76] Harbor Defenses Rpt of Opns, p. 17. Later, on 16 December, limited use of the lighthouse on Corregidor was allowed.

[77] Ibid.; Hart, Narrative of Events, Asiatic Fleet, pp. 39–40.

[78] Rockwell, Naval Activities in Luzon Area, pp. 5–6.

[79] Japanese Naval Opns in Phil Invasion, pp. 7–8.

was decided to use the remaining planes for reconnaissance in order to conserve them as long as possible. The pursuit planes were based at Clark and Nichols, and the heavy bombers were withdrawn to Del Monte. On the morning of the 12th few American planes remained to hinder the Japanese.[80]

The enemy attack on the 12th came at noon, the hour when Clark and Cavite had been hit. Sixty-three naval bombers from Takao in Formosa arrived over Central Luzon between 1130 and 1200 and struck Iba and Clark Fields. Only a small number of planes flew over Clark; the remainder delivered the main attack against Iba, reporting the destruction of ten planes on the ground.[81]

That morning, the PBY's at Olongapo had been dispatched on a fruitless search for a nonexistent Japanese carrier reported off the Luzon coast. They were followed in by a Japanese force of Zeros which had been escorting a large number of bombers in a scheduled strike against one of the Manila fields. When the mission was canceled on account of poor weather over the target, the Zeros sought targets elsewhere. The returning PBY's offered an opportunity too good to be missed. Unseen by the Americans, the Japanese planes waited for the seven Navy patrol bombers to land, and then destroyed them at leisure.[82] These same planes then went on to attack Batangas before returning to Formosa. MacArthur reported at the end of the day that "the crescendo of enemy air offensive was rapidly rising," with attacks by at least 113 planes. "Pilots have been ordered to avoid direct combat," he explained, in order to make a "show of strength and to have air reconnaissance." [83]

The next day almost 200 Japanese planes were over Luzon. The first attack came at dawn against Del Carmen. At 1030 and at 1100 Clark Field was attacked. About the same time Baguio and Tarlac were hit. These early strikes were made by Army planes. At 1230 the naval bombers put in an appearance. During the afternoon, Del Carmen, Clark, Nichols, Cabanatuan, and Batangas were hit at least once. The fields, already strewn with wrecked planes, received further damage. Over Subic Bay additional PBY's were destroyed, leaving less than a full squadron in Patrol Wing 10. By the end of the day, American Army and Navy air power in the Philippines had been virtually destroyed.[84]

One thing was clear to Admiral Hart by this time: the United States forces in the Philippines were on their own. With the loss of air power the possibility of effective naval support was extremely limited and the sea lanes along which reinforcements could be expected to travel were closed. He felt, therefore, that he must salvage what he could of the Asiatic Fleet for later operations in the defense of the Malay Barrier. On 14 December he sent out the remaining bombers of Patrol Wing 10, together with three tenders and such extra personnel

---

[80] Craven and Cate, *The Army Air Forces in World War II*, I, 218–19; Brereton, *Diaries*, p. 51; Ind. *Bataan, The Judgment Seat*, p. 124; Hist of Fifth Air Force, p. 22.

[81] Japanese Naval Opns in Phil Invasion, p. 8. American sources do not mention an attack at Iba.

[82] *Ibid.*; Morison, *Rising Sun in the Pacific*, p. 173.

[83] Rad, MacArthur to AGWAR, 12 Dec 41, AG 381 (11–27–41 Gen) Far East.

[84] *5th Air Gp* Opns, p. 22; Japanese Naval Opns in Phil Invasion, p. 8; *The Java Sea Campaign*, ONI Narrative, p. 7.

and spare parts as could be carried southward.[85] Staff officers, including the chief of staff of the Asiatic Fleet, followed by plane and by boat. All that remained of the Asiatic Fleet in Philippine waters were 2 destroyers (1 under repair), 6 motor torpedo boats, 2 tenders, 3 gunboats, and various small craft, in addition to the 27 submarines. Admiral Hart himself decided to remain in Manila as long as the underwater craft could be operated and serviced from there.[86]

The position of the heavy bombers in Mindanao had by now become precarious. The Japanese were flying extensive reconnaissance missions in an effort to discover the remaining American aircraft. Thus far they had been unable to find the Del Monte field, but it was only a question of time before this last haven would be discovered and destroyed. Moreover, it was becoming increasingly difficult to service the B–17's with the inadequate facilities at Del Monte. There were no spare parts, engines, or propellors for the B–17's in the Philippines; B–18's and damaged B–17's had to be cannibalized to keep the bombers flying. The only tools were those in the possession of the crews. The men who worked on the planes all night often got no rest the next day because of air alerts. On some days the heavy bombers had to remain aloft during the daylight hours to avoid destruction on the ground. They dodged back and forth

between Mindanao and Luzon, playing "a game of hide-and-seek that wore out men as well as planes." [87]

Under these conditions, it was evident that the remaining heavy bombers could not operate efficiently in the Philippines. General Brereton therefore requested authority on 15 December to move the B–17's to Darwin in northwest Australia, 1,500 miles away, where they could be based safely and serviced properly. His intention was to operate from fields near Darwin, using Clark and Del Monte as advance bases from which to strike enemy targets in the Philippines. Sutherland approved the plan the same day and secured General MacArthur's concurrence. The planes were immediately prepared for the long flight southward, and two days later the first group of B–17's left Del Monte airfield. By the following evening ten of the bombers had reached Batchelor Field outside Darwin. They had left Mindanao none too soon, for on the 19th the field at Del Monte received its first major air attack from Japanese planes based on the carrier *Ryujo*.[88]

By 15 December the air strength of the Philippines had been reduced to a handful of fighters. All hopes for preventing the main Japanese landings soon to come and for keeping the supply routes open rested now on these few planes and on the submarines of the Asiatic Fleet.

---

[85] Hart, Narrative of Events, Asiatic Fleet, p. 41.
[86] *Ibid.;* rad, CINCAF to Naval Observer, Singapore, 16 Dec 41, 160755, War Diary of 16th Naval Dist, Off of Naval Rcds.

[87] Brereton, *Diaries,* p. 55.
[88] Hist of Fifth Air Force, p. 21; Brereton, *Diaries,* pp. 55, 57, 59; Craven and Cate, *The Army Air Forces in World War II,* I, 221–22. The Darwin-based B–17's flew missions against the Japanese in Mindanao on 22 and 24 December.

CHAPTER VI

The First Landings

The Japanese did not wait for the destruction of American air and naval forces to begin landings in the Philippine Archipelago. Hours before the first Japanese plane had taken off to attack targets in the Philippine Islands, three task forces had sailed south from Formosa ports under cover of darkness on the evening of 7 December (Tokyo time). Their destination was the Philippine Islands; two were to land on northern Luzon, and the third was headed for the tiny island of Batan about 150 miles to the north. The next day another task force left Palau and steamed toward Legaspi, near the southeast tip of Luzon. At the same time, a fifth task force, scheduled to seize Davao, the principal port in Mindanao, was assembling at Palau. (*Maps 1 and 4*)

Altogether, the Japanese planned six advance landings: Batan Island, Aparri, Vigan, Legaspi, Davao, and Jolo Island. All but the last two were on or near Luzon and were designed to provide the Japanese with advance bases from which short-range fighters could attack the fields of the Far East Air Force and support the main landings to follow. A base at Legaspi, the Japanese believed, would, in addition to providing an airfield, give them control of San Bernardino Strait, between Luzon and Samar, and prevent the Americans from bringing in reinforcements. The landings at Davao and Jolo Island were designed to secure advance bases for a later move southward into the Netherlands Indies. The

Japanese hoped also, by landing in Mindanao, to isolate the Philippine Archipelago from Allied bases to the south and to cut the American route of withdrawal and supply.

The forces assigned to these landings were small, even for such limited objectives. But to secure so many detachments for the advance landings, General Homma had had to weaken seriously the two combat divisions *Imperial General Headquarters* had allotted to him for the Philippine invasion. Not one of the advance landing detachments was strong enough to withstand a determined counterattack; the largest was only about as large as a regiment, and the smallest was hardly stronger than a company. Moreover, the timetable for invasion was a complicated one and could easily be upset by any unexpected event.

It has been claimed that the preliminary landings were part of a clever Japanese scheme to draw the American forces toward widely separated points and then cut them off by later landings.[1] There is no evidence for such a view. General Homma had no intention of drawing the American troops to the landing points and was not naive enough to hope to deceive the Americans by so obvious a ruse. Nor did he have the troops to spare for such an effort. The size of the forces assigned to the preliminary

---

[1] Japanese Land Opns, 8 Dec 41–8 Jun 42, Campaign Study 3, 18 Nov 42, MIS; Wainwright, *The Wainwright Story*, p. 27; Hunt, *MacArthur and the War Against Japan*, p. 36.

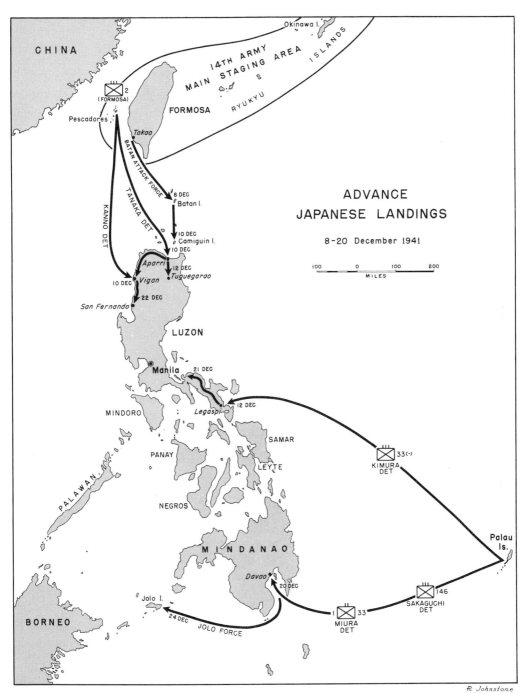

CHINA

Okinawa I.

14TH ARMY
MAIN STAGING AREA

RYUKYU   ISLANDS

FORMOSA

Pescadores

2
(FORMOSA)

Takao

ADVANCE
JAPANESE LANDINGS

8-20 December 1941

100   0   100   200
MILES

BATAN ATTACK FORCE

TANAKA DET

KANNO DET

8 DEC
Batan I.

10 DEC
Camiguin I.
10 DEC

Aparri

10 DEC   Vigan

12 DEC
Tuguegarao

22 DEC

San Fernando

LUZON

Manila   21 DEC

MINDORO

Legaspi   12 DEC

SAMAR

33 (-)
KIMURA
DET

PANAY

LEYTE

PALAWAN

NEGROS

Palau
Is.

MINDANAO

Davao

20 DEC

146
SAKAGUCHI
DET

Jolo I.

1   33
MIURA
DET

BORNEO

24 DEC   JOLO FORCE

R. Johnstone

MAP 4

landings and the places selected for the landings revealed their true purpose almost immediately to the American command.

Batan Island

The first Japanese invaders on Philippine soil went ashore on Batan Island in Luzon Strait, midway between Formosa and Luzon, at dawn 8 December. The invasion force, which had left the Formosan ports of Takao and Hozan on the evening of the 7th, consisted of 2 transports escorted by 1 destroyer, 4 torpedo boats, and a large number of other small vessels. Aboard the transports was a naval combat unit of 490 men as well as air corps troops who were to establish an airbase on the island. The combat troops quickly seized the airfield near Basco, and air force troops came ashore to inspect the field. It was found to be barely suitable for fighter and reconnaissance planes, but to require expansion for large-scale operations. The next day, while construction crews worked on the field, planes of the *24th* and *50th Fighter Regiments* began operations from the Basco base.

When the success of the attack on Clark Field became known, the Japanese discontinued work on the Batan Island field. Such a base was now unnecessary. Early on the morning of the 10th, the men of the *3d Gunboat Division,* part of the *Batan Attack Force,* seized Camiguin Island to the south. A seaplane base was immediately established on the island by the naval base force, thus providing the Japanese with an airbase only thirty-five miles north of Aparri.[2]

The Americans did not oppose the Batan Island landing and seem to have been entirely unaware of it. In fact, General MacArthur reported on the 9th after the Batan Island landing, that the enemy had not yet landed.[3] It is extremely unlikely that even if USAFFE had been warned of the assault any effort would have been made to meet it. On the morning of the 8th, American planes were being sent aloft to intercept reported enemy flights over Luzon. By the 10th the Far East Air Force had already been reduced to half strength, and the Japanese had begun to land on the island of Luzon itself.

The Landings on North Luzon

Luzon is a curiously shaped island. The northern part of the island is about 125 miles wide, with only one major indentation along the west coast, at Lingayen Gulf. Mountain ranges extend along the east and west coasts to the central plains just above Manila. The range on the east extends southward to Tayabas Bay. To the west of the central plain are the Zambales Mountains which face the South China Sea across a narrow coastal plain. The southern portion of Luzon is narrow and irregular in shape, trailing away in a southeasterly direction for 180 miles.

North of Manila, the island of Luzon is shaped like a mittened, giant right hand, palm down, with the index finger pointing directly at Formosa. Lingayen Gulf lies between the thumb and the forefinger. From Lingayen south across the top of the hand, like so many veins, are the highways and roads leading to Manila. At the tip of the ring finger lies Aparri, and midway

---

[2] *14th Army* Opns, I, 40; Japanese Naval Opns in Phil Invasion, p. 11; *5th Air Gp* Opns, pp. 12, 16; Morison, *Rising Sun in the Pacific,* pp. 161, 174.

[3] Rad, MacArthur to AGWAR, No. 1135, 9 Dec 41, AG 381 (11–27–41 Gen) Far East.

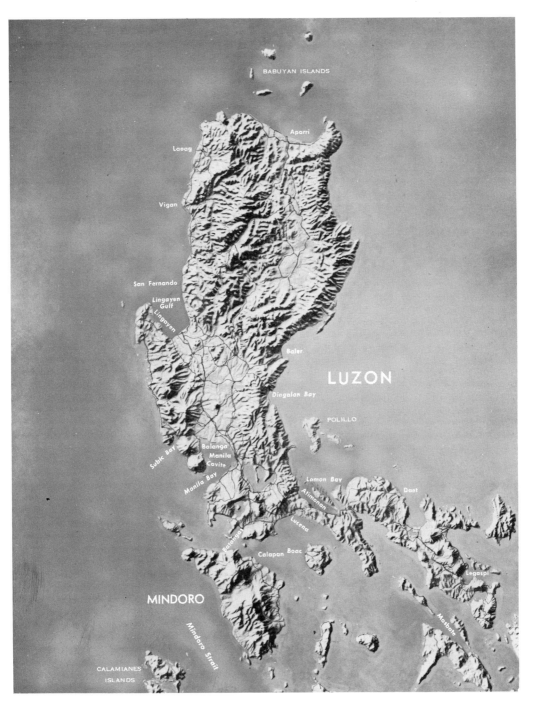

LUZON

along the forefinger is Vigan. Both were
next on the Japanese timetable for invasion.

Aparri was, before the war, a fairly large
port with a population of 26,500. Located
at the mouth of the Cagayan River and at
the head of the Cagayan valley, with
formidable mountain ranges to the east,
west, and south, Aparri could be reached
from the central plains only by way of
Balete Pass from the south or by the coastal
road around the northern tip of Luzon.
The most direct route from Manila to
Aparri, along Route 5 through the pass,
was 275 miles long; the more circuitous
route along the coast was 100 miles longer.
The Americans could safely assume that
any force landing at Aparri would not have
Manila as its destination. The Cagayan
valley was not the route of invasion.

Vigan, the capital of Ilocos Sur Province,
lies on the western shore of Luzon, about
220 miles north of Manila on Route 3. To
the east lie the Cordillera Mountains separating the Cagayan valley from the narrow
coastal plain. About three miles south of
Vigan is the mouth of the Abra River, one
of the five principal waterways of Luzon.
The port for Vigan is Pandan, on the north
bank of the river's mouth, linked to the
provincial capital by a hard-surface, all-
weather road.

Both Aparri and Vigan were in the area
defended by General Wainwright's North
Luzon Force. With only three Philippine
Army divisions, a Philippine Scout cavalry
regiment and infantry battalion, one battery of field artillery, and a quartermaster
troop, General Wainwright had to defend
an area about 625 miles long and 125 miles
wide at its widest point. The most he could
spare for the entire northern portion of

Luzon was one partially trained and
equipped Philippine Army division, the
11th, commanded by Col. William E.
Brougher. His task was made even more
difficult by the absence of headquarters personnel and corps troops necessary to direct
and support operations in so large an area.

The 11th Division, like the other Philippine Army reserve divisions, had begun to
mobilize in September. At the start of the
war, its infantry regiments were only at two-
thirds their authorized strength of 1,500
men per regiment; its artillery was in the
process of mobilization and had not yet
joined the division; service elements had
joined, but had not yet been organized or
trained as units. Transportation was practically nonexistent. The division suffered
from a serious shortage of equipment. Individual training, especially in rifle marksmanship, scouting, and patrolling, was inadequate. Only one regiment of the
division had begun to train in units larger
than company or battery size.[4]

The 11th Division, with responsibility for
the entire area north of Lingayen Gulf, was
spread butter thin. Most of the division
was in position along the gulf as far north
as San Fernando, La Union.[5] Beyond that
point it maintained only small patrols. One
battalion of the division, the 3d Battalion,
12th Infantry, was assigned to defend all
of the Cagayan valley. This battalion had
its command post at Tuguegarao, with one

---

[4] NLF and I Corps Rpt of Opns, pp. 3–5, Annex
IV, USAFFE-USFIP Rpt of Opns; USAFFE-
USFIP Rpt of Opns, p. 10.
[5] There are two towns named San Fernando in
northern Luzon, both of which figure largely in the
campaign. One is in La Union Province, along
the shore of Lingayen Gulf. The other is in
Pampanga Province, and is the gateway to Bataan.

company posted fifty miles to the north, at Aparri. There were no troops at Vigan.[6]

For the landings in north Luzon General Homma organized two forces from the *48th Division's 2d Formosa Infantry Regiment.* The force which was to land at Aparri numbered approximately 2,000 men. Its main infantry element was the regimental headquarters, the *2d Battalion,* and half of the *1st Battalion.* In command was Col. Toru Tanaka, the regimental commander, hence the name *Tanaka Detachment.* The unit scheduled to take Vigan was known as the *Kanno Detachment,* after the commander of the *3d Battalion, 2d Formosa.*[7] It was of approximately the same size and composition as the *Tanaka Detachment,* and included the rest of the *2d Formosa—* half of the *1st Battalion* and the *3d Battalion.*[8]

The Japanese attached a great deal of importance to the success of the Vigan and Aparri landings, and what they lacked in ground troops they made up in naval escort. As a cover force, Vice Adm. Ibo Takahashi personally led a flotilla consisting of two heavy cruisers, the *Ashigara* and *Maya,* one light cruiser, two destroyers, and a converted seaplane tender. He left Mako on 8 December with his fleet, and on the morning of the 10th was about 200 miles west of Vigan.[9]

The transports left Mako on the evening of 7 December, about the same time as the *Batan Island Attack Force.* The *14th Army* staff watched them sail with misgivings. The success or failure of these preliminary landings would have a tremendous effect upon the main landings to follow, and the Japanese feared that the Americans might discover and heavily damage, if not destroy, the two detachments.[10]

Careful provision had been made for air support. With the first light of day, planes of the *24th* and *50th Fighter Regiments* appeared overhead to protect the convoy from air and naval attack. All that day and the next, *5th Air Group* planes covered the two convoys.[11] In the early morning hours of the 10th, the convoys had arrived at their anchorages. Not a single American aircraft had been sighted during the entire trip. "It was a miracle," stated the Japanese, "that it [the convoy] wasn't detected by the enemy."[12] Before dawn the *Tanaka Detachment* was waiting off

---

[6] NLF and I Corps Rpt of Opns, pp. 6–8; Capt Wayne C. Liles, 12th Infantry (PA), p. 4, Chunn Notebooks, OCMH. The notebooks of Capt Calvin E. Chunn, an officer of the 45th Infantry (PS), contain a large number of brief unit histories. These were compiled in prison camp where Captain Chunn interviewed officers from many of the units which had fought in the campaign and then wrote the information in his notebooks. Copies of the unit histories are on file in OCMH where they are collected in a folder entitled Chunn Notebooks. References to these histories throughout this volume specify their location in Chunn Notebooks.

[7] Full name and rank of Kanno is unknown. He was either a lieutenant colonel or major.

[8] *14th Army* Opns, I, 32–33. Interrogs, Col Nakajima, *14th Army* staff officer, 25 Apr 47; Col Haba, *14th Army* staff, Apr 47; Lt Gen Susumu Morioka, comdr of *16th Div,* 24 Apr 47; Maj Kotoshi Doba, *5th Air Gp* staff, 19 Apr 47, all in Interrogations of Former Japanese Officers, Mil Hist Div, GHQ FEC, I.

[9] Japanese Naval Opns in Phil Invasion, pp. 10–11; Morison, *Rising Sun in the Pacific,* pp. 161, 174; interrog of Capt Kawakita Ishihara, *3d Fleet* Staff, 22 Oct 45, USSBS, *Interrogations of Japanese Officials,* I, 83.

[10] *14th Army* Opns, I, 43.

[11] *5th Air Gp* Opns, pp. 9, 16. Captain Morison states that the converted seaplane tender *Sanyo Maru* provided air patrol for the Aparri landings. *Rising Sun in the Pacific,* p. 176. There is some evidence from *2d Demob Bureau,* Interrogations of Former Japanese Officers, G-2, FEC, that the *Sanyo Maru* was still in port being fitted out at the time of the Aparri landing.

[12] *14th Army* Opns, I, 43.

Aparri; the *Kanno Detachment* was off
Vigan. The wind was strong and the seas
high. The next few hours would be the
most critical and hazardous of the entire
voyage.

The Landings at Aparri and Gonzaga

In the first light of dawn, 10 December,
the men of the *Tanaka Detachment* began
to transfer from the transports to the landing craft. Under cover of fighter aircraft
from the recently captured field on Batan
Island, two companies made the trip to
shore successfully. But strong northeasterly winds and rough sea threatened to do
what the Americans thus far had made no
effort to do—frustrate the landings. The
convoy commander therefore decided to
land the remaining troops at Gonzaga, over
twenty miles to the east, where Cape En-
gano offered partial protection from the
heavy surf. The convoy sailed east along
the coast, leaving the two companies at
Aparri, and on reaching the new anchorage
the rest of the *Tanaka Detachment* began
to debark immediately.[13]

The first report of the landing force, estimated as a regiment in size, reached Mac-
Arthur's headquarters late in the day, and
aircraft were ordered aloft immediately to
attack the landing force.[14] The purpose of
the landing was apparently well understood. Lt. Col. James V. Collier of the

G–3 Section noted that the Japanese "most
assuredly" were attempting to seize airfields
from which fighters could support Formosa-
based bombers.[15] That night, the staff at
USAFFE prepared to take the field, and a
general plan for establishing an advance
headquarters at San Fernando, Pampanga,
with a rear echelon in Manila, was discussed.[16]

General Wainwright, the North Luzon
Force commander, first heard of the Aparri
landing, this time estimated as a reinforced
brigade of 3,000 men, while he was inspecting the beach defenses of the 11th and 21st
Divisions at Lingayen Gulf. Believing that
the landing was a feint "to pull some of my
forces up to that point and weaken the already weak defenses in the Lingayen Gulf
region," Wainwright decided not to offer
any opposition to the *Tanaka Detachment*.[17]
Since the only route south was down
the Cagayan Valley, and since he believed
that a battalion at Balete Pass could stop "a
fairly considerable force," he made no disposition to meet the attack. He was certain,
he later wrote, that the main Japanese
landings would come "in the areas where I
had the chief weight of my troops"—Lingayen Gulf.[18] But he did take the precaution of sending several scout cars of the 26th
Cavalry (PS) to the Cagayan Valley to provide communication with the 11th Division
troops in that area.[19] MacArthur's headquarters in Manila issued orders to destroy

[13] *Ibid.*, 42–43; *5th Air Gp Opns*, p. 13. The
14th Army history states that the landing at Gonzaga was completed at 0550. This is extremely unlikely in view of the change in plans made during
the Aparri landing, and the length of time it must
have taken to reach the new anchorage.
[14] Rad, MacArthur to AGWAR, No. 1148, 10
Dec 41, AG 381 (11–27–41 Gen) Far East;
USAFFE-USFIP Rpt of Opns, p. 36; Collier, Notebooks, I, 69.

[15] Collier, Notebooks, I, 69.
[16] *Ibid.* This plan was never carried out and
USAFFE headquarters remained in Manila until
the move to Corregidor at the end of December.
[17] Wainwright, *General Wainwright's Story*, p. 27.
This decision may have been made by USAFFE.
If made by Wainwright, it was undoubtedly confirmed by MacArthur's headquarters.
[18] *Ibid.*
[19] NLF and I Corps Rpt of Opns, p. 6.

bridges in the valley and to establish a block at Balete Pass.[20]

The company of the 3d Battalion, 12th Infantry, located at Aparri on the morning of 10 December was commanded by a young reserve officer, Lt. Alvin C. Hadley. When the two companies of the *Tanaka Detachment* came ashore at dawn, Lieutenant Hadley reported the landing to battalion headquarters at Tuguegarao and was ordered to attack immediately and drive the enemy into the sea. Estimating the size of the force as considerably larger than it was he prudently withdrew south along Route 5, without, so far as is known, firing a shot.[21]

The reaction of the American air forces was more spirited. As the *Tanaka Detachment* was unloaded at Gonzaga, two B-17's appeared overhead. They had taken off from Clark Field at about 0930 with orders to attack and sink the naval vessels and transports. The first plane, carrying eight 600-pound bombs, flew over the transport area dropping its bombs. Before being driven off by the Japanese fighter aircraft, the pilot reported a hit on one of the transports. In the second plane was Capt. Colin P. Kelly, Jr., the first war hero and winner of the Distinguished Service Cross. Under orders to attack a Japanese carrier mistakenly supposed to be near Aparri, Captain Kelly had taken off hurriedly in the midst of an air raid with only three 600-pound bombs. When he was unable to find a carrier, Kelly decided to attack what he

thought was a large battleship, later presumed to be the *Haruna*. Of the three bombs, one is supposed to have been a direct hit; two, near misses. As the B-17 flew away, the vessel appeared to have stopped, with black smoke rising in a heavy cloud above it.[22] On return to base, the plane was jumped by two enemy fighters and shot down. All of the crew except Kelly bailed out safely. Captain Kelly's body was later recovered in the wreckage.

Actually Captain Kelly had not attacked a battleship, and certainly not the *Haruna*. Nor had he sunk any vessel of the Japanese fleet. There were no battleships in Philippine waters at this time; the *Haruna* was hundreds of miles away supporting the Malayan invasion. Only Admiral Takahashi's cover force, with the heavy cruisers *Ashigara* and *Maya*, was in the vicinity, and it was 200 miles off the west coast of Luzon. Kelly was nowhere near this force, although the Japanese report it was attacked by heavy bombers that day.[23]

The air attacks did not seriously hinder the Japanese landing at Gonzaga. Two other attacks against shipping resulted in the reported sinking of a transport. Actually, the Japanese suffered only minor damage; one minesweeper run aground and another heavily damaged.[24]

---

[20] Rad, MacArthur to AGWAR, 10 Dec 41, AG 381 (11–27–41 Gen) Far East.

[21] Col Glen R. Townsend, CO 11th Inf (PA), The Defense of the Philippines, p. 10, OCMH. The title of this document is misleading. Actually it is an account of the operations of the 11th Infantry. According to Colonel Townsend, Lieutenant Hadley told him that 10,000 Japanese landed at Aparri that morning.

[22] Hist of Fifth Air Force, p. 18; Army Air Action in Phil and NEI, pp. 63–65.

[23] Japanese Naval Opns in Phil Invasion, p. 11; Interrog of Capt Ishihara, 22 Oct 45, USSBS, *Interrogations of Japanese Officials*, I, 83. American sources do not mention an attack against the cover force.

[24] *Japanese Naval and Merchant Shipping Losses During World War II*, Joint Army-Navy Assessment Committee, p. 1; interrog of Capt Mitsugo Ihara, 3d Fleet staff, 10 Nov 45, USSBS, *Interrogations of Japanese Officials*, I, 275; Japanese Naval Opns in Phil Invasion, p. 10.

The *Tanaka Detachment* was ashore and in Aparri by 1300, when it reported the capture of the airfield. In Aparri it was joined by the two companies that had landed there earlier. By evening elements of the detachment had penetrated six miles south to occupy the strip at Camalaniugan.[25] Construction troops and air service units moved in immediately and began to extend the airfields, establish depots, and ready the strip for operations. It had not been possible to bring much heavy equipment ashore that day because of the air attacks, and some supplies, such as drummed oil, had been lost or floated ashore because of the transport crews' anxiety to retire.[26]

Early the next morning the *Tanaka Detachment* began to march south toward Tuguegarao, along Route 5. Aircraft from the *50th Fighter Regiment* and the *16th Light Bombardment Regiment* flew over the highway, bombing likely targets. The 3d Battalion of the 12th Infantry retreated quickly down the Cagayan valley, offering no opposition, and by 0530 on 12 December elements of the *Tanaka Detachment* had reached Tuguegarao airfield, fifty miles to the south.[27]

The Landing at Vigan

Simultaneously with the landing at Aparri, the *Kanno Detachment* of 2,000 men began to debark at Pandan, near Vigan. A P–40 pilot flying reconnaissance gave the first warning of the attack at 0513 of the 10th. Alerted by this message, the

Far East Air Force readied five B–17's and escorting P–40's and P–35's to bomb the invaders. By 0600 the planes were airborne, flying north to the threatened area.[28] The reception of the *Kanno Detachment* promised to be a warm one.

As at Aparri, bad weather and heavy seas upset the landing schedule. Only a small portion of the Japanese force was able to get ashore at Pandan that morning, but these men quickly moved on to seize Vigan by 1030. Meanwhile the convoy came under attack from American planes and suspended all efforts to land the rest of the force.[29] The five B–17's, each loaded with twenty 100-pound demolition bombs, came in for their first run over the target shortly after 0600. They were covered by P–40's of the 17th Pursuit Squadron. After the B–17's had dropped their bombs, the P–40's dived through the antiaircraft fire to strafe the ships. The P–35's of the 21st Squadron now arrived on the scene and, despite the lack of armor and leakproof tanks, flew low to strafe the invaders again and again. One of the transports, hit by a B–17 bomb, exploded during the last P–35 run, destroying the squadron commander's plane.[30]

Later in the day, three more heavy bombers attacked the *Vigan Attack Force*. The first B–17 to arrive over the target dropped its bombs on what was thought to be a carrier, with no observed effect. The second attacked a cruiser unsuccessfully, but managed to score a direct hit on a transport. The last plane had had time to load only one 600-pound bomb, and this the bom-

---

[25] *14th Army* Opns, I, 42; *5th Air Gp* Opns, p. 13.

[26] Situation of Both Sides Prior to War, ATIS, Current Translation 46, 2 Jun 43; Morison, *Rising Sun in the Pacific*, p. 176.

[27] Morison, *Rising Sun in the Pacific*, pp. 174–76.

[28] Craven and Cate, *The Army Air Forces in World War II*, I, 215 and n. 60.

[29] *14th Army* Opns, I, 43; *5th Air Gp* Opns, pp. 13, 17–18.

[30] Craven and Cate, *The Army Air Forces in World War II*, I, 215; Brereton, *Diaries*, pp. 46–49.

bardier released over the water, near the transports.[31]

Despite the presence of eighteen naval fighters and planes of the Army's *24th Fighter Regiment,* the Japanese were unable to fend off the American attack. As a result of the day's action, the enemy lost the transports *Oigawa Maru* and *Takao Maru,* both badly damaged and beached, and one minesweeper, sunk. The Japanese also suffered casualties aboard the destroyer *Murasame* and the light cruiser *Naka,* Rear Adm. Shoji Nishimura's flagship, which was slightly damaged.[32]

The successful attacks of the 10th were to be the last co-ordinated effort of the Far East Air Force. On that day the Japanese attacked Nichols, Nielson, and Cavite, completing the destruction begun two days earlier at Clark. Thereafter the American fighters with few exceptions flew only reconnaissance missions over assigned areas; the 21st and 34th Squadrons covered south Luzon while the 17th and 20th patrolled the northern part of the island.[33]

There was no activity near Vigan during the night of the 10th, but from Lingayen Gulf, 100 miles to the south, came reports of another Japanese landing. Around midnight "several dark shapes" were observed approaching the mouth of the Agno River. When confirmation was received, one battery of the 3d Battalion, 21st Field Artillery (PA), opened fire. "It was like dropping a match in a warehouse of Fourth of July

fireworks," wrote the American instructor assigned to the regiment. "Instantly Lingayen Gulf was ablaze. As far as the eye could see the flashes of artillery, shell-bursts, tracer machine gun bullets and small arms. . . . Thousands of shadows were killed that night." [34] When morning came, all that was found of the supposed invasion was one life preserver with markings which may have been Japanese characters. The absence of sunken ships did not prevent the 21st Division commander, Brig. Gen. Mateo Capinpin, from reporting to Manila that an attempted hostile landing had been repulsed.[35]

What actually happened that night was that the Japanese had sent one motor boat into Lingayen Gulf on a reconnaissance mission. The Japanese had no force near Lingayen then and no plan for a landing in the area at that time. Nevertheless, the news of the frustrated enemy landing was reported in the press as a great victory and the 21st Field Artillery was officially credited with repulsing an enemy landing.[36]

Meanwhile, the *Vigan Attack Force,* unable to land troops and supplies in the face of rough seas, had moved four miles to the south. Protected by a squadron of fighters, the Japanese were finally able to put the *Kanno Detachment* ashore. A small force was immediately dispatched north, along Route 3, to Laoag, the capital of Ilocos Norte Province, fifty miles away. By the

---

[31] Craven and Cate, *The Army Air Forces in World War II,* I, 215; Edmonds, *They Fought With What They Had,* pp. 121–25.

[32] *14th Army* Opns, I, 43; Japanese Naval Opns in Phil Invasion, p. 7; *Japanese Naval Merchant Ship Losses During World War II,* pp. 1, 29; interrog of Capt Ihara, 10 Nov 45, USSBS, *Interrogations of Japanese Officials,* I, 275.

[33] Army Air Action in Phil and NEI, pp. 67–68.

[34] Mallonée, Bataan Diary, I, 52.

[35] Collier, Notebooks, I, 70.

[36] Mallonée, Bataan Diary, I, 52–53. Colonel Mallonée did not believe that the Japanese had tried to land at Lingayen on that night or on the succeeding two nights. Hunt mistakenly reported that the Japanese had twelve transports at Lingayen that night, two of which were sunk, and that the enemy was "bloodily repulsed." Hunt, *MacArthur and the War Against Japan,* p. 36.

following evening that town and its airfield had been occupied.[37]

The Japanese now had a firm foothold in northern Luzon, with planes of the *5th Air Group* operating from fields, however inadequate, at Aparri, Vigan, and Laoag.[38] Originally Homma had intended to leave the *Tanaka* and *Kanno Detachments* in position, but the American reaction had made it evident that there would be no counterattack. He decided therefore to leave only small garrisons to hold the seized airfields and to send the bulk of the two detachments, forming substantially the *2d Formosa Regiment,* to Lingayen Gulf to meet the main force of the *14th Army* when it came ashore. Colonel Tanaka was to march around the north tip of Luzon along Route 3 to Vigan, and there join forces with Kanno. The combined force would then move south along the coastal road to Lingayen Gulf. At the same time Homma sent his chief of staff, General Maeda, to Luzon for a personal inspection and to brief the commanders on the change in plans. Maeda arrived at Aparri on 14 December and after talking with Colonel Tanaka placed him in command of both detachments and gave him his new mission.[39]

By 20 December the *Tanaka* and *Kanno Detachments* had joined and were ready to move south toward Lingayen Gulf. At 1300 that day Colonel Tanaka led his reconstructed regiment (less three companies)

out of Vigan, along Route 3. Repairing destroyed bridges along the line of march, forward elements of the regiment reached Bacnotan the next evening. There they made contact with the 11th Division troops, but by a flanking movement to the left (east) were able to force part of the defenders back, while cutting off others who made their way eastward to the mountains. Colonel Tanaka finally reached San Fernando, La Union, on the morning of the 22d.[40]

Just a few hours earlier the main strength of the *14th Army* had begun to land across the beaches at Lingayen Gulf, a short distance to the south. Colonel Tanaka just missed being on the beaches to greet his comrades.

The advance landings on northern Luzon, seen in retrospect, accomplished little. The fields seized were poor and, by the time they were ready for operations, were of small value. The detachments that landed did not require close air support, since in no case did the Americans offer any determined resistance. The *5th Air Group* had planned to operate mainly from Luzon bases by 17 December, and by the following day had placed a number of Japanese air units on the recently seized fields. But they were not needed. As events turned out, Japanese misgivings were entirely unfounded; the dispersion of force entirely unnecessary. But this was small comfort for the Americans. In General Wainwright's words, "The rat was in the house." [41]

---

[37] *14th Army* Opns, I, 42–43; *5th Air Gp* Opns, p. 18.

[38] *5th Air Gp* Opns, pp. 18–20. The *5th Air Group* moved into Vigan on 11 December and into Laoag the next day.

[39] *14th Army* Opns, I, 39; On Phil Landing Opns (Amphibious), prepared by *2d Demob Bureau* in answer to a series of questions by Lt Comdr Henry Salomon, Jr., ATIS Doc 1989-6A.

[40] *14th Army* Opns, I, 42; Capt Liles, 12th Inf (PA), p. 5, and 1st Lt Raymond W. Bliss, 13th Inf (PA), pp. 8, 9, both in Chunn Notebooks; interv, author with Col Donald D. Blackburn, Apr 49; NLF and I Corps Rpt of Opns, p. 10.

[41] Wainwright, *General Wainwright's Story,* p. 27.

The Legaspi Landing

The area held by General Parker's South Luzon Force was ninety miles at its widest point and stretched from the Rosario–Infanta line, southeast of Manila, sixty miles to the Atimonan–Padre Burgos line. In this region were five bays, all suitable for landing operations, and two large lakes, Laguna de Bay and Lake Taal. Altogether there were 250 miles of possible landing beaches. The area contained a good network of roads and one railroad which extended from Manila southeast to Daraga. Along the west coast the terrain was rugged, restricting the defenders to the roads. On the east coast, which was mountainous a good part of the way to Atimonan, the terrain presented a formidable obstacle to any military force. Below Atimonan was the Bicol Peninsula, trailing away in a southeasterly direction like the tail of a downcast dog. Near its tip, in Albay Gulf and only one mile from the southern terminus of the Manila Railroad, lay Legaspi, the next Japanese objective.

To defend south Luzon, General Parker had two Philippine Army divisions. On the west was the 41st Division (PA) commanded by Brig. Gen. Vincente Lim, a West Point graduate and former deputy chief of staff of the Philippine Army. On the east was Brig. Gen. Albert M. Jones's 51st Division (PA), with its northern boundary along the line Pililla–Infanta and its southern boundary at Atimonan—Padre Burgos.

The 51st Division, like Colonel Brougher's 11th Division (PA), was poorly equipped and imperfectly trained. Presumably all the men had had five and one half months training some time during the past five years, but, said General Parker, "this was never apparent." [42] The enlisted men of the division spoke the Bicolanian dialect, and the majority of the officers, who were from central Luzon, spoke Tagalog, making training even more difficult than it would otherwise have been. One infantry regiment had had thirteen weeks' training, another five weeks, and the last none at all. In the opinion of General Jones, the only troops in his division capable of offering any effective resistance were those of the 52d Infantry.[43]

For the landing in south Luzon General Homma had organized a force of approximately 2,500 men from the *16th Division.*[44] Led by Maj. Gen. Naoki Kimura, infantry group commander of the division, this force consisted of infantry group headquarters, the *33d Infantry* (less *1st Battalion*), a battery of the *22d Field Artillery,* and engineer detachments. Accompanying the *Kimura Detachment* was the *Kure 1st Special Naval Landing Force* with 575 men.[45]

Two days before General Kimura's men boarded their transports at Palau, Rear Adm. Takeo Takagi sortied from that base with an impressive naval force. By dawn of the 8th he had reached a point about 120

---

[42] SLF and II Corps Rpt of Opns, p. 6.

[43] *Ibid.,* pp. 4–8. Diary of Maj Gen Albert M. Jones, OPD 319.1 PTO (3 Oct 45). This diary covers the operations of the South Luzon Force during the period 24 December 1941–1 January 1942, when Jones was in command. The text of the diary is reproduced as App. II to SLF and II Corps Rpt of Opns. All references to this document are to the diary itself and not to the SLF and II Corps Rpt.

[44] Ltr, Chief, Hist Div SSUSA to G–2 GHQ FEC, 9 Nov 48, 3d Ind, 16 Aug 49, OCMH.

[45] *14th Army* Opns, I, 42; Japanese Naval Opns in Phil Invasion, p. 12. The infantry regiments of a Japanese division are under an infantry group headquarters whose commander, a major general, controls the infantry elements of the division as well as other elements that may be assigned for specific missions.

miles east of Davao. From here, the carrier *Ryujo* launched the attack against Davao which the *Preston* had evaded. Following this strike Takagi turned northeast and early the next morning joined Kimura's transports, which had left Palau at 0900 the day before. Accompanying the transports was the *Legaspi Attack Force;* to the rear, en route from Palau, was the *17th Minelayer Division.*[46]

By 1100, 11 December, this combined force was 135 miles east of San Bernardino Strait. Here the minelayers broke formation. Escorted by 2 destroyers, one column headed for San Bernardino Strait; another column, accompanied by 1 light cruiser and 2 destroyers, turned south for Surigao Strait. By midnight both groups had reached their destinations and had begun laying mines. The U.S. submarines *S–39* on patrol in San Bernardino Strait, was attacked and driven off by 2 Japanese destroyers without inflicting any damage on the Japanese force.[47] From a point about 100 miles offshore, planes of the *Ryujo* covered the convoys as it moved toward the shores of Albay Gulf. Admiral Takagi's force remained behind to provide distant cover. As the convoy approached the beaches, the Japanese planes shifted operations to the Legaspi area.[48]

The *Kimura Detachment* began to land at Legaspi early on the morning of 12 December. No difficulty was experienced and there was no opposition; the nearest American and Filipino troops were 150 miles away. By 0900 the Japanese were in control of the airfield and the terminus of the Manila Railroad. A few hours later,

when he had a firm grip on Legaspi, General Kimura sent advance detachments to the northwest and southeast. The next day the huge cover force returned to Palau to prepare for the next landing.[49]

The initial report of a Japanese landing at Legaspi came from the railroad stationmaster there. The apocryphal story is told that his call was switched from the railroad central to USAFFE headquarters in Manila and the following conversation took place:

STATIONMASTER: "There are four Jap boats in the harbor, sir, and the Japs are landing. What shall I do?"
USAFFE OFFICER: "Just hang onto the phone and keep reporting."
STATIONMASTER: "There are about twenty Japs ashore already, sir, and more are coming." A pause. "Now there are about three hundred Japs outside the station, sir, What am I to do?"
USAFFE OFFICER: "Just sit tight."
STATIONMASTER: "Sir, a few of those Japs, with an officer in front, are coming over here."
USAFFE OFFICER: "See what they want."
STATIONMASTER: "Those Japs want me to give them a train to take them to Manila, sir. What do I do now?"
USAFFE OFFICER: "Tell them the next train leaves a week from Sunday. Don't give it to them."
STATIONMASTER, hanging up: "Okay sir."[50]

The subsequent conversation between the Japanese officer and the stationmaster—if it ever took place—is not recorded.

When South Luzon Force headquarters received news of the landing, it considered a proposal to send a strong force south to surprise the Japanese and push them back into the sea. There were many practical difficulties in the way of such an expedi-

[46] Japanese Naval Opns in Phil Invasion, pp. 11–13.
[47] *Ibid.;* Log of *S–39,* 11 Dec 41, cited by Morison, *Rising Sun in the Pacific,* p. 177.
[48] Japanese Naval Opns in Phil Invasion, p. 13.
[49] *Ibid.; 14th Army* Opns, I, 42.
[50] Clark Lee, *They Call it Pacific* (New York: Viking Press, 1943), p. 73; interv, author with Clark Lee, Apr 51.

tion, the most serious of which was how to surprise an enemy who had control of the air and sea. The proposal was soon dropped, but General Jones's 51st Division (PA) was ordered to send units south into the Bicol Peninsula to destroy highway and railroad bridges and to evacuate as much railroad rolling stock as possible.[51] Two companies of the 1st Battalion, 52d Infantry, each with an attached machine gun platoon, were sent south to outpost Route 1 and the Manila Railroad, the only two routes north from Legaspi, and a specially trained detachment of the 51st Engineer Battalion was ordered to prepare all bridges for demolition in order to delay the enemy advance.[52]

First American reaction to the Legaspi landing came on 12 December when 2 fighters struck the Japanese-held airfield, killing three and injuring two men. Two days later 3 of a group of 6 Del Monte-based B–17's, ordered to attack the landing force, reached the area. They attacked a Japanese minesweeper and a transport, thought to be a destroyer, with meager results, and 9 naval aircraft based on the Legaspi strip. The unescorted bombers were no match for the Japanese fighters and soon beat a hasty retreat. Only 1 of the B–17's was able to make its way back to Del Monte; the others had to crash-land short of their base. The Japanese lost at most 4 fighters.[53]

With Legaspi firmly in Japanese hands, the *Kimura Detachment* moved northwest along Route 1 toward Naga. Ground units first made contact on 17 December when a Japanese patrol ran into a demolition detachment of the 51st Engineer Battalion working on a bridge near Ragay. The engineers managed to destroy the bridge and establish themselves on the near bank of the gorge, whereupon the Japanese patrol withdrew. The next day the *Kimura Detachment* entered Naga.[54]

Pushing northwest from Naga, rebuilding bridges and repairing roads as they advanced, the Japanese reached Sipoco on the 19th with an estimated force of one battalion of infantry. Patrols were still active near Ragay, and reports reaching the Americans mentioned other Japanese elements moving along Route 1 toward Daet. By this time, the two outposted companies of the 1st Battalion, 52d Infantry, were at Aloneros and Sumulong, and had thrust strong combat patrols forward. Luzon at this point forms a very narrow neck only seven miles wide, and any force from Legaspi must pass through one of the two barrios, Aloneros on the Manila Railroad or Sumulong on Route 1. The position was an excellent one.[55]

On 21 December, the division commander, recently promoted to brigadier general, ordered Lt. Col. Virgil N. Cordero, the regimental commander, to move on Sipoco with Companies B and C of the 52d Infantry. At 0500 the next morning, a Japanese force estimated to be a company attacked Company B at Timbuyo, just east

[51] Supplement to Diary of Maj Gen Albert M. Jones, OPD 319.1 PTO (20 Nov 45). This document, though unsigned, was prepared by Col. Stuart C. MacDonald, Jones's chief of staff, and consists of three separate documents: Important Dates, SLF; Notes on Left Subsector, I Phil Corps; and Pocket Fights. It will be cited hereafter as MacDonald, Supplement to Jones Diary.
[52] Jones, Diary, p. 5.
[53] Japanese Naval Opns in Phil Invasion, p. 12; Brereton, *Diaries*, p. 54; Morison, *Rising Sun in the*

Pacific, p. 177. For a full account of the air attack against Legaspi, see Edmonds, *They Fought With What They Had*, pp. 151–60.
[54] *14th Army Opns*, I, 42; Jones, Diary, p. 6.
[55] Jones, Diary, p. 6; MacDonald Supplement to Jones Diary.

of the Negritos Camp along the highway. The Filipino troops, under the command of 1st Lt. Matt Dobrinic, were in a well-organized position and drove off the Japanese, chasing them down the road for about six miles. They inflicted heavy losses on the enemy, suffering about 15-percent casualties themselves.[56]

On 23 December General Jones ordered his troops to withdraw from the Bicol Peninsula when a Japanese invasion force appeared off Atimonan. Part of the 1st Battalion, 52d Infantry, was cut off by the Japanese landing at Atimonan that night, but some of the men made their way back into the American lines. The 51st Division had accomplished its objective. It had delayed the enemy advance and prevented an immediate juncture of the *Kimura Detachment* with the main elements of the *16th Division* soon to land at Lamon Bay.[57]

Landings in the South

The Japanese landings in the southern Philippines, in Mindanao and the Sulu Archipelago, were intended primarily to provide bases for the *16th Army's* drive on Borneo. They had no effect on Japanese plans for Luzon, except to prevent reinforcements from reaching that island from Allied bases to the south and to cut the American route of withdrawal.

Two landings were scheduled in the south, one at Davao in Mindanao, and another on Jolo Island in the Sulu Archipelago. Two detachments, both under Maj.

Gen. Shizuo Sakaguchi, infantry group commander of the *16th Army's 56th Division*, were organized for these landings. The first, originally scheduled to capture Davao alone, was led by Lt. Col. Toshio Miura and consisted of the *1st Battalion* of the *16th Division's 33d Infantry,* plus engineer and service elements. To it was later added the *Sakaguchi Detachment,* composed of the *56th Division's 146th Infantry,* an armored unit, and one battalion of divisional artillery. The strength of the entire force was about 5,000 men.[58]

This combined force was under *16th Army* control, although the date of departure from Palau was set by *14th Army* headquarters in Formosa. Once Davao was seized, the *Miura Detachment* was to revert to *14th Army* control and the *16th Army's Sakaguchi Detachment* was to move on to Jolo Island on its way to Tarakan in Dutch Borneo. For the Jolo Island operation, the *Kure 2d Special Naval Landing Force* from Legaspi and a naval airfield maintenance unit were to be added to the *Sakaguchi Detachment.*[59]

The combined force left Palau at 1400 on 17 December in fourteen transports. Admiral Takagi's force provided naval escort. Direct support was given by a destroyer squadron, while a cruiser squadron and the carrier *Ryujo* constituted a close covering force.[60] On the afternoon of the

---

[56] Jones, Diary, p. 6; ltr, Col· John R. Boatwright, formerly CO 53d Inf, to George Groce, research asst to author, 22 Mar 49; Luzon Campaign of *16th Division,* 24 Dec 41–3 Jan 42, ATIS, Enemy Publications 355, p. 2. The Japanese claimed a victory in this action.

[57] MacDonald, Supplement to Jones Diary, p. 8; ltr, Boatwright to Groce, 22 Mar 49.

[58] *14th Army* Opns, I, 31–32; interrogs of Gen Morioka, 24 Apr 47 and Col Nakajima, 25 Apr 47, in Interrogations of Former Japanese Officers, Mil Hist Div, GHQ FEC, I; Comments of Former Japanese Officers Regarding The Fall of the Philippines, pp. 25–26, OCMH.

[59] The Jolo Island Opns, Japanese Studies in World War II, No. 23, p. 1, *1st ↓Demob Bureau,* FEC; Japanese Naval Opns in Phil Invasion, p. 17.

[60] *14th Army* Opns, I, 43; Japanese Naval Opns in Phil Invasion, pp. 15–16; Morison, *Rising Sun in the Pacific,* pp. 163, 182.

19th, from a point about 200 miles east of Davao, the *Ryujo* launched six planes to attack the radio station at Cape San Augustin, the tip of the eastern arm of Davao Gulf, while the seaplane carrier *Chitose* launched its own planes to reconnoiter over Davao. The transports arrived off the city after midnight on the night of 19–20 December.[61]

At 0400 troops of the *Miura Detachment*, covered by carrier-based aircraft, began landing in the northern section of Davao while elements of the *Sakaguchi Detachment* came ashore along the coast southwest of the city. Defending this sector of the island were about 2,000 Philippine Army troops led by Lt. Col. Roger B. Hilsman, commander of the 2d Battalion, 101st Infantry.[62]

The *Miura Detachment* was momentarily mistaken for an American naval or marine force when it was first sighted. When a Japanese destroyer began shelling the beaches, this misapprehension was quickly removed. The only opposition offered to the landing force came from a machine gun squad which inflicted numerous casualties on the enemy before it was knocked out by a direct hit from a Japanese shell.[63] Thereafter Colonel Miura's men met no further opposition. The casualties suffered made it necessary to commit those elements of the *Sakaguchi Detachment* which the Japanese were saving for the Jolo Island operation.

By about 1030 that morning, Colonel Hilsman had pulled his men out of the city along the road leading northwest into the hills, leaving behind three of the eight 2.95-inch guns which constituted the artillery of the Visayan-Mindanao Force. The troops remaining in Davao were directed to withdraw also and set up defensive positions along the heights surrounding the city.[64]

The *Sakaguchi Detachment* apparently met no resistance southwest of the city. Moving northeast along the coastal road, it entered the city and made contact with Colonel Miura's force early in the afternoon. By 1500 the city and its airfield were occupied. That evening a seaplane base was established south of the city, and the next morning naval shore units began bringing Japanese nationals into Davao.[65]

General Sakaguchi lost no time in dispatching the *Jolo Force,* consisting of one infantry battalion (less two companies), with attached artillery, engineer, and communications units, and the *Kure 2d Special Naval Landing Force.* Its departure was delayed first by the unexpected casualties to the *Miura Detachment* and then by a B–17 attack. Nine of the bombers had come from Batchelor Field near Darwin, Australia, and they hit the Japanese at sunset of the 22d. The raid came as a complete surprise to the Japanese. Fortunately, for them, visibility was poor and the Jolo Force suffered only minor damage. The next morning the convoy set out from Davao, reaching its destination on Christmas Eve.[66]

---

[61] Japanese Naval Opns in Phil Invasion, pp. 15, 16.

[62] Ltr, Col Howard N. Frissell, formerly CO 3d Bn, 101st Inf, to author 5 May 49; statement of Maj Charles I. Humber, Jr., 30 Jan 42, in Gen Sharp's papers loaned by Mrs. Sharp to author and in OCMH.

[63] Humber Statement; Jolo Island Opns, p. 2.

[64] V-MF Rpt of Opns, p. 173; Humber Statement.

[65] Japanese Naval Opns in Phil Invasion, p. 16; *14th Army* Opns, I, 43.

[66] Craven and Cate, *The Army Air Forces in World War II,* I, 223–24; Japanese Naval Opns in Phil Invasion, pp. 16–17. Edmonds claims that the B–17's sank a 10,000-ton tanker. *They Fought With What They Had,* p. 180.

First warning of the approaching force reached the defenders, 300 Constabulary troops, at 1700 of the 24th. The landings began three hours later. The Constabulary were able to offer only slight resistance, and by the following morning, the Japanese were in the town of Jolo.[67] From Davao and Jolo the Japanese were in position to launch an attack against Borneo.

[67] Jolo Island Opns, p. 3; statement of 1st Lt Jose V. Valera, Jan 42, in Sharp Papers; V-MF Rpt of Opns, p. 575.

CHAPTER VII

The Impact of War

The transition from peace to war in the Philippines was a sudden one. The civilian population and the untrained Filipino soldiers were ill prepared to withstand the initial shock without displaying signs of nervousness and apprehension. Although a war with Japan had been expected for some time, bomb shelters had not been completed and the Philippine Army was still in the process of mobilization. A voluble and excitable people, the Filipinos saw danger everywhere and their fertile imagination produced reports of enemy activity that kept the USAFFE staff busy searching for the grain of truth in the wild tales that came in over the wires.

The most fantastic reports were accepted and widely circulated. During the first air raids, the belief that the Japanese bombers were "at least partially manned by white pilots" was given sufficient credence to be reported to the War Department.[1] Dewey Boulevard was supposed to be lined, the planeless 27th Bombardment Group heard, with A-20's ready to fly into combat. The same unit also reported a telephone message stating that its A-24's were at the docks being unloaded. A frantic but unprofitable rush to the water front followed.[2]

Many residents in Manila reported hearing short-wave messages to Japan, but the most careful search by Army authorities failed to reveal a short-wave transmitter. One day there was news that the fleet was sailing across the Pacific to the rescue; another day that the water supply in Manila had been poisoned and that poison gas had been spread in the port area. Again, the Japanese were supposed to have sailed into Manila Bay and put ashore 1,000 men at the mouth of the Pasig River.[3] From 9 December on, Admiral Hart wrote, "An extraordinary crop of incorrect enemy information flowed in over the warning net. Too many reports came in of enemy sightings when nothing actually was sighted. . . ."[4] "The Army," said one writer, "was travelling as much on rumors as on its stomach."[5]

Each fresh rumor made the civilian population more uneasy. No one knew what to believe. Numerous air raid alarms, all of them false, and the blackout added to the tense and foreboding atmosphere. The air alarms in Manila became so frequent that General Sutherland had to order wardens to clear through the Army headquarters before sounding the sirens.

The blackout was rigorously enforced, and the criminal element in the city took full advantage of the darkness and confusion. They were unwittingly aided by

---

[1] Rad, MacArthur to AGWAR, No. 1135, 9 Dec 41, AG 381 (11-27-41 Gen) Far East.
[2] Army Air Action in Phil and NEI, p. 74.

[3] Charles Van Landingham, "I Saw Manila Die," *Saturday Evening Post*, September 26, 1942, pp. 13, 71.
[4] Hart, Narrative of Events, Asiatic Fleet, p. 38.
[5] Quoted in Craven and Cate, *The Army Air Forces in World War II*, I, 222.

guards, sentries, and air raid wardens, who "popped up seemingly at every corner to issue a nervous challenge." [6] If not answered promptly and satisfactorily, they fired. In an effort to control crime and reported fifth-column activity, the police were given orders to shoot if the reply to a challenge was not satisfactory. Many interpreted their orders narrowly, challenging and firing at the same time. With sentries, air raid wardens, and police shooting, sometimes at each other, the confusion became even worse. Finally, USAFFE ordered all firearms turned in.

Manila showed all the signs of a modern city under attack. Shop windows were covered with adhesive tape and entrances barricaded with sandbags. Improvised bomb shelters appeared in shops and public buildings. Those fortunate enough to have cellars in their homes spent their nights there. Transportation was commandeered by the Army and gasoline was rationed. Those who drove cars had to shade their headlights in the approved fashion.[7] Street traffic became disorganized, and trucks, ambulances, and official cars raced through the streets at top speed with complete disregard for traffic signals.

Life in Manila during these days was topsy-turvy. Residents fled the city to seek safety in rural areas, and their country cousins flocked to the city for the same reason. Main thoroughfares were blocked with trucks, animal-drawn vehicles, and handcarts moving in both directions. Vehicles were loaded with household goods, trussed pigs, and chicken crates. To the rear trailed the dogs. To their barking

was added the squealing of the pigs and the clucking chatter of the fowls. The skies were watched anxiously for any sign of Japanese planes. People began to hoard food. Radio and cable offices were filled and it was impossible to handle all the messages to the outside world.[8]

With the first bombs the people rushed to the banks to withdraw their money. Frantic mobs pushed and milled outside the banks and swore at the tellers. Those banks and commercial houses that had not already done so sent their gold to Australia and the United States. After several days withdrawals were limited to 200 pesos in paper money weekly. Filipinos hoarded silver money and the result was a shortage in change. Most merchants sold only for cash, thus increasing the difficulties of the business community.[9]

During these days of confusion, military and civilian authorities worked closely to restore the confidence of the people. Bomb shelters were constructed and the people began to pay less attention to the air raid warnings when the Japanese failed to attack the city. The Commonwealth Assembly met in emergency session and made available to President Quezon the sum of 20,-000,000 pesos for defense. The United States contributed an equal sum for civilian relief. Government employees were given three months' advance in pay so that they could move their families out of the city to places supposedly safer than Manila. But it never became necessary to establish martial law, and after a week or two the Filipinos quieted down and life in the capital became more normal.

The troops were just as nervous as the civilians. Most of them were convinced

---

[6] Collier, Notebooks, I, 75. See also Amea Willoughby, *I Was on Corregidor* (New York, 1943), pp. 93–94.
[7] Van Landingham, "I Saw Manila Die," p. 13.

[8] *Ibid.*, p. 12; Collier, Notebooks, I, 75.
[9] Van Landingham, "I Saw Manila Die," p. 12.

that a well-organized Japanese fifth column existed in the Philippines. Flares, rockets, strange lights, descending paratroopers, cut wires, and interrupted communications were all observed and cited as evidences for this belief. Rumors circulated as widely among the troops as the civilians and were as firmly believed.

The assistant supply officer of USAFFE, Maj. Frank F. Carpenter, Jr., on a visit to a barrio about fifteen miles north of Manila, heard stories of American convoys, shortages of ammunition, the landings at Aparri, and other military matters, which the average American soldier did not know. He was told that Germans wearing the American uniform had been seen and that 1,500 Japanese soldiers in civilian clothes were living in Manila, "all set to take action at the proper time." It was Major Carpenter's considered judgment that fifth columnists in the uniform of the American soldier were spreading information and creating dissatisfaction, and he asked the intelligence officer to investigate.[10]

Almost all survivors of the campaign agree that they saw flares or that they know someone who did. These lights were apparently unlike signal flares; they were small, orange in color, and could be seen close to the ground or just above the trees. Other observers noted rockets rising over uninhabited areas, and series of lights forming a straight line pointing to an airfield or military target just before an attack. Colonel Collier tells this story of the predawn raid on Nichols Field on the morning of 9 December: As the sound of the Japanese planes became audible, an old automobile near Nichols burst into flames, casting a glow over the field. At the same time, about a dozen fishing boats were observed in the bay, just outside the breakwater. They formed a circle with their lights pointing toward the center. The straight line from this point to the blazing automobile formed a line which the Japanese bombers presumably followed to reach the field.[11]

Similar stories are told about the raids on Clark Field and Cavite. One witness states that he learned from an unnamed cavalry officer—since killed—that a Filipino who operated a bar near Clark Field was largely responsible for the success of the Japanese attack on 8 December. This Filipino is supposed to have had a powerful short-wave transmitter with a beam director in a room in back of the bar and to have informed the Japanese when all the B–17's were on the ground. He was discovered at the dials of his transmitter after the raid and a "grim sergeant from the 26th Cavalry went into the place with a tommy gun." [12] The presence of collaborators at Clark is also mentioned by Lt. Joseph H. Moore, commander of the 20th Pursuit Squadron, who states that he found a mirror tied to a tree above his quarters. Presumably the reflections from the mirror guided the Japanese aircraft to the field.[13]

A variation of the Clark Field story was told of the raid on the Cavite Navy Yard. Here a secret radio transmitter was also supposed to have been found. The operators, according to this account, were an American with a Japanese wife, both later discovered and arrested. At Cavite, also, an attractive girl of Japanese ancestry, who was

---

[10] Memo, Maj Carpenter, to G–2 USAFFE, 16 Dec 41, AG 383.4 Phil Rcds.

[11] Collier, Notebooks, I, 62–63; Ind, *Bataan, The Judgment Seat,* pp. 107, 110–14.
[12] Van Landingham, "I Saw Manila Die," pp. 12–13; Lee, *They Call It Pacific,* p. 45.
[13] Interv, author with Col Moore, 12 Aug 49, OCMH.

employed in a trusted position at the yard, was "caught red-handed in act of treachery." Someone decided she had to be executed immediately and the officers drew lots. The task fell, so the story goes, to a young naval officer who was in love with the beautiful spy. He led her outside and performed the sentence "without hesitation." [14] Official records do not support any of the stories told about secret radio transmitters, beautiful spies, or fifth columnist barkeepers.

Reports of paratroops were frequent also, but upon investigation all proved to be false. A drop of 20,000 paratroops about ten miles east of Clark Field was reported on 10 December. USAFFE placed enough reliability on the report to order the Philippine Division there to meet and destroy the enemy. When the reported Japanese paratroopers failed to appear, the division was ordered elsewhere.[15]

Interrogation of Japanese officers after the war and a study of Japanese and American records fail to support the belief that a Japanese fifth column existed in the Philippines. There is not a shred of evidence to indicate that any organized effort was made by the Japanese to utilize the sympathies of the Japanese population in the Islands or of Filipino collaborators. To have done so would have involved knowledge by a Japanese organization in the Philippines of the *14th Army's* detailed plans well in advance of the attack, communications with the airfields on Formosa, and an elaborate organization to receive information from agents and relay it on to Japanese headquarters on Formosa. Such an organization did not exist. If an effort

to assist the attacking Japanese was made, it must have been sporadic and on an individual basis.

It is possible to explain some of the observed phenomena on grounds other than fifth-column activity. The flares may have been caused by American and Filipino troops using faulty .30-caliber tracer ammunition of World War I vintage. No one was ever able to find any person who fired flares, and examination invariably revealed that the strange lights and flares came from an area where American troops were stationed. Sometimes those searching for the origin of the flares used lights which others reported as signs of fifth-column operations. The reports of Japanese paratroopers can be explained by parachuting pilots from damaged aircraft, by the descending burst of antiaircraft fire, or by jettisoned spare gas tanks. The heated imagination of men during the first days of war is capable of conjuring up visions far more fantastic than strange lights and descending paratroopers.

The possibility of sabotage and fifth-column activity had been anticipated in prewar plans. The Philippine Department G–2 and the Commonwealth secret service had listed enemy aliens and had kept many individuals under surveillance. Provision had been made to secure information and locate enemy agents in the event of a Japanese attack. Several FBI operators of Japanese parentage (nisei) had been brought from Hawaii before the war to circulate among the Japanese population. Many American businessmen, engineers, and planters had been enrolled secretly in the intelligence organization and provided a potential American fifth column in the event of a Japanese occupation of the Islands. The Philippine Constabulary also

[14] Lee, *They Call It Pacific* (Viking), p. 46.
[15] USAFFE-USFIP Rpt of Opns, pp. 27–29.

provided secret agents for counter-espionage.[16]

At the outbreak of hostilities, all suspected persons were quickly and quietly taken into custody. Japanese civilians living in the Japanese section of Manila were ordered to remain in their homes, and the military police took over the guard of this area.[17] On the first day of war, General MacArthur reported to the War Department that 40 percent of the enemy aliens in Manila, and 10 percent of those in the provinces had been interned.[18] The Philippine Constabulary picked up aliens wherever found—in homes, offices, clubs, and on the streets. On 13 December, two days after Germany and Italy declared war on the United States, German and Italian residents in the Philippines were also interned.[19] The aliens were first screened at Bilibid Prison in Manila and those cleared were released at once. Those not able to explain their business satisfactorily were then transferred to a camp south of the city to await examination by a board consisting of a representative of the High Commissioner and several Army officers.[20]

Although the civilian population and the untrained troops were nervous during the first days of war, the task of mobilizing the Philippine Army continued. According to the prewar plan the last units were scheduled for induction on 15 December, a week after the attack came. Some, such as the 43d Infantry, had already been brought in and, as soon as hostilities opened, all re-maining units were immediately mobilized. Those divisional elements not yet in service, usually the third infantry regiment and the field artillery regiment, were brought in immediately. A provisional Constabulary regiment, later designated the 4th, was formed and, with the 1st and 2d Regiments, became the basis for the 2d Regular Division, organized early in January and consisting entirely of Constabulary troops. The 1st Regular Division (PA), which in peacetime consisted mainly of cadres for training reservists, was brought up to strength and inducted, without an artillery regiment, on 19 December. It was assigned to the South Luzon Force and its 1st Infantry moved at once to the Mauban area along Lamon Bay.[21]

In the Visayas and in Mindanao, mobilization was about one-half completed when war came. On orders from MacArthur's headquarters, the 72d and 92d Infantry (PA) were sent to Luzon on 9 December. Numerous provisional units were organized and equipped by local commanders. These units consisted of volunteers, ROTC cadets, and reservists not yet called or who had failed to report.[22]

All reservists were ordered to report to the nearest unit or mobilization center on 8 December. As a result, some units found themselves overstrength and additional units were hastily organized. Men undergoing instruction and not yet assigned were organized into separate units. Coast artillery personnel at Fort Mills (Corregidor), for example, was organized into the 1st Coast Artillery (PA), with a headquarters battery of twenty-eight men and four gun

---

[16] Brief Hist of the G–2 Sec, GHQ SWPA, pp. 1–2.

[17] USAFFE-USFIP Rpt of Opns, p. 34; Van Landingham, "I Saw Manila Die," p. 12.

[18] Rad, MacArthur to AGWAR, No. 1133, 8 Dec 41, AG 381 (11–27–41 Gen) Far East.

[19] USAFFE-USFIP Rpt of Opns, p. 37; Collier, Notebooks, I, 65.

[20] Collier, Notebooks, I, 65.

[21] USAFFE-USFIP Rpt of Opns, p. 15; USAFFE GO's 47 and 50, 19 and 21 Dec 41.

[22] V-MF Rpt of Opns, p. 21; Notes on Phil Army, 1941–42.

batteries of one hundred men each. The coast artillery reservists at Fort Wint in Subic Bay were similarly organized.[23]

In some cases, units were formed to utilize armament or equipment lying in warehouses or elsewhere. At the suggestion of General King, MacArthur's artillery officer, the 301st Field Artillery (PA) was formed from two groups of volunteers, altogether 700 men, and equipped with 24 wooden-wheeled 155-mm. guns of World War I type, and 2 155-mm. howitzers of the same vintage. These were the 155's that had been sent to the Philippines to protect the straits leading into the inland seas and were the only weapons of this caliber in the Philippines, outside of Corregidor. Col. Alexander S. Quintard was brought from Mindanao to command the unit.[24] At about the same time, three separate provisional battalions of field artillery of four 4-gun batteries each were formed. These units were armed with 48 of the 50 75-mm. guns on self-propelled mounts that had been shipped to the Philippines in October. Personnel was secured from the Philippine Scouts, Philippine Army reservists, and the 200th Coast Artillery (AA). Two of the battalions were assigned to the North Luzon Force, and one to the South Luzon Force.[25]

Immediately upon the outbreak of war, USAFFE ordered all procurement agencies to fill their needs by purchase in the local

markets. The quartermaster bought all the new and used automobiles and trucks he could find, as well as large quantities of clothing and food. Several motor transport companies were taken over by the Army, lock, stock, and barrel. The Signal Corps purchased all available photographic, radio, and telephone equipment, and took control of the Manila Long Distance Telephone Company, commissioning its president, Joseph Stevenot, a lieutenant colonel. The Medical Corps gathered up all the medicine, bandages, and surgical equipment it could find in the Islands. Buildings of all kinds were occupied by the Army—the *Jai Alai* Club became a hospital; Rizal Stadium, a medical depot.[26] The officers assigned to the former inherited the food, chefs, and service of the club, and for a few days dined sumptuously on onion and mushroom soup, steak, broiled lobster, and Viennese pastry, served on snowy linen gleaming with silver by waiters in natty green and white uniforms. After headquarters heard of this arrangement, the medics ate Army fare.[27]

Manila, the commercial center of the Islands, was exploited for supplies to supplement existing stocks. On orders from General MacArthur the quartermaster took over from the large oil companies all their bulk petroleum products stored in the vicinity of Manila. He sought especially to procure food from local sources, for it was evident already that there would be a shortage should the campaign last long. From Chinese merchants in Manila, the Army secured thousands of 125-pound sacks of polished rice, and from ships in the

[23] Notes on Phil Army, 1941–42. For a list of units inducted with dates and stations, see Plan of Induction of Phil Army; Arrival of Units from the United States, Annex II, USAFFE-USFIP Rpt of Opns.
[24] USAFFE-USFIP Rpt of Opns, pp. 8, 22; USAFFE GO's 45 and 49, 17 and 21 Dec 41; Collier, Notebooks, II, 13–18; Col Quintard, CO 301st FA (PA), Diary, entries of 8–12 Dec 41. This diary was borrowed from Colonel Quintard and a photostat copy is on file in OCMH.
[25] Collier, Notebooks, II, 18–23.

[26] *Ibid.*, pp. 3–6; QM Rpt of Opns, pp. 13–23.
[27] Alfred A. Weinstein, *Barbed-Wire Surgeon*, (New York, 1948), pp. 5–6; Brig Gen Charles C. Drake, Comments on Draft MS, Comment 5, OCMH.

harbor large quantities of food. The quartermaster took over from Armour, Swift, and Libby large quantities of canned meats and other foods.[28]

Within a few days after the opening of hostilities, the port area in Manila had become crowded with rapidly expanding military installations. Fort Santiago, headquarters of the Philippine Department, was on the edge of this area, as was the mouth of the Pasig River, now jammed with inter-island freighters and other craft. The supply services that had warehouses and depots in the area decided it would be safest to move out, although Manila had not yet been bombed. The engineers were the first to go; they moved to the University of the Philippines. The quartermaster took over Santo Tomas University, and the other services followed. By 20 December most of the service installations in the port area had quietly moved to safer quarters.[29]

An unexpected addition to the tanks of Col. James R. N. Weaver's Provisional Tank Group was received shortly after the start of war. The Japanese attack left marooned in Manila Harbor the *Don Jose,* a vessel belonging to the Canadian Government and carrying a cargo of motor equipment for two Canadian motor battalions in Hong Kong. MacArthur immediately requested that this matériel be released for use in the Philippines, and the War Department secured the Canadian Government's consent. The cargo included fifty-seven Bren gun carriers, forty of which were made available to Colonel Weaver. Unfortunately, the guns for the carriers were not

included in the cargo, and they had to be armed by the Manila Ordnance Depot.[30]

The immediate reaction at Headquarters, USAFFE, to the first Japanese landings was one of calm. General MacArthur optimistically reported that the Philippine people had withstood the shock of war "with composure," and that there were "no signs of confusion or hysteria."[31] The Japanese moves were correctly analyzed but a counteroffensive was not launched to drive off the invaders. "We did not disperse forces," says General Sutherland, "but waited for what we felt would be the main attack."[32]

More concern was felt during the first days of the war over the rapid dissolution of the Far East Air Force than over the Japanese landings. "The present phase of énemy action," MacArthur told the War Department on 12 December, "involves a series of concentric thrusts probably intended to confuse and demoralize northern movement. Probably has the additional objective of securing airdromes for operation of land based aircraft."[33] The next day he declared that the enemy's intent was clearly revealed. The Japanese, he said, were seizing airbases outside the heavily defended area of central Luzon, and ground action could be considered sporadic and unimportant.[34]

---

[28] Alvin P. Stauffer, Quartermaster Operations in the War Against Japan, Ch. I, p. 45, a forthcoming volume in this series. This excellent manuscript was made available by the author before publication.
[29] Collier, Notebooks, II, 5–6.

[30] Memo, Asst QMG for G–4, 20 Dec 41, sub: Canadian Supplies, G–4 33817; memo for rcd, Brig Gen Brehon B. Somervell for TAG, n.d., approved by DCofS, OCS 18136-165.
[31] Rad, MacArthur to AGWAR, No. 1135, 9 Dec 41, AG 381 (11–27–41 Gen) Far East.
[32] Interv, author with Sutherland, 12 Nov 46, p. 4, OCMH.
[33] Rad, MacArthur to AGWAR, 12 Dec 41, AG 381 (11–27–41 Gen) Far East.
[34] Rad, MacArthur to AGWAR, 13 Dec 41, AG 381 (11–27–41 Gen) Far East.

This view was expressed also in Col. Charles A. Willoughby's intelligence estimate to the War Department on 13 December 1941. He expected the Japanese forces at Aparri, Vigan, and Legaspi to be reinforced, but pointed out that the landing areas were not suitable for the employment of strong forces in offensive operations. The purpose of the landing, he correctly analyzed, was to establish advance airbases. "As soon as air support is established," he warned, "a major landing effort can be expected; it is estimated after 15 days." [35]

The only change in plans made by MacArthur as a result of the Japanese landings was the new mission given the North Luzon Force on 16 December. Before that time General Wainwright had been charged with the defense of all northern Luzon, and his orders were to meet the enemy at the beaches and drive him back into the sea. The main line of resistance was the beach. Such a mission was impossible of execution with the available means and in the absence of air and naval support. On the 16th the North Luzon Force was relieved of responsibility for the defense of that portion of Luzon north of San Fernando, La Union, and required only to hold the enemy north of an east-west line through that city.[36]

Within a few days after the landings the pattern of the Japanese plan had become clear to the American command. First, Japanese air and naval forces were to cut off the Philippine Islands from all possible aid. Then, Japanese aircraft could destroy or neutralize the defending air and naval forces and gain superiority in the air and on the sea. At the same time, Japanese ground forces would secure advance bases at the northern and southern extremities of the island of Luzon and on Mindanao where the opposition was negligible or nonexistent. The major enemy effort, it was clear, was still to come. That it would come soon—Colonel Willoughby thought 28 December—there was no doubt, and when it did the objective would be Manila, the capital. Before the year was out, the worst fears of the early pessimists were to be realized. Even before the advance landings were completed, the main elements of General Homma's *14th Army* were already nearing the Luzon coast.

[35] Rad, Willoughby to War Dept G–2, 13 Dec 41, AG 381 (11–27–41 Gen) Far East.

[36] USAFFE-USFIP Rpt of Opns, p. 30.

CHAPTER VIII

The Main Landings

The first part of *Imperial General Head-quarters'* plan for the conquest of the Philippines had been successful beyond the hopes of the most optimistic. American air and naval power had been virtually destroyed. Five landings had been made at widely separated points and strong detachments of Japanese troops were already conducting offensive operations on Luzon and Mindanao. The *5th Air Group* was established on Luzon fields, and the Navy had its own seaplane bases at Camiguin Islands, Legaspi, and Davao. Army short-range fighters were in position to support Japanese ground troops when required. All this had been accomplished in less than two weeks.

The main landings, to be made on Luzon north and south of Manila, were still to come. There would be two landings: the major effort at Lingayen Gulf, and a secondary effort at Lamon Bay. (*Map 5*) The forces assigned to these landings had begun to assemble late in November. The *16th Division* (less the *9th* and *33d Infantry*) left Osaka in Japan on 25 November and arrived at Amami Oshima in the Ryukyus on 3 December. Three days later all of the *48th Division* less the *Tanaka* and *Kanno Detachments*) was concentrated at Mako, in the Pescadores, and at Takao and Kirun, on near-by Formosa. The major portion of the shipping units was in Formosa by the end of November and began to load the convoys soon after.

There was much confusion during the concentration and loading period. The greatest secrecy was observed, and only a small number of officers knew the entire plan. These men had to travel constantly between units and assembly points to assist in the preparations and in the solution of detailed and complicated problems. Unit commanders were given the scantiest instructions, and worked, for the most part, in the dark. Important orders were delivered just before they had to be executed, with little time for study and preparation. Such conditions, the Japanese later regretted, "proved incentives to errors and confusion, uneasiness and irritation."[1] Moreover, after 8 December, the Japanese lived in fear of an American bombing of Formosa ports, where the vessels were being loaded with supplies and ammunition.

Despite fears, confusions, and mistakes, the separate convoys were finally loaded and ready to sail by 17 December. The uneasiness arising from ignorance and secrecy persisted aboard ship. Even now the men were not told where they were going. Adding to the nervousness was the restriction placed on the use of maps. Only a few officers were allowed to see them. "All the units," the Japanese later observed, "were possessed of a presentiment, arising from the general atmosphere, that they were on their way to a very important theater of operations."[2] The *14th Army* staff, which did know the destination, shared the nervous-

---

[1] Phil Landing Opns (Amphibious), ATIS Doc 1989-6A.

[2] *Ibid.*

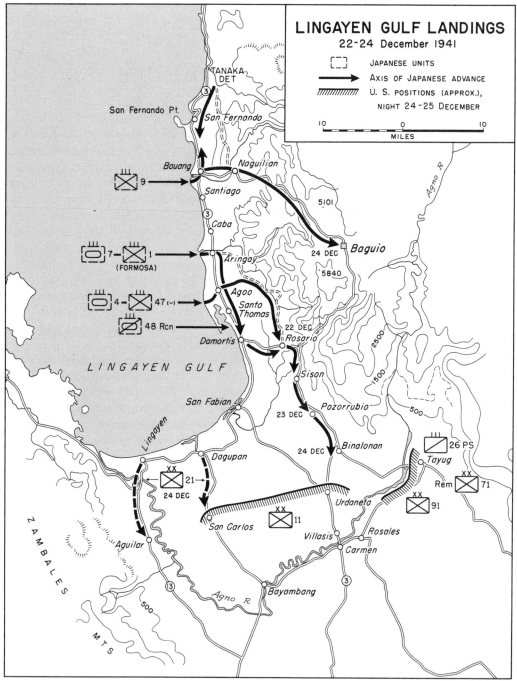

LINGAYEN GULF LANDINGS
22-24 December 1941

[⌐¬] JAPANESE UNITS

➡ AXIS OF JAPANESE ADVANCE

▨ U. S. POSITIONS (APPROX.),
NIGHT 24-25 DECEMBER

10   0   10
MILES

TANAKA DET

San Fernando Pt.

San Fernando

Bauang

Naguilian

9

Santiago

5101

Caba

24 DEC   Baguio

7- 1
(FORMOSA)

Aringay

5840

4- 47 (-)

Agoo
Santo
Thomas

22 DEC

48 Rcn

Damortis

Rosario

LINGAYEN GULF

Sison

2500

San Fabian

Pozorrubio

23 DEC

1500

500

Lingayen

24 DEC   Binalonan

26 PS

Dagupan

Tayug

21

24 DEC

Rem   71

91

Urdaneta

11

San Carlos

Z
A
M
B
A
L
E
S

Villasis

Rosales

Aguilar

Carmen

500

Agno R.

Bayambang

3

MTS

H.Damon

MAP 5

ness of the troops. Everything depended upon the success of this operation. All that had gone before was but a preliminary to these landings. If they did not succeed, the plans of the *Southern Army* and of *Imperial General Headquarters* would fail. "During all my campaigns in the Philippines," said General Homma when he was on trial for his life, "I had three critical moments, and this was number one." [3]

The Lingayen Landing

On the morning of 21 December, Filipinos near Bauang along the shores of Lingayen Gulf observed a Japanese trawler cruising leisurely offshore. Unmolested, it took soundings and then serenely sailed off to the north. [4] Late that night, seventy-six heavily loaded Army transports and nine Navy transports, all under strong naval escort, steamed into Lingayen Gulf and dropped anchor. The main assault was on.

The Landing Force

Aboard the transports was the main strength of General Homma's *14th Army,* altogether 43,110 men. [5] The major combat strength of the *Lingayen Force* was drawn from Lt. Gen. Yuichi Tsuchibashi's *48th Division.* Activated in Formosa in late 1940 and as yet untried in battle, this division was composed of the *1st* and *2d Formosa Infantry Regiments,* the *47th Infantry,* and artillery, reconnaissance, engineer, and transport regiments. Attached to it for the landing was a large number of combat and service units, but the *2d Formosa* had been lost by the establishment of the *Tanaka* and *Kanno Detachments.* Although probably the best motorized division in the Japanese Army at this time, the *48th* by American standards could hardly be said to have sufficient motor transportation. One battalion of each infantry regiment was equipped with bicycles. Divisional artillery consisted of the *48th Mountain Artillery,* similar to a standard field artillery regiment except that the basic weapon was the 75-mm. mountain gun (pack). [6]

---

[3] Proceedings of the trial, United States of America *vs.* Masaharu Homma Before the Military Commission Convened by the Commanding General, United States Army Forces Western Pacific, p. 3050, testimony of Homma.

The transcript of the trial includes 30 volumes of testimony before the military tribunal, 5 volumes of exhibits, and 1 volume of the trial review by Lt. Gen. Wilhelm D. Styer. The volumes of testimony are numbered 1 through 30—each volume covering one day of the trial, held during the period December 19, 1945, to February 11, 1946—and are paginated seriatim. They will be hereafter referred to as USA *vs.* Homma with appropriate page. The 5 volumes of exhibits include 3 kinds of documents: Prosecution Exhibits, 1–425, Defense Exhibits, A–Y, and Commission Exhibit 1, and will be hereafter cited as USA *vs.* Homma, Prosecution, Defense, or Commission Exhibits with appropriate number or letter. When used, the transcript of the proceedings of this tribunal and the exhibits were on file in the War Crimes Division of the Office of the Judge Advocate General.

[4] Interv, author with Col Blackburn, 11th Div (PA), 13 May 49. Colonel Blackburn was stationed near Bauang at this time.

[5] Ltr, Chief, Hist Div SSUSA to G–2 GHQ FEC, 9 Nov 48, 3d Ind, 16 Aug 49. The breakdown of the troops landing between 22 and 28 December 1941 is as follows:

14th Army	34,856
Shipping Units	4,633
Army Air Force	3,621
Total	43,110

[6] Order of Battle of the Japanese Armed Forces, WD G–2, 1 Mar 45, p. 108; USA *vs.* Homma, p. 3054–55, testimony of Homma; Handbook of Japanese Military Forces, TM–E–30–480, 15 Sep 44, p. 37.

In addition to the *48th Division,* the *Lingayen Force* contained the *16th Division's 9th Infantry,* and part of the *22d Field Artillery* with 8 horse-drawn 75-mm. guns. Larger caliber pieces were provided by the *9th Independent Field Artillery Battalion* (8 150-mm. guns), the *1st Field Artillery Regiment* (24 150-mm. howitzers), and the *8th Field Artillery Regiment* (16 105-mm. guns). Included in the *Lingayen Force* were between 80 and 100 light and heavy tanks distributed between the *4th* and *7th Tank Regiments.*[7] A large number of service and special troops completed the force.

The vessels that reached Lingayen Gulf on the night of 21 December were organized in three separate convoys. The first to leave had come from Kirun in northern Formosa and had sailed at 0900 of the 17th. It contained twenty-one transports and had been escorted by the *Batan Island Attack Force,* which had returned to Formosa after the landing on 8 December.[8]

The convoy loaded at Mako in the Pescadores, being second farthest from the Philippines, was the next to depart. At noon on 18 December, the twenty-eight transports of this group, accompanied by the *Vigan Attack Force,* left port. The last convoy left Takao in Formosa at 1700 on the 18th, escorted by the naval force which had supported the Aparri landing.

With each convoy went a large number of landing craft, altogether 63 small landing craft, 73 large ones, and 15 others, which the Japanese called "extra large." In addition, there were 48 small craft, best described as powered sampans. The smallest of the landing craft weighed 3 tons and was apparently used as a personnel carrier. The large landing craft, *Daihatsu* Model A (Army), was probably the one that saw most service in the Pacific war. Resembling a fishing barge in appearance, it weighed 5 tons, was 50 feet long, was capable of 6 to 10 knots, and had a draft of 3 to 4 feet and a capacity of 100 to 120 men for short hauls.[9] The "extra large" landing craft, or *Tokubetsu Daihatsu,* weighed 7 to 8 tons and was capable of carrying the later model tanks. Its end could be dropped, enabling the tanks to climb in and out under their own power.[10]

In addition to the direct support provided by the naval escorts with each convoy—altogether 2 light cruisers, 16 destroyers, and a large number of torpedo boats, minesweepers and layers, patrol craft, and miscellaneous vessels—a large naval force led by Vice Adm. Ibo Takahashi, *3d Fleet* commander, moved into position to furnish distant cover. On 19 December this force sortied from Mako and sailed to a point about 250 miles west of Luzon. There it was joined by units of Vice Adm. Nobutake Kondo's *2d Fleet,* detached from support of the Malayan invasion. Altogether, the Japanese had a force of 2 battleships, 4 heavy cruisers, 1 light cruiser, 2 seaplane

---

[7] One of these was a heavy tank regiment, whose tanks were the equivalent of the U.S. 13-ton light tank; the other was light. The Japanese do not indicate which is the heavy and which is the light tank regiment, but it appears that the *4th* contained the light tanks.

[8] *14th Army* Opns, I, 46; II, 8, Untranslated Chart 5; Japanese Naval Opns in Phil Invasion, p. 14; Morison, *Rising Sun in the Pacific,* p. 162.

[9] *14 Army* Opns, II, 1–5, 8, Untranslated Charts 1 and 5; Handbook of Japanese Mil Forces, pp. 327–30.

[10] Answers by *1st Demob Bureau* to Questionnaire on Phil Campaign prepared by author, 5 Aug 49, ATIS Doc 49692.

carriers, and some destroyers in position to meet any Allied naval attempt to disrupt the landing of the *Lingayen Force.*[11]

The Plan

The Japanese plan called for landings at three points along the shores of Lingayen Gulf, to begin at 0500 of the 22d.[12] Each of the convoys constituted a separate task force and each was to land at a different point. The southernmost landing was to be made by the Takao convoy carrying the *47th Infantry* (less one battalion), *4th Tank Regiment* (less one company), and supporting elements. This force was to land at Agoo, a small village just inland from the eastern shore of Lingayen Gulf, about five

miles north of Damortis. Starting at 0500, the troops, already loaded into the sixty-nine landing craft assigned to this force, were to head for the beach. The first wave was scheduled to touch down at 0540. The round trip time of the landing craft in this wave was to be two hours; thereafter it would be one hour. Altogether each of the craft would make ten round trips during the first day.

The landing craft of the Mako convoy, carrying the *1st Formosa* and *7th Tank Regiment,* were to move out thirty minutes after the *47th Infantry,* and at 0550 would hit the shore at Caba, seven miles north of Agoo. To carry the troops of this force ashore, 57 landing craft and 19 powered sampans were assigned. The third force, consisting of the *9th Infantry* and called the *Kamijima Detachment,* was not to start landing operations until 0700.[13] At that time the troops would be loaded into 20 landing craft and 29 sampans and would head for Bauang, about seven miles north of Caba, the first wave reaching shore at 0730. Thus, *14th Army* expected to hold a fifteen-mile stretch of beach, from Bauang on the north to Agoo on the south, along the narrow coastal plain between Lingayen Gulf and the Cordillera central range, by 0730 of D Day, 22 December.

The position chosen for the landing was an excellent one. Between the mountains and the shore was a narrow level strip along which ran Route 3, an excellent hard-surface, two-way highway. At Bauang was a road intersecting Route 3 and leading eastward through a mountain defile to Baguio, whence it turned south to join Route 3 again near Rosario. At Aringay, just above Agoo, was a river which formed

---

[11] Japanese Naval Opns in Phil Invasion, p. 14; Interrogs of Vice Adm Kazutaka Shiraichi, CofS, *2d Fleet,* 15 Oct 45, and of Capt Masamichi Fujita, *2d Fleet* staff, 20 Oct 45, USSBS, *Interrogations of Japanese Officials,* I, 26, 72; Morison, *Rising Sun in the Pacific,* p. 178.

[12] The landing plan was drawn up in Formosa on 1 Dec 41 and is reproduced in *14th Army Opns,* II, 1–5. The author used the untranslated version.

Unless otherwise noted, the account of the Lingayen landing and the consolidation of the beachhead is based on the following sources: *14th Army* Opns, I, 46–48, 51–52; *5th Air Gp* Opns, pp. 31–37; Statement of Col Moriji Kawagoe, former CofS, *48th Division,* 30 Jun 49, ATIS Doc 62707, in Statements of Japanese Officials on World War II, GHQ FEC, Mil Intel Sec, II, 124–28; Japanese Naval Opns in Phil Invasion, pp. 8–9, 13–14; Morison, *Rising Sun in the Pacific,* pp. 179–83; USAFFE-USFIP Rpt of Opns, pp. 31ff.; NLF and II Corps Rpt of Opns, pp. 7–10; Wainwright, *General Wainwright's Story,* pp. 33–35; Lt Col William E. Chandler, "The 26th Cavalry (PS) Battles to Glory," *Armored Cavalry Journal,* Nos. 2 and 3 (March–June 1947), Part 1, pp. 14–16, Part 2, pp. 7–11; ltr, Col Clyde A. Selleck to Board of Officers, 1 Feb 46, sub: Statement for Reinstatement of Rank, pp. 7–9, copy supplied author by Col Selleck, and in OCMH; and ltr, Col Halstead C. Fowler, formerly CO 71st FA(PA) to author, 30 Apr 49.

---

[13] The name Kamijima also appears as Uejima.

a small valley through the mountains. Through this valley ran a partially surfaced road which led from Aringay to Rosario, one of the key road intersections in this area. South of the landing beaches was the central plain of Luzon. Route 3 opened directly on to the road network leading into Manila.

Once ashore the troops were to destroy any American forces in the vicinity and move inland without waiting to consolidate the beachhead. Later waves would perform that task. The *Kamijima Detachment* at Bauang was to send one element north to occupy San Fernando, La Union, and another east along the Bauang–Baguio Road, to seize the Naguilian airfield and then press on to Baguio. By seizing Baguio, the Japanese would prevent an American counterattack from the east through the defile. The occupation of San Fernando to the north would effect a consolidation with Colonel Tanaka's force moving south from Vigan and would protect the rear of the Japanese southward advance.

The forces landing at Caba and Agoo were to press south toward Damortis and Rosario. Two roads would be used: the coastal highway to Damortis, and the partially surfaced road which paralleled the Aringay River and led to Rosario. Once at their objectives, these troops were to assemble and "prepare to advance" toward the bank of the Agno River, the first formidable obstacle to a force moving south from Lingayen Gulf to Manila.

The Landing

The voyage of the *Lingayen Force* to the target was uneventful. In an effort to avoid detection and to create the impression that the destination was Indochina, the transports at first followed a southwesterly course. Only a typhoon in the South China Sea hindered the approach; no American planes or ships appeared.

The combined invasion force was without air cover, such support no longer considered necessary, until the 21st when twenty planes of the *24th* and *50th Fighter Regiments,* based at Laoag, came out to meet the ships and escort them during the last leg of the journey. At the same time, six light bombers struck Fort Wint on Grande Island at the entrance to Subic Bay, hoping thus to make the real landing site. Between 0110 and 0430 on 22 December, the three convoys, after a slow voyage at an average speed of 8 knots, dropped anchor in Lingayen Gulf.[14] The weather was chill, the skies were dark, and an intermittent rain was falling.

At this point things began to go wrong. The convoy leaders, warned against stopping short of their targets, went to the other extreme. The initial anchorage was to have been between San Fernando and the Aringay River, but the lead ship, unable to locate the river in the darkness, overshot the mark, and dropped anchor off Santo Thomas, about four miles south of Agoo. The other transports followed, dropping anchor at intervals over a distance of fifteen miles. As a result, the landing craft now had to make a longer trip than anticipated to reach their designated beaches.[15]

[14] Answers to Questionnaire on Phil Campaign, 5 Aug 49, ATIS Doc 49692; Interrog of Gen Maeda, CofS, *14th Army,* 10 May 47, Interrogations of Former Japanese Officers, Mil Hist Div, GHQ FEC, I; USA *vs.* Homma, p. 3049, testimony of Homma.
[15] Interrog of Gen Maeda, 10 May 47; Phil Landings Opns (Amphibious), ATIS Doc 1989–6A.

Under cover of cruiser and destroyer gun-fire, the troops began going over the side shortly after 0200. By 0430 two battalions of the *47th Infantry* and one battalion of the *48th Mountain Artillery* were in the landing craft, ready to strike out for shore. At 0517 the first troops touched down on the beach south of Agoo. Less than fifteen minutes later, at 0530, the *1st Formosa Infantry,* the main strength of the *3d Battalion, 48th Mountain Artillery,* and tanks began landing at Aringay, about two miles south of Caba. Two hours later part of the *Kamijima Detachment* came ashore near Bauang; the rest of the *Detachment* landed at Santiago, three miles to the south, at 0830.[16]

The transfer of the troops to the landing craft had proved extremely difficult because of high seas. The light craft were heavily buffeted on the way to shore and the men and equipment soaked by the spray. The radios were made useless by salt water, and there was no communication with the first waves ashore. Even ship-to-ship communication was inadequate. The men had a difficult time in the heavy surf, and it proved impossible to land heavy equipment. The high seas threw many of the landing craft up on the beach, overturning some and beaching others so firmly that they could not be put back into operation for a full day. The northernmost convoy finally had to seek shelter near San Fernando Point, where the sea was calmer. The second wave could not land as planned, with the result that the entire landing schedule was disrupted. The infantry, mountain artillery, and some of the armor got ashore during the day, but

few of the heavy units required for support were able to land.

Luckily for the Japanese, they had been able, by skillful handling of the transports, to enter shoal waters before the American submarines could get into action. Once inside, however, the vessels were strung out for fifteen miles, presenting a perfect target for those submarines that could get into the gulf. The *S–38* pushed into shallow waters and sank the Army transport *Hayo Maru* while it was following the gunboats which were preparing to lay mines a few miles west of the anchorage. But on the whole the results obtained by the submarines were disappointing.[17]

To increase the Japanese worries, four of the B–17's that had come up from Batchelor Field to bomb the Japanese at Davao flew on to Lingayen Gulf and managed to slip through the covering screen of the *24th* and *50th Fighter Regiments* that morning to strafe the cruisers and destroyers and inflict some damage on the Japanese. Even Admiral Takahashi's cover force, now about 100 miles northwest of Lingayen Gulf, came under attack. PBY's and Army planes went for the flagship *Ashigara,* mistaking it for the *Haruna.* Although they scored no hits, the planes reported the *Haruna* sunk. The cover force finally slipped away into a rain squall.

Meanwhile, the rising sea had forced many of the Japanese ships to shift anchorage and they moved into the inner bay. There they ran into more trouble when they came into range of the 155-mm. guns of the 86th Field Artillery Battalion (PS). This battalion had two guns at San Fabian and

---

[16] Interrog of Capt Ishihara, *3d Fleet* staff, 22 Oct 45, USSBS, *Interrogations of Japanese Officials,* I, 83.

[17] Apparently many of the transports were shallow draft, converted fishing vessels, presenting difficult targets for the undersea craft.

155-MM. GUN EMPLACEMENT NEAR DAGUPAN

two at Dagupan, and these apparently opened fire on the southernmost elements of the invasion force. Although claiming to have sunk three transports and two destroyers, the coastal guns actually did no damage except to give General Homma many nervous moments.[18]

The Japanese landing at Lingayen did not surprise the high command in the Philippines. It was the logical place to land a large force whose destination was Manila. On 18 December G–2, USAFFE, had received information of the movement of a

hostile convoy of about eighty transports moving toward the Philippines from the north. This information had been relayed to naval headquarters which already had submarines in the area.[19] At 0200 of the 20th, 16th Naval District headquarters reported to USAFFE that a large convoy had been sighted forty miles north of Lingayen Gulf. On the night of 20–21 December, USAFFE, acting on information received, warned the units stationed in that area that a Japanese expedition "of from 100 to 120 vessels" was moving south and could be expected off the mouth of the gulf by

---

[18] Rad, MacArthur to AGWAR, No. 34, 22 Dec 41, AG 381 (11–27–41 Gen) Far East; account of 86th FA Bn, from diary of an unidentified officer who died at Cabanatuan as a prisoner of war, OCMH.

[19] Collier, Notebooks, II, 10. This information is not corroborated by naval sources or by the meager official accounts, but it corresponds with the known facts.

evening of the 21st.[20] The first report of
the arrival of the invasion force came from
the submarine *Stingray* which had been on
patrol off Lingayen for several days. Before any action could be taken, the landings
had begun.

Despite the warning, the Americans
seem to have been ill prepared to drive off
the invaders. At this time the 120-mile-
long coast line of Lingayen Gulf was defended by two Philippine Army divisions,
only one of which had divisional artillery.
The southern edge of the gulf where the
landing was expected and where the bulk of
the artillery was emplaced, was in the 21st
Division sector. The eastern shore, as far
north as San Fernando, was held by the 11th
Division. The 71st Infantry (71st Division), with only ten weeks' training, was attached to the 11th Division and posted in
the Bauang–Naguilian area. The 26th
Cavalry (PS), led by Col. Clinton A. Pierce,
had been moved from North Luzon Force
reserve at Rosales to Pozorrubio on Route 3
about twelve miles south of Rosario, in the
path of the Japanese advance.

Only at Bauang were Filipino troops
waiting at the beach. Here the Headquarters Battalion, 12th Infantry (PA), with
one .50-caliber and several .30-caliber machine guns, faced the oncoming Japanese.
As the *Kamijima Detachment* approached
the shore, the Filipinos took it under fire.
The .50-caliber gun caused heavy casualties
among the Japanese, but the .30's had
dropped out of the action early with clogged
firing mechanisms, due to faulty ammunition. Despite the casualties, the Japanese

pushed ahead and established a foothold on
shore, whereupon the Filipinos withdrew.[21]

Behind the beach at Bauang was Lt. Col.
Donald Van N. Bonnett's 71st Infantry
(PA). On the 21st Bonnett had been given
orders to halt Colonel Tanaka's *2d Formosa*
at San Fernando, La Union. One battalion, with a battery of 75-mm. guns
(SPM) attached, was to move up the coastal
road to meet the *2d Formosa* head on. Another battalion was to advance along a secondary road to the east and attack
Colonel Tanaka on his left flank. This
maneuver, if well executed, might have destroyed the *2d Formosa,* but the inexperienced and poorly equipped Filipinos were
not capable of a swift and sudden onslaught.[22]

Before the 71st Infantry could complete
its movement the Japanese landed. Patrols
from the *Kamijima Detachment* immediately moved north along Route 3 and at
1100 made contact with a *2d Formosa*
patrol. By 1400 the main bodies of both
units had joined. Meanwhile, Colonel
Kamijima's *2d Battalion, 14th Army* reserve, had pushed into Bauang immediately
after landing and by 1700 had secured the
town and surrounding area. The *3d Battalion,* in accordance with the plan, moved

---

[20] Mallonée, Bataan Diary, I, 58. The author
has been unable to find a copy of this radio
message.

[21] USA *vs.* Homma, p. 3054, testimony of
Homma; Interrog of Gen Maeda, 10 May 47; Phil
Landing Opns (Amphibious), ATIS Doc 1989-
6A; interv, author with Col Blackburn, 13 May
49. The ammunition had been buried in the sand.

[22] The remainder of the regiment was at Bauang.
71st Infantry (PA), extract from the diary of Maj
William J. Priestley, pp. 1, 2, copy on file in
OCMH. This diary consists of a series of notebooks prepared by Major Priestley in prison camp
after talking with the officers and men of the various units whose contribution to the Philippine
campaign he describes.

out along the Bauang–Baguio road to the east, toward the Naguilian airfield.

With Colonel Kamijima's *9th Infantry* ashore, the position of the 71st Infantry units became untenable. One battalion moved down the coastal road and the other, with elements of the 11th Division, fell back to the east in the face of the Japanese advance. Bonnett's orders now were to withdraw through Baguio to the south, clearing the Philippine summer capital by dark.[23]

Farther south Col. Hifumi Imai's *1st Formosa* and the *48th Mountain Artillery* (less *1st* and *2d Battalions*) had landed at Aringay and by 1030 had concentrated for the advance. Colonel Imai's mission was to move his force south toward Damortis and Rosario. Early in the forenoon the regiment moved out, down the coastal road, and by 1600 the column had joined the *48th Reconnaissance* and the *4th Tank Regiments,* which had come ashore at 0730, north of Damortis.

The landing at Agoo, where Col. Isamu Yanagi's *47th Infantry* with a battalion of the *48th Mountain Artillery* had come ashore, was unopposed initially. Without waiting for motor transportation, Colonel Yanagi moved inland toward the Aringay Road, thence south to Rosario. Meanwhile, Brig. Gen. William E. Brougher, 11th Division commander, had sent forward a battalion of infantry to meet the Japanese coming down the coast and, if possible, disrupt the landing at Agoo. By this time the *48th Reconnaissance* and *4th Tank Regiments* were ashore, and in the brush that followed easily routed the Philippine Army troops who beat a hasty retreat to Damortis.[24]

---

[23] *Ibid.,* p. 1.
[24] Collier, Notebooks, II, 35.

Thus, by afternoon of the 22d, the Japanese had pushed ashore elements of three infantry regiments, with supporting artillery and tanks; the main force of the *14th Army* was still aboard the transports. Hard fighting lay ahead before the initial objectives of the *Lingayen Force* would be attained and the Japanese freed from the danger of being driven back into the sea.

Consolidating the Lingayen Beachhead

While his troops at Lingayen were pushing ahead, General Homma remained aboard ship in Lingayen Gulf. He had done all he could in the planning and preparation for the invasion. Now his troops were committed and their failure or success was out of his hands. His anxieties, the lot of any commander during the amphibious stages of an operation, were increased by lack of communications with the men ashore and the confusion caused by high seas and heavy surf. He had no knowledge of the disposition of his troops, moving in many columns in all directions, and no way of controlling the action. He had pushed his infantry and approximately half his armor ashore between Bauang and Agoo, but all the artillery save one regiment was still aboard the transports in the gulf. Cut off from his troop commanders, he had no way to lessen his apprehension by assurances that all was well.

There was some basis for General Homma's fears. The position of the Japanese troops ashore, while generally favorable, might easily become precarious. The landing had been made in a narrow corridor crossed by numerous streams, each of which afforded the defender an opportunity for delaying action. Although the plain to the south provided an excellent route to Manila, it could also be used by the Americans and Filipinos as the base for a concerted counterattack against the Japanese as they streamed out of the corridor. A vigorous and well-timed attack by the four divisions of the North Luzon Force, spearheaded by the well trained and equipped Philippine Division in USAFFE reserve, might well "wipe out the invader."[25] If, at the same time, sufficient air and naval forces could be mustered to attack the transports and naval escort lying at anchor in the bay, the Japanese line of retreat would be cut and all Homma's achievements and plans brought to naught.

According to the Japanese plan, the troops, once they had landed at Lingayen, were to move on without waiting for the concentration of the entire landing force. But a difference of opinion now arose in *14th Army* headquarters. The more cautious staff officers, believing it would be suicidal to proceed with the advance as planned, argued for the establishment of a strong, well-organized beachhead before moving further. Their troops, they reasoned, were at present confined to the long, narrow coastal plain, and the Americans from their positions along the commanding heights to the east might well hold up any Japanese advance long enough to allow General MacArthur to send up his reserves. The results would be disastrous.

The more aggressive wished to execute the original plan. They argued that the American commanders would not risk an offensive in front of the Agno River line. Even if the Americans decided to attack

earlier, the bolder *14th Army* staff officers felt that the advantages gained from continuing the advance were great enough to justify the risk. If the plan succeeded, the Japanese would gain bridgeheads across the Agno and would be in position to advance rapidly on Manila. Also, it would assure the safety of the beachhead. The views of the more aggressive won out, and General Homma agreed to continue the advance as planned.[26]

As the first day passed and no word came from the advancing troops, General Homma's fears increased. With no prospect of a calm sea in which to land his artillery and heavy equipment next day, and still fearing an American counterattack, he determined to shift anchorage. At 1730 of D Day he ordered the convoy to move farther south during the night, to a point off Damortis, and continue landing operations there the next day. Fearing artillery fire at the new anchorage, he ordered General Tsuchibashi, the *48th Division* commander, to take San Fabian, where there were two 155-mm. guns, thus extending the Japanese drive southward along the Lingayen coast.[27]

Damortis and Rosario

As the Japanese invasion force made ready to land, the Americans made last-minute preparations to meet the attack. USAFFE attached twelve 75-mm. guns on self-propelled mounts to Wainwright's North Luzon Force and ordered the 192d Tank Battalion to his support, but did not place them under his command. Wainwright in turn sent Colonel Pierce's 26th

---

[25] Mallonée, Bataan Diary, I, 60. The four divisions were the 11th, 21st, 71st and 91st Divisions (PA). With the state of training, lack of equipment and transportation, and the absence of communication, such an attack was impossible.

[26] Phil Landing Opns (Amphibious), ATIS Doc 1989-6A.

[27] USA vs. Homma, pp. 3053–54, testimony of Homma.

Cavalry (PS) from Pozorrubio to Rosario and by 0500 the Scouts were on their way.

While the main body of the 26th Cavalry advanced toward Rosario, the Scout Car Platoon (less detachments) moved ahead quickly to Damortis. When it found the town unoccupied it pushed northward along the coastal road. A few miles to the north the Scout platoon ran into the forward elements of the *48th Reconnaissance* and *4th Tank Regiments* and fell back to Damortis.

Meanwhile the rest of the 26th Cavalry at Rosario had been ordered to Damortis and directed to hold that town. Upon its arrival the regiment established defensive positions, which would permit a delaying action in the event of a forced withdrawal. At 1300 the cavalrymen came under attack from Japanese ground units supported by planes of the *5th Air Group.*

Colonel Pierce, who now had, in addition to his own cavalry, a company of the 12th Infantry and one from the 71st under his command, was hard put to hold his position and called on General Wainwright for help. At about the same time Wainwright received word that an enemy force mounted on cycles or light motor vehicles was approaching Damortis. To meet this emergency, Wainwright requested a company of tanks from Brig. Gen. James R. N. Weaver, the Provisional Tank Group commander.

Because of a shortage of gasoline, Weaver could furnish only a platoon of five tanks from Company C, 192d Tank Battalion. These moved out to the threatened area and near Agoo met the enemy's light tanks. The command tank, maneuvering off the road, received a direct hit and burst into flames. The other four, all hit by 47-mm. antitank fire, succeeded in returning to Rosario but were lost by bombing later in the day. At

1600 elements of the *1st Formosa* and *48th Mountain Artillery,* which had landed earlier in the day at Aringay joined the attack. Colonel Pierce, finding himself completely outnumbered, withdrew to his first delaying position east of Damortis. By 1900, the Japanese were in complete control of the town.[28]

Earlier that afternoon Wainwright had attached the 26th Cavalry to the 71st Division and had ordered Brig. Gen. Clyde A. Selleck to take his 71st Division (less 71st Infantry), then at Urdaneta, to Damortis, a distance of about twenty-five miles, and prevent the Japanese from moving south. The 26th Cavalry was to cover the right flank of the 71st Division and hold the junction of the Rosario–Baguio road, east of Rosario, in order to permit Major Bonnett's force, the 71st Infantry (less 1st Battalion), then at Baguio, to clear that point and join the North Luzon Force.

At about 1630 General Selleck, accompanied by the 72d Infantry commander and Lt. Col. Halstead C. Fowler of the 71st Field Artillery, arrived at Rosario, which had by now become the focal point of American resistance. There he learned that Japanese troops were not only approaching from the west along the Damortis road, but also from the northwest where Colonel Yanagi's *47th Infantry* was advancing from Agoo along the Aringay River valley. On his way to Damortis, Selleck found Colonel Pierce in his defensive position and learned of the exhausted condition of the 26th Cavalry. Since 71st Division troops had not

---

[28] Miller, *Bataan Uncensored,* p. 94; ltr, Weaver to Wainwright, 20 Nov 45, copy made available to author by General Weaver, and in OCMH; Weaver, Comments on Draft MS, Comment 3, OCMH; Prov Tank Gp, Rpt of Opns 1941–42, p. 9, Annex X, USAFFE-USFIP Rpt of Opns.

yet come up, he ordered the cavalrymen to fall back slowly on Rosario.

The Japanese by this time had a sizable force advancing along the Damortis–Rosario road. With the *48th Reconnaissance Regiment* in the lead and Colonel Imai's *1st Formosa* supported by the *48th Mountain Artillery* (less *1st* and *2d Battalions*) forming the main body, the Japanese threatened to overwhelm Colonel Pierce's weary cavalry. The tankers, Company C, 192d, supporting the Scouts, claimed to have orders from General Weaver, the Provisional Tank Group commander, to fall back at 2000 to Rosario, and at the appointed time began to pull out. As the last of the tanks passed through the American lines, the rear guard of the 26th Cavalry was penetrated by Japanese tanks. In the confused action which followed, the Japanese tanks, merged in the darkness with the struggling men and the terrified riderless horses, cut up the defenders and exacted a heavy toll. Only bold action by Maj. Thomas J. H. Trapnell in blocking a bridge over a small river a few miles west of Rosario with a burning tank halted the Japanese and prevented a complete rout.

When the retreating cavalrymen reached Rosario, they discovered that Troop F, which had been defending the trails northwest of the town, had been forced back by Colonel Yanagi's troops. It was now fighting a pitched battle in the town's public square. Fortunately for the Scouts, part of Colonel Yanagi's force had just been detached and ordered back to Agoo for the drive on San Fabian. Troop F held until the rest of the regiment had passed through Rosario. Then it broke off the action and followed, leaving the Japanese in possession. There was no pursuit; the *47th Infantry* was content to wait for the *1st Formosa* and the tanks, a few miles west of the town on the Damortis road.

Things had gone no better for Major Bonnett's force at Baguio. Busily tracking down rumors of Japanese units approaching in every direction, Bonnett spent the night at Baguio instead of pushing south to Rosario. Lt. Col. John P. Horan, the commander of Camp John Hay at Baguio, kept MacArthur's headquarters informed by radio of Japanese movements in the area and of the predicament of the force under Bonnett.[29] A few minutes before midnight of the 22d Horan radioed that the Japanese were "reported in Rosario" and that Bonnett desired "to move south at once if way is clear." "Can you contact Selleck by radio," he asked, "and inform us?"[30]

Although Horan received no reply, Wainwright, about midnight of the 22d, ordered Pierce to hold the junction of the Baguio and Rosario roads. Bonnett, unaware of this effort and believing that the Japanese held Rosario, remained at Baguio, and the 26th Cavalry finally had to withdraw the next morning when the position became untenable.[31] Bonnett later moved east over the mountains into the Cagayan valley, but Horan remained at his post throughout the 23d. The next morning, with the Japanese advancing from all sides, Horan pulled out after sending a final message to MacArthur: "My right hand in a vise, my nose in an inverted funnel, con-

[29] Colonel Horan's radios to MacArthur are in AG 370.2 (19 Dec 41) Phil Rcds.
[30] Rad, Horan to CG USAFFE, 22 Dec 41, AG 370.2 (19 Dec 41) Phil Rcds.
[31] Interv, author with Col Blackburn, 13 May 49; Liles, 12 Inf (PA), pp. 5–6; unsigned account of 13 Inf (PA), pp. 9–10.

stipated my bowels, open my south paw. . . ."[32] So ended the American occupation of the Philippine summer capital.

Thus, by the end of D Day, the Japanese had secured most of their objectives. They had landed safely along the beaches between Bauang and Agoo, and, pushing north, south, and east, had seized the defiles through the mountains, effected a juncture with Colonel Tanaka's force, and occupied Damortis and Rosario. The Japanese were now in position to debouch on to the central plain. Only their inability to get artillery and supplies ashore marred the day's success.

All the honors in the first day's fight had gone to the Japanese. Only the Scouts of the 26th Cavalry had offered any serious opposition to the successful completion of the Japanese plan. The untrained and poorly equipped Philippine Army troops had broken at the first appearance of the enemy and fled to the rear in a disorganized stream. Many of them, moving back along the coastal road, had passed through the 21st Field Artillery command post at the bend of the gulf. Col. Richard C. Mallonée, American instructor with the regiment, thought, "Their presence presages disaster." Although he reorganized them and sent them back to division headquarters, few of them, he felt sure, ever arrived. Their stories were always the same.

Always they were subjected to terrible, horrible mortar fire. Always the storyteller continued to bravely fire his rifle, machine gun or 75, as the case might be; always their officers ran away—or if the teller is an officer, then his superior officers ran first; always the enemy planes dropped many bombs and fired many machine guns; always there suddenly appeared many hostile tanks, headed straight for him; always he was suddenly surprised and astonished to realize that he was absolutely alone, all the others having been killed, or—despicable cowards—ran away. Then and only then, with the tanks a few feet away had he flung himself to one side where—and there the story has two variations, first he is captured but escapes that night; second he hides until night when he returns to our lines—but doesn't stop there. But from there on the threads of the story re-unite; they are very tired, they seek their companions, they are very hungry, and, Sir, could they be transferred to the Motor Transport Corps and drive a truck.[33]

The Approach to the Agno

The morning of 23 December found the 71st Division (less 71st Infantry) in position astride Route 3 south of Sison, the 72d Infantry and the 71st Engineers in the front lines, with the 71st Field Artillery in support to the rear. The 26th Cavalry, which had suffered heavily, was under orders to fall back through the 71st Division line to Pozorrubio to reorganize. The 91st Division, USAFFE reserve at Cabanatuan, had been attached to the North Luzon Force, and its 91st Combat Team had been ordered north to reinforce the 71st Division. It was to arrive at noon and occupy a position north of Pozorrubio, along the road leading south from Rosario.

The action on the 23d opened when two battalions of the *47th Infantry,* moving south from Rosario, struck General Selleck's line near Sison. Largely because of Colonel Fowler's artillery, the Japanese advance was held up until noon. During the early afternoon the *47th Infantry* was joined by the *48th Reconnaissance* and *4th Tank Regiments.* Aided by planes of the *10th*

---

[32] Rad, Horan to CG USAFFE, 24 Dec 41, AG 370.2 (19 Dec 41) Phil Rcds.

[33] Mallonée, Bataan Diary, I, 62–63. See also Collier, Notebooks, II, 35–38.

26TH CAVALRY (PS) MOVING INTO POZORRUBIO *pass a General Stuart light tank, M3.*

Independent and *16th Light Bombardment Regiments,* the Japanese now began a concerted attack.

The Filipinos of the 71st Division, like those of the 11th, broke and fled to the rear, leaving the artillery uncovered. The line might have held if the 91st Combat Team, en route from Cabanatuan, had reached Sison in time. But the 91st had run into bad luck. Japanese light bombers ranging far in advance of the ground troops had knocked out a bridge across the Agno River in the path of the 91st advance. The 91st Combat Team was forced to detour and at this critical moment was far from the scene of combat.

The situation was serious. A meeting of the American commanders was hastily called and it was agreed that the 71st Division would have to withdraw to a line just north of Pozorrubio. The 91st Combat Team, it was hoped, would reach that place in time to set up a line there. The 26th Cavalry in 71st Division reserve at Pozorrubio was to retire to Binalonan where it would set up an outpost line through which the remainder of the division could fall back if necessary.

At 1900, as the Japanese entered Sison, the 26th Cavalry began to move out toward Binalonan and the 91st Combat Team reached Pozorrubio. That night the enemy attacked the 91st and drove it out of the town. With its rout, all hopes of holding a line at Pozorrubio came to an end.

Even before the Japanese had entered

Sison that afternoon, General Wainwright had telephoned MacArthur's headquarters at Manila. After explaining that further defense of the Lingayen beaches was "impracticable," he requested permission to withdraw behind the Agno River. This request was readily granted. Believing that he could launch a counterattack if he had the Philippine Division, then in USAFFE reserve, Wainwright also asked for the division and for permission to mount an attack from the Agno. He was directed to submit his plans. "I'll get my plans there as soon as possible," he replied, but asked for an immediate answer on whether he would get the Philippine Division. After a slight delay, he was told that his chances of securing the division were "highly improbable." Nevertheless he began to make his plans for a counterattack.[34]

The action of 24 December placed the Japanese in position for the final drive toward the Agno River. At about 0500, with the *4th Tank Regiment* in the lead, the Japanese made contact with the 26th Cavalry outposts north and west of Binalonan. Although the Scouts had no antitank guns, they were able to stop the first attack. The tanks then swung west to bypass the American positions, leaving the infantry to continue the fight for Binalonan. By 0700 the 26th Cavalry had blunted the assault and inflicted many casualties on the enemy. Pursuing their advantage, the Scouts counterattacked and the Japanese had to send in more tanks to stop the 26th Cavalry. Even with the aid of tanks, the Japanese made no progress. Sometime during the morning the *2d Formosa* joined the attack, and the cavalrymen found themselves in serious trouble. Too heavily engaged to break off

the action and retire, they continued to fight on.

At this juncture, General Wainwright arrived at Binalonan to see Selleck. He found neither General Selleck, who had gone to Wainwright's command post to report, nor any 71st Division troops, but did find the 26th Cavalry, which now numbered no more than 450 men. He ordered Pierce to get his wounded men and supply train out as quickly as possible and to fight a delaying action before withdrawing southeast across the Agno to Tayug. For more than four hours the cavalrymen held their position against overwhelming odds, and at 1530 began to withdraw. By dusk the last elements had reached Tayug and the *2d Formosa* entered Binalonan. "Here," said General Wainwright, himself a cavalryman, "was true cavalry delaying action, fit to make a man's heart sing. Pierce that day upheld the best traditions of the cavalry service."[35]

Despite the heroic struggle by the 26th Cavalry, the Japanese had secured their initial objectives and had established a firm grip on northern Luzon. They were now in position to march south to Manila along the broad highways of the central plain of Luzon. Only the southern route to the capital remained to be seized. That task was the mission of the *Lamon Bay Force,* already moving into position.

The Lamon Bay Landings

Simultaneously with the departure of the *Lingayen Force* from Formosa, Lt. Gen. Susumu Morioka, *16th Division* commander, had left Amami Oshima in the Ryukyus on 17 December to begin his six-

[34] Wainwright, *General Wainwright's Story,* pp. 35–36.

[35] *Ibid.,* p. 39.

day voyage southward to Lamon Bay, 200 road miles southeast of Lingayen. With the landing of his force, the Japanese plan to place troops in position to attack Manila from the north and south would be complete.

Organization and Preparation

The *Lamon Bay Force* had a secondary role in the seizure of Luzon and was consequently much smaller than the *Lingayen Force*. Its combat elements consisted primarily of General Morioka's *16th Division* (less the *9th* and *33d Infantry* and some supporting elements) and numbered 7,000 men. In addition, it contained a number of attached service and supporting units. General Homma did not expect much from this force; in his opinion, the *16th Division*, which had seen action in China, "did not have a very good reputation for its fighting qualities." [36]

The plan for the Lamon Bay landing had been prepared during November, while the division was still in Japan. The original objective had been Batangas Bay on the southwest coast of Luzon, where the beaches were suitable for landings and where a direct route led through favorable terrain toward Manila to the north.[37] (*Map 6*) But when the number of aircraft assigned to the Philippine operation was reduced,

and when intelligence sources reported American reinforcements in bombers and submarines, the target had been changed to Lamon Bay on the southeast coast.

The new landing site was undesirable on two grounds. First, the line of advance to Manila from Lamon Bay lay across the Tayabas Mountains, and secondly, Lamon Bay offered poor landing sites during the winter months because of prevailing winds. Despite these objections, Lamon Bay was chosen as the target of the *16th Division*.

The final plan developed by Morioka called for landings at three points along the shore of Lamon Bay—at Mauban, Atimonan, and Siain. General Morioka expected to take the Americans by surprise, but was ready, if necessary, to make an assault landing. His troops were to rout any American forces on the beaches, rapidly cross the Tayabas Mountains, and then concentrate in preparation for an expected counterattack. In order to avoid congestion on the narrow beaches and during the crossing of the mountains, the troops were to move ahead rapidly in several columns immediately after landing, without waiting for supporting troops or for the consolidation of the beachhead. The main force of General Morioka's division was to advance west along Route 1, then sweep around Laguna de Bay to drive on to Cavite and Manila from the south.

The force scheduled to land at Mauban was the *2d Battalion, 20th Infantry*, and a battery of the *22d Field Artillery* under Lt. Col. Nariyoshi Tsunehiro. After landing, it was to strike out to the west to Lucban, where it would be in position to move southeast to support the Atimonan force. If such support proved unnecessary, Tsunehiro was to turn northwest to Laguna de Bay, skirt

---

[36] USA *vs.* Homma, p. 3232, testimony of Homma. The strength of the division at this time is computed from Order of Battle information and from Japanese tables of organization.

[37] Except as otherwise noted the account of the Lamon Bay landings is based upon: *14th Army Opns*, I, 28, 32, 54–55; II, 6–7; *Luzon Campaign of 16th Division*, 24 Dec 41–3 Jan 42, ATIS Enemy Pub 355, pp. 1–3; *Japanese Naval Opns in Phil Invasion*, p. 15; Jones, *Diary*, pp. 8–11; and *SLF and II Corps Rpt of Opns*, pp. 12–15.

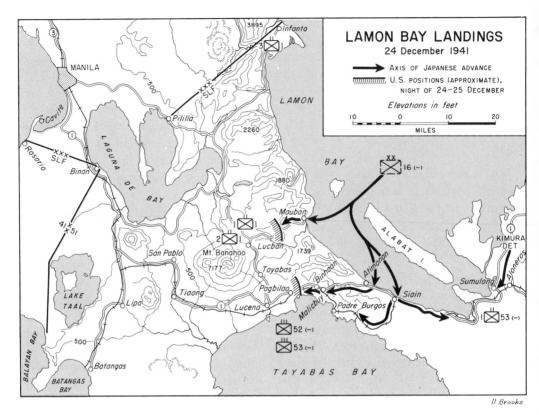

MAP 6

the southern shore, then strike north along Route 1 to Manila.

The main force of the *16th Division,* under direct command of General Morioka, was to make the assault on Atimonan. Included in this force were the *20th Infantry* (less than *2d* and most of the *1st Battalion*); the *16th Reconnaissance Regiment,* with one company of light armored cars; the *16th Engineers;* and the *22d Field Artillery* (less *2d Battalion* and one battery of the *1st*). Once ashore, these troops were to move west across the mountains along Route 1, then north along the shore of Laguna de Bay and on to Manila. American troops and positions encountered along

the way were, so far as possible, to be bypassed and mopped up later. The main advance was not to be held up.

Simultaneously with the landing at Atimonan, the *1st Battalion, 20th Infantry* (less one company), with artillery support, was to land near Siain to the south, and cover the left flank of the main force. Having fulfilled this mission, the Siain force was to pass into division reserve.

The 24 transports carrying the invasion force left the staging area at Amami Oshima in the Ryukyus at 1500 on 17 December, six hours after the first Lingayen convoy pulled out of Kirun Harbor in northern Formosa. The transports were escorted initially by 4 destroyers and 4 minesweepers, but they had not gone far before they were joined by Rear Adm. Kyuji Kubo's force of 1 light cruiser, 2 destroyers, 2 minesweepers, and 1 minelayer from Legaspi.

The voyage from Amami Oshima was smooth and uneventful until the 23d, when the American submarine *Sculpin* forced the convoy to adopt evasive tactics. No damage was caused. At 0130 of the following morning, after the *Lingayen Force* had already been ashore for two days, the transports dropped anchor in Lamon Bay. An hour later the troops were ready to move to shore.[38]

The Landing

From the American point of view, the Japanese could not have landed at a more inopportune moment. Maj. Gen. George M. Parker's South Luzon Force was badly dispersed. The 41st Division (PA) on the west coast was in position, but elements of the 51st Division along the east coast were in the process of movement. The South Luzon Force had been reinforced during the past few days by the recently inducted 1st Regular Division (PA), but only the 1st Infantry of this division had actually moved into the area. Its orders were to relieve the 3d Battalion, 52d Infantry, north of Mauban. By evening of the 23d the relief had been accomplished, and one battalion of the 1st Infantry was in position at Mauban, another at Infanta; the remaining battalion was in reserve at a road junction northeast of Lucban. This move had just been completed when MacArthur's headquarters transferred the 1st Infantry to North Luzon Force. General

Parker—and General Jones—protested the order vigorously, and it was finally rescinded, but the movement of the 3d Battalion, 52d Infantry, was in progress when the enemy landed.

That same evening the 51st Division troops, who had moved south to delay the movement northward of the *Kimura Detachment* from Legaspi, were pulled back and were in the process of moving when the Japanese landed. The results for them were more tragic; many of them were cut off and never returned to the American lines.

Not only were the forces along the east coast dispersed at the moment of the landing, but those units in position were handicapped by the absence of artillery. The South Luzon Force included two batteries of the 86th Field Artillery with 6 155-mm. guns, and a battalion of 16 75-mm. guns on self-propelled mounts. But none of these pieces were emplaced in the Lamon Bay area. They were all on the west coast—at Batangas, Balayan, and Nasugbu Bays. General Jones had requested that at least 2 of the 155-mm. guns be moved to Atimonan, and Parker, concerned over this lack of artillery along the east coast, had twice asked MacArthur's headquarters for additional artillery. Both times he had been turned down, despite the fact that he used "the strongest arguments possible." [39]

The failure to move some of the guns from the west coast to Lamon Bay, especially after the Japanese landing at Legaspi, can be explained only by the fact that MacArthur's headquarters feared to uncover the west coast beaches which offered a direct route to Manila across favorable terrain.

---

[38] American sources do not confirm the attack by the *Sculpin*.

[39] SLF and II Corps Rpt of Opns, p. 13; ltr, Jones to Ward, 3 Jan 52, OCMH; ltr, Col S. C. MacDonald to Jones, 21 Dec 51, OCMH.

By accepting the difficulties of a Lamon Bay landing, the Japanese unconsciously gained a great advantage.

Thus, during the night of 23–24 December, as the Japanese were loading into the landing craft, the Lamon Bay area was without artillery support and was the scene of confusion, with several units in the process of movement from one place to another. Fortunately, the 1st Battalion, 1st Infantry, was in position at Mauban, and Headquarters and Company A of the 1st Battalion, 52d Infantry were at Atimonan.

News of the approach of the Japanese reached the defenders at 2200 on the night of the 23d, when the transports off Atimonan were sighted. Four hours later troops were reported debarking there and at Siain. First word of a landing at Mauban was received by General Jones of the 51st Division at 0400. All these reports greatly overestimated the strength of the Japanese force. The Atimonan force was thought to be a reinforced division, and the troops coming ashore at Mauban were estimated as a reinforced brigade.

Under cover of aircraft from the seaplane carrier *Mizuho*, Colonel Tsunehiro's *2d Battalion, 20th Infantry*, came ashore at Mauban, northernmost of the three landing sites, in the first light of dawn. Immediately it ran into an effective crossfire from the 2d Battalion, 1st Infantry, dug in along the beach. At about this time, American planes struck the Japanese, inflicting heavy casualties on the troops and causing considerable damage to the ships.[40] By 0800, after much

heavy fighting, the Philippine Army regulars had been pushed back into Mauban. Thirty minutes later Colonel Tsunehiro's troops were in control of the village. The 2d Battalion, 1st Infantry, fell back five miles to the west, where it set up a defensive position. At 1430 the Japanese reached this position and there the advance came to a halt before the stubborn defense of the Filipinos.

The *1st Battalion, 20th Infantry*, landed at Siain without difficulty. At 0700 one company moved out to the southwest along the Manila Railroad toward Tayabas Bay while the rest of the battalion pushed southeast on Route 1 to effect a juncture with General Kimura's troops moving northwest. Both columns made satisfactory progress during the day. By evening the company moving toward Tayabas Bay was within five miles of Padre Burgos. The rest of the force ran into sporadic opposition from Colonel Cordero's 52d Infantry troops in the Bicol Peninsula, and it was not until three days later that the *1st Battalion, 20th Infantry*, joined with the *Kimura Detachment*.

General Morioka's main force came ashore on the morning of 24 December about two and one half miles southeast of its target. The first troops landed were held up by Company A, 52d Infantry. The next wave containing the *16th Reconnaissance Regiment*, landed beside the infantry but avoided action by moving off to the side, in accordance with instructions not to delay the main advance. The regiment then

---

[40] Craven and Cate, *The Army Air Forces in World War II*, I, 224, states that 12 P–40's and 6 P–35's attacked a Japanese landing force at San Miguel Bay, 85 miles from Lamon Bay, on the morning of the 23d. There was no such landing,

and it is possible that Lamon Bay is meant. Japanese sources state that there was an American air attack at the time of the Mauban landing. General Jones denies that American aircraft hit the Japanese at this time. Ltr, Jones to Ward, 3 Jan 52, OCMH.

LT. GEN. MASAHARU HOMMA, *14TH ARMY* COMMANDER, *coming ashore at Lingayan Gulf, 24 December 1941.*

struck off into the mountains, bypassing Atimonan. The town itself was secured by 1100, although the Philippine Army troops fought stubbornly.

The *16th Reconnaissance Regiment* pushed along Route 1 toward Malicbuy, where the 2d Battalion, 52d Infantry, was frantically setting up defensive positions. Planes of the *8th Air Regiment* (light bombers) provided cover for the advancing Japanese and attacked Malicbuy several times during the morning, destroying a number of vehicles and impeding the efforts of the troops to establish an adequate defense. When the *16th Reconnaissance* reached the town, the 2d Battalion, 52d

Infantry, already weakened by air attacks, fell back after a short fight. The Japanese entered Malicbuy without further interference.

The American forces set up their next defensive position along a river near Binahaan, about four miles to the west. Here they were joined by the 53d Infantry (less two battalions) and the 3d Battalion (less one company) of the 52d Infantry. Late in the afternoon, when the Japanese at Atimonan had completed mopping-up operations in the town, they joined the main body at Malicbuy. The entire force then struck the delaying position at Binahaan. Under cover of darkness the defenders withdrew

797–257 O–66—11

along Route 1 toward Pagbilao, the next objective of the *16th Division*.[41]

By the evening of 24 December the Japanese had successfully completed the first and most difficult part of their plan for the conquest of the Philippines. In the south, at a cost of 84 dead and 184 wounded, General Morioka had landed his reduced division of 7,000 men. American resistance had held up the advance of some units, but the main force of the *16th Division* had swept ahead, with the armored cars of the *16th Reconnaissance* in the van. Unloading had progressed satisfactorily, and many of the service and supporting units had already landed. The roads leading westward through the Tayabas Mountains had been secured, and the troops of the *Lamon Bay Force* were in position to reach Tayabas Bay the following morning. General Homma had not expected much from this force.

Its success came, therefore, as "quite a surprise" to *14th Army* headquarters at Lingayen Gulf, and, as the Japanese later confessed, "The result realized was more than expected." [42]

North of Manila the *Lingayen Force* stood ready to drive on to the Agno River. After several days of difficulties, the beachhead had been organized and heavy supplies and equipment brought ashore. San Fabian to the south had been occupied and the American artillery there driven out. The north and east flanks of the coastal corridor had been secured, and Japanese troops were pouring out on to the central plain to add their weight to the advance on Manila, 100 miles away. That day, 24 December, General Homma brought his staff ashore at Bauang, where he established *14th Army* headquarters. The Japanese were evidently in the Philippines to stay.

[41] 1st Lt John Shaw, 52d Inf (PA), p. 1, Chunn Notebooks, OCMH.

[42] Phil Landing Opns (Amphibious), ATIS Doc 1989-6A.

CHAPTER IX

Strategy and Logistics

The success of the Japanese after 7 December had been phenomenal. Not only had they won air and naval supremacy in the western Pacific and landed a large number of troops on Luzon and Mindanao, but they had taken Guam on 10 December and Wake two weeks later; Hong Kong was to surrender on Christmas Day. In the Malay States, Gen Tomoyuki Yamashita's *25th Army* was advancing steadily in two parallel columns down the east and west coasts. By 23 December it had reached a point about 250 miles from the tip of the peninsula. Once there, the Japanese would be in position to bring Singapore under assault. On the 24th a small Japanese force landed at Kuching and a week later another force landed at Brunei in British Borneo, thus inaugurating the two-pronged offensive against the Netherlands Indies. By the end of the year the Japanese had established themselves at Davao, on Jolo Island, and on British Borneo, astride the Allied line of supply between the southern Philippines and northwest Australia.

The electrifying news of Pearl Harbor, followed by the declaration of war by Germany and Italy, united the American people as nothing else could have done. The attention of the country, until then centered on the war in Europe, focused now on the Pacific and Far East where American troops were putting up a valiant defense. There was a strong feeling that everything possible should be done to aid the beleaguered forces

in the Philippines, and General MacArthur's name became a symbol of American resistance to a foe who was meeting with success everywhere.

At the very start of the war there was a general acceptance among military and naval authorities in Washington of the view that the Philippines would soon be lost. Acceptance of this view did not mean, however, that every effort should not be made to reinforce General MacArthur. The President, the Secretary of War, and the Chief of Staff all felt strongly, with the American people, that the country had an obligation, no matter what the risks, to do all in its power to aid the Philippine people. Only final defeat would end that obligation. The question was what could be done and how much could be spared from the more important task, the defense of the United States.

The Pensacola *Convoy*

The question of reinforcing the Philippines arose on the first day of war. Already on the high seas in the South Pacific when the Japanese opened hostilities was a convoy of seven ships, escorted by the heavy cruiser *Pensacola* and the subchaser *Niagara*, en route to Manila via the southern route. Aboard the vessels were badly needed planes for the pilots of the 27th Bombardment Group, two regiments of artillery, and large quantities of ammunition and supplies.[1] The convoy was immediately ordered to put in at Suva in the Fiji Islands until a decision could be made on its ultimate destination.

The decision was made on 9 December at a meeting of the Joint Board. The chief planners of the Army and Navy, General Gerow and Rear Adm. Richmond K. Turner, wanted the convoy brought back immediately to˙ Hawaii to reinforce that badly battered garrison. General Gerow's position was more extreme than that of his naval counterpart. He suggested that if the convoy was not sent to Hawaii it should be brought back to the United States. Following discussion, the Joint Board approved the plan to recall the *Pensacola* convoy to Hawaii.[2]

While the safety of the Hawaiian Islands was undoubtedly of prime importance, the decision to bring back the *Pensacola* convoy was, in effect, an abandonment of the Philippine Islands. General Marshall was willing to concede the importance of Hawaii, but felt keenly the obligation to send help to General MacArthur. He had already assured the USAFFE commander on the afternoon of 7 December that he had "the complete confidence of the War Department," and that he could expect "every

possible assistance within our power."[3] On the morning of the 10th, "concerned with just what to say to General MacArthur," he discussed the Joint Board decision with Mr. Stimson. He confessed that "he did not like to tell him [MacArthur] in the midst of a very trying situation that his convoy had had to be turned back, and he would like to send some news which would buck General MacArthur up."[4]

At a White House meeting later that day, the question of the *Pensacola* convoy was again discussed, and the President indicated his desire that the vessels should continue to the Far East. He referred the matter back to the Joint Board, and at its meeting that afternoon the Board decided to send the convoy on to Brisbane, Australia. The Army members reversed their stand of the previous day and expressed the opinion that Hawaii could be supplied from the United States. They now wished, they said, to make every effort to send aircraft, ammunition, and other critical material to the Philippines.[5]

On 12 December the commander of the *Pensacola* convoy was ordered to proceed to Brisbane, his later movements to be determined "following arrival and depending upon the situation."[6] At the same time, the U.S. military attaché in Melbourne, Col. Van S. Merle-Smith, was notified of the impending arrival of the vessels and given instructions to be passed on to the senior Army commander in the convoy, Brig. Gen. Julian F. Barnes. In these instructions

---

[1] The seven vessels were the *Holbrook, Republic, Meigs, Bloemfontein, Admiral Halstead, Farmer,* and *Chaumont.* The vessels carried a field artillery brigade with 20 75-mm. guns; the ground elements of the 7th Heavy Bombardment Group; 18 P–40's; and 52 A–24's, 500,000 rounds of 50-caliber armor-piercing and tracer ammunition; 9,600 rounds of high explosive for 37-mm. antiaircraft guns; 2,000 500-pound and 3,000 30-pound bombs; and miscellaneous vehicles and equipment. The total number of U.S. troops aboard was 4,600. Rad, Marshall to MacArthur, No. 776, 12 Dec 41, WPD 4628.
[2] Min, JB Mtg, 9 Dec 41, OPD Reg Doc.

[3] Rad, Marshall to MacArthur, No. 736, 7 Dec 41, WPD 4544-20.
[4] Min, mtg in OCS, 10 Dec 41, Notes on Conf, WDCSA, CofS Confs, II.
[5] *Ibid.,* 12 Dec 41.
[6] *Ibid.,* 12 Dec 41.

General Barnes was ordered to place himself under MacArthur's command and told that his principal task was to get the aircraft, men, and supplies in the convoy to the Philippines as quickly as possible. Upon arrival in Australia, he was to assemble the A–24's immediately and send them north to the Philippines. Before unloading the other troops and supplies, he was to find out from the Navy if the vessels could be escorted northward. If they could not, they were to be unloaded in Brisbane and used "as the situation dictates," with first priority given to the defense of the Philippines.[7]

General MacArthur received the welcome news that reinforcements were on the way on 13 December.[8] Immediately he conferred with Admiral Hart on the possibility of escorting the ships from Brisbane to Manila. He emphasized to Hart the necessity for bringing in supplies and reinforcements and explained how limited were the resources at his disposal. "I suggested," he reported to the Chief of Staff, "that he [Hart] should endeavor with his own surface forces and with assistance of Australian and Dutch naval and air forces to bring in the present convoy and keep my line open."

But Admiral Hart's answer was extremely discouraging. He pointed out that the British and Dutch were fully engaged trying to hold Singapore and the Malay Barrier and that he could not take the responsibility of protecting the convoy with the weak forces at his disposal. The Japanese, he believed, would have established a complete blockade of the Philippine Islands before the convoy could arrive. "In effect," Mac-

Arthur reported, "he [Hart] seemed to be of the opinion that the islands were ultimately doomed." [9] MacArthur's own view was that there was no serious obstacle to the safe convoy of vessels from Brisbane to Manila "provided reasonable naval and air protection are furnished." [10]

While the matter of the *Pensacola* convoy was being settled in Washington, MacArthur made specific requests for reinforcements based upon his ideas for offensive action. On the recommendation of General Brereton he asked for 300 pursuit planes, together with air warning equipment. If the aircraft in the *Pensacola* convoy could be ferried to Luzon and be ready for operations by 1 January, he felt he could meet the immediate situation with 250 dive bombers. At this time, 14 December, he first advanced the idea that the planes be brought within operating distance of the Philippines by means of aircraft carrier. He asked also for additional .50-caliber ammunition and suggested that it be brought in by the dive bombers or by Pan American Airways planes shuttling between Australia and the Philippines. Altogether, he declared, he had or would soon have fourteen airfields capable of accommodating the aircraft he was requesting.[11]

The receipt of these specific requests in Washington resulted in immediate action. General Gerow, in a personal note to General Marshall, pointed out that the *Pensacola* convoy was due in Brisbane very shortly and an immediate decision on the

[7] Memo, CofS for Comdr D. H. Harries, RAN, Australian Naval Attaché, 12 Dec 41, sub: Msgs for U.S. Mil Attaché, WPD 4628-1; rad, OPNAV to COM TF 15, 10 Dec 41, WPD Msg File.
[8] Rad, Marshall to MacArthur, No. 776, 12 Dec 41, WPD 4628.

[9] Rad, MacArthur to Marshall, 13 Dec 41, OPD Exec O; ltr, Hart to Ward, 19 Dec 51, OCMH.
[10] Rad, MacArthur to Marshall, 13 Dec 41, OPD Exec O.
[11] Memo, Brereton for MacArthur, 14 Dec 41, cited in Craven and Cate, *The Army Air Forces in World War II*, I, 222; rad, MacArthur to Marshall, 14 Dec 41, OPD Exec O.

Navy's willingness to convoy the vessels northward was necessary. "If the ships can go directly to Manila, the supplies, except aircraft, should not be unloaded in Australia," Gerow noted. "Admiral Stark is the only one that can make the decision." [12]

Marshall had already discussed this problem with Stimson, who felt that to abandon the Philippines would "paralyze the activities" of the Allied forces in the Far East. The question was discussed at the White House, and the President instructed the Navy to do all in its power to assist the Army in reinforcing General MacArthur.[13] General Marshall thereupon assured MacArthur that there would be "no wavering in the determination to support you." Although naval losses had complicated the problem of reinforcement, he declared that fighters and bombers would be rushed to the Philippines as quickly as possible.[14]

Quick action followed the President's instructions to send help to the Philippines. Orders were issued to load the transport *Polk* in San Francisco harbor and the *Coolidge,* due in port soon, with pursuit planes and ammunition and dispatch them immediately to Australia. Two additional shipments were scheduled to reach Brisbane early in January. The arrival of these vessels would place in Australia 230 aircraft.[15] At the same time, two Pan American clippers were loaded with .50-caliber ammunition and dispatched to Australia via the

South Atlantic–Africa route. Fifteen heavy bombers were also immediately diverted to MacArthur, and a flight schedule was established which would give him three planes a day until the new year. The sum of $10,000,000 was made available to the future commander of the base in Australia to enable him to carry out his mission of supporting the defense of the Philippines. By 18 December Marshall was able to inform MacArthur that the War Department "is proceeding with utmost expedition to provide necessary supplies at base with early emphasis on most critical items." [16]

On 22 December the *Pensacola* convoy with its valuable cargo of aircraft, artillery, and ammunition arrived in Brisbane. It was still a long way from Manila, but the first leg of the journey had been completed. A way now had to be found to send the planes and supplies from Australia to the Philippines.

The program to reinforce the Philippines was in full swing. The necessity for reaching a decision on the destination of the *Pensacola* convoy had raised the question of reinforcement immediately on the outbreak of war and brought the issues into sharp focus. But the settlement of this question had raised broader strategic problems. These were not so easily solved.

Far East and Pacific Strategy

The basic strategy of the war had been established during staff talks with the British between January and March 1941 and was embodied in the RAINBOW plan. This

---

[12] Note, Gerow to Marshall on WPD copy of rad, MacArthur to Marshall, 15 Dec 41, OPD Exec O.

[13] Stimson and Bundy, *On Active Service,* pp. 395–96.

[14] Rad, Marshall to MacArthur, No. 787, 15 Dec 41, WPD 4544-31.

[15] Memo for Rcd by Gen Gerow, 15 Dec 41, OPD Exec O; memo, Arnold for CofS, 15 Dec 41, sub: Aerial Reinf for Hawaii and Phil, WPD Msg File; rad, Marshall to MacArthur, No. 824, 18 Dec 41, WPD 4622-28.

[16] Rad, Marshall to MacArthur, No. 824, 18 Dec 41, WPD 4622-28; ltr, Maj Gen Richard C. Moore, DCofS, to Maj Gen George H. Brett, 19 Dec 41, OCS 18136-161. The way in which the $10,000,000 was spent is described in Chapter XXII, below.

strategy provided that the principal effort of the Allies would be made against Germany and that the decisive theater would be in the Atlantic and Europe. Except for certain limited offensive operations assigned the Pacific and Asiatic Fleets, the most important of which were the defense of Hawaii and the Philippines and the capture of positions in the Japanese mandated islands, operations against Japan were to be defensive. The destruction of the Battle Force of the Pacific Fleet and the attack against the Philippines made it evident that a different strategy for the Far East would have to be evolved to meet the new situation.

As soon as the results of the Pearl Harbor attack were assessed, the Navy knew that it could not execute the missions assigned in RAINBOW 5. At the 8 December meeting of the Joint Board, the Navy members had pointed out that as a result of the losses at Pearl Harbor the Pacific Fleet would not be able to advance across the Central Pacific.[17] Two days later, when the decision was made to send the *Pensacola* convoy on to Brisbane, Admiral Stark, Chief of Naval Operations, told the Joint Board that the Navy had decided that the Asiatic Fleet should be withdrawn from the Philippines, "in view of the destruction at Cavite and the untenability of Manila as a fleet anchorage." Admiral Hart was to be left free to execute the withdrawal and to select a future base of operations.[18]

The Navy Department's views on Far East strategy did not include any strong measures for the defense of the Philippines. Admiral Stark declared that he was not surprised by the success of the Japanese but only by the vigor of the attack, which had

resulted in such unexpectedly rapid advances. He expected that with the fall of Singapore and Luzon—which he seemed to regard as inevitable—the Japanese would move into the Netherlands Indies. To him, the essential problem was to hold the Malay Barrier—the line Malay Peninsula–Sumatra–Java–Australia—long enough to build up the defenses of northwest Australia. Apparently the defense of Luzon did not, in his opinion, contribute to this mission.[19]

Stark approved Hart's orders sending the major surface units of the fleet to Borneo, and cautioned the Asiatic Fleet commander not to delay his own withdrawal lest the Japanese mine the exits of Manila Bay. There was no indication in his messages to Manila of any intention to carry out offensive operations against the Japanese Navy or of a determination to hold the Philippines, although Hart was reminded of his obligation to support the Army's defense of Luzon as long as it was practicable.

On the all-important question of getting reinforcements to the Philippines, Admiral Stark merely told Hart what he already knew—that a convoy was soon to arrive in Brisbane and that he was to get in touch with General MacArthur "as to present orders for this force." The Chief of Naval Operations pointed out that the convoy carried aircraft and artillery which, he added significantly, "may be very important for the defense of Port Darwin and vicinity." He said nothing about the necessity of bringing the convoy to Manila. This is a surprising omission, since the reinforcements were intended for MacArthur, and every effort was being made in

---

[17] Min, JB Mtg, 8 Dec 41, OPD Reg Doc.
[18] *Ibid.,* 10 Dec 41.

[19] Rad, OPNAV to CINCAF, 14 Dec 41, copy in AG 381 (11–27–41 Gen) Far East.

Washington to provide safe convoy of the vessels northward from Australia. He further suggested to Hart that the minesweepers and small craft in Manila would be useful at Darwin, and concluded by placing the U.S. naval observer there under Hart's command.[20]

The Army planners shared the Navy's pessimism about the fate of the Philippines and on 9 December had been as anxious as the Navy members of the Joint Board to bring back the *Pensacola* convoy. While still feeling that there was little hope for the Philippine garrison, they reversed their views after 10 December and supported strongly the program for reinforcement. Mr. Stimson, after the war, explained his reasons for supporting General MacArthur as follows:

I laid before them [his three civilian assistants] the issue which was now pending before us, namely as to whether we should make every effort possible in the Far East or whether, like the Navy, we should treat that as doomed and let it go. We all agreed that the first course was the one to follow; that we have a very good chance of making a successful defense, taking the southwestern Pacific as a whole. If we are driven out of the Philippines and Singapore, we can still fall back on the Netherlands East Indies and Australia; and with the cooperation of China—if we can keep that thing going—we can strike good counterblows at Japan. While if we yielded to the defeatist theory, it would have had not only the disastrous effect on our material policy of letting Japan get strongly ensconced in the southwestern Pacific . . . but it would psychologically do even more in the discouragement of China and in fact all of the four powers who are now fighting very well together. Also it would have a very bad effect on Russia. So this theory goes. It has been accepted by the President, and the Army is

taking steps to make a solid base at Port Darwin in Australia.[21]

It was admitted by Army and Navy planners that the Philippines were no longer defensible, and some urged that the limited resources of the United States should be used to "defend the defensible." But the issue was not entirely a military one. "Politically," says Stimson, "it was still more important that this defense be supported as strongly as possible, for neither the Filipino people nor the rest of the Far Eastern world could be expected to have a high opinion of the United States" if it abandoned the Philippines at this critical moment.[22] It was because of these considerations that Stimson and Marshall strongly supported General MacArthur and firmly opposed any signs of a defeatist attitude in the General Staff. In this effort they had the support of the President.

In the Philippines there was strong disagreement between the Army and Navy commanders. Admiral Hart agreed with his Washington superiors that his fleet should be withdrawn and had already sent the major portion of his surface forces southward. He was still resolved, he told Admiral Stark, to use his submarines and small craft in the defense of the Philippines, but pointed out that the undersea craft could not prevent enemy landings or the blockade of the Islands.[23]

MacArthur, unlike his naval colleague and many officers in Washington, refused to accept the inevitability of the loss of the

---

[20] *Ibid.*

[21] Stimson's Diary, 17 Dec 41, cited in Stimson and Bundy, *On Active Service,* pp. 396–97.

[22] *Ibid.,* p. 395.

[23] Rads, CINCAF to OPNAV, 101330 and 131026, 10 and 13 Dec 41, War Diary, 16th Naval Dist, Off of Naval Rcds.

Philippines. Instead, he urged upon the War Department an offensive strategy in the Far East. The enemy, he asserted, was overextended, presenting the Allies with a "golden opportunity . . . for a master stroke." The "master stroke" he had in mind was a strong air attack against the Japanese home islands from the north. If successful such an attack would inflict great damage on the enemy and force him to pull in his widely dispersed air forces to protect the homeland.[24] The aircraft and carriers needed to carry out such a raid were not available at this time, and MacArthur's bold plan was shelved. But it is of more than passing interest to note that the Halsey-Doolittle raid against Tokyo on 18 April 1942, five months later, conformed to General MacArthur's suggested offensive against Japan, although it came too late to achieve the results he had hoped for.[25]

General MacArthur reacted strongly to Hart's pessimistic attitude. After the meeting on 13 December, when MacArthur asked Hart to escort the *Pensacola* convoy to Manila, the general wrote that he was greatly concerned over the Navy's estimate since "he [Hart] is charged with the security of the Army's supply lines." The acceptance of the view that the Philippines could not be reinforced, General MacArthur pointed out, meant the virtual abandonment of the Philippine Islands and the Philippine people. "If the suspicion of such action ever materializes," he warned the

Chief of Staff, "the entire structure will collapse over my head." [26]

MacArthur's reaction to Hart's views brought immediate results. The President on the 14th told the Acting Secretary of the Navy that "he was bound to help the Philippines and the Navy has got to help in it." [27] Thus prodded by the White House, the Navy was forced to modify its attitude somewhat. Recognizing Hart's inability to guarantee safe transport of the *Pensacola* convoy to Manila, the Chief of Naval Operations suggested an "effort when appropriate to pass through such support as may be practicable." With this lukewarm injunction, Admiral Stark also directed Hart to "cooperate with the Army" in the transportation by air of particularly needed supplies "when practicable." His authority to transfer his headquarters farther south was reiterated, but he was told to "assure MacArthur" that he would continue his "full support" of the defense of the Philippines. He was further instructed to turn over all naval stores to the Army on his departure from Manila and to place all marines and bluejackets under MacArthur's command.[28]

In the firm belief that the Philippines could be defended successfully against the Japanese, General MacArthur argued for a review of the strategic situation "lest a fatal mistake be made." Despite assurances of support from the War Department he felt that the importance of the Islands was not appreciated and that not enough was being done to support him. "The Philippine theater of operations," he as-

[24] Rad, MacArthur to Marshall, No. 198, 10 Dec 41, WPD 4544-26.

[25] Morison, *Rising Sun in the Pacific,* pp. 389–90, credits Admiral King with the idea of proposing the raid and initiating studies for its execution in January 1942. Actually, the President suggested the raid at a White House meeting on 28 January. WDCSA 334 Mtgs and Confs (1–28–42).

[26] Rad, MacArthur to Marshall, 13 Dec 41, OPD Exec O.

[27] Stimson and Bundy, *On Active Service,* p. 396.

[28] Rad, OPNAV to CINCAF, 170105, 17 Dec 41, War Diary, 16th Naval Dist, Off of Naval Rcds.

serted categorically, "is the locus of victory or defeat." "If the Philippines and the Netherlands East Indies go," he warned, "so will Singapore and the entire Asiatic continent." [29]

MacArthur's solution was to concentrate the resources of the Allies against Japan and so reverse the basic strategic decision of the war. Japan, he pointed out, was isolated from her Allies and "completely susceptible to concentrated action." He proposed therefore that the combined resources of the United States and its allies should be employed in the Pacific to delay Japan's advance. This delay, he argued, could be accomplished by sending more pursuit and bombardment aircraft to the Philippines. The retention of the Islands, he concluded, fully justified the diversion of the entire air production and other resources of the United States to the Philippines.[30]

The final answer to MacArthur's plea for a reversal of strategy and the concentration of Allied resources in the Far East was provided by the first of the wartime U.S.-British conferences, held in Washington between 24 December and 14 January. With the Pacific Fleet in ruins at Pearl Harbor and with the Philippines under strong attack, the British had good reason to fear that the United States would now abandon the earlier informal agreement to exert its principal effort against Germany. Their fears were groundless. The Washington conference reaffirmed the thesis that Germany was the main enemy and that the major effort must be made in the North At-

lantic and Europe.[31] MacArthur's efforts to secure a change in basic strategy had failed.

The Base in Australia

The discussions over strategy did not interrupt the efforts to send supplies to the Philippine garrison. These efforts inevitably involved the use of Australia as a base of operations for American forces. With the line of communications across the Central Pacific cut by the Japanese, the only way remaining to reach the Philippines was northward from Australia. Such a possibility had not been anticipated in prewar plans except as an air ferry route; the Australian base developed simply as a result of improvisation during the first days of the war. Once the *Pensacola* convoy was routed to Brisbane and it was decided to support General MacArthur, American effort in the Southwest Pacific turned to the build-up of supplies in Australia and the establishment of a line of communications northward.

To supervise the establishment of an advanced American base in Australia General Marshall selected Brig. Gen. Dwight D. Eisenhower. Having served on MacArthur's staff for three years, Eisenhower was peculiarly qualified for the task. He knew the situation in the Far East well, understood General MacArthur's plans and requirements, and could be presumed to have the confidence of the USAFFE commander. From his post as Chief of Staff,

[29] Rad, MacArthur to Marshall, 13 Dec 41, OPD Exec O.
[30] *Ibid.*

[31] This meeting, called the Arcadia Conference, is discussed in full in Maurice Matloff and Edwin M. Snell, *Strategic Planning for Coalition Warfare, 1941–1942,* UNITED STATES ARMY IN WORLD WAR II (Washington, 1945).

Third Army, at Fort Sam Houston, Eisenhower was called to Washington on 12 December and reported to General Marshall two days later. After outlining for Eisenhower the situation in the Far East, Marshall abruptly asked what our line of action should be. Evidently his reply would determine his worth, and Eisenhower asked for and secured time to prepare an answer. He returned to his desk in the War Plans Division to work out his reply, resolved that it "should be short, emphatic, and based on reasoning." [32]

After some hours of thought, Eisenhower returned to the Chief of Staff with his answer. He admitted that there was little chance that the garrison in the Philippines could hold out for long, but declared that everything possible should be done to support it. The risks and the money involved should not deter the United States from making a determined effort to help the Philippine Commonwealth. The trust and friendship of the people of Asia were important to the United States; failure might be excused, but never abandonment. To aid General MacArthur, Eisenhower believed, it would be necessary to convert Australia into a military base from which supplies might be ferried northward to the Philippines. [33]

Eisenhower's views coincided exactly with those of Marshall and Stimson and had already been approved by the President. Eisenhower had passed the test, and Marshall told him to do his best to save the Philippines. During the next few months,

first as head of the Pacific Section of the War Plans Division and then as chief of the division, he devoted himself almost exclusively to the task of reinforcing the Philippines.

By 17 December Eisenhower had developed and Marshall had approved a plan for establishing the base in Australia. [34] The forces in the *Pensacola* convoy were to form the nucleus for the new commands which was to be essentially an air base. Barnes, when he arrived in Brisbane, was to be relieved by Brig. Gen. Henry B. Claggett, then commanding the Interceptor Command in the Philippines. Clagett was ordered to Australia immediately. Ultimately, the base, to be known as U.S. Army Forces in Australia, was to be commanded by Maj. Gen. George H. Brett, who was in Chungking attending an Allied conference. Col. Stephen J. Chamberlin, a highly qualified G-4 officer on duty with the General Staff, was sent to Australia to serve as Brett's chief of staff.

While the establishment of this new command implied a larger purpose than the support of the forces in the Philippines, the War Department made it clear that the primary mission of U.S. Army Forces in Australia was to get vitally needed supplies to General MacArthur. General Brett was informed that his command was to be considered as an advanced base of a communications zone "for the support of USAFFE" and that he would operate under the orders of General MacArthur. He was further instructed to co-operate with U.S. naval authorities "in assuring the safety of sea routes used," and to fly the planes in the *Pensacola* convoy northward

---

[32] Gen. Dwight D. Eisenhower, *Crusade in Europe* (New York, 1948), p. 18.

[33] *Ibid.*, p. 21–22. An unsigned and undated paper entitled Assistance to the Far East, OPD Exec O, is probably the one prepared by Eisenhower on 14 December.

[34] Memo, WPD for CofS, 17 Dec 41, sub: Plan for Australian Base, WPD 4628–1.

with all the ammunition they could carry. Any course that would achieve these results was authorized.[35]

On 22 December, the same day the *Pensacola* convoy reached Brisbane, General Claggett arrived from the Philippines. He was immediately handed the instructions for the new base by Colonel Merle-Smith, the military attaché. Already General MacArthur had indicated that the convoy should proceed to the Philippines and that the aircraft should be assembled and flown north. Every attempt was made to comply with these instructions, but the situation was changing rapidly and there were numerous obstacles to be overcome in unloading and rerouting the ships.

General Marshall had done all he could to assure the arrival of the supplies in the convoy to MacArthur. He had reminded both Claggett and Barnes repeatedly of the urgent necessity of getting the planes and .50-caliber ammunition to the Philippines and told them to spare neither effort nor expense to accomplish this task.[36] The Navy had also instructed its representatives in Australia to assist in every way, and the Chief of Naval Operations asked Admiral Hart, still in Manila, to "impress upon the Australian Naval Board the importance of their full cooperation" in keeping open Torres Strait as a route for U.S. reinforcements to the Philippines and northwest Australia.[37]

MacArthur had been kept fully informed of these measures. "The President has seen all of your messages," Marshall told him, "and directs Navy to give you every possible support in your splendid fight."[38]

Despite these assurances and the efforts of the men in Australia, the aircraft, reinforcements, and supplies failed to get through. When the planes were brought ashore and assembled, they were found to lack parts such as trigger motors, gun sights, and self-sealing gas tanks, all of which would be required in combat.[39] The field artillery brigade and the naval supplies were placed aboard the two fastest ships in the convoy, the *Holbrook* and *Bloemfontein,* which sailed from Brisbane on 28 December. By that time the Japanese had established bases in Borneo, and it was realized that the ships would not be able to get through the blockade. General Brett, who had arrived in Australia on 31 December, therefore ordered the troops debarked. Most of the artillerymen came ashore at Darwin; the rest went on to Surabaja in Java. None of the planes, men, or supplies of the *Pensacola* convoy ever reached the Philippines.

But General MacArthur had not yet given up hope that the planes might be brought into the Philippines. On the 14th he had suggested that air reinforcements be brought in by carrier, thus eliminating the problem of bases between Australia and Luzon. On the 22d, the day on which the Japanese landed at Lingayen Gulf, he observed that enemy air and naval forces were threatening his line of communications southward and called for some American

---

[35] Ltr, R. C. Moore to Brett, 19 Dec 41, OCS 18136-161; rad, Marshall to Military Attaché, Melbourne for Brett, No. 31, 17 Dec 41, WPD 4628-1. See also the Administrative Order dispatched to CG USAFIA, 20 Dec 41, AG 381 (12–20–41) MSC–D–M.

[36] Rad, Marshall to Military Attaché, Melbourne, No. 36, 22 Dec 41, WPD 4630-2. General MacArthur received copies of the radios sent to Australia.

[37] Rad, OPNAV to CINCAF, 222302, 23 Dec 41, War Diary, 16th Naval Dist, Off of Naval Rcds.

[38] Rad, Marshall to MacArthur, No. 855, 22 Dec 41, AG 381 (11–27–41 Gen) Far East.

[39] Hist of Fifth Air Force, Part I, p. 44 and App. 2, Doc 67; Arnold, *Global Mission,* p. 290.

naval effort to limit the enemy's freedom of movement along the vital sea lanes. Pointedly he asked for "any inkling" of the strategic plans for the Pacific Fleet and reminded Marshall that carriers could bring pursuit planes within operating radius of the Philippines. "Can I expect anything along that line," he asked.[40]

The answer was no. Admiral Stark asserted that the use of aircraft carriers as transports was "impracticable in the existing strategic situation," and Marshall was forced to tell MacArthur that he would have to rely on the ability of cargo ships and aircraft to make their way northward from Australia by way of Torres Strait and the Netherlands Indies.[41]

Apparently MacArthur's suggestion that a naval threat be made against Japan brought an inquiry from the Chief of Naval Operations to Admiral Hart. The Asiatic Fleet commander explained that MacArthur had sent his message without consulting him, and that the reference "was meant to apply forces other than this [Asiatic] fleet."[42] The next day, 24 December, Hart received another message from his chief in Washington asking for a full report of his operations in support of the Army, "as my information on this subject is meager." The Army, Stark explained, was "bringing heavy pressure for greater naval activity in Philippine waters."[43]

By the time Hart received this message he had already determined to join his surface forces in the Indies.[44] The next morning, 25 December, he turned over to Admiral Rockwell full command of all naval activities in the Philippines and at 0200 of the 26th left Manila aboard the submarine *Shark*. The two remaining destroyers followed the next day, when General MacArthur reported to the War Department that "Admiral Hart has left Manila to join naval forces in the south, destination to be reported later. Admiral Rockwell now in command of naval forces with headquarters on Corregidor."[45]

Before he left, Hart made available to General MacArthur all naval personnel, including the marines. The submarines were to continue to operate in Philippine waters as long as "practicable and profitable," and then retire southward. All that was to remain in the Philippines were 3 gunboats, 3 minesweepers, 6 motor torpedo boats, and a few tugs and yachts for inshore patrol. Orders were issued for the destruction of all oil and gasoline in storage in Manila, the evacuation of the Cavite Navy Yard and Sangley Point, and the shipment of all remaining stores to Corregidor and Mariveles, at the southern tip of Bataan.[46]

The submarines began to withdraw after Christmas and by the 31st the last one had

---

[40] Rads, MacArthur to Marshall, Nos. 22 and 40, 22 Dec 41, AG 381 (11–27–41 Gen) Far East.
[41] Memo, Stark for Marshall, 23 Dec 41, sub: Transportation of Aircraft to Phil, AG 381 (11–27–41 Gen) Far East; rad, Marshall to MacArthur, 23 Dec 41, OPD Exec O.
[42] Rad, CINCAF to OPNAV, 220830, 22 Dec 41, War Diary, 16th Naval Dist, Off of Naval Rcds.
[43] Rad, OPNAV to CINCAF, 231601, 23 Dec 41, War Diary, 16th Naval Dist.
Hart's reply, dated the 24th, was that until he received reports from the submarines still at sea he

would be unable to give a full report. Rad, CINCAF to OPNAV, 241225, 24 Dec 41, War Diary, 16th Naval Dist.
[44] Hart, Narrative of Events, Asiatic Fleet, pp. 45–46; rad, CINCAF to OPNAV, 241225, 24 Dec 41, War Diary, 16th Naval Dist.
[45] Rad, MacArthur to AGWAR, 26 Dec 41, AG 381 (11–27–41 Gen) Far East; Rockwell, Naval Activities in Luzon Area, pp. 6–8; ltr, Hart to MacArthur, 25 Dec 41, sub: Move of Comd Post, War Diary, 16th Naval Dist.
[46] Rockwell, Naval Activities in Luzon Area, p. 7.

left Manila Bay.[47] Thus ended the activities of the underwater craft in Philippine waters. Constituting the largest single undersea force in the Navy, the submarines were expected to exact an impressive toll from any approaching Japanese fleet. In the eight separate landings the Japanese made in the period between 8 and 25 December, the submarines proved unable to impede the enemy or even inflict any serious damage. Their record, like that of the B–17's, was most disappointing.

The withdrawal of the Asiatic Fleet coincided with the movement southward of the Far East Air Force whose heavy bombers were already based in Australia. On 24 December, General Brereton was called to MacArthur's office and told that he was to go to Australia with his headquarters to "organize advanced operating bases from which . . . you can protect the lines of communication, secure bases in Mindanao, and support the defense of the Philippines." [48] Brereton offered to stay on, but MacArthur told him that he would be more useful in Australia.

Brereton closed his headquarters at Fort McKinley at 1600 of the 24th, and in a PBY left that evening to join his bombers at Batchelor Field near Port Darwin. To the War Department General MacArthur radioed "Operations heavy bombardment no longer possible from bases here. B–17's have been moved to Australia and Netherlands East Indies bases. Brereton with skeleton staff departed on 24th." [49]

With Brereton's departure, the small number of fighters, all that remained of the once formidable Far East Air Force, came under the command of Col. Harold H. George, formerly chief of staff of the Interceptor Command. Fighter fields were established on Bataan and preparations were made to continue operations from there. The 650 men of the 19th Bombardment Group left Luzon before the end of December to join their planes in Australia. Their comrades in the 24th and 27th Groups were not as fortunate. They remained behind and, since few men were required to fly and service the planes still in operation, eventually became infantry soldiers on Bataan.[50]

All hopes of reinforcing the Philippines with pursuit planes were now at an end. Even if these planes could be flown from Australia northward, there were no longer any fields on Luzon outside Bataan on which they could base. The War Department told General MacArthur frankly that its plans for sending fighter aircraft to him were now jeopardized and that "the day to day situation" in the Philippines and Borneo—where the Japanese had landed on the 24th—would determine what could be done. He could draw what small comfort he could from fresh assurances that the United States would develop a strong air force in the Far East and that the Secretary of War approved fully his plans and orders.[51]

General Brett, still in Chungking when news of the decision to withdraw reached Washington, was directed to get to Australia as quickly as possible. He was informed

[47] Rpt, COMSUBS to COMINCH, War Activities, Submarines, U.S. Asiatic Fleet, 1 Dec 41–1 Apr 42, Off of Naval Rcds.

[48] Ltr Order, USAFFE to CG FEAF, 24 Dec 41, reproduced in Brereton, *Diaries*, p. 62.

[49] Rad, MacArthur to AGWAR, 25 Dec 41, AG 381 (11–27–41 Gen) Far East.

[50] Craven and Cate, *The Army Air Forces in World War II*, I, 224–25; Brereton, *Diaries*, p. 62; Ind, *Bataan, The Judgment Seat*, passim.

[51] Rad, Marshall to MacArthur, No. 879, 24 Dec 41, AG 381 (11–27–41 Gen) Far East.

of the changed situation and asked to submit recommendations on the "location, composition, and future operations of U.S. Forces in Australia." [52] The air forces in Australia, he was told, were to be built up in the hope that long-range bombers would be able to aid the Philippine garrison and that the entire force would be useful in supporting the Allied attempts to halt the Japanese advance along the Malay Barrier.[53]

By 24 December every effort to bring supplies and reinforcements to General MacArthur had failed. The *Pensacola* convoy had reached Australia, but no way had been found to move its cargo northward. General MacArthur had not received a single piece of equipment or one additional man to reinforce his garrison. The supplies and men destined for the Philippines remained in Australia, which was rapidly being developed into an advanced Allied air and supply base.

Within a period of three weeks, from 8 December to 25 December, the Japanese had achieved astounding results in the Philippines. They had completed one major amphibious assault and at least seven minor landing operations; they had placed a large number of troops ashore on Luzon, north and south of Manila, and were ready to move on the capital; they had cut the line of communications between the Philippines and Australia.

During this three-week period, the Japanese had also established complete aerial and naval supremacy in the Philippines and forced the Asiatic Fleet and the Far East Air Force to retire to the line Surabaja–Darwin, 1,500 miles from Manila. General MacArthur summed up his situation on 27 December as follows: "Enemy penetration in the Philippines resulted from our weakness on the sea and in the air. Surface elements of the Asiatic Fleet were withdrawn and the effect of the submarines has been negligible. Lack of airfields for modern planes prevented defensive dispersion and lack of pursuit planes permitted unhindered day bombardment. The enemy has had utter freedom of naval and air movements." [54] To these reasons, he could have added the unsatisfactory performance of the ill-trained and poorly equipped Philippine Army reservists.

---

[52] Rad, Marshall to Military Attaché, Melbourne for Brett, No. 41, 25 Dec 41, WPD 4628-3.

[53] *Ibid.*

[54] Rad, MacArthur to AGWAR, 27 Dec 41, AG 381 (11–27–41 Gen) Far East; see Brereton's views on the same subject in his *Diaries,* pp. 64–67.

PART THREE

THE WITHDRAWAL TO BATAAN

CHAPTER X

The Withdrawal Begins

The success of the Japanese landings at Lingayen Gulf and Lamon Bay ended all hopes for an American victory in the Philippines. Only one day after the landing to the north, on 23 December, General MacArthur decided that he would have to fall back to Bataan and fight a delaying action there until help could arrive. This decision, made only under the greatest necessity, was the basic strategic decision of the campaign in the Philippines.

"WPO–3 Is in Effect"

Before the war, General MacArthur had determined that he would meet a Japanese attack by offensive action, not by what he considered to be the passive defense provided for in WPO–3. Accordingly, he had ordered his force commanders to meet the Japanese at the beaches and to drive them back into the sea. There was to be "no withdrawal from beach positions." The first Japanese landings between 8 and 10 December had caused no change in this strategy.

Once the Japanese had landed, General MacArthur had to consider seriously the prospect of an eventual withdrawal to Bataan and the evacuation of Manila. To prepare President Quezon for the worst, he sent word to him on the morning of the 12th to be ready to move to Corregidor on four hours' notice.

Shocked and wholly unprepared for this "startling message," Quezon arranged a

conference with MacArthur that night at the Manila Hotel. At the meeting, MacArthur explained that there was no immediate cause for concern, and that he was only "preparing for the worst in case the Japanese should land in great force at different places." In such an event, it would be unwise, he told Quezon, to have his forces scattered. He intended to concentrate his army on Bataan, and to move his headquarters, the High Commissioner's office, and the Commonwealth Government to Corregidor and declare Manila an open city. "Do you mean, General," asked Quezon, "that tomorrow you will declare Manila an open city and that some time during the day we shall have to go to Corregidor?" MacArthur's answer was an emphatic "No." He did not seem to be certain that the move would even be necessary, and was evidently only preparing the President for such a possibility. The meeting closed with Quezon's promise to consider the matter further. Later he consented, with reluctance, to move to Corregidor if necessary.[1]

The possibility of a withdrawal seems to have been in the minds of other officers in MacArthur's headquarters before the main Japanese landings. During an inspection of the 21st Field Artillery sector along Lingayen Gulf, Col. Constant L. Irwin, MacArthur's G–3, showed little interest in the

---

[1] Quezon, *The Good Fight,* pp. 194–98. Present at the meeting also were Col. Manuel Nieto, the President's aide, and Lt. Col. Sidney L. Huff, MacArthur's aide.

tactical placement of the guns. He seemed concerned, instead, with the location of the ammunition and supply routes, selected to conform with the mission of holding at the beaches. "He took a look at our ammunition disposition and the dangerous supply routes," wrote Colonel Mallonée, instructor of the 21st Field Artillery, "and very violently announced that it would be impossible to withdraw the ammunition in time to save it. . . ."[2] This was the first time, remarked Mallonée, that he heard the word "withdraw." He explained to Colonel Irwin that his orders were to hold at all costs, and repeated Wainwright's order: "We must die in our tracks, falling not backward but forward toward the enemy." The answer of the G–3 officer was, "Don't believe everything you hear."[3]

Colonel Mallonée, as well as the chief of staff and senior instructor of the 21st Division, was now thoroughly confused about the mission and after a conference decided to request clarification from General Wainwright's headquarters. They were told that the mission was still to hold at all costs, but, added Colonel Mallonée, "by the manner in which it was issued it was evident that there is considerable doubt in the minds of the North Luzon Force command as to whether the mission is actually as given."[4]

As early as 12 December, then, General MacArthur was preparing the ground for measures that would have to be taken if he decided that it was necessary to withdraw to Bataan. When General Homma landed his *14th Army* at Lingayen Gulf ten days later, on 22 December, MacArthur still made no change in his plan. But his message to General Marshall on that date shows that he now believed he might have to withdraw quickly. He estimated that the Japanese disembarking from the seventy to eighty transports in Lingayen Gulf had a strength of 80,000 to 100,000 men, and reported that he had on Luzon only about 40,000 men "in units partially equipped." He anticipated that "this enormous tactical discrepancy" would force him "to operate in delaying action on successive lines through the Central Luzon plain to final defensive position on Bataan."[5] When forced to do so, he told General Marshall, he would declare Manila an open city to save the civilian population and move his headquarters, together with the Philippine Commonwealth Government and the High Commissioner's office, to Corregidor, which, he said, "I intend

---

[2] Mallonée, Bataan Diary, I, 56; see also ltr, Brig Gen. Constant L. Irwin, ret., to Ward, 13 Jun 51, OCMH. The author discussed the question of the withdrawal with Generals Sutherland and R. J. Marshall and with Colonel Collier.

[3] Mallonée, Bataan Diary, I, 56. The conversation between Irwin and Mallonée took place in the presence of the senior American instructor of the 21st Division (PA), Col. Ray M. O'Day, the division chief of staff, and several other officers. Colonel O'Day did not get the idea of a withdrawal from Irwin, but did say that such a remark was made in reference to the ammunition. Ltr, O'Day to author, 16 Nov 49, OCMH.

[4] Mallonée, Bataan Diary, I, 57.

[5] Rad, MacArthur to Marshall, No. 3, 22 Dec 41, AG 381 (11–27–41 Gen) Far East. Although MacArthur stated that he had only 40,000 men on Luzon, an analysis of the units present indicates that the number of troops was actually much higher. The strength of the American garrison, even without the air force, could not have been less than 20,000, including the 12,000 Philippine Scouts. To this figure must be added the strength of seven Philippine Army reserve divisions and one regular division, as well as the Constabulary, inducted into the service of the United States in December. Many of the units were undoubtedly at two-thirds strength, but even at half strength, the total number of troops on Luzon at this time could not have been less than 75,000–80,000. The number of Japanese troops who landed at Lingayen between 22 and 28 December was about 43,000.

to hold." [6]   General Marshall immediately replied that his proposed line of action was approved and that he was doing his utmost to send aid.[7]

The fighting in North Luzon on 22 and 23 December and the rapid advance by the Japanese to Rosario apparently convinced MacArthur that the time had come to put the scheme for withdrawal into effect. General Wainwright's request on the afternoon of the 23d for permission to withdraw behind the Agno River must have confirmed this decision. To these military considerations must be added General MacArthur's desire to save the city of Manila from destruction.

But the chief reason for the withdrawal order was the failure of the troops to hold the enemy. Up to this time General MacArthur seems to have had the greatest confidence in the fighting qualities of the Philippine Army reservists and in the ability of his forces to hold the central Luzon plain. The events of the 22d and 23d forced a revision of this view. "General MacArthur, viewing the broken, fleeing North Luzon Force," wrote Colonel Collier, a sympathetic observer, "realized that his cherished plan of defeating an enemy attempt to advance toward Manila from the north was not now possible. . . ." [8]

MacArthur's position on 23 December 1941 was somewhat akin to the position in which General Yamashita found himself three years later, when the victorious Americans were preparing to invade Luzon. Realizing that his opponent's air and naval forces were far superior to his own, that American ground forces were free to land on any beaches they chose, and that their superior mobility and fire power were too great for him, he concluded that the Japanese would be unable "to conduct warfare on flat land." Yamashita, therefore, decided to withdraw from Manila and the central Luzon plain, and to fight a delaying action to "divert American forces in Luzon so as to keep them from attacking Japan as long as possible." Unlike General MacArthur, Yamashita hoped to accomplish his objective by withdrawing into the mountains of northern Luzon.   He might have been more successful if he had retired to Bataan, as the Americans had four years earlier. From there he could have maintained his forces intact and have denied the Americans, for a time at least, the use of Manila Bay.[9]

The decision having been made to withdraw to Bataan, USAFFE notified all force commanders that "WPO–3 is in effect." [10] Nothing more was required. WPO–3 was an old plan, well known to all U.S. Army officers who had been in the Philippines six months or more.   Under it, the Philippine Department headquarters, after the experience of numerous maneuvers, had selected

[6] *Ibid.*

[7] Rad, Marshall to MacArthur, 22 Dec 41, AG 381 (11–27–41 Gen) Far East.   This message implied approval of MacArthur's plans by the President, for it contained the statement that the President had seen all of MacArthur's messages.

[8] Collier, Notebooks, II, 38.

[9] A. Frank Reel, *The Case of General Yamashita* (Chicago, 1949), pp. 21–22. Most of the Japanese officers who read this volume in manuscript form did not agree with the author that a withdrawal to Bataan by Yamashita would have resulted in a more successful defense.   Comments of Former Japanese Officers Regarding The Fall of the Philippines, p. 41, OCMH.

[10] Wainwright, *General Wainwright's Story*, p. 36. Wainwright received the order on the night of the 23d, but General Parker did not get the order until about 1000 of the 24th, when he was ordered to Bataan to organize the Bataan Defense Force. Ltr, Parker to Ward, 16 Jan 52, OCMH.

certain delaying positions along the central Luzon plain. These positions had been reconnoitered and were considered fairly strong defensive lines along the route of withdrawal to Bataan. It only remained to issue written orders to supplement the announcement that WPO–3 was in effect.

The next morning, 24 December, at 1100, the USAFFE staff was called to a conference. General Sutherland announced the decision and stated that the headquarters was to be moved to Corregidor that evening. Each man was to take with him only field equipment and one suitcase or bedroll. By special order all officers in the headquarters, except those of high rank who had been promoted a few days earlier, were promoted one grade. To the War Department General MacArthur sent news of his decision, as well as the further information that the Japanese had landed at Atimonan and Mauban that morning.[11] "Tonight I plan to disengage my forces under cover of darkness," he wrote. "For the present, I am remaining in Manila, establishing an advanced headquarters on Corregidor." After evacuating the High Commissioner and the Commonwealth Government, he told the Chief of Staff, he would declare Manila an open city.[12]

On the afternoon of the 24th, President Quezon and High Commissioner Sayre, with their personal and official families, sailed to Corregidor aboard the interisland steamer *Mayan*. Many Philippine officials simply packed a few belongings and left the city, despite the order that all Commonwealth officials would remain at their posts.[13]

The headquarters began to move out on the *Don Esteban* after 1900 that day. "It was a beautiful moonlit night," wrote Colonel Collier, "and the cheerful, peaceful murmuring of the rippling waves from the cutting prow of the ship belied the havoc of war."[14] It was Christmas Eve, and the men sat around on deck talking in hushed tones and watching the flames rising from the Navy's fuel dump where over 1,000,000 gallons of oil had been fired earlier in the day. The *Don Esteban* docked at Corregidor at 2130, and the next morning Headquarters, USAFFE, opened on the island. That day, MacArthur reported to the War Department that his headquarters had moved.[15] A rear echelon, headed by Brig. Gen. Richard J. Marshall, Deputy Chief of Staff, remained behind in Manila to close out the headquarters and supervise the shipment of supplies and the evacuation of the remaining troops.[16]

There was much to do in the days that followed to prepare Bataan for the troops destined to make their last stand there. On the morning of the 24th, Col. Lewis C. Beebe, G–4, USAFFE, and Brig. Gen. Charles C. Drake, Quartermaster, were called to General Marshall's office and there told of the decision to withdraw all troops on Luzon to Bataan and to evacuate Manila. General Drake was instructed to move his base of operations to Bataan immediately and to check on the reserves at Corregidor

---

[11] Rad, CG USAFFE to AGWAR, 24 Dec 41, AG 381 (11–27–41 Gen) Far East. MacArthur mistakenly reported that the Japanese were standing off Nasugbu. No landing was ever made there.
[12] Rad, MacArthur to Marshall, 24 Dec 41, AG 381 (11–27–41 Gen) Far East.

[13] Collier, Notebooks, I, 80–81; II, 40.
[14] *Ibid.*, II, 42.
[15] *Ibid.*, 44; rad, MacArthur to AGWAR, 25 Dec 41, AG 381 (11–27–41 Gen) Far East.
[16] USAFFE-USFIP Rpt of Opns, pp. 33, 40; interv, author with R. J. Marshall, 7 Apr 48.

to be sure that there was enough to supply 10,000 men for six months. Small barges and boats required to move the supplies from Manila to Corregidor and Bataan were quickly gathered, and within twenty-four hours Corregidor was completely stocked with the supplies for a six months' campaign. At the same time, all supplies were immediately started on their way to Bataan by every available means—water, truck, and rail. Ammunition had already been stored in the peninsula, together with certain defense reserves including 300,000 gallons of gasoline, lubricating oil, and greases, and about 3,000 tons of canned meats and fish.[17]

In Manila, the rear echelon worked valiantly to get all the supplies out of the city before the Japanese moved in. Those small craft not transferred to Corregidor and Bataan were destroyed; demolitions were carried out with efficiency and dispatch. By the time General Marshall and his men moved out on New Year's Eve, most of the supplies that might possibly be of value to the enemy had been destroyed.[18]

At the same time that a revised supply plan was put into effect, a revised plan of operations was quickly worked out. The object of these plans was to gain time to prepare defenses on Bataan and to permit an orderly withdrawal into the peninsula.

Wainwright's North Luzon Force was to hold the Japanese north of the key city of San Fernando, Pampanga—where Route 7, the main highway leading into the Bataan peninsula, began—until 8 January, then withdraw into Bataan.[19] This would provide time for the South Luzon Force to move up past Manila and into Bataan and give those troops already on Bataan an opportunity to establish a line. The withdrawal was to be in five phases, or along five lines. On each line Wainwright's men were to hold only long enough to force the enemy to prepare for an organized attack. The object was to delay, not defeat, the enemy and to reach Bataan intact.[20]

General Parker's South Luzon Force was to withdraw west and north along successive defense lines through and around Manila, across the Pampanga River, spanned by the two bridges known collectively as the Calumpit Bridge, to San Fernando, and then to Bataan. All of the South Luzon Force was to clear the bridge before 8 January. The Calumpit Bridge therefore became a critical point in the plan for withdrawal. It had to be held until all the troops in the South Luzon Force passed over.[21]

To prepare defensive positions on Bataan, the Bataan Defense Force was organized on the 24th. General Parker was placed in command and given two Philippine Army divisions, the 31st and 41st (less 42d Infantry), in addition to the troops already in Bataan to do the job. Command of the South Luzon Force, which consisted during

---

[17] QM Rpt of Opns, pp. 20–21.

[18] Interv, author with R. J. Marshall, 7 Apr 48; Carlos P. Romulo, *I Saw the Fall of the Philippines* (New York: Doubleday & Company, Inc., 1942), pp. 68–90.

The first specification in the charge against General Homma when he was tried as a war criminal in Manila in 1946 was the violation of an open city. Since Manila was used as a base of supplies, and since a U.S. Army headquarters was based in the city and troops passed through it after 26 December, it is difficult to see how Manila could be considered an open city between 26 and 31 December 1941. Nevertheless, the charge against General Homma stood. USA *vs.* Homma, specification of charges.

[19] The date was later changed when it was found that North Luzon Force could not hold until the 8th.

San Fernando, Pampanga, should not be confused with San Fernando, La Union.

[20] USAFFE-USFIP Rpt of Opns, p. 33; Collier, Notebooks, II, 47.

[21] *Ibid.;* ltr, Sutherland to CG 51st Div (PA), 24 Dec 41, sub: Opns Orders, AG 371 Phil Rcds.

the withdrawal of the 51st Division (PA), one regiment of the 1st Division, the 42d Infantry, plus supporting tanks and SPM's, passed to General Jones.[22]

The only troops in Bataan when Parker reached there at 1700 of the 24th were the Philippine Division (less 57th Combat Team and one battalion of the 45th Infantry) and a provisional air corps regiment. The 14th Engineers (PS) marked out the defensive positions and the Philippine Army troops, when they arrived on the peninsula, moved into these positions and began to dig foxholes and put up wire. Brig. Gen. Clifford Bluemel's 31st Division (PA), stationed along the Zambales coast was the first into Bataan. Its movement was completed by 26 December. Two days later the 41st Division (PA), less elements, took up its position along the skeleton line.[23]

The plan for the withdrawal of the forces in north and south Luzon called for a difficult maneuver requiring accurate timing and the closest co-ordination. Should the forces in north and south Luzon fail to pull back to Bataan, or should the Japanese seize the road net leading into the peninsula, then the strategic objective of the withdrawal, the denial of Manila Bay to the enemy, would be jeopardized.

The North Luzon Force Plan

The North Luzon Force plan of withdrawal was based on the five delaying positions or lines selected and reconnoitered during peacetime. Separated by the estimated distance which could be covered in one night's march, these lines utilized the

terrain features advantageous in defense—rivers, high ground, and swamps. Each was anchored on high ground and took full advantage of natural barriers. They lay across the face of the central Luzon plain and covered the main approaches to Manila, Routes 3 and 5. (*Map 7*)

The first defensive line, known as D–1, extended in an easterly direction from Aguilar, south of Lingayen Gulf on Route 13, through San Carlos to Urdaneta on Route 3. As Col. William F. Maher, Wainwright's chief of staff, has observed, the D–1 line "was simply a line on which we hoped to be able to reorganize the badly disorganized forces north of the Agno River." [24]

The second position, the D–2 line, extended in general along the arc of the Agno River, one of the formidable natural barriers in the central plain. After holding for one day on this line, the troops were to retire next to the D–3 line, stretching from Santa Ignacia on the west through Gerona and Guimba to San Jose on the east. The D–4 line was approximately twenty-five miles long and extended from Tarlac on the left (west) to Cabanatuan on the right. Small rivers and streams intersected this line, which, at Cabanatuan, was anchored on the Pampanga River.

The final and most southerly position, called the D–5 line, stretched from Bamban in front of Mt. Arayat, across Route 5 to Sibul Springs. Southeast of Mt. Arayat, between the Pampanga River and Route 5, was the Candaba Swamp, which broke the central plain into two narrow corridors leading toward Manila. Of the five lines, only the last, the D–5 line, was to be organized for a protracted defense. Plans called for a stand here until the South Luzon

---

[22] USAFFE GO 54, 27 Dec 41; SLF and II Corps Rpt of Opns, pp. 16, 19.
[23] SLF and II Corps Rpt of Opns, p. 19; USAFFE-USFIP Rpt of Opns, pp. 33–35.

[24] Ltr, Maher, formerly NLF CofS, to author, 11 Nov 49, OCMH.

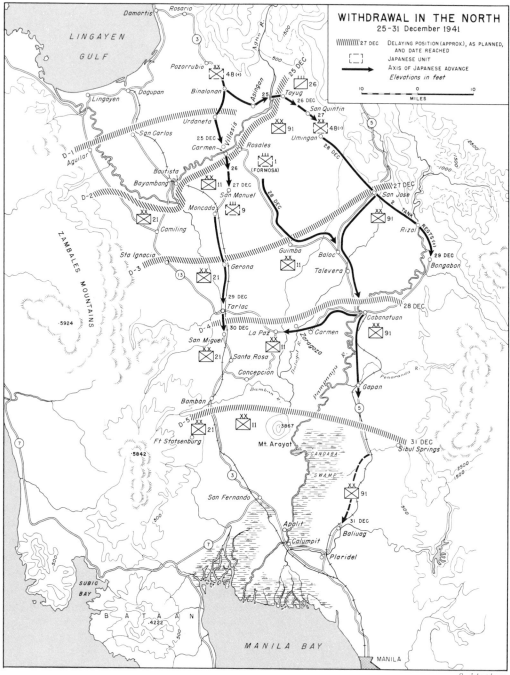

WITHDRAWAL IN THE NORTH
25–31 December 1941

|||||||| 27 DEC DELAYING POSITION (APPROX.), AS PLANNED, AND DATE REACHED

[___] JAPANESE UNIT

→ AXIS OF JAPANESE ADVANCE

Elevations in feet

10   0   10
MILES

MAP 7

R. Johnstone

Force could slip behind the North Luzon Force, up Route 3, into San Fernando.[25]

During its withdrawal to Bataan, the North Luzon Force was to be supported by General Weaver's Provisional Tank Group, whose job it would be to cover the withdrawal, sweep enemy avenues of approach, and halt hostile mechanized movement. The tanks were deployed on alternate sides of the road, at curves and bends, to achieve maximum sweep of their weapons with a minimum of exposure. Always they were to take care that they left themselves a route of escape. When required to withdraw, the tanks were to move back one at a time, under cover of the forward tank. The tankers were to select their positions after a careful reconnaissance, and with an eye to fields of fire, alternate positions, avenues of approach, and emergency escape routes.[26]

The success of the withdrawal would depend to a large degree on the engineers. Their task was twofold: to maintain roads and bridges ahead of the retreating columns, and to destroy the bridges and block the roads already passed to halt the enemy advance. Demolitions and the construction of obstacles before the D–1 line were to be accomplished by the front-line units; North Luzon Force engineers, consisting principally of the engineer battalion of the 91st Division (PA), were made responsible for all work south of that line. The destruction of railroad bridges was left to a special detachment of demolition experts from MacArthur's headquarters, attached to North Luzon Force. Demolitions were to be exe-

cuted by the engineers when ordered by the division or covering force commander and when the tanks and vehicles of the last elements of the rear guard had cleared the bridge.[27]

The term *line,* applied to the five delaying positions, is misleading. Actually the front was too wide to be held continuously by the forces available to General Wainwright. Unit commanders were given considerable leeway in occupying their positions and usually could do little more than place their troops so as to cover the most likely routes of approach. Each line was to be occupied before dawn, held during the day, and evacuated at night, the troops withdrawing to the next line. Their withdrawal would be covered by a shell, a small part of the retiring force, which was to remain in position until just before dawn when it was to pull back hastily to rejoin its parent unit on the line below. This shell, in theory, would consist of an infantry-artillery team, but in practice often included only one of these arms.

By occupying these positions successively and holding them with a shell while the bulk of the force retired to the safety of a prepared position to the rear, MacArthur hoped to force the enemy to halt and deploy for an attack before each position. By the time he was ready to attack, the line would be evacuated. In this way, the Japanese advance southward would be considerably delayed, and time would be gained to prepare defenses on Bataan and to permit the South Luzon Force to pass into the penin-

---

[25] Collier, Notebooks, II, 82; NLF and I Corps Rpt of Opns, p. 11.

[26] Prov Tank Gp Rpt of Opns, pp. 10–11; ltr, Col Ernest B. Miller to Ward, 31 Dec 51, copy in OCMH.

[27] Memo, NLF Engineer for CofS NLF, 1 Aug 42, sub: Orgn and Opns of NLF Engineers 8 Dec 41–6 Jan 42, pp. 1–10, copy made for author by Col Harry A. Skerry, the NLF Engineer, and on file in OCMH. This memo will hereafter be cited as Skerry, NLF Engineer Rpt of Opns.

sula behind the North Luzon Force. The danger of the scheme lay in the Japanese control of the air, which made it possible for them to play havoc with the retiring road-bound tanks and artillery. The risk was a calculated one, but the danger was minimized by limiting important movements to the hours of darkness.[28]

The supply of the troops during the withdrawal would be difficult. The problems ordinarily encountered in supplying large bodies of mobile troops during a retrograde movement would be complicated by the shortage of supplies and trained supply officers, the necessity of moving a large amount of equipment to Bataan, and the destruction of those supplies which could not be saved. The fact that most of the men were inadequately trained, poorly equipped, and often undisciplined would add considerably to the difficulties.[29]

To the Tarlac–Cabanatuan Line

On Christmas Eve the North Luzon Force stood generally along a line extending from Tayug on the east through Urdaneta and San Carlos to Aguilar on the west. (*Map 5*) All units were under orders to hold for twenty-four hours before falling back to the Agno.

On the right (east) was the 26th Cavalry (PS). That afternoon the Scouts had been forced to retreat from Binalonan across the Agno River to Tayug, thus actually anchoring the North Luzon Force at the start of the withdrawal on the D–2 line. At Tayug, the cavalrymen had relieved the 71st Engineer Battalion (PA) covering the river

crossing and had joined the 91st Division (PA) and the remnants of the 71st.[30]

West of Tayug, holding the center of the North Luzon Force line from Urdaneta to San Carlos, was General Brougher's 11th Division (PA). Also in the center was the 192d Tank Battalion, at this time the only armor in support of the North Luzon Force. On the afternoon of the 24th it was moving south toward the Agno, under orders to deploy along the south bank. Already on its way toward the river was the 194th, which had left Manila that morning with orders to assemble in the vicinity of Carmen.[31]

Extending the North Luzon Force line west from San Carlos to the Zambales Mountains, straddling the Agno, was General Capinpin's 21st Division (PA). Stationed initially along the southern shore of Lingayen Gulf, this division had not yet come in contact with the enemy. Its orders were to withdraw at 1900 on the 24th in two columns along the two roads, one on each side of the river.

Withdrawal to the Agno

At the appointed hour, 1900 of 24 December, the 21st Division began to withdraw.[32] Wire communication between the

---

[28] Ltr, Maher to author, 11 Nov 49, OCMH; Collier, Notebooks, II, 82; Mallonée, Bataan Diary, I, 67; NLF and I Corps Rpt of Opns, p. 14.

[29] QM Rpt of Opns, pp. 4–5.

[30] Lt. Col. William E. Chandler, "26th Cavalry (PS) Battles to Glory," Part 2, *Armored Cavalry Journal* (May–June 1947), p. 11; Skerry, NLF Engineer Rpt of Opns, pp. 3, 5, 9.

[31] Miller, *Bataan Uncensored*, pp. 88–91; Prov Tank Gp Rpt of Opns, pp. 10–11; 11th Inf (PA), Beach Defense and Delaying Action, 8 Dec 41–5 Jan 42, p. 19, OCMH. The latter is Part 2 of an unsigned and undated account entitled The 11th Infantry Regiment (PA). Part I is entitled Mobilization and Training.

[32] The plan of withdrawal of the 21st Division (PA) can be reconstructed in some detail from personal papers loaned to the author and on file in OCMH. Mallonée, Bataan Diary, I, 62, 67–70;

division command post and front-line units was discontinued and signal troops began reclaiming the wire for later use. The first units to move out were the 22d Infantry and the 1st Battalion, 21st Field Artillery. Blowing the large bridges to the rear, they retired down the road toward San Carlos.

West of the Agno, the 21st Infantry began to withdraw from its beach positions at about 1900. By 2130 of Christmas Eve, division headquarters had reached its new command post on Route 13, eleven miles south of San Carlos. So quiet had the night been that Col. Ray M. O'Day, division instructor, turning on his radio to hear the midnight mass, "looked up at Heaven and could hardly believe it was a war-torn world." [33]

The withdrawal continued all through the night. By about 0400 of 25 December the bulk of the 21st Infantry had reached Aguilar and, when the sun rose, its 3d Battalion moved across the Agno in bancas to take up positions along the east-west road to San Carlos. It was not until late afternoon that the last covering units reached the D-1 line. They had been held up by delays in the destruction of many small bridges, and in one case, premature demolition of a bridge had forced the abandonment of precious vehicles. There had been no hostile contact during the withdrawal.

The rest of the North Luzon Force spent a less peaceful Christmas. The enemy, prevented from reaching the Agno on 24 December by the stiff defense of the 26th Cav-

alry, continued his efforts the next day. With Binalonan in his possession, General Tsuchibashi, the *48th Division* commander, could now split his force into two columns. One he sent south on Route 3 to Urdaneta, where the 11th Division was posted; the other went east toward Tayug. (*Map 7*) The column along Route 3 would consist of the *1st* and *2d Formosa Infantry* with the *4th Tank Regiment*. The remainder of the *48th Division* (less *1st Battalion, 47th Infantry* at Damortis), concentrated in the Pozorrubio–Binalonan area during the night of 24–25 December.[34]

At 0200 of Christmas morning, the *1st* and *2d Formosa* and the *4th Tank Regiment* moved out against Urdaneta, which was defended by elements of the 11th Division's 13th Infantry (PA). The fight lasted all morning but the Japanese proved too strong for the Filipinos and by noon had control of the town. The 11th Division then began falling back toward the Agno.[35]

Meanwhile, on the right flank of the North Luzon Force there had been a shuffling of units. The 71st Division, ordered to San Fernando, Pampanga, for reorganization, was moving out of the line. The 91st Division, with the 26th Cavalry attached, was under orders to pull back to the next line at 2100, leaving a shell on the river until dawn of the 26th. The cavalry was to hold the river line at Tayug to cover General Stevens' withdrawal and to protect the force right flank. A shell from the 91st Division, the 92d Combat Team, was to take up a

---

O'Day, 21st Div (PA), II, 10–11; Brief History of 22d Infantry (PA), p. 3; Rpt on Opns of 21st Inf (PA), 7 Dec 41–9 Apr 42, p. 2; Capt Grover C. Richards, Outline of Steps to a POW Camp, pp. 3–4; ltr, [CO, 21st Inf] to TAG PA, 30 Dec 45, sub: Opns of 21st Inf (PA), 7 Dec 41–9 Apr 42, p. 2.

[33] O'Day, 21st Div (PA), II, 11.

[34] *14th Army Opns*, I, 52–53; Answers to Questionnaire on Phil Campaign, 5 Aug 49, ATIS Doc 49692; Statement of Col Moriji Kawagoe, CofS 48th Div, in Statements of Japanese Officials on World War II, II, 126–27.

[35] *14th Army Opns*, I, 53; Col Glen R. Townsend, CO, 11th Inf (PA), Defense of the Philippines, p. 12, OCMH; O'Day, 21st Div (PA), II, 11.

VILLASIS–CARMEN BRIDGE *over the Agno River on Route 3. (Photograph taken in 1935.)*

position to Pierce's left, along the Agno as far south as Carmen.[36]

By evening of 25 December, the 11th Division, in the center, stood on the Agno River and was in its D–2 positions. Defense of Carmen and its important bridge, rebuilt by the 91st Engineer Battalion, was assigned to the 1st Battalion, 21st Infantry, in force reserve since the second week of hostilities. To its left (west) along a 2,000-yard front west of Carmen, was the 13th Infantry. The rest of the 11th Division sector, extending to Bautista, was held by the 11th Infantry. The 21st Division was on the left, the 92d Combat Team and the 26th Cavalry on the right of the D–2 line. Spread thin along the Agno River between Carmen and Route 13, a distance of twenty-five miles, was the 194th Tank Battalion (less Company C) which had reached the river at 1900 the previous night. Tank support on the right side of the line was provided by the 192d Tank Battalion, which covered the sixteen miles from Carmen to Tayug.[37]

[36] Maj William E. Chandler, An Outline History of the 26th Cavalry (PS), p. 4, OCMH; see also the same author's article, "26th Cavalry (PS) Battles to Glory," Part 2, *Armored Cavalry Journal* (May–June 1947), pp. 11–12; ltr, Selleck to Board of Officers, 1 Feb 46, sub: Reinstatement of Rank, p. 9, OCMH; unsigned account of 92d Inf (PA), p. 1, OCMH.

[37] Prov Tank Gp Rpt of Opns, p. 11; Miller, *Bataan Uncensored,* pp. 89–91; *Engineers of the Southwest Pacific 1941–1945,* Vol. I, *Engineers in Theater Operations* (Washington, 1947), p. 6 illustration, and p. 15 n. 24; NLF and I Corps Rpt of Opns, p. 8; 11th Inf (PA) Beach Defense and Delaying Action, p. 19, OCMH; ltr [CO, 21st Inf] to TAG PA, Opns 21st Inf (PA), p. 2.

AGNO RIVER *between Bayambang and Carmen. Bayambang, foreground, stretches along the southwestern bank of the river.*

Carmen

Bautista

Bayambang

When the move was completed and all of the North Luzon Force had reached D–2, General MacArthur reported to Washington, "Our position now along the Agno River." [38] Thus far, the withdrawal had proceeded satisfactorily. The Japanese had attacked at only one point and had achieved their objective, but had not disrupted the American scheme of withdrawal. Already the important bridges across the Agno, at Bayambang and Villasis, were ready for destruction.

Fight on the Agno

The D–2 line, from three to twelve miles behind the D–1 line, depended primarily on the curving Agno River for its strength. Both flanks were guarded by high ground. The two critical points on the line were Tayug and Carmen, both important road junctions. A break-through at Tayug would open the right of the North Luzon Force to a hostile flanking movement; a Japanese penetration at Carmen would split the defenses in the center. Failing to hold either of these vital points, the North Luzon Force would have to abandon its position and perhaps its plan of withdrawal.

While Wainwright was pulling back to the Agno, the Japanese had not been idle. Shortly after noon on 25 December, an advance element of Lt. Col. Kuro Kitamura's *48th Reconnaissance Regiment,* moving east from Binalonan, met patrols of the 26th Cavalry at Asingan, across the river from Tayug. By 1900 Kitamura's troops had driven the Scouts back to the river where the 2d Squadron was already in position on the opposite shore. Only the soft mud of the riverbank had prevented the Japanese tanks

from crossing immediately. The struggle continued into the night and at 0200 the next morning, when the Japanese finally reached the opposite shore, the Scouts broke off the action. By 0400 Tayug was in enemy hands. Since further opposition was futile, Colonel Pierce withdrew to the 91st Division line at Umingan, ten miles to the southeast. Blowing eight bridges between Tayug an San Quintin as it retired, the decimated 26th Cavalry passed through General Stevens' line at 0545. Later in the day, under North Luzon Force orders, it continued south toward Bataan as force reserve. [39] The Scouts had fought with great effect in the five days since the Japanese landings and had contributed in a large degree to the enemy delay. Their discipline and courageous stands at Damortis, Rosario, and Binalonan had shown that the Philippine soldier, properly trained, equipped, and led, was the equal of any.

While the *48th Reconnaissance Regiment* was attacking the 26th Cavalry at Tayug, the second of General Tsuchibashi's columns—consisting of the *2d Formosa,* a battalion of the *1st Formosa,* and the *4th Tank Regiment*—was moving due south against Carmen. During the evening of 25 December, this force entered unoccupied Villasis on Route 3, only a mile north of Carmen and the Agno River. After a preliminary air strike behind the lines by twelve planes of the *8th* and *16th Light Bombardment Regiments,* the Japanese opened the assault against Carmen, crossing the Agno near Villasis after sunset of the 26th. The *2d Formosa* and the *4th Tank Regiment,* with artillery in support, met opposition

[38] Rad, CG USAFFE to TAG, 26 Dec 41, AG 381 (11–27–41 Gen) Far East.

[39] *14th Army* Opns, I, 53; Chandler, "26th Cavalry (PS) Battles to Glory," p. 12; ltr, Maher to author, 11 Nov 49, OCMH; rads, Maj Lomuntod to USAFFE, Nos. 29 and 31, 26 Dec 41, AG 370.2 (19 Dec 41) Phil Rcds.

TARLAC RAILROAD STATION *after Japanese bombing, above; salvaging a carload of .30-caliber ammunition, below.*

from the 37-mm. guns of the 194th Tank Battalion, which, having only armor-piercing shells, was unable to hold up the Japanese advance.[40]

Late in the afternoon of the 26th, when news of the withdrawal of the 26th Cavalry on the right reached Wainwright, he ordered the 11th Division to fall back through Carmen to Route 3, then south to the D-3 line. Before the move could get under way, the Japanese shattered the 1st Battalion, 21st Infantry, at Carmen, inflicting two hundred casualties and capturing Maj. Robert Besson, the battalion commander. By 1930 Carmen was in enemy hands. The Japanese pushed on vigorously, a battalion of the *1st Formosa* striking the 92d Combat Team on the right of the 11th Division line. Two hours later the enemy was in Rosales, three miles to the east of Carmen.

With Route 3 in Japanese hands, the 11th Division was forced to fall back via the Manila Railroad, which extended along the western (left) edge of its sector. There was no other route of retreat in this area. Behind the division front was a large, roadless area covered with rice fields. The only routes leading to the rear were on the division flanks—Route 3 on the east and the Manila Railroad on the west. Swift action on the part of General Brougher in commandeering and dispatching a locomotive and several freight cars from Tarlac that night made possible the escape of the troops.[41]

The Provisional Tank Group encountered greater difficulty in withdrawing than had the infantry. Col. Ernest B. Miller, the 194th Tank Battalion commander, had told General Weaver at 1830 of the 26th that the enemy might soon cross the Agno and that there remained "nothing but the tanks to stop it." [42] Actually, the Japanese were already across the river. Weaver ordered Miller to hold at the D-2 line until 0500 the following day. The 192d Tank Battalion to the east was also ordered to hold, but Colonel Miller as the senior tank officer was authorized to withdraw both battalions sooner if Japanese action threatened to cut their line of retreat.[43]

In the 192d Tank Battalion area the tactical situation made compliance with General Weaver's order impossible. Around dusk on 26 December, Col. John H. Rodman, commanding the 92d Combat Team, informed Col. Theodore Wickord, the 192d commander, that the infantry was pulling back on the right to form a line from Carmen to Umingan. When the 92d pulled back at about 2100, Wickord's battalion also moved out. It moved east past Carmen, then south, before the Japanese could block-

[40] *14th Army Opns*, I, 53; *5th Air Gp Opns*, p. 39; Statement of Gen Kawagoe, ATIS Doc 62707, Statements of Japanese Officials on World War II, II, 128; Answers to Questionnaire on Phil Campaign, 5 Aug 49, ATIS Doc 49692; Miller, *Bataan Uncensored*, p. 95.

[41] *14th Army Opns*, I, 53; 11th Inf (PA) Beach Defense and Delaying Action, pp. 19–20, OCMH; 2d Lt Louis I. Bentz, Jr., 82d Inf (PA), p. 1, Chunn Notebooks; O'Day, 21st Div (PA), I, 4.

Brougher, Notes on Withdrawal of 11th Infantry from Agno River Position, pp. 1–2, copy in OCMH.

[42] Miller, *Bataan Uncensored*, p. 97.

[43] Prov Tank Gp Rpt of Opns, p. 11; Miller, *Bataan Uncensored*, pp. 97–98; ltr, Miller to Ward, 31 Dec 51, OCMH; Weaver, Comments on Draft MS, Comment 13, OCMH. Miller claims he was given no authority to withdraw earlier if necessary. He also claims that no holding orders were issued to the 192d. Weaver stated that his orders were given to both battalion commanders. The 192d has prepared no reports and efforts by the author to secure additional material on this question from the battalion commander have been unsuccessful. Colonel Miller intimates that General Weaver was keeping the tanks in a "rat trap." There is no direct evidence other than Colonel Miller's published statements to substantiate such a view.

ade the route of escape, and reached the D-3 line without difficulty.[44]

Meanwhile, the 194th Tank Battalion made its own way south as best it could. The tanks of Company A fought their way through a Japanese roadblock at the edge of Carmen and retreated down Route 3. Above San Manuel, about six miles south, Colonel Miller, the battalion commander, organized a roadblock with three tanks; all the others he sent to the rear. Shortly after, a single half-track with a 75-mm. gun (SPM), commanded by Capt. Gordon H. Peck, came down the road after having cut its way through the cane fields. Placing himself under Colonel Miller's orders, Peck took his place at the roadblock. At about 2300, General Brougher, the 11th Division commander, arrived at San Manuel. He explained that his division was moving back by rail and asked that the tanks cover the railroad until the Filipino troops could pass through to safety. It was finally agreed that the block would be held as long as possible before the tanks and the SPM fell back five miles to Moncada, where the railroad crossed Route 3. The troop trains carrying the 11th Division were expected to pass through that town at 0400 on 27 December.[45]

All was quiet at the roadblock until a few hours before dawn. At about 0245, after the last stragglers had cleared the block, a Japanese armored column, apparently advance elements of the *4th Tank Regiment,* reached the spot. Fire from the American tanks and

SPM's swept the highway and adjoining ditches. The Japanese were taken completely by surprise and after fifteen minutes pulled back. Fearing encirclement by Japanese infantry, Miller and Peck then struck out for Moncada.[46]

The tanks and the SPM that had formed the roadblock moved slowly down Route 3 in the dark hours before dawn. They reached the rail crossing in Moncada only a scant ten minutes before the 11th Division troop trains entered the town. Once the trains had cleared the danger point, Colonel Miller continued his march south and reached the D-3 line at Gerona at about 0830 on the morning of 27 December. Here he was joined by the survivors of the battalion's Company D. Cut off from retreat, the company had come south along an old carabao cart trail, the Manila Railroad tracks, and Route 3. It found the bridge just below Moncada destroyed and was forced to leave its fifteen tanks north of the stream. This decision had been made in the hope that some of the men could return later with guides and bring the tanks south. This expectation could not be fulfilled and the tanks were lost for the rest of the campaign.[47]

---

[44] Prov Tank Gp Rpt of Opns, p. 12; ltr, Weaver to Wainwright, 20 Nov 45, OCMH; Miller, *Bataan Uncensored,* p. 98.

[45] Miller, *Bataan Uncensored,* pp. 97–102; GO 10, Hq Prov Tank Gp in the Field, 14 Feb 42, copy given the author by General Weaver and on file in OCMH. Prov Tank Gp Rpt of Opns, p. 12; ltr, Miller to Ward, 31 Dec 51, OCMH; Weaver, Comments on Draft MS, Comment 14, OCMH.

[46] Miller, *Bataan Uncensored,* pp. 102–03; GO's 5 and 10, Hq Prov Tank Gp in the Field, 13 Jan and 14 Feb 42.

[47] Miller, *Bataan Uncensored,* pp. 103–04, 108–09; Prov Tank Gp Rpt of Opns, p. 12; Capt Jack C. Altman, 194th Tank Bn, p. 3, Chunn Notebooks; Weaver, Comments on Draft MS, Comment 15, OCMH. During an interrogation at the end of the war General Homma stated that the *9th Infantry* had reported the capture of twenty-three tanks stranded north of a river above Paniqui after the bridge had been blown. Interv, Col Walter E. Buchly with Homma, Manila, Mar 46, copy in OCMH.

There was an investigation of the blowing of the bridge and the loss of the tanks in prison camps in Formosa and Manchuria in 1944 and 1945. It was

The D–3 Line

Approximately forty miles in length, the D–3 line stretched across the Luzon central plain midway between Lingayen Gulf and San Fernando, Pampanga, from a point just west of Santa Ignacia on Route 13 to San Jose in Nueva Ecija Province, at the junction of Routes 5 and 8. Deployed along this line were the 91st, 11th, and 21st Divisions (PA), supported by the Provisional Tank Group and the 75-mm. guns (SPM).

The right (east) flank, resting on the foothills of the Sierra Madre, was held by the 91st Division which had taken up positions across Route 5 and on the south bank of a small river in the vicinity of San Jose.[48] Between Route 5 and Gerona on Route 3 were the 11th Division and the bulk of the Tank Group—the 194th at Gerona and the 192d to its right. The 21st Division, whose two columns had reunited at Camiling, was in position between Gerona and Santa Ignacia at the edge of the Zambales Mountains.[49]

Despite occasional alarms there was no action on the D–3 line on 27 December. That night the North Luzon Force made ready to fall back to the D–4 line. The 91st Division began pulling out at about 1730 and by 0430 had reached the south bank

of the Pampanga a few thousand yards below Cabanatuan. Two hours later the entire unit was ordered into the line between Cabanatuan and Carmen, Nueva Ecija, a barrio on the road ten miles west of Cabanatuan and not to be confused with the village of the same name on the Agno. At Carmen the 91st Division tied in with units of the 11th Infantry that had withdrawn from the D–3 line during the night and were deployed from Carmen west to La Paz. The 21st Division stood on the left of the 11th Division, extending the line to Tarlac, where Route 13 joined Route 3 and the main track of the Manila Railroad. The tanks were in general support.

On the Agno River the Japanese halted to consolidate their position and bring up more troops. During the 27th, artillery, armor, and service troops moved forward to join the *48th Division*. The *47th Infantry* and a battalion of artillery, in reserve near Pozorrubio since 24 December, together with the *7th Tank Regiment*, were dispatched to Tayug. Infantry and artillery units occupied San Quintin to the south and patrols pushed forward into undefended Umingan. On the *48th Division* right (west), the *1st Formosa* consolidated its hold on Rosales. One battalion of the regiment remained at Urdaneta, and another went on to Carmen to relieve Colonel Tanaka's troops who then moved back across the Agno to Villasis for rest.[50]

By 28 December the North Luzon Force was on the D–4 line. In the face of a well-trained and better equipped enemy, it had fulfilled its mission—to hold the Agno line until the night of 26–27 December and to withdraw to the Tarlac–Cabanatuan line. Now, from positions along this line, the

---

then shown that Company D had reached the Moncada bridge fifteen hours after the last tanks of its battalion headquarters and fourteen hours after the last infantry elements had crossed. No tank guides from either Company A or Battalion Headquarters, 194th Tank Battalion, had been left behind to direct the withdrawal of Company D. Comments of Col Skerry on Draft MS, Comment 4, OCMH.

[48] Bentz, 92d Inf (PA), pp. 1–2, Chunn Notebooks.

[49] O'Day, 21st Div (PA), II, 12; Mallonée, Bataan Diary, I, 82; Miller, *Bataan Uncensored*, p. 107; Weaver, Comments on Draft MS, Comment 16, OCMH.

---

[50] *14th Army Opns*, I, 50, 53–54.

troops in North Luzon awaited the next attack.

Supply

As the front-line units moved back, the troops to the rear began to carry out the supply plan. On 24 December General MacArthur's headquarters had ordered the evacuation of Fort Stotsenburg and the destruction of its 300,000 gallons of gasoline and large amounts of high octane fuel. Lt. Col. Wallace E. Durst, Post Quartermaster, was able to save about 50,000 gallons of gas by shipping some of it to the rear and issuing the rest to vehicles in the immediate area. "No material amount of gasoline," reported Durst's assistant, Lt. Col. Irvin Alexander, "was abandoned to the enemy."[51] In addition to gasoline, Stotsenburg stocks included 8,000 pounds of fresh beef, about 100,000 components of dry rations, large supplies of clothing, and air corps ammunition and equipment. When the post was finally abandoned, almost nothing of value was left, according to Colonel Alexander. All supplies, he said, had been shipped to Bataan or issued to troops in the Stotsenburg area.[52]

The evacuation of Fort Stotsenburg long before the approach of enemy forces, aroused much criticism from officers who disagreed sharply with Colonel Alexander's optimistic statements on the amount of supplies saved. Colonel Collier exaggeratedly described the evacuation of Stotsenburg as a "frenzied departure" in which "warehouses filled with food, clothing, and other military supplies were left intact." Also left behind, he reported, were 250,000 gallons of gasoline and several obsolete but serviceable planes.[53] General Drake, MacArthur's quartermaster, reported that only a portion of the reserve supplies stocked at Stotsenburg had been removed before its evacuation.[54]

On the afternoon of 25 December, as North Luzon Force fell back to the D–2 line, Lt. Col. Charles S. Lawrence, commanding the Tarlac Depot, had informed Drake that evacuation of the depot would be necessary very soon. In the absence of orders to the contrary, he said, he would issue all his supplies, including five days' subsistence for the North Luzon Force, at one time and head for Bataan with his men.[55] That night he learned from Lt. Col. Gyles Merrill, Wainwright's supply officer, that the line through Tarlac would be occupied on the night of 27 December. Merrill suggested that Lawrence place his remaining rations in dumps at Tarlac, to be picked up by the troops as they withdrew. With Wainwright's approval Lawrence placed the supplies in separate dumps, one for each division or separate unit. Troops of the 21st Division Headquarters Company were posted as guards.

---

[51] Col Alexander, Narrative Rpt of QM Activities at Fort Stotsenburg, pp. 1–2, App. A to QM Rpt of Opns.

[52] *Ibid.*, pp. 2–3; Col Alexander, Personal Recollections of Bataan and Later, pp. 48–50, copy in OCMH.

[53] Collier, Notebooks, II, 84; III, 2. See also ltr, Lt Col John E. Olson to author, 10 Jan 52, OCMH. In his comments on this manuscript, Colonel Alexander insisted that the supplies had been evacuated and that nothing was left behind. Ltr, Alexander to Ward, 25 Dec 51, OCMH.

[54] QM Rpt of Opns, p. 22; see also Mallonée, Bataan Diary, I, 108; O'Day, 21st Div, I, 12–13; Drake, Comments on Draft MS, Comment 8, OCMH.

[55] Col Lawrence, Tarlac Advance QM Depot Rpt of Opns, p. 6, App. A to QM Rpt of Opns.

This done, Lawrence and his men left for Bataan.[56]

The evacuation of Stotsenburg and Tarlac was typical of the hurried movement of supplies once the plan of withdrawal had gone into effect. "The troops withdrew so fast," reported General Drake, "that we could not put into operation any of our withdrawal plans to cover this movement." [57] There was scarcely time to remove "a few defense reserve supplies" from McKinley and Stotsenburg and no time to evacuate the depots established before the war at Tarlac and Los Banos. Fortunately, many of the supplies left behind were picked up by the units as they withdrew, and much of the remainder was destroyed.

Closely related to the difficulty of supply and evacuation was the scarcity of motor vehicles on Luzon. Even the addition of civilian vehicles did not solve this problem. "The fact is," wrote Colonel Lawrence, "that there was not sufficient motor equipment in the Philippines to begin to meet fully all the requirements." [58] This shortage was made more serious by the failure of commanders to return the vehicles which brought their supplies. Even more reprehensible was the hijacking and commandeering of vehicles along the highways, often by commanders who feared that they would not have the transportation to move their troops and equipment in an emergency. These practices "resulted in confusion and caused a complete interruption in motor transport service during the period of evacuation of supplies to Bataan." [59]

The Tarlac–Cabanatuan Line

The original plan of withdrawal called for only a brief halt at the D–4 line, just long enough to force the enemy to stop and prepare for a co-ordinated attack. A determined stand would be made on the D–5 line. On 27 December General Wainwright changed this plan. Fearing that a quick withdrawal from D–4 would leave too little margin for error between his last defensive line and the vital bridges across the Pampanga River at Calumpit, over which the South Luzon Force would have to pass, he decided to hold at Tarlac and Cabanatuan, the D–4 line. Late that night he issued new orders to his North Luzon Force abandoning D–5 as the final line of defense. "D–4 will be held at all costs until ordered withdrawn," he announced. "Maximum delay will be effected on each position. Withdrawal plan later." [60]

The final plan for holding the D–4 line and for the withdrawal to follow utilized the existing deployment of units already on the line. The 91st Division was assigned the eastern edge of the central plain, the zone between the Pampanga River, which paralleled Route 5, and the mountains to the east. The critical point in this sector was Cabanatuan, where the roads from the north converged into Route 5 which led south toward Manila. When ordered to withdraw, the division would move down Route 5 to Plaridel, a distance of forty-five miles, thence west to Calumpit where Route 3 crossed the Pampanga River.

---

[56] *Ibid.*

[57] Qm Rpt of Opns, p. 22.

[58] Lawrence, Tarlac Advance QM Depot Rpt of Opns, pp. 7–8, App. A to QM Rpt of Opns.

[59] QM Rpt of Opns, p. 66.

[60] This order is quoted in Mallonée, Bataan Diary, I, 90. See also O'Day, 21st Div (PA), II, 12. The author has been unable to find the original of this order. It is entirely possible that the change in mission of North Luzon Force was initiated by MacArthur's headquarters.

The 11th Division was on the left of the 91st, in the area between Carmen and Route 3. It was to retire along the secondary roads in its sector. The 21st Division was on the western edge of the central plain, covering Tarlac and Route 3. Its line of retreat was along Route 3 to Angeles, thence to Bataan by Route 74.[61] As a further protection to the Calumpit bridges and the South Luzon Force route of withdrawal, the 194th Tank Battalion, reduced to twenty tanks, was pulled out of the D–4 line by MacArthur's headquarters on the 29th and ordered back to Apalit, three miles northwest of Calumpit, to a position of readiness. The day before, Company A of the 192d had been shifted from the 91st Division sector to the area west of the Pampanga and now, with a platoon of the 194th, formed the only tank support between the Pampanga and Route 3. The rest of Colonel Wickord's battalion remained in position east of the Pampanga, in support of the 91st Division.[62]

When all units were on the line, General MacArthur reported to the War Department that he was "endeavoring to temporarily hold hard in the north" until the North and South Luzon Forces could join at San Fernando after which he would "pivot on my left into Bataan." American and Filipino troops were "tired but well in hand." In this report, MacArthur mistakenly estimated that his North Luzon Force alone was facing three Japanese divisions. These enemy troops, he pointed out, were excellent, and their equipment "modern and extensive." Although the Japanese were not then exerting heavy pressure against his line, MacArthur believed that this inactivity would soon end. The enemy, he warned, was "undoubtedly setting up a powerful attack both north and south simultaneously designed to pin me down in place and crush me." [63]

General MacArthur's estimate of the enemy's intentions was correct. The arrival of the 48th Division at the Agno River had completed the landing phase of the operation. General Homma was now ready to drive on through Cabanatuan and Tarlac to Manila.

As of noon, 27 December, the North Luzon Force position seemed to the Japanese to favor a rapid advance. American air power had been knocked out and the Philippine garrison was effectively cut off from reinforcement. Three of the divisions which had opposed their landings, the 11th, 71st, and 91st, as well as armor and cavalry, the Japanese believed, had suffered decisive defeats. The Japanese were also aware of General MacArthur's move to Corregidor and of the transfer of at least one division— the 31st—to Bataan. On the basis of his intelligence estimate General Homma reasoned correctly that MacArthur planned a delaying action "in one corner of Bataan" and on Corregidor.[64]

Despite this correct evaluation of American intentions, the consensus in the 14th Army staff was for a continuation of the drive on Manila. The mission assigned by Imperial General Headquarters was to take Manila, and it is doubtful that Army had the authority to divert any of its forces from that mission. As Lt. Col. Yoshio Nakajima, 14th Army intelligence officer, wrote: "Since the mission of the 14th Army was to occupy Manila, the main force proceeded

---

[61] NLF and II Corps Rpt of Opns, p. 12.
[62] Prov Tank Gp Rpt of Opns, p. 13; Miller, Bataan Uncensored, p. 111.

[63] Rad, CG USAFFE to TAG, 28 Dec 41, AG 381 (11–27–41 Gen) Far East.
[64] 14th Army Opns, I, 55–56.

to that city." [65] Some even felt that, since Manila was the main objective, the withdrawal to Bataan "expedited the completion of our mission." [66]

The plan finally adopted for the advance from the Agno River utilized one division, reinforced, supported by armor and aircraft. The main effort was to be made on the east, along Route 5, and the immediate objective was Cabanatuan. The *48th Division* would jump off from the Agno River on the 28th and advance toward that town. Simultaneously, the *Kamijima Detachment,* consisting of elements of the *9th Infantry* and supporting artillery, would move from its positions along the Lingayen coast to Carmen to protect the right flank of the *48th Division.* From there it would presumably advance down Route 3 toward Tarlac. The only concession made to the obvious American withdrawal to Bataan was to order General Tsuchibashi to send an infantry regiment with heavy artillery support to Tarlac to assist the *9th Infantry* in its effort to move speedily down the central plain and seize the road net leading into the peninsula. Supporting the *48th Division* advance were the *4th* and *7th Tank Regiments, 14th Army* artillery, and the *5th Air Group.*[67]

Threat on the East

The key to the right flank of the D–4 line was Cabanatuan. Situated on the banks of the Pampanga River, the town is an important road junction on Route 5. The river, about 100 yards wide at this point, and unfordable by motor vehicles, flows

swiftly in its twisting and irregular course. Approaching Cabanatuan from the mountains to the northeast, the Pampanga passes the town about 3,000 yards to the north then turns sharply south to flow west of the town and continue its errant way in a southwesterly direction toward Manila Bay. At Cabanatuan two bridges span the swiftly flowing river: one to the north and another to the west. It was in the general vicinity of these bridges that the Japanese first attacked the D–4 line.

The *14th Army* advance from the Agno began on schedule on the morning of 28 December, at the same time that General Homma moved his command post to Binalonan. In the lead were the *4th* and *7th Tank Regiments,* a battalion of the *2d Formosa,* and a battalion of the *48th Mountain Artillery* which advanced through San Quintin to San Jose. From there, they struck southeast, crossed the Pampanga at Rizal, and by 29 December had reached Bongabon, in position to threaten the right flank of the D–4 line.

The *48th Division* followed in two columns. The west column, consisting of the *1st Formosa* supported by a battalion of artillery, left Rosales before dawn of the 29th and marched southeast through Guimba, then east to Baloc on Route 5, north of Cabanatuan. The east column, consisting of the *2d Formosa, 47th Infantry, 48th Reconnaissance,* and artillery and engineer units, followed behind the tank regiments to San Jose, where Route 5 intersected Route 8, and then followed the former toward Cabanatuan.[68]

At Cabanatuan, the main strength of the 91st Division, the 92d Combat Team,

[65] Interrog of Col Nakajima, 25 Apr 47, Interrogations of Former Japanese Officers, I, Mil Hist Div, GHQ FEC.
[66] Interrog of Col Motoo Nakayama, Apr 47, *ibid.*
[67] *Ibid.; 14th Army* Opns, I, 56–57, 61–64.

[68] *14th Army* Opns, I, 60–61, 83; Statement of Gen Kawagoe, ATIS Doc 62707, Statements of Japanese Officials on World War II, pp. 128–30.

waited for the attack. In and around the town were the 2d and 3d Battalions, and to the left extending to the Pampanga, was the 1st Battalion. Both bridges had been blown and were considered impassable for wheeled traffic, but not for foot troops. Moreover, the river was fordable north of Cabanatuan.[69] On the morning of 29 December, the left (east) column of the *48th Division* reached the Pampanga northwest of Cabanatuan, but it was the tanks, driving down from Bongabon, that reached the town first. As the tankers approached, the *47th Infantry*, under cover of an artillery bombardment, began crossing the river. It was now late in the afternoon, and the 92d Combat Team, outflanked and faced by a superior enemy, fell back. That night the Japanese entered Cabanatuan.[70]

The Japanese did not stop at Cabanatuan. Led by Maj. Gen. Koichi Abe, *48th Division* infantry group commander, they continued south along Route 5 on 30 December. Followed by two battalions of the *48th Mountain Artillery* and a battalion of 150-mm. howitzers of the *1st Field Heavy Artillery Regiment,* the *47th Infantry* pursued the withdrawing 91st Division toward Gapan, about fourteen miles below Cabanatuan. Just north of that village the defenders crossed the Penaranda River, destroying the steel highway bridge over that stream. Urged on by Lt. Louis I.

Bentz, Jr., about sixty-five Filipinos of the 92d Infantry formed a line along the south bank of the river, while the remainder of regiment, bolstered by three hundred high school ROTC boys who had arrived that morning from Manila, occupied a mile-long line from the village west to the Pampanga. The *47th Infantry* hit this line late in the afternoon and broke through with little difficulty. By nightfall the enemy had entered the town. The remnants of the 91st Division withdrew toward Baliuag, twenty-five miles south on Route 5, where they planned to reorganize.

The rapid advance of the Japanese along Route 5 jeopardized the American right and resulted in a shortening of the D–5 line. The North Luzon Force right flank would now have to be anchored on Mt. Arayat, west of Route 5, instead of Sibul Springs to the east. Route 5 lay open and the enemy was well on his way toward the Calumpit area. Unless he was held, the withdrawal of the South Luzon Force would be threatened.

Advance in the Center

The center of the D–4 line, from the Pampanga to Tarlac, was held by the 11th Division. Paralleling the front was an east-west road. The critical points in the line were Zaragoza and La Paz, held by the 11th Infantry. The 2d Battalion was in front of La Paz, the 3d Battalion to the east above Zaragoza, and the 1st Battalion in reserve about 5,000 yards to the south. Company A, 192d Tank Battalion, was in general support near Zaragoza. The only route of withdrawal was down a secondary road from La Paz to Concepcion, about thirteen miles, then west to Route 3.

In the initial deployment of the 11th Infantry no provision had been made for

[69] Bentz, 92d Inf (PA), p. 2, Chunn Notebooks; Skerry, Comments on Draft MS, Comment 6, OCMH. The 192d Tank Battalion was in the area, but there is no information on its position or employment at this time.

[70] The American sources for this action are sketchy and vague as to times and places. Where doubts exist or where the records are irreconcilable, the Japanese account of the action has been used. *14th Army* Opns, I, 63, 83. Ltr, Luther R. Stevens to Capt Edwin B. Kerr, 30 Dec 52; ltr, Col John H. Rodman to Maj Gen Orlando Ward, 1 Feb 52, both in OCMH.

guarding the eastern entrance to the critical east-west road which ran behind the line. The 92d Infantry on the right was supposed to protect that flank, but Maj. Russel W. Volckmann, acting 11th Infantry commander, was uneasy about this arrangement. Recognizing the importance of the road and the vulnerability of his position he shifted his line so that troops of his 3d Battalion were in position to guard the road. A roadblock was established on the west side of the bridge across the Dalagot River, leading into Zaragoza, and a platoon of tanks placed in position there. The bridge was prepared for demolition, but the river was easily fordable by foot troops. The organization of the roadblock was a wise precaution, for the Tarlac–Cabanatuan road had already been exposed on the east by the withdrawal of the 91st Division.[71]

The assault against the 11th Division was made by the *Kanno Detachment,* consisting of the *3d Battalion, 2d Formosa,* supported by a battalion of the *48th Mountain Artillery,* substantially the same force which had landed at Vigan on 10 December. This force was the one which General Tsuchibashi had assigned to assist the *Kamijima Detachment* in its drive toward San Fernando. Its mission was to move south along Route 5 to Cabanatuan, then push west to outflank Tarlac, which Colonel Kamijima was approaching from the north. This maneuver would cover the right flank of the *48th Division* and, if executed speedily and successfully, would turn the North Luzon

line and cut off the retreat of the American troops in the center.[72]

The *Kanno Detachment* jumped off from Talevera, north of Cabanatuan, at 0100 on 30 December. Preceded by bicycle-mounted infantry, the unit cleared Cabanatuan, already in Japanese hands, shortly after and pushed on along the Cabanatuan-Tarlac road, disregarding security measures. At 0315 an alert tanker of the 192d Tank Battalion observed a large number of cyclists in column approaching Zaragoza. When the Japanese reached the American position they were greeted by point-blank fire from the alerted tanks. At the mercy of the tanks, the cyclists lost an estimated eighty-two men before they could make their escape.

It was still dark when the action ended. The tank commander, fearing infiltration by enemy infantry, withdrew his platoon across the Zaragoza bridge, then insisted that the bridge be blown though the 11th Infantry troops were still on the other side. The commander of the engineer detachment had no choice but to comply and lit the time fuses. So surprised was the troop commander when the bridge was blown that he ordered an investigation immediately and incorrectly concluded

. . . that the engineer lieutenant had left the destruction of the bridge to his platoon sergeant and departed for the rear. The platoon sergeant detailed a private and departed with the rest of the men. The private, not to be outdone, had found a civilian, instructed him how to light the dynamite, paid him one peso and then left to join his platoon. The civilian, after hearing the shooting, became excited and blew the bridge.[73]

---

[71] Interv, author with Col Volckmann, May 48; Maj W. J. Lage, Opns of 3d Bn, 11th Inf (PA) at Zaragoza, 28–29 Dec 41 (paper prepared for Advanced Infantry Officers Course, 1947–48, The Infantry School) ; Weaver, Comments on Draft MS, Comments 18 and 19, OCMH. Major Lage's account is one day off, and the author has made necessary corrections.

[72] *14th Army* Opns, I, 83.

[73] Lage, Opns of 3d Bn, 11th Inf (PA), p. 16. Another explanation of these events is to be found in the report of the 11th Engineer Battalion, a portion of which is quoted in Skerry, Comments on Draft MS, Comment 10, OCMH.

BICYCLE-MOUNTED JAPANESE TROOPS

The premature destruction of the bridge took the tanks out of the action and left the infantry, still on the far side of the shallow river, without the support of the armor.

When daylight came the *Kanno Detachment* struck the roadblock with heavy rifle and mortar fire. Part of the detachment had swung around to the north and now began to exert pressure from that direction. Fearing that his battalion might be outflanked, the commander pulled his men back across the river. By noon, they were established in positions along the west bank. Despite heavy casualties and the presence of a strong hostile patrol above La Paz, the battalion commander felt he could hold the enemy at the river line.

Shortly after noon the Japanese artillery opened fire against the 3d Battalion, pre-

paratory to an infantry attack. After a twenty-minute barrage by 75-mm. guns of the *48th Mountain Artillery*, the *Kanno Detachment* began to cross the river. Unable to halt the enemy, the 3d Battalion moved west along the Zaragoza–La Paz road. Colonel Kanno brought his men safely across, then halted the advance until he could get his heavier weapons across the river. The 3d Battalion, about 500 yards to the west and supported by tanks, awaited the attack. At 1415 a Japanese antitank gun moved into the Japanese line and directed its fire against the Americans. It was finally knocked out, but only after it had destroyed the lead American tank.

With the lead tank gone and their location known to the enemy, the tanks began to pull back. Since they were not under 11th

Infantry control, there was no way to keep them in position. The Japanese immediately unleashed a heavy barrage, threatening the American positions. Major Volckmann, who was on the scene, organized a counterattack with the battalion reserve. The counterattack opened at 1500 and, although no ground was gained, it evidently surprised the Japanese and led them to believe the defenders were stronger than they actually were. When the Japanese fire slackened, the 3d Battalion withdrew again, this time about 1,500 yards to the west along the La Paz road. By 1360 the men were in their new positions.

No sooner had the 3d Battalion taken up its new position than it received orders to pull back. These orders originated in Wainwright's headquarters, where it had become apparent during the day that the entire line was threatened by the *48th Division's* breakthrough at Cabanatuan. Division commanders were ordered to pull back to the D–5 line. General Brougher, accordingly, directed his men holding the center of the line to withdraw through La Paz to Concepcion. The 11th Infantry immediately began to assemble at La Paz. By 1730 the 3d Battalion had fallen back across the bridge just east of that point, the remainder of the regiment retiring before it. When all the troops were across, the bridge was destroyed. At this moment the *Kanno Detachment* appeared along the Zaragoza road and was met with machine gun fire. With its rear momentarily secure, the battalion retired toward the D–5 line.

Of the 550 men of the 3d Battalion only 156 remained. Many of these were wounded. But the Japanese had been stopped effectively. By delaying Kanno for twenty-four hours, the 3d Battalion had prevented him from reaching Tarlac on 30

December in time to join in the attack on that town. It had thus frustrated a maneuver which might well have turned the left anchor of the North Luzon Force line.

Fight on the West

At the western end of the D–4 line stood the ruined city of Tarlac, its streets a shambles from the repeated strikes of enemy bombers. Just south of the city, the 21st Division, as yet untried in battle, awaited the advance of the Japanese. On the gently sloping ground to the west was the 21st Infantry guarding the bridge where Route 13 crossed the Tarlac River. The 22d Infantry, on its right, straddled Route 3. In reserve was the 23d Infantry, eight miles south of Tarlac at Santa Rosa. The terrain, except for the area in which the 21st was deployed, was low and level, consisting largely of rice fields and offering little opportunity for cover. The infantry derived what protection it could from dry cornstalks, bamboo trees, and swamps. The only consolation the rifleman could draw from his position was that he had a clear field of fire.[74]

The *Kamijima Detachment*, which was assigned the mission of assaulting Tarlac, had shown a curious reluctance to advance below the Agno River. Heavy casualties during the landings had made Colonel Kamijima, in the words of *14th Army* Chief of Staff Maeda, "very cautious." [75] Such reluctance might well expose the right

---

[74] O'Day, 21st Div (PA), II, 12–13; ltr, [CO, 21st Inf] to TAG PA, Opns of 21st Inf (PA), p. 2; Brief Hist of 22d Inf (PA), p. 3; Hist of 21st Div (PA), pp. 18–19. This last document was obtained from General Capinpin and like the others is on file in OCMH.
[75] Interrog of Gen Maeda, 10 May 47, Interrogations of Former Japanese Officers, Mil Hist Div, GHQ FEC, I.

(west) flank of *48th Division,* and General Maeda, whose interest in Bataan had led him to emphasize the importance of the advance on Tarlac, took steps to correct the situation. He reprimanded Kamijima for his excessive caution and ordered him to move across the Agno.[76]

By 29 December the *Kamijima Detachment* had apparently progressed to a point just north of Tarlac. On that day the 3d Battalion, 21st Infantry, reported that it had been fired on by Japanese patrols. The 23d Infantry was ordered to reconnoiter and organize a position along the high ground between Santa Rosa and San Miguel, east of Route 3. At the same time the rear of the 22d Infantry was strengthened. That night the men of the 22d found occasion to open fire against Japanese patrols. Their fire was not returned, and it is possible that the imagination of the men in combat for the first time was responsible for the many Japanese patrols reported south of Tarlac.[77]

Shortly after noon of the 30th, advance elements of the *9th Infantry* led by Colonel Kamijima himself entered Tarlac. With only two companies of infantry Kamijima refused to push on. At about 1500 the remainder of the *9th Infantry* (less the *3d Battalion*) and the two batteries of the *22d Field Artillery* reached the area. Thus reinforced, Colonel Kamijima felt strong enough to attack and sent his men against the 22d Infantry positions along Route 3. The defenders held firm, inflicting severe losses on the *9th Infantry* and killing Colonel Kamijima himself.[78]

During the course of the action, the 22d Infantry noted a number of men advancing down the road from Tarlac. These men were first thought to be 13th Infantry troops retiring from positions east of the city, but just before they reached the stream in front of the American line they were identified as enemy troops and fired upon. A few minutes later, five American tanks and two SPM's broke out of Tarlac and fought their way down toward the stream. Their retreat had been cut off by Colonel Kanno's advance along the Cabanatuan–Tarlac road, and after much difficulty they had pushed their way through enemy-held Tarlac. The 21st Division troops recognized the tanks and half-track and furnished them with artillery support in their flight to the stream. But here they met an insuperable obstacle and the men had to abandon their vehicles. With the exception of one crew whose tank was hit, all the men reached the 21st Division lines safely. Attempts to rescue the vehicles were unsuccessful and the artillery was ordered to destroy them.[79]

Late in the afternoon the 21st Division received orders to withdraw under cover of darkness to the D–5 line. That evening units began moving out of their D–4 positions. Pressure on the 22d Infantry had died down, but now the 21st Infantry came under heavy attack. As the division pulled back, this regiment supported by the 3d Battalion, 21st Field Artillery, covered the withdrawal alone. During the fight the 21st Infantry received many casualties and was badly battered. Finally, still intact but greatly weakened, the regiment began to pull back. The artillery battalion remained

[76] *Ibid.; 14th Army* Opns, I, 60–61.
[77] O'Day, 21st Div (PA), II, 13; Richards, Steps to a POW Camp, p. 6.
[78] *14th Army* Opns, I, 63; Interrog of Gen Maeda, 10 May 47, Interrogations of Former Japanese Officers, Mil Hist Div, GHQ FEC, I; USA *vs.* Homma, p. 3055; Mallonée, Diary, I, 100; Brief Hist of 22d Inf (PA), p. 3.
[79] Mallonée, Bataan Diary, I, 101–02; O'Day, 21st Div (PA), II, 13–14; separate, unsigned one-page history, entitled 194th Tank Battalion, OCMH; Miller, *Bataan Uncensored,* p. 111. The identity of the tanks is not clear in the sources.

in position to cover the infantry's withdrawal. Long after its scheduled hour of retirement, the artillerymen, led by their American instructor, 1st Lt. Carl J. Savoie, continued to fire.

To the rear the division covering force waited impatiently and anxiously for the 3d Battalion to pass through its line. When the trucks and guns of the battalion finally came down the road, Colonel Mallonée noted that the men "were tired, worn, hungry—but cocky, proud, aggressive." [80] They had good reason to feel cocky. The battalion, unaided, had held up the Japanese advance and made possible the successful withdrawal of the 21st Infantry.

". . . every man of the 21st Infantry who came out of Tarlac . . . alive should get down on his knees and thank God for that redheaded son of a bitch [Savoie]. He was everywhere he was needed at the right time. . . . He kept the guns in almost three hours after he could have withdrawn to give us a chance to break off. We were all out and the enemy back into Tarlac before he pulled up a gun." [81]

By dawn, 31 December, the 21st Division was on the D–5 line. The 21st Infantry at Bamban, fifteen miles south of Tarlac, was here joined by its 1st Battalion. This battalion had been detached and placed in North Luzon Force reserve earlier and had seen action on the Agno line in the fighting around Carmen. The Japanese *9th Infantry* was also reinforced when its *3d Battalion* caught up with the rest of the regiment. The enemy force at Tarlac was further strengthened on the 31st by the arrival of the *Kanno Detachment* and by Lt. Col.

Katsumi Takahashi's *8th Field Heavy Artillery Regiment.* This greatly increased Japanese force spent the day preparing to push south along Route 3.[82]

In the brief period of seven days, from Christmas Eve to the year's end, there had been a radical change in the situation in northern Luzon. The Japanese, who on 24 December had just secured their beachhead, now threatened Manila and the road net into Bataan. The enemy had broken out of his initial lodgment and was now moving rapidly in two columns down the broad central plain of Luzon.

The North Luzon Force had withdrawn approximately fifty miles from its first defense line to its D–5 positions at Bamban and Arayat. The left and center had retired with moderate success, but the right flank was in grave danger. On that flank, General Homma had placed the main strength of the *48th Division* supported by two regiments of tanks and increasing amounts of artillery and other supporting arms. Should the right flank give way, the withdrawal of the South Luzon Force to Bataan might well be imperiled.

The first part of the withdrawal had been completed. Although it had been successful, there had been difficult moments. Communications had broken down at times, supply had proved difficult, and some of the bridges had been blown too soon. The defense lines had sometimes been hastily and inadequately manned, or not occupied at all. "Not a single position," wrote the assistant G–3 of USAFFE, "was really occupied and organized for defense. Troops were barely stopped and assigned defensive sec-

[80] Mallonée, Bataan Diary, I, 105; O'Day, 21st Div (PA), II, 14.
[81] Mallonée Bataan Diary, I, 105, quoting Lt Col William A. Wappenstein, CO, 21st Infantry.
[82] 14th Army Opns, I, 64.

tors before they stampeded into farther withdrawal, in many instances without firing a shot." [83] This view portrays the withdrawal at its worst. Not all troops stampeded, and there were numerous instances of heroism under fire and determined stands. For the most part, the withdrawal was conducted as well as it could be with the untrained and ill-equipped Philippine Army troops.

---

[83] Collier, Notebooks, II, 83.

CHAPTER XI

Withdrawal in the South

The withdrawal of the American and Philippine troops south of Manila began at the same time that General Wainwright's forces evacuated the D–1 line. At about 1000, 24 December, General Parker had turned over command of the South Luzon Force to General Jones and left for Bataan. Jones, who retained command of the 51st Division (PA), inherited four American officers from Parker's staff. It was fortunate that he did, for there were none on his division staff.[1]

Jones' orders when he assumed command of the South Luzon Force were to "block the enemy advance" and, "when forced to do so," withdraw past the open city of Manila and join Wainwright's forces north of the city.[2] While USAFFE orders directed General Jones to "harass and delay to the utmost the advance of the enemy," they made clear that his primary mission was to get his troops out of south Luzon and into Bataan.[3]

The force under General Jones's command was much smaller than Wainwright's North Luzon Force. It consisted primarily of the 1st Infantry of the 1st Division (PA) and the inadequately trained and poorly equipped 51st Division (PA), which had for its artillery component only one battalion of eight British 75's. The 42d Infantry, 41st Division (PA), was assigned to beach defense on the west side of the island. The rest of the division had gone with General Parker to Bataan. Artillery support for the South Luzon Force was provided by the three batteries of 155-mm. GPF's of the 86th Field Artillery, defending the beaches in southwest Luzon, and three batteries of 75-mm. guns (SPM) organized into the 2d Provisional Group.[4] Armored support was limited to one company—Company C of the 194th Tank Battalion—detached from the parent organization with the North Luzon Force.

The Japanese force in south Luzon was numerically smaller than the composite American and Philippine force defending the area. Drawn from the *16th Division* and led by the division commander, Lt. Gen. Susumu Morioka, it consisted of the *20th Infantry*, the *16th Reconnaissance Regiment*, and supporting arms and services.

---

[1] Interv, author with Jones, 25 Oct 49, OCMH; Jones, Diary, p. 10; ltr, Parker to Ward, 16 Jan 52, OCMH; USAFFE-USFIP Rpt of Opns, p. 33.

[2] Opns Orders, USAFFE to CG 51st Div, 24 Dec 41, AG 381, Phil Rcds.

[3] Quoted in Diary of Lt Col Arthur L. Shreve, Arty Officer, SLF, p. 10, copy lent to author and on file in OCMH; interv, Stanley Falk, research asst to author, with Jones, 15 Dec 49. General R. J. Marshall, in a letter to the author, states that the "final evacuation of the headquarters in Manila and cessation of transfer of supplies was governed by the length of time that the South Luzon Force was able to delay the approach of the Japanese." Ltr, Marshall to author, 31 Oct 49, OCMH.

---

[4] The 155-mm. GPF batteries had two guns in each battery. The GPF (Grande Puissance Filloux) 155-mm. gun is a weapon designed by a French officer, Col. L. J. F. Filloux, before the first World War and furnished to the American troops in France.

General Morioka's route to the Philippine capital was not as broad or as smooth as that followed by General Tsuchibashi in the north. The Japanese in northern Luzon had the wide central plain to traverse; the path of the *16th* Division was blocked by mountains and broad lakes. (*Map 8*) Immediately after landing at Lamon Bay, Morioka had crossed the steep Tayabas Mountains with the major part of his force. Before him were the towering heights of Mt. Banahao. To reach Manila he would have to skirt the southern slopes of this obstacle and follow Route 1 westward. Once beyond Mt. Banahao he could turn north toward the huge inland lake called Laguna de Bay, follow Route 1 along its western shore, thence through the narrow corridor between the lake and Manila Bay into the city of Manila itself. The smaller force which had landed at Mauban would have to skirt the northern foothills of Mt. Banahao, move along the south shore of Laguna de Bay to Route 1, then northward to the capital city. The two enemy forces would have to act independently until they were halfway to Manila.

If the Japanese advance westward in two columns made mutual support of the two columns impossible once Mt. Banahao was reached, it also presented General Jones with a serious problem: to maintain contact between his units in order to avoid hostile flanking movements. He solved his problem by assigning a half-track patrol from Company C, 194th Tank Battalion, to patrol the north-south road in front (east) of Mt. Banahao. This patrol was charged with maintaining contact between the 1st Infantry to the north and the 52d and 53d Infantry on the south.[5]

Withdrawal From Mauban

Of the two Japanese columns moving west from Lamon Bay, the northernmost, which had landed at Mauban, was the weaker, its mission the less important. This force, led by Colonel Tsunehiro, was numerically small, about the size of a battalion combat team, and consisted of the *2d Battalion, 20th Infantry,* supported by a battery of the *22d Field Artillery.* Unless it was allowed to advance entirely unchecked, Tsunehiro's force could have no decisive effect on the outcome of the action. Its mission was merely to advance along the south shore of Laguna de Bay toward Manila. If necessary, Tsunehiro could turn south shortly after capturing Lucban to aid the main force of the *16th Division* advancing from Atimonan.[6]

Opposing Colonel Tsunehiro was the 1st Infantry (less 3d Battalion) of the 1st Regular Division (PA), dug in near Sampaloc, seven miles west of Mauban. At 0300 on Christmas Day it began an unauthorized withdrawal toward Lucban, about eight miles to the west. General Jones did not learn of this move until noon when, as he was about to begin his Christmas dinner, a motorcycle messenger from the half-track patrol of Company C, 194th Tank Battalion, came in with the news. He immedi-

---

[5] Interv, author with Jones, 25 Oct 49, OCMH; Jones, Diary, p. 11.

797-257 O-66—14

[6] In addition to the sources cited below, the account of the withdrawal from south Luzon is based upon: Jones, Diary, pp. 11–16; MacDonald, Supplement to Jones Diary, pp. 11–13; Shreve, Diary, pp. 9–18; Maj Alfredo M. Santos, CO 1st Inf, The 1st Regular Div (PA) in Battle of Phil (paper prepared for School of Logistics, Command and General Staff College, 7 Jun 47), pp. 32–34; ltr, Col Boatwright to Groce, research asst to author, 25 Mar 49, OCMH; intervs, author and Falk with Jones, 25 Oct 49, 15 Dec 49, 15 Mar 50, 5 Apr 50, and on other occasions; *14th Army Opns,* I, 54–55, 69–70; II, 12; *16th Div Opns,* 24 Dec 41–3 Jan 42, ATIS Enemy Pub 355, pp. 4–9.

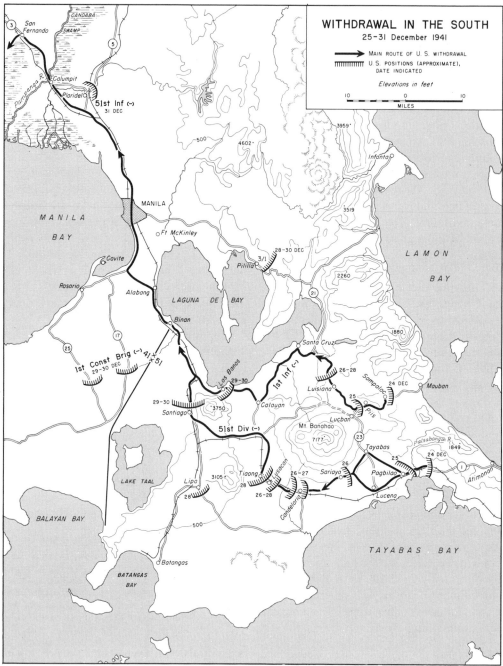

WITHDRAWAL IN THE SOUTH
25-31 December 1941

→ MAIN ROUTE OF U.S. WITHDRAWAL

U.S. POSITIONS (APPROXIMATE),
DATE INDICATED

Elevations in feet

MAP 8

MOTORCYCLE MESSENGER CATNAPPING

ately went forward to stop the retreat. Meanwhile, the Japanese reached Sampaloc, which they took without opposition. From there they pushed on toward the barrio of Piis, four miles distant.

General Jones located the headquarters of the 1st Infantry near Luisiana, about six miles northwest of Lucban on Route 23. Angered by the retreat, he demanded of Maj. Ralph E. Rumbold, the senior American instructor, "just what the devil" he meant by pulling back. Rumbold replied that he had been ordered to do so by the commander of the South Luzon Force, "General Parker." Jones thereupon informed him that he, Jones, now commanded the South Luzon Force, and that the 1st Infantry was to establish contact with the enemy immediately.[7] With a half-track from the tank company General Jones set out in his own vehicle ahead of the 1st Infantry to seek a suitable delaying position. At about 1900, near Piis, he met an enemy patrol. The Japanese, equipped with machine guns, opened fire on Jones's party and disabled the half-track. The patrol was finally dispersed and Jones returned to the 1st Infantry, the half-track crew hiking back carrying its machine gun. By this time Rumbold had pushed forward toward Piis but

---

[7] One possible explanation for the confusion was the fact that the 1st Infantry had been ordered to north Luzon on the night of 23–24 December by USAFFE, and then later, before it could move, the order had been rescinded.

had been halted by a combination of rain, darkness, and enemy fire.[8]

On his return to the 1st Infantry lines late that night General Jones ordered Major Rumbold to fight a delaying action until he was forced to withdraw. He was to retire northwest along Route 23 to a point above Luisiana and hold there until further notice.

The next morning, 26 December, Rumbold ordered the 2d Platoon, Company C, 194th Tank Battalion, which General Jones had attached to the 1st Infantry the previous evening, to attack the Japanese in Piis. Lt. Robert F. Needham, the platoon leader, suggested a reconnaissance first, but was told that it would be unnecessary since the enemy was understood to have nothing larger than .50-caliber machine guns. Advancing in column along the narrow road, the tanks ran into a strong Japanese roadblock consisting of antitank guns, 75-mm. guns, and several machine guns. The enemy block had been prepared the previous evening, after the fight with General Jones's half-track, in expectation of an American mechanized attack. During the action that followed, the platoon's lead and rear tanks were knocked out, immobilizing the others on the narrow road, and Lieutenant Needham and his crew in the lead tank killed. The surviving tankers managed to escape, to drift back finally into the American lines at the end of the month.[9]

Deprived of tank support, the 1st Infantry fell back to the junction of the Mauban road and Route 23. Here it was joined shortly before noon by more than three hundred retired Philippine Scouts led by Maj. Montgomery McKee, a retired Scout officer. These grizzled veterans, trained and disciplined by a lifetime in the Scouts, had long since served their time. Called on to bolster the raw Filipino troops, they assembled hurriedly near Fort McKinley and, in a fleet of taxicabs, rushed to the front. General Jones immediately attached them to the 1st Infantry and replaced Major Rumbold with McKee, their commander. These "seasoned, trained men," wrote Col. Stuart C. MacDonald, South Luzon Force chief of staff, "definitely stiffened the green 1st Infantry." [10]

Meanwhile, Colonel Tsunehiro had been advancing along the Mauban road. When he reached the road junction where the 1st Infantry and the Scouts were dug in, he was met by determined resistance. For several hours there was a hard fight; finally at about 1400 the defenders were forced to pull out and fall back along Route 23 toward Luisiana to the northwest. The Japanese did not follow immediately but continued southwest to Lucban, only a short distance away, which they reached at dusk.

The next morning reports of Japanese troop movements northward began to reach the 1st Infantry. These reports were accurate. Minor elements of the *16th Reconnaissance Regiment,* which had landed at Atimonan, had come west and north along Route 23 to join Tsunehiro in Lucban about noon. The 1st Infantry thereupon continued to withdraw that day and the next. Part of Tsunehiro's force was pushing northwest toward Luisiana along Route 23 and another column had struck out along an unimproved road west of Lucban. The first and stronger element entered Luisiana

---

[8] The general recommended decorations for all participants. Miller, *Bataan Uncensored,* p. 122; Prov Tank Gp Rpt of Opns, p. 13.

[9] Miller, *Bataan Uncensored,* pp. 117–21; Weaver, Comments on Draft MS, Comment 21, OCMH.

[10] MacDonald, Supplement to Jones Diary, p. 11.

about noon of the 28th while the column to the west occupied Majayjay at about the same time.

The Japanese advance in two columns constituted a real threat to the 1st Infantry. If the element to the west pushed on rapidly it might reach the south shore of Laguna de Bay before the Philippine regulars and cut their line of retreat. The 1st Infantry, therefore, at 1000 on 28 December, began to fall back to Calauan on Route 2 which paralleled the south shore of Laguna de Bay. Withdrawal to Calauan meant a circuitous march of twenty-five miles, first north and northwest along Route 23 to Santa Cruz, then southwest along Route 21. The regiment began its march at 1000 on 28 December, but before it could reach its destination and set up defensive positions it was directed to proceed to Los Banos, seven miles farther along Route 21. From Los Banos it was a short distance to Route 1, the main road northward to Manila.[11] The 3d Battalion of the 1st Infantry, stationed originally to the north, pulled back at the same time to Pililla on the north shore of the lake, where it was in position to halt an enemy advance to Manila from that direction.

By 29 December the 1st Infantry, forming the north flank of the South Luzon Force, had withdrawn successfully from Mauban on Lamon Bay to Los Banos along the south shore of Laguna de Bay, a distance of thirty-five miles. It was now in position to move quickly around the lake and northward past Manila through San Fernando, thence to Bataan.

Withdrawal From Atimonan

The withdrawal from Atimonan had begun at the same time, on Christmas Day, as the 1st Infantry's withdrawal from Mauban and General Wainwright's stand at the Agno River. At Atimonan the Japanese had landed a force consisting of the *16th Reconnaissance Regiment,* more than a battalion of the *20th Infantry,* a comparable force from the *22d Field Artillery,* almost all of the *16th Engineers,* and other service units. To oppose this Japanese force, which by 25 December had crossed the mountains west of Atimonan and was advancing along Route 1 toward Pagbilao, General Jones had initially the equivalent of a reinforced regiment of infantry. From Col. Virgil N. Cordero's 52d Infantry he had the 2d and 3d Battalions (less one company); and from Col. John R. Boatwright's 53d Infantry, the 1st Battalion. A detachment from Lt. Col. David S. Babcock's 2d Provisional Group of SPM's was in support. Only Cordero's men were in contact with the enemy along Route 1.[12]

Pagbilao, fifteen miles inland from Atimonan on Route 1 and the immediate Japanese objective, is an important road junction in south Luzon. From there a road leads northwest to Tayabas, about seven miles away, where it joins Route 23, along which the 1st Infantry, farther north, was withdrawing. Route 1 turns southwest at Pagbilao to join that village with Lucena. The road then changes direction sharply to travel northwest to meet the road linking Tayabas with Sariaya. Route 1 then continues west through Sariaya and Candelaria

[11] Major Santos asserts that he was ordered to proceed without delay to Bataan and that he did so. Other evidence indicates that the regiment was not ordered to Bataan immediately, but to Los Banos. Santos, 1st Reg Div (PA), p. 34.

[12] Jones states in his diary, pages 11–12, that the 155-mm. GPF's were in support here, but these guns were actually to the west, according to Colonel Shreve. Shreve, Diary, pp. 9–13, OCMH.

to Tiaong, where it turns north toward Manila. Tayabas and Lucena are linked by the southern portion of Route 23. The road net between Pagbilao and Sariaya is shaped like a kite, with its tail (Route 1) stretching eastward to Atimonan. Before Pagbilao, flowing due south, is the Palsabangon River, intersecting Route 1 about 3,000 yards east of the village.

On Christmas Day Colonel Cordero's 52d Infantry was ordered to hold the Pagbilao–Tayabas road, and Colonel Boatwright's one battalion of the 53d was posted on the east shore of the Palsabangon River to cover the east-west road and Cordero's line of retreat. When the Japanese reached the river they were halted briefly by Boatwright's 53d Infantry troops to permit final preparations for the demolition of the bridge and the crossing of Cordero's men. The last 52d Infantry troops crossed under enemy fire and the bridge was blown almost in the face of the pursuing Japanese. Colonel Cordero continued through the 53d Infantry lines to positions about 2,000 yards northwest of Pagbilao, along the Tayabas road. Boatwright remained at the river line to oppose the expected Japanese crossing.

The Japanese were held up only briefly at the Palsabangon River. During the afternoon, they forced a crossing and established a bridgehead on the west bank of the river. Colonel Boatwright's battalion withdrew quickly along Route 1 through Pagbilao. The Japanese who had forced the crossing, the *16th Reconnaissance Regiment,* reinforced, did not pursue Boatwright but turned northwest toward Tayabas instead to follow Cordero's 52d Infantry. The pursuit of the 53d Infantry along Route 1 fell to the *3d Battalion, 20th Infantry,* which had crossed the Palsabangon behind the *16th Reconnaissance.* By evening of the 25th the Japanese were in possession of Pagbilao and in full pursuit of the two American columns withdrawing rapidly toward Tayabas and Lucena.

The Japanese were too close for comfort. To cover the retirement of the 52d and 53d Infantry, General Jones hurriedly made new dispositions the next day. He pulled back the 3d Battalion, 53d Infantry, from its position on beach defense along Tayabas Bay and attached it to the provisional infantry battalion formed earlier from the 51st Field Artillery (less two batteries). This unit, led by Col. Hamilton F. Searight, Jones further strengthened by attaching a platoon of Company C, 194th Tank Battalion. He then ordered Searight to dig in along Route 1 at the eastern edge of Sariaya and to hold there until the troops of the two infantry regiments moving back from Tayabas and Lucena passed through his lines.

The two Japanese columns, meanwhile, were pushing forward determinedly. Along Route 1, the *3d Battalion, 20th Infantry,* followed Boatwright's battalion, which passed through Lucena early on the 26th to reach Sariaya about 1530 that afternoon. The Japanese battalion, which had had a late start, did not enter Lucena until 2100 that night. To the northwest Colonel Cordero's 52d Infantry pulled back through Tayabas early in the morning, then turned southwest toward Sariaya, blowing bridges as it retired. The regiment passed through Searight's lines that evening, some hours after the 53d Infantry. The *16th Reconnaissance,* delayed by obstacles and blown bridges, reached Tayabas at 1600. From there it sent forward a patrol northward along Route 23 to establish contact with Colonel Tsunehiro's force nearing Lucban. By nightfall of the 26th General Morioka held the entire area east of Sariaya, with its important network of roads, and was in position to drive west along Route 1 or north on Route 23.

General Jones's position, while far from desperate, was not favorable. Unlike Wainwright in the north, who by evening of the 26th was on the D-3 line, he had no phase lines or previously reconnoitered positions to fall back to. In the absence of these, he improvised a system of delaying positions. Along terrain favorable to defense, he set up his front lines. To the rear he established a secondary line, behind whatever obstacles the terrain offered. Since it was practically impossible, as one staff officer noted, "to rally our troops . . . without a considerable lapse of time" after a line had been hit hard, the stragglers from the front lines were collected at the secondary line, re-formed, and put into position along a third line.[13] To make matters more difficult and confusing, the units became so mixed during the withdrawal that it was practically impossible to call them by their proper designations. They were identified instead, in the Japanese manner, by their commander's name. "Our tactics," observed Colonel Shreve in his diary, "have been unique." [14]

The evacuation of supplies and equipment proved as difficult in south Luzon as it did in the north, and for the same reasons. The quartermaster supply depot at Los Banos was never evacuated, probably because of the shortage of transportation. Eventually, division trains moving through Los Banos picked up all the supplies they could carry; the remainder was reported destroyed. The shipment to Bataan of the six 155-mm. GPF's, emplaced along the

west coast, proved extremely difficult. USAFFE's order directing that the prime movers, 10-ton tractors, be sent to Bataan left the GPF's without transportation. Finally, by changes in orders and desperate improvisations, the 155's were moved out of position. By the evening of the 26th, they were on their way to Bataan.[15]

At 1900 on 26 December General Jones established his foward command post at Candelaria, seven miles west of Sariaya, on Route 1. Here he organized his first line of defense. Along the two rivers which bracketed the town on the east and west, Jones posted Colonel Boatwright's 53d Infantry (less 3d Battalion). The main line of resistance was established along the river west of the city, with an outpost line on the river to the east. The bridges over both rivers were prepared for destruction. At the same time, General Jones set up a secondary line six miles behind Candelaria, at Lusacan, with Colonel Cordero's 52d Infantry. Troops of the 53d Infantry would fall back through Cordero's line when they withdrew from Candelaria.

With two lines across the enemy's route of advance, Jones pulled Searight back from Sariaya to Tiaong, about 3,000 yards west of Lusacan, where Route 1 turns north toward Laguna de Bay. Searight broke contact with the enemy at 0100 on the 27th, his troops moving to the rear in buses.

General Morioka, meanwhile, had concentrated his forces at Lucena, sending the *16th Reconnaissance Regiment* in pursuit of the retreating South Luzon Force. The destruction of the four large bridges be-

---

[13] Shreve, Diary, p. 15.
[14] *Ibid.*

[15] QM Rpt of Opns, p. 22. Shreve's original orders had been to destroy the guns, but he was determined to get them out "by hook or crook." Shreve, Diary, p. 9.

CAMOUFLAGED 155-MM. GUN M1917 (GPF), *towed by a 10-ton tractor.*

tween Tayabas and Sariaya held up the vehicles, and the reconnaissance regiment was forced to advance toward Candelaria on foot. On the afternoon of the 27th the Japanese finally reached the town and broke through the outpost line. Passing through the town quickly, they hit the main line of resistance about dusk. The Filipinos, failing to recognize their own troops falling back before the advancing Japanese, opened fire on their comrades. Fortunately, little damage was done and few lives lost. Behind the retreating troops came the Japanese. Despite determined opposition, they forced a crossing of the river and by 2030 of the 27th the 53d Infantry (less 3d Battalion) was in full retreat. On General Jones's orders, Colonel Boatwright's troops continued on to the rear for much needed rest and reor-

ganization, and the following day moved out of southern Luzon to Bataan.[16]

The Japanese did not stop at Candelaria. Pushing ahead aggressively, they reached Lusacan, six miles away, on the morning of the 28th. Here they ran into Colonel Cordero's 52d Infantry, deployed along the secondary line of defense. The Japanese were able to outflank Cordero's position quickly and at 0915 the American commander abandoned his position and retired toward Tiaong.

The American position at Tiaong, guarding the defile through which Route 1 led north, was a strong one. Protected on both flanks by high ground, it was ideal for a prolonged stand, and General Jones decided

[16] Capt William Cummings, 53d Infantry (PA), pp. 3–4, Chunn Notebooks.

that he would make a determined effort to hold here. In the line he placed about four battalions of infantry, a battery of field artillery, and all his tanks and self-propelled artillery. The SPM's were deployed so as to provide direct support for the infantry, and the eight guns of the 51st Artillery were placed on high ground to the left of the main defenses, enfilading the path of the Japanese advance. To secure the rear, Jones withdrew the Philippine Scout detachment under Major McKee from the 1st Infantry and placed it in position about eight miles north of Tiaong. The 51st Infantry (less 1st Battalion) was placed at Lipa, eleven miles to the west, in position to cover the approaches from that direction. The 2d Philippine Constabulary Regiment, part of the 1st Constabulary Brigade, was in general reserve. From Santiago, about six miles southwest of Los Banos, it could support either the Tiaong position or the troops along the lake.

Despite these elaborate preparations no stand was made at Tiaong. By the evening of the 28th General MacArthur had apparently become apprehensive about the right flank of Wainwright's North Luzon Force which was now on the D–4 line. He therefore ordered General Jones to hurry his withdrawal and to get out of South Luzon in time to pass safely behind Wainwright's lines. The entire South Luzon Force was to be across the Calumpit bridges by 0600 of the first day of the new year.

These orders meant the abandonment of the strong position at Tiaong, and it was with reluctance that Jones, shortly after midnight, 28–29 December, ordered the troops there to fall back to Santiago. Colonel Cordero's 52d Infantry with a battery of the 51st Field Artillery left at 0200, and reached the bivouac area north of Santiago four hours later. By midnight Cordero was

on his way to Bataan. The 51st Infantry at Lipa also withdrew to Santiago on the 29th and then continued north along the lake to Alabang where it went into mobile reserve. Brig. Gen. Simeon de Jesus' 1st Constabulary Brigade (less the 2d Regiment), part of the 2d Division formed from the Constabulary on the outbreak of war, relieved the 42d Infantry, still on beach defense, and took up positions covering Routes 17 and 25 leading into Manila. The 42d Infantry withdrew by bus to Bataan. That night South Luzon Force headquarters moved to Fort McKinley.[17]

By evening of 29 December the South Luzon Force stood in position at Santiago, with flank guards at Los Banos and on Routes 17 and 25, and a mobile reserve at Alabang to the north. Approximately half of the 51st Division was already on its way to Bataan. The rest of the South Luzon Force was ready to follow. To the south the van of the Japanese forces, the *16th Reconnaissance Regiment,* was just entering Tiaong.

Out of South Luzon

Not long after the South Luzon Force had started hurriedly for Bataan, it was halted by orders from the rear echelon headquarters of USAFFE in Manila. About 1030 of the 30th General Jones was notified by Lt. Col. Jesse Traywick, G–3 of that headquarters, that he was to withdraw no farther unless forced to do so by enemy pressure.[18] Probably the change in orders was an attempt to delay the final evacuation of Manila, thus gaining time for the transfer

---

[17] The 1st Brigade (PC) consisted of the 1st and 2d Philippine Constabulary Regiments.

[18] Ltr, Gen. R. J. Marshall to author, 31 Oct 49, OCMH.

of additional equipment to Bataan and Corregidor. Jones, unaware of the situation to the north, was puzzled by the new order, coming as it did but thirty-six hours after the order calling for a top-speed withdrawal. But without question and happy for an opportunity to meet the enemy, he immediately made his plans. He went forward to Santiago where the bulk of his force was and arranged an ambush. The position was an excellent one, the force adequate, and time sufficient to prepare the trap. Except for a few patrols, the Japanese were still around Tiaong and Candelaria, consolidating and moving up equipment and supplies, the last of which had been landed about noon of the 28th. Those elements advancing were doing so slowly and cautiously.

Again Jones was to be deprived of his chance to pick a fight with the Japanese. General Homma's main force of infantry, tanks, and artillery in northern Luzon had broken through at Cabanatuan and was pressing down Route 5. With Wainwright's right flank exposed and the North Luzon Force "in a very precarious position" there was a real possibility that the Japanese would succeed in driving a wedge between the North and South Luzon Forces.[19] General MacArthur on Corregidor immediately saw the danger to his scheme for withdrawal to Bataan and, through his deputy chief of staff in Manila, General Marshall, made plans to meet the emergency. On the evening of the 30th, Marshall telephoned the South Luzon Force command post at McKinley and spoke to Colonel MacDonald, the chief of staff, who took the call in General Jones's absence. Marshall directed MacDonald to return immediately to the original plan of withdrawal so as to clear the Calumpit bridges not later than 0600 of 1 January. He

stressed the importance of covering the bridges from the north and east by holding Plaridel seven miles to the east and made the South Luzon Force responsible for this task. When informed that the 51st Infantry was "ready to roll" Marshall "seemed quite relieved." "Very evidently," wrote MacDonald, "something very bad had happened in NLF, just what the situation is there, we still didn't know."[20]

Unable to reach General Jones at Santiago, MacDonald issued the necessary orders for the withdrawal. The 2d Philippine Constabulary was returned to General de Jesus, the brigade commander, who was ordered to relieve all other elements of the South Luzon Force and to cover their withdrawal. He placed one of his regiments in position to block Routes 17 and 25, and the other to cover Routes 1 and 21. The 1st Infantry was now free to continue its withdrawal and moved around Manila to Bataan. The force at Santiago was ordered to fall back through the Constabulary and the mobile reserve—51st Infantry (less 1st Battalion) plus a battery of the 51st Field Artillery—to proceed immediatley to Plaridel to meet General Marshall's requirements for more troops in that area. When these units had cleared Manila, General de Jesus was to pull his brigade back first to Fort McKinley and then, on the night of 31 December–1 January, to Bataan, clearing the Calumpit bridges by 0600 of New Year's Day.[21]

---

[19] USAFFE-USFIP Rpt of Opns, p. 37.

[20] MacDonald, Supplement to Jones Diary, pp. 13–14; Hunt, *MacArthur and the War Against Japan*, pp. 44–45.

[21] The Army Transport Service was prepared to ferry the South Luzon Force headquarters from Manila or Cavite if the situation demanded, but South Luzon Force headquarters was never informed of this possibility. QM Rpt of Opns, p. 23; interv, author with Jones, 5 Apr 50.

General Jones returned to his command post from Santiago as the units began to move to their new locations. Unaware as yet of the change in orders, the general "was astonished to find that the greater part of the CP was already on the road to Plaridel," and hastened after it.[22] Lt. Col. Arthur L. Shreve, the G–3 and artillery officer, and Capt. Arthur G. Christensen, intelligence officer, had left McKinley in an old taxi shortly before midnight. Stopping in Manila for sandwiches, beer, and ice cream, they arrived at Plaridel and opened the new command post in a schoolhouse at 0400, 31 December. Colonel Shreve noted in his diary that he telephoned Fort McKinley to report, "We are set up. Check in to USAFFE and wait."[23]

General Jones arrived in Plaridel a short time later. After a brief search he found his new command post just before daylight. He immediately phoned MacDonald and instructed him to close the command post at McKinley. Captain Christensen went forward with a North Luzon Force staff officer to learn the exact location of troops in the area.

Many of the 51st Division units cleared the Calumpit bridges before dawn of 31 December, and other elements crossed during the day. The first battalion of the mobile reserve, the 51st Infantry, under Lt. Col. Loren P. Stewart, arrived at Plaridel at 0600, and the other battalion came up three hours later. During the morning these two 51st Infantry battalions were placed in position astride Route 5, northeast of Plaridel. Colonel Babcock's 75-mm. SPM's were placed north of the town to oppose the Japanese tanks known to be approaching from

Cabanatuan. About twelve miles south of Plaridel, on Route 3, Company C of the 194th Tank Battalion held the road against enemy pursuit from the south. Below Manila, at Fort McKinley, General de Jesus' 1st Brigade (PC) was preparing to withdraw toward Bataan under cover of darkness. "Manila," reported General MacArthur to the War Department, "will be uncovered by nightfall."[24]

The withdrawal of the South Luzon Force had been eminently successful. With little loss, the Filipino and American troops had retreated approximately 140 miles through rugged terrain from Lamon Bay to Plaridel. Most of the South Luzon Force had already gone to Bataan. Although Jones had inflicted no major damage on the enemy, he had shown great skill in hampering Morioka's pursuit. After the 28th of December the Japanese had been unable to maintain contact with the withdrawing South Luzon Force. Indeed, on New Year's Day, their advance elements were still near Santiago and in no position to influence the struggle for Luzon. So effective had been Jones's destruction of highway and railroad bridges that he thought "the South Luzon Force could have effectively delayed the enemy's advance on Manila for a considerably longer period had it been necessary."[25] The correctness of this conclusion is amply confirmed by General Morioka, who complained frequently of his inability to bring up armored cars, artillery, and supplies because of the destruction of roads and bridges

---

[22] MacDonald, Supplement to Jones Diary, p. 14.
[23] Shreve, Diary, p. 17.

[24] Rad, MacArthur to TAG, 31 Dec 41, AG 381 (11–27–41) Far East; Prov Tank Gp Rpt of Opns, p. 14; ltr, Maj John Curtiss, Jr., To Whom It May Concern, 5 Jun 45, written in Manchukuo while Curtiss was a prisoner of war. A copy of this letter was obtained from General Jones.
[25] Jones, Diary, pp. 17–18.

and the back-breaking task confronting his overworked engineers.[26]

By the last day of the year most of Luzon was in the hands of the enemy, but General MacArthur's forces were still intact. The first part of the double retrograde movement to Bataan had been successfully accomplished, and the USAFFE commander could report to Washington that "the South Luzon Force had made firm contact with the North Luzon Force in the San Fernando area." [27] All that now remained to complete the withdrawal of the troops east of the Pampanga River was the difficult maneuver across that river and the movement north through San Fernando then south into Bataan, while the troops along the D-5 line fell back along the roads leading into Bataan. It would be a hazardous operation, for enemy air and ground forces were an ever-growing menace as the area of maneuver became smaller. But the greatest test, the complicated movement of thousands of men and tons of supplies from north and south Luzon toward San Fernando, had gone well. The success of the withdrawal would be decided during the next few days.

---

[26] Morioka reported Japanese casualties from 24 December through 1 January as 128 killed and 260 wounded in action. *16th Div* Opns, 24 Dec 41–3 Jan 42, ATIS Enemy Pub 355, p. 11.

[27] Rad, MacArthur to Marshall, 1 Jan 42, AG 381 (11–27–41 Sec 1) Far East.

CHAPTER XII

Holding the Road to Bataan

On 30 December 1941 the Philippine Commonwealth reaffirmed its faith in the future with the inauguration of President-elect Manuel Quezon at a brief ceremony on the island fortress of Corregidor. Across the bay, the American and Filipino troops were making ready for their last stand before withdrawing to Bataan. Despite Quezon's brave inaugural words, the future of the nascent republic never appeared darker.[1]

Almost all of the troops on Luzon were now north of Manila. The North Luzon Force stood on the D–5 line, from Bamban to Arayat, in front of San Fernando and the road leading into Bataan. (*Map 9*) Fifteen to twenty miles long, this line was the shortest of the five defensive lines used by General Wainwright's forces. Guarded on the left (west) by the steep heights of the Zambales Mountains and on the right by the rugged 3,367-foot high Mt. Arayat and the twenty-mile-long Candaba Swamp, it was susceptible only to frontal attack by the Japanese force moving south from Tarlac along Route 3.

Ten miles south of Bamban, the west anchor of the D–5 line, an unimproved road, Route 74, branched off from Route 3 to the southwest to give access to Bataan. The main road into the peninsula, Route 7, began at San Fernando, ten miles farther south. Troops north and south of San Fernando would have to pass through that town to get to Bataan; only the left elements of the troops on the D–5 line would be able to use Route 74.

General Homma's main striking force was not aimed at the D–5 line, but at Manila. This force, which had broken through at Cabanatuan on the 30th, was moving rapidly down Route 5, east of the Candaba Swamp. Once it reached Plaridel, where a road led westward to Route 3, it would be only a short distance east of the two bridges at Calumpit. If the Japanese secured Plaridel and the bridges quickly enough, they would cut off the retreat of the troops still south of Calumpit and, by gaining a position west of the Pampanga River in the rear of the D–5 line, compromise the execution of the withdrawal into Bataan.

General MacArthur had foreseen this contingency as soon as the Japanese had broken through at Cabanatuan and had quickly sent reinforcements from the North and South Luzon Forces to hold Plaridel and the road to the north as far as Baliuag. Defending Plaridel was as essential to his plan for withdrawal to Bataan as holding the D–5 line. Possession of this barrio meant that the Calumpit bridges over which the forces east of the Pampanga must pass to get to San Fernando were safe. The task of the forces on Luzon was, then, twofold: to hold in the north along the D–5 line and on the east at Plaridel. Failure to

---

[1] Quezon, *The Good Fight*, pp. 227–35. General MacArthur and High Commissioner Sayre also spoke briefly and feelingly at the ceremony. MacArthur's speech is printed in Hunt, *MacArthur and the War Against Japan,* pp. 48–49.

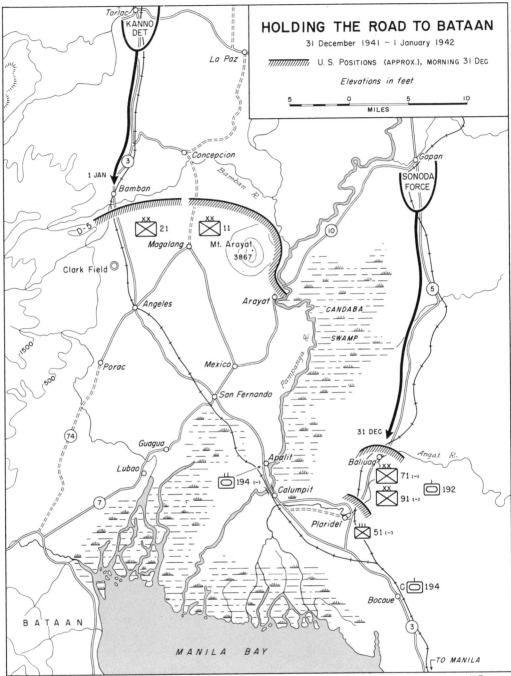

HOLDING THE ROAD TO BATAAN

31 December 1941 — 1 January 1942

///////// U. S. POSITIONS (APPROX.), MORNING 31 DEC

Elevations in feet

MILES

Tarlac

KANNO DET

La Paz

Concepcion

Bamban R.

1 JAN

Bamban

D-5

Magalang

Clark Field

XX 21

XX 11

Mt. Arayat 3867

Angeles

Arayat

Gapan

SONODA FORCE

CANDABA

SWAMP

Pampanga R.

Porac

Mexico

San Fernando

31 DEC

Guagua

Apalit

Baliuag

Angat R.

XX 71 (−)

192

Lubao

194 (−)

Calumpit

XX 91 (−)

Plaridel

XX 51 (−)

Bocaue

C 194

BATAAN

MANILA BAY

TO MANILA

H. Damon

MAP 9

MOUNT ARAYAT, *looking west.*

hold long enough at either point spelled the doom of the entire plan.

The Defense of Calumpit

For the defense of the Calumpit bridges MacArthur placed every unit that could be spared east of the Pampanga. From the South Luzon Force came the 51st Infantry (less 1st Battalion) and the 75-mm. guns of Colonel Babcock's SPM provisional battalion, both stationed at Plaridel. The 194th Tank Battalion (less Company C) was posted at Apalit, on the west bank of the Pampanga two miles above Calumpit, in position "to insure the exit" of those forces east of the river. If necessary, the tank battalion was to move to Bocaue, between Manila and Plaridel, to reinforce Company C, part of the South Luzon Force, which was to hold that barrio "until the extrication of North and South Luzon Forces was insured." [2] At least one company of the 192d Tank Battalion was in the Plaridel–Baliuag area.

The 91st Division, retreating down Route 5 from Cabanatuan, reached Baliuag at daybreak of the 31st. It was joined shortly by elements of the 71st Division— the 71st Field Artillery and the 71st and 72d Infantry—which had been ordered there the night before by General Wainwright. The 71st Division units took up positions north of Baliuag and the 91st Division went into reserve south of the town.

---

[2] Prov Tank Gp Rpt of Opns, p. 14.

Before 1000 Wainwright's headquarters warned the two divisions that they would have to withdraw from Baliuag in time to clear the Calumpit bridges, nine miles away, by 0400 the next morning.[3]

At approximately 1000 that morning, General Sutherland, MacArthur's chief of staff, telephoned Jones, commander of the South Luzon Force, and placed him in command of all forces east of the Pampanga. In effect, this made Jones commander of the troops holding the Calumpit bridges. Sutherland ordered Jones to hold the bridges until the 1st Brigade (PC) had passed over and warned him that all troops would have to be west of the Pampanga River by 0600 of 1 January, for at that time the bridges would be blown. Apparently General Wainwright was not informed of the change in command.[4]

The Fight for Plaridel

The defense of the Baliuag–Plaridel area was of the greatest importance. Baliuag, a town of rambling houses and nipa huts scattered along Route 5 and the north bank of the Angat River, commands the approaches to Plaridel, six miles to the south. Plaridel is located at the intersection of Route 5 and several secondary roads, two of which extend along opposite banks of the Angat River to Route 3 and the Calumpit bridges, some eight miles to the northwest. The South Luzon Force

and those elements of the North Luzon Force in the area would have to pass through Plaridel and along these secondary roads to cross the Calumpit bridges. South of Plaridel lay the invader's route to Manila.

General Tsuchibashi, *48th Division* commander, was fully aware of the importance of Calumpit and the Baliuag-Plaridel area. On the 30th he had ordered two tank regiments and a battalion of infantry to advance from Cabanatuan to the Angat River and cut the route from Manila to San Fernando. This force, led by Col. Seinosuke Sonoda, commander of the *7th Tank Regiment,* and assisted by a company of engineers to repair roads and bridges, was marching unopposed down Route 5 toward Plaridel on the night of the 30th.[5]

On the morning of 31 December an advance detachment of Colonel Sonoda's force reached the outskirts of Baliuag. The engineers, protected by tanks, attempted to repair the bridge across the stream north of the town, but were met by fire from the 71st Field Artillery. Shortly after, the enemy tanks were brought under fire by a platoon of Company C, 192d Tank Battalion, which lay in concealed positions below the stream. The Japanese broke off the action and withdrew to the east where they effected a crossing around noon. It was at this time that the 91st Division left its reserve position below Baliuag and started for Bataan, leaving the 71st Division elements alone in the town.[6]

---

[3] NLF and I Corps Rpt of Opns, p. 13; USAFFE-USFIP Rpt of Opns, p. 39; ltr, Selleck to Board of Officers, 1 Feb 46, sub: Reinstatement of Rank; ltr, Col Fowler, CO 71st FA, to author, 30 Apr 49, OCMH; Capt Albert W. Erickson, 71st Inf (PA), pp. 2–3, and Bentz, 92d Inf (PA), pp. 1–2, both in Chunn Notebooks.

[4] Jones, Diary, p. 16. These instructions were passed on to General de Jesus, commander of the 1st Brigade (PC), for his was the only unit not yet in position to clear Calumpit rapidly.

[5] *14th Army* Opns, I, 84; statements of Col Moriji Kawagoe, CofS *48th Div,* 9 Mar 50, ATIS Doc 56354 and of Maj Makoto Nakahara, Opns Officer, *48th Div,* 13 Mar 50, ATIS Doc 56372, in Interrogations of Former Japanese Officers, Mil Hist Div, GHQ FEC, II.

[6] USAFFE-USFIP Rpt of Opns, p. 39; NLF and I Corps Rpt of Opns, p. 13; Prov Tank Gp Rpt of Opns, p. 14; ltr, Fowler to author, 30 Apr 49, OCMH.

By 1330 the Japanese tanks had reached the eastern outskirts of Baliuag and were awaiting infantry reinforcements before making an all out assault against the town. Meanwhile, the 71st Infantry prepared to pull out of Baliuag in accordance with orders. The two infantry regiments and the engineers left in buses around 1400, but the artillery regiment remained behind.[7]

At about this time General Wainwright arrived at Jones's command post in the Plaridel schoolhouse. The North Luzon Force commander, unaware of the fact that Jones now commanded all troops east of the Pampanga, ordered him to take up positions for a close-in, perimeter defense of the Calumpit bridge. Jones informed Wainwright of his orders from Sutherland and explained that he intended to hold the enemy at Baliuag rather than at the bridge. While Jones and Wainwright were talking, General Stevens, 91st Division commander, entered the command post, followed a short time later by a South Luzon Force staff officer who announced that the 71st Division had moved out of Baliuag. Jones then ordered Stevens to stop the 71st and put it in position west of Plaridel, along the road leading to Calumpit. Wainwright left soon after for his own command post.[8]

Stevens' efforts to halt the withdrawal of the 71st Division infantry elements proved futile. By 1500 the main body of Sonoda's

mechanized force was standing in front of Baliuag and it was perfectly evident that the Japanese were massing for an attack. Deeply concerned over the effect of an attack on the untried 51st Infantry, Jones ordered two platoons of Company C, 192d Tank Battalion, to cross the river and attack the enemy concentration at the east end of Baliuag. The tanks were to be supported by about a half dozen of Colonel Babcock's 75-mm. SPM's which were to fire on Baliuag and its northern approaches when the tanks broke off the attack. After a hasty reconnaissance, Babcock placed his guns on the dry, baked fields a few thousand yards west of Baliuag and sent a forward observer to a position 500 yards west of the town. For communications with the tanks Babcock had a radio-equipped scout car of Company C.

At about 1700 the tanks of Company C, led by Lt. William Gentry, moved out to the attack. As the two platoons approached the enemy, the covering artillery fire, presumably supplied by the 71st Field Artillery, lifted. A bitter fight ensued. The American armor made a shambles of that part of Baliuag in Japanese hands. The tanks rolled through the streets, firing into bahays, smashing through the nipa huts as if they were so many toy houses, and scattering hostile infantry right and left. A brief but wild tank-versus-tank action followed. In the fading daylight American and Japanese tanks chased each other up and down the narrow streets, while enemy foot soldiers, in a futile gesture, fired small arms at the tankers. The SPM's and artillery remained idle, unable to fire for fear of hitting their own tanks. When Company C finally broke off the action, it had knocked out eight Japanese tanks with little loss to itself. As the tanks pulled back, the SPM's and

---

[7] USAFFE-USFIP Rpt of Opns, p. 39; ltr, Fowler to author, 30 Apr 49. Official reports do not record the fact that the 71st Field Artillery remained in Baliuag. This fact is established by the artillery commander, Colonel Fowler.

[8] General Jones was unaware that the 71st Field Artillery was still at Baliuag. Interv, author and Falk with Jones, 1 Nov 49 and 6 May 50. See also, Jones, Diary, pp. 16–17; NLF and I Corps Rpt of Opns, pp. 13–14; USAFFE-USFIP Rpt of Opns, p. 39; ltr, Fowler to author, 30 Apr 49, OCMH; MacDonald, Supplement to Jones Diary, p. 15.

artillery opened up on Baliuag and continued to fire until 2200 when Fowler and Babcock pulled their men back to Plaridel and then west across the Pampanga. The last of the tanks crossed the Calumpit bridge at about 0230 on 1 January.[9]

Holding the unimproved road from Plaridel to Calumpit was the untried 51st Infantry. When at 0300 the 1st Brigade (PC) cleared the Calumpit bridge General Jones sent his chief of staff to Plaridel with orders for the 51st to withdraw immediately. The retirement began at 0400, 1 January. Meanwhile, the Japanese had entered Baliuag and were pushing cautiously toward Plaridel. At 0400 they were close enough to hear the sound of motors as the 51st Infantry began to pull out, and immediately rushed forward to attack. Firing into the truck column the Japanese hit the rearmost vehicles but inflicted no damage. Lacking motor transportation they were unable to follow. Colonel Stewart pushed ahead rapidly and crossed the Pampanga with his 51st Infantry at about 0500 on the morning of the 1st, the last unit to cross the Calumpit bridge.[10]

---

[9] The account of this action is based on the following sources, many of them in conflict with each other: Prov Tank Gp Rpt of Opns, p. 14; ltr, Weaver to author, 30 Jan 50; Jones, Diary, p. 17; interv, author and Falk with Jones, 31 Oct and 1 Nov 49, 24 Jan 50; ltr, Maj Curtiss (forward observer for the 75-mm. SPM's), To Whom It May Concern, 5 Jun 45, copy in OCMH; Collier, Notebooks, II, 78–80; Lt Col Thomas Dooley, The First U.S. Tank Action in World War II (paper prepared for Advanced Officers Class No. 1, The Armored Force School, 1 May 48), p. 12; ltr, Weaver to Wainwright, 20 Nov 45, copy in OCMH; 14th Army Opns, I, 84.

[10] Jones, Diary, p. 17; 14th Army Opns, I, 84; ltr, Col Skerry, NLF Engineer, to Lt Col George A. Meidling, 4 Jun 49, Comment 9. Col Skerry's comments, altogether numbering twenty-one, pertain to Chapter II of Combat Engineer Operations, a projected volume in the series Engineers of the

"Blow the Bridges"

What the Japanese could not accomplish on the ground they might have accomplished with their air force. On 31 December the highway and railroad bridges spanning the Pampanga at Calumpit presented to the Japanese air force the most inviting target since Clark Field. Heavily laden with dynamite charges for rapid demolition and protected by only two gun batteries of the 200th Coast Artillery (AA), the bridges were extremely vulnerable to air attack.[11] Indeed, like marriage, in Shaw's classic definition, they combined the maximum of temptation with the maximum of opportunity.

The Japanese failed to take advantage of this opportunity for a decisive blow from the air. The 48th Division urged that the Calumpit bridges be bombed and there were heated discussions over this question, but the view of Col. Monjiro Akiyama, 14th Army air officer, that the destruction of the bridges would prove of little value, prevailed. The 14th Army's order of the 30th, therefore, directed the 5th Air Group simply to attack the retreating enemy and to make an effort to destroy the bridges west of Lubao, just above the base of the Bataan peninsula.[12]

Even with this limited mission, the Japanese air forces made only a desultory effort. Col. Harry A. Skerry, the North Luzon

---

Southwest Pacific 1941–1945. These comments were sent to the author by Colonel Skerry and are on file in OCMH. They are hereafter cited as Skerry, Comments on Engineer Hist, with appropriate number.

[11] Interv, author with Gen Sage, 28 Feb 51; USAFFE-USFIP Rpt of Opns, p. 39.

[12] Statements of Cols Kawagoe, CofS, 48th Div, and Akiyama, in Statements of Japanese Officials on World War II, GHQ FEC, Mil Intel Sec, I, 19, II, 134.

CALUMPIT BRIDGES *spanning the Pampanga River.*

Force engineer and the man directly responsible for blowing the bridges, later wrote that he was "amazed" by the "weak air efforts" the Japanese made and "the few planes seen in the sky, despite the previous almost total destruction of our air force and the resulting enemy air superiority." [13]

At about 0500 on New Year's Day, as the 51st Infantry cleared the Calumpit bridge, General Wainwright asked Generals Jones, Stevens, and Weaver if all their units were safely across. He received affirmative

replies from these three, but Colonel Skerry pointed out that a platoon of demolition engineers under Lt. Col. Narciso L. Manzano (PS) was still on the road south of Calumpit. Nothing had been heard from Manzano since the previous noon, and Colonel Skerry requested that destruction of the bridges be delayed as long as the tactical situation permitted, to enable Manzano's group to escape. Wainwright assented, but all final preparations for demolition were made and orders were issued to fire the charges at 0600.

It was still dark. There was no Japanese air bombardment or artillery fire, but from the south came the sounds of rifle fire. The nervous Filipino troops fidgeted in their positions and stared apprehensively across the river. At 0545, when there was still no sign

---

[13] Skerry, Comments on Engineer Hist, No. 9, p. 5; interrog of Lt Col Hikaru Haba, Intel Officer, *14th Army,* Apr 47, Interrogations of Former Japanese Officers, Mil Hist Div, GHQ FEC, I.

The account of the blowing of the bridge is based on Colonel Skerry's Comment 9; Wainwright, *General Wainwright's Story,* p. 44; and interv, author with Jones and Sage, 28 Feb 51.

of Manzano's detachment, Wainwright extended the time for blowing the bridges to 0615.

As dawn broke, the noise of enemy rifle fire from the south increased. General Wainwright, unaware that the main Japanese force was pushing toward Manila and that less than a regiment had been sent toward Calumpit, believed that this fire presaged a major Japanese effort to cross the Pampanga. Blowing the bridges would place the deep, unfordable river squarely in the path of the advancing enemy and give the Bataan forces time to prepare for defense. Wainwright then made his decision; Manzano and his men would have to reach Bataan by other routes. He turned to his engineer. "Skerry," he said, "we cannot wait any longer. Blow the bridges."

The covering force withdrew to a safe distance, the explosives were checked, and at 0615 the charges were detonated. The air was filled with a roar and a rushing noise, a flash lit up the sky, and the Calumpit bridges disappeared in a mass of falling debris. In front of the defenders flowed the deep Pampanga; to their rear lay San Fernando, where the road to Bataan began.

The D–5 Line: Bamban–Arayat

By the first day of the new year the bulk of the American and Filipino forces had escaped from the enemy pincer movement designed to trap them on the plain before Manila. Calumpit had been passed successfully and the troops from the south had side-stepped the Japanese and withdrawn in good order across the Pampanga. MacArthur's men no longer faced the main strength of Homma's *14th Army,* which was pushing rapidly toward Manila.

San Fernando, nine miles north of Calumpit, was as vital to the successful completion of the plan of withdrawal as Plaridel. Not only did the South Luzon Force have to pass through it before turning southwest to Bataan, but almost the entire North Luzon Force would funnel through that town also.

Thirty-five miles northwest of Manila, and strategically second in importance only to the capital, San Fernando is an important road and rail junction. It is there that Route 7, the main road to Bataan, joins Route 3. The troops from Calumpit would have to travel northward along Route 3 to reach San Fernando; those on the D–5 line would withdraw south along this road and Route 10. At San Fernando both groups would pick up Route 7 for the final lap of their journey to Bataan.

The 21st Division on the west flank of the D–5 line was the only unit which could escape into Bataan without going through San Fernando. At Angeles, midway between Bamban and San Fernando, it would leave Route 3 and follow Route 74 to Bataan. All other units north and south of San Fernando would reach Bataan via San Fernando and Route 7.

Even if the enemy did not impede the march to Bataan, the roads over which the tired soldiers must travel to reach the peninsula would present many obstacles. From Calumpit north to San Fernando, and from there south to Bataan, the road was packed with a "solid stream of traffic," military and civilian.[14] Vehicles of all types—cars, buses, trucks, artillery, and tanks—filled the center of the road. In some places, there were stretches of several miles

---

[14] Collier, Notebooks, I, 73–74.

SAN FERNANDO, *looking northwest. Route 3 from Calumpit runs diagonally through the photograph; Route 7 leading to Bataan is in upper left. Zambales Mountains are visible in background.*

where the vehicles were lined up almost bumper to bumper. On each side was an endless line of pedestrians, mostly civilians fleeing from the invading army.

The enemy air force could hardly be expected to overlook so obvious and inviting a target on their way to other, more important military missions. The primary objective of the thirty-two light bombers of the *5th Air Group* that day was ammunition dumps, but the Japanese pilots reported that they also dive-bombed American vehicles and "motorized units." [15] Colonel Collier noted that "hostile bombers, with the rising sun glistening on wing tips, flying at low and high altitudes, crossed and re-crossed the road." [16] But he saw no dive-bombing or strafing attacks. "Had the bombers struck the jammed columns with bombs and strafing," he wrote, "our withdrawal into Bataan would certainly have been seriously crippled." [17]

Since 30 December General Homma had been strengthening his forces in front of the D–5 line. By New Year's Eve he had on Route 3, in and around Tarlac, the entire *9th Infantry Regiment*, the *Kanno Detachment* (*3d Battalion, 2d Formosa*), *8th Field Artillery* (less one battalion), two batteries of the *22d Field Artillery*, and a battalion of the *48th Mountain Artillery*. The mis-

---

[15] *5th Air Gp* Opns, p. 43.

[16] Collier, Notebooks, I, 74.
[17] *Ibid.*, 76.

sion of this force was to drive south toward Bataan.[18]

Along the D–5 line stood two Philippine Army divisions, the 11th on the right and the 21st on the left. Between the high ground on each end of the line the terrain was flat, the vegetation consisting of cane fields and uncultivated grassland. As the troops reached this position they began to clear fields of fire and, when they could get the wire, erect barbed-wire entanglements.[19]

The 21st Division held the left (west) portion of the flatlands along the south bank of the Bamban River from the Magalang–Concepcion road to the Zambales Mountains. On the right was the 22d Infantry; to its left was the 21st Infantry, with the 3d Battalion on the right and the 2d Battalion on the left. Along the front, between the two battalions, were two high multiple-span steel bridges (one railroad and one highway) fording the Bamban River. The engineers had destroyed both bridges, but the river, practically dry at this season of the year, presented no obstacle to advancing infantry and only a slight one to vehicles. To strengthen the river line, therefore, Company C, 23d Infantry, was posted on the high ground north of the Bamban River and west of Route 3, in position to dominate the road and railroad south of the town. The 21st Field Artillery was in general support.[20]

The wisdom of placing Company C in this position was soon confirmed. At about

0130 New Year's Day, a Japanese force mounted on bicycles and estimated as of company size was observed pedaling down the road from Bamban toward the destroyed bridge between the 2d and 3d Battalions, 21st Infantry. The enemy troops were part of the *Kanno Detachment*, which had been caught in the open by American tanks at Zaragoza two days earlier. Their reception at Bamban was no less warm. As the Japanese cyclists advanced along the short stretch of road paralleling the river east of the bridge, Company C delivered a punishing fire in their midst. After some minutes of confusion and milling about, the surprised and badly hit Japanese force retreated, having suffered thirty-five casualties. Company C gained an assortment of bicycles, swords, and miscellaneous equipment, as well as a wounded Japanese noncom. Since he spoke no English and no one present understood Japanese, he proved useless as a source of information. By the time he had been evacuated to the rear he had died of his wounds.[21]

By 0900 the remainder of the *Kanno Detachment* had reached Bamban. The infantry soon began an attack against the river line and Company C; the artillery joined in the action about noon. That afternoon the fighting was brisk, with heavy shelling on both sides and with Japanese aircraft participating in the action. But all efforts by the Japanese to cross the river met with failure and Company C was still in position late in the day.

At division headquarters reports of Japanese troop movements south from Tarlac

[18] *14th Army* Opns, I, 64, 71–72.

[19] Mallonée, Comments on Draft MS, 8 Jan 52, OCMH; ltr, Townsend to Ward, 8 Jan 52, OCMH; Central Luzon, Allied Geographical Sec (AGS) GHQ SWPA, Terrain Study 94, I, 48; Skerry, NLF Engineer Rpt of Opns, p. 9.

[20] Brief Hist of 22d Inf (PA), p. 2; Mallonée, Bataan Diary, I, 106; O'Day, 21st Div (PA), II, 14.

[21] The account of 21st Division operations at Bamban is based upon O'Day, 21st Div (PA), II, 15; Brief Hist of 22d Inf (PA), p. 4; Opns of 21st Inf (PA), p. 2; Richards, Steps to a POW Camp, pp. 7–8; *14th Army* Opns, I, 65 84; ltr, O'Day to Ward, 14 Jan 52, OCMH.

to Bamban had been received earlier in the day, one scout noting "that one of our own tanks was being driven around Tarlac to the hilarity of the enemy troops." [22] These reports were accurate. The *9th Infantry* and supporting troops were moving forward to reinforce the *Kanno Detachment.* As the Japanese came within artillery range they were brought under fire by guns of the 21st Field Artillery. Although suffering losses in personnel and equipment, the *9th Infantry* by 1600 had joined the *Kanno Detachment* on the north bank of the river.

But the Japanese for some inexplicable reason failed to attempt a crossing. At nightfall the 21st Division began to move out, Company C wading the shallow Bamban to rejoin the division. The entire division withdrew down Route 3 to Angeles, then turned southwest along Route 74 to Porac. The enemy followed cautiously and it was not until 1130 of the 2d that the *Kanno Detachment* reached Angeles. The Japanese now had possession of the Clark Field area.

It was now the turn of the 11th Division to extricate itself and withdraw into Bataan. This division had recently been strengthened by the return from the Cagayan valley of about 1,000 of its men, drawn largely from the 12th and 13th Infantry Regiments. Its sector of the D–5 line extended from the Magalang–Concepcion road eastward to the Pampanga River. On the right (east) was the reorganized 12th Infantry, holding a front from Mt. Arayat to the Pampanga River and the town of Arayat. It was in position to guard against an unexpected Japanese advance toward San

Fernando along Route 10, which connected Gapan on Route 5 with that town.

The western portion of the 11th Division line, from the Magalang road to Mt. Arayat, was held by the 11th Infantry under the command of Col. Glen R. Townsend, who had led the Cagayan valley force. At Magalang a north-south road from Concepcion branched off, one section leading to Angeles on Route 3 and another to Mexico, a few miles northeast of San Fernando. The 2d Battalion, 11th Infantry, was posted across the Magalang road, a few miles north of the town and directly in the path of a Japanese advance from Concepcion. The 3d Battalion extended the line east to the mountains, and the 1st Battalion, recovering from its hard fight at Zaragoza on the 30th, was in reserve.[23]

Early on 1 January General Brougher, the division commander, ordered Colonel Townsend to withdraw his 11th Infantry, starting at 2000 that day. The regiment was to retire along the Magalang road through Mexico and San Fernando to Guagua, about fifteen miles from Bataan.

While the 11th Infantry was preparing to move, an enemy force estimated as a reinforced battalion of infantry with artillery support was pushing south along the Magalang road from Concepcion. At 1630 this Japanese force attacked Townsend's line. Maj. Helmert J. Duisterhof's 2d Battalion, composed of Igorot troops, bore the brunt of the assault. Despite repeated attacks, the Igorots, supported by two 75-mm. SPM

---

[22] O'Day, 21st Div (PA), II, 15.

[23] NLF and I Corps Rpt of Opns, p. 12; Townsend, Defense of Phil, OCMH; 11th Inf (PA), Beach Defense and Delaying Action, pp. 21–22, OCMH; Capt Liles, 12th Inf (PA), p. 13, Chunn Notebooks.

guns, held firm, inflicting heavy losses on the enemy. A Japanese attempt to outflank the 11th Infantry line by pushing elements through dense fields of sugar cane met with failure. At 2000, the appointed hour, the 11th Infantry broke contact and began its withdrawal, passing through the 194th Tank Battalion in position east of San Fernando. By 0200 of the 2d the regiment had reached Guagua. During the night it was joined by the 12th Infantry and remaining elements of the 13th Infantry.[24] With the successful withdrawal of the 11th Division, the troops on the D–5 line had made good their escape through San Fernando. Meanwhile the remaining troops south of that town were doing the same.

Escape Through San Fernando

The blast that destroyed the Calumpit bridges in the early hours of 1 January signaled the end of the South Luzon Force. Its mission completed, the force moved on to Bataan where General Jones rejoined the 51st Division. At the same time General Stevens of the 91st Division and General Weaver, commander of the tank group, went on to San Fernando to join their units.[25]

When the debris had stopped falling at the Pampanga crossing, the covering force of 71st and 91st Division elements, originally organized by Stevens, returned to its positions along the river bank. A second force, the 3d Battalion of the 23d In-

fantry, with a battery of the 21st Field Artillery, moved into position near Apalit, about 4,000 yards to the north on the west bank of the Pampanga. The mission of this battalion, led by Maj. Charles A. McLaughlin, was to "assist in delaying the enemy advance on San Fernando," by preventing a hostile crossing before 2000. In support of both forces was the tank group, posted just below San Fernando.[26]

Late on the morning of 1 January the Japanese reached Calumpit. The *Tanaka Detachment* (*2d Formosa,* less *3d Battalion,* and a battalion of the *48th Mountain Artillery*) had moved cautiously from Plaridel during the night and now faced the covering force across the wide, unfordable Pampanga. The sight of the Japanese at such close proximity was extremely disconcerting to the poorly trained Filipino troops. Their nervousness was increased by the sight of the Japanese bombers which passed overhead that morning on their way to bomb installations on Bataan.

During the day the Japanese made numerous attempts to push a force across the swiftly flowing Pampanga, but to no avail.[27] The covering force on the river line pulled out for San Fernando during the afternoon, followed that evening by McLaughlin's battalion. The remnants of the 71st and 91st Divisions which constituted the first of these forces were "so badly disorganized and in need of equipment" that they were sent directly to Bataan. McLaughlin's battalion

---

[24] Ltr, Townsend to Ward, 8 Jan 52, OCMH; O'Day, 21st Div (PA), II, 15. See also ltr, Col Miller to Ward, 31 Dec 51, OCMH. There is no Japanese confirmation of this action.

[25] Jones, Diary, p. 17; Skerry, Comments on Engineer Hist, No. 9, p. 10; Miller, *Bataan Uncensored,* pp. 122–23.

[26] NLF and I Corps Rpt of Opns, p. 14; Skerry, Comments on Engineer Hist, No. 9, p. 10; McLaughlin to author, 14 Jun 49, OCMH; Mallonée, Bataan Diary, I, 113; O'Day, 21st Div (PA), II, 6.

[27] NLF and I Corps Rpt of Opns, p. 14, *14th Army* Opns, I, 65, 84; USA *vs.* Homma, p. 3055, testimony of Homma.

rejoined the 21st Division at Porac on the morning of 2 January. The last elements to pass through San Fernando were the tanks. Reaching the town at 0200 on the 2d, after all the others had left, they found it to be "truly a ghost town." The tankers gave the order to blow the bridge across the San Fernando River and in the darkness moved down Route 7 toward Guagua and the American line being formed there.[28]

The Japanese did not cross the Pampanga until the afternoon of 2 January when at 1600 the *Tanaka Detachment* finally got its artillery over the swiftly flowing river. Once across, Colonel Tanaka moved forward rapidly and by 1830 had reached San Fernando. There he made contact with

the *Kanno Detachment* which had pushed down Route 3 from Angeles.[29]

In the few days from 30 December 1941 to 2 January 1942 the North and South Luzon Forces had completed successfully the most complicated and difficult maneuver of the campaign thus far. They had held at Plaridel and along the D–5 line. A part of the force had crossed the Calumpit bridge, marched through San Fernando, and down Route 7 toward Bataan. Another part had withdrawn from the D–5 line, along the flat grassland west of Mt. Arayat to Mexico and San Fernando to join the others retreating down Route 7. The remainder had moved down Route 3 to Angeles and then along Route 74 to Porac. Everywhere the enemy had been held and the route of escape kept open until the last unit was on its way into Bataan.

---

[28] NLF and I Corps Rpt of Opns, p. 14; Mallonée, Bataan Diary, I, 114; Miller, *Bataan Uncensored*, p. 124; Prov Tank Gp Rpt of Opns, p. 15; Dooley, First U. S. Tank Action in World War II, p. 13; ltr, Miller to Ward, 31 Dec 51, OCMH.

[29] *14th Army* Opns, I, 84; USA *vs.* Homma, p. 3055, testimony of Homma.

CHAPTER XIII

Into Bataan

By the first week of January 1942 the American and Filipino troops withdrawing from both ends of Luzon had joined at San Fernando and begun the last lap of their journey to Bataan. In ten days they had retired from Lingayen Gulf and Lamon Bay to Guagua and Porac, on the two roads leading into Bataan. There they had halted and established a line only fifteen miles from the base of the peninsula. The longer they could hold, the more time would be available to prepare the final defenses in Bataan.

The Guagua–Porac Line

Along the ten-mile line from Guagua to Porac, paralleling the road between the two barrios, General Wainwright had placed the 11th and 21st Divisions (PA), as well as armor and cavalry. (*Map 10*) On the left (west), around Porac, was the 21st Division with the 26th Cavalry (PS) to its rear, in force reserve. On the east was the 11th Division, its right flank covered by almost impenetrable swamps crisscrossed by numerous streams. In support of both divisions was General Weaver's tank group.

The troops along this line, the best in the North Luzon Force, though battle tested and protected by mountains on the west and swamps on the east, felt exposed and insecure. They were convinced that they were opposing the entire Japanese *14th Army*, estimated, according to Colonel Mal-

lonée, to number 120,000 men.[1] Actually, Japanese strength on Luzon was about half that size, and only two reinforced regiments with tanks and artillery faced the men on the Guagua–Porac line.

From Cabanatuan, where Homma had moved his headquarters on New Year's Day, *14th Army* issued orders to attack the line before Bataan.[2] A force, known as the *Takahashi Detachment* after its commander, Lt. Col. Katsumi Takahashi, and consisting of the *9th Infantry* (less two companies), two batteries of the *22d Field Artillery,* and the *8th Field Heavy Artillery Regiment* (less one battalion), was to strike out from Angeles along Route 74, smash the American line at Porac, and go on to seize Dinalupihan, an important road junction at the entrance to Bataan. To support Takahashi's drive down Route 74, Homma ordered the *9th Independent Field Heavy Artillery Battalion,* then approaching Tarlac, to push on to Porac.

A second force, drawn largely from the *48th Division,* was organized for the drive down Route 7 through Guagua to Hermosa, a short distance southeast of Dinalupihan. This force, organized at San Fernando and led by Colonel Tanaka, was composed of the *2d Formosa* and a battalion of the *47th Infantry* supported by a company of tanks and three battalions of

---

[1] Mallonée, Bataan Diary, I, 113. This estimate came from G–3 USAFFE.
[2] *14th Army* Opns, I, 66.

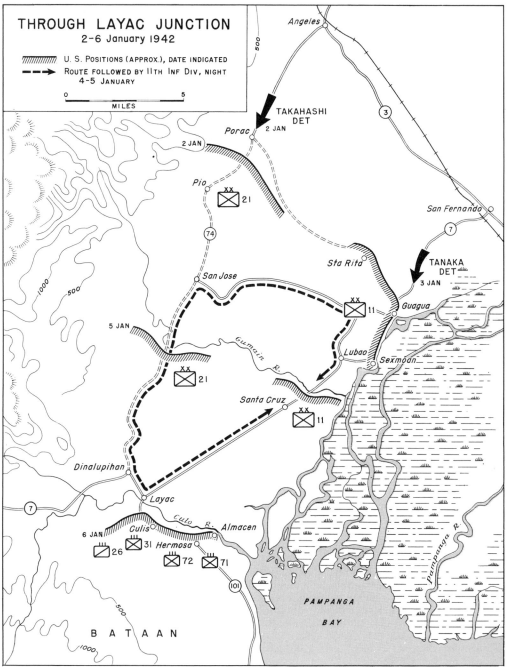

THROUGH LAYAC JUNCTION
2–6 January 1942

////// U. S. Positions (approx.), date indicated
━ ━▶ Route followed by 11th Inf Div, night
4–5 January

0 _____ 5
MILES

MAP 10

artillery. Both detachments were to receive support from the *5th Air Group,* which was also to strike at targets on Bataan. The attack would begin at 0200 on 2 January.[3]

The Japanese expected to smash the defenses before Bataan easily and to make quick work of the "defeated enemy," who, in General Morioka's striking phrase, was like "a cat entering a sack." [4] General Homma fully intended to draw the strings tight once the Americans were in the sack, thereby bringing the campaign to an early and successful conclusion. He was due for a painful disappointment.

The Left Flank

In the 21st Division sector, just below Porac, two regiments stood on the line. On the west (left), from the mountains to Route 74, was the 21st Infantry, spread thin along the entire front. On the right, behind the Porac–Guagua road, was the 22d Infantry. The 23d Infantry, organized at the start of hostilities, was in reserve about five miles to the rear. The division's artillery regiment was deployed with its 3d Battalion on the left, behind the 21st Infantry, and the 1st Battalion on the right. The 2d Battalion was in general support, but placed immediately behind the 3d Battalion which was short one battery.[5]

Seven miles south of Porac, at San Jose, was the force reserve, the 26th Cavalry, now partly rested and reorganized after its fight in the Lingayen area. Its mission was to cover the left flank of the 21st Division and extend it westward to the Zambales Mountains. Colonel Pierce, the cavalry commander, dispatched Troop G, equipped with pack radio, forward toward Porac, to the left of the 21st Infantry. The rest of the regiment he kept in readiness at San Jose. The 26th Cavalry was not the only unit in San Jose; also there were the 192d Tank Battalion and the headquarters of the 21st Division. The place was so crowded that Colonel Mallonée, who wanted to establish the command post of the 21st Field Artillery there, was forced to choose another location because "the town was as full as the county seat during fair week." [6]

The expected attack against the Guagua–Porac line came on the afternoon of 2 January, when an advance detachment from the *9th Infantry* coming down Route 74 hit the 21st Infantry near Porac. Although the enemy detachment was small, it was able to force back the weakened and thinly spread defenders about 2,000 yards to the southwest, to the vicinity of Pio. Stiffened by the reserve, the regiment finally halted the Japanese advance just short of the regimental reserve line. Efforts to restore the original line failed, leaving the artillery exposed to the enemy infantry, who were "about as far from the muzzles as outfielders would play for Babe Ruth if there were no fences." [7]

Division headquarters in San Jose immediately made plans for a counterattack using a battalion of the reserve regiment, the

[3] *Ibid.,* 64, 71–72, 85; *5th Air Gp* Opns, p. 41.
[4] Interrog of Lt Gen Susumu Morioka, 24 Apr 47, Interrogations of Former Japanese Officers, Mil Hist Div, GHQ FEC, I, 71.
[5] The account of action on the left flank is based upon NLF and I Corps Rpt of Opns, pp. 14–15; O'Day, 21st Div (PA), II, 15–20; Mallonée, Bataan Diary, I, 114–20, 123–25; Chandler, "26th Cavalry (PS) Battles to Glory," Part 2, *Armored Cavalry Journal* (May–June 1947), pp. 12–13; Prov Tank Gp Rpt of Opns, p. 15; Brief Hist of 22d Inf (PA), p. 4; Richards, Steps to a POW Camp, pp. 9–12; *14th Army Opns,* I, 73, 85.

[6] Mallonée, Bataan Diary, I, 115.
[7] *Ibid.,* 116.

23d Infantry. But darkness fell before the attack could be mounted and the 2d Battalion, 23d Infantry, the unit selected for the counterattack, was ordered to move up at dawn and restore the line on the left. When the 2d Battalion moved into the line, the 21st Infantry would regroup to the right, thus shortening its front.

That night the stillness was broken only by fire from the Philippine artillery which had pulled back about 600 yards. When morning came the enemy was gone. Reports from 21st Infantry patrols, which had moved forward unmolested at the first sign of light, encouraged division headquarters to believe that the original main line of resistance could be restored without a fight and orders were issued for a general advance when the 2d Battalion, 23d Infantry, tied in with the 21st Infantry.

American plans for a counterattack were premature. The evening before, the main force of the *Takahashi Detachment* had left its assembly area midway between Bamban and Angeles and marched rapidly toward Porac. The *8th Field Heavy Artillery Regiment* (less one battalion), with its 105-mm. guns, had accompanied the force and by morning was in position to support the infantry attack. Thus, when the 2d Battalion, 23d Infantry, began to advance it was met first by punishing small-arms fire from the infantry, then by fire from the 105-mm. guns of the *8th Field Artillery*. At the same time three Japanese aircraft swung low to strafe the road in support of the enemy attack. The momentum of the advance carried the Japanese below Pio, where they were finally stopped.

When news of the attack reached General Wainwright's headquarters, the most alarming item in the report was the presence of Japanese medium artillery, thought

to be heavy guns, on the left of the American line. This artillery represented a serious threat, and the 21st Division was ordered to "hold the line or die where you are." [8] General Capinpin did his best, but he had only two battalions of the 23d Infantry, an unseasoned and untrained unit, left in reserve. One of these battalions was in North Luzon Force reserve and it was now ordered to move to the 11th Division sector near Guagua where a heavy fight was in progress.

Meanwhile, Colonel Takahashi had launched an assault against the 21st Infantry. First the battalion on the left gave way and within an hour the reserve line also began to crumble. By noon the left flank of the 21st Infantry was completely disorganized. The right battalion, though still intact, fell back also lest it be outflanked. This withdrawal exposed the left flank of the 22d Infantry on its right.

Colonel Takahashi lost no time in taking advantage of the gap in the American line. Elements of the *9th Infantry* drove in between the two regiments, hitting most heavily the 1st Battalion, 22d Infantry, on the regimental left. The action which followed was marked by confusion. The noise of artillery fire and the black smoke rising from the burning cane fields reduced the troops to bewildered and frightened men. At one time the 21st Infantry staff was nearly captured when the onrushing enemy broke through to the command post. A group of tanks from the 11th Division sector, ordered to attack the Japanese line in front of the 21st Division, showed a marked disinclination to move into the adjoining sector without orders from the tank group commander. Before the ferocity of the Jap-

---

[8] O'Day, 21st Div (PA), II, 16.

anese attack the defending infantry line melted away.[9]

Had it not been for the artillery the Japanese attack might well have resulted in a complete rout. Fortunately, the 21st Field Artillery acted in time to halt Takahashi's advance. The 1st Battalion on the right, behind the 22d Infantry, covered the gap between the two regiments and fired directly against the oncoming Japanese at a range of 600–800 yards. The 2d and 3d Battalions delivered direct fire up the draw leading through Pio. Notwithstanding the punishing artillery fire, the *9th Infantry* continued to attack. For six hours, until darkness closed in, the left portion of the 21st Division line was held by the guns of the 21st Field Artillery alone, firing at close range across open fields. "As attack after attack came on, broke, and went back," wrote Colonel Mallonée, "I knew what Cushing's artillerymen must have felt with the muzzles of their guns in the front line as the Confederate wave came on and broke on the high water mark at Gettysburg." [10]

Quiet settled down on the 21st Division front that night. The *Takahashi Detachment,* its attack halted by the effective fire of the artillery, paused to reorganize and take stock of the damage. The next day, 4 January, there was no action at all on the left and only intermittent pressure on the right. The Japanese did manage to emplace one or two of their 105-mm. guns along the high ground to the west and dur-

ing the day fired on the rear areas. Fortunately, their marksmanship was poor and although they made life behind the front lines uncomfortable they inflicted no real damage.

On the afternoon of the 4th, as a result of pressure on the 11th Division to the east, General Wainwright ordered the 21st Division to withdraw under cover of darkness to the line of the Gumain River, about eight miles south of Porac. That night the division began to move back after successfully breaking contact with the enemy. Despite the absence of enemy pressure there was considerable confusion during the withdrawal. By daylight of the 5th, however, the troops were across the Gumain where they began to prepare for their next stand. Division headquarters, the 23d Infantry, the division signal company, and other special units were at Dinalupihan, with the 21st Field Artillery located just east of the town.

The Right Flank

Along the east half of the Guagua–Porac line stood the 11th Division (PA). The 11th Infantry was on the left, holding the Guagua–Porac road as far north as Santa Rita. The regiment, in contact with the 21st Division on the left only through occasional patrols, had three battalions on the line. The 2d Battalion was on the left, the 1st in the center, and the 3d on the right. Next to the 11th was the 13th Infantry, which held Guagua and was in position across Route 7. Extending the line southeast from Guagua to Sexmoan were two companies of the 12th Infantry. The 11th Field Artillery, for the first time since the start of the war, was in support of the di-

---

[9] Lt. Grover C. Richards, 21st Infantry (PA), states that he was sent to bring the tanks in and finally had to walk in front of the lead tank in order to get it to advance. Richards, Steps to a POW Camp, pp. 9–10. See also Weaver, Comments on Draft MS, Comment 22, OCMH.

[10] Mallonée, Bataan Diary, I, 120.

vision. Part of the 194th Tank Battalion and Company A of the 192d provided additional support.[11]

The Japanese attack on the right flank of the Guagua–Porac line came on 3 January. Leaving San Fernando at 0400 the reinforced *Tanaka Detachment* had advanced cautiously along Route 7. At about 0930 the point of the Japanese column made contact with a platoon of tanks from Company C, 194th, posted about 1,000 yards north of Guagua. Under tank fire and confined to the road because of the marshy terrain on both sides, the Japanese halted to await the arrival of the main force. About noon, when the force in front became too formidable, the American tanks fell back to Guagua. The Japanese continued to advance slowly. Forced by the nature of the terrain into a frontal assault along the main road and slowed down by the numerous villages along the line of advance, the attack, the Japanese admitted, "did not progress as planned." [12] Artillery was brought into support and, late in the afternoon, the 75-mm. guns opened fire, scoring at least one hit on the 11th Infantry command post. The defending infantry were greatly cheered by the sound of their own artillery answering the Japanese guns. Organized after the start of the war and inadequately trained, the men of the 11th Field Artillery, firing from positions at Guagua and Santa Rita, made up in enthusiasm what they lacked in skill.[13]

The Japanese artillery fire continued during the night and increased in intensity the next morning, 4 January, when a battalion of 150-mm. howitzers joined in the fight. In the early afternoon an enemy column spearheaded by tanks of the *7th Tank Regiment* broke through the 13th Infantry line along Route 7 and seized the northern portion of Guagua. Another column hit the 3d Battalion, 11th Infantry, to the left of the 13th, inflicting about 150 casualties. The two units held on long enough, however, for the 1st and 2d Battalions of the 11th Infantry to pull out. They then broke contact and followed the two battalions in good order.[14]

During this action Company A, 192d Tank Battalion, and elements of the 11th Division attempted to counterattack by striking the flank of the Japanese line before Guagua. This move almost ended in disaster. The infantry on the line mistook the tanks for enemy armor and began dropping mortar shells on Company A, and General Weaver, who was in a jeep attempting to co-ordinate the tank-infantry attack, was almost hit. The mistake was discovered in time and no serious damage was done.

---

[11] The account of the action around Guagua is based on Townsend, Defense of Phil, p. 13; 2d Lt James, 11th Inf (PA), p. 8, and Liles, 12th Inf (PA), p. 13, both in Chunn Notebooks; 11th Inf (PA), Beach Defense and Delaying Action, pp. 22–23; Miller, *Bataan Uncensored*, pp. 124–32; Prov Tank Gp Rpt of Opns, pp. 15–16; Dooley, The First U.S. Tank Action in World War II, p. 13; Mallonée, Bataan Diary, I, 124–25.

[12] *14th Army* Opns, I, 85.

[13] 11th Inf (PA), Beach Defense and Delaying Action, pp. 22–23; Townsend, Defense of Phil, p. 13.

[14] The account of this action and those that follow are reconstructed from a large number of records which present at best a confusing picture. The main sources used in this reconstruction are: NLF and I Corps Rpt of Opns, pp. 14–15; Prov Tank Gp Rpt, p. 15–16; Miller, *Bataan Uncensored*, pp. 126–32; Rpts of S–2 and S–3, 194th Tank Bn in Diary of Col Miller, copy in OCMH; *14th Army* Opns, I, 86; Weaver, Comments on Draft MS, Comments 22–25, OCMH.

When news of the Japanese break-through at Guagua reached General Wain-wright on the afternoon of the 4th he decided it was time to fall back again. The next line was to be south of the Gumain River, and orders were issued to the 11th, as well as the 21st Division, to withdraw to the new line that night.

General Brougher's plan of withdrawal called for a retirement along Route 7 through Guagua and Lubao to the new line. The rapid advance of the *Tanaka Detachment* through Guagua and down Route 7 toward Lubao late that afternoon, however, cut off this route of retreat of the 11th Infantry and other elements on the line. A hasty reconnaissance of the area near the highway failed to disclose any secondary roads or trails suitable for an orderly retirement. To withdraw cross-country was to invite wholesale confusion and a possible rout. The only course remaining to the cutoff units was to traverse a thirty-mile-long, circuitous route through San Jose, in the 21st Division sector, then down Route 74 to Dinalupihan. There the men would turn southeast as far as Layac Junction and then north along Route 7 to a point where they could form a line before the advancing *Tanaka Detachment*.

That evening, 4 January, the long march began. Those elements of the 11th Division cut off by the Japanese advance, and Company A, 192d Tank Battalion, reached San Jose without interference from the enemy but not without adding to the confusion already existing in the 21st Division area.

Meanwhile at San Jose, General Brougher, the 11th Division commander, had collected all the trucks and buses he could find and sent them forward to carry his men. With this motor transportation, the 11th Infantry was able to take up a posi-tion along Route 7, between Santa Cruz and Lubao, by about 0600 of 5 January. This line was about one mile southwest of the Gumain River, the position which the division had originally been ordered to occupy. Troops arriving on this line found themselves under small-arms fire from the *Tanaka Detachment,* which had entered Lubao the previous evening.

A short distance north of this line, an outpost line had already been established the previous afternoon by General Brougher with those troops who had been able to withdraw down Route 7. The infantry troops on this line were from the 12th Infantry, part of which had pulled back along Route 7. Brougher had rounded up about two hundred men from the regiment, together with the ten guns of the 11th Field Artillery and some 75-mm. SPM's, and formed a line on Route 7 between Lubao and Santa Cruz. For fourteen hours, from the afternoon of 4 January to the morning of 5 January, these troops under the command of Capt. John Primrose formed the only line between the enemy and Layac Junction, the entrance into Bataan. Early on 5 January when the new line was formed by the troops who had withdrawn through San Jose, Primrose and his men pulled back to join the main force of the division.

The withdrawal of the 194th Tank Battalion from Guagua had been accomplished only after a fierce fight. Colonel Miller, the tank commander, had ordered the tanks to pull out on the morning of the 4th. Under constant enemy pressure, the tanks began a slow withdrawal, peeling off one at a time. Guarding their flank was a force consisting of a few tanks of Company C, 194th, and some SPM's from Capt. Gordon H. Peck's provisional battalion posted at a block along the Sexmoan–Lubao road. At about 1600 Peck and Miller had observed a large enemy force approaching. This force, estimated as between 500 and 800 men, supported by machine guns, mortars, and artillery, was led by three Filipinos carrying white flags, presumably under duress. The tanks and SPM's opened fire, cutting the Japanese column to pieces. The 194th Tank Battalion then left burning Guagua and Lubao and moved south to positions a mile or two above Santa Cruz. The tanks and SPM's at the block covered its withdrawal.

Some time after midnight, between 0200 and 0300 on 5 January, the covering force was hit again, this time by infantry and artillery of the *Tanaka Detachment*. Attacking in bright moonlight across an open field and along the road, the enemy came under direct fire from the American guns. Driven back with heavy casualties, he attacked again and again, and only broke off the action about 0500, at the approach of daylight. Later in the day the *Tanaka Detachment*, seriously depleted by casualties, was relieved by Col. Hifumi Imai's *1st Formosa Infantry* (less one battalion) to which were attached Tanaka's tanks and artillery.

By dawn of 5 January, after two days of heavy and confused fighting, the Guagua–Porac line had been abandoned and the American and Filipino troops had pulled back to a new line south and west of the Gumain River. The 21st Division on the west had retired to a position about eight miles below Porac and was digging in along the bank of the river; to the east the 11th Division had fallen back six miles and stood along a line about a mile south of the river. But the brief stand on the Guagua–Porac

797-257 O–66—16

line had earned large dividends. The Japanese had paid dearly for the ground gained and had been prevented from reaching their objective, the gateway to Bataan. More important was the time gained by the troops already in Bataan to prepare their positions.

Behind the Gates

The only troops remaining between the enemy and Bataan—the 11th and 21st Divisions, the 26th Cavalry, and the tank group—were now formed on their final line in front of the peninsula. This line, approximately eight miles in front of the access road to Bataan and generally along the Gumain River, blocked the approach to Bataan through Dinalupihan and Layac Junction.

Both Dinalupihan and Layac Junction lie along Route 7. This road, the 11th Division's route of withdrawal, extends southwest from San Fernando to Layac where it joins Route 110, the only road leading into Bataan. At Layac, Route 7 turns sharply northwest for 2,000 yards to Dinalupihan, the southern terminus of Route 74 along which the 21st Division was withdrawing. Route 7 then continues west across the base of the peninsula to Olangapo on Subic Bay, then north along the Zambales coast to Lingayen Gulf, a route of advance the Japanese had fortunately neglected in favor of the central plain which led most directly to their objective, Manila.

Layac Junction, where all the roads to Bataan joined, was the key point along the route of withdrawal. Through it and over the single steel bridge across the Culo River just south of the town would have to pass the troops converging along Routes 7 and 74. The successful completion of this move would require the most precise timing, and, if the enemy attacked, a high order of road discipline.

Through the Layac Bottleneck

The withdrawal from the Gumain River through Layac Junction, although made without interference from the enemy, was attended by the greatest confusion. On the east, where the 11th Division was in position astride Route 7, there were a few skirmishes between patrols on 5 January but no serious action. General Brougher had received a battalion of the 71st Infantry to strengthen his line but the battalion returned to its parent unit at the end of the day without ever having been engaged with the enemy.[15]

In the 21st Division area to the west there was much milling about and confusion on the 5th. Work on the Gumain River position progressed very slowly during the morning, and the troops showed little inclination to extend the line eastward to make contact with the 11th Division. During the day contradictory or misunderstood orders sent the men forward and then pulled them back, sometimes simultaneously. Shortly before noon General Capinpin, needlessly alarmed about the situation on the 11th Division front and fearful for the safety of his right (east) flank, ordered a withdrawal to a point about a mile above Dinalupihan. The movement was begun but halted early in the afternoon by an order from General Wainwright to hold the Gumain River line until further orders.

By midafternoon the division had once more formed a line south of the river.

Thinly manned in one place, congested in another, the position was poorly organized and incapable of withstanding a determined assault. In one section, infantry, artillery, and tanks were mixed together in complete disorder. "Everyone," said Colonel Mallonée, "was in everyone else's lap and the whole thing resembled nothing quite as much as the first stages of an old fashioned southern political mass meeting and free barbecue."[16]

Fortunately for General Capinpin, the *Takahashi Detachment* on Route 74 did not advance below Pio. This failure to advance was due to an excess of caution on the part of the colonel who, on the 4th, had been placed under the *65th Brigade* for operations on Bataan.[17] It is entirely possible that Japanese caution and lack of vigor in pressing home the attack may have been due to a mistaken notion of the strength of the defending forces and a healthy respect for American-led Filipino troops. Had Takahashi chosen this moment to launch a determined attack against the 21st Division he would almost certainly have succeeded in trapping the forces before Bataan.

The troops had hardly taken up their positions behind the Gumain River when General Wainwright issued orders for the withdrawal into Bataan through Layac Junction, to begin at dark. First to cross the bridge over the Culo River below Layac would be the 11th Division, followed closely by the 21st. To cover the withdrawal of the 11th, one battalion of the 21st Division was to sideslip over in front of the 11th Division, while the 26th Cavalry would protect the left flank of the 21st during its withdrawal.[18]

[15] 11th Inf (PA), Beach Defense and Delaying Action, p. 24; ltr, Selleck to Board of Officers, 1 Feb 46, sub: Statement for Reinstatement of Rank, p. 10, OCMH.

[16] Mallonée, Bataan Diary, I, 131. See also pp. 127–30, and O'Day, 21st Div (PA), II, 19.
[17] See below, Ch. XV, p. 21.
[18] O'Day, 21st Div (PA), II, 20.

The execution of such a maneuver seemed impossible under the conditions existing along the front. The 23d Infantry, in division reserve, was already at Dinalupihan and Colonel O'Day, senior American instructor in the 21st Division, proposed instead to place a battalion of this regiment astride Route 7 behind the 11th Division. General Brougher's troops could then fall back through the covering battalion. This proposal was accepted, and after considerable difficulty "the equivalent of a battalion" was placed in position by dark.[19]

When night fell the 11th Division withdrew from its positions and moved southwest along Route 7 toward Layac Junction and the road to Bataan. Soon the town was crowded with men and vehicles and as the withdrawal continued became a scene of "terrible congestion," of marching men, trucks, buses, artillery, tanks, horses, and large numbers of staff and command cars. "It looked," remarked one observer, "like the parking lot of the Yale bowl." [20]

At about 2030 Col. John Moran, chief of staff of the 11th Division, reported that his division had cleared Layac and was across the Culo bridge. The 21st Division was now ordered across. Observing the passage of men, Colonel O'Day wrote: "It was a painful and tragic sight—our soldiers trudging along, carrying inordinate loads of equipment and personal effects. Many had their loads slung on bamboo poles, a pole between two men. They had been marching almost since dark the night before, and much of the daylight hours had been spent in backing and filling. . . ." [21]

By about midnight of the 5th, the last guns of the 21st Field Artillery had cleared the bridge, and within the next hour all of the foot troops, closely shepherded by the Scouts of the 26th Cavalry, were across. Last to cross were the tanks, which cleared the bridge shortly before 0200 of the 6th. General Wainwright then ordered Capt. A. P. Chanco, commanding the 91st Engineer Battalion, to blow the bridge. The charges were immediately detonated and the span demolished. All of the troops were now on Bataan, and the last gate slammed shut. The Japanese had lost their opportunity again to cut off the retreat. Colonel Imai was still at Santa Cruz and Takahashi still hung back at Porac.[22]

Holding Action Below Layac Junction

Already formed below Layac Junction when the Culo bridge was blown was another line designed to delay the enemy and gain more time for the Bataan Defense Force. The idea for a delaying action at Layac Junction was contained in WPO–3, the plan that went into effect on 23 December, and General Parker, commander of the Bataan Defense Force, had sent the 31st Infantry (US) there on the 28th to cover the junction.

The importance of this position was stressed by Col. Hugh J. Casey, MacArthur's engineer officer, who, on 2 January, pointed out to General Sutherland that the defense lines then being established on Bataan left to the enemy control of Route 110 which led south from Layac into the peninsula. This road, he felt, should be de-

---

[19] *Ibid.*, pp. 18, 20.

[20] Mallonée, Bataan Diary, I, 138. See also O'Day, 21st Div (PA), II, 20; Prov Tank Gp Rpt of Opns, p. 16; 11th Inf (PA), Beach Defense and Delaying Action, p. 24.

[21] O'Day, 21st Div (PA), II, 20.

[22] *14th Army* Opns, I, 73, 86; O'Day, 21st Div (PA), II, 21; Skerry, Comments on Engineer History, No. 9, p. 11; Chandler, "26th Cavalry (PS) Battles to Glory," Part 2, *Armored Cavalry Journal* (May–June 1947), p. 13.

nied the Japanese as long as possible. He recommended to General Sutherland, therefore, that a strong delaying action, or, failing that, "definite reference to preparing strong delaying positions . . . should be made." [23]

These recommendations were apparently accepted, for the same day General MacArthur ordered Wainwright to organize a delaying position south of Layac Junction along Route 110. On completion of this position, control would pass to General Parker, who was to hold until forced to withdraw by a co-ordinated enemy attack. [24]

Responsibility for the establishment of the Layac Junction line was given to General Selleck who had just reached Bataan with his disorganized 71st Division (PA). The troops assigned were the 71st and 72d

---

[23] Memo, Casey for CofS USAFFE, 2 Jan 42, sub: Defense of Bataan, AG 381, Phil Rcds; ltr, Parker to Ward, 16 Jan 52, OCMH; ltr, Col Olson to author, 10 Jan 52, OCMH. Colonel Maher, Wainwright's chief of staff, states that the Layac Junction position would have been occupied "as a matter of course," and that Colonel Casey had nothing to do with its use. Ltr, Maher to Ward, 24 Dec 51, OCMH.

[24] Except where otherwise indicated this section is based upon: ltr, Selleck to CG II Corps, 3 Feb 43, sub: Action at Layac Junction, in Selleck, Notes on the 71st Div (PA), pp. 20–22. Attached to this letter are accounts of the 31st Infantry (US) by Col. Charles L. Steel and of the 26th Cavalry (PS) at Layac Junction by Lt. Col. Lee C. Vance, and a memo, Weaver for Selleck, 1 Feb 43, sub: Action Prov Tank Gp in Connection with Layac Delaying Position; ltr, Selleck to Board of Officers, 1 Feb 46, sub: Statement for Reinstatement of Rank, OCMH; USAFFE-USFIP Rpt of Opns, pp. 41–42; SLF and II Corps Rpt of Opns, pp. 22–27; and Chandler, "26th Cavalry (PS) Battles to Glory," Part 2, Armored Cavalry Journal (May–June 1947), pp. 13–14; Weaver, Comments on Draft MS, Comments 29 and 30, OCMH; ltr, Miller to Ward, 31 Dec 51, OCMH; Skerry, Comments on Draft MS, Comment C, OCMH. Japanese sources for this action are scanty and the author had to rely on 14th Army Opns, I, 86, and the American sources cited.

Infantry from Selleck's 71st Division, totaling approximately 2,500 men; the 26th Cavalry, now numbering 657 men; and the 31st Infantry (US) of the Philippine Division, the only infantry regiment in the Philippines composed entirely of Americans. Of this force, the 31st was the only unit which had not yet been in action. Artillery support consisted of the 71st Field Artillery with two 75-mm. gun batteries and four 2.95-inch guns; the 1st Battalion of the 23d Field Artillery (PS) with about ten 75's; and the 1st Battalion, 88th Field Artillery (PS) with two batteries of 75's. The tank group and two SPM battalions were also in support.

On 3 and 4 January the 71st Division elements and the 31st Infantry moved into position and began stringing wire and digging in. General Selleck had been denied the use of the 71st Engineers by North Luzon Force, with the result that the construction of defenses progressed slowly. When Colonel Skerry inspected the line on the 4th and 5th he found that the tired and disorganized 71st and 72d Infantry had made little progress in the organization of the ground and that their morale was low. In the 31st Infantry (US) sector, however, he found morale high and the organization of the ground much more effective.

At that time Selleck's forces were spread thin along a line south of Layac Junction across Route 110, which ran southeast and east between Layac and Hermosa. On the right was the 71st Infantry, holding a front along the south bank of Culis Creek—not to be confused with the Culo River immediately to the north. This line, parallel to and just north of Route 110, extended from Almacen, northeast of Hermosa, to a point northeast of Culis, where Culis Creek turned south to cross Route 110. The eastern extremity of the 71st Infantry sector was protected by swamps and a wide river; on the west was the 72d Infantry, straddling Route 110. Its sector was about 1,000 yards below Layac Junction and faced north and east.

Next to the 72d Infantry was the 31st Infantry, with the 1st and 2d Battalions extending the line to the southwest, about 3,000 yards from the nearest hill mass. This exposed left flank was to be covered by the 26th Cavalry, then pulling back through Layac Junction with the 11th and 21st Divisions. In reserve was the 3d Battalion, 31st Infantry, about 1,000 yards to the rear. Supporting the 31st was the 1st Battalion, 88th Field Artillery, on the west, and the 1st Battalion, 23d Field Artillery, to its right, west of Route 110. The 71st Division infantry regiments each had a battalion of the 71st Field Artillery in support.

At approximately 0330 of the 6th of January the 26th Cavalry reached the new line south of Layac Junction and fell in on the left of the 31st Infantry, to the foothills of the Zambales Mountains. It was followed across the bridge by the tanks, which took up supporting positions southwest of Hermosa—the 194th Battalion on the left (west) and the 192d on the right. The 75-mm. SPM's, which withdrew with the tanks, were placed along the line to cover possible routes of advance of hostile tanks.

The line when formed seemed a strong one. In Colonel Collier's opinion, it had "a fair sized force to hold it," and General Parker declared, referring probably to the 31st Infantry sector, that it "lent itself to a good defense . . . was on high ground and had good fields of fire." [25]

General Selleck did not share this optimism about the strength of his position. To him the front occupied by his troops seemed excessive, with the result that "all units except the 26th Cavalry were over-extended." [26] Colonel Skerry's inspection on the 5th had led him to the conclusion that the length of the line held by the disorganized 71st and 72d Infantry was too extended for these units. Selleck thought that his line had another, even more serious weakness, in that part of the right portion faced northeast and the left portion northwest, thus exposing the first to enfilade from the north and the second to enfilade from the east.

Admittedly the position chosen had weaknesses, but no more than a delaying action was ever contemplated along this line. As in the withdrawal of the North Luzon Force from Lingayen Gulf, all that was expected was that the enemy, faced by an organized line, would halt, wait for artillery and other supporting weapons, and plan an organized, co-ordinated attack. By that time the objective—delay—would have been gained, and the line could pull back.

At 0600, 6 January, when all the troops were on the line, Wainwright released General Selleck from his command to Parker's control. After notifying MacArthur of his action he withdrew to Bataan, stopping briefly at Culis where Selleck had his command post. North Luzon Force had completed its mission. Like the South Luzon Force it was now in position behind the first line on Bataan. Only the covering force at Layac Junction denied the enemy free access to Bataan.

Action along the Layac line began on the morning of 6 January with an artillery

[25] Collier, Notebooks, III, 11; SLF and II Corps Rpt of Opns, p. 25; ltr, Parker to Ward, 16 Jan 52, OCMH.

[26] Ltr, Selleck to CG II Corps, 3 Feb 43, Action at Layac Junction, in Selleck, Notes on 71st Div (PA), p. 25.

barrage. At about 1000 forward observers reported that Japanese infantry and artillery were advancing down Route 7 toward Layac Junction. This column was part of the *Imai Detachment* which consisted of the *1st Formosa Infantry*, one company of the *7th Tank Regiment,* two battalions of the *48th Mountain Artillery* armed with 75-mm. guns, and one battalion of the *1st Field Heavy Artillery Regiment* with eight 150-mm. howitzers. By 1030 the Japanese column was within artillery range of the defenders and the 1st Battalions of the 23d and 88th Field Artillery Regiments opened fire. The first salvo by the Philippine Scout gunners was directly on the target. Switching immediately to rapid volley fire, the two battalions, joined by the 71st Field Artillery, searched the road from front to rear, forcing the enemy to deploy about 4,200 yards northeast of Layac.[27]

The Japanese now moved their own artillery into position. The 75's of the *48th Mountain Artillery* and the 150-mm. howitzers of the *1st Field Artillery,* directed by unmolested observation planes, began to drop concentrated and effective fire on the Americans and Filipinos. It was during this bombardment that Jose Calugas, the mess sergeant of Battery B, 88th Field Artillery, won the Medal of Honor.

General Selleck, without antiaircraft protection, was unable to prevent aerial reconnaissance, with the result that the Japanese 150's, out of range of the American guns, were able to place accurate and punishing fire upon the infantry positions and upon the artillery. Around noon, therefore, Selleck ordered his artillery to new positions, but the observation planes, flying as low as 2,000 feet, reported the changed positions, and the

Japanese artillery shifted fire. It enfiladed the 31st Infantry and inflicted great damage on the 71st Infantry and the 1st Battalion, 23d Field Artillery, destroying all but one of the latter's guns. The 88th Field Artillery, in a more protected position, did not suffer as great a loss. That day General MacArthur informed the War Department that the enemy was using his "complete command of the air . . . to full effect against our artillery." [28]

The intense Japanese artillery barrage was the prelude to an advance by the infantry. MacArthur had warned that the Japanese were "apparently setting up a prepared attack in great strength," and, except for his estimate of the strength of the enemy, his analysis was correct.[29] At about 1400 a Japanese force of several battalions of infantry crossed the Culo River below Layac Junction and pushed forward the American line. Another force turned north at Layac and moved toward Dinalupihan, entering that undefended town at 1500. An hour later the Japanese who had continued south on reaching Layac hit Selleck's line between the 31st Infantry and the 72d Infantry. Company B, on the right of the 31st line, had been badly shaken by the artillery barrage and fell back in disorder to higher ground about 800 yards to the rear, leaving a gap between Company C on its left and the 72d Infantry on the right. Japanese troops promptly infiltrated. Attempts by the rest of the 1st Battalion, 31st Infantry, to fill the gap failed and Col. Charles L. Steel, the regimental commander, secured his 3d Battalion from Selleck's reserve and ordered it into the line.

[27] Collier, Notebooks, II, 12–14; ltr, Fowler to author, 30 Apr 49, OCMH.

[28] Rad, MacArthur to TAG, No. 14, 6 Jan 42, AG 381 (11–27–41 Sec 1) Far East.
[29] *Ibid.*

The Japanese, supported by artillery fire, continued to push into the gap, hitting the right of Company C, 31st Infantry, and Company A of the 72d on the left. Lt. Col. Jasper E. Brady, Jr., the 3d Battalion commander, ordered Companies I and L, 31st Infantry, into the sector previously held by Company B. As Company I moved forward, it was caught in the enemy's artillery fire, badly disorganized, and forced back to the rear. Company L, however, continued to press forward. Within thirty minutes from the time it had jumped off to the attack, it had succeeded in restoring the line.[30]

Outwardly the situation seemed well in hand. But General Selleck was in serious trouble. His overextended line had been partially penetrated, his reserves had been committed, and his artillery was practically out of action. The Japanese were continuing to press south across the Culo River. Should they attack successfully through the 72d Infantry line, they would gain control of the road and cut off Selleck's route of escape. Colonel Steel recommended withdrawal and General Selleck informed Parker that he would not be able to hold out without artillery and infantry reinforcements and that a daylight withdrawal might prove disastrous. At 2200 of the 6th, General Parker ordered a withdrawal under cover of darkness.

Although both the American and Japanese commanders had tanks at their disposal neither had employed them that day. Possibly the Japanese had failed to use armor because there were no bridges over the Culo River. Some of the American tanks had been hit by the Japanese artillery, but not seriously enough to prevent their use. They had not been used to support the attack by the 3d Battalion, 31st Infantry, General Selleck noted caustically, because "the terrain was not considered suitable by the tank commander." [31]   At about 1830, when it appeared that the Japanese might cut off the route of escape, Colonel Miller, senior tank commander in the area, had moved the tanks toward the highway. They arrived there about 2100, and were met by General Weaver's executive with orders for a further withdrawal southward into Bataan.[32]

The tanks were already well on their way when the units on the line received orders to pull back. The 71st Division elements experienced no difficulty in withdrawing down the road. The 31st Infantry, leaving three companies on the line as a covering shell, pulled out about 0130 on the morning of the 7th. An hour later, as the shell began to move out, the Japanese launched an attack against Hermosa, cutting off Company E and almost destroying it. The Japanese reached their objective by 0500, but the survivors of Company E

---

[30] Maj Donald G. Thompson, Opns of Co L, 31st Inf (US) in Battle of Layac Junction (paper prepared for Advanced Infantry Officers Course, 1947–48, The Infantry School), pp. 10–14. Major Thompson commanded L Company during this action.

[31] Ltr, Selleck to Board of Officers, 1 Feb 46, sub: Statement for Reinstatement of Rank, p. 11, OCMH. General Weaver does not mention this matter in his memo to Selleck, cited above, or in his report. Colonel Miller speaks of the impossibility of tank action in this area in *Bataan Uncensored*, p. 139. In his comments on a draft of this manuscript, General Weaver states that no request for tanks was ever made to him. Comment 29, OCMH.

[32] Miller, *Bataan Uncensored*, pp. 140–41; Prov Tank Gp Rpt of Opns, pp. 16–17; ltr, Miller to Ward, 31 Dec 51, OCMH; Weaver, Comments on Draft MS, Comments 29 and 30, OCMH.

did not rejoin the regiment until a few days later.[33]

The 26th Cavalry, which had not been under attack that day, had lost contact with the 31st Infantry on its right. Radio communication proved inadequate; messages were garbled and, in some cases, indecipherable. The code had been changed during the night and no one had informed the 26th Cavalry. Consequently the Scout regiment was not aware of the order to withdraw during the night. It was not until the approach of daylight that the 26th learned of the withdrawal. It began to pull back at 0700 of the 7th. By this time the Japanese controlled the road as far south as Hermosa and the Scouts were compelled to move overland across the mountainous jungle to reach the American line. With the departure of the 26th Cavalry the Layac line disappeared.

At Layac Junction the American and Philippine troops had paid dearly to secure one day of grace for the forces preparing to defend Bataan. Against the longer range Japanese guns the Americans had been defenseless. The line had been penetrated at the first blow, only to be restored and then abandoned. The Japanese had once more failed in their attempt to follow up their advantage.

The withdrawal into Bataan was now complete. Under desperate circumstances and under constant pressure from the enemy, General MacArthur had brought his forces from the north and south to San Fernando and Calumpit. There, in a most

difficult maneuver, he had joined the two forces and brought them safely into Bataan, fighting a delaying action all the way. All this had been accomplished in two weeks, during which time positions had been prepared on Bataan and supplies shipped there from Manila and elsewhere. Not a single major unit had been cut off or lost during the withdrawal, and only once, at Cabanatuan, had the American line failed to hold long eough to permit an orderly withdrawal. The success of this complicated and difficult movement, made with ill-equipped and inadequately trained Filipino troops, is a tribute to the generalship of MacArthur, Wainwright, and Jones and to American leadership on the field of battle.

The withdrawal had been a costly one on both sides. General Wainwright's North Luzon Force of 28,000 men had been reduced to about 16,000 largely by the desertion of Filipino soldiers who returned to their homes. Only a small portion of the 12,000 men lost were battle casualties or captured by the enemy. General Jones's South Luzon Force fared much better. Of the 15,000 men in his force originally, General Jones had 14,000 left when he reached Bataan.[34] The Japanese suffered close to 2,000 casualties during the period since the first landing. This number included 627 killed, 1,282 wounded, and 7 missing.[35]

The men who reached Bataan were tired

---

[33] Thompson, Opns of Co L, 31st Inf (US), p. 15; Maj Eugene B. Conrad, Opns of 31st Inf (US), pp. 10–11, and Maj Everett V. Mead, S–4 of 31st Inf (US), Opns and Mvmts of 31st Inf (US), p. 15. Both papers prepared for Advanced Officers Course in 1946–47 and 1947–48, respectively, at The Infantry School.

[34] Wainwright, General Wainwright's Story, pp. 45, 48; interv, Falk with Jones, 2 Dec 49. The strengths as given are rough approximations at best. No official figures are available for the campaign or any part of it.

[35] Comments of Former Japanese Officers Regarding The Fall of the Philippines, pp. 50, 124; USA vs. Homma, Defense Exhibit Y. See also the testimony of Colonel Nakajima, who said at the trial of General Homma that there were 4,500 casualties, including 1,300 wounded and 2,700 sick, in the 14th Army thus far. USA vs. Homma, p. 2573, testimony of Nakajima.

and hungry. Before the fight began again they were accorded a brief rest while the enemy reorganized. To Colonel Collier this interlude seemed but an intermission between the acts of a great tragedy entitled "Defense of the Philippines." But before the curtain could go up on the second act, certain off-stage arrangements had to be completed. While these did not directly affect the action on-stage, they exerted a powerful influence on the outcome of the drama.

CHAPTER XIV

The End of an Era

On 26 December, Manila was declared an open city. All newspapers published the text of the proclamation and radio stations broadcast the news through the day. A huge banner bearing the words *Open City* and *No Shooting* was strung across the front of the city hall. That night the blackout ended and Manila was ablaze with lights.[1]

With the evacuation of the government and the army, a feeling of foreboding and terror spread through the city, and the exodus, which had ceased after the first confusion of war, began again. "The roads back into the hills," noted one observer, "were black with people striving to reach their native villages . . . . The few trains still running into the provinces were literally jammed to the car tops."[2] The business district was deserted and there were few cars along Dewey Boulevard.

Here and there a few shops made a brave attempt at a holiday spirit with displays of tinsel and brightly wrapped gifts. On the Escolta, two Santa Clauses with the traditional white beards and red costumes looked strangely out of place. One walked up and down as if dazed while the other, more practical, piled sandbags before the entrance to his shop. "No girls in slacks and shorts were bicycling along the water front," wrote Maj. Carlos Romulo reminiscently, "and there

were no horseback riders on the bridle path . . . the Yacht Club, the night clubs and hotels . . . all looked like funeral parlors."[3] "Let it be known," reported NBC correspondent Bert Silen, "that our Christmas Eve was the darkest and gloomiest I ever hope to spend."[4]

Late on the night of 26 December Radio Tokyo acknowledged receipt of the Manila broadcasts declaring the capital an open city.[5] Official notification to *14th Army* came later, either on the 28th or after, when *Imperial General Headquarters* forwarded the information from Tokyo. Apparently MacArthur made no attempt to notify the Japanese forces in the Philippines of his intentions, but a mimeographed announcement of the open city declaration was in the hands of the Japanese troops by 31 December.[6]

General Maeda commented later that "Imperial General Headquarters did not recognize the declaration of Manila as an open city. Manila had to be taken. Even if it were an open city, Japanese troops had to occupy it." Interrog of Maeda, 10 May 47, Interrogations of Former Japanese Officers, Mil Hist Div, GHQ FEC, I.

[1] USA *vs.* Homma, pp. 271, 283, 291, testimony of Abelardo L. Valencia, correspondent, and Don Bell, news commentator; Lee, *They Call It Pacific* (Viking), p. 125.
[2] Lee, *They Call It Pacific,* pp. 126–27; USA *vs.* Homma, pp. 264–355.
[3] Romulo, *I Saw the Fall of the Philippines,* pp. 73–74, 77.
[4] John Hersey, *Men on Bataan* (New York, 1942), p. 41.
[5] USA *vs.* Homma, pp. 283–86, testimony of Don Bell.
[6] *Ibid.,* pp. 2573–74, testimony of Col Nakajima; p. 3067, testimony of Homma; pp. 357–58, testimony of Yoshiaki Nakada, a chaplain on the *14th Army* staff; Defense Exhibits M and N, affidavits by the Spanish and Swiss Consuls; Statement of Nakajima, 6 Feb 50, ATIS Doc 56349, Interrogations of Former Japanese Officers, Mil Hist Div, GHQ FEC, II, 5.

THE OPEN CITY (*Japanese photograph*).

Either the Japanese in the Philippines were unaware of the open city declaration or they chose to ignore it, for enemy aircraft were over the Manila area on 27 December. The Army's *5th Air Group* sent 7 light and 4 heavy bombers against Nichols Field, and at least 2 fighters over the port district that day.[7] But the main bombing strikes, directed against the Manila Bay and Pasig River areas, were made by naval aircraft. For three hours at midday, successive waves of unopposed bombers over Manila wrought great destruction on port installations and buildings in the Intramuros, the ancient walled city of the Spaniards. The attacks against shipping continued the next day, with additional damage to the port area.[8]

By New Year's Eve the rear echelon of USAFFE headquarters under General Marshall had completed its work and was prepared to leave the "open city." The capital was subdued but ready to greet the New Year. Hotels, nightclubs, and cabarets were opened, a dance was held at the Fiesta Pavilion of the Manila Hotel, and many women donned evening gowns for the first time since the start of the war. But no sirens were sounded as in the past to herald the new year; there was no exploding of firecrackers, no tooting of horns, and no bright lights from naval ships in the bay lighting the sky. The only fireworks came from burning military installations. Along Manila streets the uncollected garbage of many days lay almost unnoticed.[9]

While a few citizens drank and danced, most of the bars closed at 2100. A large number of bartenders, in what someone termed a "scotched-earth policy," smashed the remaining bottles to prevent their falling into Japanese hands.[10]

The next morning the quartermaster stores in the port area were thrown open to the public and great crowds hurried towards the piers. About to be burned, the sheds yielded a wide assortment of booty to the delighted Filipinos. The ice plant, filled with frozen food, was also thrown open. Not all the residents were at the piers; many attended church services, for the Japanese were expected that afternoon.[11]

For almost forty years Manila had been the outpost of American civilization in the Orient. Now the badly mauled port area was quiet and dead as the old year. From the waters of Manila Bay rose the funnels of sunken ships and along the waterfront stood the blackened, empty walls and the battered piers, mute epitaph to one of the finest harbors in the Far East.[12]

The city was surrounded by an inferno of flame, noise, and smoke. Fuel supplies at Fort McKinley to the southeast, installations that survived the bombing at Nichols Field to the south, and the ruins of Cavite across Manila Bay were demolished in great bursts of flame and explosion. The bewildered and frightened population was further panic-stricken by the soaring flames from the oil tanks at Pandacan, which ate up surrounding warehouses and buildings

---

[7] *5th Air Gp* Opns, p. 39.

[8] *Ibid.;* Sunday *Tribune* (Manila), December 28, 1941, in USA *vs.* Homma, Prosecution Exhibit 20, and pp. 267–355, *passim.*

[9] Philippines *Herald* (Manila), December 31, 1941; Manila *Bulletin,* January 1, 1942; Romulo, *I Saw the Fall of the Philippines,* pp. 85–89.

[10] Hersey, *Men on Bataan,* p. 237.

[11] Van Landingham, "I Saw Manila Die," *Saturday Evening Post,* September 26, 1942, p. 70.

[12] Romulo, *I Saw the Fall of the Philippines,* p. 74; Philippines *Herald* (Manila), December 31, 1941.

and sent up black clouds of smoke. The flaming oil floated along the Pasig and set other fires along the banks. And from the air the enemy continued to drop bombs, adding even more fuel to the great conflagration which swept huge areas in and around the city. "To the native population of Manila," commented one observer, "it seemed like the end of the world." [13]

The Occupation of Manila

On the first day of the New Year the Japanese *48th Division* and the *4th* and *7th Tank Regiments* were twelve miles above the northern outskirts of Manila. To the south that night advance elements of General Morioka's *16th Division* reached Manila Bay at a point less than ten miles from the capital city.[14] With two divisions "ready to go," Homma stopped the advance on the outskirts of the capital over the protests of both divisional commanders. "If those divisions went in together from south and north," he explained later, "anything might happen." [15]

Both divisions could have entered Manila on New Year's Day and expected to do so. When the order to advance did not come, Lt. Gen. Yuichi Tsuchibashi, *48th Division* commander, sent Homma an urgent message at 1040, pointing out that the great fires had dissipated "the Army's hope of

preserving the city of Manila" and that "to rescue Manila from this conflagration" he planned to enter the capital in force. From Homma he requested approval for his plan.[16] This was followed by a plea from the division's chief of staff, who wrote: "I beseech you at the order of my superior to promptly approve the previously presented plan." [17]

Immediately after the *14th Army* command post completed its movement from Binalonan to Cabanatuan, a staff conference was held at 1900 on New Year's Day to decide on the method of entry into Manila. Two plans were discussed: one to send a force into the city immediately, as proposed by the *48th Division* commander; the other to dispatch a "military commission" to the capital to urge its surrender while the troops remained outside the city.

The former plan was finally adopted, and at 2000 the *48th Division* was ordered to seize Manila and prevent its destruction. Similar orders were given the *16th Division* at 1000 on 2 January. General Morioka would also occupy Cavite and Batangas.[18] The line of the Pasig River, which flowed through the capital and into Manila Bay, was set as operational boundary between the two divisions. That night supplementary orders from General Homma fixed the size of the force entering Manila from the north at three infantry battalions of the *48th Division*. The *16th Division* was seemingly left free to determine the number of its troops entering Manila. Further orders apparently directed that the city was not to

---

[13] Van Landingham, "I Saw Manila Die," *Saturday Evening Post,* September 26, 1942, p. 70.

[14] *14th Army* Opns, I, 65. *The 2d Formosa* and two battalions of the *48th Mountain Artillery* were not with the *48th Division* at this time.

[15] USA *vs.* Homma, p. 3056, testimony of Homma. General Maeda, Homma's chief of staff, declared that the *48th Division,* for one, "was told to wait so that it could spruce up and reorganize." Interrog of Maeda, 10 May 47, Interrogations of Former Japanese Officers, Mil Hist Div, GHQ FEC, I.

[16] *14th Army* Opns, I, 67. The telegram was dated 1040, but it did not reach Homma until 1710. The nearly five hours it required to reach Army headquarters is unexplained.

[17] *Ibid.*

[18] *Ibid.,* 68–69.

be entered until the 2d, for no entry was made that night.[19]

Inside the city a newspaper extra at noon on New Year's Day declared the enemy to be on the verge of entry and advised inhabitants to remain in their homes and await further orders from the Philippine authorities in control. Anticipating confinement in internment camps, American residents immediately packed toilet articles and a change of clothing.[20] Word of the impending entry of the Japanese reached Corregidor quickly. MacArthur reported to the War Department on the morning of the 2d that Japanese troops would enter Manila that afternoon. His information was accurate enough to enable him to predict that the force would be small and that its duties would be limited to the maintenance of law and order, "which would indicate that there will be no violence." [21] That morning Japanese nationals were released from custody. The crowds, laden with stores from the quartermaster warehouses, began to break into business establishments and wholesale looting began.[22] The once proud city, covered with the ashes and filth of destruction, was difficult to recognize as the beautiful and orderly metropolis it had been less than a month before.

Finally, at 1745 on Friday, 2 January 1942, the Japanese entered Manila. Maj. Gen. Koichi Abe, *48th Division* infantry

group commander, led one battalion of the *1st Formosa* and two of the *47th Infantry* into the northern sector of the capital. Simultaneously, from the south, the *16th Reconnaissance Regiment* and a battalion of the *20th Infantry* also entered.[23] Accompanied by released Japanese civilians, who acted as interpreters, the occupying troops posted guards at strategic points and set about securing the city.[24] "The joyful voices of the Japanese residents," reported General Morioka, "were overwhelming." [25]

The voices of the other residents were not so joyful. Throughout the city at important intersections Japanese officers and interpreters set up card tables and checked pedestrians. All "enemy aliens," British and Americans, were ordered to remain at home until they could be registered and investigated. The only Caucasians who walked the streets unmolested were Germans, Italians, and Spaniards.[26]

All that night Japanese trucks poured into the city, their occupants taking over private hotels and some public buildings as billets. Enemy troops moved into the University of the Philippines and other school buildings. The next morning the only cars on the street were those driven by Japanese officers and civilians. From their radiators flew the flag of the Rising Sun. Spanish, French, Italian, German, Portuguese, and Thai flags could also be seen. The vault of the national treasury at the Intendencia Building was sealed and a large placard announced the building and its contents to be the property of the Japanese Government. The banks remained closed and the doors

[19] *Ibid.,* 76. Homma later claimed that "arrangements were made to enter the city . . . with only two battalions from each division, and the rest of the divisions must stay out of the city." Neither Generals Tsuchibashi nor Morioka limited the entering units to two battalions. USA *vs.* Homma, p. 3056, testimony of Homma.

[20] Van Landingham, "I Saw Manila Die," *Saturday Evening Post,* September 26, 1942, p. 70.

[21] Rad, MacArthur to AGWAR, No. 5, 2 Jan 42, AG 381 (11–27–41 Sec 1) Far East.

[22] Manila *Bulletin,* January 3, 1942.

[23] *14th Army* Opns, I, 70, 84.

[24] Manila *Bulletin,* January 3, 1942.

[25] *16th Div* Opns, 24 Dec 41–3 Jan 42, ATIS Enemy Pub 355, p. 9.

[26] Margaret Utinsky, *Miss U* (San Antonio, Tex., 1948), p. 1; Hersey, *Men on Bataan,* p. 154.

JAPANESE LIGHT TANKS *moving toward Manila on the day the city was entered.*

of Manila restaurants were also shut. News-paper publication was briefly suspended and then began again under Japanese con-trol. The few stores that were open did a land-office business with Japanese officers who bought up brooches and watches with colorful occupation pesos.[27]

Governmental departments of the Philip-pine Commonwealth were placed under "protective custody." The courts were tem-porarily suspended, utilities were taken over by the Japanese, and a bewildering list of li-censes and permits was issued to control the economic life of the Islands. Japanese sick and wounded were moved into the Chinese General Hospital and three wards of the Philippine General Hospital. All British and Americans were ordered to report for intern-ment, and nearly 3,000 were herded to-gether on the campus of Santo Tomas Uni-versity. "Thereafter," reported the Japa-nese, "peace and order were gradually re-stored to Manila."[28]

The restoration of "peace and order" re-quired the Japanese to place many restric-tions on the civilian population. On 5 Janu-ary a "warning" appeared in heavy black type across the top of the Manila *Tribune.* "Any one who inflicts, or attempts to in-flict, an injury upon Japanese soldiers or in-dividuals," it read, "shall be shot to death"; but "if the assailant, or attempted assailant,

[27] The Sunday *Tribune* (Manila), January 4, 1942; Utinsky, *Miss U,* p. 4.

[28] Hersey, *Men on Bataan,* pp. 152–54; *14th Army Opns,* I, 77.

cannot be found, we will hold ten influential persons as hostages who live in and about the streets or municipalities where the event happened." The warning concluded with the admonition that "the Filipinos should understand our real intentions and should work together with us to maintain public peace and order in the Philippines." [29]

With the occupation of Manila, General Homma had successfully accomplished the mission assigned by *Imperial General Headquarters*. But he could draw small comfort from his success, for MacArthur's forces were still intact. The newly formed Philippine Army, the Philippine Scouts, and the U.S. Army garrison had successfully escaped to Bataan and Corregidor. So long as they maintained their positions there, the Japanese would be unable to enter Manila Bay or use the Manila harbor. The Japanese had opened the back door to Manila Bay but the front door remained firmly closed.

Strategic Views on the Philippines

To the civilians who watched quietly from behind closed shutters as the Japanese entered their city it seemed incredible that the war was less than a month old. In that brief span of time, the enemy had made eight separate landings on widely dispersed beaches. He had driven out of the Philippines the Far East Air Force and the Asiatic Fleet. On Luzon he had marched north and south from each end of the island to join his forces before Manila. Casualties had been comparatively light and the main objective was now in his hands.

In that same time the Japanese had secured a foothold in Mindanao to the south and had gained control of the important harbor at Davao. Brig. Gen. William F. Sharp's forces on that island were still intact, however, and held the airfield at Del Monte, the only field in the archipelago still capable of supporting heavy bombers. In the Visayas the Japanese had made no landings. There the scattered American and Philippine garrisons on Panay, Cebu, Bohol, Leyte, and other islands fortified their defenses and made plans for the day when the enemy would appear off their shores.

Elsewhere, the Japanese forces had set about exploiting their initial gains. Hong Kong had fallen to the *23d Army* on Christmas Day. General Yamashita's *25th Army,* which had landed on the Malay Peninsula on the first day of war, was now pushing ever closer to Singapore. Japanese forces in the Sulu Archipelago and Borneo consolidated their positions and prepared to move into the Netherlands Indies. The *South Seas Detachment,* which had seized Guam, was now ready to move on to Rabaul, while other units staged for operations in the Celebes–Ambon area. Important Burmese airfields had been attacked on 25 December and at the year's end the *15th Army* was concentrating in Thailand for its invasion of Burma. After the first rapid gains, the enemy was ready for further offensives. The Allies had little left to challenge the Japanese bid for supremacy in the Southwest Pacific and Southeast Asia.

General MacArthur attributed the success of the Japanese to American weakness on the sea and in the air. The enemy, he pointed out, now had "utter freedom of naval and air movements" and could be expected to extend its conquests southward into the Netherlands Indies, using Mindanao as a base of operations.[30] If the Jap-

---

[29] Sunday *Tribune* (Manila), January 5, 1942; see also USA *vs.* Homma, Prosecution Exhibit 16.

[30] Rad, MacArthur to TAG, 27 Dec 41, AG 381 (11–27–41) Far East.

anese were able to seize the Netherlands Indies, he warned, the Allies would be forced to advance from Australia through the Dutch and British islands to regain the Philippines. He regarded it as essential, therefore, to halt the Japanese drive southward, and proposed that air forces should be rushed to the Southwest Pacific. Operating from advance bases, these planes could prevent the Japanese from developing airfields. Concurrently, with strong naval action to keep open the line of communication to Mindanao, Japanese air forces were to be neutralized by Allied air power, and then ground forces would be landed there. He had already done all he could to support such action, MacArthur told the War Department, by sending his air force to Australia and the Netherlands Indies and by supporting Mindanao with reinforcements and ammunition. "I wish to emphasize," he concluded, "the necessity for naval action and for rapid execution by land, sea, and air." [31]

Receiving no reply to this message, General MacArthur took the occasion, on 1 January, when asked about the evacuation of President Quezon, to emphasize his isolated position and to remind the Chief of Staff of his strategic concept for a combined effort by land, sea, and air forces through the Netherlands Indies to Mindanao. Quezon's departure, he warned, would undoubtedly be followed by the collapse of the will to fight on the part of the Filipinos, and he pointedly added that, aside from 7,000 combat troops (exclusive of air corps), his army consisted of Filipinos. "In view of the Filipinos effort," he declared, "the United States must move strongly to

their support or withdraw in shame from the Orient." [32]

Just a week later, as his forces withdrew behind the first line of defenses on Bataan, MacArthur outlined for the Chief of Staff the preparations he was making for the arrival of an expeditionary force in Mindanao. These included transfer of equipment for one division, the movement of nine P–40's and 650 men of the 19th Bombardment Group to Del Monte, and plans to develop additional landing fields there. It was essential, he wrote, to inaugurate a system of blockade-running to Mindanao since supplies were low.

Our air force bombardment missions from south should quickly eliminate hostile air from Davao and our pursuit should go into Del Monte without delay. Establishment of air force will permit immediate extension into Visayas and attacks on enemy forces in Luzon. . . . An Army Corps should be landed in Mindanao at the earliest possible date. . . . Enemy appears to have tendency to become overconfident and time is ripe for brilliant thrust with air carriers.[33]

MacArthur's pleas for a major Allied effort in the Southwest Pacific were received with sympathy in Washington, where the first wartime United States-British conference on strategy was in session. The British recognized the importance of the threat in the Far East and agreed that munitions and supplies should go there, even though such shipments represented a diversion from the agreed strategy that the main effort should be made against Germany first. "The President and Prime Minister, Colonel

---

[31] *Ibid.* For the measures taken to strengthen Mindanao, see V–MF Rpt of Opns, Part I, *passim,* Annex XI, USAFFE-USFIP Rpt of Opns.

[32] Rad, MacArthur to Marshall, Nos. 2 and 3, 1 Jan 42, WPD 4639-2. Apparently MacArthur excluded from his estimate of combat strength the 12,000 Philippine Scouts who, though Filipinos, were part of the U.S. Army.

[33] Rad, MacArthur to Marshall, No. 20, 7 Jan 42, AG 381 (11–27–41) Far East.

Stimson and Colonel Knox, the British Chiefs of Staff and our corresponding officials," General Marshall told MacArthur, "have been surveying every possibility looking toward the quick development of strength in the Far East so as to break the enemy's hold on the Philippines."

Though all were agreed on the need for action in the Southwest Pacific, little could be done. The loss in capital ships, Marshall explained, prevented naval convoys for heavy reinforcements and the concentration of strong naval forces in the Southwest Pacific such as MacArthur was requesting. Heavy bombers were on the way, via Africa and Hawaii, and pursuit planes were being sent by every ship, so that the Allies should soon have aerial supremacy in the Southwest Pacific. "Our great hope," Marshall told MacArthur, "is that the rapid development of an overwhelming air power on the Malay Barrier will cut the Japanese communications south of Borneo and permit an assault in the southern Philippines." The naval carrier raids MacArthur was asking for were not ruled out entirely but little hope was offered for such an effort. Marshall closed his message on a note of encouragement for the future and the assurance that "every day of time you gain is vital to the concentration of overwhelming power necessary for our purpose." [34]

Actually, the American and British staffs in Washington had already agreed upon the strategy for the Far East: to hold the Malay Barrier from the Malay Peninsula through Sumatra and Java to Australia. This line was considered the basic Allied defensive position in the Far East, and the retention of its east and west anchors, Australia and Burma, was therefore regarded as essential.

The latter had additional strategic importance because it was essential to the support of China and the defense of India. The Allies were agreed that land, sea, and air forces should operate as far forward of the barrier as possible in order to halt the Japanese advance southward. The support of the Philippine garrison and the re-establishment of the line of communications through the Netherlands Indies to Luzon apparently came after the more important task of holding Australia and Burma.[35]

During the first week in January the War Plans Division of the General Staff, which had been studying the possibility of sending an expedition to the relief of the Philippine garrison, came to the conclusion that the forces required could not be placed in the Far East in time. While this reason was probably the overriding consideration in its recommendation that operations to relieve the Philippines not be undertaken, the War Plans Division went on to point out that the dispatch of so large a force would constitute "an entirely unjustifiable diversion of forces from the principal theater—the Atlantic." The greatest effort which could be justified on strategic grounds was to hold the Malay Barrier while projecting operations as far north as possible to provide maximum defense in depth. This view was essentially that already agreed upon by the Combined Chiefs of Staff. The War Plans Division therefore recommended that, "for the present," operations in the Far East should be limited to these objectives.[36]

[34] Ibid.

[35] Rpt of U.S.-British CsofS, 31 Dec 41, sub: Supporting Measures for SWPA (ABC 4/3), OPD Reg Doc. General MacArthur was informed of the substance of this report on 31 December 1941.
[36] Memo, Brig Gen L. T. Gerow for CofS, 3 Jan 42, sub: Relief of Phil, WPD 4639-3.

The War Plans Division study is of considerable interest, not only for the effect it may have had on MacArthur's requests for a joint advance through the Netherlands Indies to Mindanao, but also for its realistic appraisal of the strategic situation in the Far East and the importance of the Philippine Islands. Accepting General MacArthur's estimate of Japanese strength in the Philippines and of the length of time he could hold out against serious attack—three month—the Army planners agreed that the loss of the Philippines, "the key to the Far East position of the Associated Powers," would be a decisive blow, followed probably by the fall of the Netherlands Indies and Singapore.[37] Australian and British trade routes would then be seriously threatened, while Japan's strength would be increased by control of the raw materials in the Indies. The isolation of China was "almost certain to follow." [38] This analysis coincided with MacArthur's, as did the plan of operations outlined to recover the Philippines.

It was when the planners considered the means necessary to carry out these operations that they found themselves in disagreement with General MacArthur. They estimated that 1,464 aircraft of various types, only about half of which were available, would be necessary to advance from Australia to Luzon. The difference would have to come from other areas—Hawaii, Panama, and the United States—and from lend-lease aircraft already committed. Additional airfields would have to be built in

Australia and along the line of advance. The line of communications to Australia would have to be made secure and a logistical organization developed to support the drive northward. Such an effort, the planners estimated, would require very large naval resources. With the vessels already in the area, the Allies would have to transfer 7 to 9 capital ships, 5 to 7 carriers, about 50 destroyers, 60 submarines, and the necessary auxiliary vessels from the Atlantic and Mediterranean to the Pacific and Far East. The diversion of naval forces might well result in the loss of the supply routes to Europe and the Middle East and would severely limit the defense of the Western Hemisphere. It was not surprising, therefore, that the War Plans Division concluded that the relief of the Philippine garrison could not be accomplished in the three months left, and that the allocation of such sizable forces to the project would represent a major and unjustifiable diversion from the main effort.[39]

There is no record of any formal approval of the conclusions of the War Plans Division. Both Secretary Stimson and General Marshall noted the study but made no comment. If there had ever been any serious consideration given to MacArthur's proposals to send an expedition to the relief of the beleaguered Philippine garrison, the War Plans study put an end to such hopes. But there was no relaxation of the determination to send General MacArthur whatever aid was within the means of the United States and its Allies. President Roosevelt had time and again stated his desire to do so and as late as 30 December had written Stimson that he wished the War Plans Division to explore every possible means of re-

---

[37] *Ibid.* MacArthur estimated that the Japanese had six divisions on Luzon, one at Davao, and a small force at Jolo. There were only two Japanese divisions in the Philippines. The planners, for lack of more definite information, accepted MacArthur's estimate.

[38] *Ibid.*

[39] *Ibid.*

lieving the Philippines. "I realize great risks are involved," he said, "but the objective is important." [40]

While the President's stated desire remained the official policy of the government and the hope of the American people, the strategy evolved by the Allies placed more realistic limits to the objectives they hoped to attain. The conference then meeting in Washington agreed that the Allies must hold the Malay Barrier and established a theater of operations known as the ABDA (American-British-Dutch-Australian) area, with Gen. Sir Archibald P. Wavell in command, to co-ordinate the efforts of the various national forces in that region. This command, the first Allied command of the war, included the Philippines, the Netherlands Indies, Malaya, and Burma. Wavell's mission was to hold the Malay Barrier against the advancing Japanese, but he was also directed to re-establish communications through the Netherlands Indies with Luzon and to support the Philippine garrison. Thus, General MacArthur was placed under Wavell's command, but, explained General Marshall, "because of your present

isolation this will have only nominal effect upon your command. . . ." [41]

Actually, the organization of the ABDA area had no effect on operations in the Philippines, and aside from a formal acknowledgement between the two commanders there was no communication between the two headquarters. Although General Marshall pointed out that the new arrangement offered "the only feasible method for the eventual relief of the Philippines," [42] it was already clear to General MacArthur that the Allies were not going to make a determined effort to advance to his rescue.

It was perhaps just as well that the Americans and Filipinos who crowded into Bataan and took their positions behind the lines already established did not know how serious was the Allied position in the Far East and how remote were their chances for relief. Ahead of them were long, dreary months of starvation and hard fighting before they would be herded into prison camps. At least they could hope that help was on the way. Only General MacArthur and his immediate staff knew the worst.

[40] Quoted in Robert E. Sherwood, *Roosevelt and Hopkins: An Intimate History* (New York, 1948), p. 454.

[41] Rad, Marshall to MacArthur, No. 93, 11 Jan 42, WPD 4639-14.
[42] *Ibid.*

PART FOUR

THE SIEGE OF BATAAN

CHAPTER XV

Setting the Stage

Formed by the southern heights of the Zambales Mountains, the Bataan peninsula juts out from the mainland of Luzon between Subic and Manila Bay like a huge thumb pointing at the shore of Cavite Province only twelve miles away. Between Bataan and the Cavite shore lie Corregidor and several smaller islands, guarding the entrance to Manila Bay. (*Map 11*)

Only twenty-five miles long and twenty miles wide across its base, Bataan is ideally suited for defensive warfare. It is jungled and mountainous, cut by numerous streams and deep ravines, and has only two roads adequate for motor vehicles. Dominating the peninsula are two extinct volcanoes: the 4,222-foot high Mt. Natib in the north and, to the south, the Mariveles Mountains whose highest peak, Mt. Bataan, towers to a height of 4,722 feet. Along the east coast, on the Manila Bay side, the peninsula is flat and swampy near its base but becomes hilly and rugged to the south. The coastal plain on the west is extremely narrow. Here the mountains extend almost to the sea; high cliffs guard the shore and toothlike promontories jut into the water. Radiating from the two volcanic masses flow many streams which wind their way through steep ravines and gullies toward the bay and the sea.

Bataan is crisscrossed by a large number of trails, quickly overgrown by the tropical vegetation and rarely suitable for vehicular traffic. Across the base of the peninsula is Route 7, lost to the Americans by their withdrawal from Layac. South of Layac, paralleling the east coast down to Mariveles at the tip of the peninsula, then turning north to parallel the west coast as far as Moron, is Route 110. The east coast portion, called the East Road, is a single-lane, all-weather road; the stretch from Mariveles to Moron on the opposite coast, the West Road, is not as well surfaced. The only other road of importance is an east-west road from Pilar to Bagac, midway down the peninsula and across the saddle between Mt. Natib and the Mariveles Mountains. This road, called the Pilar–Bagac road and cutting Bataan like a waist belt, was the only vehicular road providing lateral communication for the forces divided by the rugged heights of central Bataan.[1]

No better place than Bataan could have been chosen for a final stand. There were compensations for the inhospitable countryside. "Taking it all in all," noted Colonel Skerry, the North Luzon Force engineer, "the rugged terrain of the Bataan Peninsula, covered as it was by a thick jungle, concealed the works of the defender even when the enemy had constant air superiority and air observation." [2] And after two weeks of withdrawal the men were glad to reach a position that was not to be abandoned the next day. Morale was good. "The general feeling seemed to be," wrote Colonel Col-

---

[1] Bataan–Zambales, AGS, GHQ SWPA, Terrain Handbook 42, pp. 23–39, 76.

[2] Skerry, Comments on Engineer Hist, No. 10.

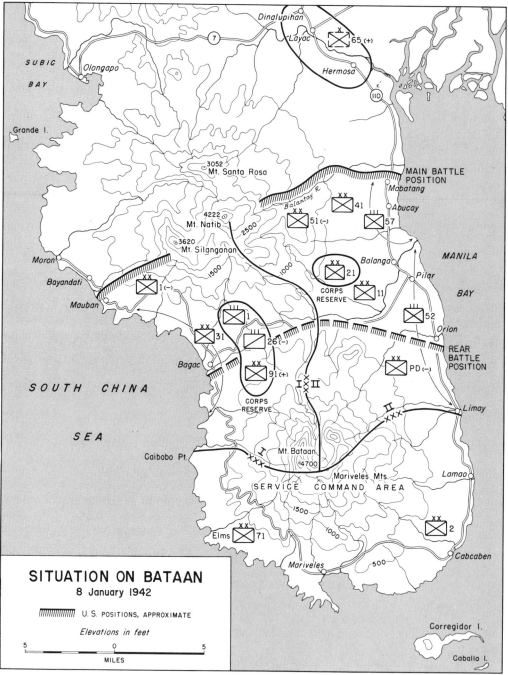

SUBIC BAY

Olongapo

Grande I.

7

Dinalupihan

Layac

X
65 (+)

Hermosa

110

Mt. Santa Rosa
3052

Balantay R.

MAIN BATTLE
POSITION

Mabatang

XX
41

Abucay

4222
Mt. Natib

2500

XX
51 (—)

XX
57

Moron

3620
Mt. Silanganan

1500

1000

XX
21

Balanga

CORPS
RESERVE

Pilar

MANILA

BAY

Bayandati

XX
1 (—)

Mauban

III
1

III
31

III
26 (—)

XX
91 (+)

XX
11

XX
52

Orion

REAR
BATTLE
POSITION

Bagac

CORPS
RESERVE

X
I · II

XX
PD (—)

SOUTH   CHINA

SEA

Caibobo Pt.

I
XXX

Mt. Bataan
4700

II
XXX

Limay

Mariveles Mts.

Lamao

SERVICE   COMMAND   AREA

1500

1000

XX
2

Elms

XX
71

Mariveles

500

Cabcaben

Corregidor I.

Caballo I.

SITUATION ON BATAAN
8 January 1942

  U. S. POSITIONS, APPROXIMATE

Elevations in feet

5   0   5
MILES

MAP 11

U. Brooks

lier, the assistant operations officer of USAFFE, "we have run far enough; we'll stand now and take 'em on." [3]

The American Position

The defense of Bataan began officially on 7 January 1942. On that day Wainwright assumed command of the West Sector of the Bataan Defense Force, which became I Philippine Corps, and the East Sector, redesignated II Philippine Corps, came under General Parker, till then commander of the entire Bataan Defense Force. The boundary between the two corps bisected the length of the peninsula from Mt. Natib to the Mariveles Mountains. The tip of Bataan south of the Mariveles Mountains was designated the Service Command Area and responsibility for its defense given to Brig. Gen. Allen C. McBride, MacArthur's deputy for the Philippine Department. To Wainwright's corps was assigned the defense of the western half of Bataan; Parker's corps was on the Manila Bay side.[4] Both corps were under MacArthur's headquarters on Corregidor, which by 5 January had established a Bataan echelon under Brig. Gen. R. J. Marshall. Through Marshall's headquarters, consisting of officers from the general and special staff sections of USAFFE, it was possible for MacArthur to exercise close control over operations on Bataan.[5] "I am on my main battle line," MacArthur told the War Department on 7 January, "awaiting general attack." [6]

The defense of Bataan was conceived as a defense in depth. The first line, called the main battle position, extended from Mabatang, a short distance north of Abucay, on the east, across Mt. Natib to Mauban on the west coast, a distance of twenty miles. A strong outpost line of resistance was established in front of the main battle position and defenses to a depth of several miles were prepared to the rear. Along the beaches on both coasts troops were posted to guard against amphibious envelopment.[7]

In Wainwright's corps on the west were three Philippine Army divisions, the 1st, 31st, and 91st, to which was attached the combat elements of the 71st Division (PA); the 26th Cavalry (PS); a battery each of field artillery and 75-mm. guns (SPM), and miscellaneous troops—altogether about 22,500 men. On the right (east), in Parker's corps, were four more Philippine Army divisions, the 11th, 21st, 41st, and 51st; supporting artillery; and the 57th Infantry (PS) from the Philippine Division. General Parker had about 25,000 men in his corps.[8]

Eight miles behind the main battle position, paralleling the Pilar–Bagac road, was the rear battle position which in prewar plans had formed the main line of the Bataan defenses. On 7 January this line was not yet fully organized; while the forces along the main battle position held back the enemy, other troops would prepare this position. Posted along this line and assigned

---

[3] Collier, Notebooks, III, 10.

[4] USAFFE FO 1, 6 Jan 42, AG 300.4 (28 Dec 41) Phil Rcds; ltr, Parker to Ward, 16 Jun 52, OCMH.

[5] Interv, author with Marshall, 7 Apr 48; memo, Marshall for CofS USAFFE, 13 Jan 42, AG 370.2 (19 Dec 41) Phil Rcds.

[6] Rad, MacArthur to TAG, No. 20, 7 Jan 42, AG 381 (11–27–41 Sec 1) Far East.

[7] USAFFE FO 1, 6 Jan 42, AG 300.4 (28 Dec 41) Phil Rcds.

[8] Ibid.; USAFFE GO 3, 7 Jan 42, AG 320.2 (6 Jan 42) Phil Rcds. This general order was erroneously issued as GO 56, 6 January 1942, and was corrected by GO 4, 7 January 1942. Strengths given are estimates by the author, based on scattered strength figures. See especially those in Luzon Force Rpt of Opns, 12 Mar 42 to 9 Apr 42, Annex VI, USAFFE-USFIP Rpt of Opns.

the task of organizing it for a last-ditch defense was the USAFFE reserve, the Philippine Division (less 57th Infantry), the tank group, and a group of 75-mm. SPM's. Corps and USAFFE artillery was emplaced to cover the front lines as well as the beach defenses in all sectors.[9]

South of the rear battle position was the Service Command Area. Under McBride's command was a variety of troops: the 2d Division (PC), organized on 7 January and composed of Constabulary troops, the remaining elements of the 71st Division (PA), including the division headquarters, provisional infantry units formed from air corps troops, and a provisional battalion of bluejackets and marines.[10]

The Mabatang–Mauban line, or Abucay–Mauban line, as it was more generally called, the main battle position, occupied on 7 January, was not a continuous line. Separating and forming an almost impenetrable barrier between the left portion held by I Corps and the right portion held by II Corps was the northernmost of the two extinct volcanoes, covering an area about fifteen by fifteen miles. Around the crater are steep and jagged peaks rising to a height of 3,000 to 4,000 feet. The northernmost peak, Mt. Santa Rosa, is 3,052 feet high. About three and a half miles southeast is the highest point on the crater's edge, Mt. Natib. In a distance of 2,000 yards this 4,222-foot-high mountain drops to half its height. Mt. Silanganan, to the southwest, is 3,620 feet high. On its west escarpment this land mass drops a thousand feet in as many

yards. Though the military crests of these mountains provided ideal defensive positions—one officer called them "an infantryman's dream"—they made effective mutual support between the two corps impossible. The Mt. Natib position was selected, despite its known limitations, because strategy required that a stand be made here to gain time to prepare the rear battle position and to retain as long as possible the lateral communication provided by the Pilar–Bagac road.

I Philippine Corps

The sector defended by General Wainwright's I Philippine Corps on the west "was practically all wooded and almost wholly uninhabited." [11] The terrain was extremely rugged and a bolo was a necessity for a man on foot. From the South China Sea, wrote Colonel Skerry, Wainwright's engineer officer, after a reconnaissance, this side of the peninsula "presented a most formidable appearance of very high timbered banks with a solid mass of woods stretching east to a high mountain rainge, heavily timbered throughout, except for the break at Bagac and Moron." [12]

Communications in this area were poor. That portion of the West Road which stretched from Mariveles to Bagac was poorly surfaced. Northward from Bagac as far as Moron the road had been improved and had a crushed rock surface which made it passable in all weather. The only method of continuing northward from Moron where the West Road ended was by a series of roundabout trails. "By and

[9] USAFFE FO 1, 6 Jan 42, AG 300.4 (28 Dec 41) Phil Rcds.

[10] USAFFE FO 2, 7 Jan 42, and amendment of 10 Jan 42, AG 300.4 (28 Dec 41) Phil Rcds; Collier, Notebooks, III, 6.

[11] Collier, Notebooks, III, 21.

[12] Skerry, Comments on Engineer Hist, No. 10.

large," said Skerry, "this was an area where an American needed a map, compass and bolo even in the dry season.[13]

The main line of resistance on this side of the peninsula followed Mauban Ridge from Mauban on the coast to Mt. Silanganan. Holding the western portion of this line was the 3d Infantry, 1st Division (PA); to its right was a battalion of the 31st Field Artillery of the 31st Division (PA), equipped and organized as an infantry unit. On the extreme right, on the slopes of Mt. Silanganan, was Company K, 1st Infantry. Its mission was to establish contact with the 51st Division on the left of II Corps—an apparently impossible task in that uncharted, mountainous country. Only that portion of the main line of resistance held by the 3d Infantry was reinforced; it had a double apron of barbed wire. The rest of the line "was unprotected by obstacles other than the natural jungle." [14]

The selection of Mauban as the western anchor of the main line of resistance had been debated before the war. In January 1941, at General Grunert's direction, officers of the 26th Cavalry (PS) had made a reconnaissance of a proposed Mt. Natib–

Moron line. When their report was in, Grunert ordered Wainwright, then commanding the Philippine Division, to prepare plans for a line from Mt. Natib to the west coast of Bataan, in the vicinity of Moron or Mauban. Officers of the 45th Infantry (PS) had then visited the area and decided to place the western anchor of the line at Mauban, where a 50- to 75-foot ridge commanded the beach and offered a clear field of fire for several hundred yards. The line established when the troops moved into Bataan, therefore, utilized the plans developed before the war, and the first draft of the field order outlining positions on Bataan at the beginning of January 1942 anchored the line at Mauban.[15]

In commenting on the first draft of the field order establishing this line, Colonel Casey, MacArthur's engineer officer, urged that the main line be placed further north, at Moron. Noting the excellent beach between Moron and Mauban and recognizing the danger of envelopment at Moron, he pointed out that "if the rear position [Mauban] only is held, it permits the concentration of enemy on these beaches for attack on this flank." [16] He had recommended therefore that Moron be "organized and defended" and the Mauban line used as a switch position.

Although Mauban remained the anchor of the main line of resistance when the final plan was drawn up, an effort was made to meet Casey's objections. Two units, Company I of the 1st Infantry and Troop G, 26th Cavalry, were posted at Moron and along the stretch of sandy beach to the south

<hr>

[13] *Ibid.*

[14] NLF and I Corps Rpt of Opns, pp. 16–17; SLF and II Corps Rpt of Opns, p. 28; Santos, The 1st Reg Div (PA) in Battle of Phil, p. 36; ltr, Brig Gen Kearie L. Berry, ret., formerly CO 1st Inf (PA), to author, 9 Jun 49, OCMH.

General Bluemel, who commanded the west sector before Wainwright's arrival, had ordered Brig. Gen. Fidel V. Segundo, the 1st Division (PA) commander, to establish contact with the left unit of the east sector. Segundo was unable to do so, and explained that there was no water on Mt. Natib and that he could not keep troops there. Bluemel finally sent a patrol led by his G–2 to establish contact with the troops to the east. The patrol was gone three days and failed to establish contact. Bluemel, Comments on Draft MS, Comment 15, OCMH.

[15] Bluemel, Comments on Draft MS, Comment 11, OCMH; interv, Groce with Lt Col Edgar Wright, Jr., formerly with 45th Inf (PS), 2 Feb 49, OCMH.

[16] Memo, Casey for CofS USAFFE, 2 Jan 42, sub: Defense of Bataan, AG 381, Phil Rcds.

to prevent enemy landings and to deny the landing beaches at Moron to the enemy.[17]

The outpost line of resistance in the I Corps sector extended from the barrio of Bayandati, a mile and a half northwest of Mauban, eastward to a point about halfway up the slopes of Mt. Silanganan. The 3d Infantry held this line, which paralleled its sector on the main line of resistance. To the rear, behind the main line, was the 2d Battalion, 1st Infantry, forming a regimental reserve line which stretched from the beach defense below Mauban across the West Road.[18]

Artillery support for Wainwright's corps was provided by the 71st Field Artillery (less 1st Battalion), two batteries of the 91st Field Artillery, one battery of the 23d Field Artillery, a battery of 75-mm. guns (SPM), and two 155-mm. guns. Colonel Fowler, who commanded this force, had altogether thirty-three pieces, all but two of which were 75-mm. guns or 2.95-inch mountain howitzers. The 75's were emplaced along Mauban Ridge, just behind the main line of resistance, and along the high ground to the northeast. The SPM's were disposed along a ridge about 300 yards to the south, and the shorter range 2.95-inch guns placed farther forward. The two 155-mm. guns were emplaced along the high ground near Mauban Point to cover the sea approaches as well as those by land. Secondary positions for the artillery, located about 3,000 yards

to the rear, were selected, "but due to the excellent cover of the dense jungle around the primary positions," Colonel Fowler noted, "were not occupied until the last day and night." [19]

Defense of the beach south of the main battle position was assigned to Brig. Gen. Clifford Bluemel's 31st Division (PA). The division was responsible for a stretch of approximately ten miles, from the regimental reserve line on the north to Saysain Point, with one battalion of the 45th Infantry (PS) at Bagac Bay. Actually, Bluemel's southern flank was extended south of the assigned limit by one battalion of the 31st Infantry (PA). In support of the 31st Division was a battery of the 92d Coast Artillery (PS), which had gone into Bataan with Bluemel and been assigned to cover Saysain Point with its two 155-mm. guns. Another battery of that regiment was located near Bagac.[20]

For corps reserve General Wainwright had the remnants of Selleck's 71st Division and Stevens' 91st Division, both badly mauled by their fight in northern Luzon. In an effort to secure one effective unit from these two divisions, the combat troops of the 71st were placed under Stevens' command and the entire force reorganized.[21] The 26th Cavalry (PS), which had joined the I Philippine Corps after a difficult overland march from Layac junction, was also tired

---

[17] Santos, 1st Reg Div (PA), p. 36; Chandler, "26th Cavalry Battles to Glory," Part 2, *Armored Cavalry Journal* (May–June 1947), p. 15.

[18] NLF and I Corps Rpt of Opns, p. 17; Santos, 1st Reg Div (PA), p. 36; Chandler, "26th Cavalry (PS) Battles to Glory," Part 2, *Armored Cavalry Journal* (May–June 1947), p. 15; Col K. L. Berry, Hist of 3d Inf, 1st Reg Div (PA), 19 Dec 41–9 Apr 42, p. 2, copy lent author by Gen Berry, OCMH.

[19] Ltr, Fowler to author, 11 Mar 49, OCMH; NLF and I Corps Rpt of Opns, p. 18.

[20] NLF and I Corps Rpt of Opns, pp. 18–19; Bluemel, 31st Div (PA), Rpt of Opns, pp. 7–8; Bluemel, Comments on Draft MS, Comment 13, OCMH; Harbor Defenses Rpt of Opns, p. 18.

[21] NLF and I Corps Rpt of Opns, pp. 18–19; Selleck, Notes on 71st Div (PA), p. 55. The 71st Division, although it remained a division on paper, ceased to function as one after 6 January.

and disorganized. Since there were no replacements for its animals and only a limited supply of forage, it was shortly reorganized into a motorized squadron of riflemen and a mechanized unit equipped with scout cars and Bren carriers.[22]

II Philippine Corps

Defending the eastern half of the Bataan peninsula was General Parker's II Philippine Corps, holding a line approximately 15,000 yards in length from Manila Bay to the I Corps boundary at Mt. Natib.[23] Unlike the western half of Bataan, the eastern coast was low and swampy and devoted largely to the growth of rice. Here the cleared ground provided good fields of fire, and when the troops reached their position the flat ground to the front, consisting mainly of rice paddies, was flooded. The East Road was an excellent highway compared to the West Road and passed through many small, thriving communities such as Cabcaben, Lamao, Orion, Pilar, and Abucay. Inland, the II Corps sector became more mountainous and rugged as it approached the high volcanic mass in the center of the peninsula.[24]

The main battle position in the II Corps sector, as in the I Corps sector, consisted of a main line of resistance, with an outpost and a regimental reserve line. The main line extended westward from Mabatang on the coast to the heights of Mt. Natib. The right flank, including the coastal plain and the East Road, was considered the most

critical portion of the line. The enemy, advancing unopposed down the East Road, was expected to make his first attempt to breach the main battle position at this point. In this sector, therefore, Parker placed the fresh, well-trained Scouts of the 57th Infantry. They were to hold a line from Manila Bay across the road and approximately 2,000 yards inland as well as a portion of the beach as far south as Balanga.[25]

Next to the 57th Infantry, extending the main line of resistance 6,500 yards to the west, was Brig. Gen. Vincente Lim's 41st Division (PA). One of the first units to reach Bataan, the division was as yet untried in battle. Its three infantry regiments were disposed abreast to give maximum protection to the division front, which extended along the precipitous heights of the gorge above the shallow Balantay River.[26] The rest of the II Corps main line, from the left of the 41st Division to the slopes of Mt. Natib, was held by Jones's 51st Division which had reached Bataan during the night of 3–4 January. The division, less its 52d Infantry, which was on beach defense until 11 January, held a front of more than 5,000 yards along the Balantay River. On the right was the 51st Infantry. On the west, holding down the corps left flank and trailing off into scattered foxholes, was the 53d

---

[22] NLF and I Corps Rpt of Opns, p. 19; Chandler, "26th Cavalry (PS) Battles to Glory," Part 2, *Armored Cavalry Journal* (May–June 1947), p. 15.

[23] SLF and II Corps Rpt of Opns, p. 20 and map, App. 5.

[24] Collier, Notebooks, III, 21, 23; Skerry, Comments on Engineer Hist, No. 10.

[25] USAFFE FO 1, 6 Jan 42, AG 300.4 (28 Dec 41) Phil Rcds; SLF and II Corps Rpt of Opns, p. 23; Maj John E. Olson, Opns of 57th Inf (PS) at Abucay, 10–23 Jan 42, pp. 9, 11, and Maj Ernest L. Brown, Opns of 57th Inf (PS), Abucay, Jan 42, p. 8 (papers prepared for Advanced Officers Course, in 1947–48 and 1946–47, respectively, The Infantry School); Phil Div Rpt of Opns, pp. 10–11, Annex XII, USAFFE-USFIP Rpt of Opns.

[26] SLF and II Corps Rpt of Opns, p. 21 and map, App. 5; ltr, Col Malcolm V. Fortier to Hist Rcds Sec Bd, Hq Fourth Army, 14 May 46, sub: Opns of 41st Div (PA), p. 1, copy sent to the author by Colonel Fortier, formerly senior instructor of the 41st Division, OCMH.

Infantry. The 52d was placed in reserve when it rejoined the division.[27]

Fortifications along the II Corps line were far stronger than in Wainwright's sector. At least as far west as the 51st Division there was a double apron of barbed wire. Working with only a small number of picks, shovels, and axes, and substituting bayonets and the covers of mess kits for individual entrenching tools, the men were able to clear fields of fire, dig foxholes, trenches, and gun emplacements, and construct camouflage overhead. The Japanese later wrote that they found "the strongest sort of field fortifications on the II Corps line." "Covered rifle pits and machine gun emplacements had been constructed," they reported, "and these formed the main structure of the fire network; between them were placed foxholes. . . . The fields of fire had been cleared of cover; camouflage was thorough; the rear communications network had been carefully and thoroughly laid." [28]

Only in the 51st Division sector, on the corps left, were the fortifications inadequate. Here the establishment of a military line along the jungled slopes of Mt. Natib proved impossible in the time and with the tools available. No regular line was organized in this area where patrols operated with the greatest difficulty. Mt. Natib remained an insuperable barrier to the establishment of physical contact between the two corps.[29]

Long-range artillery support in Parker's sector was provided by the 86th Field Artillery Battalion (PS), with twelve 155-mm. guns (GPF), and the 301st Field Artillery Regiment (PA), with sixteen guns of the same type and two 155-mm. howitzers. Emplaced west of Abucay, these pieces were in position to cover all of the main battle positions and the East Road. Providing direct support to the 57th Infantry along the coastal road and the beach was the 1st Battalion, 24th Field Artillery (PS), with one battery on the main line of resistance and two more near Abucay. Additional support was furnished by a battery of the 88th Field Artillery (eight 75-mm. guns) and the 2d Battalion of the 24th, which also supported the 41st Division from a position southeast of Abucay. Each of the divisions had its own divisional artillery in support as well, with the 2.95-inch howitzers of the 41st in position to back up the 51st Division. That division had only eight 75-mm. guns of a type unsuitable for use in the rugged country to which it was assigned.[30]

Defense of the Manila Bay coastline in the II Corps sector, from Balanga, where the 57th line ended, as far south as Limay, after 11 January was assigned to the 11th Division (PA). In addition to its own artillery regiment, it had the support of the

---

[27] SLF and II Corps Rpt of Opns, pp. 21, 31; interv, Falk with Jones, 13 Jun 50; Jones, Chronological Order of Events, 51st Div (PA), 29 Dec 41–26 Jan 42, pp. 1–2, copy lent the author by General Jones, OCMH.
[28] 65th Brig, Combat in the Mt. Natib Area, Bataan 9–27 Jan 42, ATIS Enemy Pub 151, 13 Jul 44, p. 1; SLF and II Corps Rpt of Opns, p. 20.
[29] SLF and II Corps Rpt of Opns, p. 20; Jones, 51st Div (PA) Order of Events, p. 2.

[30] SLF and II Corps Rpt of Opns, pp. 21–23, 29 and App. 5; Shreve, Diary, pp. 21–22; Col Alexander S. Quintard, The 301st FA (PA), p. 4, OCMH; ltr, Capt Willard A. Smith to author, 23 May 49, OCMH; copy of parts of a narrative by Col Quintard, CO 301st FA, p. 2; 2d Bn, 24th FA (PS), extract from Priestley Diary, Notebook 1, p. 15; Olson, 57th Inf (PS) Opns at Abucay, pp. 11, 12; Brown, 57th Inf (PS) Opns at Abucay, p. 9; ltr, Lt Col Charles E. N. Howard, Jr., to TAG, n.d., sub: Unit Hist, 2d Bn, 88th FA (PS), 7 Dec 41–9 Apr 48, pp. 2, 5–6, copy of this letter and a longer draft sent to author and on file in OCMH.

FORTIFICATIONS ON BATAAN. *Tank obstacles and double-apron fence entanglements, above; below, roadblock near the Mauban line.*

21st Field Artillery, detached from its parent unit for beach defense. The rest of the 21st Division was in corps reserve.[31]

By the end of the first week in January the main battle position on Bataan was organized and the troops in place. The Japanese, who on the 7th had taken Layac Junction, the gateway to Bataan, were already in position to move against the American line. "It was felt," wrote Colonel Collier, "that the enemy would continue his close follow up of our troops and launch an early push against the right of the II Corps [along] the East Road." [32] Unlike the rest of Luzon, Bataan offered no room for maneuver and little space for withdrawal. The Japanese would have to be held as long as possible at each position. Except for the few who would be fortunate enough to reach Corregidor, there was no retreat from Bataan.

The Status of Supply

The supply situation on Bataan was serious from the start and became steadily worse through the campaign. Originally, under the ORANGE plan, supplies for 43,000 men for a period of six months were to have been moved to the peninsula on the outbreak of war. MacArthur's order to fight it out on the beaches had invalidated this plan, and when war came supplies and equipment were moved forward to advance depots to support the troops on the front lines. At that time there were stored on Bataan 2,295,000 pounds of canned salmon, 152,000 pounds of fruits and vegetables, 6,000 pounds of miscellaneous foods, and 400,000 gallons of gasoline.[33]

Full-scale movement of supplies to Bataan did not begin until the decision was made on 23 December to withdraw to Bataan. By that time the number of troops to be supplied during the siege of Bataan had increased from the planned 43,000 to almost 80,000, in addition to about 26,000 civilians who had fled to Bataan to escape the invading army. Moving to Bataan enough food and supplies to keep so large a force in action for a period of 180 days would have been extremely difficult under the most favorable circumstances. To accomplish it in about one week, during the confusion of war and retreat, proved to be an impossible task.

Some preparations had been made for the transfer of supplies to Bataan even before the orders for a general withdrawal had been issued on the evening of 23 December. Lt. Col. Otto Harwood, a quartermaster officer, had gone to Limay on Bataan on 14 December to disperse the defense reserves stored there the previous summer, and Col. Alva E. McConnell of the Philippine Quartermaster Depot had begun to ship small quantities of food and petroleum products to Bataan some days before the 23d. Altogether Harwood received from Manila for storage on Bataan approximately 750,000 pounds of canned milk, 20,000 pounds of vegetables, 40,000 gallons

---

[31] Mallonée, Bataan Diary, II, 18–20; SLF and II Corps Rpt of Opns, p. 23.

[32] Collier, Notebooks, III, 18.

[33] Col Otto Harwood, Storage of Supplies on Bataan, p. 1, App. A, QM Rpt of Opns; Stauffer, Quartermaster Operations in the War Against Japan, Ch. I. Mr. Stauffer's chapter, plus the QM Rpt of Opns, Annex XIII, USAFFE-USFIP Rpt of Opns, and the appendixes to this report, especially the narratives in Appendix A, have been used in the preparation of this section.

of gasoline, and 60,000 gallons of lubricating oils and greases. The *Si-Kiang*, bound for Indochina with 5,000,000 pounds of flour and large quantities of petroleum, was seized and brought to Bataan, but unfortunately was bombed and sunk before the flour could be unloaded.[34]

The large-scale movement of supplies to Bataan and Corregidor began after 23 December. First Corregidor was stocked with enough reserves to supply 10,000 men for six months. This task required only one day since the island already had rations for 7,000 men. The movement of supplies to Bataan was more difficult, largely because of transportation problems, the brief period of time in which to accomplish the task, and the size of the shipments.

The only land route to Bataan was the one being used by the retreating troops. Until 31 December the roads to San Fernando and into the peninsula could be used, but with difficulty. The shortage of motor vehicles further limited the quantities of supplies that could be dispatched by this means. After that date the land route from Manila to Bataan was closed. The rail net north of Manila, the best in the archipelago, proved of limited value because of the shortage of rolling stock and the desertion of train and engine crews.

There was no time to evacuate the depots in northern Luzon and scarcely time to get out part of the reserves from Forts McKinley and Stotsenburg. Many of the troops became afflicted with "withdrawal fever" and left behind much that they could have taken. At Stotsenburg, long before the Japanese were within striking distance, the post was evacuated. Food, clothing, and other supplies, it is reported, were left behind by post personnel, to be picked up later by the withdrawing troops. The same thing is supposed to have happened at Clark Field, adjacent to Stotsenburg, where 250,000 gallons of aviation gasoline and several obsolete but serviceable planes were left behind.[35] North and South Luzon Force commanders were instructed to pick up whatever food they could on their way to Bataan, and to turn their supplies in when they reached the peninsula. "Not an ounce" was turned in, noted the quartermaster, although the divisions brought in between ten and twenty-five days' supply of food.[36]

Most of the supplies for Bataan came from Manila, where the port area with its large warehouses and loaded ships was filled with stores of all kinds. Bataan, only thirty miles away across the bay, could be reached easily by almost every type of vessel. With the shortage of motor and rail transportation, water transport become the chief means of getting supplies from the capital to Bataan. The quartermaster's Army Transport Service, led by Col. Frederick A. Ward and staffed largely by civilian volunteers, took over all the available barges, tugs, and launches and used them for the journey. The first two were slow, but they had the advantage of being easily unloaded at the three piers on Bataan where dock facilities were primitive.

At the Manila end loadings were hampered by the Japanese bombings of the port area between the 27th and 30th and the shortage of stevedores. The latter was partially overcome by the use of some two hundred American and British civilians who volunteered to work as dock hands. Altogether, a total of approximately 30,000

---

[34] Harwood, Storage of Supplies on Bataan, pp. 1–3, and Lt Col Irvin Alexander, Supply Problems, p. 2, both in App. A, QM Rpt of Opns.

[35] See above, Ch. X, p. 18.
[36] QM Rpt of Opns, p. 23.

tons of supplies was shipped to Bataan and Corregidor by barge and unloaded by the time the Japanese occupied Manila on 2 January.

Also loaded, but still lying out in the bay at this time, were another 150 barges and 3 freighters. These vessels were unloaded during the weeks that followed at times when they would be safe from Japanese attack, usually at night. But large quantities of food, supplies of all kinds, and gasoline were left behind on the docks and in commercial storage. What the civilians in Manila did not take away with them just before the Japanese entered the city, the conquerors appropriated.[37]

At the time the decision was made to withdraw to Bataan, ammunition and food appeared to be the most critical items of supply and they were accorded first priority. Second priority went to defense materials and to gasoline. All other supplies were given third priority. When rations and ammunition had been shipped, medical supplies, demolitions, barbed wire, and gasoline moved to the top of the priority list.

The movement of ammunition and ordnance supply to Bataan progressed swiftly. Before the war all units had been issued one unit of fire and a second was issued when units moved into defensive positions along the beach. Some ordnance materials had been stored at Forts Stotsenburg and McKinley, but two thirds of the ammunition reserves, about 15,000 tons, as well as six carloads of replacement parts for the tanks, were already in Bataan on 8 December. During the last week of the year another 15,000 tons of ammunition and ordnance

supplies were shipped to Bataan. An inventory of 5 January revealed that the supply of ammunition was satisfactory and that the shortages anticipated would not develop.[38]

The shortage of rations proved to be even more serious than expected, and from the start the scarcity of food was the most alarming fact in the situation of the 80,000 troops on Bataan. The transfer of rice to Bataan had proved difficult because of Commonwealth regulations which stipulated that neither rice nor sugar could be removed from one province to another. When the time came to move supplies to Bataan, authority was requested to take these commodities but permission was not received in time. In this way 10,000,000 pounds of rice at the Government Rice Central at Cabanatuan was lost.[39] Even the seizure of Japanese-owned stocks was prohibited. At Tarlac Lt. Col. Charles S. Lawrence, commander of the depot there, planned to take over about 2,000 cases of canned food, mostly fish and corned beef, as well as a considerable quantity of clothing that belonged to Japanese firms. He was informed by MacArthur's headquarters that he had no right to do so and that he would be court-martialed if he did. These supplies were later destroyed during operations.[40]

On 3 January an inventory of the food in the hands of the quartermaster on

---

[37] Col Ward, ATS Activities, Lt Col Michael A. Quinn, Motor Transport Service Activities, and Lt Col Richard G. Rogers, Traffic Control Opns, Apps. B, C, and E, QM Rpt of Opns.

[38] Gen McBride, Notes on the Fall of Bataan; Weaver, Comments on Draft MS, Comment 34, OCMH. General McBride, Service Command Luzon Force commander, died in prison camp. A copy of this report was borrowed from Colonel Selleck and is on file in OCMH. It will be hereafter cited as McBride, Notes on Bataan Service Command.

[39] QM Rpt of Opns, pp. 19–23.

[40] Lawrence, Tarlac Advance QM Depot Rpt of Opns, pp. 4–5, App. A, QM Rpt of Opns.

Bataan was prepared. This inventory revealed that there was only a 30-day supply of unbalanced field rations for 100,000 men, including a 50-day supply of canned meats and fish, 40 days of canned milk, 30 of flour and canned vegetables (string beans and tomatoes), and 20 of rice, the most important element of the Philippine diet. There were some staples such as sugar, salt, pepper, lard, and syrup, but almost no fresh meat or fruit and only limited quantities of canned fruits, coffee, potatoes, onions, and cereals.[41]

The necessity for drastic action was apparent. On 5 January MacArthur approved the recommendation of his quartermaster, General Drake, that the troops and civilians on Bataan and Corregidor be placed on half-rations, and the necessary instructions were issued to the local commanders.[42]

The half-ration, containing about 2,000 calories, half the normal requirements of an active man, was obviously inadequate to the needs of fighting troops who had to work as much as twenty hours a day, under the most difficult conditions and in the worst kind of climate and terrain. Fortunately many of the men had accumulated food during the withdrawal and this supply was used to supplement the meager diet. Colonel Mallonée, instructor of the 21st Field Artillery (PA), for example, had a case and a half of mixed canned goods, forehandedly purchased before the withdrawal. On his way past Fort Stotsenburg he picked up another half case. Although he gave part of his private stock to some of his fellow officers, he kept a large portion of the two cases for himself. Yet, with this additional sup-

ply of food, he wrote, "I had to do a tailoring job on my waistband twice. . . ."[43]

Heroic measures to augment the food supply were obviously necessary if the troops on Bataan were to hold out for the required six-month period. No sooner had the withdrawal been completed than the quartermaster began to exploit every possible resource on the peninsula to increase his stores. Fortunately, it was the harvest season and the rice stood ripe in the fields. It was only necessary to bring it to the mills, which the engineers were ordered to build near Limay. Plans were made to secure fresh meat by slaughtering carabao, the Philippine draft animal, and a large abattoir was established by the veterinarians. In addition, the units in the field butchered whatever carabao or other animals they could capture. A fishery was established at Lamao, and plans were made to utilize the catch of the local fishermen who went out each night until prevented from doing so by Japanese fire. Salt was secured by boiling sea water in large iron cauldrons. Before the troops had been on Bataan long, no local resource that would yield any additional amount of food was being overlooked.[44]

So serious was the shortage of food after the first few weeks on Bataan that the search for food assumed more importance than the presence of the enemy to the front. Every man became a hunter, and rifle shots could be heard at all hours far from the Japanese lines. Lt. Col. Irvin Alexander, a quartermaster officer, wrote:

Any carabao which was encountered in the jungle was classed as wild and neither his an-

---

[41] Inventory of Rations, 3 Jan 42, AG 430.2 (3 Jan 42) Phil Rcds.

[42] Rad, MacArthur to CG Bataan Service Command, 5 Jan 42, AG 430 (25 Dec 41) Phil Rcds.

[43] Mallonée, Bataan Diary, II, 12.

[44] Frank Hewlett, "Quartermasters on Bataan," *Quartermaster Review*, XXI (May–June 1942), 64; Capt Harold A. Arnold, "The Lesson of Bataan," *Quartermaster Review*, XXVI (November–December 1942), 14.

cestry nor his ownership was investigated. The wild game was not too numerous and it was very shy so that only the cunning and lucky hunters were successful in bringing in meat. Lack of success did not discourage the hunters. . . . One Filipino . . . caught a snake and ate it one day to die unpleasantly the next. There were always plenty of experimenters ready to try any kind of native flora or fauna which might prove edible . . . although the experimenting individual frequently paid a high price.[45]

The supply of clothing on Bataan, while not as alarming as the shortage of food, was just as limited. It had been scanty at the beginning of the war and was almost gone by the time the men reached Bataan. The regular garrison of U.S. Army troops and Philippine Scouts had been comparatively well clad when they took the field, but the Philippine Army had been only partially clothed and equipped. Those who had been inducted before the war were far more fortunate than the Filipinos mobilized after hostilities began. The uniforms and equipment of these men consisted of odds and ends, whatever was on hand for issue and whatever they could salvage or buy. Early in January the Quartermaster had only 10,000 pairs of trousers and shorts and an equal number of shirts and blue denim suits. Obviously this amount of clothing was hardly enough for 80,000 men fighting in heavy jungle and mountains, in a wet climate where days were hot and nights cold, and where tangled vegetation quickly tore shirts and trousers. The army service shoe, of which there were 50,000 pairs on Bataan, was of little use to the Filipino soldier whose feet were too narrow for footgear built on American lasts.

The absence of mosquito netting, shelter halves, blankets, and sun helmets was as

serious as the shortage of clothing. The physical deterioration of the troops and the high incidence of malaria, hookworm, and other diseases were caused as much perhaps by the lack of proper protection against the weather and the jungle as the unbalanced and deficient diet.

Provision had been made in war plans for a general hospital on Bataan. At Limay, where the defense reserves were stored, all supplies for the hospital were already assembled when the order to withdraw was given. General Hospital No. 1 was established on 23 December and before the end of the month another general hospital was organized not far from Cabcaben. The medical depot in Manila, where supplies and equipment for a 10,000-bed hospital center had been established at the start of the war, began to transfer this vast accumulation of medical supplies to Bataan after the 23d. But only enough was brought in to assure an adequate supply of drugs and medical equipment for the first part of the siege of Bataan. By the end of February a critical shortage of several drugs, the most important of which was quinine, had already developed.[46]

The supply of petroleum products on Bataan was adequate for several months if strict economy was practiced. During the first week or two on Bataan there was no control over the use of gasoline. When it was discovered that stocks were being depleted at the rate of 14,000 gallons a day, the supply was closely rationed. Ultimately the consumption of gasoline was reduced to 4,000, then 3,000 gallons daily.

---

[45] Alexander, Supply Problems, p. 5, App. A, QM Rpt of Opns.

[46] Col Wibb E. Cooper, Medical Dept Activities in Phil, pp. 54–56, 57, 78, Annex XIV, USAFFE-USFIP Rpt of Opns; McBride, Notes on Bataan Service Command, pp. 113–14; ltr, Col Harold W. Glattly to Ward, 8 Jan 52, OCMH.

Motor vehicles were much sought after on Bataan. The various services and units commandeered vehicles for their own use and hijacking of both vehicles and loads was common. The provost marshal did his best to stop this practice, with little success. Finally, all vehicles except those organic to units were ordered into motor pools. When the order failed to bring in the vehicles, a search and seizure system was inaugurated. The military police stopped vehicles and if the drivers could not prove that they were on a legitimate mission they were directed to one of the motor pools. But most of the vehicles had been well hidden and the most careful search failed to locate them. Only later, when gasoline was rationed and the units could not operate the vehicles, were they turned in.[47]

Engineer supply, like that of the other services, was limited and carefully controlled. The engineers had managed to ship to Bataan and Corregidor more than 10,000 tons of their supplies, in addition to organizational equipment, by the end of December.[48] These included 350 tons of explosives, 800 tons of valuable barbed wire, 200 tons of burlap bags for use as sandbags, and large quantities of lumber, construction material, and depot stocks. During the withdrawal, engineer supplies had been evacuated from advance depots along the route of retreat and moved to Lubao, a short distance north of Bataan. From there they were to be transferred to two locations on Bataan. Despite congestion along the roads, the shortage of transportation, and the confusion of retreat, the final evacuation of engineer supplies from the Lubao depot was completed by 6 January.

The first engineer troops to reach Bataan were put to work immediately on airfield construction to accommodate the few fighter craft still left and those which, it was hoped, might yet arrive from the United States. Work was also begun on access roads to the main highway along the east coast of Bataan and on a lateral road from east to west across the slopes of the Mariveles Mountains.[49]

The main work on fortifications along the front was performed by the infantry and artillery, but the engineers improved these positions, strung wire, and laid mines. They maintained roads and bridges and prepared demolition charges where necessary. In addition to serving the troops along the front, they built camps for the 26,000 civilians who had taken refuge on Bataan, sawmills to provide lumber for buildings and bridges, and rice mills to feed the men. The greatest handicap to engineer activity was the lack of trained engineer troops. Civilian labor was used wherever possible, but there was no substitute for trained engineer officers. So small was their number that in one instance a civilian served for a time as the commander of an engineer battalion.[50]

The shortage of supplies of all types, and especially of food, had a greater effect on the outcome of the siege of Bataan than any other single factor. "Each day's combat, each day's output of physical energy," wrote one officer in his diary, "took its toll of the human body—a toll which could not be repaired. . . ."[51] When this fact is understood, he added, the story of Bataan is told.

[47] McBride, Notes on Bataan Service Command, p. 113.

[48] The material on engineer supply is derived from Engineers in the Southwest Pacific, 1941–1945, Vol. I, Engineers in Theater Operations, p. 19, and Vol. III, Engineer Supply, pp. 6, 9, and 11.

[49] Engineer Supply, p. 9, n. 6.

[50] Engineers in Theater Operations, p. 19.

[51] Mallonée, Bataan Diary, II, 16.

BRIDGES ON BATAAN. *Top left, straw ready to be set on fire is piled over a wooden bridge; top right, remains of a steel bridge; bottom, foundation for a temporary bridge is prepared.*

The Enemy and His Plan

While General MacArthur's force on Luzon was preparing the defenses of Bataan, the enemy *14th Army* was being reorganized. Original Japanese plans had called for the reduction of Luzon fifty days after the start of war. At that time the *48th Division,* Homma's best unit, and most of the *5th Air Group* were to leave the Philippines for operations elsewhere. The mop-up would be left to a garrison unit, the *65th Brigade,* and the *16th Division.* The brigade, with attached service and supply troops, was to reach Luzon on the forty-fifth day of operations, 22 January.[52]

Sometime late in December, Gen. Count Hisaichi Terauchi, *Southern Army* commander, and Admiral Kondo, commanding the *2d Fleet,* jointly recommended to *Imperial General Headquarters* that *16th Army*'s invasion of Java be advanced about one month ahead of schedule. This suggestion found willing listeners in Tokyo. Reasoning that such a move would result in the rapid occupation of the Southwest Pacific while the Allies were still off balance, and noting the success of Homma's forces in the Philippines, *Imperial General Headquarters* approved the Terauchi-Kondo proposal and ordered the transfer of the *48th Division* to *16th Army* at a much earlier date than originally planned. On 2 January, as *14th Army* units entered Manila, General Homma received notice from *Southern Army* that the *48th Division* would soon be transferred. Orders for the transfer of the division as well as the *5th Air Group* reached Manila during the next few days, and on 5 January staff officers of

Southern Army arrived in the Philippines to supervise the transfer.[53]

In the opinion of *14th Army* the transfer of ground and air troops from the Philippines showed a lack of understanding of the situation by higher headquarters.[54] Actually, both *Southern Army* and *Imperial General Headquarters* recognized that this early redeployment might jeopardize operations in the Philippines, but they were willing to take this risk in order to hasten the attack on Java and free themselves for any move by the Soviet Union. "Difficulties would undoubtedly arise in the future in the Philippines," the Japanese believed, "but the *Southern Army* thought that the Philippines could be taken care of after the conclusion of the campaign in Java." [55]

The removal of the *48th Division* from Homma's command at a date earlier than originally planned might well have left him with only the *16th Division* to open the attack against Bataan. Fortunately for the Japanese cause, Homma had ordered the *65th Brigade* to make ready for departure from Takao in Formosa only a week after the start of hostilities. This decision to embark the brigade somewhat sooner than scheduled was made without reference to the early departure of the *48th* but was apparently based on the unexpected lack of American resistance to the initial landings

[52] *14th Army* Opns, I, 24–25.

[53] *14th Army* Opns, I, 73, 75, 77; Statement of Maeda, 2 Mar 50, ATIS Doc 56234, Interrogations of Former Japanese Officers, Mil Hist Div, GHQ FEC, II; USA *vs.* Homma, p. 3225, testimony of Homma; Hist *Army Sec, Imperial GHQ,* pp. 40, 41; *Southern Army* Opns, p. 16.

[54] *14th Army* Opns, I, 75; Interrog of Col Motoo Nakayama, *14th Army* Senior Opns Officer, Apr 47, Interrogations of Former Japanese Officers, Mil Hist Div, GHQ FEC, I.

[55] *Southern Army* Opns, p. 16.

in northern Luzon.[56] On 27 December, Homma ordered Lt. Gen. Akira Nara, the brigade commander, to sail from Takao with all the troops then scheduled to reinforce *14th Army*. Delayed in his departure by a typhoon, Nara finally set sail with his convoy of fourteen ships and naval escort on 30 December. At 1400 on New Year's Day the troops began to debark at Lingayen Gulf.[57]

The day the *65th Brigade* landed in the Philippines it was ordered to move by foot to Tarlac. Within three days advance elements had entered the town. On the 6th the brigade reached Angeles and began to concentrate along Route 74, as far south as Porac.[58] "They had made their march," remarked General Nara proudly of his troops, "but were footsore and exhausted." [59]

Southern Army had stripped General Homma of some of his best ground and air units just before the start of the battle of Bataan. All he had left was the *16th Division*, which "did not have a very good reputation" for its "fighting qualities," the *65th Brigade*, the *7th Tank Regiment*, supporting arms and services, and a small air unit of less than seventy fighters, bombers, and reconnaissance planes.[60] Only in the air were the Japanese assured of superiority.

The brigade which replaced the well-trained and equipped *48th Division* was, in the words of its commander, "absolutely unfit for combat duty." [61] Organized in

early 1941 as a garrison unit, it had a total strength of about 6,500 men. Its three infantry regiments, the *122d, 141st* and *142d Infantry*, consisted of but two battalions, each organized into three rifle companies and one machine gun company. The brigade had few vehicles and no artillery unit, but at least one of the regiments and possibly the others had a battery of field artillery. Organic to the brigade was a field hospital, an engineer unit, and a signal unit no larger than a "telegraph platoon." The majority of the enlisted men were conscripts and the month of training at Formosa was entirely inadequate. Unit training had progressed only as far as the company.[62]

General Homma and the majority of the *14th Army* staff believed that American resistance on Bataan would be weak and that operations there would be quickly concluded. The plan for the attack, therefore, was conceived of as a pursuit rather than an assault against a strongly fortified position in depth.[63]

This conception was confirmed by intelligence reports. The *14th Army* staff estimated that MacArthur had 40,000 to 45,000 men, about 40 tanks, and a few fighter planes on Bataan and Corregidor. On Bataan alone, Homma was told by his intelligence officer, there were only 25,000 men. The American "regular" 31st Division and the "fortress unit" on Corregidor were believed to total 35,000 while the remnants of the Philippine Army units altogether comprised 5,000 to 10,000 more. Reports received from air reconnaissance gave

[56] *14th Army* Opns, I, 39.
[57] *Ibid.,* 32, 60–61, 65. One regiment of the brigade landed at Laoag or Vigan. The rest of the force landed between San Fabian and Mabilao.
[58] *Ibid.,* 66, 73, 75–76, 91; *65th Brig* Opns Rpt, Mt. Natib, pp. 2–3.
[59] *65th Brig* Opns Rpt, Mt. Natib, p. 2.
[60] The quotation is from USA *vs.* Homma, p. 3057, testimony of Homma. See also p. 3232; and *5th Air Gp* Opns, pp. 50–51.
[61] *65th Brig* Opns Rpt, Mt. Natib, p. 3.

[62] *Ibid.;* *14th Army* Opns, I, 66, 73, 97.
[63] Statement of Maeda, 2 Mar 50, ATIS Doc 56234, Interrogations of Former Japanese Officers, Mil Hist Div, GHQ FEC, II. No orders dealing with the forthcoming operation were received from *Southern Army* or *Imperial General Headquarters* at this time.

no reason to believe that the Americans and Filipinos had constructed any strong installations on Bataan.

The physical condition of the troops on Bataan was believed to be poor. All units in combat had been badly cut up, rations had been reduced by half, and the entire American-Filipino army was on a skimpy two-meals-a-day diet. Desertions by Filipino troops were believed to be heavy and the Japanese fully believed that the Americans had taken strong measures to halt these desertions and the surrender of individuals. In support of these conclusions they pointed out that the bodies of Philippine soldiers had been found tied to trees.[64]

With this picture of the enemy, it is not surprising that General Homma believed the capture of the peninsula would be an easy task. His estimate of the American scheme of defense was that MacArthur's forces would make their strong stand around Mariveles and then withdraw to Corregidor. Seizure of the island fortress would not be easy and a "sea blockade" might be necessary before the island would be reduced. On the whole, "the threat of enemy resistance was taken lightly" by *14th Army*.[65]

On the theory that the campaign would be a light one, Homma assigned the seizure of Bataan to the inexperienced and untrained *65th Brigade*. His plan was to have the brigade advance in two columns, one along the east coast through Abucay to Balanga and the other down the opposite shore through Moron to Bagac. Once these objectives had been taken, Nara was to send the main force of his brigade south from Balanga, while a smaller force drove on from Bagac. Both were to push towards Mariveles, the *14th Army* operation order read, "with the annihilation of the enemy on Bataan Peninsula as their objective." [66]

Attached to the *65th Brigade* for the Bataan operation were infantry, artillery, armor, and service units of all types. From the *16th Division* came the *9th Infantry*, a battalion of field artillery (75-mm. guns), an engineer regiment, and a medical unit. The *48th Division* supplied two battalions of artillery (75-mm. mountain guns), which were pulled out a short time later. Armored support consisted of the *7th Tank Regiment*, and artillery support was furnished by Army: *1st Field Heavy Artillery Regiment* (150-mm. howitzers), the *8th Field Heavy Artillery Regiment* (105-mm. guns), and the *9th Independent Heavy Artillery Battalion* (150-mm. howitzers). Service and support units from Army completed the force available to General Nara for the forthcoming operation.[67]

Direct support for the *65th Brigade's* operations on Bataan was to be provided by the air unit under Col. Komataro Hoshi.[68] This unit was made responsible for reconnaissance, artillery spotting, and support missions. Starting on 10 January it was to base at Clark Field and from that date through the 13th was to attack I Corps artillery positions, the airstrips on Bataan, and

---

[64] *14th Army* Opns, I, 87, 89; USA vs. Homma, p. 3057, testimony of Homma.

[65] Interrog of Maeda, 10 May 47, Interrogations of Former Japanese Officers, Mil Hist Div, GHQ FEC, I. "General Homma," remarked his chief of staff, "thought only in terms of continuing the pursuit."

[66] *14th Army* Opns Order, Series A, No. 155, 1200, 11 Jan 42, and *65th Brig* Opns Order, Series A, No. 42, 1800, 8 Jan 42, both in *65th Brig* Opns Rpt, Mt. Natib, Apps. 20 and 3, respectively.

[67] *Ibid.*, p. 7, and *14th Army* Opns Order, Series A, No. 138, 0800, 7 Jan 42, App. 1.

[68] *5th Air Gp* Opns, pp. 47–51. The air unit consisted of 11 fighters, 21 reconnaissance, liaison, and artillery observation planes, 36 light bombers, and a number of service units.

installations in the Mariveles area.[69] The *16th Division* was to "cooperate" with the *65th Brigade* by "sending a portion of the division to occupy the strategic ground in the vicinity of Ternate and Nasugbu." [70] The occupation of Ternate, on the south shore of Manila Bay, and of Nasugbu to its south would have the effect of cutting communication between Corregidor and southern Luzon.

At noon 4 January General Homma had ordered the *65th Brigade* to move down Route 74 to the main battle position to relieve the *48th Division* and take command of the *Takahashi Detachment* and the *9th*

Independent Heavy Artillery Battalion. Nara apparently understood then that his unit was to relieve the *48th Division*, for his orders were to "destroy the enemy," send his main force toward Balanga, and make a secondary effort toward Olongapo.[71] Final orders for the relief of the *48th Division* were issued at 0800 of the 7th. At that time General Nara was again instructed to move toward Olongapo and Balanga. By 1800 of 8 January the brigade had completed its relief of the *48th* and was concentrated between Dinalupihan and Hermosa, preparing to attack.[72] The next afternoon the assault would begin.

---

[69] *14th Army* Opns, I, 89.
[70] *14th Army* Opns Order, Series A. No. 155, 1200, 11 Jan 42.

[71] *14th Army* Opns, I, 73–74.
[72] *65th Brig* Opns Order, Series A, No. 42, and *14th Army* Opns Order, Series A, No. 138, both cited above; *14th Army* Opns, I, 91.

CHAPTER XVI

The First Battle of Bataan

The Japanese opened the battle for Bataan at 1500 on 9 January with a concentrated barrage directed against II Corps. As "the roar of artillery . . . shook the northern portion of the Bataan peninsula," the Japanese infantry moved out to the attack.[1]

General Nara's plan of attack, based on *14th Army*'s order to make the main effort on the east, rested on two misconceptions: first, that the American and Filipino troops had been so weakened during the withdrawal that opposition would be light; and second, that the II Corps line was farther north than was actually the case. General Nara's misapprehension on the first point was quickly corrected when II Corps artillery replied, "particularly ferociously," to the opening barrage. Tons of explosive hurtling down on the advancing Japanese, ranged along the East Road and backed up four miles on Route 7, made abundantly clear the American determination to stand and fight.[2]

The initial Japanese error in locating the II Corps line was corrected only as the battle developed. In drawing up his plan of attack, General Nara had placed Parker's left flank in the vicinity of Mt. Santa Rosa, about three miles above its actual location. The American outpost line, he estimated, extended along the high ground immediately below Hermosa, an error of three to four miles. Thus, in making his plans for the major drive down the east side of the peninsula, Nara assumed he would meet the II Corps outposts soon after the attack opened. On these assumptions he ordered his troops to advance to a line extending east and west of Album, with the main effort on the west to "overwhelm the enemy's left flank." At the same time, a part of the force was to swing wide in an encircling movement to take II Corps in the rear. Simultaneously, a secondary thrust by a smaller force would be made down the west side of the peninsula against I Corps.[3]

For the attack General Nara organized his reinforced brigade and attached units into three regimental combat teams and a reserve. Against II Corps he sent two regiments supported by tanks and artillery. Forming the brigade left (east) was Col. Takeo Imai's *141st Infantry*, supported by a battalion of mountain artillery, a battery of antitank guns, plus engineer and signal troops. Starting from positions near Hermosa, Colonel Imai's force was to advance southward down the East Road as far as the Calaguiman River. It would have strong support, if needed, from the *7th Tank Regiment* which had spearheaded the attack against Baliuag and Plaridel at the end of December. In this first attack on Bataan, the tanks would remain in the rear until the

---

[1] *65th Brig* Opns Rpt, Mt. Natib, p. 15.

[2] Quintard, 301st FA (PA), p. 5; Quintard, CO 301st FA (PA), Diary p. 5; Shreve, Diary, pp. 21–22.

[3] Description of the Japanese plan is based on *65th Brig* Opns Order, Series A, No. 42, 1800, 8 Jan 42, *65th Brig* Opns Rpt, Mt. Natib, App. 3, pp. 44–48.

engineers had repaired the bridges and removed the roadblocks along the East Road.

General Nara's hopes for a quick victory rested on the combat team that was sent against the western portion of the II Corps line. This force, under Col. Susumu Takechi, consisted of the experienced *9th Infantry,* reinforced by a battalion of artillery, an antitank gun battery, plus service and support troops. Takechi's orders were to "overwhelm" Parker's left flank, take Album, then send an encircling force around the flank to join Colonel Imai's *141st Infantry* coming down the East Road. To assure the success of this maneuver Nara placed his reserve, the *142d Infantry,* behind the *9th* along the narrow trail leading from Dinalupihan to Album, in position to exploit the expected breakthrough of Takechi's troops.

Artillery support for the advance against II Corps would be provided by Col. Gen Irie's *Army* artillery, attached to the brigade for the operation.[4] The guns were initially emplaced north of Hermosa, in position to fire direct support and counterbattery missions. As the battle progressed the artillery would be displaced forward to Orani. Additional support for the *9th Infantry* would be furnished by a field artillery battalion advancing eastward from Olongapo along Route 7.

Against I Corps on the western side of Bataan, General Nara sent his third regimental combat team, built around the *122d Infantry,* and led by Col. Yunosuke Watanabe. Watanabe's mission was to advance west along Route 7 to Olongapo, then south to Moron. From there he would prepare to advance on Bagac, western terminus of the one lateral road across Bataan. Nara

apparently did not expect any resistance above Bagac and was not even certain that he would meet any there.

By early afternoon of 9 January all troops were in position, tensely awaiting the zero hour. General Nara himself was at Dinalupihan. At 1500 the big guns opened up.

Attack Against II Corps: The Abucay Line

The II Corps line, called the Abucay line, extended from Mabatang on Manila Bay to the northeast slopes of Mt. Natib. (*Map 12*) On the east, guarding the East Road, stood the well-trained Scouts of the 57th Infantry. To their left was the untried 41st Division (PA), once briefly part of the South Luzon Force and now in position along the Mt. Natib trail and Balantay River, defending the center of the Abucay line.[5] Holding the western portion of the corps line was General Jones's 51st Division (PA), weakened by the long withdrawal from south Luzon. With its left resting on the jungled slopes of Mt. Natib, the division held a line along the north bank of the Balantay River as far east as Abucay Hacienda, a raised clearing in the jungle about five miles west of the town of Abucay. At its western extremity the line consisted of little more than scattered foxholes.

The Japanese attack began on schedule. At 1500 Colonel Imai's men started down the East Road but had not advanced far

---

[4] The attached artillery consisted of the *1st* and *8th Field Heavy Artillery Regiments* and the *9th Independent Heavy Artillery Battalion.* Colonel Irie was commander of the first-named unit.

[5] The Mt. Natib trail extended from Mabatang westward to the slopes of Mt. Natib. The 57th Infantry and part of the 41st Division had placed their main line of resistance along this trail. Farther west the trail ran below the main line of resistance. The Balantay River appears in many sources and on some maps as the Lavantan or Labangan River. A tributary of the Calaguiman River, it is formed by two streams joining about a mile west of Abucay Hacienda; it then flows northeast until it joins the Calaguiman. The Balantay is shallow and easily fordable; its virtue as a military obstacle was due to the fact that it flows through a deep gorge.

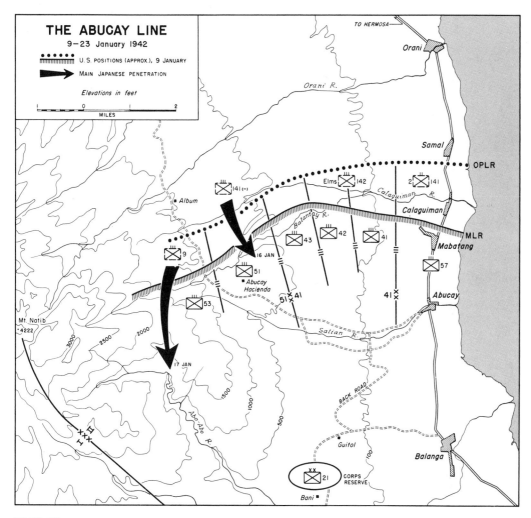

MAP 12

before they were met by punishing fire from
II Corps artillery which had the road under
interdiction.[6] To the west the movement of
the *9th Infantry* was unopposed and
Colonel Takechi reached the vicinity of Album without any difficulty or opposition.

The only infantry contact during the day
came when a reconnaissance patrol of the
57th Infantry met a Japanese patrol below
Hermosa. After a brief fire fight the Scouts
had withdrawn.

---

[6] Probably more has been written on the fight at
Abucay than on any other episode in the Philippine
campaign. The sources for the action of each unit
will be cited in the appropriate place but the fight
as a whole can be reconstructed from *65th Brig*

Opns Rpt, Mt. Natib, pp. 15–30; *14th Army* Opns,
I, 88–92; SLF and II Corps Rpt of Opns, pp. 29–
35; Lt Col Edmund J. Lilly, Jr., Rpt of Opns, 57th
Inf (PS), 8 Dec 41–9 Apr 42, pp. 3–4, copy in
OCMH; Jones, 51st Div (PA) Order of Events,
pp. 2–4.

INSPECTION. *General MacArthur and Brig. Gen. Albert M. Jones with members of their staffs, 10 January 1942.*

General Nara, who had expected to hit the II Corps outpost line on the first day of the battle, was greatly encouraged by the progress of his units. Both the *141st Infantry* and the *9th Infantry* sent back optimistic reports of their advances, and Nara incorrectly concluded that the Americans had "made a general withdrawal" and "fled into the jungle without putting up a fight." [7]

On the evening of the 9th Wainwright and Parker received orders from Corregidor to have all their general officers assembled to receive an important visitor the next morning.[8] At the first light of dawn a PT boat carried General MacArthur and

his chief of staff, Maj. Gen. Richard K. Sutherland, across the channel from Corregidor to Mariveles. From there they drove up the East Road to Parker's headquarters where they talked with II Corps officers and inspected positions in that sector. Moving west across the Pilar–Bagac road MacArthur met Wainwright and inspected I Corps installations. When Wainwright offered to show MacArthur his 155-mm. guns, MacArthur replied, "I don't want to *see* them. I want to *hear* them." [9]

The Japanese unwittingly chose the day of MacArthur's visit to Bataan to make their first demand for surrender. In a mes-

---

[7] *65th Brig* Opns Rpt, Mt. Natib, p. 16.

[8] Wainwright, *General Wainwright's Story*, p. 49. Only Wainwright mentions the order directing him to assemble the general officers. It is assumed that Parker received similar orders.

[9] *Ibid.*, p. 50; Hunt, *MacArthur and the War Against Japan*, pp. 52–53; USAFFE-USFIP Rpt of Opns, p. 45. Colonel Mallonée recalls MacArthur's answer to Wainwright as, "Don't need to see 'em. I hear 'em." Mallonée, Bataan Diary, II, 31.

sage addressed to the American commander and dropped from the air behind the American lines, General Homma told MacArthur that his men were doomed and the end near. "The question," he declared, "is how long you will be able to resist. You have already cut rations by half. . . . Your prestige and honor have been upheld. However, in order to avoid needless bloodshed and save your . . . troops you are advised to surrender. . . . Failing that our offensive will be continued with inexorable force. . . ." [10]

The only answer the Japanese received to their request for surrender was an increase in the volume of artillery fire from II Corps.

To avoid the interdiction fire on the East Road, Colonel Imai shifted the bulk of his *141st Infantry* to the west on the 10th, with the result that his regiment split into two columns. The easternmost column, consisting of the *2d Battalion* (less two companies), continued to advance down the East Road toward the 57th Infantry; the western column, containing the rest of the regiment, advanced against the 41st Division. Late on the afternoon of the 10th, the *2d Battalion* struck the 57th Infantry outpost line just below Samal, and after a brief fire fight the Scouts fell back. Though unopposed by infantry, the *2d Battalion,* hindered by artillery fire, was able to advance only as far as the narrow Calaguiman River, about 1,800 yards below Samal. To

the west the rest of the *141st Infantry,* under less intense artillery fire but delayed by the rugged terrain, finally reached the 41st Division outpost line along the Calaguiman River four miles west of the East Road, sometime during the night of 10–11 January. [11]

The 57th Infantry, under the command of Col. George S. Clarke, was the first unit on the II Corps line to come under heavy infantry attack. Along the main line of resistance were the 1st Battalion on the right and the 3d Battalion on the left. The 2d Battalion was in reserve. On 11 January a reinforced company of the reserve battalion, which had established an outpost line south of the Calaguiman, came under attack by the advance elements of Colonel Imai's eastern column, the *2d Battalion, 141st Infantry.* Soon the Japanese began to cross the Calaguiman, about one mile north of the main line of resistance. By 2300 the Japanese battalion had reached a cane field on the left front of the 57th's 3d Battalion, directly before Company I. This cane field, about 150 yards in front of the main line of resistance, had not been cleared on the

---

[10] MacArthur quoted the Japanese message in a radio to the War Department, 27 Jan 42, WPD, Ready Reference File. On the reverse side of his message to MacArthur, General Homma later wrote a separate warning for the Philippine troops. In it he advised the Filipinos to save their "dear lives" by throwing away their weapons and surrendering before it was too late. "MacArthur had stupidly refused our proposal," declared Homma, "and continues futile struggle at the cost of your precious lives."

[11] The account of the action on the right of the II Corps line is based upon: Olson, Opns of the 57th Inf (PS) at Abucay, pp. 10–17; Brown, Opns of 57th Inf (PS) at Abucay, pp. 9–12; Capt William C. Anderson, Hist of 57th Inf (PS), pp. 2–5, Chunn Notebooks; Capt Harry J. Stempin, Opns of Co G, 57th Inf (PS), 7 Dec 41–30 Jan 42, pp. 9–12, and Maj William E. Webb, Opns of 41st Inf (PA) in Defense of Abucay Line, 10–18 Jan 42, pp. 15–21 (both are papers prepared for Advanced Officers Course in 1946–47 and 1949–50, respectively, The Infantry School); Lt Col Harold K. Johnson, "Defense Along the Abucay Line," *Military Review* (February 1949), pp. 50–51; Col Malcolm V. Fortier, Notes on 41st Div (PA), pp. 1–2; memo, Lt Col Frank F. Carpenter, Jr., Asst G–4 USAFFE, for G–4 USAFFE, 14 Jan 42, sub: Rpt of Inspection Trip, 13 Jan 42, AG 319.1 (8 Jan 42) Phil Rcds; unsigned account of the 41st Div (PA), pp. 2–4.

assumption that artillery would effectively prevent its use by the enemy as a route of approach.

That night the Japanese in the cane field moved out against the main line of resistance. First came an artillery and mortar barrage, which was answered by concentrated fire from the 75-mm. guns of the 24th Field Artillery (PS). Hardly had the 24th opened fire than the Japanese infantry jumped off in a banzai attack across the moonlit patch of ground in front of Company I. Wave after wave of screaming Japanese troops hurled themselves forward in the face of intense fire. Men in the leading wave threw themselves on the barbed wire entanglements, forming human bridges over which succeeding waves could pass.

Despite the appalling effects of the point-blank fire from the 75's, the Japanese continued their ferocious attack until Company I, its commander seriously wounded and its executive officer killed, finally gave ground. Company K on the right immediately refused its flank and the battalion commander threw his reserve, Company L, into the fight. When this force failed to halt the Japanese, Colonel Clarke committed a company of the reserve battalion and the Japanese attack stalled. At the approach of dawn, the Scouts began a counterattack which took them almost to the original line. When the action was broken off on the morning of the 12th, there were an estimated 200 to 300 dead Japanese on the field of battle.

During the night a number of Japanese had infiltrated into the 3d Battalion area, on the left of the regimental line. The 57th Infantry spent most of the next day routing out the infiltrators, man by man, in hand-to-hand combat. After a number of Scouts had been killed, a more efficient scheme for

the elimination of the infiltrated Japanese was devised. Sniper parties consisting of riflemen assisted by demolition engineers were formed and these began to comb the 3d Battalion area systematically. By the end of the day most of the Japanese had been found and killed. It was as a result of his action as the leader of one of these sniper parties that 2d Lt. Alexander R. Nininger, Jr., was posthumously awarded the Medal of Honor. His was the first of World War II, although Calugas received his award for heroism in the earlier fight at Layac Junction.

The Japanese advance in other sectors had been even less successful than that of the *2d Battalion, 141st Infantry.* The remainder of Imai's regiment in front of the 41st Division had begun to exert pressure against the outpost line on the night of 10–11 January. Unable to make progress here, it had continued to move westward in search of a soft spot in the line. By late afternoon of the 11th Colonel Imai stood before the 43d Infantry on the left of the 41st Division line.

The *9th Infantry* had also drifted far from its original axis of advance. Despite the lack of opposition Takechi's advance through the jungle of central Bataan was slow. By the morning of the 11th his *2d Battalion* had progressed only as far as the Orani River, two miles from the 51st Division line. The rest of the regiment had taken the wrong road and marched east until it was now only a few thousand yards northwest of Samal, almost behind the *141st* instead of to its right.

It is not surprising that the Japanese had become lost during the advance. Not only were they hindered and confused by the difficult terrain, but they were further handicapped by the lack of adequate maps.

"Imperfect maps," General Nara later wrote, "were the greatest drawback as far as directing the battle was concerned." He had difficulty also in maintaining communications with his forward units, largely because his signal unit was inexperienced and the men frequently became lost in the jungle. American artillery imposed further difficulties on communications and he complained that "an hour of [radio] conversation a day was considered good, but even this was not always possible." [12]

It was not until the evening of 11 January that General Nara received enough information to form an approximately correct estimate of his position. It was clear by now that the Americans intended to resist his advance and that this resistance would be far stronger than he had expected. His units had strayed from their original paths, their gains had been small, and they were becoming disorganized. "Besides the fact that the front line force was hampered by the terrain and that the control of the heavy weapons and artillery forces was very poor," lamented Nara, "the line forces . . . did not know each other's intentions and positions." [13] He decided, therefore, to revise his plans. Modifying an earlier plan he ordered the *141st Infantry*, Colonel Imai's regiment, to continue its westward movement until it became the brigade right flank instead of the left, which it had been originally. The *142d*, formerly brigade reserve, was reinforced with artillery and ordered to advance down the east coast to become the brigade left flank. Colonel Takechi's *9th Infantry*, less one battalion, was designated as the "encircling unit" and directed to strike at Parker's left flank and take the

corps line from the rear. The remaining battalion of the regiment was ordered into brigade reserve. To get his artillery forward Nara was forced to order the construction of a new road since II Corps artillery effectively denied him the use of the East Road. Zero hour for the attack was set for noon of the 13th, when the *9th Infantry*, the "encircling unit," would jump off; the remainder of the brigade was to move out at dusk of the same day. [14]

On the 12th, as the Japanese moved into position for the attack, all units on the II Corps line found themselves under increasingly heavy pressure. On the right, in front of the 57th Infantry, the Japanese succeeded in establishing themselves again on the south bank of the Calaguiman; in the center they pushed back the outpost line before the 43d Infantry. [15] It was on the left of the corps line that the Japanese made their most important gains on 12 January, when they tore a gap in the 51st Infantry sector. A counterattack by a reserve battalion regained some of the lost ground but at a heavy cost. By nightfall it was evident that the Japanese, thwarted in their advance on the east, were shifting their effort westward.

The threat to the eastern anchor of the line was still too serious to be ignored. Though the 57th Infantry had beaten back all attempts by the *2d Battalion, 141st Infantry*, to pierce the main line of resistance, it was still hard pressed on the left and was beginning to feel pressure on its right. Late on the evening of the 12th, therefore, General Parker released the two-battalion 21st

---

[12] *65th Brig* Opns Rpt, Mt. Natib, pp. 6, 26.
[13] *Ibid.*, p. 21.

797-257 O—66—19

[14] *65th Brig* Opns Orders, Series A, Nos. 49 and 53, 11 and 12 Jan 42, *65th Brig* Opns Rpt, Mt. Natib, Apps. 6 and 7.
[15] Ltr, Col Loren A. Wetherby to author, 23 Oct 50, OCMH.

Infantry (PA) from corps reserve and gave it to Colonel Clarke. With these fresh troops Clarke made plans for an attack the next morning with the 21st Infantry's 2d Battalion and the same numbered battalion of the 57th. That night the 2d Battalion, 21st Infantry, took over the left of the line and the 3d Battalion went into reserve to free the 2d Battalion, 57th Infantry, for the counterattack.[16]

At 0600, 13 January, on the heels of a rolling artillery barrage, the 2d Battalion, 21st Infantry, jumped off in the counterattack. Its task was made more difficult by the fact that the Japanese had pushed a deep salient into the left of the 57th line during the night. The Filipinos advanced quickly and aggressively, pushing the Japanese back across the bloodied ground. It soon became evident to Capt. Philip A. Meier, the battalion's American instructor, that the gap was too large to be filled by his men alone and he moved east to tie in with the 1st Battalion, 57th Infantry, on his right, thus creating a hole between his men and the 41st Infantry on his left. Colonel Clarke, the 57th commander, thereupon ordered the 3d Battalion of the 21st Infantry from reserve to plug the gap. As the battalion began to move up at about 1300 it came under Japanese artillery fire and was pinned down. When the artillery

fire ceased three hours later, the 2d Battalion, 57th Infantry, counterattacked and advanced to within 150 yards of the original line. By late afternoon the gap had been closed and the Japanese were left in possession of only a small salient on the left of the 57th Infantry line, a meager return indeed for four days of hard fighting.[17]

The counterattack by the 21st Infantry on the morning of the 13th had forestalled the Japanese offensive in that sector, leading General Nara to complain that "the battle did not develop according to plan." [18] Elsewhere along the II Corps front he was more successful. His artillery and air attacks that morning had caused damage along the entire front and had caught a battalion of the 23d Infantry, moving from reserve into position behind the 43d Infantry, inflicting from sixty to seventy casualties. Farther west the *141st Infantry* had begun to push against the right of General Jones's line, in the 51st Infantry sector, during the morning, and had forced Jones back to his main line of resistance along the high ground on the north bank of the Balantay. The advance of the *9th Infantry* down the center of the peninsula, "hampered by the terrain" and, Colonel Takechi reported, considerable resistance, had failed to reach the main line of resistance on the 13th.[19]

Japanese pressure next day, the 14th, was heaviest on the left of the Abucay line. Here the *141st Infantry* hit the 43d Infantry, forcing the outposts along the Balantay back across the river. The 51st Di-

---

[16] The date of the attachment of the 21st Division units to the 57th is variously given in the sources used. The weight of evidence as well as the sequence of events and Japanese sources point to the evening of the 12th as the most likely date. On this point as well as the action which follows, in addition to the sources already cited in note 11, see: O'Day, 21st Div (PA) I, Part 2, 1–2, II, 23–25; ltr [CO 21st Inf] to TAG (PA), Opns 21st Inf (PA), p. 4; Richards, Steps to a POW Camp, pp. 14–20; Capts Roy Oster and Grover C. Richards, 21st Inf (PA), p. 2, Capt John C. Ellis, 23d Inf (PA), p. 8, and Lt Col Eugene T. Lewis, 43d Inf (PA), p. 30, all in Chunn Notebooks.

[17] Brig Gen Arnold J. Funk, Comments on Draft MS, 12 Jan 52, p. 2, OCMH. For Clarke's views on this action, see his interview with a G–2 WDGS officer on his return to the United States, 14–15 August 1942. Mil Intel Library.

[18] *65th Brig* Opns Rpt, Mt. Natib, p. 22.

[19] *Ibid.*

vision to the left thereupon abandoned the main line of resistance and pulled back to positions on the south bank of the Balantay. Farther west the *9th Infantry* continued its effort to encircle the corps left flank, but failed again to reach the main line of resistance. The reports reaching Nara that night were generally favorable, but they could not obscure the fact that the attack had failed or that "the enemy's established fire net was increasing in intensity . . . and enemy artillery was concentrating fire on [the east] front without a minute's respite." [20]

By 15 January the Japanese drive no longer constituted a serious threat to the eastern anchor of the Abucay line, and Col. Arnold J. Funk, who had relieved Clarke at about 1200 on the 13th, replaced the 21st Infantry with the 22d, which had been made available by corps. But in the center, where the 43d Infantry had been reinforced by the 23d, the threat of a break-through became serious. It was here, at the boundary between the 41st and 51st Divisions, that the main enemy blow came on the 15th with a strong attack by Imai's *141st Infantry*. The reinforced 43d, on the left of the 41st Division, held firm, but General Jones had to commit his division reserve as well as his service troops to maintain his position on the Balantay. The fight continued throughout the day and at about 1600 a small party of Japanese troops crossed the river in the face of heavy fire and occupied a hill between the 51st and the 43d Infantry. The Filipino troops sought determinedly to drive the enemy back across the river, but, despite claims by Parker and Jones that the 51st line was unbroken, the

Japanese, at the end of the day, still retained their foothold on the south bank of the Balantay. With the *9th Infantry* in position about 1,000 yards to the west, the prospects for the next day were distinctly unfavorable. [21]

General Jones was in a serious position. Although his division was still in place, his troops were "very perceptibly weakening." [22] Unless he received reinforcements, he told General Parker, he might have to fall back from the main line of resistance. To meet this demand for more men, the II Corps commander, who had already committed his reserve, was forced to request additional troops from MacArthur's headquarters.

This request had apparently been anticipated. The center of the Abucay–Mauban line, where the fight was now becoming critical and where the terrain made physical contact between the two corps extremely difficult if not impossible, had been a matter of concern to high-ranking officers in MacArthur's headquarters from the very start. After his visit to Bataan with MacArthur on the 10th, General Sutherland had criticized the disposition of the troops and expressed the fear that the enemy "would attack down the center of the penin-

---

[20] *Ibid.*, p. 23; see also Apps. 8 and 9, pp. 53, 55.

[21] The account of the action on the left of the II Corps line is reconstructed from: Jones, 51st Div (PA) Order of Events, pp. 1–4; Col Virgil N. Cordero, *My Experiences During the War with Japan* (Nuremburg, privately printed, n.d.), pp. 20–23; MacDonald, Supplement to Jones Diary, pp. 16, 17; 52d Inf (PA), p. 36; Bluemel, 31st Div (PA) Rpt of Opns, pp. 8–9; Phil Div Rpt of Opns, pp. 11–12; Maj William R. Nealson, Opns of a Prov Bn, 41st Div (PA) at Abucay, 15–25 Jan 42 (paper prepared for Advanced Officers Course, 1947–48, The Infantry School), pp. 9–11; Cummings, 53d Inf (PA), p. 4, Chunn Notebooks; Funk, Comments on Draft MS, p. 3, OCMH.

[22] MacDonald, Supplement to Jones Diary, p. 16.

sula over the roughest terrain and not along the coast where the roads were located." [23] The bulk of the forces on Bataan, he noted, was not deployed to meet such an attack, and he had suggested to the two corps commanders that they shift their troops so as to strengthen their interior flanks. The following day, 11 January, the subject had been raised again in an order which directed that contact between the two corps "be actual and physical" and that all avenues of approach, including "the rough area in the center of the Bataan Peninsula," be covered.[24]

After an inspection of the front line on 12 January, General R. J. Marshall, USAFFE deputy chief of staff and commander of the Bataan echelon of that headquarters, also became concerned over the weakness of the center of the line. He discussed the problem with General Wainwright who, he wrote, "did not agree entirely, saying that he thought that the center of our position was too difficult terrain for the major attack." [25] Seriously disturbed, Marshall turned to Sutherland for aid. "I don't believe," he declared, "we can over-estimate the importance of denying observation of both our battle positions, which would be available to the enemy were he in possession of Mt. Natib." [26]

Parker's request for reinforcements, therefore, came as no surprise to Sutherland and Marshall who had already ordered various units into the II Corps area. From USAFFE reserve came the Philippine Division (less 57th Infantry) and from Wainwright's corps came the Philippine Army 31st Division (less elements). When Parker learned of these reinforcements he made plans to use the former when it arrived for a counterattack to restore the line and the latter initially as corps reserve and later to relieve the Philippine Division after the counterattack.

While the reserves were moving into position on the night of 15–16 January, General Parker decided to make an immediate effort to regain the ground lost on his critical left flank, and ordered the 51st Division to counterattack on the morning of the 16th. To strengthen the division for this venture he gave General Jones the 3d Battalion, 21st Infantry, which had already seen action in the fight along the East Road.[27] Jones vigorously protested the order to counterattack, pointing out to his corps

---

[23] Sutherland made this statement in an interview with the author on 14 November 1946, five years after the events. Contemporary sources support Sutherland's foresight in predicting Japanese intentions.

[24] Ltr Order, USAFFE, 11 Jan 42, sub: Plans for Counterattack, AG 381 (10 Nov 41) Phil Rcds. General Parker did not recall later any discussion with Sutherland on this subject, but added that he, too, was greatly concerned at the time and never able to work out a satisfactory solution to the problem. "There were just not enough units . . . to cover the front effectively," he later wrote. Those in the line were already overextended and lacked sufficient deployment in depth. He felt then and still did after the war that it would have been unwise to weaken his line at any point to shift troops to the west, to the center of the peninsula. Ltr, Parker to Ward, 16 Jan 52, OCMH.

[25] Memo, Marshall for CofS USAFFE, 13 Jan 42, AG 370.2 (19 Dec 42) Phil Rcds.

[26] *Ibid.* In this memorandum Marshall stated that he was sending Colonel Funk, who had not yet assumed command of the 57th Infantry, to see Wainwright again to find out what was being done to protect the right flank of I Corps. When Funk took command of the 57th, the visit was canceled.

[27] The battalion was to arrive at Abucay Hacienda at about 0400 of the 16th. There is a difference of opinion in the source as to the identity of the unit given Jones. Some claim it was the 21st Engineers; others, the 3d Battalion, 21st Infantry. This confusion may arise from the fact that the 21st Engineers got into the fight in this sector later, and that the battalion of the 21st was late in reaching the 51st Division.

commander that his main line of resistance was tactically unsound and that "the weakened condition of his division from continuous combat and heavy losses during the past month" made the ordered counterattack "extremely hazardous." "Moreover," he asserted, "the present position was being held only with great difficulty." [28] His protests were unavailing and it was with little hope of success that he made his preparations.

The 51st Division attack began on schedule at dawn of the 16th and immediately ran into strong enemy resistance. The Japanese considered this area to be, in Nara's words, "the pivot point of the entire enemy position" and apparently expected the counterattack. [29] Despite the heavy opposition the 51st Infantry on the division right succeeded in beating back the Japanese in its sector. So successful was the regiment that it pushed ahead of the units on its right and left, thereby creating a dangerous salient in the line.

The enemy was quick to take advantage of Jones's exposed position. About noon elements of the *141st Infantry* pressed in against the right (east) of the salient and began infiltrating between the 51st Infantry and the 43d Infantry to its right. At about the same time the *9th Infantry* which had been approaching Parker's left flank from the north struck the left side of the salient and pressed in between the 51st and 53d Infantry. The 51st was thus threatened by a double envelopment.

Under pressure from three directions, the entire 51st regimental line gave way and the Filipino troops fled to the rear in disorder, exposing the 43d to envelopment by the *141st Infantry*. Colonel Imai recognized the danger as well as the advantage of his

own position immediately. Should he push ahead after the 51st he might well leave his own left flank exposed to attack by the 43d Infantry, whose strength he did not know. He decided against this risk and after a brief pause for reorganization sent the bulk of his regiment eastward against the 41st Division. The 43d Infantry, on the left, was now forced to refuse its flank back to the reserve line, where, under the calm guidance of Lt. Col. Eugene T. Lewis, regimental instructor, it held against the repeated onslaughts of Imai's men. Lewis was given additional men to hold the refused flank when a hastily organized provisional battalion, consisting of the 41st Engineer Battalion, signal and quartermaster troops, and stragglers, was thrown into the action.

While a portion of the *141st Infantry* was pressing the attack against the 43d and 51st Infantry, other elements of Colonel Imai's regiment were pushing the 42d Infantry, on the east (right) of the 43d, threatening to drive between the two. To halt the Japanese here, a battalion of the 23d Infantry was attached to the 42d and the attackers were beaten off. Farther east elements of the *142d Infantry* joined with the *2d Battalion, 141st Infantry,* which had borne the brunt of the fighting in the 57th Infantry sector earlier, in an attack against the 41st Infantry, on the division right flank. Here the Japanese were repulsed only after the 3d Battalion, 32d Infantry, the first element of the reserve 31st Division (PA) to reach II Corps, was sent into action.

The disintegration of the 51st Infantry had exposed not only the left flank of the 43d but also the right of the 53d Infantry, westernmost unit on the II Corps line. Colonel Boatwright, 53d Infantry commander, attempted to maintain contact with the 51st on his right by pulling back his regimen-

---

[28] Jones, 51st Div (PA) Order of Events, p. 3.
[29] *65th Brig* Opns Rpt, Mt. Natib, p. 24.

tal flank to conform to that of the adjacent unit. This effort proved unsuccessful.

Behind and to the left rear of the 51st Infantry was the 3d Battalion, 21st Infantry, in position to support the 53d and available for a counterattack if necessary. This battalion, which had been given General Jones by corps as division reserve before the counterattack, had arrived in the 51st Division sector late on the morning of the 16th, and without Jones's knowledge had taken up a position behind the critical portion of the line. Throughout the action of the 16th, Jones was unaware of its presence and firmly believed that he was operating without a reserve.[30] Consequently the 3d Battalion, 21st, saw little action during the 16th and withdrew later to Guitol.

Though the situation in the 53d Infantry sector appeared desperate, it was not as dangerous as it seemed, partly because of the presence of the 3d Battalion, 21st Infantry, and partly because of the Japanese dispositions. Neither Boatwright nor General Jones knew that Colonel Imai had decided to throw the bulk of the *141st Infantry* against the 43d Infantry rather than against the 53d. Nor did either know that the *9th Infantry,* which was in front and to the right of the 53d, had halted at this critical moment to reorganize after its long march through the jungled heights of central Ba-

taan. Instead, the 51st Division staff was convinced that disaster was imminent and the situation too precarious to permit the 53d to remain in place." In Jones's absence at the front, the division chief of staff therefore ordered Boatwright to fall back to the southwest farther up the slopes of Mt. Natib and establish physical contact with I Corps, a task that thus far had proved impossible.

The withdrawal of the 53d Infantry across the precipitous slopes of Mt. Natib was made under the most trying conditions and proved a harrowing experience. The men became separated in the jungle and along the winding trails and the regiment failed either to establish a position on Mt. Natib or to tie in with I Corps. The majority of the men finally reached Guitol, tired, hungry, and footsore; but others, after a march through some of the most difficult country in the Philippines during which they subsisted on leaves, shrub roots, and boiled snails, reached Bagac on the west coast.[31]

With the troops that succeeded in making their way south General Jones organized a covering force late on the afternoon of the 16th. This force he placed astride the Guitol trail, approximately 4,000 yards south of the Balantay River line from which he had launched his counterattack that morning.

It was not this covering force that saved the II Corps line but the failure of the Japanese to exploit their advantage. The two Japanese units in position to envelop the left flank of the corps chose instead to

---

[30] There is a good deal of confusion and controversy in contemporary records and in diaries and interviews over the movements and action of the 3d Battalion, 21st Infantry. Since it did not take an important part in the counterattack of the 16th, the activities of this battalion have not been covered in detail here. Richards, Steps to a POW Camp, pp. 17–19; Jones, 51st Div (PA) Order of Events; O'Day, 21st Div (PA), II, 25; Oster and Richards, 21st Inf (PA), p. 3, Chunn Notebooks; ltr, Jones to Ward, 3 Jan 52, OCMH; ltr, MacDonald to Jones, 21 Dec 51, OCMH.

[31] One officer in Boatwright's party states that all he ate for three days was a can of pineapple, which he shared with several other officers. 1st Lt Eugene Forquer, 53d Inf (PA), p. 42, Chunn Notebooks; ltr, Boatwright to George Groce, research asst, 22 Mar 49, OCMH; ltrs, Boatwright and MacDonald to Jones, 12 and 6 Nov 50, lent to author by General Jones.

pursue other, less profitable objectives. The *141st Infantry* had flung itself against the left flank of the 41st Division instead of attempting to take it in the rear. With the 51st Division in retreat, such a maneuver might well have been more rewarding than the attack against the 43d Infantry, which had successfully refused its left flank. The *9th Infantry*, Nara's "encircling unit," was under orders to move southeast down the Salian River valley, a short distance behind the II Corps line. Had Colonel Takechi moved through the gap between the 51st and 41st Divisions he could have reached the Salian River quickly and turned the corps left flank. Instead, misled by poor maps which confused the Abo-Abo and the Salian, he began a wide sweep around Parker's left in preparation for an advance south and southeast down the Abo-Abo River valley. At the critical moment, therefore, when he should have been pushing down the Salian River valley, Takechi was preparing for the march down the Abo-Abo, a course that would take him out of the action for the next few days.

General Parker had recognized the gravity of his position almost as soon as the 51st sector gave way. At about 1200 of the 16th he had ordered Brig. Gen. Maxon S. Lough to move his Philippine Division (less the 57th Infantry) to the left of the 41st Division and to counterattack the next morning with two regiments abreast. The 31st Infantry (US)—not to be confused with the 31st Infantry (PA), a regiment of the Philipine Army's 31st Division which was also in the II Corps sector at this time—moved out early in the afternoon and about 1900 reached its destination, approximately one mile east of Abucay Hacienda. The 45th Infantry (PS) left its bivouac area at 1700 of the 16th but lost its way and when

the counterattack began the next morning it was about 5,000 yards to the southeast.[32]

By the evening of 16 January, just one week after he had opened his attack, General Nara was in position to turn the left flank of II Corps. Though forced to change his plans repeatedly and held up by unexpectedly strong resistance, he had made considerable progress. Repulsed on the east by the 57th and 21st Infantry and in the center by the 41st Division, he had shifted the axis of attack to the west and concentrated his forces against the weakened 51st Division whose 51st Infantry had finally broken. This disaster had completely unhinged the II Corps line and left it open to a dangerous flanking attack. If Nara could press his advantage and push his men south and southeast quickly enough he would envelop the entire corps and push it against Manila Bay. He would also make Wainwright's position untenable and force him to withdraw. Already the Japanese had driven a wedge between the two corps. The fate of the entire line, from Mabatang to Mauban, depended on the counterattack of the 31st Infantry scheduled for the morning of 17 January. If the regiment was successful II Corps might remain in position for some time; if it was routed the entire line would be forced to fall back in disorder. Should the 31st delay the Japanese temporarily,

---

[32] Ltr, Parker to Ward, 16 Jan 52, OCMH. For the movements of the 31st and 45th Infantry, see: Phil Div Rpt of Opns, p. 12; Conrad, 2d Bn, 31st Inf, Opns of 31st Inf (US), pp. 12–13; Maj John I. Pray, former CO Co G, Action of Co G, 31st Inf (US) Abucay Hacienda, 15–25 Jan 42, pp. 6–7, Maj Louis B. Besbeck, Opns of 3d Bn, 45th Inf (PS) at Abucay Hacienda, 15–25 Jan 42, pp. 10–12, and Maj Henry J. Pierce, Opns of Co L, 45th Inf (PS) at Abucay Hacienda, p. 7. All three papers prepared for Advanced Officers Course, the first two in 1946–47 and the last in 1949–50, at The Infantry School.

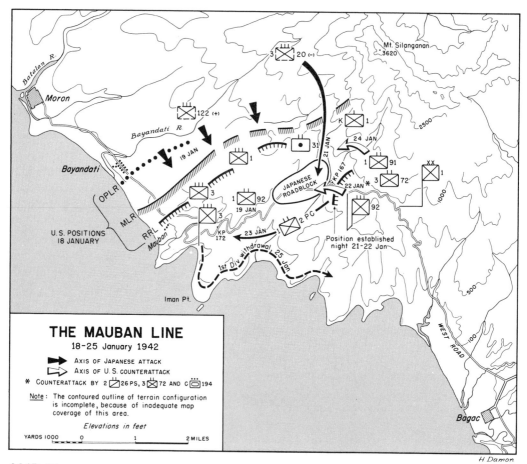

MAP 13

H. Damon

then the corps might yet gain time for a planned and orderly withdrawal.

Attack Against I Corps: The Mauban Line

The Mauban line along which Wainwright's I Corps was posted extended from the slopes of Mt. Silanganan on the east, westward along Mauban Ridge, to the small coastal village which gave the line its name. (*Map 13*) Along the steep and rugged slopes of the mountain was Company K of the 1st Infantry (PA) which had been

ordered to establish contact with II Corps on the right. It was never successful in accomplishing its mission, an impossible one in the view of many officers. To its left was a battalion of the 31st Field Artillery, 31st Division (PA), organized and equipped as infantry. The rest of the line was held by the 3d Infantry of Brig. Gen. Fidel V. Segundo's 1st Division (PA).

About three quarters of a mile in front of the main line of resistance, from Bayandati to a point about midway up the mountain, was the outpost line, manned by elements of the 3d Infantry. Defending Moron, two miles north of Bayandati, and the sandy stretch of beach between it and the outpost line was Company I, 1st Infantry, and Troop G, 26th Cavalry. In corps reserve was the 91st Division (PA), with combat elements of the 71st Division attached; the 26th Cavalry; and the 1st Infantry (less detachments).

In drawing up his plans for the conquest of Bataan, General Nara had correctly estimated that decisive results could be obtained most quickly in the II Corps sector and had sent the bulk of his troops down the eastern side of Bataan. Against Wainwright's I Corps he had sent a relatively weak force, consisting of a combat team composed of the *122d Infantry* (less two companies), a battalion of field artillery, a platoon of engineers, and a squad of signalmen. This force, led by Colonel Watanabe, was under orders to advance westward from Dinalupihan to Olongapo, then south through Moron toward Bagac.[33]

Leaving Dinalupihan at 1900 of the 9th, Colonel Watanabe led his men along Route 7 toward undefended Olongapo. Delayed only by destroyed bridges and demolitions planted earlier by the American engineers, he reached Olongapo at 1400 the next day. His field artillery was still at Dinalupihan where it was to remain until the road could be repaired. Two days later, on 12 January, under orders from *14th Army*, the *122d Infantry* embarked in native boats and quickly seized Grande Island, at the entrance to Subic Bay.

In occupying Grande Island the Japanese acquired possession of Fort Wint, the "little Corregidor" of Subic Bay. Strategically situated to guard the entrance to the bay and control the northwest shore of Bataan, this fort had been part of General Moore's Harbor Defenses and had been manned by coast artillery personnel under Col. Napoleon Boudreau. On 24 December Colonel Boudreau had been ordered to abandon the fort by the next day and join the troops then entering Bataan. He had completed the evacuation in time, but only at the expense of several thousand rounds of 155-mm. ammunition, some mobile guns, and the fixed guns of larger caliber.[34]

While the support or retention of Fort Wint was probably impossible once the decision had been made to fall back on the Mabatang–Mauban line, its evacuation without a struggle gave the Japanese an important objective at no cost. An American garrison on Grande Island, even if it was ultimately lost, might well have paid substantial dividends and certainly would have given the Japanese many uncomfortable moments. From Fort Wint the Americans with their large guns could have disputed Japanese control of the bay and of Olongapo, which later became an important enemy supply base, and would have constituted a threat to the flank of any Japanese

---

[33] As in the section preceding, the Japanese side of the story has been reconstructed from *65th Brig* Opns Rpt, Mt. Natib, pp. 25–28 and *14th Army* Opns, I, 92–97. The plan outlined above is derived from the *65th Brig* Opns Order, Series A, No. 42, 1800, 8 Jan 42, App. 3, *65th Brig* Opns Rpt, Mt. Natib, p. 44.

[34] Collier, Notebooks, II, 48–49; ltr, Boudreau to author, 12 Dec 47, OCMH; Harbor Defenses Rpt of Opns, p. 23. Neither Boudreau nor General Moore mentions the loss of armament or ammunition but Colonel Collier states there was such a loss and the Japanese claim that they captured a number of guns and a large supply of ammunition when they seized the island. *14th Army* Opns, I, 88–92. General Bluemel states that four 155-mm. guns were moved to Olongapo and from there moved by tractor into Bataan. Bluemel, Comments on Draft MS, Comments 14 and 16, OCMH.

force advancing down the west coast of Bataan.

It was not until 14 January that Watanabe began his advance southward along the west coast of the peninsula.[35] Wainwright had dispatched a battalion of the 1st Infantry to Moron at the first news of the occupation of Olongapo, but had withdrawn it two days later when the Japanese failed to advance. On the 14th, when the Japanese began to move toward Moron, the battalion was in corps reserve. Part of the *122d Infantry* came down the narrow trail between Olongapo and Moron; the rest of the regiment embarked in boats for Moron where the West Road began. Watanabe hoped in this way to advance more rapidly down the west coast toward Bagac and avoid the delay inevitable if the entire regiment followed the winding trail north of Moron. Unfamiliar with the coast line and handicapped by poor maps, the water-borne elements of the *122d* came ashore at a small barrio midway between Olongapo and Moron and prepared to march the rest of the distance on foot.

Wainwright received word of the Japanese advance almost as soon as the forward elements of the *122d Infantry* landed. In an effort to contain the enemy

he dispatched the entire 1st Infantry, as well as the 1st Engineer Battalion and two battalions of artillery, to Moron. He also relieved Troop G of the 26th Cavalry, which had been on patrol since the 10th, and replaced it with the composite Troop E–F of the same regiment. In command of these forces was General Segundo, commander of the 1st Division. Major McCullom,[36] commander of the 1st Infantry, exercised tactical control.

On 15 January the two elements of the *122d Infantry* joined and by the following morning the regiment was within a mile of Moron. When it crossed the Batalan River, just north of the village, opposed only by fire from an American patrol, Wainwright hastened to Moron where he organized and directed an attack by the 1st Infantry and Troop E–F of the 26th Cavalry. In this first engagement in I Corps the honors went to the Filipinos who forced the Japanese back to the river line. Unfortunately, the cavalrymen suffered heavily in men and animals and had to be withdrawn. During the course of the action Major McCullom was wounded in the head and Col. Kearie L. Berry, commander of the 3d Infantry, on the main line of resistance, was placed in command of the 1st Infantry as well.

The Japanese continued the attack against Moron during the 17th and by late afternoon penetrated the town in force. Wainwright's men thereupon withdrew to a ridge about a mile and a half to the south. It is possible that from this position they could have delayed the enemy advance but already strong Japanese reinforcements were moving against the Mauban line.

The decision to commit additional troops to the attack against I Corps had been made by General Homma, the Army commander,

---

[35] In addition to the sources cited below, this account of the fight in I Corps is based upon: USAFFE-USFIP Rpt of Opns, p. 48; NLF and I Corps Rpt of Opns, pp. 17–21; Berry, Hist of 3d Inf, 1st Reg Div (PA), 19 Dec 41–9 Apr 42, pp. 2–5; Chandler, "26th Cavalry (PS) Battles to Glory," Parts 2 and 3, *Armored Cavalry Journal* (May–June 1947), p. 15, (July–August 1947), pp. 15–16; Col John H. Rodman, Engagement of 91st Div (PA) on Moron–Bagac Road, p. 1, copy borrowed from Rodman, OCMH; ltr, Col Fowler to author, 11 Mar 49, OCMH; ltr, Lt Col Houston P. Houser, Jr., to author, 18 Mar 49, OCMH; ltr, Rodman to author, 30 Mar 49, OCMH; Prov Tank Gp Rpt of Opns, p. 18; ltr, Berry to Ward, 11 Jan 52, OCMH.

[36] First name unknown.

not General Nara, who was responsible for the assault against the Abucay–Mauban line. Homma had made this decision on 13 January, by which time he had correctly estimated that Nara's attack against II Corps "was not progressing favorably" and that the advance of Watanabe's force was meeting no resistance.[37] By strengthening the force on the west coast Homma apparently hoped to overwhelm the two corps simultaneously. His revised plan called for a continuation of the drive against II Corps by the *65th Brigade* and an increased effort on the west by a larger force than originally contemplated. This force would not only advance to Bagac but would also push east along the Pilar–Bagac road to take II Corps from the rear.

To secure the troops for his revised plan of operations against I Corps, General Homma drew on the *16th Division.* On the 13th he ordered the division commander to send to Bataan two infantry battalions and as many regimental guns of 75-mm. caliber and rapid-fire 37-mm. guns as possible. This force, when finally organized, consisted of *Headquarters, 16th Infantry Group,* the *20th Infantry* (less one battalion), an antitank battery, and half the regimental gun battery of the *33d Infantry.* Led by Maj. Gen. Naoki Kimura, *16th Division* infantry group commander, it left Manila for San Fernando on 15 January. Late that night General Homma created the *Kimura Detachment* and placed it directly under the control of *14th Army,* thus relieving Nara of responsibility for operations against I Corps. In addition to the units he had brought with him, Kimura was also placed in command of the troops already operating along the west

coast of Bataan. Altogether he had a force of about 5,000 men.[38]

On the morning of 18 January General Kimura reached Moron and assumed control over operations. For the assault against Wainwright's line along the ridge south and southeast of the town he organized three forces. The *122d* was to attack frontally down the West Road; the *3d Battalion, 20th Infantry,* was to swing east of Moron in an attempt to take the ridge position on the flank. The third force, one company of the *3d Battalion,* was sent far up the mountain around the I Corps flank to cut the Pilar–Bagac road and did not participate in the ensuing action. The *2d Battalion, 20th Infantry,* Kimura held in reserve.

In the belief that his force was not strong enough for a successful stand along the ridge, Wainwright on the 18th directed a withdrawal. The 1st Infantry and the 1st Engineers fell back through the outpost line to take up a position along the main line of resistance between the 3d Infantry and the battalion of the 31st Field Artillery on the slopes of Mt. Silanganan. The Japanese followed closely and that night drove in the corps outpost line "without much effort."[39] A counterattack the next morning restored the line but another Japanese assault on the night of the 19th gave the Japanese final and permanent possession of the outpost line.

As the *122d Infantry* continued to push against the 1st Division troops on the left of the Mauban line, the *3d Battalion, 20th Infantry* (less one company), which had been sent around the east flank of the ridge

---

[37] *14th Army* Opns, I, 92, 96.

[38] *14th Army* Opns Order, Series A, No. 167, 2200, 15 Jan 42, App. 21, *65th Brig* Opns Rpt, Mt. Natib, p. 75. For a description of the regimental and rapid-fire guns, see Handbook of Japanese Military Forces, TM–E 30–480, 1 Oct 44, pp. 217–18, 220.

[39] Berry, Hist of 3d Inf, 1st Reg Div (PA), p. 3.

line on the 18th, swung back to the south-west into the I Corps area. Unopposed, the battalion, led by Lt. Col. Hiroshi Nakanishi, either infiltrated through the I Corps line along the slopes of Mt. Silanganan or advanced through a gap between the 1st Infantry and 31st Field Artillery. At about 1000 of the 21st it reached the West Road, three miles east of Mauban in the vicinity of Kilometer Post (KP) 167, and established a roadblock behind the 1st Division.[40] By this move the Japanese placed themselves squarely athwart the only major road suitable for transporting heavy equipment and supplies. Though the enemy force was a small one, less than a battalion, the danger to Wainwright's position was a grave one.[41]

To meet the threat Wainwright was obliged to shift units in his sector. The transfer five days before of the 31st Division (less 31st Field Artillery) to II Corps had left Wainwright with no reserves, and the commitment of the Philippine Division made it impossible to secure reinforcements from USAFFE. He would have to fight the battle with what he had. Most of the 91st Division, including the attached elements of the 71st, had replaced the 31st on beach de-

fense when that division had gone to Parker. One battalion of the 92d Infantry had been attached to the 1st Division and was in place along the reserve line, north of the roadblock. When, on the 19th, word reached General Segundo, the 1st Division commander, that a Japanese force was infiltrating into the line from Mt. Silanganan, he sent three company-size patrols from the battalion of the 92d Infantry forward to block the trails. They quickly became involved in action along the slopes of Mt. Silanganan and were not available to meet the threat behind the line. The remainder of Wainwright's force, the 26th Cavalry and elements of the 71st Division, were already committed to the defense of the Pilar–Bagac road and could not be shifted without endangering the security of that vital highway.

When the Japanese roadblock was first discovered, therefore, the only unit available to throw against it from the north was a reinforced platoon of the 92d Infantry. Col. John H. Rodman, the regimental commander, ordered 1st Lt. Beverly N. Skardon to lead the platoon into action. After an advance of a few hundred yards it came under fire and was forced to halt. Meanwhile, south of the roadblock, a provisional platoon was being readied for action. This platoon was organized and led personally by General Wainwright who, on his way to the front that morning, had heard firing to the north and had hastily gathered about twenty men from the Headquarters Company, 92d Infantry, to meet this unexpected threat. With these men he attacked the block from the south, but after two hours, realizing he could make no progress with so few men, he left the platoon with another officer and continued forward by another route to organize a larger force.

---

[40] Locations along the roads and trails on Bataan are frequently given in terms of the distance from Manila in kilometers. In the absence of towns and villages on Bataan, this description sometimes is the only way to fix a point precisely on a map. These locations corresponded to road and trail markers which read simply "KP" and the number of kilometers from Manila.

[41] There is some disagreement as to the date the road was cut. Some officers gave the date as 20 January; Wainwright and other officers say the block was established on the 21st. The Japanese give the 21st as the date, and that date has been accepted in this account. The time is fixed by the evaluation of Japanese and American sources. See especially Rodman, Engagement of 91st Div (PA) on Moron–Bagac Road; ltr, Rodman to author, 30 Mar 49, OCMH; ltr, Skerry to author, 15 Jul 52, with incls, OCMH.

The initial Japanese block had been established by only a portion of the *3d Battalion, 20th Infantry*. During the day the rest of the battalion picked its way along circuitous routes around blocked trails and down the steep slopes of Mt. Silanganan to join in the defense of the roadblock. Meanwhile, the build-up on the American side continued as additional forces from the 91st Division were released for the impending battle. Scouts of the 26th Cavalry and Company C, 194th Tank Battalion, were also ordered to the threatened area in an all-out effort to clear the road. Colonel Rodman, 92d Infantry commander, was placed in command of the entire force.

The attack opened on the morning of the 22d with an attempt by a platoon of tanks to break through the block and establish contact with the 1st Division to the north. By this time the Japanese had constructed antitank obstacles and laid mines, which, with the fire from their 37-mm. antitank guns, effectively held up the tankers. When the two lead tanks of the 194th were disabled by mines, the remaining tanks of the platoon were held up and the attack stalled.

Next, Rodman sent an understrength motorized squadron of the 26th Cavalry and the 3d Battalion, 72d Infantry, against the roadblock. This attack was initially successful and the Filipinos reached a ridge near the roadblock. But all efforts to eliminate the block met with failure. Meanwhile, the *122d Infantry* continued to engage Colonel Berry's 1st Division troops along the main line of resistance.

During the next few days Rodman attempted again and again to drive out the Japanese, first by frontal assaults and then by flanking attacks. A general attack by all units in contact with the enemy was delivered at daylight of the 23d but failed to gain any ground. Later in the day the 1st Battalion, 2d Constabulary, in an effort to outflank the enemy and establish contact with 1st Divsion units, slipped through the jungle south of the roadblock and at nightfall emerged in the vicinity of KP 172, from where it could attack the enemy from the west. Without explanation, however, the Constabulary withdrew during the night to its former position. The next morning, 24 January, the 1st Battalion, 91st Infantry, and the 3d Battalion of the 72d attacked the roadblock from the east. Despite support from the Constabulary, which delivered a limited attack from the south, this effort to penetrate the block also proved unsuccessful.

Rodman's inability to make progress against the roadblock could not have been due to a shortage of troops. By 24 January he had under his command the 2d Battalion, 92d Infantry; 1st Battalion, 91st Infantry; 3d Battalion, 72d Infantry; the 2d Squadron, 26th Cavalry; two battalions and a howitzer company from the 2d Constabulary, attached to I Corps on 22 January; as well as other mixed detachments. All of these units, it must be added, were understrength, tired, poorly fed, and, except for the 26th Cavalry squadron and the howitzer company, had no automatic weapons at all.

Against this array of units Colonel Nakanishi had only a single battalion, less one company. Moreover, the Japanese probably suffered greater hardships than their opponents. It is extremely doubtful that Kimura was ever able during this period to establish a supply route over the mountains and through the I Corps line to the men at the roadblock. Nor is there any definite evidence of enemy air drops to Nakanishi's troops. His men probably had no supplies other than those they had carried across the mountain. Their staunch defense of the roadblock in the face of such strong opposition was therefore the more remarkable, explainable only by the difficulty of the terrain, which favored the defender, by training, and by determination.

While the fight for the roadblock was being fought to a standstill, the Japanese continued to push against the main line of resistance. Their advance was contested by Colonel Berry's 3d Infantry and elements of the 1st Infantry, but by evening of the 24th the "situation was desperate and rapidly growing worse." [42] The line was under attack from the north, ammunition was short, and the supply route had been cut. The 1st Division troops, whose food stocks were low when the roadblock was established, were suffering from a real shortage of rations. Under the circumstances there was little for Colonel Berry, who for all practical purposes was now commanding the 1st Division, to do except to abandon the main line of resistance. His position was untenable, his supplies gone, his men exhausted and hungry. He could not even rely on continued artillery support since Colonel Fowler's ammunition was exhausted. On his own responsibility, after consultation with Colonel Fowler and Maj. A. L. Fitch and without permission from General Wainwright, Berry made the "inevitable" decision to withdraw.[43]

---

[42] Berry, Hist of 3d Inf, 1st Reg Div (PA), p. 4.

[43] Ltr, Berry to Ward, 11 Jan 52, OCMH; ltr, Fowler to author, 11 Mar 49, OCMH. Wainwright confirms Berry's responsibility and the fact that he was acting without orders. Ltr, Wainwright to TAG, 27 Jun 47, sub: Recommendation for DSC for Col Berry, copy in OCMH.

Colonel Collier tells an entirely different story about the withdrawal of the 1st Division but this account has not been accepted in the absence of corroborating testimony. Collier, Notebooks, III, 36.

Having made his decision, Berry still had a difficult problem to face. By what route would his men withdraw and what equipment could he save? On his front was the *122d Infantry;* to his rear was the *3d Battalion, 20th Infantry,* firmly in position along the roadblock. With the West Road blocked, Colonel Berry had only one route southward, the narrow beaches paralleling the South China Sea coast line. If he used this route, he would have to abandon his vehicles, Colonel Fowler's artillery, and all heavy equipment. Moreover, he would be without cover from air attack while he was on the exposed beaches. Knowing all this, Berry had no choice but to withdraw along this route.

On the morning of the 25th the order to withdraw was issued. All guns, trucks, and equipment which could not be moved along the beaches were to be destroyed. "My officers and myself," wrote Colonel Fowler, the artillery commander, "destroyed the guns with tears in our eyes." [44] At 1030 the withdrawal began, with men bearing the wounded on improvised litters leading the way. Covering the withdrawal was the 1st Battalion, 3d Infantry, blocking the West Road along the slopes of Mauban Ridge. Colonel Rodman's men kept the beaches clear of Nakanishi's patrols by pressing in against the roadblock from the west.

The withdrawal of the 1st Division from the main line of resistance was made by battalion, from east to west. The route of withdrawal ran westward through the battalion support area to the West Road and then along it to the 3d Infantry command post. From here the troops scrambled down trails to the water's edge, where a station was established to direct the men on their way toward Bagac. By noon of the 25th an esti-

---

[44] Ltr, Fowler to author, 11 Mar 49, OCMH.

mated 1,000 men had "infiltrated south";
of this number about one fourth were clad
only in underwear, carried no arms, and
passed as civilians.[45] By nightfall the main
force had reached the beach from where the
men made their way south as best they
could. The withdrawal continued during
the night, the covering troops pulling back
under cover of darkness to join their comrades in the flight to safety.

The difficult task of disengaging the
enemy and moving a large number of men
to the rear along a dangerously exposed and
inadequate route of withdrawal was accomplished with a minimum of loss and confusion. The maneuver had been well planned
and executed. Only one tragic fact marred
the success of the withdrawal—the loss of the
artillery. Altogether, twenty-five pieces, of
which fifteen were 2.95-inch mountain guns
and the rest 75's, had to be left behind.
These had been emplaced just behind the
infantry when the line was set up. Their destruction by the retreating artillerymen left
I Corps with but two 155's and four 75-mm.
guns (SPM).[46] At least the destruction was
accomplished with the greatest efficiency for
the Japanese failed to report the capture of
any large number of guns.

Presumably when the 1st Division elements and the artillery withdrew from the
Mauban line, the other units to its right, the
31st Field Artillery and Company K of the
1st Infantry, also pulled back. There is no
record of their movement beyond scattered

references to Filipino troops infiltrating to
the south.[47]

By evening of the 25th the Mauban line
had been evacuated. That night MacArthur
reported to the War Department that enemy
pressure on the left had forced him "to give
ground with some loss including guns of
the obsolete 2.95 type." [48] The situation, he
asserted, had been stabilized and "for the
present the immediate danger is over." At
the time he sent these reassurances to Washington, the enemy had already scored a
great victory against II Corps and the withdrawal of both corps was in progress.

The Abucay Line Is Turned

A week before the withdrawal from the
Mauban line, it will be recalled, the situation in the II Corps area on the east had
already become serious. The disintegration
of the 51st Infantry on the 16th had unhinged the left flank of Parker's corps and
had left the line exposed. "Unless the 51st
Division sector could be regained," wrote
General Parker later, "it was evident that
my left flank would be enveloped and the
position would be lost." [49] To recover the
lost ground and fix firmly the western anchor of his main battle position, Parker had
ordered the Philippine Division (less 57th
Infantry) to counterattack at daylight of
the 17th. The 31st Infantry (US) had

[45] USAFFE G–4 Journal, Bataan Echelon, 25–26
Jan 42, Extract from G–2 Rpt of 1200, 25 Jan 42
[erroneously written as 24 Jan], AG 461 (25 Dec
41) Phil Rcds.

[46] There is some confusion as to the exact number
of pieces lost as a result of the withdrawal and the
figures given are the best that could be worked out
from the conflicting sources.

[47] General Berry stated in an interview that there
was not a single American officer with the 31st Field
Artillery and that it withdrew without orders from
Mt. Silanganan. No light is cast on this subject by
General Bluemel's report since the 31st Division at
this time was in II Corps. Interv, author with Berry,
Jan 48; Bluemel, 31st Div (PA) Rpt of Opns,
passim.

[48] Rad, MacArthur to TAG, No. 119, 25 Jan 42,
AG 381 11–27–41 Sec 1) Far East.

[49] SLF and II Corps Rpt of Opns. p. 32.

moved into position near Abucay Hacienda the evening before; the 45th Infantry (PS) was still moving up and was about 6,000 yards southeast of that barrio when zero hour came. Thus, the attack, when it was made, was a piecemeal one. (*Map 12*)

At 0815, 17 January, the American troops of the 31st Infantry, led by Col. Charles L. Steel, jumped off from the line of departure and advanced north along Trail 12, nearly a mile east of Abucay Hacienda. On the left was the 1st Battalion; next to it, astride and to the right of the trail, was the 2d Battalion. The 3d Battalion was in reserve. The 1st Battalion on the left met little opposition and was able to reach the Balantay River by nightfall. The 2d Battalion on the right was not so fortunate. About 400 yards from the line of departure it encountered enemy resistance and, despite numerous attempts to break through, was unable to advance farther that day. To fill the gap between the 1st and 2d Battalions, which had developed as a result of the unimpeded advance on the left, Company K from the reserve battalion was sent into the line.[50]

Plans for the next day's action were drawn up at a predawn conference held at the 41st Division command post. Present at the meeting were General Lough, Philippine Division commander; Col. Malcolm V. Fortier, 41st Division senior instructor; Col. Thomas W. Doyle, commander of the 45th Infantry, which had finally reached the scene; and Colonel Steel of the 31st. After some discussion it was agreed that a co-ordinated attack by all present would be made that morning. The 31st Infantry was to attack north, and the 45th, echeloned by battalion to the right rear, would deliver the main assault between the 31st and 43d to the right. The 43d Infantry was to maintain its position along the regimental reserve line. Artillery support for the advance would be furnished by 41st Division artillery.

As his 45th Infantry moved forward to the line of departure early on the morning of the 18th, Colonel Doyle learned that the 1st Battalion of the 31st was under strong enemy pressure and in danger of being outflanked. A hurried conference between Doyle and Steel produced a revised plan of operations. The 3d Battalion, 45th Infantry, was now to move to the left of the 31st Infantry, supporting the 1st Battalion of that regiment on the extreme left of the Abucay line. The rest of the units would continue the attack as planned.

The 45th Infantry attack began later than planned, but proceeded without major mishap. The regiment—less the 3d Battalion, which had lost its way and overshot the mark—advanced between the 31st and 43d but was unable to reach its objective, the Balantay River, before dark. The 3d Bat-

---

[50] The account which follows is based on the following sources: On the Japanese side, *65th Brig Opns Rpt, Mt. Natib,* pp. 25–31; *14th Army Opns,* I, 94–98. On the American side, SLF and II Corps Rpt of Opns, pp. 32–37; Phil Div Rpt of Opns, pp. 12–13; Lt Col Jasper E. Brady, Jr., Diary, pp. 2–3, in Brady Papers, OCMH; Pray, Co G, 31st Inf (US) Abucay Hacienda, pp. 9–17; Besbeck, Opns 3d Bn, 45th Inf (PS) at Abucay Hacienda, pp. 12–27; H. J. Pierce, Opns of Co L, 45th Inf (PS) at Abucay Hacienda, pp. 7–14; Conrad, Opns of 31st Inf (US) 8 Dec 41–9 Apr 42, pp. 14–15; Fortier, Notes on 41st Div (PA), p. 2; Bluemel, 31st Div (PA) Rpt of Opns, p. 10; O'Day, 21st Div (PA), II, 27–29; Jones, 51st Div (PA) Order of Events, 29 Dec 41–26 Jan 42, pp. 4–5; Richards, Steps to a POW Camp, pp. 20–21; Mead, Opns and Mvmts of 31st Inf (US), p. 21; Maj Clarence R. Bess, Opns of Service Co, 31st Inf (US), 5 Jan 42–9 Apr 42, pp. 22–23, and Maj Kary C. Emerson, Opns of II Phil Corps on Bataan, 10 Jan–8 Apr 42, pp. 18–19 (both papers prepared for Advanced

Officers Course in 1947–48 and 1949–50, respectively, The Infantry School); interv, Stanley Falk, research asst, with Col Wright, formerly S–3 45th Inf (PS), 5 Oct 50; ltr, Doyle to Ward, 8 Jan 52, OCMH.

talion, after a false start which found it "climbing the backs" of the 31st Infantry's left company, finally reached the river by 1630. There it settled down to hold a front of 1,400 yards, with no protection on its left except that offered by the jungle. The 1st Battalion, 31st Infantry, to its right was at the river line, but the 2d Battalion was still short of the river, as were the 45th Infantry elements to its right. Thus at the end of the second day of counterattack the Japanese still held the salient above Abucay Hacienda.

The situation was still threatening. In addition to the danger presented by the westward movement of Imai's *141st Infantry,* Parker was receiving reports from artillery spotters of Japanese, still out of range, moving down the Abo-Abo River valley in a southeasterly direction. These were the men of Takechi's *9th Infantry,* sweeping wide around Parker's left end toward the positions now held by the remnants of Jones's 51st Division and the reserve 31st Division near Guitol.

On the 19th the American and Scout regiments resumed the attack. Starting just before noon the 31st Infantry hit the enemy salient only to be repulsed. Time after time the American infantrymen re-formed and attacked, but with no success. Efforts to bring tanks into the action failed when Parker's request for tank support was refused on the ground that the terrain was unsuitable for tank operations. Sending armor into such an engagement, wrote Weaver, would be "like sending an elephant to kill flies." [51] On the west, the 3d Battalion, 45th Infan-

try, now attached to the 31st Infantry, was under fire throughout the day from troops of the *141st Infantry* who had infiltrated into the American line. Only on the right did the Philippine Division make progress that day. There, elements of the 1st and 2d Battalions, 45th Infantry, were able to reach the Balantay early in the afternoon.

Despite this limited success the prospects for the Philippine Division counterattack were distinctly unfavorable on the evening of the 19th. Enemy pressure against the left flank had become extremely strong and the 3d Battalion, 45th Infantry, was under fire from the enemy's automatic weapons. More ominous was the report from a 45th Infantry patrol that an enemy force—presumably the *9th Infantry*—had already passed around the II Corps flank. But General Parker did not know that Nara, abandoning all hope for success along the coastal road, had ordered the *2d Battalion, 141st Infantry,* to rejoin Colonel Imai at the opposite end of the line. Nara had further strengthened the *141st* by attaching to it a company of the *9th Infantry.* These arrangements completed, Nara directed Colonel Imai to launch an all-out attack against Parker's left flank and rear "to drive the enemy southeastward and annihilate them." The attack was to open at noon of the 22d, by which time all the units would be in place and all preparations completed. [52]

On 20 and 21 January the Americans and the Scouts again made numerous unsuccessful efforts to restore the original line. The terrain, dense vegetation, and the lack of accurate information about the enemy

[51] Ltr, Weaver to Wainwright, 20 Nov 45. Weaver, in his comments on this manuscript, states that his remark was made with reference to the use of tanks in the earlier action in the 57th Infantry area and that no request for tanks was made by General Parker at this time. Comment 41, OCMH.

[52] *65th Brig* Opns Order, Series A, No. 82, 1800, 19 Jan 42, App. 11, *65th Brig* Opns Rpt, Mt. Natib, pp. 58–60. The order gives the date 21 January for the attack, but this is evidently a misprint since there is no indication of a delay.

prevented effective co-ordination and made contact between front-line units extremely difficult and sometimes impossible. During these two days the Japanese made their preparations for the scheduled offensive. Leaving enough men in position to contain the two Philippine Division regiments, Colonel Imai gradually shifted the bulk of his men westward to the extreme left of the II Corps line. At dawn of the 22d these men began crossing the Balantay northwest of Abucay Hacienda, to the left of the 3d Battalion, 45th Infantry. By 1000 enough men and heavy weapons had been put across to begin the attack.

The offensive opened shortly before noon with an air attack and an artillery barrage, directed mainly against the 1st Battalion, 31st Infantry, immediately adjacent to the 45th Infantry's 3d Battalion on the corps left flank. Colonel Imai then sent his men into the attack. Whether by chance or design, the weight of the infantry attack fell upon the same battalion that had suffered most from the artillery preparation, and the 1st Battalion, 31st Infantry, began to fall back slowly. Under the threat of envelopment from the east and west, the 3d Battalion, 45th Infantry, broke contact with the enemy and also moved back. The 3d Battalion, 31st, was also exposed by the withdrawal, for on its right was the enemy salient and on its left was the gap left by the 1st Battalion. It, too, began to fall back, refusing its left flank. By late afternoon the 31st Infantry and the attached 3d Battalion of the 45th had formed a new line east and south of Abucay Hacienda. The 2d Battalion remained in place about 1,000 yards east of the Hacienda, along the east-west road leading to that barrio. To its left was the 3d Battalion, 31st Infantry, then the 1st Battalion with its flank sharply re-

fused and facing almost due west. The 3d Battalion, 45th Infantry, was in support about 100 yards behind the 31st Infantry line.

By nightfall on the 22d, the 31st and 45th Infantry were in approximately the same place they had been five days earlier when they began the counterattack. The physical condition of the men, however, had greatly deteriorated. They had been in action almost continuously during these five days and the strain of combat was clearly evident. The men on the front line had received little water or food and practically no hot meals during the battle. Many had been forced to rely on sugar cane to satisfy their thirst and hunger. All the men showed the effects of sleepless nights spent in beating off an enemy who preferred to attack during the hours of darkness. Casualties had been heavy, and the men were particularly bitter about Japanese air bombardment, against which the Americans had no weapon.

The infiltration tactics of the Japanese, which carried them into and behind the American positions, also did much to wear down physical resistance and lower morale. Japanese artillery fire had been unopposed for the most part, largely because the terrain prevented close artillery support. When the guns to the rear had offered support, they had been quickly forced into silence by enemy dive bombers which buzzed around the offending weapons like bees around a hive. Against an enemy well equipped with mortars and grenade dischargers, and supported by artillery and aircraft, the Americans had only a limited number of improvised hand grenades and 3-inch Stokes mortars with ammunition that contained a very high proportion of duds. "It was only through maximum effort and determination," wrote one company commander, "that we were able to attack, and later, defend as long as we did." [53]

General Nara misread entirely the significance of the advance of his men on the 22d. He felt that the action had not gone well and that progress had been slow. "Indignant in a towering rage," he could see no hope of victory in sight.[54] General Parker made a more accurate estimate of the situation. "It was now evident," he wrote, "that the MLR [main line of resistance] in the 51st Division Sector could not be restored by the Philippine Division." [55] The counterattack of the Philippine Division, on which Parker had based his hopes for restoring the left portion of his line, had failed.

Not only had the Japanese driven in the II Corps left flank but they now threatened to envelop the entire line and pin the corps against the sea. On the 17th, the *9th Infantry* (less two companies) had entered the Abo-Abo River valley on its journey southeast toward Orion, far behind the line. Though handicapped by inadequate maps, lack of communications with brigade headquarters, shortage of rations, and the difficult terrain, Colonel Takechi's men had, by 19 January, reached a position on the flank and in the rear of the line.[56] Their advance, though observed, had been unchallenged.

All General Parker had to meet this new threat was Bluemel's 31st Division (less elements), the 3d Battalion, 21st Infantry, and the remnants of Jones's 51st Division. These units were in the vicinity of Guitol, about four miles south of Abucay Hacienda. Still in position astride the Guitol trail, which joined Guitol with Abucay Hacienda, was the covering force consisting of remnants of the 51st Infantry and most of the 21st Engineer Battalion. So weak was this covering force that it could do little more, in Jones's words, than hold the trail "with both flanks open." [57]

By the morning of 19 January the commanders at Guitol were receiving reports of the approaching enemy force. Patrols of the 21st Infantry attempted to hold up advance elements of the *9th Infantry* but were easily routed. During the middle of the afternoon the Japanese met and engaged elements of the 21st and 31st Divisions before Guitol. The former promptly withdrew, but the green untried 31st Division troops remained in place to fire indiscriminately at friend and foe through the night. The small enemy force withdrew the next morning and was gone when General Bluemel finally quieted his hysterical troops and organized a counterattack with the 3d Battalion, 31st Infantry.[58]

On 21 January Takechi's men appeared behind the covering force along the Guitol trail and seized the high ground, from which they could dominate the Abo-Abo River

[53] Conrad, 31st Inf (US), p. 15. Conrad commanded Company F.

[54] *65th Brig* Opns Rpt, Mt. Natib, p. 29.

[55] SLF and II Corps Rpt of Opns, p. 34.

[56] The maps used were drawn to the scale 1:200,-000. Takechi was not sure where he was and may not even have known he was following the Abo-Abo River. General Nara was not even aware that Takechi had entered the Abo-Abo valley. *65th Brig* Opns, Mt. Natib, pp. 26–31; *14th Army* Opns, I, 98.

[57] Jones, 51st Div (PA) Order of Events, p. 4.

[58] The reasons for the withdrawal of the 21st Division (PA) elements on the afternoon of the 19th is not clear. One explanation given is that its task was to reorganize stragglers of the 51st Division (PA). O'Day, 21st Div (PA), II, 28. This does not seem a compelling enough reason for a withdrawal. Col Robert J. Hoffman, and Bluemel, Comments on Draft MS, Comments 9 and 18, OCMH.

valley. An attempt, first by the 51st Infantry on the north, and then from the south by General Jones, to recapture the hill proved unsuccessful. The covering force, cut off from direct access to Guitol via the trail, was forced to move north that night to Abucay Hacienda, then south by another route to rejoin the division near Guitol. The Japanese were now in position to make good their threat to envelop II Corps. With his left flank driven in and with the Japanese in possession of the high ground dominating the left and rear of his line, General Parker was in a most vulnerable position.

The Withdrawal

On Corregidor MacArthur and his staff had been receiving full and complete reports each day on the progress of the campaign from General Marshall and his assistants in the Bataan echelon of USAFFE. These reports had proved most disquieting, and on 22 January General Sutherland on MacArthur's orders went to Bataan himself to get "a clear picture of the situation." [59] His first stop was Limay, near where General Parker had his headquarters. There he discussed the situation with the II Corps commander before moving on to visit General Wainwright. Actually, Sutherland's trip to I Corps was unnecessary for, after his talk with General Parker, he had decided that "a withdrawal from the Abucay–Mt. Natib position was essential." [60] He gave both corps commanders verbal warning orders to prepare for a general withdrawal to the reserve battle position behind the Pilar–Bagac road and told them

they would receive written orders that night.

Sutherland's decision, approved by MacArthur, was based on a clear and correct understanding of the tactical situation. The disintegration of the 51st Division, coupled with the failure of the Philippine Division to restore the main line of resistance, had opened a wide gap on the left flank of II Corps through which the enemy had pushed an unknown number of troops. The wedge that now existed between the two corps left both exposed to envelopment and made the entire line untenable. Moreover, the route of withdrawal in I Corps had been jeopardized by the enemy's establishment of a roadblock behind the line on the West Road. With USAFFE reserve and the reserves of the two corps committed, Sutherland realized that failure to withdraw at this time might well result in disaster.

The decision made, General MacArthur alerted the War Department to the impeding move. "The enemy," he wrote, "seems to have finally adopted a policy of attrition as his unopposed command of the sea enables him to replace at will." He pointed out that his losses had been very heavy and "now approximate 35 percent of my entire force" with some divisions showing a loss "as high as sixty percent." His diminishing strength, he explained, would soon force him to fall back to a new line, where he planned to make his final stand. "I have personally selected and prepared this position," he told the Chief of Staff, "and it is strong." [61]

---

[59] USAFFE-USFIP Rpt of Opns, p. 48.

[60] SLF and II Corps Rpt of Opns, p. 37. See also General Parker's letter to author, 14 Feb 48, in OCMH, in which he states that Sutherland did not announce the decision to him at this time.

[61] Rad, MacArthur to Marshall, No. 108, 23 Jan 42, AG 381 (11–27–41 Sec 1) Far East. The losses which MacArthur mentions in this message refer to the entire campaign since 8 December and not to the action on Bataan alone. Since there are no casualty tables for this campaign, it is not possible to state what the losses for the action along the

That General MacArthur viewed the situation on Bataan with the greatest concern is evident from the tone of the message and from his specific request to the Chief of Staff that the "fame and glory" of the men on Bataan "be duly recorded by their countrymen." While his army was still intact, MacArthur declared that he wished to pay tribute "to the magnificent service it has rendered. No troops have ever done so much with so little." The final pessimistic note came when MacArthur raised the question of his successor "in case of my death." In such an event he recommended that his chief of staff, General Sutherland, be appointed to succeed him. "Of all my general officers," MacArthur declared, "he has the most comprehensive grasp of the situation." [62]

The order for the withdrawal, issued on on the night of 22 January, called for the progressive evacuation of the line, to be completed by daylight of the 26th. The troops would start to withdraw under cover of darkness the following day, 23 January, and would continue the withdrawal on each succeeding night until all troops had reached the reserve battle position. [63] The speed with which these detailed orders were issued indicates that they had already been prepared, an assumption which is entirely reasonable in view of the fact that the Abucay–Mauban line was never intended as the place where the troops would make their last stand. It had been occupied primarily to keep the Pilar–Bagac road in American possession as long as possible and to allow time to prepare the final line to the rear. [64] That line extended generally along the Pilar–Bagac road, "a baked clay road with a double track," crossing it at various points to take advantage of favorable terrain. [65]

Under the withdrawal plan, II Corps was to move first, on the night of the 23d–24th, leaving only one night for the withdrawal of I Corps. As Wainwright's men had been moving back since the 22d, little difficulty was expected in this sector. The withdrawal of II Corps required a complicated plan, calling for the shift of the 45th Infantry and the 11th Division (less artillery) from Parker's to Wainwright's sector.

The first elements to abandon their position would be the heavy artillery and service installations which would begin to move out the first night, 23–24 January, and would arrive at their new positions by daylight of the 25th. A covering force, led by General Lough of the Philippine Division, was to protect the retirement of II Corps' combat elements from the main line of resistance by establishing a thin line extending from the vicinity of Balanga westward to Guitol. Along this line, from east to west, would be posted the remnants of the 51st Division, the 33d Infantry (PA), a battalion of the 31st Infantry (PA), one third of the 57th Infantry (PS), and one third of the

Abucay–Mauban line were. It is extremely doubtful that they were serious enough to force a withdrawal, as implied in the message cited. The reasons for the withdrawal were tactical.

[62] *Ibid.* The author has been unable to find in the records any response to this message.

[63] USAFFE FO 9, 22 Jan 42, AG 300 (28 Dec 41) Phil Rcds.

[64] This supposition is supported by Colonel Collier, who, in his notebooks and in an interview with the author, declared that the orders had been prepared in advance. Collier, Notebooks, III, 37; interv, author with Collier, 20 Nov 46.

[65] The quotation is from a poem entitled "Abucay Withdrawal" in Henry G. Lee, *Nothing But Praise* (Culver City, Calif., 1948). Lieutenant Lee was in Headquarters Company, Philippine Division, and wrote the poems included in this small volume during the campaign and in prison camp. He was killed when the prison ship on which he was being transferred to Formosa was hit by an American bomb. The poems had been buried in the Philippines and were recovered after the war.

BRIG. GEN. MAXON S. LOUGH, *left, with Col. Harrison C. Browne (CofS Phil Div) and Capt. Joseph B. Sallee (ADC), near the front lines.*

31st Infantry (US). General Lough would be supported by Weaver's tank group and the 75-mm. guns (SPM).

From right to left, the front line units would begin to fall back through the covering force at 2300 of the 24th, leaving behind a shell to hold the original position. This shell, consisting of one rifle company and one machine gun platoon for each battalion, with the addition of a battery of 75-mm. guns for each regiment—would start its own withdrawal at 0300 of the 25th. At 2330 on the 25th the covering force would fall back rapidly and by daylight of the 26th, if the movement was completed as planned, all units would be in position along the new line.[66]

During the night of 23–24 January the artillery and service elements withdrew successfully, while all other units made hurried preparations to follow the next night. The covering force took its position during the day, with the tanks, scheduled to be the last to pull out, deployed along the East Road and the so-called Back Road southeast of Abucay Hacienda. The night of 24–25 January was one of confusion. On the extreme right of the line, troops of the 21st Division in the 57th Infantry sector began to fall back from positions above Abucay along the East Road. In the center of the line the 41st Division withdrew along the Back Road.

The intersection of the Back Road with the east-west road connecting Abucay with Abucay Hacienda was the scene of the greatest confusion. Troops poured into the road leading south from all directions. Efforts to organize the men and keep the units intact were fruitless. There were no military police to regulate the traffic and it proved impossible to maintain any semblance of order or organization. At times movement of vehicles and men stopped altogether, despite the best efforts of American and Philippine officers. "It was impossible," wrote Colonel Miller, commander of a tank battalion, "to do anything but keep the mass moving to the rear—praying—hoping—talking to yourself out loud—gesticulating—and trying to make yourself understood. It was a nightmare.[67] Had the enemy chosen this moment to register artillery on the road junction, the cost in lives would have been shocking and the withdrawal might well have ended in a rout.[68]

On the left of the line the pressure which had been building up against the Philippine Division on the 23d and 24th reached its climax just as the Scouts and Americans began their withdrawal that night. As the men began to move out of the line, heading east toward Abucay and the East Road, the Japanese hit the thin covering shell. Against determined Japanese onslaughts the shell held long enough to permit the bulk of the men to withdraw. At about 0300 of the 25th the last of the Americans of the 31st Infantry, covered by heavy fire from the 194th Tank Battalion, staggered out of their positions, looking "like walking dead men." "They had a blank stare in their eyes,"

---

[66] USAFFE FO 9, 22 Jan 42; SLF and II Corps Rpt of Opns, p. 30; Phil Div Rpt of Opns, p. 14.

[67] Miller, *Bataan Uncensored,* p. 156. For the withdrawal of each unit the author used the sources relating to the various units already cited. See also ltr, Doyle to Ward, 8 Jan 52, OCMH, in which Colonel Doyle states that at about 0230 of the 25th he "took over this mess of men and trucks" and "cleared the congested area."

[68] In prison camp Maj. Kary C. Emerson of the Philippine Division and II Corps staff talked with many small unit commanders and they all agreed that "coordination was poor, that all roads were clogged with troops and vehicles, and that had the Japanese artillery fired on the roads . . . our losses would have been very severe . . . in fact, mass slaughter." Emerson, Opns of II Phil Corps, p. 19.

wrote an officer of the regiment, "and their faces, covered with beards, lacked any semblance of expression." Unwashed and unshaven, their uniforms in shreds, "they looked like anything but an efficient fighting force. . . ." [69]

The withdrawal continued throughout the night of 24–25 January, all the next day and on through the night, with the Japanese in full pursuit. On the 25th Japanese aircraft were out in full force, bombing and strafing the retreating soldiers. From early morning until dusk, enemy planes buzzed unopposed over the long columns of men, dropping bombs and diving low to spray the road with machine gun bullets. The Philippine Army soldier, in dusty blue denims, coconut hat, and canvas shoes, watched "with apprehensive eyes" for the first far speck of approaching planes. When the attacks came and the road erupted "in a sheet of death," the "untrained denim men" milled "like sheep in a slaughter pen." [70] The reaction of the American infantryman, with his scarred and tilted helmet and shredded khaki trousers black with dirt, was more expressive. At the first alarm, he threw himself to the ground and "in a tone of hurt disgust" cursed

. . . the noble Japanese
With four letter Saxon obscenities. . . . [71]

As the II Corps units moved into positions along the new line on the morning of 26 January, they were covered by the two tank battalions. The tanks of the 194th were stretched out for nearly a mile along the north-south Back Road, near Bani, with instructions to hold until two disabled tanks along the narrow road could be moved back.

Atop a knoll at the southern end of the column were the 75-mm. guns (SPM), which, with the tanks, were designated as the last elements of the covering force to withdraw. Between 0930 and 1030 that morning the tankers came under attack from the *141st Infantry*, which moved in on the column from the west. In the fight that followed, the SPM's added their accurate fire power to the armor-piercing 37-mm. shells of the 194th. Unable to advance, Colonel Imai called for artillery support and soon enemy shells were falling near the road-bound tanks. The enemy's mortars joined the battle and by noon shells were falling dangerously close to the Americans. Though the two disabled tanks had not yet been pulled out, the tank column was forced to fall back and leave the two behind. Pursued by low-flying aircraft, the SPM's and then the tanks withdrew to the safety of the new line. Though they had delayed the Japanese only a few hours, they had given the disordered units a chance to dig in for the expected onslaught. [72]

While II Corps was withdrawing under heavy pressure, I Corps fell back with little difficulty. Cut off from the corps commander, Colonel Berry, it will be recalled, had independently decided to withdraw from the Mauban line. Wainwright, in the meantime, had received instructions from General Sutherland to evacuate the Mauban position and fall back behind the Pilar–Bagac road. As he was going forward, he met Colonel Berry who, by his decision, had anticipated Sutherland's order for a general withdrawal. Wainwright thereupon

[69] Mead, Opns of 31st Inf (US), p. 21.
[70] Lee, "Abucay Withdrawal," *Nothing But Praise*, p. 25.
[71] *Ibid.*

[72] Miller, *Bataan Uncensored*, pp. 161–70; Prov Tank Gp Rpt of Opns, pp. 21–22; USAFFE-USFIP Rpt of Opns, p. 50. General Nara claimed to have "routed the American tanks." *65th Brig* Opns Rpt, Mt. Samat, 26 Jan–29 Feb 42, ATIS Enemy Pub 289, 19 Jan 45, p. 7.

directed Berry to continue to withdraw but to take his men all the way back to the Pilar–Bagac road. By morning of the 26th, I Corps was in position along the new line to the left of II Corps.[73]

Though they had finally been forced to give ground and abandon the first line of defense, the American and Filipino troops had inflicted heavy casualties on the enemy. The 65th Brigade had entered combat on 9 January with a strength of 6,651 officers and men. By 24 January it had suffered 1,472 combat casualties, almost all of which were in the three infantry regiments. Attached units probably suffered proportionate losses and at the end of the Abucay fight General Nara wrote that his brigade had "reached the extreme stages of exhaustion." [74]

When the troops of I and II Corps reached the reserve battle position, they were on the final line. Since 24 December, a month earlier, they had fallen back from position after position to reach the safety of Bataan. Here they had held off the overconfident enemy along a line which, because of the terrain in the center, was soon turned. After two weeks of hard fighting the American and Filipino troops had fallen back again. Bataan had been saved,

. . . . . saved for another day
Saved for hunger and wounds and heat
For slow exhaustion and grim retreat
For a wasted hope and a sure defeat. . . .[75]

There was no further retreat from the new line. "With its occupation," MacArthur wrote to the Chief of Staff, "all maneuvering possibilities will cease. I intend to fight it out to complete destruction." [76]

---

[73] Ltr, Wainwright to TAG, 27 Jun 47, sub: Recommendation for DSC for Col Berry, copy in OCMH; USAFFE-USFIP Rpt of Opns, pp. 48–49.
[74] 65th Brig Opns Rpt, Mt. Natib, pp. 33, 38. Each infantry regiment entered combat with 1,919 men. The 122d Infantry, which fought on the west coast, suffered 108 casualties; the 141st, 700; and

the 142d, 613. American and Filipino casualties for this same period are unknown.
[75] Lee, "Abucay Withdrawal," Nothing But Praise, p. 26.
[76] Rad, MacArthur to Marshall, No. 108, 23 Jan 42, AG 381 (11–27–41 Sec 1) Far East.

CHAPTER XVII

The Battle of the Points

On the same day that General Mac-Arthur made his decision to withdraw from the Abucay–Mauban line, 22 January, the Japanese set in motion a new series of operations potentially as dangerous to the American position on Bataan as General Nara's assault against II Corps. Begun as a limited and local effort to exploit the break-through at Mauban, this fresh Japanese attack soon broadened into a major effort by *14th Army* headquarters to outflank I Corps and cut the West Road. It was to be an end run, amphibious style, with its objectives far to the south, in the Service Command Area. Altogether the Japanese landed at three separate places, each a finger of land—a point—jutting out from the rocky coast line of western Bataan into the South China Sea. The first landings came on 23 January, as the American and Filipino troops began to fall back to the reserve battle position; the last, on 1 February, four days after the new line along the Pilar–Bagac road had been established. Although the Japanese committed only two battalions to this amphibious venture, it posed a threat out of all proportion to the size of the forces engaged. (*Map 14*)

The Service Command Area

When the American line was first established on Bataan on 7 January, defense of the southern tip of the peninsula, designated the Service Command Area, had been assigned to Brig. Gen. Allan C. McBride,

MacArthur's deputy for the Philippine Department. McBride's command included, roughly, all of Bataan south of the Mariveles Mountains (the line Mamala River–Paysawan River formed the northern boundary), and was divided into an East and West Sector by the Paniguian River which flows southward into Mariveles Bay. Excluded from his control was the naval reservation near the town of Mariveles which was under the control of the Navy and defended by naval troops.[1]

The Service Command Area covered over 100 square miles. The distance around the tip of Bataan along the East and West Roads, from Mamala River on the Manila Bay side to the Paysawan River on the South China Sea coast, is at least forty miles. Inland, the country is extremely rugged and hilly, with numerous streams and rivers flowing rapidly through steep gullies into the surrounding waters. The coast line facing Manila Bay is fairly regular but the west coast, where the Japanese landings came, is heavily indented with tiny bays and inlets. The ground on this side of the peninsula is thickly forested almost to the shore line where the foothills of the central range end in abrupt cliffs. Sharp points of land extend from the "solid curved dark shore line" to form small bays. A short distance inland, and connected with a few of the more prominent points by jungle trail, was the single-

---

[1] USAFFE FO 2, 7 Jan 42, AG 300.4 (28 Dec 41) Phil Rcds; USAFFE-USFIP Rpt of Opns, p. 44.

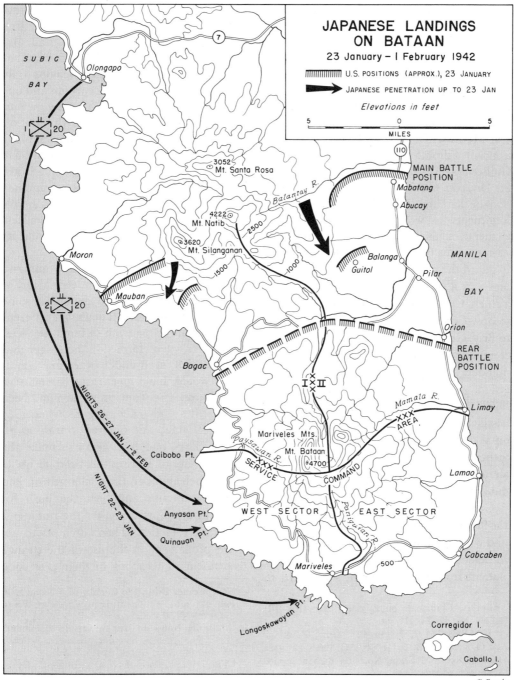

**JAPANESE LANDINGS
ON BATAAN**
23 January – 1 February 1942

|||||||||| U.S. POSITIONS (APPROX.), 23 JANUARY

➤ JAPANESE PENETRATION UP TO 23 JAN

Elevations in feet

5   0   5
MILES

SUBIC
BAY

Olongapo

MAIN BATTLE
POSITION

3052
Mt. Santa Rosa

Balantay R.

Mabatang

Abucay

4222
Mt. Natib

2500

3620
Mt. Silanganan

Moron

1500

1000

Balanga

Guitol

MANILA

Mauban

Pilar

BAY

Orion

Bagac

REAR
BATTLE
POSITION

I × II
× ×

Mamala R.

Limay

XXX
AREA

NIGHTS 26-27 JAN, 1-2 FEB

Mariveles Mts.

Paysawan R.

Caibobo Pt.

Mt. Bataan

4700

Lamao

SERVICE

COMMAND

NIGHT 22-23 JAN

WEST SECTOR

EAST SECTOR

Pariguan R.

Anyasan Pt.

Quinauan Pt.

Cabcaben

Mariveles

500

Longoskawayan Pt.

Corregidor I.

Caballo I.

U. Brooks

MAP 14

lane, badly surfaced West Road, which wound its tortuous way northward from Mariveles.[2]

An adequate defense of this long and ragged coast line would have been difficult under the best of circumstances. With the miscellany of troops assigned to him, the task was an almost impossible one for General McBride. Defending the east coast was a small Filipino force under Maj. Gen. Guillermo B. Francisco, commander of the 2d Division (PA). To accomplish his mission he had the 2d and 4th Constabulary Regiments, as well as other miscellaneous elements of his division, and one battery of 75-mm. guns (SPM). All that was available to guard the west coast against hostile landings was a mixed force of sailors, marines, airmen, Constabulary, and Philippine Army troops. Command of this sector was given to Brig. Gen. Clyde A. Selleck, 71st Division commander, on 8 January. Both sector commanders, Francisco and Selleck, had similar orders: to construct obstacles and station their troops along those beaches suitable for hostile landings, maintain observation posts on a 24-hour schedule, and make arrangements for a mobile reserve of battalion size, alerted and ready to move by bus on thirty minutes' notice.[3]

General Selleck reported to McBride on the 9th and was told then "what I was to do and what I had to do it with." [4] His task was to defend ten miles of the western coast of Bataan from Caibobo Point southward to Mariveles, where the Navy's responsibility began. The orders that had brought Selleck to the Service Command Area had also taken from him practically all of the combat elements of his 71st Division, leaving only the headquarters and service troops and one battalion of artillery (two 75-mm. guns plus one battery of 2.95-inch guns). In addition to these troops he had the 1st Constabulary Regiment from Francisco's division and five grounded Air Forces pursuit squadrons. From Comdr. Francis J. Bridget, commanding the naval battalion at Mariveles, he received the assurance that the bluejackets would move in the West Sector should its southern extremity be threatened.[5]

The troops assigned to Selleck's command constituted a curious force indeed. Many of the men had no infantry training and some had never fired a rifle. They wore different uniforms and came from different services. Altogether, they formed a heterogeneous group which, even under peacetime conditions, would have given any commander nightmares. The planeless airmen had been issued rifles and machine guns when they reached Bataan and ordered to train as infantry. They had two weeks to make the transformation. During this time, to quote one of their number, they "charged up and down mountains and beat the bush for Japs" in an effort to master the rudiments of infantry tactics.[6] Their attempts to acquire proficiency in the use of the strange assortment of weapons in their possession

---

[2] Skerry, Comments on Engineer Hist, No. 10; Collier, Notebooks, III, 21.

[3] USAFFE FO 2, 7 Jan 42; memo, Funk for Asst G–3 USAFFE, 8 Jan 42, AG 300.6 (24 Dec 41) Phil Rcds; McBride, Notes on Bataan Service Command, p. 106.

[4] Ltr, Selleck to Board of Officers, 1 Feb 46, sub: Statement on Reduction in Rank, p. 11, OCMH.

[5] Rpt, Comdr Bridget to Comdt, 16th Naval Dist, 9 Feb 42, sub: Action at Longoskawayan Point, p. 2, Off of Naval Rcds; memo, Selleck for McBride in McBride, Notes on Bataan Service Command, p. 131. The precise boundary between Selleck's sector and the Navy was at Apatot Bay.

[6] The Dyess Story by Lt. Col. William E. Dyess, p. 38. Copyright, 1944, by Marajen Stevick Dyess. Courtesy of G. P. Putnam's Sons. Ind, Bataan, The Judgment Seat, p. 215.

were hardly more successful. Some had the .30-caliber World War I Marlin machine gun; others, air corps .50-caliber guns on improvised mounts, Lewis .30-caliber machine guns, and Browning automatic rifles (BAR). In a group of 220 men there were only three bayonets, but, wrote one of their officers, "that was all right because only three . . . men knew anything about using them."[7]

The Constabulary had had little training as infantry, having served as a native police force prior to their induction into the Army in December. The naval battalion consisted of aviation ground crews left behind when Patrol Wing Ten flew south, sailors from the *Canopus,* men from the naval base at Mariveles, and from forty to sixty marines of an artillery unit. Of this group, only the marines had any knowledge of infantry weapons and tactics.[8]

With this force Selleck made his plans to resist invasion. He set up his command post along the West Road at KP 191, midway between the northern and southern extremities of his sector and about 5,000 yards inland from Quinauan Point. After a reconnaissance, he set his men to work cutting trails through the jungle and forest to the tips of the more important promontories along the coast. Barbed wire was strung, machine guns emplaced, lookouts posted, and wire and radio communications established. Selleck had four 6-inch naval guns, but had time to place only two of them, manned by naval gun crews, into posi-

tion. One was at the northern extremity of his sector; the other, in the south. The third was to have been put in at Quinauan Point but the cement base was still hardening when the Japanese attacked. The road cut through the jungle to bring the gun in, however, proved invaluable later. Selleck also planned to install searchlights atop prominent headlands to forestall a surprise night landing but never received the equipment.[9]

On 22 January Selleck was still frantically seeking more men and more weapons for his sector, but the critical ten miles of beach, which had been practically undefended only two weeks before, was now manned by troops and organized into battalion sectors for defense. On the north was the 17th Pursuit Squadron, about two hundred men strong. Below it, down to the Anyasan River, was the 1st Battalion, 1st Constabulary Regiment. The 34th Pursuit Squadron, with 16 officers and 220 men, occupied the next sector of the beach which included Quinauan Point. Following in order from north to south were the 2d Battalion of the Constabulary regiment, the 3d Pursuit Squadron, and then the naval battalion. In reserve Selleck had the 3d Battalion of the Constabulary regiment and the 20th and 21st Pursuit Squadron.[10] There was little more he could do but wait and trust that his inexperienced and poorly equipped men would perform well if the Japanese should come ashore at any of the tiny inlets in the West Sector.

[7] Dyess, *The Dyess Story,* p. 39.

[8] Morison, *Rising Sun in the Pacific,* p. 200. Morison states there were one hundred marines but this number is too high. Lt. William F. Hogaboom, who commanded these marines, put the number at forty. Hogaboom, "Action Report: Bataan," *Marine Corps Gazette* (April 1946), p. 27.

[9] Memo, Selleck for McBride, in McBride, Notes on Bataan Service Command, p. 131; intervs, author with Selleck at various times in 1947 and 1948; ltr, Selleck to Board of Officers, 1 Feb 46, sub: Statement on Reduction in Rank; Col Alexander, Personal Recollections of Bataan, pp. 52–53, copy in OCMH.

[10] Memo, Selleck for McBride in McBride, Notes on Bataan Service Command, p. 131.

Longoskawayan and Quinauan Points

The Japanese scheme for a landing behind the American lines, a maneuver which
General Yamashita was then employing
with marked success in Malaya, originated
with General Homma. On 14 January,
when General Kimura, commander of the
force driving down the West Road against
Wainwright's I Corps, came to call on him,
Homma had expressed his concern over the
unexpected resistance along the east coast
and the "stalemate" on the west coast.
Though he did not apparently issue orders
for an amphibious move, he pointed out to
Kimura the advantages of a landing to the
enemy's rear and told him that landing
barges had already been ordered from Lingayen to Olongapo.[11] With his detachment
of about 5,000 men, including most of the
20th and *122d Infantry,* Kimura had then
advanced down the west coast and on 21
January—when the *3d Battalion* of the *20th
Infantry* established itself firmly on the West
Road behind Wainwright's main line of resistance—appeared to be in an excellent position to reach Bagac from where he could
move east to take II Corps from the rear.[12]

That his drive on Bagac could be continued "without difficulty" seemed certain
to Kimura. But to forestall a possible enemy
reaction south of Bagac and to protect his
right (south) flank once he started to move
east along the Pilar–Bagac road, Kimura
decided to follow Homma's suggestion and
send a portion of his detachment by water
from Moron to Caibobo Point, five air miles
below Bagac. Selected to make this amphib-

ious hop was Colonel Tsunehiro's *2d Battalion, 20th Infantry,* then in reserve at
Mayagao Point.[13] This move, if properly reinforced and supported, might have had disastrous consequences for the American position on Bataan. It might well render Bagac,
the western terminus of the Pilar–Bagac
road, untenable for the Americans, cut off
all of the American and Filipino forces north
of Bagac, and present a serious threat to II
Corps on the east and Mariveles to the
south.

That it did not was due to chance, poor
seamanship, and the lack of adequate maps
and charts. When the *2d Battalion* embarked
in barges at Moron on the night of 22 January, it was ill prepared for the journey.
Lack of time ruled out preparations ordinarily required to insure the success of an
amphibious operation. The only map available was scaled at 1 : 200,000, virtually useless for picking out a single point along the
heavily indented coast line.[14] So deceptively
does the western shore of Bataan merge into
the looming silhouette of the Mariveles
Mountains that it is difficult even in daylight to distinguish one headland from another, or even headland from cove. At night
it is impossible.

Once afloat the Japanese found themselves in difficulty. The tides were treach-
erous and the voyage a rough one for the
men crowded into the landing barges. Unexpected opposition developed when the U.S.
Navy motor torpedo boat, PT 34, commanded by Lt. John D. Bulkeley and on a
routine patrol mission, loomed up in the
darkness. After a fifteen-minute fight, PT
34 sank one of the Japanese vessels. Unaware of the presence of other enemy ves-

---

[11] Statement of Lt Col Shoji Ohta, Intel Officer,
16th Div, in Comments of Japanese Officers Regarding The Fall of the Philippines, pp. 58, 130,
copy in OCMH.

[12] For a full discussion of this action, see above,
Ch. XVI, pp. 278–285.

[13] *14th Army* Opns, I, 97.

[14] USA *vs.* Homma, pp. 3060–61, testimony of
Homma.

sels in the area, the torpedo boat continued on its way. About an hour later Bulkeley encountered another of the Japanese landing craft and dealt it a fatal blow. Before it sank he managed to board and take two prisoners and a dispatch case with Japanese documents.[15]

By this time the Japanese invasion flotilla had not only lost its bearings but had split into two groups. Not a single Japanese soldier reached Caibobo Point. The first group, carrying about one third of the battalion, came ashore at Longoskawayan Point, ten air miles southeast of the objective. The rest of the battalion, by now a mélange of "platoons, companies, and sections," landed seven miles up the coast, at Quinauan Point.[16] At both places the Japanese achieved complete tactical surprise, but only at the expense of their own utter, though temporary, bewilderment.

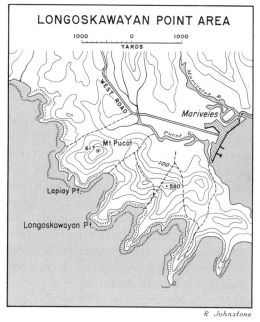

R. Johnstone

MAP 15

The Landings

Longoskawayan Point, a fingerlike promontory jutting out into the South China Sea and only 3,000 yards west of Mariveles Harbor, is the southern coast of a small bay whose northern shore is formed by Lapiay Point. (*Map 15*) Four hundred yards wide at its tip and twice that at the base, Longoskawayan Point is only 700 yards long. Skirting its narrow coast are rocky cliffs about 100 feet high, covered with tall hardwood trees and the lush vegetation of the jungle.

Visibility on the ground is limited by creepers, vines, and heavy undergrowth to a few yards; travel, to the narrow footpaths. The base of the point is less than 2,000 yards from Mariveles, the major port of entry for Bataan.

Just inland from Lapiay Point is the 617-foot high Mt. Pucot, dominating the West Road and the harbor of Mariveles. Though within range of Corregidor's heavy guns, its possession by the enemy would enable him to control the southern tip of Bataan with light artillery. This fact had been recognized early by the Navy and Commander Bridget had posted a 24-hour lookout on the summit of Mt. Pucot. He had, moreover, by agreement with General Selleck, promised to send his naval battalion into the area should the Japanese make an effort to seize the hill.[17]

---

[15] Rpt, Comdr, Torpedo Boat Sq Three, to Comdt, 16th Naval Dist, 27 Feb 42, sub: Action of PT 34, 22–23 Jan 42, Off of Naval Rcds; ltr, Comdr John D. Bulkeley to author, 5 Mar 48 OCMH; White, *They Were Expendable*, p. 11.

[16] USA *vs.* Homma, pp. 3060–61, testimony of Homma; *14th Army* Opns, I, 94, 97; Lt Col Irvin Alexander, Narrative of Quinauan Point Landing, p. 1, App. A, QM Rpt of Opns.

---

[17] Bridget, Action at Longoskawayan Point, p. 2, Off of Naval Rcds; interv, Groce with Maj John McM. Gulick, 20 Apr 48.

The presence of a Japanese force in the vicinity of Mt. Pucot was first reported by the naval lookout at 0840 of the 23d. The 300 Japanese, first estimated as a force of 200 by the Americans, had by this time moved inland from Longoskawayan and Lapiay Points and were approaching the slopes of the hill. Though Bridget had 600 men at Mariveles, only a portion of this force was available initially to meet the Japanese threat. As soon as he had dispatched a small force of marines and sailors to the hill he therefore requested reinforcements from Selleck, who promptly dispatched one pursuit squadron and a 2.95-inch mountain pack howitzer, with crew, from the 71st Division. Later in the day Bridget was further reinforced by a portion of the American 301st Chemical Company.[18]

When the first elements of Bridget's battalion reached Mt. Pucot they found an advance detachment of Japanese already in possession. Before the enemy could dig in, the marines and bluejackets cleared the summit, then mopped up the machine-gun nests along the slopes. The 3d Pursuit Squadron to the north suffered a few casualties the first day, when a squad, sent to investigate the firing, ran into a Japanese patrol. That night the men of the 301st Chemical Company took up a position along the north slope of Mt. Pucot and established contact with the 3d Pursuit. Marines and sailors were posted on Mt. Pucot and along the ridges to the south. The

howitzer was emplaced on a saddle between the two ridges southeast of the hill.[19]

When the sun rose the next morning, 24 January, the Americans discovered that during the night the Japanese had reoccupied their former positions along the west and south slopes of Mt. Pucot. This was the sailors' and marines' first experience with the Japanese penchant for night attacks. The Americans normally halted their attack about an hour before sunset, for the light faded quickly in the thick jungle where even during midday the light was muted. As the troops along the Abucay line had discovered, the Japanese frequently launched a counterattack shortly after dark. Unless a strong defense had been established before darkness, they were often able to regain the ground lost during the day. At the end of such a counterattack the Japanese usually settled down for the night and by daybreak were dug in along a new line. The Filipinos had displayed considerable nervousness during night attacks and had showed a tendency to fire intermittently through the night at the last known Japanese positions to their front. In their first encounter with the Japanese the men of Bridget's battalion reacted in the same manner.

For the Japanese, this first encounter with the untrained bluejackets was a confusing and bewildering one. A Japanese soldier recorded in his diary that he had observed among the Americans a "new type of suicide squad" dressed in brightly colored uniforms. "Whenever these apparitions reached an open space," he wrote, "they would attempt

---

[18] Bridget, Action at Longoskawayan Point, pp. 2–3; Selleck, Comments on Draft MS, 8 Jan 52, OCMH. The number of men Bridget committed initially is not known but at the end of five days he had two hundred men from his naval battalion in action. The information on the number of Japanese in the area was secured from a prisoner of war and reported by Bridget, page 2.

[19] Bridget, Action at Longoskawayan Point, pp. 3–4; Hogaboom, "Action Report: Bataan," *Marine Corps Gazette* (April 1946), pp. 27–28; Lt Herb S. Ellis, Hist of 3d Pursuit Sq, p. 48, Chunn Notebooks. The action at Longoskawayan Point is based upon the first two sources.

to draw Japanese fire by sitting down, talking loudly and lighting cigarettes." [20] The brightly colored uniforms the Japanese noted were the result of an effort by the sailors to dye their whites khaki, an effort which produced a uniform of a "sickly mustard yellow" color.

During the 24th, in a day of vigorous patrol action, the marines and sailors succeeded in driving the Japanese back to Longoskawayan and Lapiay Points. By nightfall they were in control of Mt. Pucot and dug in along the ridges commanding the Japanese positions. But it was evident that the enemy force was too well entrenched and too strong to be expelled by less than a full battalion with supporting weapons.

Quinauan Point, where the remaining 600 men of Colonel Tsunehiro's *2d Battalion, 20th Infantry,* landed, is about midway between Mariveles and Bagac. Like Longoskawayan Point, it is a heavily timbered promontory with trees sixty to eighty feet high and with a thick jungle undergrowth. Two roads suitable for motor vehicles and tanks connected the points with the West Road. As in the landing to the south, the Japanese had by chance come ashore in an area where they could move inland rapidly, cut the I Corps line of communication, and threaten the southern tip of the peninsula. (*Map 16*)

Guarding the beaches along which the bulk of the *2d Battalion* landed was the 34th Pursuit Squadron. Some salvaged .50-caliber machine guns with improvised firing mechanism had been emplaced along Quinauan Point, but evidently the airmen had failed to make proper provision for security for there was no warning of the presence of

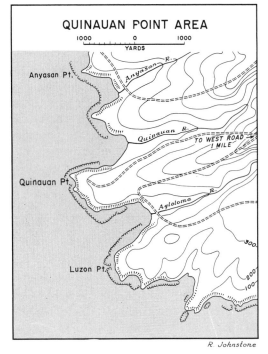

MAP 16

the enemy. The gun crews, awakened by the sound of the Japanese coming ashore in pitch blackness and unable to fire their .50-caliber machine guns, put up no resistance. After giving the alarm, they "crept back to their CP." [21] By the time the squadron was alerted the enemy had completed the hazardous landing and was safely on shore.

News of this landing reached General Selleck at his command post at KP 191 at 0230, six hours before the Longoskawayan landing was reported. He immediately dispatched Colonel Alexander, recently assigned American instructor of the 1st Philippine Constabulary, with the 3d Battalion of that regiment to drive the enemy back into

---

[20] Capt Earl L. Sackett, USN, Hist of USS *Canopus,* p. 14, Off of Naval Rcds.

797-257 O—66—21

[21] Lt Paulger (first name unknown), Hist of 34th Pursuit Sq, p. 52, Chunn Notebooks; Selleck, Comments on Draft MS, 8 Jan 52, OCMH.

the sea.[22] In the time it took the Constabulary to reach the scene of action, the Japanese dug in and constructed defensive positions near the base of the point. When the Constabulary attacked at about 1000 of the 23d, therefore, it ran into strong opposition and was finally halted about 600 yards from the tip of the 1,000-yard-long peninsula. Alexander then tried to flank the Japanese position but that move, too, proved unsuccessful. Before the end of the day Alexander had reached the conclusion that he was facing a reinforced battalion, about seven hundred Japanese, and called on Selleck for tanks, artillery, and more infantry, preferably Americans or Scouts.[23]

Back at Selleck's headquarters on the West Road, the 23d was a hectic day. McBride was there and so was General Marshall, MacArthur's deputy chief of staff. By that time news of the landing at Longoskawayan Point had been received and Sutherland had telephoned from Corregidor to say that the Japanese were landing at Caibobo Point. This last report, evidently based on the documents picked up by Lieutenant Bulkeley, was quickly proved erroneous. The three men were discussing plans for containing the Japanese at the two points and driving them back into the sea when Alexander's request for reinforcements was received. McBride turned to Marshall and asked for tanks to send to Quinauan Point, but the urgent need for armor to cover the withdrawal from the Abucay line, scheduled to begin that night, made it impossible for Marshall to grant this request. The USAFFE deputy chief of staff left shortly for his own headquarters and late that night telephoned Selleck to relay MacArthur's orders that he, Selleck, was to take personal charge of the attack on Quinauan Point the next morning.[24]

Meanwhile Colonel Alexander's force had been augmented by the addition of two Bren gun carriers, sent in lieu of the tanks, and by elements of the 21st Pursuit Squadron, a company of Constabulary troops, and a provisional company formed from Selleck's 71st Division headquarters company. Despite these reinforcements, attacks made during the 24th were unsuccessful and evening found the heterogeneous force in a holding position at the base of the peninsula.[25] Present during the day's action was Col. Charles A. Willoughby, intelligence officer on MacArthur's staff. When Colonel Alexander was hit in the hand at 1600 it was Willoughby who accompanied the wounded man off the field.[26]

During the day there had been a change in command in the West Sector. General Marshall, who believed that only a small number of Japanese had come ashore at

---

[22] Ltr, Selleck to Board of Officers, 1 Feb 46, sub: Statement on Reduction in Rank, p. 12; Alexander, Quinauan Point Landings, pp. 1–2; Alexander, Personal Recollections of Bataan, pp. 54–55; NLF and I Corps Rpt of Opns, p. 24; Collier, Notebooks, III, 43.

[23] Alexander, Quinauan Point Landings, p. 2; Paulger, 34th Pursuit Sq, p. 52, Chunn Notebooks; Col Gilmer M. Bell, CofS South Sector, Opns in the South Subsector, p. 2, copy in OCMH; Alexander, Personal Recollections of Bataan, p. 61.

[24] Ltr, Selleck to Board of Officers, 1 Feb 46, sub: Statement on Reduction in Rank, p. 13; Selleck, Comments on draft chapter prepared by author, OCMH; interv, author with Marshall, 7 Apr 48.

[25] Alexander, Quinauan Point Landings, p. 2; Alexander, Personal Recollections of Bataan, p. 62; Bell, Opns in South Subsector, p. 2; Dyess, *The Dyess Story*, p. 41. Dyess, then a captain, commanded the 21st Pursuit Squadron.

[26] Melville Jacoby, "Corregidor Cable No. 79," *Field Artillery Journal* (April 1942), p. 267; ltr, Maj Gen Charles A. Willoughby to Ward, 17 May 51, OCMH; Notebook of Col Alexander, copy in OCMH; Selleck, Comments on Draft MS, 8 Jan 52, OCMH.

Quinauan Point, had come to the conclusion that the offensive was not being pushed aggressively enough.[27] He passed this estimate on to General Sutherland sometime during the night of 23–24 January, and, as a result, it was decided at USAFFE to relieve Selleck and send Col. Clinton A. Pierce to the West Sector to take over command. Pierce had earned high praise and an enviable reputation for his handling of the 26th Cavalry (PS) since the start of the campaign and he seemed the right man for the job. In the early morning hours of the 24th, Colonel Pierce, who was to be promoted to brigadier general in six days, appeared at Selleck's headquarters with the information that he had been ordered to assume command of the West Sector. This was the first intimation Selleck had that he was to be relieved. Later that day, after he received official notice of his relief from General McBride, Selleck took Pierce to Quinauan Point, turned over to him command of the sector, and left for the Service Command.[28]

The change in command of the West Sector occurred almost simultaneously with a reorganization of the command on Bataan following the withdrawal to the reserve battle position. On 25 January McBride was relieved of responsibility for beach defense and that mission was assigned by USAFFE to the two corps commanders. Francisco's command along the east coast was merged with Parker's corps, and the West Sector was redesignated the South Sector of Wainwright's corps on the west. Pierce, as commander of the South Sector, now came directly under Wainwright's command.[29]

Despite these administrative changes and the arrival of additional reinforcements—including the rest of the 21st Pursuit Squadron—the situation on Quinauan Point remained the same on the 25th and 26th. It was evident that trained infantry troops supported by artillery and tanks would be required to clear out the entrenched Japanese on both Quinauan and Longoskawayan Points. On the 26th USAFFE ordered the 2d Battalion, 88th Field Artillery (PS), which had withdrawn to I Corps from the Abucay line, to the west coast to support the troops on beach defense. One battery of the Scout battalion's 75-mm. guns went to Longoskawayan Point; another battery, to Quinauan Point.[30]

The dispatch of trained infantry troops into the threatened area was hastened when, on 27 January, the Japanese attempted to reinforce their stranded men at Quinauan. MacArthur's headquarters quickly concluded that this move presaged a major enemy drive to cut the West Road and ordered Wainwright to clear the area as soon as possible. Wainwright thereupon ordered two Scout battalions, released from USAFFE reserve the day before, to move in and take over these sectors. The 2d Battalion, 57th Infantry, was to go to Longoskawayan Point; the 3d Battalion, 45th, to Quinauan Point.[31] When the movement of

---

[27] Interv, author with Marshall, 7 Apr 48.

[28] *Ibid.;* ltr, Selleck to Board of Officers, 1 Feb 46, sub: Statement on Reduction in Rank, p. 13; ltr, Pierce to Ward, 5 Jan 52, OCMH; Bell, Opns in the South Subsector, p. 2. Selleck was reduced to colonel on 25 January. *Official Army Register,* 1947.

[29] USAFFE FO 10, 25 Jan 42, AG 300.4 (28 Dec 41) Phil Rcds.

[30] Ltr, Col Howard to TAG, sub: Unit Hist 2d Bn, 88th FA (PS), p. 5. A copy of the letter, as well as a lengthier draft, is on file in OCMH.

[31] *14th Army* Opns, I, 107; Collier, Notebooks, III, 42; USAFFE-USFIP Rpt of Opns, p. 49; Capt Clifton A. Croom, Hist, 3d Bn, 45th Inf (PS) 8 Dec 41–9 Apr 42, p. 8, and Anderson, Hist of 57th Inf (PS), p. 3, both in Chunn Notebooks. The Japanese attempt to reinforce on the 27th is described below, pp. 21–23.

these units was completed Wainwright hoped to wind up the action on both points in short order.

The Fight for Longoskawayan Point

The Americans on Longoskawayan Point had made little progress since 24 January. On that day Bridget had called up more of his men from Mariveles and had received from the 4th Marines on Corregidor two 81-mm. mortars and a machine-gun platoon. By morning of the 25th the two guns were in position on a saddle northwest of Mt. Pucot. Aided by an observation post on the hill, they had lobbed their shells accurately into the Japanese positions on both Longoskawayan and Lapiay Points. When the mortar fire lifted, patrols had moved in to seize both points. Lapiay had been abandoned and was occupied with no difficulty. But the men who attempted to reach Longoskawayan were driven back. There the Japanese were strongly entrenched and supported by machine guns and mortars. All efforts to drive them out that day failed and Bridget called for support from Corregidor.[32]

Since the morning of the 25th the crew of Corregidor's Battery Geary (eight 12-inch mortars) had been waiting eagerly for permission to open fire on the Japanese. At 1000 this permission had been denied and Col. Paul D. Bunker, commander of the Seaward Defenses on Corregidor, had gone back to his quarters "inwardly raving with disappointment." [33] Finally, late that evening

word had come from Maj. Gen. Edward P. King, Jr., USAFFE artillery officer, that the battery could fire in support of the naval battalion. At about midnight the men began their "first real shoot of the war." [34] Using 670-pound land-attack projectiles with superquick fuzes, "which worked beautifully," Battery Geary fired sixteen rounds at a range of 12,000 yards, only 2,000 short of extreme range. The results were most gratifying. After the fourth shot the forward observer on Mt. Pucot reported that such large fires had been started on Longoskawayan Point that he could no longer see the target.[35]

This bombardment, the first hostile heavy caliber American coast artillery fire since the Civil War, made a strong impression on the Japanese. One of them later declared: "We were terrified. We could not see where the big shells or bombs were coming from; they seemed to be falling from the sky. Before I was wounded, my head was going round and round, and I did not know what to do. Some of my companions jumped off the cliff to escape the terrible fire." [36]

Even with the aid of the heavy guns from Corregidor, Bridget's battalion was unable to make any headway against the Japanese on the point. Unless reinforcements were received, not only was there little likelihood of an early end to the fight but there was a possibility that the enemy might even launch a counterattack. Fortunately, the reinforcements sent by Wainwright began to arrive. On the evening of the 26th the battery of 75-mm. guns from the 88th Field

---

[32] The account of the fight at Longoskawayan Point to 28 January is based on Bridget, Action at Longoskawayan Point, pp. 3–5, and Hogaboom, "Action Report: Bataan," *Marine Corps Gazette* (April 1946), pp. 27–31.

[33] Diary of Col Bunker, entry of 25 Jan 42. Colonel Bunker died in prison camp and the diary was

lent to the author before it was given to the U. S. Military Academy at West Point. A photostat copy is in OCMH.

[34] *Ibid.*

[35] *Ibid.*

[36] USAFFE G–3 Info Bulletin, 3 Feb 42, quoted in Harbor Defenses Rpt of Opns, p. 31.

Artillery arrived and next morning the guns were in place, ready for action.[37]

At 0700, 27 January, all the guns that could be brought to bear on Longoskawayan Point—the 75-mm. battery of the 88th Field Artillery, the two 81-mm. mortars of the 4th Marines, the 2.95-inch pack howitzer from the 71st Field Artillery, and the 12-inch mortars of Battery Geary—opened fire with a deafening roar. The barrage lasted for more than an hour and when it lifted the infantry moved out to take the point.

Though it seemed that nobody "could be left alive" after so heavy a shelling, the marines and sailors who attempted to occupy Longoskawayan found the Japanese active indeed.[38] Not only were all attempts to push ahead repulsed but, when a gap was inadvertently left open in the American line, the Japanese quickly infiltrated. For a time it appeared as though they would succeed in cutting off a portion of the naval battalion and only the hasty action of the 81-mm. mortars and the pack howitzer saved the situation. At the end of the day Bridget was no nearer success than he had been before the attack opened.

Prospects for the next day were considerably improved when, at dusk, the 500 Scouts of the 2d Battalion of the 57th Infantry, led by Lt. Col. Hal C. Granberry, reached Longoskawayan Point. That night they relieved the naval battalion and early the next morning moved out to the attack.[39] In the line were Companies E and G, with F in reserve. The Scouts advanced steadily

during the morning but halted when it became apparent that the artillery, its field of fire masked by Mt. Pucot, could not support the attack. A platoon of machine guns was set up on an adjoining promontory to the left to cover the tip of the point, and a platoon of the 88th Field Artillery moved to a new position from which it could fire on the Japanese.[40] By nightfall the Scouts had advanced about two thirds of the length of Longoskawayan Point.

At dawn of the 29th, the Scouts moved back to their original line of departure to make way for a thirty-minute artillery preparation, to begin at 0700. Again the 12-inch mortars on Corregidor joined the guns off the point.[41] A unique feature of this preparation was the participation by the minesweeper USS *Quail* which stood offshore and fired at specified targets on land.[42] Still supported by the *Quail,* which continued firing until 0855, the Scouts moved out again at 0730 only to discover that the Japanese had occupied the area won the day before. It was not until 1130 that the Scouts regained the line evacuated earlier in the morning. That afternoon Colonel Granberry put Company F into the line and within three hours the 2d Battalion was in possession of the tip of Longoskawayan Point. Except for mopping up, a job left largely to the naval battalion and to armored launches, the fight for Longoskawayan Point was over.[43] Next day the Scout

---

[37] Ltr, Howard to TAG, sub: 2d Bn, 88th FA (PS), p. 5; Collier, Notebooks, III, 41–42; USAFFE-USFIP Rpt of Opns, p. 49.

[38] Bunker, Diary, entry of 27 Jan 42.

[39] The account of the last days of fighting at Longoskawayan Point is based on Anderson, Hist of the 57th Inf (PS), pp. 3–4, Chunn Notebooks.

[40] Ltr, Howard to TAG, sub: 2d Bn, 88th FA (PS), p. 5.

[41] Bunker, Diary, entry of 29 Jan 42; Harbor Defenses Rpt of Opns, p. 31.

[42] Rockwell, Naval Activities in Luzon Area, p. 14, and ltr, CO, USS *Quail* to Comdt, 16th Naval Dist, 30 Jan 42, sub: Action at Longoskawayan Point, 29 Jan 42, both in Off of Naval Rcds.

[43] For an account of the activities of the armored launches, see Sackett, Hist of USS *Canopus,* pp. 16–17.

battalion rejoined its regiment at sector headquarters on the West Road, carrying with it a supply of canned salmon and rice, the gift of a grateful Commander Bridget.[44]

The cost of the action had not been excessive. In wiping out a force of 300 Japanese the Americans had suffered less than 100 casualties; 22 dead and 66 wounded. Half of the number killed and 40 of the wounded had been Scouts. Once again the Americans had learned the lesson, so often demonstrated during the campaign, that trained troops can accomplish easily and quickly what untrained soldiers find difficult and costly. But had it not been for the prompt action of the naval battalion, Mt. Pucot might well have been lost during the first day of action.

Although the Americans had not known it, the Japanese on Longoskawayan had never had a chance to inflict permanent damage for their location was unknown to higher headquarters. Indeed, neither Kimura, who had sent them out, nor Tsunehiro, the battalion commander, seems to have been aware, or even to have suspected, that a portion of the 2d Battalion had landed so far south. Later, the Japanese expressed amazement and disbelief when they learned about this landing. One Japanese officer would not be convinced until he was shown the Japanese cemetery at Longoskawayan Point.[45] Thus, even if they had succeeded in gaining Mt. Pucot, there was little likelihood that the small force of 300 Japanese

at Longoskawayan Point could have exploited their advantage and seriously threatened the American position in southern Bataan.

The Fight for Quinauan Point

While the Japanese were being pushed off Longoskawayan Point, the battle for Quinauan Point, seven miles to the north, continued. By 27 January the Japanese landing there had been contained but the fight had reached a stalemate. Against the 600 Japanese of Colonel Tsunehiro's *2d Battalion, 20th Infantry,* Pierce had sent a miscellaneous and motley array of ill-assorted and ineffective troops numbering about 550 men and drawn from a wide variety of organizations: the V Interceptor Command, the 21st and 34th Pursuit Squadrons, headquarters of the 71st Division (PA), the 3d Battalion, 1st Philippine Constabulary, and Company A, 803d Engineers (US).[46] It is not surprising, therefore, that little progress had been made in pushing the enemy into the sea.

On 27 January, it will be recalled, Wainwright had been ordered to bring the fight on the beaches to a quick conclusion and had dispatched the 3d Battalion, 45th Infantry (PS), to Quinauan Point. By 0830 of the 28th, the entire Scout battalion, numbering about 500 men and led by Maj. Dudley G. Strickler, was in position at the point ready to start the attack. All units except the V Interceptor Command (150 men), which

[44] Lt Col Harold K. Johnson, Anyasan and Silaiim Points (paper prepared for School of Combined Arms, 1946–47, Command and General Staff College), p. 12.

[45] USA vs. Homma, p. 3060, testimony of Homma; ltr, Col Stuart Wood to author, 23 Mar 48, OCMH; interv, Groce with Selleck, 2 Apr 48.

[46] Bell, Opns in South Subsector, p. 2; Dyess, *The Dyess Story*, p. 42; 1st Lt John A. Goodpasture, V Interceptor Comd Combat Unit 1, p. 43, Paulger, Hist of 34th Pursuit Sq, p. 52, and 1st Lt Lawrence N. Parcher, Hist of 21st Pursuit Sq, p. 50, all three in Chunn Notebooks.

remained to cover the beaches below the cliff line, were relieved.[47]

The Scouts advanced three companies abreast in a skirmish line about 900 yards long, their flanks protected by the grounded airmen. Attached to each of the rifle companies was a machine-gun platoon, placed along the line at points where it was thought enemy resistance would be stiffest. The line stretched through dense jungle where the visibility was poor and the enemy well concealed. "The enemy never made any movements or signs of attacking our force," wrote the Scout commander, "but just lay in wait for us to make a move and when we did casualties occured and we still could not see even one enemy." [48]

Under such conditions it is not surprising that the battalion was unable to make much progress during the day. Despite the fact that the machine guns were set up just to the rear of the front line and "shot-up" from top to bottom those trees that might conceal enemy riflemen, advances during the day were limited to ten and fifteen yards at some points. Progress along the flanks was somewhat better and in places the Scouts gained as much as 100 yards. By 1700, when the battalion halted to dig in for the night and have its evening meal of rice and canned salmon, Major Strickler had concluded that it would be impossible for his Scouts, aided only by the airmen, to take the point. He asked for reinforcements and that night Company B, 57th Infantry (PS), was attached to his battalion.[49]

On the 29th, shortly after dawn, the attack was resumed. Two platoons of Company B, 57th Infantry, were in position on the battalion right flank; the rest of the reinforcing company was in reserve. Despite the strengthened line no more progress was made on this day than had been made the day before. Again casualties were heavy, especially in the center where resistance was strongest.

The battle continued throughout the 30th and 31st, with about the same results. The Japanese were being pushed slowly toward the sea, but only at very heavy cost. No headway could be made at all against the enemy positions along the cliff and on the high ground about 200 yards inland from the tip of the point.

Hindering the advance as much as the enemy was the jungle. The entire area was covered with a dense forest and thick undergrowth that made all movement difficult and dangerous. Even without enemy opposition the troops could move through the jungle only with great difficulty, cutting away the vines and creepers that caught at their legs and stung their faces and bodies. The presence of concealed enemy riflemen and light machine-gun nests, invisible a few feet away, added immeasurably to the difficulty of the attacking troops. In such terrain, artillery, mortar, and armor could be of slight assistance and the advance had to be made by the rifleman almost unaided. It was a slow and costly process.

At daylight, 1 February, in an effort to reduce the opposition in the center, the infantry attack was preceded by a heavy but ineffective mortar operation. When it lifted the two center companies moved in quickly but were able to advance only a short distance before they were halted. Major Strickler then went forward to the front lines to

[47] Croom, Hist, 3d Bn, 45th Inf (PS), pp. 8–14, Chunn Notebooks; Bell, Opns in South Subsector, p. 3; Lilly, 57th Inf (PS) Opns Rpt, p. 5. The account which follows is based on these sources.
[48] Croom, Hist, 3d Bn, 45th Inf (PS), pp. 9–10, Chunn Notebooks.
[49] Lilly, 57th Inf (PS) Opns Rpt, p. 5.

make a personal reconnaissance. He was last seen in the vicinity of Company B, 57th Infantry. After an intensive search during the day battalion headquarters regretfully reported that its commander was missing, presumably killed in action. Capt. Clifton A. Croom, battalion adjutant, assumed command.[50]

By now the battalion was sadly reduced in strength, with casualties estimated as high as 50 percent. The men, "dead tired from loss of sleep and exposure," would need help soon if the attack was to be pushed aggressively.[51] On the afternoon of the 2d Captain Croom asked General Pierce for tanks, a request, happily, that Pierce was now in a position to grant, for on the night of 31 January, on orders from MacArthur's headquarters, General Weaver had sent the 192d Tank Battalion (less one company) to the west coast. In less than two hours a platoon of three tanks from Company C was in position on the line.[52]

Late on the afternoon of the 2d, with the aid of tanks, the attack was resumed. General Weaver, arriving as the tanks were making their third attack, was on hand to observe the action. This attack, like the others, failed to make any headway, and on Weaver's insistence two more attacks, preceded by artillery preparation, were made, with little success. Late in the afternoon Col. Donald B. Hilton, executive officer of the 45th Infantry, arrived and assumed control of all troops on the point.[53]

The next morning the Scouts and tankers resumed the attack, but with little success. Stumps and fallen trees impeded the advance of the tanks whose usefulness was further limited by the absence of proper co-ordination between infantry and armor, and faulty communication and control. When the battalion halted at 1700 it was not far from its original line of departure. That night it was joined by Captain Dyess and seventy men from the 21st Pursuit Squadron which had been in the fight earlier but had been relieved when the Scouts had taken over the line on the 28th. "On our return," wrote Dyess, "we found that the Scouts had occupied fifty yards more of the high jungle above the bay—at terrible cost to themselves. Their casualties had run about fifty percent. The sight and stench of death were everywhere. The jungle, droning with insects, was almost unbearably hot."[54]

For the attack of the 4th Colonel Hilton received two additional tanks and a radio control car. Deploying his tanks across the narrow front and stationing men equipped with walkie-talkie sets with each tank, Hilton moved his reinforced battalion out early in the morning. The line moved forward steadily, the tanks, guided by directions from the radio control car, spraying the area to the front with their machine guns and knocking out strong points.

Success crowned this co-ordinated infantry-tank attack. By the end of the day the Japanese had been crowded into an area 100 yards wide and only 50 yards from the cliff at the edge of the point. Plainly visible to the Scouts were the Japanese soldiers and beyond them the blue water of the South China Sea. Suddenly the men wit-

[50] Strickler's body was recovered on the 7th. Memo, QM Hq Phil Dept to QM USAFFE, sub: Supply Situation, 7 Feb 42, AG 319.1 (29 Jan 42) Phil Rcds.
[51] Croom, Hist, 3d Bn, 45th Inf (PS), p. 12, Chunn Notebooks.
[52] Prov Tank Gp Rpt of Opns, p. 20–21; NLF and I Corps Rpt of Opns, p. 24.
[53] Croom, Hist, 3d Bn, 45th Inf (PS), p. 12, Chunn Notebooks; Prov Tank Gp Rpt of Opns,

p. 21; Weaver, Comments on Draft MS, Comment 44, OCMH.
[54] Dyess, *The Dyess Story*, p. 43.

nessed a remarkable sight. Screaming and yelling Japanese ripped off their uniforms and leaped off the cliff. Others scrambled over the edge and climbed down to prepared positions along the rock ledges. Down on the beach Japanese soldiers ran up and down wildly. "I'll never forget the little Filipino who had set up an air-cooled machine gun at the brink and was peppering the crowded beach far below," wrote one eyewitness. "At each burst he shrieked with laughter, beat his helmet against the ground, lay back to whoop with glee, then sat up to get in another burst." [55]

Though the Americans reached the edge of the cliff the next morning, the fight was not yet over. The Japanese had holed up in caves along the cliff and in the narrow ravines leading down to the beaches. Every effort to drive them out during the next few days failed. Patrols which went down the ravines or the longer way around the beach to polish off the enemy only incurred heavy casualties. Though their cause was hopeless the Japanese steadfastly refused to surrender. "The old rules of war," wrote General Wainwright, "began to undergo a swift change in me. What had at first seemed a barbarous thought in the back of my mind now became less unsavory. I thought of General U. S. Grant's land mine at Petersburg and made up my mind." [56]

First he made arrangements to bring a small gunboat close in to shore to shell the area. Then, at dawn of the 6th, he sent in a platoon of the 71st Engineer Battalion (PA) under the supervision of Colonel Skerry, the North Luzon Force engineer, to assist the attacking troops—the 3d Battalion, 45th Infantry, and Company B, 57th

Infantry (PS)—in routing out the holed-up Japanese. Fifty-pound boxes of dynamite fired with time fuzes were lowered over the cliff to the mouth of the caves. After a Scout engineer sergeant was fatally wounded while lowering one of the boxes, this method was abandoned in favor of throwing dynamite hand grenades (four sticks of dynamite with a 30-second time fuze) along the length of the cliffs close to the bottom edges from where the Japanese fire had come. By this means most of the Japanese (about fifty) were forced into one large cave that was completely demolished by dynamite. All of the enemy had not yet been exterminated and when patrols entered the area, they encountered spasmodic fire. [57]

It was not until 8 February that the Japanese were finally exterminated. The job was done from the seaward side, as at Longoskawayan Point. Two armored naval motor launches armed with 37-mm. and machine guns, and two whaleboats, each with ten men from the 21st Pursuit Squadron on board, sailed from Mariveles at 0600 that morning. In command of the boats was Lt. Comdr. H. W. Goodall; Captain Dyess led the landing parties. At about 0800 the small flotilla arrived off Quinauan Point and the navy gunners took the beach under fire. Sheets lowered over the face of the cliff marked the Japanese positions. When the opposition on shore had been neutralized, the whaleboats, waiting a mile off the coast, came in to land the airmen. One group landed on the northern side of Quinauan Point, the other along the southern beaches. Both moved cautiously toward the tip of the peninsula while Scout patrols from the battalion on the cliffs above worked their way

---

[55] *Ibid.,* pp. 43–44.
[56] Wainwright, *General Wainwright's Story,* p. 57.

[57] Skerry, Comments on Draft MS, Comment D, OCMH.

down through the ravines. Despite attacks by three enemy dive bombers which hit the small boats and the men on shore, the operation was successfully concluded during the morning.[58]

The end of resistance on Quinauan Point marked the destruction of the *2d Battalion, 20th Infantry*. Three hundred of that battalion's number had been killed at Longoskawayan; another 600, at Quinauan. In the words of General Homma, the entire battalion had been "lost without a trace." [59] But the cost had been heavy. The 82 casualties suffered at Longoskawayan were less than one fifth of the number lost at Quinauan. On 28 January when the 3d Battalion, 45th Infantry, took over that sector it had numbered about 500 men. It marched out with only 200; 74 men had been killed and another 234 wounded. The other Scout unit, Company B, 57th Infantry, left Quinauan Point with 40 men less than it had had ten days earlier. Other units suffered correspondingly high losses. Total casualties for the Quinauan Point fight amounted to almost 500 men.[60] It was a heavy price to pay for the security of the West Road, but there was still a payment due, for the Japanese, on 27 January, had landed at yet another point on the west coast behind Wainwright's front line.

---

[58] Ltr, Capt H. W. Goodall, USN, to George Groce, 17 Aug 48, OCMH; Dyess, *The Dyess Story*, p. 44; rad, Comdt, 16th Naval Dist, to OPNAV, 8 Feb 42, War Diary, 16th Naval Dist, Off of Naval Rcds. On the way back, the boats were attacked again by dive bombers. Among the casualties that day was Commander Goodall, seriously wounded.
[59] USA *vs.* Homma, p. 3061, testimony of Homma; rpt, Graves Registration Unit, 7, 8, 9, and 11 Feb 42, AG 319.1 (29 Jan 42) Phil Rcds.
[60] Bell, Opns in South Subsector, p. 4; Paulger, 34th Pursuit Sq, p. 52, Croom, Hist, 3d Bn, 45th Inf (PS), p. 14, and Parcher, 21st Pursuit Sq, pp. 50–51, all three in Chunn Notebooks.

Anyasan and Silaiim Points

General Kimura's success against Wainwright's Mauban line between 20 and 23 January had led *14th Army* headquarters to revise its estimate of the situation and to prepare new plans for the occupation of Bataan. Originally, the main effort had been made against II Corps on the east. In view of Kimura's success, General Homma now decided to place additional forces on the west and increase pressure against I Corps in the hope that he might yet score a speedy victory. On the 25th, therefore, he directed Lt. Gen. Susumu Morioka, *16th Division* commander, who had come up from southern Luzon and was now in Manila with a portion of his division, to proceed to western Bataan with two battalions of infantry and the headquarters of the *21st Independent Engineer Regiment* and there assume command of the operations against I Corps.[61]

The First Landing

Homma's order of the 25th, though made two days after the landings at Longoskawayan and Quinauan, contained no reference to this effort to outflank I Corps by sea. Homma was not yet convinced that this amphibious venture should have the full support of *14th Army*. The decision to reinforce Tsunehiro's *2d Battalion* at Quin-

---

[61] Morioka's *16th Division* was scattered at this time. The *9th Infantry* was under General Nara's control on the east coast of Bataan; two battalions of the *20th Infantry* were already in Bataan and operating under General Kimura, infantry group commander of the division. The third regiment of the division, the *33d Infantry*, was split: one battalion was in Manila, one in southern Luzon, and the third was on Mindanao. *14th Army Opns*, I, 98–99.

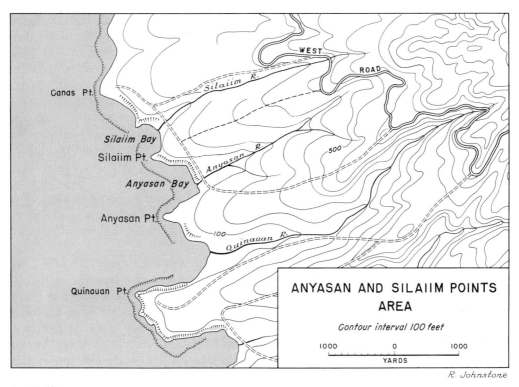

MAP 17

auan, the only landing of which the Japanese had knowledge, was made by General
Morioka, Kimura's immediate superior. To
him, as to Kimura, the landing held out the
promise of large results. Even before he left
Manila, he ordered one company of the
small force at his disposal to go to the aid
of the *2d Battalion, 20th Infantry*. The company selected was from the same regiment's
1st Battalion. It was to move with all speed
from Manila to Olongapo and there pick up
supplies for the trapped and hungry men
"fighting a heroic battle" against a "superior enemy" on Quinauan Point.[62]

The reinforcing company reached Olongapo at the head of Subic Bay on the night
of 26 January. At midnight it embarked in

landing craft loaded with ammunition,
rations, and supplies, and set sail for Quinauan. Once more poor seamanship and the
lack of navigation charts and large-scale
maps led the Japanese astray. This time
they landed about 2,000 yards short of the
objective, between the Anyasan and Silaiim
Rivers, in the sector guarded by the 1st Battalion, 1st Philippine Constabulary.[63] (*Map
17*)

The beach on which the Japanese craft
ran aground was little different from that
at Longoskawayan and Quinauan. The
coast line here presented the same irregular
appearance as that to the south. Dense
tropical forest and thick undergrowth extended almost to the shore line, and the foot-

[62] *Ibid.*, 107–08.

[63] *Ibid.*; Collier, Notebooks, III, 42.

hills of the Mariveles Mountains formed steep cliffs about 100 feet high just in front of the beach. The two rivers, Silaiim on the north and Anyasan about 1,000 yards to the south, emptied into shallow bays, each bearing the name of the river. Separating the two bays was Silaiim Point, a narrow headland which formed the upper shore of the southern bay. The lower coast of the bay received its name from the southernmost of the two rivers. Thus, from north to south, presenting a confusion of identically named geographic features, were: Silaiim Bay, Silaiim River, Silaiim Point, Anyasan Bay, Anyasan River, and Anyasan Point. This confusion of points, when combined with those to the north and south, was as bewildering to the troops as it is, probably, to the reader. Their plight was most aptly expressed by one member of a wire crew, perched atop a telephone pole who, when asked where he was, replied, "For Christ's sake, sir, I don't know. I am somewhere between asinine and quinine points." [64]

Inland, the ground was even more difficult than at Longoskawayan and Quinauan. Small streams branched off from the two rivers, dry at this time of the year, to create additional hazards to troop movements and to provide cover for the enemy. With only one access trail from the West Road to the beach, the task of maintaining communications and supplying troops to the front would be a difficult one. The absence of roads would also limit the effective use of tanks in formation and require their employment singly or in small numbers at isolated points. Similarly, the dense forest, by restricting observation and increasing the

hazards of tree bursts, would limit the use of artillery and mortars. Like the fights then in progress at Longoskawayan and Quinauan, the struggle to drive off the Japanese between the Anyasan and Silaiim Rivers would be a job for the rifleman. [65]

In MacArthur's headquarters, the new landing was regarded as the prelude to a major enemy offensive. Should this hostile force, thought to be of "considerable size," establish contact with the Japanese on Quinauan Point to the south or advance as far as the West Road, only 2,700 yards away, it would present "a threat of no mean importance." [66]

Coming ashore at about 0300 of the 27th, the confused and lost Japanese of the *1st Battalion, 20th Infantry,* numbering about two hundred men, met no more resistance than had their fellows in the *2d Battalion.* The Constabulary troops on beach defense promptly took flight at the first approach of the enemy and the entire Constabulary battalion was soon dispersed. At dawn, when General Pierce received news of the landing, he immediately dispatched the 17th Pursuit Squadron, then in sector reserve, to meet the invaders. [67]

The grounded airmen moved out shortly after dawn. At the abandoned Constabulary command post, where breakfast still simmered in the pots, they discovered a smashed switchboard and an aid station complete with stretchers. After breakfasting on the food and reporting the situation to sector headquarters, the airmen set off jauntily for

---

[64] Maj Achille C. Tisdelle, Diary, entry of 6 Feb 42, copy in OCMH. Major Tisdelle was aide to General King, Chief of the Artillery Section, USAFFE.

[65] Johnson, Anyasan and Silaiim Points, pp. 2–3. Colonel Johnson states that the percentage of the tree bursts was as high as 50 percent.

[66] Collier, Notebooks, III, 42.

[67] Bell, Opns in South Subsector, p. 5; 2d Lt Stephen H. Crosby, Hist of 17th Pursuit Sq, p. 48, Chunn Notebooks; NLF and I Corps Rpt of Opns, p. 25.

the coast. As they did so, some men were heard inquiring how to fire their rifles.

More than a mile inland from the beach and about 400 yards distant from the vital West Road, the 17th Pursuit Squadron met the enemy's advance patrols. The Japanese pulled back without offering serious resistance and the squadron was able to advance along the path between the two rivers until it was about 1,000 yards from the shore line. The Japanese had apparently established their front line positions here and the Americans' easy march came to an abrupt halt. Joined at this point by the 2d Battalion, 2d Philippine Constabulary, which had just been in the fight against the Japanese roadblock to the north, the Americans dug in for the night.[68] This was to be the easiest advance by the troops in the Anyasan-Silaiim sector.

The next day, 28 January, the airmen and Constabulary attacked during the morning. Either because the Japanese had pulled back or shifted position during the night, the Constabulary battalion was able to advance almost to the coast at Anyasan Bay. That night, when the Japanese appeared ready to counterattack, the Constabulary pulled back leaving the 17th Pursuit to fend for itself. The threat to the West Road now seemed serious, for there was every indication that the Japanese force, whose size and precise location were still not known, might burst out of the beachhead and create havoc behind the American lines.[69]

The situation was saved the next day when the Scouts of the 2d Battalion, 45th Infantry, arrived on the scene, led by their executive officer, Capt. Arthur C. Biedenstein. General Pierce placed Biedenstein in

charge of the operation and gave him the 1st Battalion, 1st Philippine Constabulary, and the 1st Battalion, 12th Infantry (PA)—both of which had just been relieved at Quinauan Point—to clear out the Japanese. To guard the West Road and insure the safety of the line of communication, he placed Company A, 57th Infantry (PS), on patrol to the rear.[70]

On 30 January, after a personal reconnaissance to locate the Japanese, Captain Biedenstein opened the attack. Calling for support from the 75-mm. guns of the 88th Field Artillery, whose Battery D was in position to assist the men in both the Quinauan and Anyasan–Silaiim sectors, he sent his Scouts out to regain the beach near the mouth of the Silaiim River. Either the battalion's front line had been incorrectly reported to the artillery or plotted inaccurately, for the result of the preparation was almost disastrous. Without adequate communication between infantry and artillery and with high trees limiting observation and causing tree bursts, the Scouts soon found themselves under fire from their own guns. Before the artillery command post could be reached, four Scouts had been killed and sixteen more wounded. The offensive of the 30th came to an end even before it had fairly begun.[71]

---

[68] Crosby, 17th Pursuit Sq, pp. 48–49, Chunn Notebooks.

[69] Ibid.; Bell, Opns in South Subsector, p. 5.

[70] Ibid.; Capts Ralph Amato, Jr., and Louis Murphy, Hist of 2d Bn, 45th Inf (PS), 8 Dec 41–9 Apr 42, p. 9, Chunn Notebooks; NLF and I Corps Rpt of Opns, p. 25; Lilly, 57th Inf (PS) Opns, p. 5; Maj Harold K. Johnson, 57th Inf (PS) Diary, pp. 11–12, copy in OCMH. There is considerable disagreement among the sources on the dates for operations in this sector. The conflicting sources cannot be reconciled and the dates used in this account were determined after an evaluation of all the sources.

[71] Amato and Murphy, 2d Bn, 45th Inf (PS), p. 10, Chunn Notebooks; Johnson, 57th Inf (PS) Diary, pp. 11–17; Johnson, Anyasan and Silaiim, pp. 6–13; ltr, Howard to TAG, sub: 2d Bn, 88th FA (PS), p. 11; Lilly, 57th Inf (PS) Opns, p. 5;

That night the 57th Infantry (less detachments) was moved to South Sector headquarters on the West Road with orders to prepare for operations in the Anyasan–Silaiim sector. Hardly had the regiment arrived when General Pierce called for a volunteer—a lieutenant colonel or major—to co-ordinate the activities of the troops already engaged on that front. Maj. Harold K. Johnson, who had been relieved as S–3 of the regiment a week earlier and had "nothing else specific to do," volunteered for the job. "When I reported to General Pierce at 7:30 P. M.," he wrote in his diary, "I found about as complete a lack of knowledge of conditions on the coast along which the Japanese had landed as could be imagined." [72]

A personal reconnaissance on the night of the 30th did not greatly increase his knowledge of the enemy but it did give him a clearer picture of the disposition of the units now under his control. On the north, between the Silaiim River and Canas Point, was the 1st Battalion, 12th Infantry (PA), facing almost due north and with its right flank on the sea. Facing west and holding a line from the Silaiim River to the trail leading from Silaiim Point to the West Road, was the 2d Battalion, 45th Infantry. Below it, to the left of the trail and extending the line south as far as the Anyasan River, was the 1st Battalion, 1st Constabulary. To the rear, along the trail, was the 17th Pursuit. Since there were no troops south of the Anyasan River, Johnson asked for and received permission to relieve Company A of the 57th Infantry from its patrolling mission along the West Road and send it to Anyasan

Point, the promontory south of the river bearing the same name. Its new mission was to establish contact with the enemy on the point in an effort to determine his strength and locate his positions.

Johnson's efforts on the 31st were directed primarily toward securing information about the strength and disposition of the enemy. While Company A of the 57th Infantry reconnoitered Anyasan Point to the south, the 1st Battalion, 12th Infantry, pivoted on its right (west) flank and swept in on the beaches of Silaiim Bay. At the same time the Scouts and Constabulary between the Anyasan and Silaiim Rivers pushed westward toward the sea. The 17th Pursuit remained in place, keeping open the line of supply and communications. Unopposed, the Scout and Philippine Army battalions cleared the area north of the Silaiim River during the morning, thus reducing the beachhead by about one third. The Constabulary troops, however, were stopped cold after an advance of about 100 yards. The Scout company moving out toward Anyasan Point failed to make any contact that day. Johnson now knew where the Japanese were dug in. But he still had no knowledge of their strength or defenses.

With this scanty information, Major Johnson concluded that there was no hope of clearing the area with the force he had. His 2d Battalion, 45th Infantry, was in poor shape. It had reached the Anyasan–Silaiim sector after a grueling march from Abucay where it had been badly mauled. One of its companies had been hard hit and disorganized by fire from friendly artillery and casualties throughout the battalion had been heavy. The unopposed Scout company to the south could not be expected to make rapid progress through the jungle and it was too weak to attack alone if it should meet

---

Bell, Opns in South Subsector. The present account is based on these sources in addition to those cited below.

[72] Johnson, 57th Inf (PS) Diary, p. 11.

an enemy force. Of the rest of his troops Johnson had no high opinion. He did not believe that the 17th Pursuit would be "particularly helpful in an assault," or that the Constabulary would contribute much in an offensive. On the evening of the 31st, therefore, he asked General Pierce for more troops, and asserted that in his opinion only his own regiment, the 57th Infantry, then at sector headquarters, would be able to clear the Japanese out of the area. "No other troops," he declared, "would make the necessary attacks." [73] That night the 57th Infantry was released to General Pierce, who immediately ordered it into the Anyasan–Silaiim area. Next morning Lt. Col. Edmund J. Lilly, Jr., commander of the 57th Infantry, assumed control of operations there and Major Johnson resumed his former post as S–3.

By the end of January the enemy had been isolated and contained. A strong force was assembling for a determined effort to root out the Japanese hiding in the canebrakes, thickets, and creek bottoms of the Anyasan and Silaiim Rivers. The Japanese at Longoskawayan Point had been killed or driven into the sea. At Quinauan Point the slow costly process of attrition was under way. To General Pierce the situation everywhere in the South Sector seemed generally favorable. But appearances were deceptive, for already the Japanese had launched a desperate and final effort to reinforce their beachheads on the west coast.

The Second Landing

At the time it was made, USAFFE's estimate that the first landing in the Anyasan–Silaiim sector presaged a major enemy effort

to cut the West Road was incorrect. Events soon proved it prophetic, however, for on the evening of 27 January General Homma had for the first time lent his support to the landings. That day, in an order to General Morioka, he had directed that the beachhead at Quinauan Point be reinforced and that the augmented force drive inland to seize the heights of Mariveles and then the town itself.[74]

Morioka's first efforts to comply with Homma's orders were limited to attempts to drop rations, medicine, and supplies from the air to his beleaguered forces on the beaches. But the Japanese aircraft were unable to locate their own troops in the jungle. Supplies fell as often on Americans and Filipinos as they did on the starved Japanese. The Scouts of the 45th Infantry one day picked up twelve parachute packages containing food, medicine, ammunition, and maps. The rations consisted of a soluble pressed rice cake, sugar, a soy bean cake, a pink tablet with a strong salty taste, and "other ingredients [which] could not be determined." [75]

While these efforts to supply the troops by air were in progress, Morioka assembled the troops he would require to reinforce the beachhead and push on to Mariveles. On 31 January he ordered the *1st Battalion, 20th Infantry,* one company of which was already in the Anyasan–Silaiim area, to undertake this dangerous mission. Maj. Mitsuo Kimura, battalion commander, immediately

---

[73] *Ibid.,* p. 13.

[74] *14th Army* Opns Order, Series A, No. 220, 27 Jan 42, *65th Brig* Opns Rpt, Mt. Samat, ATIS Enemy Pub 289, Supp. 24.

[75] Memo, QM Phil Dept to QM USAFFE, sub: Status Rpt, 1 Feb 42, AG 319.1 (29 Jan 42) Phil Rcds. See also, USA *vs.* Homma, p. 3061, testimony of Homma; ltr, Col Wood to author, 23 Mar 48, OCMH; Amato and Murphy, 2d Bn, 45th Inf (PS), pp. 10–11, Chunn Notebooks.

made his preparations to sail the next night.[76]

By this time Morioka had tipped his hand. First warning of the impending Japanese move had reached the Americans on the 28th when a Filipino patrol on the opposite side of Bataan had found a mimeographed order on the body of a slain Japanese officer. When translated, it revealed the Japanese intention to reinforce the beachheads and drive toward Mariveles. Thus warned, USAFFE took measures to counter the expected landings. Observers on the west coast were alerted and General Weaver, the tank commander, was directed to send one of his two tank battalions (less one company) to the threatened area. The few remaining P–40's were gassed, loaded with 100-pound antipersonnel bombs and .50-caliber ammunition, and ordered to stand by for a take-off at any time.[77]

The night of 1–2 February was clear, with a full moon. As the enemy flotilla sailed south it was spotted by American observers and a warning was flashed to MacArthur's headquarters. The land, sea, and air forces so carefully prepared for just this moment, were immediately directed to meet and annihilate the enemy. The result was the first large co-ordinated joint attack of the campaign. While the motor torpedo boats sought targets offshore, the 26th Cavalry moved out from I Corps reserve to Caibobo Point to forestall a landing there. The four P–40's, all that remained of the Far East Air Force, took off from the strip near Cabcaben, cleared the Mariveles Mountains, and headed for the enemy flotilla of twelve or

more barges. Sighting the target, they swooped low to release their 100-pound antipersonnel bombs, then turned for a strafing run over the landing boats.

By now the Japanese were nearing Quinauan Point. Their reception from the men on shore, themselves under fire from a Japanese vessel thought to be a cruiser or destroyer, was a warm one. Artillery shell fragments churned the sea around the landing boats as Battery D of the 88th Field Artillery and Battery E of the 301st let go with their 75's and 155's. Together, the two batteries fired a total of 1,000 rounds that night. Fire from the heavy machine guns and small arms of the Scout battalion on the point peppered the small boats and caused numerous casualties among the luckless men on board.

While the landing boats were being attacked by air, artillery, and infantry weapons, PT 32 moved in to attack the Japanese warship, actually a minelayer, stationed off Quinauan Point to cover the landing of Major Kimura's battalion. The enemy vessel turned her searchlight full on the patrol boat and let go with four or five salvos from two guns, thought to be of 6-inch caliber. The PT boat sought unsuccessfully to knock out the searchlight with machine gun fire, and then loosed two torpedoes. As she retired the men on board observed explosions on the enemy vessel, which later reported only slight damage from shore batteries.[78]

[76] *14th Army Opns*, I, 107–08.

[77] Collier, Notebooks, III, 44; Bluemel, 31st Div (PA) Rpt of Opns, p. 15; ltr, Bluemel to Groce, 15 Jun 48, OCMH; Prov Tank Gp Rpt of Opns, pp. 20–21.

[78] USAFFE-USFIP Rpt of Opns, p. 52; ltr, Howard to TAG, Hist, 2d Bn, 88th FA (PS), p. 13; NLF and I Corps Rpt of Opns, p. 25; Croom, Hist, 3d Bn, 45th Inf (PS), pp. 12–12, Chunn Notebooks; Collier, Notebooks, III, 45–46; rad, 16th Naval Dist to OPNAV, 2 Feb 42, War Diary, 16th Naval Dist, Off of Naval Rcds; Rockwell, Naval Activities in Luzon Area, p. 15; ltr, Bulkeley to author, 5 Mar 48, OCMH; Chandler, "26th Cavalry (PS) Battles to Glory," Part 3, *Armored Cavalry*

For the Americans and Filipinos who witnessed the battle in the clear light of the full moon, it was a beautiful and heartening sight to see the remnants of the enemy flotilla, crippled and badly beaten, turn away and sail north shortly after midnight. Homma's plan to reinforce his troops on Quinauan Point had failed and in the first flush of victory the Americans believed the surviving Japanese had returned to Moron. But Major Kimura either had no intention of admitting defeat or was unable to make the return journey in his battered boats. With about half his original force he landed instead in the Anyasan–Silaiim area where he was joined by his battalion's advance company.[79] Once more, against an alerted and prepared foe, the Japanese had landed behind Wainwright's line. All hope for an early end to the fight for Anyasan and Silaiim Points was now gone.

Colonel Lilly, who had assumed command of operations in the Anyasan-Silaiim sector on 1 February, spent the day in a thorough reconnaissance of the area. On the evening of the 1st he still had no knowledge of the strength of the Japanese, but he had concluded that he would be more likely to encounter the enemy in the jungle than along the river beds. The arrival of Japanese reinforcements apparently led to no change in plans formed the previous night, and on the morning of the 2d he launched an attack with three Scout battalions abreast. On

the north, its right flank resting on the dry bed of the Silaiim River, was the 2d Battalion, 45th Infantry, now led by its commander, Lt. Col. Ross B. Smith. To its south (left) was the 3d Battalion, 57th, and next to it the 1st Battalion (less Company B, at Quinauan) of the same regiment. The mission of the northernmost battalion was to seize the mouth of the river and the north side of Silaiim Point. The center unit, between the two rivers, would take the point itself while the 1st Battalion on the south was directed to take Anyasan Point. Guarding the north flank of the advance was the 1st Battalion, 12th Infantry, assigned to beach defense above Silaiim River. The 17th Pursuit Squadron remained astride the trail to the West Road to secure the line of communication. In reserve was the 2d Battalion of Colonel Lilly's 57th Infantry, recently arrived from Longoskawayan Point, and the Constabulary battalion.

The attack jumped off at daybreak, as the first rays of light filtered through the leafy branches of the high hardwood trees. Advancing cautiously through the luxuriant undergrowth, the two right (northern) battalions met resistance almost immediately. The southernmost battalion, however, met no opposition that day or during the four days that followed. But its progress was slow for the ground before it was exceedingly rough and difficult. The battalions to the north, after small gains, concluded that the force opposing them was a strong one and spent the rest of the day developing the hostile position.

On the 3d tanks joined in the action. In answer to a request of the day before, Company C, 192d Tank Battalion (less one platoon at Quinauan), consisting of nine tanks, had been sent forward from sector headquarters. Colonel Lilly placed them between

---

Journal (July–August 1947), p. 17; Ind, *Bataan, The Judgment Seat,* pp. 278–79; USA *vs.* Homma, p. 3061, testimony of Homma; *14th Army* Opns, I, 102–08, II, Maps 2 and 3; rpt, Comdr, Motor Torpedo Boat Div Nine, to Comdt, 16th Naval Dist, 3 Feb 42, sub: Attack of PT 32 on Enemy Cruiser, Off of Naval Rcds; White, *They Were Expendable,* pp. 77–82; Comments of Former Japanese Officers Regarding The Fall of the Philippines, p. 60, OCMH.

[79] *14th Army* Opns, I, 108.

the two rivers, the only area even remotely suitable for tank operations. Restricted to the narrow trail and hampered by heavy jungle, the tanks were forced to advance in column and were utilized essentially as moving pillboxes.

At the outset tank-infantry co-ordination was poor, the foot soldiers having been directed to remain 100 to 150 yards behind the tanks. With their limited fields of fire and in column formation, the tanks were particularly vulnerable to enemy mine and grenade attack. It is not surprising, therefore, that on the first day the armor was used the results obtained were disappointing. In at least one case the result was tragic. The enemy, unimpeded by the Scouts who were well behind the tanks, disabled one of the tanks, set it on fire, then filled it with dirt. The crew never had a chance and was first cremated, then buried.[80] After this experience the riflemen were instructed to work closely with the armor and four infantrymen were assigned to follow each tank. When the Japanese dropped down into their foxholes now to allow the tanks to pass, the foot soldiers picked them off before they could get back on their feet.

The greatest threat to the tanks came from enemy mines. The Japanese would dash from cover, fix a magnetic mine against the front of the tank and scurry for the trees. Or they would attach a mine to a string and drag it across the trail in front of an advancing tank. Had not the infantry provided close support, the tanks would not have lasted long in the Anyasan–Silaiim fight.

The employment of artillery also presented a difficult problem, as Colonel Lilly quickly discovered. The ground sloped up from the beach and there were no com-

manding heights along which to emplace the guns so that they could support the first-line troops. Tree bursts from the 75-mm. shells represented a real danger to friendly troops. The one battery of 155-mm. howitzers that was available had no fire direction equipment of any kind and could not be used for infantry support. In the absence of artillery forward observers, infantry rifle company commanders observed fire in front of their own lines and sent corrections to the artillery command post which had established communications directly with the assault companies.

The 2d Battalion, 88th Field Artillery (PS), which was assigned the task of providing support for all the troops in Pierce's South Sector, had to emplace its two four-gun batteries in pairs. To co-ordinate its fire the battalion had to lay thirty-eight miles of wire, in addition to utilizing the infantry communications net. The problem of firing from an altitude of 800 feet, through trees averaging 60 to 80 feet in height, at an enemy on an elevation of 100 feet or less and at a distance of about 4,000 yards, without hitting friendly front-line troops was a difficult one, and one that was never entirely solved. In the fight for Quinauan and Anyasan–Silaiim, the artillery battalion expended about 5,000 rounds, without appreciably affecting the course of the action.[81]

Machine guns, though available, were not employed widely in the fight for Anyasan and Silaiim Points, first, because the undergrowth limited the field of fire, and second, because of the difficulty of ammunition resupply. There was no way of bringing up ammunition except by hand and it was hard enough to keep the riflemen supplied. Machine gunners, therefore, were employed as

---

[80] Prov Tank Gp Rpt of Opns, pp. 21–22.

[81] Ltr, Howard to TAG, sub: 2d Bn, 88th FA (PS), p. 5.

ammunition carriers for the riflemen. Their use thus, observed Major Johnson, "outweighed the advantages of their supporting fire." [82]

Although the Scout units had both 60- and 81-mm. mortars, they had little or no ammunition for these weapons. They did use the 3-inch Stokes mortar ammunition in the 81-mm. weapon, but, in addition to the limitations imposed by the terrain, the efficiency of this weapon was severely curtailed by the abnormally high percentage of duds. To the end, the fight for Anyasan and Silaiim Points remained primarily a rifleman's fight.

While infantry-tank and infantry-artillery co-ordination were worked out during the 3d and 4th of February, the advance of the two right battalions—the 2d Battalion, 45th Infantry, and the 3d Battalion, 57th Infantry—proceeded slowly. Until the southern battalion fought its way through the jungle and established contact with the enemy on Anyasan Point, thus securing the left flank, the rest of the line had to proceed cautiously. Finally, on the 7th, this battalion reached the Japanese positions, but was roughly repulsed. American Air Corps troops and the Constabulary battalion were then sent in to join the fight. The Constabulary was placed on the right (north) of the 1st Battalion, 57th, with orders to maintain contact with the 3d Battalion to the north. The Air Corps troops went in on the left and established contact with the Scouts on Quinauan Point, thus completing a continuous line from the northern edge of Silaiim Bay to the southern extremity of Quinauan Point, a distance of about 4,000 yards.

The troops all along the front now began to advance more rapidly. Progress was facilitated when, on the 8th, a platoon of

37-mm. guns was released from Quinauan, where the fight ended that day. The guns were emplaced on a promontory overlooking Anyasan Point from where they would take the Japanese supply dumps under fire. The end of resistance at Quinauan also made possible the return of Company B, 57th Infantry, to the heavily engaged 1st Battalion on Anyasan Point. [83]

By this time the debilitating effects of the half ration instituted a month earlier were becoming apparent. Some of the men grew listless and less eager to fight. Each day it became more difficult to push the front-line troops into aggressive action, and after the first five days it became necessary to rotate the assault battalions. Even the procurement of additional rations by the 57th Infantry, a Scout unit of high *esprit de corps,* did not improve matters much.

The necessity of feeding the troops during the daylight hours imposed further restrictions on combat efficiency by shortening the fighting day. The two meals were served shortly after daybreak and just before dark so that the action was usually broken off in time to set up defensive positions against night attacks and eat the last meal of the day. Even when operations were proceeding favorably, it was necessary to follow this procedure for, with the meager ration, it was essential that every man get his full share to maintain his efficiency in combat.

Fortunately, even with the half ration, the morale of the Scouts did not deteriorate. They understood, as many did not, that they were receiving all the food that a determined commander could get for them, and there was little looting or stealing from the kitchens. But the effect of the ration on the performance of troops in combat was

[82] Johnson, Anyasan and Silaiim Points, p. 11.

[83] Bell, Opns Rpt, 8–9 Feb 42, AG 370.2 (19 Dec 41) Phil Rcds.

undeniable. "A prolonged period of reduced rations," concluded Major Johnson, "destroys the will to fight almost entirely, and . . . may even destroy the will to survive." [84]

On 9 February, the 3d Battalion, 57th Infantry, in the center of the line, was replaced by the rested and refreshed 2d Battalion, with the result that the attack that day was pushed more aggressively. One enemy strongpoint which had held up the 3d Battalion was taken during the afternoon, but the Japanese counterattacked that night to recapture the position. The following day, 10 February, the 2d Battalion resumed its march, retook the strongpoint, and then continued to move forward steadily. By evening of the next day it had reached the mouth of the Anyasan River, squeezing out the Japanese and forcing them on to Silaiim Point, between the two rivers, and in front of the 45th Infantry Scouts who were advancing more slowly. The situation of Major Kimura's remaining troops was desperate and their defeat a certainty.

As early as the 7th the Japanese had apparently realized that their forces on the west coast beachheads were doomed. From Major Kimura, commander of the troops at Silaiim, General Morioka received word that a "bitter battle" was in progress and that the enemy was attacking with tanks and artillery. "The battalion," wrote Kimura, "is about to die gloriously." [85] General Morioka responded to this message by ordering the *21st Engineer Regiment* to rescue the trapped men. On the night of the

7th the engineers, in thirty boats of varying sizes, left Olongapo for the beachheads. As they came in to shore to search for their stranded fellows they were met by artillery and machine-gun fire, as well as bombs from two P–40's. In the face of this strong opposition they returned empty-handed to Olongapo. The next night they tried again and this time succeeded in evacuating thirty-four of their wounded comrades. This was their last trip. [86]

Unable to evacuate his men, Morioka finally decided to relieve them from their assignment so that they could make a last desperate effort to save themselves. In orders sealed in bamboo tubes and dropped from the air, he instructed Major Kimura to bring his decimated battalion out by sea, on rafts or floats, and get them to Moron. If no other means were available the men would have to swim. Included in the orders was detailed information on tides, currents, the time of the rising and setting of the sun and moon, and directions for the construction of rafts. Unhappily for Kimura, copies of the orders fell into American hands, were quickly translated, and circulated to the troops on the front line. Thus alerted, riflemen along the beaches north of Silaiim got valuable target practice firing at Japanese swimmers and machine gunners were on the watch for rafts and floats. Only a few of the enemy were able to escape by sea. Most of those who were not shot or captured probably drowned. [87]

But before his final annihilation Major Kimura made one last effort to break out of

---

[84] Johnson, Anyasan and Silaiim Points, p. 12.

[85] Tactical Situation Rpt, *14th Army,* ATIS Doc 56113, 3 Mar 50, p. 4, in Translation of Japanese Documents, GHQ FEC, Mil Intel Sec, 2 vols., II, No. 15.

[86] *14th Army* Opns, I, 102, 108; Bell, Opns Rpt, 8–9 Feb 42. The Japanese reported a PT attack but American records contain no mention of such an attack.

[87] Ltr, Col Wood to author, 23 Mar 48, OCMH.

the cordon which held him tight on Silaiim Point. At dawn, 12 February, with about two hundred men, he launched a counterattack against the 2d Battalion, 45th Infantry. A gap about 100 yards wide had opened in that battalion's line, between Companies E and F, on the 9th, but this fact had never been reported to Colonel Lilly. An effort had been made to close it but when the Japanese counterattacked it was covered only by patrol. Driving in through the two companies, the Japanese met only scattered resistance in their pell-mell rush to escape. The weight of the attack was met by a machine gun section which fought heroically but unavailingly to stop the Japanese. One gun crew made good its escape after all its ammunition was gone, but the other, except for one man who had left to get more ammunition, was killed. The two gun crews together accounted for thirty Japanese.

Once they broke through the line the Japanese turned north toward the Silaiim River. At the mouth of the river were the command posts of the 17th Pursuit, which was patrolling the beach along Silaiim Bay, and of Company F, 45th Infantry. The Japanese attacked both command posts, wounding Capt. Raymond Sloan, commander of the 17th Pursuit, who died later.[88]

A hurried call for aid was sent to Colonel Lilly, and at about 1000, just as the 2d Battalion, 45th Infantry, command post came under heavy machine gun fire, the 3d Battalion, 57th Infantry, reached the threatened area. Two of its companies formed a skirmish line to fill in the gap left

by the routed 17th Pursuit and finally tied in with the north company of the 2d Battalion, 45th Infantry. About noon the Scouts attacked the Japanese and during the afternoon advanced steadily against stiff but disorganized resistance. The next morning the attack was resumed and by 1500 all units reached the beach, now littered with the equipment and clothing of those Japanese who had taken to the water to escape. The only enemy left were dead ones, and the beach was befouled with bloated and rotting bodies.

Few of the Japanese had been taken prisoner. As at Longoskawayan and Quinauan they showed a reluctance to surrender though their cause was hopeless. MacArthur's headquarters, in its first effort to use psychological warfare, made available a sound truck and two nisei and urged Colonel Lilly to broadcast appeals to the Japanese to give themselves up. But the higher headquarters failed to provide a script for the nisei and placed on the regiment responsibility for the truck and the interpreters.

To the regiment's reluctance to accept this responsibility was added its disinclination to take prisoners. The Scouts had found the bodies of their comrades behind Japanese lines so mutilated as to discourage any generous impulse toward those Japanese unfortunate enough to fall into their hands. Some of the bodies had been bayoneted in the back while the men had had their arms wired behind them. One rotting body had been found strung up by the thumbs with the toes just touching the ground, mute evidence of a slow and tortured end. Nor did the Japanese show any signs of gratitude when their lives were

---

[88] Crosby, 17th Pursuit Sq, p. 48–49, Chunn Notebooks.

spared. When one of them was brought to a battalion headquarters he had promptly attempted to destroy both himself and the headquarters with a hand grenade. It is not surprising, therefore, that "a passive resistance to the use of the sound truck developed and there were sufficient delays so that it was not used." [89]

About eighty of the enemy had made good their escape from the beachhead during the counterattack of the 12th. Hiding out in the daytime and traveling only at night, they made their way northward by easy stages. Four days later they were discovered about seven miles from Silaiim Point and only one mile from the I Corps main line of resistance. Their undetected four-day march through the congested area behind I Corps can be attributed to the wildness of the country and to their skill in jungle warfare. Only the defensive barbed wire and cleared fields of fire along the front had prevented them from reaching their own lines. A squadron of the 26th Cavalry was sent from corps reserve on the 16th to root them out. It took two days and the help of troops from the 72d and 92d Infantry to do the job. [90]

The three-week-long struggle to destroy the Japanese who had landed by accident at Anyasan and Silaiim Points was over. The cost on the American side was about 70 killed and 100 wounded. The 2d Battalion, 45th Infantry, which had been in action continuously since 29 January and had borne the brunt of the final counterattack, lost 68 men: 26 killed and 42 wounded. The 57th Infantry's 2d Battalion suffered fewer casualties; the remaining units even less. [91]

As at Longoskawayan and Quinauan Points the Americans and Filipinos had wiped out an entire enemy battalion, about 900 men. A large percentage of these had been lost on the night of 1 February when they had tried to reinforce their fellows at Quinauan; almost 400 had been killed on the beachhead, 80 had been caught by the 26th Cavalry, and an undetermined number had been drowned at sea trying to escape. Only 34 Japanese had been evacuated. [92]

Since 23 January, when General Kimura had launched his amphibious attack to cut the West Road and take I Corps from the rear, the *20th Infantry* had lost two infantry battalions. Committed piecemeal, inadequately prepared, attacked during the approach and disorganized before the landing, the Japanese who finally came ashore had presented a real threat to the American positions on Bataan. Had it not been for the prompt action of all units involved, the Japanese, weak as they were, might well have succeeded in their design. Fortunately, they were contained at each threatened point, and by the time the beachheads had been consolidated USAFFE had concentrated enough troops to hold them in place, and finally to destroy them. By the middle of February the danger along the west coast was over.

[89] Johnson, Anyasan and Silaiim Points, p. 14.

[90] Maj James C. Blanning, CO 2d Sq, 26th Cavalry (PS), War Diary, pp. 11–18, OCMH; Chandler, "26th Cavalry (PS) Battles to Glory," Part 3, *Armored Cavalry Journal* (July–August 1947), pp. 18–19.

[91] For estimated casualties in each unit see the reports cited for each unit above. The totals given are estimates reached by the author.

[92] It is extremely difficult to establish the exact number of Japanese in the *1st Battalion, 20th Infantry,* or to account precisely for their fate. Various estimates are given in all the sources cited. The author has estimated the strength on the basis of all known factors plus the fact that the battalion had seen little action and had suffered few casualties.

CHAPTER XVIII

Trail 2 and the Pockets

During the three weeks that the Battle of the Points raged along the west coast, another hard-fought battle was being waged along the front lines. No sooner had the troops completed their withdrawal from the Abucay–Mauban line to the reserve battle position then the Japanese struck again. In II Corps the Japanese blow came in the center where, in the confusion which accompanied the establishment of the new line, there was a dangerous gap during the critical hours before the attack. Fortunately it was closed before the Japanese could take advantage of the opening. I Corps, where a similar gap developed, was not so fortunate. Here the Japanese poured through the hole before it could be plugged and set up strong pockets of resistance behind the line. For the next three weeks, simultaneously with the Battle of the Points and the fight in II Corps, Wainwright's troops were engaged in a bitter struggle to contain and reduce these pockets. Thus, in the period from 23 January to 17 February, the American positions on Bataan were under strong attack in three places: along the west coast beaches and at two points along the reserve battle line, now the main line of resistance, in I and II Corps.

The Orion–Bagac Line

By the morning of 26 January most of the American and Filipino troops were in place along the reserve battle position, their final defense line on Bataan. The new line extended from Orion westward to Bagac, following a course generally parallel to and immediately south of the Pilar–Bagac road which it crossed in the center. (*Map 18*) Having left behind Mt. Natib, "that infernal mountain which separated our corps," the troops were able now for the first time to form a continuous line across Bataan and to establish physical contact between the two corps.[1] They were also able to tighten the defenses along the front and at the beaches, for the withdrawal had reduced the area in American hands by almost 50 percent.

The area into which the 90,000 men on Bataan were now compressed covered about 200 square miles. On the north, in the saddle between Mt. Natib and the Mariveles Mountains was the Pilar–Bagac road which extended across the peninsula like a waist belt. To the east, west, and south was the sea. As Mt. Natib had dominated the Abucay–Mauban line, so did the imposing mass of the Mariveles Mountains dominate southern Bataan. Except for the narrow coastal strip along Manila Bay, the entire region was rugged and mountainous, covered with forest and thick undergrowth. The temperature averaged about 95 degrees. Even in the shaded gloom of the jungle the heat during midday was intense. Any physical exertion left a man bathed in perspiration and parched from thirst. As it was the dry season there were no rainstorms to afford any relief. "The heat," complained

---

[1] Wainwright, *General Wainwright's Story*, p. 52.

General Nara, "was extreme and the men experienced great difficulty in movement." [2] When the sun set the temperature dropped sharply and those who had sweltered in the tropical heat during the day shivered with cold under their army blankets.

Forming the boundary between the two corps was the Pantingan River which flowed generally northward from the Mariveles peaks. On the east side of the river, in the II Corps area, was 1,920-foot-high Mt. Samat, four miles from the coast and a short distance south of the Pilar–Bagac road. Along its slopes and on its summit were high hardwood trees, luxuriant creepers, and thorny vines. Though movement through this jungled fastness was difficult, the heights of Mt. Samat afforded excellent observation of the entire battlefield below.

North of Mt. Samat, as far as the Pilar–Bagac road, the ground was similar to that on the slopes. Beyond, in the area held by the enemy, it was low and swampy. To the east of the mountain lay a plateau and along the coast were sugar-cane fields, thickets, and a plain. Flowing from the high ground in the center, through the coastal plain, were several large rivers and numerous small streams, many of them dry at this time of the year. But their steep, forested banks provided natural barriers to the advance of a military force.

Wainwright's I Corps was west of the Pantingan River. Here there were no plains or sugar-cane fields. The ground sloped sharply from the Mariveles Mountains al-

most to the sea, and the undergrowth was even more luxuriant and forbidding than on the east coast. Nowhere on Bataan was the terrain less suitable for military operations.

In moving to the new line, the Americans had relinquished control of the Pilar–Bagac road, the one lateral highway across Bataan. However, they had denied the enemy complete use of that valuable road by selecting commanding positions from which it could be brought under fire, and by extending the main line of resistance across the road in the center of the peninsula. A four-mile-long branch road, or cutoff, had been constructed from Orion to the Pilar–Bagac road, and the eastern portion of the II Corps line extended along this cutoff rather than along the road itself. To provide lateral communication behind the lines, the engineers were directed to link the east-west trails, a task that was completed by mid-February. The Americans still had possession of the southern portions of the East and West Roads and continued to use them as the main arteries for vehicular traffic. All other movement behind the line was by footpath and pack trail.

The organization of the new line differed in one important respect from that established for the Abucay–Mauban line. Because of the reduced size of units, the shortage of trained combat officers, and the difficulty of communications, the troops on the Orion–Bagac line were placed under sector commanders who reported directly to corps. Under this arrangement unit designations lost much of their validity and some divisions functioned only as headquarters for a sector. Thus, one sector might consist of three or more units, all under a division commander who retained only his division staff. This organization simplified control by

---

[2] 65th Brig Opns Rpt, Mt. Samat, ATIS Enemy Pub 289, p. 2. The description of the terrain and the line is based upon SLF and II Corps Rpt, pp. 38–42; Collier, Notebooks, III, 37–39; Bataan–Zambales, AGS, GHQ SWPA, Terrain Handbook 42; Skerry, Comments on Engineer Hist, No. 15; Trail Map, Bataan, 15 Feb 42, AG 400.41 (29 Dec 41) Phil Rcds.

corps also, for divisions and lesser units reported now to the sector commanders. There was, it is true, a natural tendency toward building up a large staff in the sectors, but this inclination was quickly discouraged by MacArthur's headquarters, which explained that the sector organization had been adopted "for the purpose of decreasing rather than increasing overhead." [3]

General Parker's II Corps line stretched from Orion on the east coast westward for about 15,000 yards. Initially the corps was organized into four sectors, lettered alphabetically from A through D. Sector A on the right (east), which comprised the beach north of Limay to Orion and 2,500 yards of the front line, was assigned to the Philippine Division's 31st Infantry (US) which was then moving into the line. To its left and continuing the line another 2,000 yards was Sector B, manned by the Provisional Air Corps Regiment. This unit was composed of about 1,400 airmen equipped as infantry and led by Col. Irvin E. Doane, an experienced infantry officer from the American 31st Infantry. Sector C was under the command of Brig. Gen. Clifford Bluemel and consisted of his 31st Division (PA), less elements, and the remnants of the 51st Division (PA), soon to be organized into a regimental combat team. Together, these units held a front of about 4,500 yards. The remaining 6,000 yards of the II Corps line in front of Mt. Samat and extending to the Pantingan River constituted Brig. Gen. Maxon S. Lough's Sector D. Lough, commander of the Philippine Division, had under him the 21st and 41st Divisions (PA) and the 57th Infantry (PS)—not yet in the

line—from his own division. Both Bluemel and Lough retained their division staffs for the sector headquarters. A final and fifth sector, E, was added on 26 January when General Francisco's beach defense troops were incorporated into II Corps and made a part of Parker's command. In reserve, Parker kept the 1st Battalion, 33d Infantry (PA), from Bluemel's 31st Division, and a regiment of Philippine Army combat engineers.

The emplacement of artillery in II Corps was made with a full realization of the advantages offered by the commanding heights of Mt. Samat. On and around the mountain, in support of General Lough's sector, were the sixteen 75-mm. guns and eight 2.95-inch pack howitzers of the 41st Field Artillery (PA). Along the high ground east of the mountain, in support of the other sectors, were the artillery components of the 21st, 31st, and 51st Divisions (PA), with an aggregate of forty 75-mm. guns, and two Scout battalions equipped with 75's and 2.95's. The Constabulary troops on beach defense, in addition to the support furnished by the 21st Field Artillery, were backed up by about a dozen naval guns. Corps artillery consisted of the 301st Field Artillery (PA) and the 86th Field Artillery Battalion (PS), whose 155-mm. guns (GPF) were emplaced in the vicinity of Limay.[4]

General Wainwright's I Corps line, organized into a Right and Left Sector, extended for 13,000 yards from the Pantingan

---

[3] Ltr, USAFFE to Corps Comdrs, etc., 3 Feb 42, sub: American Officers with Combat Troops Units, AG 210.31 (3 Feb 42) Phil Rcds; Emerson, Opns of II Phil Corps, p. 19.

[4] SLF and II Corps Rpt of Opns, pp. 41, 44; Bluemel, 31st Div (PA) Rpt of Opns, pp. 11–12; Collier, Notebooks, III, 39; Capt Robert N. Chapin, Hist of 33d Inf (PA), 3–9 Apr 42, p. 3, prepared at author's request, OCMH; Lt Sheldon H. Mendelson, Opns of Prov Air Corps Regt (paper prepared for Advanced Officers Course, 1946–47, The Infantry School); Quintard, 301st FA (PA), OCMH.

River westward to the South China Sea. Separating the two sectors was the north-south Trail 7. The Right Sector, with a front of about 5,000 yards to and including Trail 7, was held by the 11th Division (PA) and the attached 2d Philippine Constabulary (less one battalion). Brig. Gen. William E. Brougher commanded both the 11th Division and the Right Sector. Between Trail 7 and the sea was the Left Sector, commanded by Brig. Gen. Albert M. Jones, who had led the South Luzon Force into Bataan. The eastern portion of his sector was held by the 45th Infantry (PS); the western by Brig. Gen. Luther Stevens' 91st Division (PA). Like Parker, Wainwright was given responsibility for the beach defenses in his area and on the 26th he established a South Sector under General Pierce. For corps reserve, Wainwright had the 26th Cavalry (PS) which had helped cover the withdrawal from the Mauban line.

I Corps had considerably less artillery than the corps on the east. Corps artillery consisted of one Scout battalion, less a battery, equipped with 75-mm. guns. Jones had for his Left Sector the guns of the 91st Field Artillery and attached elements of the 71st which had lost most of its weapons at Mauban. Supporting the Right Sector was the artillery component of the 11th Division and one battery of Scouts. Only a few miscellaneous pieces had been assigned initially to beach defense but after the Japanese landings Pierce obtained additional guns and two 155-mm. howitzers.[5]

When it established the Abucay–Mauban line early in January, USAFFE had kept in reserve the Philippine Division (less the 57th Combat Team). During the course of the battle on that line both the 31st Infantry (US) and the 45th Infantry (PS) had been assigned to II Corps and committed to action. When the withdrawal order was prepared, Col. Constant L. Irwin, USAFFE G–3, had placed the Philippine Division regiments in reserve since, he explained, "these were the only units that we had upon which we could depend and which were capable of maneuver, especially under fire."[6] This provision of the withdrawal plan was immediately changed by General Sutherland who believed that the corps commanders "needed all available help in order to successfully occupy the new line and at the same time hold the attackers."[7] Both corps commanders therefore assigned their Philippine Division units to critical points along the new line, and USAFFE approved this assignment. It made no provision, however, for a reserve of its own, on the assumption that "after the withdrawal was accomplished an Army Reserve could be formed."[8]

Sometime during the 25th of January USAFFE reversed its stand and decided that it would require a reserve after all. The unit selected was the Philippine Division with its one American and two Scout regiments. This action was based, apparently, on the danger arising from the Japanese landings at Longoskawayan and Quinauan Points. General Sutherland felt, Colonel Irwin later explained, that the three regiments might be needed to contain the Japanese at the beaches and push them back into the sea.[9] When the corps commanders

[5] Phil Div Rpt of Opns, p. 16; Jones, 51st Div (PA) Order of Events, p. 6; Col Stuart C. MacDonald, Notes on Left Subsector, I Phil Corps, p. 2, OCMH; ltr, Howard to TAG, 2d Bn, 88th FA (PS), p. 5.

[6] Ltr, Irwin to Ward, 13 Jun 51, OCMH.
[7] Ltr, Collier to author, 2 May 51, OCMH. See also ltr, Sutherland to author, 29 May 51, OCMH.
[8] Ltr, Sutherland to author, 29 May 51, OCMH.
[9] Ltr, Irwin to Ward, 13 Jun 51, OCMH.

received the orders to send the three regiments to an assembly area to the rear, they were thrown "into somewhat of a tailspin." [10] The new line was already being formed and the departure of the three regiments or their failure to take up their assigned positions would leave large gaps in the line. Corps plans, so carefully prepared, would have to be hastily changed and shifts accomplished within twenty-four hours. [11]

The shifting of units which followed USAFFE's order was as confusing as it was dangerous. In II Corps, where the 57th Infantry (PS) had been assigned the extreme left and the 31st Infantry (US) the right flank of the line, General Parker sought to fill the gaps by sending elements of General Bluemel's 31st Division (PA) to both ends of the line. The Philippine Army 31st Infantry (less 1st Battalion) was fortunately on the east coast in the vicinity of Orion, and it was ordered to take over Sector A in the place of the American 31st Infantry. The 33d Infantry (PA), assigned to Sector C but not yet in position, was sent to the left of the line being formed to replace the 57th Infantry. In the confusion no one remembered to inform General Bluemel of these changes, although the 31st and 33d Infantry were a part of his division and assigned to his sector.

In I Corps, where the 45th Infantry had been assigned to the important area between the Camilew River and Trail 7 in General Jones's Left Sector, Wainwright was forced to fill the gap with elements of the reduced and disorganized 1st Division (PA). Two hastily reorganized battalions of the 1st Infantry were ordered into the line on the 26th as a stopgap until the rest of the division

could be brought in, but it was not until the next day that the troops actually occupied their positions.

When these shifts were completed the line-up along the main battle position was as follows: In II Corps, from right to left: Sector A, 31st Infantry (PA); Sector B, Provisional Air Corps Regiment; Sector C, unsettled but temporarily held by the 32d Infantry, one battalion of the 31st, and the 51st Combat Team; Sector D, 21st and 41st Divisions (PA) and the 33d Infantry (less 1st Battalion). In I Corps: Right Sector, 2d Philippine Constabulary and 11th Division (PA); Left Sector, elements of the 1st Division (PA) and the 91st Division. The reserve of the two corps remained unchanged but was backed up now by the Philippine Division in USAFFE reserve. The American 31st Infantry was located just north of Limay on the east coast, from where it could support II Corps should the need arise. The 45th Infantry was in bivouac near the West Road, about three miles south of Bagac, in position to aid I Corps. The 57th Infantry was near Mariveles, ready for a quick move to either corps. [12]

Opposing the Filipino troops—the entire line, except for Sector B, was now held by the Philippine Army—were the same Japanese who had successfully breached the Abucay–Mauban line in the first battle of Bataan. On the east, before Parker's II Corps, was General Nara's *65th Brigade* and attached *9th Infantry;* facing Wainwright was the *Kimura Detachment.* While General Kimura's force of approximately 5,000 men was comparatively fresh, Nara's troops

[10] Collier, Notebooks, III, 38.
[11] Ltr, Collier to author, 2 May 51, OCMH.

[12] Collier, Notebooks, III, 39; Phil Div Rpt of Opns, p. 16; Col Thomas W. Doyle, CO 45th Inf (PS), copy of lecture delivered at Army War College, 30 Jul 42, p. 6, OCMH.

had been hard hit during the Abucay fight. By 25 January, with reinforcements, he had built up his two regiments, the *141st* and *142d,* to a strength of about 1,200 men each.[13]

Flushed with victory and anxious to end the campaign quickly, the Japanese hardly paused before attacking the Orion–Bagac line. Some time earlier they had found a map purportedly showing the American scheme of defense. On it, marked in red, were lines denoting the positions occupied by the American and Philippine troops. The main line of resistance was shown some miles south of its actual location, extending from Limay westward to the Mariveles Mountains. The positions from Orion westward, shown on the map and corresponding to the line actually occupied, were sketchy and the Japanese concluded that they were merely outposts. On the basis of this map General Homma made his plans. He would push his troops through the outpost line—actually the main line of resistance—and strike for Limay, where he conceived the main line to be and where he expected the main battle for Bataan would be fought.

At 1600, 26 January, General Homma issued his orders for the attack. The *65th Brigade* was to sweep the supposed outpost line into Manila Bay, then proceed south to the presumed main line of resistance. General Kimura was ordered to drive down the west coast as far as the Binuangan River, which Homma apparently believed to be an extension of the Limay line. No difficulty was expected until this line was reached. So confident was Homma that his estimate was correct and so anxious was he to strike before the Americans could establish strong positions near Limay that he decided against

waiting for the artillery to move into position to support the attack.[14]

Unfortunately for the Japanese their captured map was incorrect or they read it incorrectly. The first line they met was not the outpost at all but the main line of resistance. The Japanese did have the good fortune, however, to hit the line where it was weakest and at a time when the disorganization resulting from the withdrawal of the Philippine Division was greatest.

The Fight for Trail 2

It was General Bluemel's Sector C which bore the brunt of the *65th Brigade* attack against II Corps. For three quarters of its total length of 4,500 yards, the front line of this sector followed roughly the Orion cutoff to its intersection with the Pilar River and at that point straddled the north end of Trail 2 which led southward along the east slopes of Mt. Samat through the American lines. With the exception of the East Road this trail offered the easiest route of advance to the Japanese.

Bluemel had organized the defense of his sector on the assumption that he would have most of his 31st Division and what was left of the 51st to put into the line. Accordingly, he had assigned the right (east) portion of the line, from Sector B to Trail 2, to his own division; the left to the 1,500 men of the 51st Division. On each side of Trail 2, for a distance of about 600 yards, foxholes had been dug and wire had been strung.[15]

---

[13] *65th Brig* Opns Rpt, Mt. Samat, pp. 6, 34.

[14] USA *vs.* Homma, p. 3059, testimony of Homma; *14th Army* Opns Order, Series A, No. 212, 26 Jan 42, *65th Brig* Opns Rpt, Mt. Samat, p. 83; *14th Army* Opns, I, 100.
[15] Unless otherwise noted, the account which follows is based on Bluemel, 31st Div (PA) Rpt of Opns, pp. 11–17, and two of its appendixes: Col Loren A. Wetherby, Activities of 41st Inf (PA),

On the morning of 26 January General Bluemel set out to inspect his front lines. On the way he met the 1st Battalion, 31st Infantry, heading east away from its assigned positions. With understandable heat, and some profanity, he demanded an explanation from the battalion commander, who replied that he had received orders from his regimental commander to move the battalion to Sector A to join the rest of the regiment. This was apparently the first time the general learned that his 31st Infantry had another assignment. Bluemel peremptorily ordered the battalion commander back into line and told him to remain there until relieved by his, Bluemel's, orders.[16]

The general had another unpleasant surprise in store that morning. He had hardly resumed his tour of inspection when, at about 1000, he discovered that the 33d Infantry was not in its assigned place on the right of Trail 2 and that this vital area was entirely undefended. For four hours Bluemel sought to locate the missing regiment and finally, at 1400, learned that this regiment also had been taken from him and was now assigned to the left flank of the corps line instead of the 57th Infantry. There was nothing else for him to do then but spread his troops even thinner and he immediately ordered the 2d Battalion, 32d Infantry, and the sixty men of the headquarters battery

of the 31st Field Artillery, acting as infantry and armed only with Enfields, into the unoccupied area. It was not until 1730, however, that these units were able to complete their move. Thus, for a period of almost ten hours on the 26th, there had been no troops east of the important Trail 2. Only good fortune and the action of the tanks of the covering force averted disaster. Had General Nara pushed his men down the trail during these hours he might have accomplished his mission and reached Limay even more rapidly than the misinformed Army commander expected him to.

Bluemel's troubles were not yet over. Only thirty minutes after he had closed the gap left by the transfer of the 33d Infantry, he received orders at 1800 from General Parker to transfer the 1st Battalion, 31st Infantry (PA), which he had sent back into the line early that morning, to Sector A. Bluemel had no choice now but to allow the battalion to leave. Parker promised him the 41st Infantry (less 1st Battalion) from the adjoining sector, but that unit would not reach him until late the next day. In the meantime he would have to fill the new gap with one of his own units. He finally decided to use the reserve battalion of the already overextended 32d Infantry. Thus, on the night of 26 January, the entire 31st Division area was held by only the three battalions of the 32d Infantry and the artillery headquarters battery. In reserve was the 31st Engineer Battalion with 450 men whose armament consisted exclusively of rifles.

The shifts in the line had been completed none too soon, for by 1900 of the 26th advance patrols of the *65th Brigade* had penetrated down the Orion cutoff to Trail 2, almost to the main line of resistance.

General Nara received Homma's orders for the attack on the morning of the 27th,

---

1–9 Apr 42, pp. 1–4, and Col Adlai C. Young, Rcd of Events 51st Div (PA), 25 Jan–9 Apr 42, p. 1; ltr, Bluemel to Groce, 18 Feb 49, OCMH; Maj Brice J. Martin, Regtl Hist, 51st Inf (PA), p. 5; Cordero, *My Experiences During the War with Japan*, pp. 23–24; O'Day, 21st Div (PA), I, Part 2, p. 3 and II, 31; SLF and II Corps Rpt, pp. 39–44.
For Japanese plans and operations the following sources were used: *14th Army* Opns, I, 109–16; *65th Brig* Opns Rpt, Mt. Samat, pp. 7–15, 20, and the appendixes and supplements consisting of the orders issued by *14th Army* and *65th Brigade*.
[16] Interv, author with Bluemel, 14 Apr 48, OCMH.

too late to take advantage of the confusion in the American line. At that time the bulk of his force was concentrated in front of Sector C. Colonel Takechi's *9th Infantry,* the "encircling unit" of the Abucay fight, was in position to advance down Trail 2, and the *141st Infantry* was bivouacked about one mile to the east. Above Orion probing Parker's right flank was the *1st Battalion, 142d Infantry.* The remainder of the regiment was south of Pilar, along the Pilar–Bagac road. Too far to the rear to support the attack was the artillery.

At 1100, 27 January, Nara issued his own orders for the forthcoming attack. These were based on *14th Army's* erroneous assumption that the American positions in front of him constituted an outpost line and that the main objective was a line at Limay. Nara's plan was to make the main effort in the area held by Bluemel's men. The center of the attack was to be Capot, a small barrio near Trail 2 in front of the main line of resistance. Making the attack would be two regiments, the *9th* on the right (west) and the *141st* on the left. They were to advance as far as the Pandan River where they would make ready for the assault against the supposed main line of resistance near Limay. The advance of these two regiments would be supported by Col. Masataro Yoshizawa's *142d Infantry* (less *1st Battalion*) on the brigade right, which was to drive southeast across the slopes of Mt. Samat to the Pandan River. Having reached the river, Yoshizawa was to shift the direction of his attack and advance down the river in a northeasterly direction to take the defenders in the rear. The regiment's initial advance would bring it to the American main line of resistance at the junction of Sectors C and D.

The attack jumped off at 1500, 27 January, with a feint by Maj. Tadaji Tanabe's *1st Battalion, 142d Infantry,* down the East Road. Although the Japanese claimed to have met "fierce" fire from the Filipinos in this sector, the 31st Infantry (PA) was not even aware that an attack was being made. At 1600 the rest of Colonel Yoshizawa's regiment attacked in the area between Sectors C and D, where the 51st Combat Team and 21st Division were posted. Without any difficulty the regiment occupied the outpost line, but was stopped cold at the main line of resistance. (*Map 19*)

The main attack by the *9th* and *141st Infantry* against Capot began as darkness settled over the battlefield. With the exception of a single battalion of Takechi's *9th Infantry,* which managed to cross the Pilar River and entrench itself in a bamboo thicket about seventy-five yards north of the main line, this attack, like that of the *142d,* failed to achieve its objective. General Nara was forced to conclude after the returns were in that a stronger effort would be required to drive the enemy into Manila Bay. But he still believed that the line he had unsuccessfully attacked on the night of the 27th was an advanced position or outpost line.[17]

Meanwhile the 41st Infantry, promised to General Bluemel on the 26th, had begun to arrive in Sector C. Advance elements of the regiment reported in on the evening of the 27th and by the following morning, after a twenty-four-hour march over steep trails carrying its own arms, equipment, and rations, the regiment, less its 1st Battalion, was on the line. The 3d Battalion took over a front of about 1,200 yards east of Trail 2, relieving the 2d Battalion, 32d Infantry. Since it had no machine guns, it was reinforced by Company H of the 32d, and the

---

[17] *65th Brig* Opns Rpt, Mt. Samat, p. 10.

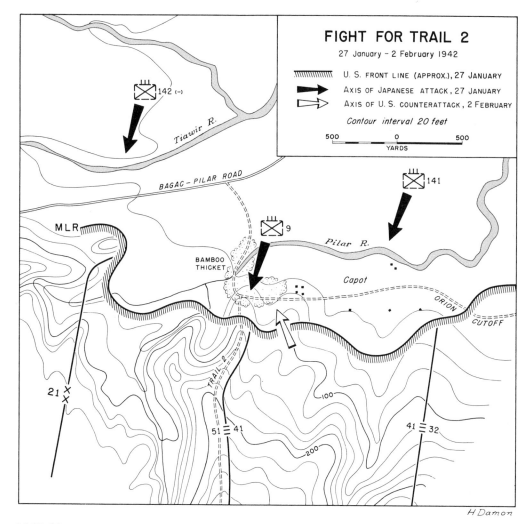

FIGHT FOR TRAIL 2

27 January – 2 February 1942

U. S. FRONT LINE (APPROX.), 27 JANUARY

AXIS OF JAPANESE ATTACK, 27 JANUARY

AXIS OF U. S. COUNTERATTACK, 2 FEBRUARY

Contour interval 20 feet

500   0   500

YARDS

H Damon

MAP 19

headquarters battery of the 31st Field Artillery (PA). One company of the 41st, Company F, was placed on Trail 2, well behind the main line of resistance, in position to support the troops on either side of the trail. The 2d Battalion (less Company F) went into regimental reserve.

When all units were in place, Bluemel's sector was organized from right to left (east to west), as follows: 32d Infantry (less Company H); 41st Infantry reinforced by Company H, 32d Infantry, and Headquarters Battery, 31st Field Artillery; and the remnants of the 51st Division. To the rear, on Trail 2, was Company F, 41st Infantry.

On the afternoon of the 28th General Nara ordered his troops to continue the attack. This time, however, he placed more emphasis on the northeast slopes of Mt. Samat where he conceived the enemy strongpoints to be, and requested support from the artillery. The *141st Infantry*, which was east of the *9th*, was directed to move west of that regiment, between it and the *142d*, thus shifting the weight of the attack westward. Tanabe's battalion remained on the East Road.

As before, the attack began at dusk. At 1830 of the 29th the *142d Infantry* on the brigade right waded the Tiawir River, in front of the 22d Infantry (Sector D), but was stopped there. The *141st*, which was to attack on the left (east) of the *142d*, failed to reach its new position until midnight, too late to participate in the action that night.

Colonel Takechi's *9th Infantry* was hardly more successful than the *142d* in its advance down Trail 2. Most of the regiment had crossed the Pilar River during the day to join the battalion in the bamboo thickets just in front of Bluemel's sector. From there the regiment had advanced by sapping operations as far as the wire entanglements on the front line. Thus, when Takechi's men moved out for the attack, after an hour-long preparation by the artillery, they were already at the main line of resistance.

The fight which followed was brisk and at close quarters. The 41st Infantry east of Trail 2, supported by machine gun fire from Company H, 32d Infantry, held its line against every onslaught, with Company K, on the trail, meeting the enemy at bayonet point. West of the trail, elements of the 51st Combat Team were hard hit and in danger of being routed. Fortunately, reinforcements arrived in time to bolster the extreme right of its line, closest to the trail, and the enemy was repulsed. Next morning when a count was made the Filipinos found about one hundred dead Japanese within 150 yards of the main line

of resistance. Some of the bodies were no more than a few yards from the foxholes occupied by the Filipinos, who suffered only light casualties. Again General Nara's attempt to pierce what he thought was an outpost line had failed.

Action during the two days that followed was confusing and indecisive. The Japanese, after nearly a month of continuous combat, were discouraged and battle weary. Losses, especially among the officers, had been high. "The front line units," complained General Nara, "notwithstanding repeated fierce attacks . . . still did not make progress. . . . Battle strength rapidly declined and the difficulties of officers and men became extreme." When "the greater part of the Brigade's fighting strength," the *9th Infantry*, was ordered by General Homma to join its parent unit, the *16th Division*, General Nara's situation became even more discouraging.[18] With commendable tenacity, however, he persisted in his efforts to break through the remarkably strong "outpost line," and on 31 January ordered his troops to attack again that night. This time he made provision for air and artillery support. The *9th Infantry*, scheduled to move out that night, Nara replaced by Major Tanabe's battalion.

At 1700, 31 January, the assault opened with an air attack against II Corps artillery below the Pandan River. An hour later the artillery preparation began, and "Bataan Peninsula," in General Nara's favorite phrase, "shook with the thunderous din of guns." The Japanese laid fire systematically on both sides of Trail 2 and down the trail as far back as the regimental reserve line. At about 1930 the barrage lifted and the infantry made ready to attack. At just this moment the artillery in Bluemel's sector

---

[18] *Ibid.*, pp. 12–13.

opened fire on the ford over the Pilar River and the area to the north in what the Japanese described as "a fierce bombardment." Simultaneously, according to the same source, "a tornado of machine gun fire" swept across the right portion of the Japanese infantry line assembling for the attack, effectively ending Japanese plans for an offensive that night. The careful preparation by aircraft and artillery had been wasted and the attack, mourned General Nara, "was frustrated." [19]

That night Colonel Takechi began to withdraw his *9th Infantry* from the bamboo thicket in front of the main line of resistance near Trail 2. Casualties in the regiment had been severe and the withdrawal was delayed while the wounded were evacuated. By daybreak, 1 February, only one of the battalions had been able to pull out of its position. The rest of the regiment, unable to move during the hours of daylight, remained concealed in the thicket until darkness. Then a second battalion began to pull back, completing the move that night. On the morning of the 2d, only one battalion of the *9th Infantry* remained in the thicket.

Meanwhile General Nara had been receiving disquieting reports of heavy troops movements behind the American line. His information was correct. General Bluemel was making preparations for a counterattack. His first effort on the 30th to drive the Japanese from the bamboo thicket had failed because the artillery had been unable to place its shells on the target. What he needed to hit the thicket was high-angle fire, but he had had no light mortars and the

ammunition of the 3-inch Stokes mortar had proved "so unreliable as to be practically worthless." [20] Since then General Parker had given Bluemel a battery of 2.95-inch mountain pack howitzers and ordered him to attack again. By the morning of the 2d he was ready. The 2.95's, 300 to 400 yards from the thicket, were in position to deliver direct fire and the 31st Engineer Battalion (PA), drawn from reserve to make the attack, was in readiness behind the main line of resistance.

At 0800 the counterattack opened. While the pack howitzers laid direct fire on the target, the 31st Engineer Battalion crossed the main line of resistance and headed toward the enemy concealed in the thicket. They were supported in their advance by rifle and machine gun fire from the front-line units near Trail 2. The engineers had not gone far before they encountered stiff resistance from the single battalion of the *9th Infantry* still in position. After a small gain the attack stalled altogether, and elements of the 41st Infantry were sent into the fight. The advance then continued slowly and by dusk the Filipinos, at a cost of twenty casualties, had reached the thicket. There they halted for the night.

Next morning, 3 February, when the engineers and infantry, expecting to fight hard for every yard, resumed the attack, they found their advance entirely unopposed. During the night the last of the *9th Infantry* had slipped out of the thicket and across the Pilar River. Bluemel's troops thereupon promptly moved the outpost line forward to a ditch about 150 yards below the Pilar–Bagac road. The danger of a break-through along Trail 2 was over.

General Nara's ill fortune was matched only by his persistence. Although he had

---

[19] *Ibid.,* p. 14, contains the quotations in this paragraph. Bluemel's account of the artillery fire by his guns is from his letter to Groce, 18 Feb 49, OCMH.

[20] Bluemel, 31st Div (PA) Rpt of Opns, p. 15.

been repulsed with very heavy casualties three times and had lost his strongest regiment, he was still determined to push the "outpost line" into the bay. During the next few days, while activities along the front were limited to patrol and harassing action by both sides, he reorganized his brigade, replenished his supplies, and sent out reconnaissance parties. By 8 February he was ready to resume the offensive and that afternoon told his unit commanders to stand by for orders. Before they could be issued, however, he received a telephone call from *14th Army* headquarters at San Fernando suspending the attack. Late that night, at 2330, he received another call from San Fernando canceling his plans altogether and directing him to withdraw the brigade to a position north of the Pilar–Bagac road and there await further instructions.

General Homma's orders were based only partially on Nara's inability to reach Limay. Everywhere on Bataan the Japanese offensive had stalled. The landings along the west coast had by this time proved disastrous and had resulted in the destruction of two infantry battalions Homma could ill afford to lose. But even more serious was the situation along the I Corps line in western Bataan where General Kimura had launched an offensive on 26 January.

The Pocket Fights

In western Bataan, as in the east, the Japanese had followed closely on the heels of MacArthur's retreating troops. General Homma's orders on 26 January had directed Kimura, as well as Nara, to push ahead rapidly without giving the enemy an opportunity to dig in. Nara, it will be recalled, had been ordered to drive toward Limay, where, according to the captured

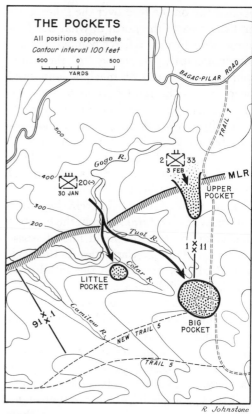

MAP 20

map, the new American line was located. Homma's orders to Kimura called for an advance as far as the Binuangan River, along which Homma believed Wainwright had established his main line as an extension of the Limay line to the east. (*Map 20*)

To make the attack General Kimura had the *122d Infantry* (less two companies) of the *65th Brigade* and Col. Yorimasa Yoshioka's *20th Infantry, 16th Division.* Actually, all Yoshioka had for the fight to follow was the regimental headquarters, service elements, and the *3d Battalion* (less one company)—altogether about 1,000 men. The rest of the regiment was already committed or stationed elsewhere.

Even before he issued orders for the attack, General Homma had made arrangements on 25 January to increase the size of the force arrayed against I Corps. Hoping to take advantage of Kimura's easy victory on the Mauban line, he had directed General Morioka in Manila to hasten to Olongapo and assume command of operations in western Bataan. Morioka, *16th Division* commander, was to take with him two battalions of infantry—one of which was the *1st Battalion, 20th Infantry,* later lost in the Battle of the Points—and the *21st Independent Engineer Regiment* headquarters. This move, Homma directed, was to be completed on 27 January. Thus, in the attack against I Corps that followed, command quickly passed from Kimura, who initiated the fight, to General Morioka.

Wainwright's main line of resistance, it will be recalled, was organized into two sectors, a Right Sector under General Brougher and a Left Sector commanded by General Jones. Brougher's line extended from the Pantingan River to Trail 7, which led southward from the Pilar–Bagac road through the American positions to join the intricate network of trails to the rear. Responsible for both the river and the trail on his flanks, Brougher placed the Constabulary on the right to guard the approach by way of the river and to tie in with the left flank of II Corps. Next to it was the 13th Infantry (PA) of the 11th Division and on the left of Brougher's sector, defending Trail 7, was the 11th Infantry led by Col. Glen R. Townsend.

Responsibility for the area west of Trail 7 rested with General Jones. On the left he placed General Stevens' 91st Division. The eastern portion of the sector, from the Cami-

lew River to but not including Trail 7, was initially assigned to the 45th Infantry (PS), but when that regiment was withdrawn on 26 January, on orders from USAFFE, Wainwright assigned the area to General Segundo's 1st Division (PA). Although two hastily organized battalions of the 1st Infantry and one of the 3d Infantry moved into the line vacated by the 45th, a gap still remained in the center. The next afternoon, 27 January, the 2d Battalion, 1st Infantry, was withdrawn from its position on beach defense near Bagac and sent in to fill the gap.[21]

Wainwright's new main line of resistance ran through a thick jungle where it was extremely difficult for units to establish physical contact. Flowing in every direction through this area was a confusing network of streams. The Gogo River flowed into the Bagac River to form one continuous stream along the Left Sector main line of resistance. South of this east-west water line were three tributaries of the Gogo—the Tuol, Cotar, and Camilew Rivers. Behind the line was an equally confusing network of trails, intersecting each other as well as the main trails running south from the Pilar–Bagac road. New Trail 5 paralleled the main line of resistance and connected the West Road with

---

[21] In addition to the sources cited below, this section is based on two reports by General Jones: The Pocket Fights, pp. 1–3, and Pocket Battles, pp. 1–4; Townsend, 11th Inf (PA), pp. 2–4, and Part II, The Tuol Pocket, pp. 6–16, copy in OCMH; MacDonald, Notes on Left Subsector, I Phil Corps, pp. 1–6; Berry, Hist of 3d Inf (PA), pp. 5–6; Lt Col Adrianus Van Oosten, Opns of 1st Bn, 45th Inf (PS) in Battle of Tuol Pocket (paper prepared for Advanced Officers Course, 1947–48, The Infantry School), pp. 8–18; Lt Col Leslie T. Lathrop, Notes on Tuol Pocket, copy in OCMH; Collier, Notebooks, III, 51–52; *14th Army* Opns, I, 100–102, 107–15; *65th Brig* Opns Rpt, Mt. Samat, Opns Orders in Supps. 23 and 27; intervs, author with Gens Jones and Berry at various times.

Trail 7. Below it and generally parallel to it was another trail, called Old Trail 5. So bewildering was the river and trail system, especially in the 1st Division area, that few of the troops knew precisely where they were at any given moment. It was in this area that the Japanese penetration came.

Establishment of the Pockets

The Japanese opened the offensive against I Corps on 26 January. Anxious to capitalize on his successful drive down the west coast, General Kimura sent his troops along the West Road against the 91st Division, on the extreme left of the line in the vicinity of Bagac. For two days, on the 26th and 27th, the Japanese sought to break through the new main line of resistance along the coast but the 91st held ground firmly. Repelled on the west, the Japanese, as they had done at Abucay, then began to probe the line in search of a soft spot. On the night of 28–29 January they found one in the 1st Division area.

The 1st Division had been badly disorganized and had lost much of its equipment in the first battle of Bataan and during the withdrawal along the beach. First sent to the rear for reorganization and a much needed rest, the division had then been hurriedly sent to the front on 26 and 27 January to replace the 45th Infantry. Since then the men had worked frantically to make ready for an attack. They dug trenches and cleared fields of fire but the work progressed slowly. Lacking entrenching tools and axes, many of the men had been forced to dig holes with their mess kits and clear the underbrush with their bayonets.

Before the men of the 1st Division could complete their preparations and while they were still stringing wire, they were hit by Colonel Yoshioka's *20th Infantry* troops. The 1,000 men of the *20th Infantry* first seized the high ground before the still unwired 1st Infantry sector. From this vantage point they pushed in the outpost line late on the 28th, drove back one company on the main line of resistance, and during the night moved rapidly through the gap up the valleys of the Cotar and Tuol Rivers, throwing out patrols as they advanced.

It is hard to imagine heavier, more nearly impenetrable or bewildering jungle than that in which Colonel Yoshioka's men found themselves. It is covered with tall, dense cane and bamboo. On hummocks and knolls are huge hardwood trees, sixty to seventy feet in height, from which trail luxuriant tropical vines and creepers. Visibility throughout the area is limited, often to ten or fifteen yards. There were no reliable maps for this region and none of the sketches then in existence or made later agreed. Major terrain features were so hazily identified that General Jones asserts that to this day no one knows which was the Tuol and which the Cotar River.[22]

Under such conditions it was virtually impossible for either side to maintain contact or to know exactly where they were. The Japanese moved freely, if blindly, in the rear of the 1st Division line, cutting wire communications and establishing strong points from which to harass the Filipinos. Segundo's men were almost as confused as the Japanese. They believed that only small enemy patrols had penetrated the line and sought blindly to find these patrols, sometimes mistaking friend for foe.

Before long, Colonel Yoshioka found his force split in two groups. One of these, less than a company, was discovered by 1st Divi-

---

[22] Interv, author with Jones.

sion patrols in a defensive position atop a hill just southeast of the junction of the Cotar and Gogo Rivers in the middle of the 1st Division area. This position, which became known as the Little Pocket, was about 400 yards below the main line of resistance and about 1,000 yards west of Trail 7.[23]

The bulk of Yoshioka's force continued to move east and soon was established along Trail 7 in the area held by Colonel Townsend's 11th Infantry. Its presence there was discovered on the morning of the 29th when the Provisional Battalion of the 51st Division led by Capt. Gordon R. Myers, moving north along Trail 7 to the aid of the 1st Division, met a Japanese force moving south. After a brief exchange of fire followed by a bayonet fight the Japanese broke off the action and withdrew. Not long after, 11th Infantry troops moving south from the front line along the same trail were fired on and killed. An American sergeant, sent forward from Colonel Townsend's 11th Infantry headquarters to investigate, met the same fate and his body was discovered about 200 yards north of the junction of Trails 5 and 7. It was clear now that an enemy force had established itself across the trail and the junction, nearly a mile behind the main line of resistance. From this position, which later came to be called the Big Pocket, the Japanese could block north-south traffic along Trail 7 and hinder the movement of troops westward along Trail 5.

There was as yet no indication of the size of the Japanese force in the pocket. Under the impression that only a strong patrol was blocking the trail, Colonel Townsend, on the afternoon of the 29th, ordered two reserve companies of the 11th Infantry to clear the area. The reaction of the Japanese to the attack quickly corrected Townsend's

impression and a hasty call was put in for additional troops. USAFFE made available to corps the 1st Battalion of the 45th Infantry (PS) and by 2000 that night advance elements of the Scout battalion had reached the trail junction, ready to join in the fight the next day.

Attacks against the Big Pocket during the next few days by the Scouts on the South and the 11th Infantry troops on the north made little progress and only confirmed the fact that the enemy was strong and well entrenched. Yoshioka's troops had by now dug their foxholes and trenches and connected them with tunnels so that they could move freely without fear of observation. They had skillfully emplaced their machine guns behind fallen trees and had taken every advantage of the jungle to strengthen and conceal their defenses. They had even taken the precaution to dispose of the earth from the foxhole so as to leave no telltale signs of their position.

Artillery availed the Americans as little here as it had in the Battle of the Points. Poor visibility, inadequate maps, and the lack of high trajectory weapons resulted in shorts, overs, and tree bursts, some of which caused casualties among friendly troops. So dense was the jungle that one 75-mm. gun, originally emplaced to provide antitank defense at the trail junction, was unable to achieve any observable results though it poured direct fire on the enemy at a range of 200 yards. The value of the mortars was limited by the high percentage of duds as well as the thick jungle. Again, as on the beaches, the fight was to be a rifleman's fight backed up by BAR's and machine guns whenever they could be used.

The location of the Big Pocket created difficulties of an administrative nature. Although the pocket blocked the trail in the

[23] Santos, 1st Regular Div (PA), pp. 39–40.

11th Infantry area, on the internal flank of Brougher's Right Sector, it extended over into Jones's Left Sector, where the 1st Division was having difficulties of its own with the Japanese in the Little Pocket. Moreover, the pockets were not entirely surrounded and Yoshioka's men moved at will from one to the other. Just where the Big Pocket ended and the Little Pocket began was not yet clear and the 1st Division was as much engaged against the former as was the 11th Infantry. To clarify this situation, General Wainwright, who was present almost daily at the scene of the fighting, placed General Brougher, Right Sector commander, in charge of all troops operating against the Big Pocket. Colonel Townsend was given command of the forces immediately engaged.

The position of the Japanese in the two pockets was not an enviable one. Since 31 January, when 1st Division troops had shut the gate behind them, Colonel Yoshioka's men had been cut off from their source of supply. Though they had successfully resisted every effort thus far to drive them out, and had even expanded the original Big Pocket westward, their plight was serious. Without food and ammunition they were doomed. General Morioka attempted to drop supplies to them, but, as had happened during the Battle of the Points, most of the parachute packs fell into the hands of the Filipinos and Americans, who were grateful for the unexpected addition to their slim rations.

Only one course remained to Morioka if he was to save the remnants of Yoshioka's regiment. He must break through the main line of resistance again and open the way for a retreat—or further advance. All efforts by the *122d Infantry,* which had been pushing against the 1st and 11th Divisions since the start of the attack, had thus far

proved unavailing. But by 6 February Morioka had received reinforcements. One of the two battalions he had brought with him from Manila, the *2d Battalion* of his own division's *33d Infantry,* was now in position before the I Corps line, and the remnants of Colonel Takechi's *9th Infantry* (less *3d Battalion*) had reached western Bataan, after its fight on the east with Nara's brigade, to join its parent unit, the *16th Division,* for the first time in the campaign.

With these forces Morioka launched a determined effort to relieve and reinforce the men in the pockets. The *2d Battalion, 33d Infantry,* he sent down Trail 7. The *122d Infantry* he strengthened by attaching two battalions of the *9th Infantry* so that it could increase its pressure against the two Philippine divisions in the center of the line. The attack began late on the 6th, and shortly after midnight those Japanese advancing down Trail 7 overran a platoon of Company F, 11th Infantry, which was holding the critical sector across the trail. Eighteen of the twenty-nine men in the platoon were killed in their foxholes. For the moment it seemed as though the Japanese would be able to advance unhindered down Trail 7 to take the Filipinos on the north side of the Big Pocket in the rear. Only the quick action of Maj. Helmert J. Duisterhof, commanding the 2d Battalion, 11th Infantry, prevented this catastrophe. Organizing a containing force from the men in headquarters and from stragglers, he kept the Japanese to a gain of 600 yards, 800 short of the Big Pocket. The troops on each side of the penetration held firm so that what had promised to be another break-through became a fingerlike salient, referred to as the Upper Pocket.

Morioka had failed to reach Yoshioka but

he had broken the main line of resistance at still another point and attained a position which posed a real threat to the security of Wainwright's I Corps. The formation of the pockets—one of them actually a salient, for the main line of resistance was not restored—was now complete.

Reduction of the Pockets

While Morioka had been making preparations for the attack which gained for him the Upper Pocket, Wainwright had been laying his own plans to reduce the pockets. Thus far all attacks against them had failed. Though General Segundo had sent in all the troops he could spare to destroy the Little Pocket in the middle of the 1st Division area, he had been unable to wipe out the small force of Japanese entrenched there. Against the larger force in the Big Pocket Brougher had pressed more vigorously but with as little success. On the north and northeast he had placed two companies, G and C, of the 11th Infantry; on the south the 1st Battalion, 45th Infantry. Guarding Trail 5, south and west of the pocket, was the Provisional Battalion, 51st Division, which had made the initial contact with Yoshioka's men on Trail 7.

On 2 February Brougher had tried to reduce the pocket with tanks. After a reconnaissance had revealed that the jungle would not permit an unsupported armored attack, a co-ordinated infantry-tank attack was made with a platoon of four tanks from Company A, 192d Tank Battalion, closely supported by a platoon from the 1st Battalion, 45th Infantry. The armored platoon ran the enemy gantlet along Trail 7 and emerged on the north side of the pocket after losing one tank. The infantry, however, made only slight gains. An attack the

next day brought similar results and the loss of another tank.

It was during that day's action that Lt. Willibald C. Bianchi won the Medal of Honor. Though assigned to another unit he had volunteered to accompany the supporting platoon sent out to destroy two machine gun positions. Leading part of the platoon forward he was wounded in the left hand. Refusing to halt for first aid he continued on, firing with his pistol. One of the enemy machine guns he knocked out with grenades. Meanwhile the tank, unable to lower the muzzle of its 37-mm. gun sufficiently, had been having difficulty reducing the other machine gun near by. Bianchi, who now had two more bullets in his chest, clambered to the top of the tank and fired its antiaircraft gun into the enemy position until the impact of a third bullet fired at close range knocked him off the tank. He was evacuated successfully and after a month in the hospital was back with his unit.[24]

By 4 February three of the four tanks of the Company A platoon had been destroyed and it was necessary to assign to Brougher's force another platoon from Company B of the 192d Tank Battalion. The attack was continued that day with as little success as before, and on the night of the 4th the Japanese were still in firm possession of the pockets. It was evident that a co-ordinated and stronger offensive than any yet made would be required for victory and General Wainwright called a meeting of the major commanders concerned to discuss plans for such an offensive.

The conference opened at about 1000 of the 5th at the command post of the 1st Divi-

---

[24] Lt Arthur A. Holland, 192d Bn, pp. 44–45, Chunn Notebooks; Prov Tank Gp Rpt of Opns, p. 22; Van Oosten, Opns of 1st Bn, 45th Inf (PS) in Battle of Tuol Pocket, p. 2.

sion. Present were Generals Jones, Brougher, and Segundo, Col. William F. Maher, Wainright's chief of staff, and Col. Stuart C. MacDonald, Jones's chief of staff. First Wainwright made the point that though the pockets overlapped sector boundaries the forces engaged would have to be placed under one commander and be treated as a single operation. All available forces, including the reserves, he asserted, would have to be thrown into the fight. Brougher was to be relieved and Jones would take command of all troops already engaged against the pockets. This decision gave the new commander the following force: 1st Battalion, 45th Infantry; the Provisional Battalion, 51st Division; Companies C and G, 11th Infantry; the 1st and 2d Battalions, 92d Infantry; the 1st Division; and the remaining tanks.

General Jones had a plan ready. First he would isolate the pockets and then throw a cordon of troops around each. The main attack against the Little Pocket would follow, and after it had been reduced he would throw all his troops against the Big Pocket. The entire operation would be a co-ordinated one with the main attacks against each pocket delivered along a single axis of advance. Wainwright approved the plan and directed that it be put into effect not later than 7 February.

Jones immediately made preparations for the reduction of the two pockets. All 1st Division troops who could be released from their posts along the main line of resistance were given to Colonel Berry, commander of the 1st Infantry, who was directed to make his own plans to take the Little Pocket. Lt. Col. Leslie T. Lathrop, commander of the 1st Battalion, 45th Infantry, was given tactical command of the troops for the assault against the Big Pocket. Jones himself worked

out the plan for that attack. The main effort was to be made by the 1st Battalion, 92d Infantry, from the west. To its south would be the Provisional Battalion, 51st Division; to its north Company G, 11th Infantry. Company C, 11th Infantry, and the 1st Battalion, 45th Infantry, were to remain northeast and east of the pocket to prevent a breakout in that direction. The offensive against the two pockets would begin at 0900, 7 February.

The night before the attack Morioka opened his own offensive which by morning of the 7th had resulted in the salient called the Upper Pocket. Brougher, fearing a Japanese break-through at the salient, took from the forces Jones had gathered for the attack Company A, 92d Infantry, the reserve company of the battalion which was to make the main effort against the Big Pocket, and the tank platoon. At 0730, when Jones learned of the unauthorized transfer of his troops, he was forced to delay the hour of the attack against the Big Pocket to bring in more troops. It was not until 1500 that the replacement, Maj. Judson B. Crow's 2d Battalion, 92d Infantry, arrived.[25]

The attack against the Big Pocket began as soon as Major Crow's battalion was in place. By that time only a few hours of daylight remained and few gains were made. Moreover it was discovered late in the day that the 92d Infantry troops on the west had failed to establish contact with Company G, 11th Infantry, to its left (north) and that the pocket was not surrounded. Next morning the cordon around the Big Pocket was completed when these units tied in their flanks. Jones now waited

---

[25] Maj Beverly N. Skardon, Opns of Co A, 92d Inf (PA), paper prepared for Advanced Officers Course, 1946–47, The Infantry School, p. 10.

for the completion of the action against the Little Pocket before beginning his final assault against Yoshioka's men on Trail 7.

The attack against the Little Pocket had begun on schedule at 0900 of the 7th. Colonel Berry organized his 1st Division troops so that they approached the pocket from all sides, and then began to draw the noose tight. Evening of the first day found the Little Pocket only partially surrounded and it was not until nightfall of the 8th that Berry was ready to make the final attack from the southeast. Even then the pocket was not entirely enclosed, for a small gap remained on the east. The attack next morning was anticlimactic. When Berry reached the area that the Japanese had so stoutly defended for ten days he found only the bodies of the slain and discarded equipment. The enemy had escaped during the night by way of the one opening in the otherwise tight cordon of Filipino troops. The Little Pocket had been reduced but now there were Japanese loose somewhere behind the 1st Division line.

The small Japanese force which had escaped from the pocket was soon discovered near the main line of resistance on the west of Trail 7, evidently seeking to make its way back into the Japanese line. By accident it had stumbled into a trap, for in holding firm the west shoulder of the salient created by the Japanese attack of the 7th, the troops had so sharply refused their flank that the line resembled a horseshoe with the opening facing west. It was into this horseshoe that the Japanese from the Little Pocket stumbled on the morning of the 9th. Offered an opportunity to surrender, they replied with gunfire and in the brief fight which followed were entirely annihilated.

With the reduction of the Little Pocket and the destruction of the escaping Japa-

nese on the morning of the 9th, General Jones was free to concentrate his entire force on the Big Pocket. But the situation had changed radically for earlier that morning General Morioka had received orders to pull back his troops to the heights north of Bagac.[26] Immediately he directed Colonel Yoshioka to discontinue his efforts to hold the pocket and to fight his way back through the American lines. To cover the retreat, the *2d Battalion, 33d Infantry,* in the Upper Pocket was to redouble its efforts to break through the holding force and join Yoshioka's men. Thus, as General Jones was making ready for the final attack against the Big Pocket, Yoshioka was hurriedly making his own preparations for a withdrawal.

On the American side the 9th and 10th were busy days. Colonel Berry, who now commanded the 1st Division, brought his force from the Little Pocket into the fight against the Big Pocket. On Jones's orders he placed his men in position to prevent a juncture between the enemy in the Upper Pocket and Yoshioka's troops. The rest of the 1st Division spent these days selecting and preparing a more favorable line along the south bank of the Gogo River. Meanwhile units surrounding the Big Pocket kept pressing in until they were so close that fire from one side of the pocket became dangerous to friendly units on the other side. Pushing in from the west were the two battalions of the 92d Infantry; on the opposite side of the pocket were the Scouts and Company C of the 11th Infantry. The Provisional Battalion, 51st Division, was pressing northward along Trail 7, while Company G, 11th Infantry, pushed south down the trail. The weakest link in the chain encircling the

---

[26] The decision was made at *14th Army* headquarters on the 8th and is discussed below in Chapter XIX.

pocket was on the north and northeast where the almost impenetrable jungle prevented close contact between the two 11th Infantry companies and the adjoining flank of the 45th Infantry. It was against this link, where a break was already evident, that Yoshioka's men would have to push if they hoped to escape.

Yoshioka's position was critical. A withdrawal in the face of these converging attacks would be a difficult and dangerous maneuver under the most favorable circumstances. With his exhausted troops the task would be even more hazardous. His men, who had been living on a diet of horseflesh and tree sap for days, were half starved, sick, and utterly worn out by two weeks of continuous fighting in the jungle. Until the 10th Yoshioka had been able to draw a plentiful supply of water from the Tuol River, but the advance of the 92d Infantry had closed off this source to him and he was feeling the effects of the shortage. Over one hundred of his men were wounded and would have to be carried or helped out during the withdrawal. Many of his officers had been killed and the maintenance of march discipline in the thick jungle promised to be a difficult task.

On 11 February the Filipinos were remarkably successful in pushing in the pocket. By 1000 that day all of Trail 7 had fallen to the Scouts. On the south the Provisional Battalion made excellent progress during the day while the two battalions of the 92d continued to push eastward against light opposition. By evening, wrote Jones's chief of staff, "it was quite obvious that the end was in sight." [27] The attackers, unaware that Yoshioka had begun his weary trek northward, attributed their suc-

cess to the enemy's lack of water and to the steady pressure exerted by the troops.

Only on the north had the Filipinos failed to register any great successes on the 11th. Here the two companies of the 11th Infantry and the northernmost element of the 45th Infantry, converging toward Trail 7, had failed to establish physical contact and one of them had lost its bearings and become dispersed. It was through these units that Yoshioka took his men. [28]

Command of the forces engaged in the Big Pocket fight changed again on 11 February. General Jones had come down with acute dysentery on the afternoon of the 11th and had been evacuated to the rear on a stretcher. Colonel MacDonald, his chief of staff, assumed command temporarily until General Wainwright placed Brougher in command the next day, 12 February.

By this time the fight for the pocket was almost over. On the afternoon of the 12th the unopposed Filipinos reached the junction of Trails 5 and 7 and on the following day moved through the entire area systematically to mop up whatever opposition they could find. There was none. The only living beings in the pocket were a number of horses and mules which the Japanese had captured earlier in the campaign. Three hundred of the enemy's dead and 150 graves were counted, and a large quantity of equipment, weapons, and ammunition—some of it buried—found. [29] The Japanese

---

[27] MacDonald, Notes on Left Subsector, I Phil Corps, p. 6.

[28] Ltr, Berry to Jones, with note by Jones to author, 11 Jan 52, OCMH; interv, author with Lt Col Russell Volckmann, formerly Exec Officer, 11th Inf (PA); Maj Archie L. McMasters, Memoirs of Tuol Pocket, pp. 5–6, copy was borrowed from Col Van Oosten, OCMH.

[29] The sources do not agree on the number of enemy dead and the figure given is an estimate by the author. The estimates of the number of Americans and Filipinos killed and wounded vary so widely that it is impossible to arrive at any reason-

made good their escape but they were traveling light.

The exhausted remnants of the *20th Infantry* worked their way north slowly, pausing frequently to rest and to bring up the wounded. In the dense foliage and heavy bamboo thickets, the withdrawing elements often lost contact and were forced to halt until the column was formed again. Passing "many enemy positions" in their march north through the American lines, the Japanese on the morning of 15 February finally sighted a friendly patrol.[30] About noon Colonel Yoshioka with 377 of his men, all that remained of the 1,000 who had broken through the American line on 29 January, reached the *9th Infantry* lines and safety, after a march of four days.

Colonel Yoshioka's *20th Infantry* had now ceased to exist as an effective fighting force. Landing in southern Luzon with 2,881 men, the regiment had entered the Bataan campaign with a strength of 2,690. Comparatively few casualties had been suffered in the fighting along the Mauban line. The amphibious operations that followed on 23 January, however, had proved disastrous for Yoshioka. First his *2d Battalion* had been "lost without a trace" at Longoskawayan and Quinauan, then the *1st Battalion,* sent to its rescue, had been almost entirely destroyed at Anyasan and Silaiim Points. The pocket fights had completed the destruction of the regiment. It is doubtful if the ill-fated *20th Infantry* by the middle of February numbered more than 650 men, the majority of whom were sick or wounded.[31]

---

able estimate. For a list of the captured equipment, see Supp. Rpt to G–2 Rpt, 11th Div (PA), 19 Feb 42, copy in OCMH.

[30] *14th Army* Opns, I, 115.

[31] Ltr, Chief, Hist Div, SSUSA, to G–2 GHQ FEC, 9 Nov 48, 3d Ind, 16 Aug 49, *16th Div*

With the fight for the Big Pocket at an end, General Brougher turned his attention to the Upper Pocket, the enemy salient at the western extremity of the 11th Division line. All efforts to pinch out the Japanese and restore the main line of resistance had failed. Since its formation on 7 February the salient had been contained by a miscellaneous assortment of troops. On the west were three companies of the 3d Infantry, one from the 1st Infantry, and the remnants of the platoon from Company F, 11th Infantry, which had been overrun in the initial attack. Holding the east side of the penetration was Company A, 92d Infantry, which Brougher had taken from Jones on the morning of the 7th, and five platoons from the disorganized 12th Infantry. The 2d Battalion, 2d Constabulary, was south of the salient. Not only had this conglomerate force held the Japanese in check, but it had pushed them back about fifty yards before the fight for the Big Pocket ended.

On 13 February Brougher sent forward a portion of the force that had participated in the fight against Yoshioka to join the troops holding back the Japanese in the salient. The 1st Battalion, 45th Infantry, took up a position to the south while the Provisional Battalion, 51st Division, and troops from the 92d Infantry attacked on its left in a northeasterly direction. At the same time, 11th Infantry units and the Constabulary pushed in from the east. By evening of the 14th, despite stubborn resistance and the difficulties presented by the jungle, the salient had been reduced by half and was only 350 yards long and 200 yards wide. An attack from the South the next day cut that area in half.

Opn, ATIS Enemy Pub 355, p. 11. This figure includes the detached company of the *3d Battalion* which did not engage in the pocket fights.

The infantry was aided here, as in the Big Pocket fight, by tanks of the 192d Tank Battalion. Hampered by the dense undergrowth and lost in the confusing maze of bamboo thickets, vines, and creepers, the tankers would have been impotent had it not been for the aid of the Igorot troops of Major Duisterhof's 2d Battalion, 11th Infantry. Hoisted to the top of the tanks where they were exposed to the fire of the enemy, these courageous tribesmen from north Luzon chopped away the entangling foliage with their bolos and served as eyes for the American tankers. From their position atop the tanks they fired at the enemy with pistols while guiding the drivers with sticks.[32]

As a result of these tactics combined with

steady pressure from the troops to the southwest and west, the Japanese were slowly pushed back. At least that was what the Americans and Filipinos believed. Actually, it is more likely that the Japanese in the salient were withdrawing to their own lines now that the necessity of providing a diversion for Yoshioka's retreat from the Big Pocket had ended. Once the 20th Infantry survivors had escaped it was no longer necessary for the men in the salient to hold their position. They had accomplished their mission and could now fall back, in accordance with Morioka's orders of the 9th. By the 16th the salient measured only 75 by 100 yards. An unopposed attack the next morning restored the main line of resistance and ended the fight which had begun on 26 January. The fight for the pockets was over.

---

[32] *New York Times*, February 23, 1942.

CHAPTER XIX

The Japanese Withdrawal

At the end of January, the time by which, according to the prewar plans of *Imperial General Headquarters,* the conquest of Luzon was to have been completed, Homma had to face the bitter realization that he was still far from his objective. The Battle of the Points and the pocket fights were still in progress, but it was already clear that the offensive begun on 26 January had failed miserably. General Nara's efforts to advance against II Corps on the east had been unsuccessful and expensive for the *65th Brigade* and the attached *9th Infantry* of the *16th Division.* One battalion of the *20th Infantry* had already been lost in the abortive landings along the west coast; another was trapped at Anyasan and Silaiim Points. The remainder of the regiment was cut off behind Wainwright's line and encircled in the pockets. Finally, the attacks against I Corps by elements of the *122d, 33d,* and *9th Infantry*—the last of which had rejoined the *16th Division* during the first week of February—were producing no results. Reluctant as he was to call off the offensive, Homma realized that to continue with it might well lead to disaster. The time for a decision had come.

The crucial question was debated heatedly by the *14th Army* staff at San Fernando on 8 February. During the discussions two points of view emerged. The first, presented by Col. Motoo Nakayama, senior operations officer of Homma's staff, held that the offensive should be pushed aggressively. The main effort, he argued, should

be made along the east coast rather than the west and should be closely controlled by *14th Army.* Lt. Gen. Masami Maeda, Homma's chief of staff, spoke for those who believed that offensive operations on Bataan should be discontinued, and that the blockade should be tightened while the remainder of the Philippines were occupied. By the time this was accomplished, the Americans and Filipinos would have been starved into submission. Thus the victory would be gained at little cost.

Homma listened carefully to both views and then made his decision. Forced by necessity to accept Maeda's argument for the cessation of operations on Bataan, he agreed to break off the action and withdraw his troops to a more secure position. But he did not agree to wait for famine and hunger to bring him victory. Instead he decided to call on *Imperial General Headquarters* in Tokyo for reinforcements with which to launch a final offensive to capture Bataan. Meanwhile, he would rest his men, reorganize the Army, and tighten the blockade. That night he issued orders for a general withdrawal.[1]

Homma's order of the 8th was the one which halted Nara's operations against Sector C in II Corps and prompted Morioka to order the troops at Anyasan and Silaiim

---

[1] Interrog of Maeda, 10 May 47, and Statement of Maeda, 2 Mar 50, ATIS Doc 56234, both in Interrogations of Former Japanese Officers, Mil Hist Div, GHQ FEC, I and II; interv, Col Walter E. Buchly with Homma, Manila, Mar 46, notes in OCMH; USA *vs.* Homma, p. 3062, testimony of Homma.

Points and those in the pockets to escape as best they could. General Nara was directed to withdraw his brigade to the area above the Tiawir and Talisay Rivers; Morioka, to the high ground north of the Bagac and Gogo Rivers. There they would establish defensive positions, reorganize, and prepare for the next offensive.[2]

Nara experienced little difficulty in carrying out his orders, but Morioka's troops were too closely engaged to withdraw easily. Moreover, the entire *20th Infantry* was behind the American line, either at the points or in the pockets. On about 13 February, therefore, Homma ordered the *65th Brigade* and the Army reserve unit to launch a diversionary attack against II Corps to relieve pressure on the *16th Division*. At the same time Army artillery and supporting aircraft would open an attack of their own to cover Morioka's withdrawal. As soon as Morioka had extricated his troops, General Nara would break off the diversionary attack and fall back again, this time to a line near Balanga, a short distance south of the old Abucay line.

The attack opened on 15 February after a careful preparation by the artillery and bombardment from the air. To create the impression of heavy troop movements, vehicles of all types were sent along the road between Abucay and Dinalupihan to the north. While the artillery and aircraft continued their activity, the ground troops moved out. Skeleton units less than a battalion in size advanced toward the American lines, reconnoitered, deployed as though for attack, opened fire, but made no effort to advance farther. The Americans, who

reported this activity as heavy patrol action, were not deceived and made no disposition to meet a general offensive against II Corps. Homma, however, believed that troops had been moved from I to II Corps and that the diversion was successful. On 2 February, after Morioka had completed his withdrawal, Nara was ordered to pull back also and occupy the line near Balanga.[3]

Thus, less than one month after the start of the offensive, *14th Army* had been halted and forced back to a defensive line to await reinforcements. "The enemy has definitely recoiled," wrote General MacArthur. "He has refused his flank in front of my right six to ten kilometers and in other sectors by varying distances. His attitude is so passive as to discount any immediate threat of attack."[4]

While these operations were in progress on Bataan Homma put into effect his plan to tighten the blockade. Col. Tatsunosuke Suzuki, whose *33d Infantry* (less *1st* and *2d Battalions*) occupied all of Luzon south of Manila, was given the *16th Reconnaissance Regiment* (less one company) and ordered to guard the southern coast of Manila Bay to prevent friendly Filipinos from sending food to Corregidor and Bataan. At the same time the four 105-mm. guns and two 150-mm. cannons stationed earlier in the same area were ordered to intensify their bombardment of the fortified islands at the entrance to the bay.[5]

---

[2] *14th Army* Opns Order, Series A, No. 273, 14 Feb 42, Supp. 29, and Plans for Feint Mvmts by Nara Inf Gp, 14 Feb 42, App. 31, both in *65th Brig* Opns Rpt, Mt. Samat; *14th Army* Opns, I, 115, 117.

[3] USAFFE-USFIP Rpt of Opns, p. 54; Bluemel, 31st Div (PA) Rpt of Opns, p. 17; *65th Brig* Opns Rpt, Mt. Samat, pp. 28–29; *14th Army* Opns, I, 116.

[4] Rad, MacArthur to TAG, No. 371, 26 Feb 42, AG 381 (11–27–41 Sec 2C) Far East.

[5] *14th Army* Opns, I, 96, 104, 113–15; *14th Army* Opns Order, Series A, No. 270, 13 Feb 42, Supp. 28, *65th Brig* Opns Rpt, Mt. Samat. For a day-by-day account of this bombardment see Harbor Defenses Rpt of Opns, pp. 34 ff; Bunker, Diary, daily entries after 6 Feb 42.

TABLE 7—WEAPONS AND EQUIPMENT CAPTURED BY *14th Army*, AS OF 20 FEBRUARY
1942

Item	Quantity	Item	Quantity
Vehicles:		Fuel (in litres) :	
Tank_____	31	Motor car fuel_____	1, 402, 954
Motor truck_____	844	Mobile gas_____	837, 994
Passenger car_____	1, 132	Aviation gas_____	107, 964
Other _____	340	Tank oil, light_____	396, 800
Arms:		Heavy oil_____	7, 900, 000
Rifle _____	27, 412	Petroleum_____	4, 776, 000
Pistol_____	1, 161	Ammunition (in rounds) :	
Machine gun, light_____	42	Rifle _____	6, 627, 599
Machine gun, heavy_____	176	Pistol_____	132, 318
Rifle, automatic_____	68	Machine gun, heavy_____	72, 496
Artillery, heavy_____	5	Artillery, field_____	426, 669
Artillery, field_____	37	Artillery, pack _____	714
Artillery, pack_____	32	Mortar, trench _____	1, 067
Mortar, trench_____	35	Mortar _____	1, 055
Mortar _____	8		
Grenade, hand_____	2, 071		
Bayonet _____	9, 371		

Source: Tactical Situation *14th Army,* ATIS Doc 56113, App. II, in translation of Japanese Doc II,
No. 15, GHQ FEC, Mil Intel Sec.

To seal off the approaches to Manila Bay from the inland seas Homma decided also to occupy the island of Mindoro, off the southwest coast of Luzon, just below Batangas Province. On the 15th he directed Colonel Suzuki to prepare for an amphibious operation and on the 22d issued final orders for the landing. Four days later, Suzuki, with a force called the *Suzuki Detachment* and consisting of the *3d Battalion, 33d Infantry,* plus a battery of the *22d Field Artillery,* left Olongapo under naval escort. On the morning of the 27th, the detachment landed on the northeast tip of the island and occupied a town and near-by airfield without any opposition. No effort was made to occupy the south end of the island where there was an airstrip and a small garrison of fifty men.[6]

This local success against an undefended island and the seizure of much booty could not disguise the fact that Homma's fortune had by the end of February reached its nadir. (*Table 7*) From 6 January to 1 March *14th Army* casualties had totaled almost 7,000 men. Twenty-seven hundred men had been killed and over 4,000 wounded. Between 10,000 and 12,000 more were down with malaria, beriberi, dysentery, and tropical diseases. Literally, *14th Army* had ceased to exist as an effective force, and its two combat elements, the *16th Division* and *65th Brigade,* had been reduced to impotence. Of the three infantry regiments in Morioka's division, one, the *20th,* had been

---

[6] Ind, *Bataan, The Judgment Seat,* pp. 148, 273, 329, 343–44; rad, Beebe (Fort Mills) to Mac-Arthur (Melbourne), 18 Mar 42, USFIP G–3 Journal. On 8 March a Japanese destroyer appeared offshore and the Mindoro garrison of fifty men set fire to 50,000 gallons of aviation gasoline before taking to the hills. A week later the Japanese landed there.

virtually destroyed. The single battalion of the *33d Infantry* that participated in the offensive had lost 125 men in the Upper Pocket. The *9th Infantry* had seen action on both sides of the peninsula and had suffered about 700 casualties. By 24 February the effective infantry strength of the *16th Division* on Bataan did not exceed 712 men.[7]

The *65th Brigade* had not fared much better than the *16th Division*. Entering Bataan early in January with about 5,000 infantrymen, its three two-battalion regiments, the *122d, 141st,* and *142d,* had been in continuous combat until the last week of February. The brigade had borne the brunt of the fighting in the first battle of Bataan and had lost a large number of men before 26 January. Between 25 January and 15 February, the *122d Infantry* had been attached to Morioka's force and had sustained over 300 casualties. During the same period the *141st Infantry* lost 80 killed and 253 wounded. Casualties in the *142d* were somewhat lighter. By the middle of February the brigade and its attachments had lost altogether over 4,000 men: 1,142 killed and 3,110 wounded. Many of those who survived were exhausted and sick and could hardly be considered effective troops.[8]

The *14th Army* was indeed, as Homma remarked at his trial in Manila four years later, "in very bad shape." Altogether Homma had in his army at that time, he estimated, only three infantry battalions capable of effective action. Had MacArthur chosen that moment to launch a large-scale counterattack, Homma told the Military

Tribunal which sentenced him to death, the American and Filipino troops could have walked to Manila "without encountering much resistance on our part." [9]

The Japanese failure in the offensive against the Orion–Bagac line raised American morale and led to an upsurge of optimism. So jubilant were the troops that they accepted unquestioningly, as did MacArthur's headquarters, the report that General Homma had committed suicide because of his failure to take Bataan. To heighten the dramatic effect, or for some obscure reason attributable to Oriental psychology, Homma was thought to have selected General MacArthur's apartment in the Manila Hotel for the act. The fictious funeral rites were reported to have been held there also.[10]

Officers were unanimous in their judgment that morale was never higher and the troops never imbued with a more aggressive spirit. "The morale of our front line troops," wrote Lt. Col. Nicoll F. C lbraith to his chief, Col. Lewis C. Beebe, G–4 on MacArthur's staff, "appears very high and they want to take the offensive. At the moment there appears to be nothing on our right except dead Japs and tons of abandoned equipment, which is being collected. . . . Prisoners give the impression that Jap morale is away down." [11] Wainwright, too,

---

[7] *14th Army* Opns, I, 116; USA *vs.* Homma, Defense Exhibit Y.

[8] *65th Brig* Opns Rpt, Mt. Natib, p. 111; *65th Brig* Opns Rpt, Mt. Samat, p. 114.

[9] USA *vs.* Homma, pp. 3062–63, testimony of Homma; pp. 2450, 2457, testimony of Lt Gen Takaji Wachi, formerly Chief of Staff, *14th Army*. Col. Yoshio Nakajima estimated that as of 1 March there were 3,000 effectives in *14th Army,* USA *vs.* Homma, p. 2576.

[10] *Ibid.,* p. 3063, testimony of Homma; rad, MacArthur to TAG, No. 438, 7 Mar 42, AG 381 (11–27–41 Sec 3) Far East; Bunker, Diary, entry of 10 Mar 42. General Yamashita, conqueror of Singapore, was reported as the new Japanese commander in the Philippines, a command he did not assume until October 1944.

[11] Ltr, Galbraith to Beebe, 5 Feb 42, AG 319.1 (8 Jan 42) Phil Rcds.

USAFFE HEADQUARTERS ON BATAAN, FEBRUARY 1942. *Left to right: Brig. Gen. Spencer B. Akin, Maj. Paul R. Wing (photographic officer), Lt. Col. Nicoll F. Galbraith, and Brig. Gen. Richard J. Marshall.*

thought that the morale of his men reached its highest point after the Battle of the Points and the pocket fights.[12] A naval intelligence officer, whose opinion of the Philippine army was not high, wrote to his superior in Washington on 11 February:

Army morale on Bataan is higher in the past ten days than at any time since the beginning of the war. . . . The opinion here is that the army has improved by many discharges and thousands of desertions, by the realization that it has to fight its own battle with little if any substantial aid. . . . Lastly, fighting qualities have improved by experience. [13]

The victories of February had made hardened veterans of the front-line troops on Bataan and they were eager to pursue the enemy. Men on patrol moved forward aggressively and Colonel Galbraith wrote that he expected at any moment to hear that "they were in San Fernando next." [14] One patrol from General Bluemel's sector in II Corps actually pushed as far forward as the former Abucay line whereupon the general proposed to Parker that a reconnaissance in force be made to that line preparatory to a restoration of the first main line of resistance. He was not alone in urging a general counteroffensive; many officers favored

[12] NLF and I Corps Rpt of Opns, p. 27.
[13] Rad, Intel Officer, 16th Naval Dist, to Chief of Naval Intel, 11 Feb 42, AG 319.1 (8 Jan 42) Phil Rcds.

[14] Ltr, Galbraith to Beebe, 5 Feb 42, AG 319.1 (8 Jan 42) Phil Rcds.

a return to the Abucay position and some wished to go even further, to Layac Junction at the base of the peninsula.[15]

Bluemel's proposal met with a flat rejection at corps headquarters, and undoubtedly would have received even less consideration from MacArthur's staff. What the proponents of a general counteroffensive failed to consider was the fact that a local victory could not change the strategic situation in the Philippines. So long as the Japanese controlled the sea and air MacArthur's forces would be unable to gain a decisive victory. Even if they fought their way back to Abucay, Layac, or Manila, they would ultimately have to retire to Bataan again, for the Japanese could reinforce at will.

The effort required for a general offensive might well have jeopardized the primary mission of the Philippine garrison—to hold Manila Bay as long as possible. To accomplish this task it was necessary to conserve carefully all human and material resources. Troops on the defensive in a static situation required less food, less gasoline, less ammunition, and less of all other supplies than those who chose to attack. Moreover, the advance, if it proved successful, would bring additional problems: it would lengthen the front line, increase the area to be defended and the line of communication, leave exposed beaches to the rear, and greatly complicate an already difficult supply situation. It was for these reasons that all proposals for an offensive, while feasible tactically and desirable for reasons of morale, were strategically unsound. The proper task for the front-line troops was to strengthen their defenses in the hope that when the next Japanese attack came it could be turned back as had the last.[16]

Thus, by the end of February, the Americans and Japanese were dug in behind their defensive positions on Bataan. Separating the two lines was a no man's land, the exclusive hunting preserve for the opposing patrols. Over the entire peninsula settled a lull as both sides prepared for the final assault.

---

[15] Ltr, Bluemel to Groce, 18 Feb 49, OCMH; Mallonée, Bataan Diary, II, 54.

[16] Mallonée, Bataan Diary, II, 54–58.

CHAPTER XX

Command

While the situation on Bataan was never more favorable to the Allied cause than it was in mid-February, there was little hope in Washington that the Philippine garrison could withstand the Japanese assault for more than a few months. What would happen to General MacArthur then? Was he to be allowed to fall into Japanese hands or should he be saved for the Allied war effort still to come? The decision reached in Washington, presumably early in February, was that the general's services were too valuable to be sacrificed in a hopeless cause, that he must be rescued to lead other forces in the war against Japan.

But there were difficulties to this solution. MacArthur would undoubtedly raise objections to any orders which might affect his reputation. And he might show an understandable reluctance to desert his troops in the midst of battle. Brig. Gen. Patrick J. Hurley, former Secretary of War and an old friend of MacArthur's, summarized these difficulties when he told General Wavell during a trip to the Indies that MacArthur would not leave the Philippines until "both the public and the troops were assured that command had passed to competent leadership." He explained also "that it would be necessary for the President to definitely order MacArthur to relinquish command and proceed elsewhere, and that even if such orders were issued MacArthur might feel that he had destroyed himself by leaving his beleaguered command." Mac-

Arthur's departure from the Philippines, Hurley concluded, would have to be arranged in such a way that "his honor and his record as a soldier" would not be compromised.[1] The settlement of these delicate questions formed the substance of the lengthy negotiations which preceded General MacArthur's departure from Corregidor on 12 March 1942.

The Evacuation of MacArthur

The subject of MacArthur's evacuation from the Philippines and his future role in the war against Japan was first raised by the Chief of Staff in an oblique fashion on 2 February. The occasion was an inquiry about MacArthur's plans for his wife and young son who were on Corregidor with him.[2] General Marshall followed up this inquiry two days later with the statement that "continuous consideration" was being given to the evacuation of officials from the Philippines. For the first time mention was made of the possibility of MacArthur's transfer to another command should Bataan fall, leaving only "the fortress defense of Corregidor" in American hands. "Under these conditions," Marshall explained, "the need for your services there might well be

---

[1] Memo, Hurley for Marshall, Melbourne, 21 Feb 42, OPD 381 SWPA, Sec 1, Case 21.

[2] Rads, MacArthur to Marshall, No. 187, 2 Feb 42, and Marshall to MacArthur, 2 Feb 42, both in WPD 3251-74.

less pressing than at other points in the Far East." [3]

Marshall outlined two possibilities for MacArthur's future employment. The first was his transfer to Mindanao. The length of his stay there would depend on the success of guerilla operations and the effectiveness of the program to bring in supplies from Australia. The second alternative was for MacArthur to go directly to Australia and there resume command of all Army forces in the Far East. After describing the situation in Australia and outlining what was being done to establish a strong base in that area, Marshall went on to say that his purpose in raising the question of MacArthur's evacuation from the Philippines was to secure from him a "highly confidential statement" of his views before a decision was made. "It is to be understood," he concluded, "that in case your withdrawal from immediate leadership of your beleaguered forces is to be carried out it will be by direct order of the President to you."

This request for MacArthur's views was not answered immediately, and when it did come was made in connection with an entirely different matter. On 8 February, four days after Marshall's inquiry, the War Department received a message for President Roosevelt from Manuel Quezon. In this message Quezon proposed that the United States immediately grant the Philippines their independence; that the Islands be neutralized; that American and Japanese forces be withdrawn by mutual consent; and that the Philippine Army be disbanded.

Quezon's disquieting proposal was accompanied by a supporting message from General MacArthur, couched in the form of a military estimate of the situation. [4] From this estimate the War Department learned for the first time that the Philippine garrison had sustained a casualty rate of 50 percent, and that divisions were reduced to the size of regiments and regiments to battalions. Although morale was good the men were "badly battle worn" and "desperately in need of rest." "There is no denying the fact," MacArthur told Marshall, "that we are near done," and warned him to be prepared for "the complete destruction of this command" at any time. It was up to the United States to decide whether the time the Allies so badly needed could be attained better through Quezon's plan or by continuing the hopeless battle. After summarizing the attitude of the Filipinos as one of "almost violent resentment against the United States," MacArthur stated that, from the military point of view, "the problem presents itself as to whether the plan of President Quezon might offer the best possible solution of what is about to be a disastrous debacle." If the plan was accepted, he pointed out, "we lose no military advantage because we would still secure at least equal delay."

The reaction from Washington was prompt and emphatic. On 9 February, one day later, President Roosevelt in a personal message to Quezon repudiated the scheme and declared that the United States Government would never agree to such a solution to the war in the Philippines. [5] At the

[3] Rad, Marshall to MacArthur, 4 Feb 42, WDCSA 370.05 (3–17–42) Phil.

[4] Rad, MacArthur to Marshall, Nos. 226 and 227, CofS Phil Situation File. The first part of the message was addressed to Roosevelt and signed Quezon; the second portion was addressed to Marshall and signed by MacArthur.

[5] Rad, Roosevelt to MacArthur, No. 1029, 9 Feb 42, CofS Phil Situation File. The message was addressed to MacArthur alone because it went through Army channels.

same time he expressed his sympathy for Quezon and the Philippine people and pledged American support "whatever happens to the present American garrison." "So long as the flag of the United States flies on Filipino soil," Roosevelt assured Quezon, ". . . it will be defended by our own men to the death . . . we shall not relax our efforts until the forces which are now marshalling outside the Philippine Islands return to the Philippines and drive the last remnant of the invaders from your soil." To General MacArthur, Roosevelt sent a personal message authorizing the surrender of the Filipino troops if necessary, but forbidding the surrender of American troops, "so long as there remains any possibility of resistance." [6] The President then went on to express his belief in the importance of the fight in the Philippines and the role of that garrison in the war against the Axis.

I have made these decisions [he wrote] in complete understanding of your military estimate that accompanied President Quezon's message to me. The duty and the necessity of resisting Japanese aggression to the last transcends in importance any other obligation now facing us in the Philippines.

There has been gradually welded into a common front a globe-encircling opposition to the predatory powers that are seeking the destruction of individual liberty and freedom of government. We cannot afford to have this line broken in any particular theater.

As the most powerful member of this coalition we cannot display weakness in fact or in spirit anywhere. It is mandatory that there be established once and for all in the minds of all peoples complete evidence that the American determination and indomitable will to win carries on down to the last unit.

I therefore give you this most difficult mission in full understanding of the desperate situation to which you may shortly be re-

duced. The service that you and the American members of your command can render to your country in the titanic struggle now developing is beyond all possibility of appraisement. I particularly request that you proceed rapidly to the organization of your forces and your defenses so as to make your resistance as effective as circumstances will permit and as prolonged as humanly possible.

Both Quezon and MacArthur accepted the President's decision without question. Quezon wrote that he fully appreciated the reasons upon which the decision was based and that he was "abiding by it." [7] It was in his reply to the President's "no surrender" order that MacArthur answered Marshall's inquiry of a week earlier for his confidential views about evacuation. He and his family, MacArthur declared, had decided to remain in the Philippines and "share the fate of the garrison." [8] He planned, he said, to fight "to destruction" on Bataan and then do the same of Corregidor. "I have not the slightest intention in the world," he told the President, "of surrendering or capitulating the Filipino element of my command. . . . There has never been the slightest wavering among the troops."

General Marshall immediately expressed personal concern over MacArthur's decision to "share the fate of the garrison." He urged the former Chief of Staff to consider the possibility of an assignment that would force him to become separated from his family "under circumstances of greatly increased peril" and "poignant embarrassment." [9] In the same message Marshall made an official inquiry about antiaircraft ammunition. The reply from Corregidor

[5] *Ibid.*

[7] Rad, Quezon to Roosevelt, No. 262, 12 Feb 42, OPD Exec O.
[8] Rad, MacArthur to Roosevelt, No. 252, 11 Feb 42, OPD Exec O.
[9] Rad, Marshall to MacArthur, 14 Feb 42, WDCSA 370.05 (3–17–42) Phil.

answered the inquiry about the ammunition but pointedly omitted any reference to the personal aspects of Marshall's message.[10]

MacArthur's message was penned on 15 February, the same day that the supposedly impregnable fortress at Singapore, key to the British position in the Far East, surrendered. Already the Japanese had taken Malaya, Borneo, and the Celebes. The early loss of Sumatra and Java and the split of the ABDA area was virtually certain. Again MacArthur called for an attack against the Japanese line of communications, declaring with characteristic optimism that "the opportunities still exist for a complete reversal of the situation." [11]

To the United States and British planners in Washington the possibility of successful flank attack against the Japanese positions appeared even more remote than before. ABDA Command was clearly doomed, and there were numerous meetings held in Washington during the two weeks following the fall of Singapore to consider the effects on Allied strategy of the new Japanese victories and the imminent collapse of Wavell's command. Gradually there emerged a scheme by which the United States would accept responsibility for the eastern portion of the ABDA area, including Australia and the Netherlands Indies; the British, the western portion. It was evident by the last week in February that the broad outlines of such an agreement were mutually satisfactory and that only the details—important as they were—remained to be worked out. The American planners considered it a wise precaution, then, to select in advance a senior officer qualified to

command a large Allied headquarters in the Southwest Pacific. Inevitably the choice fell upon MacArthur.[12] On 27 February the Combined Chiefs of Staff finally ordered Wavell to dissolve his headquarters and turn command of operations in the area over to the Netherlands authorities before leaving for India. This move placed MacArthur technically under the Dutch, but he had already been told that "because of your special situation all procedures in your case remain as heretofore. You will continue to communicate directly with the War Department." [13]

Such reassurances were by now entirely unnecessary for on 22 February the President had directed MacArthur to leave the Philippines. His intention to do so had been made clear on the 21st when the Chief of Staff had told the Far East commander that the President was considering the advisability of ordering him to Mindanao to conduct the defense of the Philippines from there.[14]

There were numerous advantages to such a move. MacArthur himself had repeatedly pointed out the possibility of continuing resistance from Mindanao by means of guerrilla warfare and had already taken measures to strengthen Brig. Gen. William F. Sharp's command. If the Allies mounted an

[10] Rad, MacArthur to Marshall, 15 Feb 42, WDCSA 370.05 (3–17–42) Phil.

[11] Rad, MacArthur to Marshall, No. 297, 16 Feb 42, WDCSA 381 (3–17–42) Phil.

[12] For an account of the reorganization of the ABDA area and the establishment of the Southwest Pacific Area, see Matloff and Snell, *Strategic Planning for Coalition Warfare 1941–1942*, and Samuel Milner, *Victory in Papua*, a volume in preparation for the series UNITED STATES ARMY IN WORLD WAR II.

[13] Rad, TAG to MacArthur, No. 1083, 24 Feb 42, WPD 4639-54.

[14] Rad, Marshall to MacArthur, 21 Feb 42, WDCSA 370.05 (3–17–42) Phil. General Eisenhower, who was handling the dispatches to MacArthur during this period from his post as Chief of the War Plans Division, makes it clear that the impetus to get MacArthur out of the Philippines came from the White House. Eisenhower, Personal Notebook, entry of 23 Feb 42.

air and naval counterattack through the Netherlands Indies, as MacArthur had urged, Mindanao would be the first objective in the Philippines and the base for an invasion of Luzon. Communication with other areas in the Far East would also be more practical from Mindanao than Corregidor. "The foregoing considerations underlie the tentative decision of the President," Marshall told MacArthur, "but we are not sufficiently informed as to the situation and circumstances to be certain that the proposal meets the actual situation."

The next day, without waiting for a reply from Corregidor, the President made up his mind about MacArthur's evacuation. The USAFFE commander was to leave Fort Mills as quickly as possible and proceed to Mindanao where he would remain long enough "to insure a prolonged defense." [15] From there he was to go on to Australia. In this message MacArthur was told definitely for the first time of the President's plans for his future role in the war and of arrangements then in progress to secure Australian and British acceptance of his command in the southwest Pacific. He was urged to make all haste in his preparations, "because of the vital importance of your assuming command in Australia at an early date," and directed not to "delay in Mindanao" longer than one week and to leave sooner if transportation became available. Obviously, by this time, his movement to Mindanao was secondary to his assumption of command in Australia. Air and submarine transportation from Cor-

regidor would be provided by Washington and he was authorized to take with him his chief of staff.

The message reached Corregidor at noon on the 23d. According to Frazier Hunt, one of General MacArthur's biographers, MacArthur first decided to refuse to leave and actually drafted a blunt refusal note. When he called in the senior members of his staff to tell them of the President's orders and his decision, they all argued that he would have to obey the orders ultimately and that he ought not to send the message already drafted. If he persisted in his refusal, they pointed out, he would face court-martial charges. He had been selected to lead a rescue force back to the Philippines and he owed it to his men to accept the assignment. There was enough food and ammunition, they declared, to last into June and the Bataan force might well hold out until his return. [16]

Thus advised, says Frazier Hunt, MacArthur tore up his first message and accepted his orders, with reservations. In his reply, dated 24 February, he expressed his appreciation of the confidence "implied" in the President's orders and agreement with the objectives desired. Pointing out that the failure to send support to the Philippines had "created a very difficult situation which I have been able to meet only through the peculiar confidence placed in me by the Filipino people and Army," and that his abrupt departure might result "in collapse in the Philippine area," he asked for permission to delay his departure until the "psychological time." "Please be guided by me in this matter," he urged the Chief of Staff. "I know the

---

[15] Rad, Marshall to MacArthur, No. 1078, 22 Feb 42, CofS Supersecret File entitled MacArthur's Move to Australia. Eisenhower wrote on 22 February that he had prepared the draft of a message to MacArthur telling him to start south. The next day he noted that the message had been approved by the President and sent. Eisenhower, Personal Notebook.

[16] Hunt, *MacArthur and the War Against Japan*, p. 64. The writer has been unable to find confirmation of this conference in the official records or in interviews.

situation here in the Philippines and unless the right moment is chosen for this delicate operation, a sudden collapse might occur. . . . These people are depending upon me now . . . and any idea that might develop in their minds that I was being withdrawn for any other purpose than to bring them immediate relief could not be explained. . . ." [17]

Authority to leave at a time he considered appropriate was received immediately. "Your No. 358," Marshall told him the next day, "has been carefully considered by the President. He has directed that full decision as to timing of your departure and details of method be left in your hands." [18] Since his date of departure was indefinite, he was given authority to call on the Army and Navy commands in Australia for a submarine to take him to Mindanao and B–17's for the trip to Australia.

These arrangements, MacArthur told Marshall, were entirely satisfactory, and he added that he expected to leave about 15 March.[19] Lt. Gen. George H. Brett and Rear Adm. William A. Glassford, the Army and Navy commanders in Australia, though not given the reason, were directed to place three heavy bombers and a submarine at MacArthur's disposal. The submarine was to move to Corregidor, the planes to Mindanao. Brett and Glassford were also told to expect such a call about 15 March and enjoined to keep the entire matter "highly secret." [20] The only urging MacArthur received from Washington to hasten his departure came on 6 March when Marshall told him, at the end of a message dealing with other matters, that the situation in Australia "indicates desirability of your early arrival there." [21]

The "psychological time" for MacArthur's departure came six days later. On 24 February, when he had asked permission to delay his departure, he had pointed out that he wished to remain in the Philippines until such time as the situation on Bataan became stabilized. The enemy's intentions were not then clear, he had said, and it was entirely possible that he might soon make a major effort. MacArthur was confident that he could defeat the Japanese and "restabilize the situation." If such an attack did not materialize, his estimate was that "we may be approaching the stalemate of positional warfare." [22] By 10 March MacArthur evidently felt such a condition had been reached and that his departure would not result in a collapse.[23] Arrangements for transportation were quickly made by Rear

[17] Rad, MacArthur to Marshall, No. 358, 24 Feb 42, WDCSA 370.05 (3–17–42) Phil.

[18] Rad, Marshall to MacArthur, No. 1087, 25 Feb 42, WDCSA 370.05 (3–17–42) Phil.

[19] Rad, MacArthur to Marshall, No. 373, 26 Feb 42, WDCSA 370.05 (3–17–42) Phil.

[20] Rad, Marshall to MacArthur, 28 Feb 42, Supersecret Msgs to Gen MacArthur, OPD Exec O.

[21] Rad, Marshall to MacArthur, 6 Mar 42, WDCSA 370.05 (3–17–42) Phil. Frazier Hunt states that on 10 March MacArthur received "another peremptory order" to leave. Hunt, *MacArthur and the War Against Japan*, p. 64. No such order has been found in the records.

[22] Rad, MacArthur to Marshall, No. 358, 24 Feb 42, WDCSA 370.05 (3–17–42) Phil.

[23] Wainwright, *General Wainwright's Story*, pp. 1–5. The account given by Wainwright of the reasons for MacArthur's departure, as given him by General Sutherland, is not supported by official records. Sutherland told Wainwright, who came to Corregidor on the 10th, that "the President has been trying to get him [MacArthur] to leave Corregidor for days, but until yesterday the general kept refusing." (p. 2) MacArthur told Wainwright that same morning that he was leaving on orders from the President and that "things have gotten to such a point that I must comply with these orders or get out of the Army. I want you to make it known . . . that I'm leaving over my repeated protests." (p. 5) MacArthur also told General Moore that he had been ordered to leave over his protest. Harbor Defenses Rpt of Opns, p. 42.

Adm. Francis W. Rockwell and General Sutherland, and the officers to accompany him carefully selected. Instead of waiting for the submarine which the Navy had placed at his disposal and which could not reach Corregidor until 15 March—by which time the Japanese might have established an effective blockade—MacArthur decided to go to Mindanao by PT boat. Rockwell assigned four of these small craft to the operation and rushed preparations for the journey. Lieutenant Bulkeley, aboard the boat carrying the general, was in tactical command of the group, but Rockwell assumed personal command of the operation.[24]

During the negotiations leading to MacArthur's reassignment no mention had been made of the size or character of the staff he would take with him. It was assumed that his family would go, and Marshall had inquired specifically about them. Only two officers had been mentioned by name as being included in the official transfer: General Sutherland and General George, the latter asked for specifically by the Air Forces who were "anxious to profit by [his] experience."[25] The group finally selected to make the trip from Corregidor to Australia via Mindanao numbered twenty-one persons. In addition to his wife, young son, and the nurse for the child, MacArthur selected from his staff seventeen officers to accompany him. They included his chief and deputy chief of staff, the G–1 and G–2, the signal, engineer, antiaircraft artillery, and air officers, a public relations officer,

Sutherland's assistant, an aide, a medical officer, and a secretary. In addition to Admiral Rockwell one other naval officer accompanied the general.[26]

On 12 March, as darkness settled down over Manila Bay, the party embarked from Corregidor. Two hours later, at 2115, the four PT boats cleared the mine fields and sped south. Sailing all that night, they put in next morning at a small uninhabited island in the Cuyo group in the central Philippines. The small craft had broken formation during the night and become separated, one of them dumping its spare fuel when it mistook Bulkeley's boat for an enemy vessel. The passengers on this boat were taken aboard the others and the group continued south through the Mindanao Sea the next night, reaching the north central shore of Mindanao at daybreak of the 14th.

---

[24] Ltr, Rockwell to Ward, 18 Jan 52, OCMH; Rockwell, Supp. to Narrative of Naval Activities in Luzon Area, Folder IV (Evacuation of Gen MacArthur), Off of Naval Rcds. The orders and plans for the voyage to Mindanao are included in this report.
[25] Rad, Marshall to MacArthur, 6 Mar 42, WDCSA 370.05 (3–17–42) Phil.

[26] Ibid.; rad, Brett to Marshall, No. 760, 19 Mar 42, AG 371 (3–19–42). The group was organized as follows:

PT 41 (Lt J. D. Bulkeley)
General MacArthur
Mrs. MacArthur
Arthur MacArthur, son
Chinese nurse
General Sutherland, CofS
Capt Harold G. Ray, USN
Lt Col Sidney L. Huff, Aide
Maj C. H. Morehouse, Med O

PT 34 (Lt R. G. Kelly)
Admiral Rockwell
General Marshall, DCofS
Col Charles P. Stivers, G–1
Capt Joseph McMicking (PA), Asst G–2

PT 35 (Ens A. B. Akers)
Col Charles A. Willoughby, G–2
Lt Col LeGrande A. Diller, Aide (PRO)
Lt Col Francis H. Wilson, Aide to Sutherland
M Sgt Paul P. Rogers, Secy

PT 32 (Lt (jg) V. S. Schumacker)
Brig Gen Spencer B. Akin, Sig O
Brig Gen Hugh J. Casey, Engr O
Brig Gen William F. Marquat, AA O
Brig Gen Harold H. George, Air O
Lt Col Joe R. Sherr, Asst Sig O

They were met by General Sharp and taken to Del Monte airfield where MacArthur found only one of the B–17's Brett had sent up from Australia. Two had failed to arrive and the third had crashed. The remaining bomber MacArthur considered unfit to carry passengers. Incensed, he requested Brett to send other planes and asked Marshall to make suitable planes available if Brett did not have them. "The best three planes in the United States or Hawaii should be made available," he radioed the Chief of Staff, "with completely adequate and experienced crews. To attempt such a desperate and important trip with inadequate equipment would amount to consigning the whole party to death and I could not accept such a responsibility." [27]

Three B–17's were dispatched from Australia immediately, two of them reaching Del Monte safely by midnight of the 16th. The entire group took off shortly after and arrived at Darwin at 0900 the next morning. "This hazardous trip by a commanding general and key members of his staff through enemy controlled territory undoubtedly is unique in military annals," MacArthur reported to the Chief of Staff on his arrival. "I wish to commend the courage and coolness of the officers and men . . . who were engaged in this hazardous enterprise. It was due entirely to their invincible resolution and determination that the mission was successfully accomplished." [28]

---

[27] Rad, MacArthur to Marshall, No. 482, 14 Mar 42, WDCSA 370.05 (3–17–42) Phil. For an account of the journey, see W. L. White, *They Were Expendable*, pp. 113–43. The author has also interviewed several of the men who made the trip.
[28] Rad, MacArthur to Marshall, No. 5, 21 Mar 42, Msgs from Gen MacArthur, OPD Exec O. All the officers and men of the four PT boats received the Silver Star by order of General MacArthur. USAFFE GO 43, 15 Mar 42.

Wainwright Assumes Command

As early as 4 March, a week before his departure, General MacArthur had begun to formulate a plan for the organization and command of the forces remaining behind. On that day the composite Visayan-Mindanao Force under General Sharp was split and the islands in the Visayas transferred to the command of Brig. Gen. Bradford G. Chynoweth. Sharp continued on as commander of the forces on Mindanao, the only island south of Luzon on which a major Japanese force had landed. [29] This move was probably designed to permit General Sharp to devote all his energies to the defense of Mindanao, the base from which MacArthur still hoped to mount a counteroffensive against the Japanese.

The reorganization of the Visayan-Mindanao Force was only a part of General MacArthur's plan. He intended also, as he told General Moore at that time, to make some changes in command on Bataan and Corregidor. [30] These intentions were a closely guarded secret and the news only began to leak out to the general staff on the 10th. [31] General Wainwright was the first to learn of it officially. On the evening of the 9th he received a telephone call from Sutherland to come to Corregidor the next morning to see General MacArthur on a matter of importance. When he arrived the USAFFE chief of staff told him that MacArthur was leaving for Mindanao and Australia the next day. "The general," Sutherland explained, "plans a number of

---

[29] USAFFE-USFIP Rpt of Opns, p. 55; Gen Chynoweth, 61st Div (PA) and Visayan Force, pp. 10–11. The latter report was prepared at the request of the author and is on file in OCMH.
[30] Harbor Defenses Rpt of Opns, p. 42.
[31] Collier, Notebooks, III, 55.

changes." [32] These changes, it appeared, did not include the appointment of another commander for the forces in the Philippines. MacArthur would continue to exercise this control from Australia through his G–4, Colonel Beebe, who would be given a star and designated deputy chief of staff of USAFFE.

The entire force, Sutherland told Wainwright, would be organized into four commands. In addition to the two already created in the south and General Moore's Harbor Defenses, a new command would be established for the troops on Bataan and those still holding out in the mountains of Luzon. This command, to be known as Luzon Force, would be led by General Wainwright. General Jones, who had demonstrated his ability in guiding the South Luzon Force during its withdrawal to Bataan and in the pocket fight, was to be promoted and given Wainwright's old command, I Corps.[33] These arrangements, Sutherland concluded, would become effective the day after MacArthur's departure.

The briefing completed, Sutherland took Wainwright in to see General MacArthur. After outlining the organization to be established on his departure and asserting his determination to "come back as soon as I can with as much as I can," MacArthur cautioned Wainwright to defend Bataan "in as great depth as you can." "You're an old cavalryman, Jonathan," he said, "and your training has been along thin, light, quick hitting lines. The defense of Bataan must be deep." "And be sure," he continued, "to give them everything you've got with your artillery. That's the best arm you have." Before the cav-

alryman returned to Bataan, MacArthur promised him his third star "if you're still on Bataan." "I'll be on Bataan," Wainwright pledged, "if I'm alive." [34] It was a promise that he would be unable to keep.

In his instructions to General Moore, MacArthur explained more fully the purpose behind the reorganization. The principal function of the staff he was leaving with Colonel Beebe, he declared, would be "to try to get supplies into Corregidor and Bataan," [35] The advance command post of USAFFE at Corregidor, therefore, would be a supply not a tactical headquarters. MacArthur apparently intended to retain control of operations in the Philippines in his own headquarters in Australia.

Moore, as commander of the Corregidor garrison, was specifically enjoined to defend that island to the last. Some time earlier MacArthur had ordered Moore to set aside enough food to last 20,000 men on half rations until 30 June 1942, in the expectation that if Bataan fell the Philippine Division would be brought to Corregidor for its final stand. Moore had made preparations for such a move and MacArthur's final warning to him was to maintain this level of supply against encroachment by the commanders of his other forces. His "last instructions to me before departing," Moore wrote, "were to hold Corregidor until he returned." If that proved impossible, "I was to make sure that the armament was destroyed to such an extent that it could not be used against an American effort to recapture the Philippines." [36]

Promptly on the morning after the four PT boats sped out of Manila Bay, General

[32] Wainwright, *General Wainwright's Story,* p. 2.
[33] *Ibid.;* rad, MacArthur to Marshall, No. 3, 21 Mar 42, Msgs from Gen MacArthur, OPD Exec O.
[34] Wainwright, *General Wainwright's Story,* p. 4.
[35] Harbor Defenses Rpt of Opns, p. 42.
[36] *Ibid.,* pp. 42–43, 33.

Wainwright "lined up" the general officers in his I Corps and told them what Mac-Arthur had said to him. "They realized as well as I," he noted, "what the score was." [37] He then turned over command of the corps to General Jones and left for his new headquarters which would control both the corps on Bataan. Two days later a general order announced the creation of Luzon Force, General Wainwright commanding. [38]

Although the War Department was fully informed about MacArthur's movements from 12 March on, it was completely ignorant of the command arrangements which went into effect on his departure. Whatever the reason, MacArthur neglected to inform the War Department of his plans to control operations in the Philippines from Australia. It was therefore assumed in Washington that Wainwright, the senior officer in the islands, was now in command. All correspondence was addressed to him as commander and dispatches spoke of him as the successor to MacArthur. [39]

The War Department's ignorance of the organization of forces in the Philippines placed Colonel Beebe, promoted to brigadier general on 17 March, in a difficult situation. His own orders from General MacArthur made Wainwright a subordinate commander to USAFFE. As deputy chief of staff of USAFFE and MacArthur's representative on Corregidor he was superior to Wainwright. But higher headquarters was now directing its correspondence and orders to Wainwright as commander. His position

was an embarrassing one. Belatedly, on the 16th, a general order was published announcing his apointment as deputy chief of staff, USAFFE. [40] This did not solve the difficulty for the War Department was still unaware of the situation. Beebe thereupon told MacArthur that it was imperative the War Department be informed of the change in order to preserve morale. [41]

Events soon overwhelmed General Beebe. On the 18th (Washington time) he received a message from the Chief of Staff addressed to the commanding general of USAFFE at Fort Mills but obviously meant for Wainwright. In it General Marshall defined MacArthur's new area of responsibility as including the Philippines and explained that "he [MacArthur] retains supervisory control of you and your forces." The "CG USAFFE" was instructed to communicate directly with the War Department and to submit daily reports. "Nothing in these instructions," the message concluded, "will be construed as altering in any way your subordination to MacArthur." [42]

General Beebe was in a quandary. The message was addressed to "CG USAFFE," who he knew was MacArthur, but it was evidently meant for Wainwright. Was he authorized to deliver it to him? On his own initiative he decided to withhold the message from Wainwright and to acknowledge its receipt himself in a message to the War Department sent in MacArthur's name. To his chief he explained what he had done, declaring, "It is not clear to me who the Chief of Staff had in mind when

[37] Wainwright, *General Wainwright's Story,* p. 67.
[38] *Ibid.;* USAFFE GO 42, 14 Mar 42. The Luzon Force was "constituted effective 11 March."
[39] See AG 311.23 (4 Feb 42), GHQ SWPA. This file contains a number of messages from Beebe to General MacArthur complaining of this situation.

[40] USAFFE GO 44, 16 Mar 42. The order was effective 11 March.
[41] Rad, Beebe to MacArthur, n.d., AG 311.23 (4 Feb 42) GHQ SWPA.
[42] Rad, Marshall to USAFIA, No. 740, 18 Mar 42, OPD 381 Phil, Sec 1, Case 13. This is a paraphrase of the original message that went to Corregidor.

the message was written." Again he urged that General Marshall be informed of the command in the Philippines and asked for instructions on what to do about the Chief of Staff's order for a daily report.[43]

The next day the situation became even more confused. First came a message from President Roosevelt for General Wainwright. The President was obviously addressing Wainwright as commander of the forces in the Philippines. He told him that he had been nominated for appointment to the rank of lieutenant general "because of the confidence I have in your leadership and in the superb gallantry of the devoted band of American and Filipino soldiers under your command." There was no mistaking the President's belief that he was addressing MacArthur's successor when he told Wainwright that the whole nation realized the "extreme difficulty" and "vast importance" of his task and pledged "every possible means and method" to send him help.[44]

Later in the day Beebe received two messages from the Chief of Staff for "CG USAFFE" but clearly intended for Wainwright. In the first, Marshall told Wainwright that the Senate had confirmed his nomination to lieutenant general.[45] The second message made it clear that the War Department considered Wainwright the successor to MacArthur. No confusion was possible in the wording of this message. "Upon the departure of General MacAr-

thur," Marshall wrote, "you became commander of U.S. forces in the Philippines. You are to communicate directly with the War Department in rendering daily operational reports." These reports, he told Wainwright, "are to be dispatched over your name." [46]

Beebe had no choice now but to turn over command to Wainwright.[47] Late on the night of the 20th he telephoned the Luzon Force commander at his headquarters on Bataan and informed him of his promotion and designation as commander of U.S. forces in the Philippines. The next morning Wainwright pinned the third star on his shoulders and moved to Corregidor where Beebe turned over to him the messages from General Marshall and the President.[48]

Wainwright's first official act was to assume command of U.S. Forces in the Philippines (USFIP), the name of his new headquarters, and to make Beebe his chief of staff.[49] His command, like MacArthur's, included Navy as well as Army elements. Under Admiral Hart and for a time under his successor, Admiral Rockwell, naval forces in the Philippines had been organized as an independent command, not subject to orders from USAFFE. Joint operations had been conducted on the basis of co-ordination between the two headquarters. At the end of January General Mac-

---

[43] Rad, Beebe to MacArthur, 19 Mar 42, AG 311.23 (4 Feb 42) GHQ SWPA.

[44] Rad, Roosevelt to CG USAFFE, No. 1198, 19 Mar 42, Msgs to Wainwright, OPD Exec O. The message was sent on the recommendation of General Marshall.

[45] Rad, Marshall to Wainwright, No. 1204, 19 Mar 42, OPD 381 PI, Sec 1, Case 14. In tracing this correspondence, the reader must keep in mind the 13 hours' difference between Washington and Manila time.

[46] Rad, Marshall to Wainwright, No. 1203, 20 Mar 42, OPD 381 PI, Sec 1, Case 15.

[47] The author has been unable to find MacArthur's replies to Beebe. Internal evidence of the radios cited makes it clear that throughout he was acting under instructions from MacArthur.

[48] Wainwright, *General Wainwright's Story*, pp. 68–69.

[49] Rad, Wainwright to AGWAR, No. 538, 21 Mar 42, AG 381 (11–27–41 Sec 3) Far East. The message was sent at 0620. At the same time he accepted his appointment as lieutenant general. A similar message went to General MacArthur in Australia.

Arthur had asked that naval forces, including the marines, be placed under his command "due to restricted area of combat and the intimacy of liaison that is required." Army and Navy authorities in Washington quickly agreed to this request and on 30 January all naval forces in the Philippines had been put under MacArthur's control. Unity of command had thus been established for the first time in the campaign.[50] Wainwright inherited this arrangement, with Capt. Kenneth M. Hoeffel as naval commander.

Wainwright's assumption of command brought from General MacArthur an inquiry for the basis of the action. Wainwright explained that he had received a message from the President and instructions from the Chief of Staff, and had had no choice but to assume command. "I trust you will understand and appreciate my position in this matter," he wrote. "The appointment came as a surprise to me without any previous intimation that I was to be selected for this command."[51]

Now, on 21 March, General MacArthur for the first time informed General Marshall about his own arrangements for four separate commands and his intention to control operations in the Philippines from his headquarters in Australia through a deputy chief of staff on Corregidor.[52] This arrangement, he explained, was based upon "special problems" and "deemed most advantageous" because of "the intangibles of the situation in Philippines." As Sutherland later explained, it was never MacArthur's

intention that Wainwright should command all the forces in the Philippines.[53]

General Marshall's comments on MacArthur's plan were made to the President on 22 March. The four separate commands, Marshall pointed out, would have to report to MacArthur in Melbourne, 4,000 miles away. In the Manila Bay area alone there would be two separate commanders, and it was Marshall's opinion that MacArthur would have to arbitrate matters between these two from Australia.[54] Although the Chief of Staff did not know it, the disadvantages of the arrangements had already been noted by Wainwright, who, on the 15th, had gone to Corregidor to try to get more supplies for his Luzon Force. In this effort he had been unsuccessful. "I had no control over it [supplies]," he noted, "which irked me a bit. MacArthur had left the matter of Bataan supplies in the hands of . . . Beebe, over on Corregidor."[55]

General Marshall found MacArthur's arrangements for command in the Philippines unsatisfactory and told the President so. He was "fearful," he said, that they would have "a very depressing effect" on General Wainwright, "on whom we must now depend for the successful continuance of the fight on Bataan."[56] These arrangements, Marshall observed, were also contrary to the principle

[50] Rads, MacArthur to Marshall, No. 156, 30 Jan 42, AG 381 (11-27-41 Gen) Far East, and Marshall to MacArthur, 30 Jan 42, WPD 3251-75.

[51] Rad, Wainwright to MacArthur, 19 Mar 42, AG 311.23 (4 Feb 42) GHQ SWPA.

[52] Rad, MacArthur to Marshall, No. 3, 21 Mar 42, AG 311.23 (4 Feb 42) GHQ SWPA.

[53] Interv, author with Sutherland, 12 Nov 46. Wainwright's appointment, Sutherland said, had been made by the War Department "after MacArthur left and without his knowledge." Actually, MacArthur seems to have been informed of the War Department's intentions before Wainwright through the messages he received from Beebe.

[54] Memo, Marshall for Roosevelt, 22 Mar 42, sub: Comd in Phil, Msgs from Gen MacArthur, OPD Exec O; interv, author with Collier, 20 Nov 46.

[55] Wainwright, General Wainwright's Story, p. 67.

[56] Memo, Marshall for Roosevelt, 22 Mar 42, sub: Comd in Phil, Msgs from Gen MacArthur, OPD Exec O.

of combined command. As a supreme commander of Allied forces in Australia, MacArthur was no longer eligible to command directly U.S. forces any more than he could command those of other nations. Such command would properly be exercised through a U.S. Army headquarters.[57] Marshall therefore recommended to the President that MacArthur be informed that his plan was unsatisfactory and that Wainwright should continue in command of the Philippines. The President agreed and that day, 22 March, a conciliatory message went out to Melbourne. Refraining from specific criticism of the earlier arrangements, the message nevertheless made it clear that unless there were strenuous objections Wainwright would remain in command.[58]

MacArthur expressed no objections. He replied that he understood thoroughly the difficulties of the Chief of Staff and would accommodate himself to the arrangements already made. "Heartily in accord with Wainwright's promotion to lieutenant general," he said. "His assignment to Philippine command is appropriate." [59] Thus ended the uncertainty and confusion. General Wainwright was now confirmed as the commander of all forces in the Philippine Islands, with the large authority and heavy responsibilities formerly possessed by General MacArthur. He remained in a subordinate position to MacArthur, however, whose new command, officially sanctioned on 18 April, included the Philippine Islands

as well as Australia, New Guinea, and most of the Solomon Islands and the Netherlands Indies.[60]

Wainwright's elevation to the highest command in the Philippines left vacant the post of commander of the Luzon Force, created only ten days earlier. To fill this vacancy Wainwright selected Maj. Gen. Edward P. King, Jr.[61] He could instead have left the post vacant and dissolved Luzon Force altogether. Such a step could easily have been justified after the creation of USFIP. No such organization had existed on Bataan during MacArthur's regime and no headquarters had ever been interposed between the high command on Corregidor and the combat forces on Bataan. Instead, MacArthur had established an echelon of USAFFE on Bataan and through the officers assigned had exercised close supervision over combat elements.

Wainwright's decision to retain Luzon Force created what was in effect an Army headquarters controlling the two corps on the peninsula. This decision, MacArthur's chief of staff thought, was a serious mistake because it removed Wainwright from direct contact with the forces in front of the enemy. "Actually, there was no necessity for King's headquarters," Sutherland declared. "That headquarters had been established by MacArthur to compensate for the absence of a commander on Corregidor and to leave Wainwright free to conduct operations on Bataan. When the War Department created a command on Corregidor,

[57] This principle was well established and was incorporated in the doctrine for joint operations, Joint Action of the Army and Navy, 1927.
[58] Rad, Marshall to MacArthur, No. 810, 22 Mar 42, Msgs from Gen MacArthur, OPD Exec O. The President's agreement is assumed from the fact that the text of the message formed part of Marshall's memorandum to the President.
[59] Rad, MacArthur to Marshall, No. 19, 24 Mar 42, AG 311.23 (4 Feb 42) GHQ SWPA.

[60] For a detailed description of MacArthur's command in Australia see Milner, Victory in Papua, Ch. II. Unlike most subordinate commanders, Wainwright was authorized to communicate directly with the War Department.
[61] King assumed command 21 March 1942 on the basis of oral instructions from Wainwright. A general order followed later. Luzon Force Rpt of Opns, p. 1.

that headquarters [Luzon Force] should have been dissolved." [62]

The man chosen to lead Luzon Force, General King, was an artilleryman of wide experience with a distinguished career in the Army. After receiving a law degree from the University of Georgia he had entered the service through the National Guard in 1908. In addition to tours of duty with troops, he had been assigned to the Artillery School as student and instructor, served in the Office of the Chief of Field Artillery at three separate times, attended the Command and General Staff School, where he later taught, and the Army War College. After attendance at the Naval War College he was appointed director of the War Plans Section of the Army War College, a post he held for three years. On 14 September 1940 he was ordered to the Philippine Islands, where he had served from 1915 to 1917, to command Fort

Stotsenburg. Appointed brigadier general on his arrival, he later supervised the artillery training of the Philippine Army, commanded the North Luzon Force for a short time before the war, and served as MacArthur's artillery officer with the rank of major general. When Luzon Force was first created he had been assigned artillery officer of that command.

Soft-spoken, modest, innately courteous to all ranks, King had achieved a reputation as an extremely able soldier of high intellectual caliber. His assignment to command the Luzon Force, while a recognition of his ability and reputation, was destined to end tragically. On him fell the terrible responsibility for making the hard decision less than three weeks later to surrender his starved and defeated troops to the enemy.[63]

---

[62] Interv, author with Sutherland, 12 Nov 46.

[63] The material on General King's career is drawn from the *Official Army Register,* the standard public relations releases, and interviews with a large number of officers on his staff, including Maj. Achille C. Tisdelle, his aide.

CHAPTER XXI

The Battling Bastards

We're the battling bastards of Bataan;
No mama, no papa, no Uncle Sam;
No aunts, no uncles, no cousins, no nieces;
No pills, no planes, no artillery pieces.
. . . And nobody gives a damn.

The lot of the individual soldier on Bataan was hardly affected by changes in command. The search for food was his constant pursuit; hunger and disease his deadliest enemies. Literally, he faced starvation. When measured against this terrible and inescapable fact all else was of secondary importance.

Food and Clothing

Since 6 January, when the ration had been cut in half, the 80,000 soldiers and 26,000 civilians on Bataan had received a steadily diminishing and unbalanced allowance of food. Theoretically, the half ration supplied the American soldier with 6 ounces each of flour and canned or fresh meat daily; the Filipino with 10 ounces of rice and 4 of meat or fish. In actual fact the ration varied with time and circumstances and never on Bataan did it equal a full half ration. From January through February, the daily issue averaged less than 30 ounces, as compared to the peacetime garrison ration of 71 ounces for Americans and 64 for Filipinos.[1]

From the start it proved impossible to establish any theoretical basis for the issue

of rations. The issue varied from day to day and was based not on the number of calories required or the vitamins necessary to maintain the health and efficiency of the command, but solely on the amount of food on hand. Since rice was most plentiful it became the basic element in the diet and all other foods were rationed to last as long as it did.

As the supply of food dwindled the amount issued was steadily reduced. The inventory of 5 January had disclosed that there was only enough canned meat and fish to last 50 days, canned milk for 20, flour and canned vegetables for 30, and small amounts of sugar, lard substitutes, coffee, and fruits.[2] By the end of the month this supply had diminished to an 11-day supply of meat and fish, 6 days of flour, 5 of fruit, and 4 of vegetables.[3] On 23 February the Philippine Department quartermaster, Col. Frank Brezina, reported that he had on hand only a 2½-day supply of meat and fish, enough flour to last 4½ days, and only 228 cans of tomatoes, 48 cans of fruit, 30 pounds of coffee, 1,100 pounds of raisins,

---

[1] AR 30–2210.

[2] QM Rpt of Opns, p. 31. Rice was not included in the inventory.

[3] Memo, Gen Drake for Gen R. J. Marshall, 2 Feb 42, sub: Rations, copy in OCMH.

27,736 cans of milk, and 21,700 pounds of sugar.[4] A few days later he told Brig. Gen. Charles C. Drake, the USAFFE quartermaster, that there was no corned beef, corned beef hash, or bacon left on Bataan. "We are entirely dependent upon the shipments of salmon from Fort Mills," he declared, "as it is impossible to slaughter sufficient carabao to make an issue to all units." [5] Before the end of the campaign the amount of canned meat, usually corned beef, issued to the troops had been reduced from 6 ounces to 1.2 ounces.

The Filipinos, whose ration, except for flour, was the same as the American ration, did not suffer as much, for the allowance of rice rarely dropped below 8 ounces. The stock of canned vegetables, limited in quantity and variety from the very start, shrank steadily until its issue was virtually discontinued. Within a month after the troops reached Bataan, butter, coffee, and tea had practically disappeared from the menu. Sugar and canned milk were extremely scarce and were doled out in the most minute quantities.

By the middle of February the ration had already dropped far below the standard half ration. On the 17th of the month the men on Bataan received only 27.7 ounces, consisting of 9 ounces of rice, 4 of meat, 5 of bread, plus a small allowance of sugar, coffee, bacon, juice, and canned tomatoes and fruit, amounting altogether to 10 ounces.[6]

As the days went by the ration was cut again and again. By the end of March it had been so reduced and the fare offered had become so monotonous as to amount to little more than a token diet barely sufficient to sustain life. The bareness and inadequacy of this diet is revealed strikingly in the ration for 25 March, shown in Table 8. At that time the men were receiving less than one quarter the amount of food allotted soldiers in peacetime.

TABLE 8—RATION, 25 MARCH 1942

[Ounces]

Component	Americans	Filipinos
Rice.....................	8.5	10.00
Flour.....................	1.44	0
Canned Meat............	1.22	1.22
or		
Fresh Meat..............	6.00	6.00
Milk.....................	1.30	1.30
Salt......................	1.60	1.60
Sugar....................	.48	.48
Totals with canned meat............	14.54	14.60
Totals with fresh meat............	19.32	19.38

Based on memo, Gen Funk for CG USFIP, 25 Mar 42, sub: Status of Rations, AG 430.2 (3 Jan 42) Phil Rcds.

Hospital patients, though allotted a double ration, ate none too well. Rice was the chief component of their diet and it was extremely difficult to provide the special foods required for postoperative and intestinal cases. "It was quite a sight," wrote one doctor, "to see . . . those who should have received adequate soft and liquid diet trying to eat a gob of sticky, gummy, half-cooked rice." [7]

---

[4] Rpt, QM Phil Dept to QM USAFFE, 24 Feb 42, sub: Class I Supplies, AG 319.1 (29 Jan 42) Phil Rcds. Other reports in this file provide detailed information on the quantity and type of food in Bataan stocks.

[5] Rpt, QM Phil Dept to QM USAFFE, 27 Feb 42, sub: Class I Supplies, AG 319.1 (29 Jan 42) Phil Rcds.

[6] Rpt, QM Phil Dept to QM USAFFE, 17 Feb 42, sub: Class I Supplies, AG 319.1 (29 Jan 42) Phil Rcds.

[7] Lt Col Walter H. Waterous, Statement of Experiences and Observations concerning the Bataan Campaign . . ., p. 51, copy in OCMH.

Every effort was made to exploit the slender food resources of Bataan. The two rice mills constructed by the engineers began operations in mid-January. Under the supervision of the quartermaster foraging parties gathered the palay (unhusked rice), which stood ripe in the narrow rice belt along Manila Bay, and brought it to the mills for threshing. Before the supply was exhausted sometime in March a total of 250 tons of palay had been collected. Since the rate of consumption was fifteen tons a day, this impressive total amounted to only a seventeen-day supply. Had modern farm machinery been available the quantity of palay recovered, one officer estimated, would have been ten times greater.[8]

Since it was the most abundant food on Bataan rice ultimately replaced wheat in the diet of the American soldiers. Accustomed to potatoes and bread they found rice a most unsatisfactory substitute. Consisting mostly of starch and with scarcely any vitamins it possessed little nutritive value. Without seasoning or other foods it had little flavor of its own and tasted like "wall-paper paste." As one wit remarked, "Rice is the greatest food there is—anything you add to it improves it." [9] But it had one virtue none could deny; it filled empty stomachs, and on Bataan that was a most important consideration.

While it lasted fresh meat was issued to the troops at regular intervals, usually every third day. This meat was obtained principally from the carabao slaughtered at the recently established abattoir near Lamao and at scattered, small slaughterhouses consisting of little more than platforms over rapidly running fresh-water streams. In the absence of refrigeration the carabao were kept in enclosures until a fresh meat issue was due, then quickly slaughtered and issued to the troops. Toward the end of the campaign about 600 of the butchered carabao were sent to Corregidor for storage in the refrigeration plant and later returned to Bataan for issue. When forage for animals was exhausted, the 250 horses of the 26th Cavalry and 48 pack mules were regretfully slaughtered also. Maj. Achille C. Tisdelle, a cavalry officer and General King's aide, wrote on 15 March that the 26th Cavalry and other units had that day finished the last of their horses.[10] Altogether the amount of fresh meat slaughtered on Bataan totaled approximately 1,300 tons.[11]

For a time the meat component was supplemented by fresh fish caught by local fishermen. At one period of the campaign the daily catch reached as high as 12,000 pounds. This supply ended when Japanese and indiscriminate American gunfire discouraged the nightly fishing trips.[12]

To these sources of food must be added the amounts procured by the individual soldier. The Filipino was most adept at fending for himself in the jungle. In various localities he could secure chickens, pigs, camotes (sweet potatoes), bamboo shoots, mangoes, and bananas. He could supplement his diet with dog and monkey meat; with the chickenlike meat of the iguana lizard, so relished by the natives; and with

[8] Class I Supplies, AG 319.1 (29 Jan 42) Phil Rcds; Capt Harold A. Arnold, "The Lessons of Bataan," *Quartermaster Review,* XXVI (November–December 1946), 14.

[9] Maj. Calvin E. Chunn, ed., *Of Rice and Men* (Los Angeles: Veterans Publishing Co., 1946), p. ii.

[10] Tisdelle, Diary, entry of 15 Mar 42. This diary has been published under the title, "Bataan Diary of Maj A. C. Tisdelle," edited by present author, in *Military Affairs,* XI (Fall 1947).

[11] QM Rpt of Opns, p. 35; Luzon Force Rpt of Opns, G–4 Annex, p. 1.

[12] QM Rpt of Opns, p. 35; Tisdelle, Diary, entry of 15 Mar 42.

the meat of the large python snake whose eggs the Filipinos considered a great delicacy. On his own initiative he picked rice in the fields near him and threshed it in his foxhole. Those in the front lines could make their way through the outposts to near-by barrios and at exorbitant prices purchase food not obtainable by the quartermaster. Ofttimes patrols would return with sacks of milled rice.[13]

The Americans soon learned that hunger is a great leveler and sought the meat of dogs—which tasted like lamb—iguanas, and monkeys as avidly as their native comrades-in-arms. "Monkeys and iguanas are quite scarce," wrote one officer regretfully, "and about all we have is rice." [14] Colonel Mallonée's experience was wider. After a varied diet on Bataan, the 195-pound six-footer offered this advice to epicures: "I can recommend mule. It is tasty, succulent and tender—all being phrases of comparison, of course. There is little to choose between calesa pony and carabao. The pony is tougher but better flavor than carabao. Iguana is fair. Monkey I do not recommend. I never had snake," [15] To supplement this report there is the judgment of another gourmet who declared "that monkey meat is all right until the animal's hands turn up on a plate." [16]

The search for food sometimes had tragic results for those who could not distinguish the edible from the inedible. The wild carrot, highly toxic in its native form, caused numerous violent intestinal disturbances and frequent deaths. Some types of berry were also poisonous and resulted in illness or death. But the troops continued to eat every berry and root they could find and by April the peninsula "had been broken dry of all edible vegetation . . . which anyone thought he could eat." [17]

In addition to the food obtained from the quartermaster and that secured by individuals through their own initiative and ingenuity, men soon found other ways to supplement their ration. A large amount of fresh meat was procured by units which seized any livestock unlucky enough to come within their reach. There was always the possibility that the animals might be diseased, but men were willing to take that chance. Headquarters frowned upon this practice for reasons of health and because it curtailed the supply of fresh meat for regular issue, and early in February prohibited the slaughter of carabao "by any individual, unit, or organization . . . except at the Field Abattoir under the direct supervision of the Department Veterinarian." [18] Despite these orders about 1,000 carabao were butchered privately during the campaign.[19]

Many units had their own private reserves of food, secured in various ways, regular and irregular. The chief source of these caches was the supplies picked up at depots during the withdrawal and never turned in. One unit, investigation disclosed, had "a considerable cache of subsistence . . . well guarded behind barbed wire"; another had 8,500 C Rations in its private

[13] Memo, Lt Col James O. Gillespie for Surgeon, USAFFE, 27 Feb 42, sub: Diet of American Soldiers, AG 430.2 (11 Sep 41) Phil Rcds; memo, Asst G–4 for G–4 USAFFE, 3 Feb 42, with ind by Gen Drake, 9 Feb 42, AG 319.1 (8 Jan 42) Phil Rcds; Cooper, Med Dept Activities, pp. 98–99; Alexander, Personal Recollections of Bataan, p. 102; intervs, author with numerous officers who served on Bataan, at various dates during the preparation of this volume.
[14] Tisdelle, Diary, entry of 15 Mar 42.
[15] Mallonée, Bataan Diary, II, 11.
[16] Chunn, Of Rice and Men, p. 34.

[17] Waterous, Statement of Experiences, p. 53.
[18] Ltr Order, USAFFE, 12 Feb 42, sub: Slaughter of Carabao, AG 431 (17 Jan 42) Phil Rcds.
[19] Luzon Force Rpt of Opns, G–4 Annex, p. 1.

dump.[20] In one case the driver of a ration truck had accumulated 520 cans of tomatoes, 111 cans of evaporated milk, 297 cans of tomato sauce, 114 cans of tomato juice, 6 cans of oleomargarine, 12 sacks of rice, and three fourths of a sack of wheat.[21] So large was the private supply of one unit that MacArthur's chief of staff ordered an investigation which revealed a situation even worse than had been thought.[22] Orders had been issued at the start of the campaign directing the return of these supplies to the quartermaster, but few units obeyed. Even the requirement of a detailed, certified report of stocks from all unit commanders failed to bring in the private caches.[23]

One of the most persistent irregularities in the issue of rations was the padding of strength reports by units so that they could draw more than their share. At one time, 122,000 rations were being issued daily. "It appears," wrote Lt. Col. Frank F. Carpenter, Jr., of the Bataan echelon of USAFFE, "that many units are doubling up."[24] A warning from MacArthur brought the figure down to 94,000 for military personnel alone, which was still considerably higher than it should have been.[25] One flagrant example of padding that came to the attention of USAFFE was that of the division, with two regiments detached, which drew 11,000 rations on 6 February.

At full strength this division did not have more than 6,500 men.[26] But despite the strictest orders and the most careful procedures, the number of rations issued continued to exceed the troop strength.

Even within units rations were sometimes distributed unequally. Reports that complete ration components were not being pushed forward from division quartermaster dumps to the front-line troops reached USAFFE and on 17 January commanders were told that "in some cases subsistence has been forcibly diverted from the units for which it was intended."[27] This reminder, like most dealing with the ration, was ignored when it was safe to do so.

While such practices existed the fare of units was uneven. Some ate well, others poorly, and it is a truism of warfare that the units to the rear always live best. "There is nothing quite so controversial as the Bataan ration," wrote one reflective officer. "Some units got corned beef, others none. Some had corned beef hash in lieu of fish. Some got eight ounces of rice, others 3.7. Some got flour in place of bread, some hard tack. But there is nothing controversial about the fact that the ration was grossly inadequate."[28]

Even when no irregularity interrupted the normal distribution of rations, the confusion and hazards of war often robbed men of their food. General Stevens justly complained that his 91st Division was receiving an unbalanced ration when, by some misadventure, the quartermaster issued for his 5,600 men 19 sacks of rice, 12 cases of sal-

[20] Memos, Asst G–4 for G–4 USAFFE, 8 Jan, 9 Feb 42, AG 319.1 (8 Jan 42) Phil Rcds.

[21] Ibid.

[22] Ibid.; memo, G–4 for Asst G–4 USAFFE, 5 Feb 42, AG 430.2 (11 Sep 41) Phil Rcds.

[23] Ibid.; intervs, author with Drake at various times.

[24] Memo, Asst G–4 for G–4 USAFFE, 16 Jan 42, AG 319.1 (8 Jan 42) Phil Rcds.

[25] Memo, CG USAFFE for Corps and Div Comdrs, 17 Jan 42, sub: Noncompliance with Orders, AG 430 (8 Dec 41) Phil Rcds; memo, Asst G–4 for G–4 USAFFE, 19 Jan 42, AG 319.1 (8 Jan 42) Phil Rcds.

[26] Memo, Asst G–4 for G–4 USAFFE, 10 Feb 42, AG 319.1 (8 Jan 42) Phil Rcds.

[27] Memo, CG USAFFE for Corps and Div Comdrs, 17 Jan 42, sub: Noncompliance with Orders, AG 430 (8 Dec 41) Phil Rcds; memo, Asst G–4 for G–4 USAFFE, 15 Jan 42, AG 319.1 (8 Jan 42) Phil Rcds.

[28] Mallonée, Bataan Diary, II, 11.

mon, 3½ sacks of sugar, 4 carabao quarters, plus a few miscellaneous items. That same day another division received nothing but canned goods.[29] Sometimes a change in assignment would leave one unit without a ration for one day while another received a double issue. The movement of units from one sector to another, usually made at night when the rations were issued, resulted as frequently in a double issue as in none at all.

The long and difficult supply lines on Bataan often slowed up the delivery of food, and vehicles carrying supplies broke down on the mountain trails. The distribution of fresh meat was extremely difficult under these conditions. Since refrigeration and an adequate road net were lacking, the meat had to be transported in open trucks during the heat of the tropical day on hauls lasting as long as twelve hours. It is not surprising that the meat which reached the front-line troops was not always fresh.

Sometimes an accident could have tragic results for the starved garrison. A lucky hit by a Japanese bomber knocked out a freezing unit in the Corregidor cold-storage plant, and 194 carabao quarters—about 24,000 pounds, almost one day's supply—was thereupon sent to Bataan for immediate issue. Five successive air raids delayed the loading of the meat which did not reach Bataan until the next morning. Since it could not be unloaded during daylight the meat remained on the barge the entire day. By evening it was unfit for distribution.[30]

The difficult supply routes and the ever-present threat of starvation were responsible for large-scale pilferage, looting, and hijacking by civilians and troops alike. Supply trucks moving slowly along the narrow, tortuous trails of Bataan were ideal targets for hungry men with guns. Guards were posted but even they were not above temptation. Philippine Army military police placed along the supply routes helped themselves generously from the vehicles they halted.

Officers also sought to secure food and supplies in this way, and on one occasion two officers, an American and a Filipino, were caught red-handed looting a quartermaster dump. So serious was the situation that it was proposed that guards be instructed to shoot anyone caught looting. A similar fate was proposed for those in the vicinity of a supply dump without "proper reason or authority." [31] Despite threats of dire consequences, looting and hijacking continued. It was comparatively easy to toss off a sack of rice to a waiting friend as a truck moved forward, and the closer the ration trucks came to the front lines the less food they contained.[32]

One item of issue that created serious difficulty was cigarettes. Never present in sufficient quantity for general distribution, they were doled out to the front-line troops from time to time. No item disappeared so quickly between the point of supply and destination. The loss was a heavy one. In mid-January an officer of the Bataan echelon of USAFFE urgently recommended that cigarettes be sent from Corregidor to the men at the front, and a month later Colonel Beebe told the chief of staff that the demand for cigarettes

[29] Memo, Asst G–4 for G–4 USAFFE, 13 Jan 42, AG 319.1 (8 Jan 42) Phil Rcds.

[30] Memo, CG USFIP for G–4, 29 Mar 42, with ind, AG 431 (17 Jan 42) Phil Rcds.

[31] Memo, Asst G–4 for G–4 USAFFE, 15 Jan 42, AG 319.1 (8 Jan 42) Phil Rcds, also draft orders atchd as Incl I.

[32] Rpt, QM Phil Dept to QM USAFFE, 2 Mar 42, sub: Class I Supplies, AG 319.1 (29 Jan 42) Phil Rcds. All survivors interviewed agreed that these practices continued until the end of the campaign.

was rapidly creating "a real morale problem." [33] Finally, early in March, USAFFE authorized the issue of five cigarettes daily to men in front-line units, and 104 cases— less than one pack a man—were shipped to Bataan.[34]

This issue did not even begin to satisfy the need for cigarettes. While inspecting a battalion position, Brig. Gen. Hugh J. Casey, USAFFE engineer, took out a pack of cigarettes. He was immediately mobbed. Every Filipino within fifty yards left his foxhole and rushed to get one.[35] Rumors began to reach Corregidor that cigarettes sent from there had been hijacked, that they had been held back by rear echelons, and that favored treatment had been accorded higher headquarters. An investigation disclosed

. . . a dire lack of cigarettes among the front line units. Soldiers will pounce on any discarded cigarette stub for a single puff. There is in time of war no difference between the needs of smokers as between front and rear echelon unit, unless the need at the front is greater. It would appear only just to make an equal allocation between all officers and men, at the front, in rear echelons, and at Ft. Mills. Troops should not be in a position of paying 2 Pesos [$1.00] on the black market for a package of cigarettes and even then being unable to get them when those in the rear can secure them in plenty at ten centavos [5 cents].[36]

A visitor from Corregidor who had heard that cigarettes would bring a fantastically high price on Bataan decided to test the validity of the rumor on his Philippine Scout driver. He was able to get ten pesos ($5.00) for a single pack and the thanks of the driver as well. "I gave the soldier back his ten pesos," he wrote, "and told him that if anyone ever wanted to charge him more than twenty centavos a package for cigarettes he should shoot them." [37]

Altogether, it is estimated, only 400 cases, each consisting of fifty 200-cigarette cartons, were sent from Corregidor to Bataan between 6 January and 2 April. In concrete terms this meant that each front-line soldier received less than one cigarette a day.[38] Deprived of the solace of tobacco and coffee, the soldier living on 17 ounces of food a day could be very miserable indeed.

To the lack of food and tobacco must be added the shortage of clothing, as well as personal and organizational equipment of every kind. General Wainwright tells how, at the beginning of January, his exhausted and unshod troops stumbled into the thorny jungles of Bataan after their long withdrawal from Lingayen.[39] Regular Army units were comparatively well off at the start of the campaign, but the Philippine Army had reached Bataan with the scantiest supplies. A large percentage of the Filipinos had no raincoats, blankets, or shelter halves, and there were almost none for issue. General Stevens reported on 13 January that his men had only well-worn denims and were badly in need of underclothes and shoes. The 11th Division was in a similar plight. Its need was par-

[33] Memo, G–4 for CofS USAFFE, 28 Feb 42, AG 430 (25 Dec 41) Phil Rcds; memo, Asst G–4 for G–4 USAFFE, 13 Jan 42, AG 319.1 (8 Jan 42) Phil Rcds.

[34] Ltr Order, USAFFE, 3 Mar 42, sub: Issue of Cigs, AG 435.8 (3 Mar 42) Phil Rcds; rpt, QM Phil Dept to QM USAFFE, 2 Mar 42, sub: Class I Supplies, AG 319.1 (29 Jan 42) Phil Rcds.

[35] Skerry, Comments on Engineer Hist, No. 18.

[36] Memo, Engineer for CofS USAFFE, 8 Mar 42, AG 319.1 (5 Jan 41) Phil Rcds.

[37] S Sgt Bernard O. Hopkins, Personal and Official Notes of Btry C, 60th CA (AA), p. 15, copy in OCMH. The writer was probably the battery commander, Capt. Roland G. Ames.

[38] QM Rpt of Opns, p. 42.

[39] Wainwright, General Wainwright's Story, p. 46.

STANDING FORMATION, *10 January 1942.*

tially met by a shipment of 10,000 pairs of socks, 3,000 leggings, and 10,000 pairs of drawers. This issue, it must be noted, was for the entire force, not for the two divisions alone.[40]

As time passed, uniforms became more ragged and threadbare, offering little protection against the cold nights and the cruel thorns so abundant on Bataan. Unit commanders were instructed to limit their clothing requisitions "to minimum replacement requirements" without regard to normal army standards. Most did not secure even this minimum. In one unit, comparatively well clad, the uniforms were considered 90 percent unserviceable. Less than 25 percent of the enlisted men in this unit had blankets, shelter halves, or raincoats. Fully one quarter of the command was without shoes; the rest went about in shoes so badly worn that under normal conditions they would have been considered unfit for use.[41] For a time the most desperate needs were met by a salvage unit which "renovated, repaired, washed, and ironed" the clothing taken from patients in hospitals.[42] Such a measure merely robbed Peter to pay Paul.

The inequities in the issue of supplies favored the troops to the rear. "Morale on the front is high," wrote a visitor from Corregidor, "though the supply situation is enough to justify dissatisfaction." Many of

[40] Memos, Asst G–4 for G–4 USAFFE, 13 and 16 Jan 42, AG 319.1 (8 Jan 42) Phil Rcds; Luzon Force Rpt of Opns, G–4 Annex, p. 1; memo, QM Phil Dept for QM USAFFE, 16 Jan 42, Incl 2, AG 430.2 (3 Jan 42) Phil Rcds.

[41] Skerry, Comments on Engineer Hist, No. 20.
[42] Rpts, QM Phil Dept to QM USAFFE, 10 and 18 Mar 42, AG 319 (29 Jan 42) Phil Rcds.

the men, he noted, were without underwear and shoes and most had only one uniform—blue denims. The meals, too, he noticed, became progressively worse as one neared the front. "Supply and service troops," he concluded, "eat better than the line troops." [43]

Late in March one last effort was made to provide clothing, blankets, raincoats, and shoes for the tatterdemalion soldiers on Bataan. On the 29th Beebe, now a brigadier and Wainwright's chief of staff, asked his G–4 whether there were any supplies on Corregidor which could be released to units along the front. Since the reserve of uniforms and blankets was under the control of the Harbor Defenses commander, General Moore, the request was passed on to him. Four days later came the reply: no blankets or uniforms were available, but there were 10,000 pairs of shoes—originally sent from Bataan for safekeeping—in odd lot sizes that could be spared. On 4 April, at the height of the final Japanese attack, General King was asked whether he desired this heterogeneous mass of footgear. To this inquiry there is no recorded answer.[44]

While the men on the line believed that their comrades to the rear dined more fully and richly than they, all were convinced that those on Corregidor ate best of all. Actually such distinctions were purely relative and no one lived well. But there was enough truth in these generalizations to create a strong feeling of dissatisfaction and a serious morale problem. General Wainwright discovered this when he moved to Corregidor.

Accustomed to the omnipresent and ominous shortages of Bataan, he found Corregidor relatively a land of plenty. The troops there, it is true, ate two meals a day and subsisted on half rations, but it was a full half ration and its components provided a well-balanced diet. It included such "luxury items" as bacon, ham, fresh vegetables, and occasionally coffee, milk, and jam—foods which had long since disappeared from the Bataan diet.[45]

The disparity between the Corregidor and Bataan rations was sharply raised when the Bataan military police halted a supply truck and confiscated its waybill. This truck was delivering food to three antiaircraft batteries stationed on Bataan but receiving a Corregidor ration, to which they were entitled as organic elements of the harbor defense. What they were not entitled to was the Bataan ration, which they were also drawing. Such an irregularity would not have been surprising but when the waybill was examined it revealed a scandalous situation. The items listed in the shipment would make any Bataan soldier envious. They included a case each of ham and bacon, 24 cans of Vienna sausage, one sack of cracked wheat, 25 pounds of raisins, 33 pounds of lard substitute, 24 cans each of peas, corn, tomatoes, and peaches, 6 cans of potatoes, 24 bottles of catsup, 50 cartons of cigarettes, and even 600 pounds of ice.

The news of this sumptuous fare, so unlike the Bataan ration, spread rapidly to the front-line troops, adding fuel to their smoldering resentment. The incident was noted by all headquarters and the matter

---

[43] Hopkins, Btry C, 60th CA (AA), p. 13.

[44] Memo, CofS to G–4 USFIP, G–4 USFIP to CG Harbor Defenses, with five inds, and memo, QM USFIP to G–4 USFIP, both dated 29 Mar 42, in AG 431 (8 Oct 42) and AG 420 (2 Jan 42) Phil Rcds.

[45] Col Chester H. Elmes, QM Opns, Fort Mills, pp. 4–5, App. F, QM Rpt of Opns; memo, CG USAFFE for CG Harbor Defenses, 13 Mar 42, sub: Field Rations, Incl I, AG 430.2 (3 Jan 42) Phil Rcds.

quickly closed with a promise for remedial action.[46] The postscript was written by Colonel Carpenter in a personal note to General Beebe:

Bataan troops feel they are discriminated against. There is no way of preventing this sort of thing getting to the front line troops and you can appreciate the effect on morale. The clandestine manner of getting the so-called luxury items to the Harbor Defense troops on Bataan . . . does not seem ethical. Realize there are not sufficient luxury items for general issue but General Wainwright was assured troops assigned to Harbor Defense on Bataan received approximately the same ration components. However, such is war.[47]

Despite the admitted superiority of the Corregidor ration, no one could contend that the men on Corregidor had an adequate diet. They did not. And it is doubtful that the reduction of their ration would have materially altered the situation. The equal distribution of food between the 100,-000 men on Bataan and the 10,000 on Corregidor could not have saved Bataan and might have led to the weakening of the harbor defenses.

Health

In the wake of starvation and want came dread disease. Malaria, dengue, and the evil consequences of avitaminosis (vitamin deficiency)—scurvy, beriberi, and amoebic dysentery—made their appearance soon after the troops reached Bataan. On 10 January General King's aide wrote prematurely in his diary that the effects of the enforced diet of half rations was already becoming evident in the condition of the

men. Two weeks later he thought he saw signs of emaciation and nerve fatigue. The ration, he believed, had so reduced the stamina of the men that they were "being incapacitated by minor sickness they [formerly] had been able to throw off without medication."[48] Another layman described the symptoms of malnutrition he had noticed about the middle of February. In the morning, he observed, men's legs "feel watery and, at intervals, pump with pains that swell and go away again." Rapid movement brought an attack of vertigo and a thumping of the heart "like a tractor engine bogged in a swamp." For an hour after breakfast a feeling of normality was restored, followed by lassitude. The hour after noon, when men doubled up with intestinal pains, was the worst of the day.[49] Unknowingly, this officer was describing incipient beriberi resulting from the absence of fresh meat, vegetables, and dairy products—all rich in Vitamin B—from the diet.

Medical men began to warn commanders of the effects of the inadequate diet at the end of January. The caloric content of the ration then being issued, one medical officer reported, was "well under the requirements for the physical work demanded," and was resulting in serious loss of weight. In one unit, composed of Americans, the men had lost 15 to 25 pounds since the start of the campaign. The absence of fats and juices, as well as Vitamins A, B, and C, was evident, this medical officer declared, in "varying degrees of apathy, depression, lack of aggressiveness and irritability."[50]

---

[46] Memo, Provost Marshal for G–4 Service Comd, 19 Mar 42, with ind and incls, AG 430.2 (11 Sep 41) Phil Rcds.

[47] Ibid.

[48] Tisdelle, Diary, entries of 10 and 22 Jan and 15 Mar 42.

[49] Ind, Bataan, The Judgment Seat, p. 296.

[50] Memo, CO Far East Air Service Comd for Med Officer, Far East Air Service Comd, 2 Feb 42, sub: Ration Deficiency, AG 430 (25 Dec 41) Phil Rcds.

The alarm of medical and combat officers became so great during the next few weeks that Lt. Col. James O. Gillespie, the medical officer in the Bataan echelon of USAFFE, told his chief on Corregidor, Col. Wibb E. Cooper, that "it appears to be the consensus of surgeons attached to American front line troops that the diet provided is inadequate for the maintenance of health and combat efficiency." The lack of protein, fat, minerals, and certain vitamins, he pointed out, was resulting in common diarrhea and dysentery. The effects of the unbalanced diet on the Filipino, accustomed to the food and climate, were not as pronounced. Colonel Gillespie's recommendations included an increase in the allowance of beef, vegetables, and fruit, the issue of four ounces of evaporated milk daily, and the procurement of native fruits and vegetables. If these foods could not be secured in adequate amounts, he urged strongly that vitamin concentrates should be secured for the American troops at least.[51]

General Wainwright lent his support to these recommendations in a separate communication to General MacArthur in which he declared that if the campaign lasted two to six months longer "it is certain that a fairly high percentage of the troops will suffer from varying degrees of malnutrition. . . ."[52] By the end of February, the effects of the food shortage were clearly evident and well understood. Already MacArthur was sending urgent and eloquent pleas for aid to Washington and Australia, and efforts were being made to break through the Japanese blockade.[53]

The number of men brought down by malnutrition and vitamin deficiency diseases increased in geometric proportion with the passage of time and the successive cuts in the ration. During January, the ration had provided, in terms of energy, approximately 2,000 calories a day. The next month the figure declined to 1,500 and during March it was only 1,000 calories daily. Defense of the line on Bataan, Lt. Col. Harold W. Glattly, the Luzon force surgeon estimated, required an expenditure of energy of at least 3,500 to 4,000 calories a day for each man. He found the results of this caloric deficit alarming in the extreme. Serious muscle waste and depletion of fat reserve were evident everywhere and beriberi in its incipient stages had become almost universal throughout the command. Moreover, malnutrition had so weakened the troops that they were particularly vulnerable to even the most minor ailment. The spread of any disease, he warned, would be of epidemic proportions. Men's physical reserves had disappeared by early March; at the end of the month the men were deteriorating rapidly.[54]

Even more serious than malnutrition and avitaminosis was the spread of malaria. This disease had made its appearance shortly after the troops reached Bataan, but was kept under control by prophylactic doses of quinine. There was a small supply of atabrine but it was quickly exhausted. A malaria control program such as existed later in the war was not possible on Bataan. Most of the Filipino troops were never issued mosquito nets, and those who had them left them behind during the withdrawal for they were of a bulky and heavy type. The area

[51] Memo, Surg Bataan Ech for Surg USAFFE, 27 Feb 42, sub: Diet of American Soldiers, AG 430.2 (11 Sep 41) Phil Rcds.

[52] Ltr, Wainwright to CG USAFFE, 26 Feb 42, sub: Rations, AG 430.2 (11 Sep 41) Phil Rcds.

[53] For an account of these efforts, see Chapter XXII below.

[54] Luzon Force Rpt of Opns, pp. 1–2; memo, Surg LF to CG LF, 28 Mar 42, sub: Vitamin Deficiencies, OCMH.

occupied by the troops contained native villages where mosquitoes could breed freely, and there were always large numbers of Filipino civilians behind the lines. These civilians were "a reservoir for malaria," and nullified the effect of any limited control program adopted by the troops.[55]

Malaria did not affect the efficiency of the troops until the beginning of March, but at the end of January most of the men were already infested with malarial parasites. Medical officers made gloomy predictions for the future, when the supply of quinine would give out. "If all troops take the prescribed 5 grams prophylactic dose," wrote a medical officer to General R. J. Marshall on 26 January, "the supply will be exhausted in a month." [56] As early as the beginning of February there were signs that the disease would soon increase at an alarming rate. Only the regular dosage of quinine kept the disease in check that month, but the supply of this drug dwindled rapidly. During the first week of March, its use as a prophylactic in most units was discontinued. Thereafter the drug was administered only to those actually ill with the disease.

The consequences were frightful. The number of daily admissions to the hospitals for malaria alone jumped to 500 during the first week in March.[57] After an inspection of fortifications on Bataan, General Casey reported that the incidence of malaria was as high as 35 percent among front-line units.[58] Two weeks later Colonel Cooper declared that already there were 3,000 active cases of malaria among the troops on Bataan and that the disease was spreading with appalling rapidity.[59] Colonel Glattly took an even more pessimistic view of the situation. The relapse rate, he noted, was high and since no quinine was available for any but active cases, the command could expect a frightful increase in the morbidity rate.[60] By the end of the month the number of daily admissions to the hospitals was aproaching the fantastic figure of 1,000, and 75 to 80 percent of the men in front-line units had the disease.[61]

Every effort was made to secure quinine as well as vitamin concentrates and other medical supplies from sources outside the Philippines. Some quinine was brought to Corregidor by plane from Australia via Mindanao, and an effort was made to manufacture a drug from the bark of a tree native to the Islands that was thought to have the properties of quinine. Despite every expedient there was never a large enough supply of the drug after 1 March to permit its use as a prophylaxis. On 23 March, when the malarial rate was 750 cases daily, there was only enough quinine in the medical depot to provide inadequate treatment for about 10,000 men. "When the present stock is gone," Colonel Glattly warned General King, "a mortality rate in untreated cases

[55] Lt Col William J. Kennard, Observations on Bataan, notes taken at conf held by Lt Col Roger G. Prentiss, Jr., 22 Aug 42, pp. 5–6, copy in OCMH.

[56] Memo, Gillespie for Marshall, 26 Jan 42, sub: Med Supplies, AG 440 (26 Jan 42) Phil Rcds.

[57] Kennard, Observations on Bataan, p. 5; Luzon Force Rpt of Opns, pp. 1–2. There is a good deal of disagreement on the number of hospital admissions for malaria. The author has accepted the figures given in the report just cited.

[58] Memo, Casey for CG USAFFE, 8 Mar 42, AG 319.1 (5 Jan 42) Phil Rcds.

[59] Memo, Surg USFIP for CG USFIP, 22 Mar 42, AG 440 (26 Jan 42) Phil Rcds.

[60] Memo, Surg LF for CG LF, 22 Mar 42, AG 440 (26 Jan 42) Phil Rcds.

[61] Luzon Force Rpt of Opns, p. 1; memo, Funk to Beebe, 31 Mar 42, AG 710 (24 Mar 42) Phil Rcds; Kennard, Observations on Bataan, p. 5.

of 7 to 10 percent can be expected." [62] A week later Wainwright's surgeon reported that approximately 758,000 quinine tablets had been received by air and that the medical depot had only 600,000 left. The inadequacy of this supply can be measured against the 3,000,000 tablets which Colonel Cooper estimated as the minimum necessary each month to prevent the wholesale spread of malaria. [63]

The rapid spread of the disease can be attributed not only to the lack of quinine but also to the area in which the troops were stationed. The withdrawal from the Abucay-Mauban line late in January had placed the men in a low, malaria-infested valley between the high ground formed by Mt. Natib on the north and the Mariveles Mountains to the south. Even under the most favorable circumstances, it is probable that a large part of the command would have ultimately been debilitated by the disease endemic in this valley.

A notable disregard for sanitary precautions, combined with the natural unhealthfulness of the battle position, added greatly to the spread of malaria, as well as other diseases. Lack of training in the elementals of military hygiene was universal in the Philippine Army. Many of the Filipinos drank unboiled water from streams and pools and failed to sterilize their mess gear. Latrines were neither well constructed nor properly used. Kitchens were dirty and garbage buried near the surface. Huge flies, attracted by these malodorous dumps, swarmed everywhere. "The fly menace," wrote a medical officer, "spread beyond

comprehension." [64] "Sanitation," remarked another officer, on duty with Filipino troops, "was ghastly. Straddle trenches—when built—adjoined kitchens. . . . The calls of nature were responded to when and where heard." [65]

Even in the hospitals sanitation was far from ideal. There were no screens and the supply of lysol was limited. The hospital waste was emptied into latrine pits and the stench at times was so offensive that men relieved themselves elsewhere. Despite the desperate efforts of the nurses to keep the hospital areas sanitary, there were, one doctor thought, "undoubtedly many cross infections." [66]

Under these circumstances it is not surprising that common diarrhea and various forms of dysentery appeared soon after the troops fell back to fixed positions. While never as serious as malnutrition or malaria, the incidence of both ailments was high and their treatment limited by the shortage of drugs. Filipino troops, often barefoot, frequently developed hookworm also. Carbon tetrachloride for treatment was available only in limited quantities, the medical depot reporting fifty-one bottles on hand at the end of March. [67]

As the men on Bataan grew more gaunt and disease-ridden it became increasingly difficult to isolate the specific causes which rendered men ineffective for combat. One surgeon believed that the high malarial rate was "covering up" the prevailing "mental and physical exhaustion" caused by a pro-

[62] Memo, Surg LF for CG LF, 23 Mar 42, sub: Present Malarial Rate, borrowed from Col Glattly, copy in OCMH.

[63] Memo, Surg USFIP for G–4 USFIP, 2 Apr 42, AG 710 (24 Mar 42) Phil Rcds.

[64] Waterous, Statement of Experiences, p. 52. See also memo, Surg 21st Div (PA) for Surg Subsector D, 3 Mar 42, OCMH.

[65] Mallonée, Bataan Diary, II, 10.

[66] Waterous, Statement of Experiences, p. 52.

[67] Cooper, Med Dept Activities, p. 36; memo, CO Phil Med Depot for Surg USFIP, 2 Apr 42, AG 710 (24 Mar 42) Phil Rcds.

tracted starvation diet.[68] It was Colonel Cooper's judgment that "the basic cause of all the trouble was the lack of food, of proper food." [69] At the time he wrote, 2 April, there were no vitamin concentrates on hand in the medical depot.

Less tangible but fully as serious as any of the diseases prevalent on Bataan was nerve fatigue. The majority of the combat troops had received no rest in a rear area since the first Japanese attack on 8 December. Even reserve units behind the line had been subjected to daily air and artillery bombardment. In the opinion of Colonel Glattly, "The fatigue resulting from constant nervous tension definitely decreased the ability of these troops to endure heavy bombardment." [70] The physical signs of this ailment were observed toward the end of the campaign when many of the men proved unable to stand the nervous strain of combat. At an earlier period stragglers had been rallied and sent back into battle. Later in the campaign stragglers discarded arms and equipment and could not be returned to the front except by force. "They were surly and physically exhausted as well as mentally unequal to further combat duty," said one medical officer.[71]

The number of men hospitalized for psychotic disorders was remarkably small and presented no serious problem to the medical authorities.[72] This may have been due to the fact that there was "no possible retreat from reality," as the medical officer of USAFFE believed, or to the failure to evacuate such cases to the hospitals. Facilities for the isolation and treatment of mental patients were limited. One ward in General Hospital No. 2 was set aside for these patients, but they could not be confined and seem to have been allowed to roam the hospital area.[73]

With the exception of quinine, dysentery serum, gas antitoxin, and some sulfa drugs, the supply of medicine held out to the end of the campaign. Large amounts of blood plasma were used. The marines had brought twenty-five cases from Shanghai and these were placed in the common pool. The shortage of antitoxin led to an abnormally large number of gas gangrene cases. Wounds which ordinarily would have presented no difficulty failed to respond to treatment and became infected. If the wound did not heal after it was opened and drained, then amputation followed.[74]

There were two general hospitals on Bataan. Until the end of January one of these, General Hospital No. 1, was located at Limay and because of its proximity to the front lines took all battle casualties requiring surgery. Its eight operating tables were housed in a building 14 by 40 feet. In a period of one month more than 1,200 battle casualties requiring major surgery were admitted to the hospital, the larger number being received on 16 January when the staff performed 182 major surgical operations. Usually all the operating tables were occupied and other patients lay on litters close by awaiting surgery. "It was neces-

[68] Ltr, Bill Ruth to Col Glattly, 20 Mar 42, copy lent to author by Col Glattly, OCMH.
[69] Memo, Surg USFIP for G–4 USFIP, 2 Apr 42, AG 710 (24 Mar 42) Phil Rcds.
[70] Rpt, Surg LF, 30 Jun 42, sub: Med Aspects of the Surrender. Written in prison camp, this report was lent to the author by Colonel Glattly and a copy is on file in OCMH.
[71] Luzon Force Rpt of Opns, p. 2.
[72] Cooper, Med Dept Activities, p. 18.

[73] Waterous, Statement of Experiences, p. 100; Lt Col Stephen C. Sitter, Psychiatric Reactions Observed on Corregidor and Bataan and in Japanese Captivity, pp. 5–6, copy lent to author, OCMH.
[74] Kennard, Observations on Bataan, p. 4.

sary," one medical officer recalled, "for the nurses to walk around patients when assisting in the operations." [75] After the withdrawal, the hospital was moved back to Little Baguio, on the slopes of the Mariveles, near the ammunition and quartermaster depots. When these installations were bombed, the hospital area, though clearly marked by a large cross, was vulnerable to air attack. Twice toward the close of the campaign it was hit.

General Hospital No. 2 was located about three miles south of Cabcaben, in the bamboo thickets and jungle along the Real River. Close by was the medical supply depot. The thicket and jungle provided concealment from air observation and the river a fresh-water supply which was filtered and chlorinated, then stored in a 3,000-gallon storage tank. [76]

Evacuation of the sick and wounded was accomplished in two ways—by ambulance directly from the aid and clearing stations and by shuttle buses. There were only a few ambulances and these were sent out on special cases. The shuttle buses had about fifteen litters instead of seats and made regular trips along designated routes on schedule. Most of the wounded were brought in at night to avoid the daytime traffic and reduce the possibility of enemy air attack. Normally it took about eight hours to get a casualty from the battlefield to the hospital, but in some Philippine Army units this period was as long as thirty-six hours. [77]

The majority of the wounds treated in the hospitals were from shell fragments and small-arms fire; relatively few were from bombs. The small caliber Japanese rifle did not inflict as serious a wound as the American .30-caliber rifle. It was one doctor's opinion, after examining men with eight and ten wounds in their arms, shoulders, and chest, that these men would have been killed if similarly wounded by .30-caliber bullets. [78]

Abdominal wounds were the most common. There was no established method of treatment; each surgeon used his own judgment. But there was an adequate supply of sulfa drugs for external use and no necessity for unusual methods. It was only when gas gangrene set in that difficulties arose because of the lack of antitoxin. Wounds healed slowly because of the weakened condition of the men, and the period of hospitalization was normally longer than might otherwise have been the case if there had been enough food for a proper diet. [79]

The large and ever-increasing number of sick and wounded strained all medical installations to the utmost. Fortunately, the number of battle casualties in the period between 15 February and 3 April was small and the beds ordinarily used by the wounded could be given to the starved and malaria-ridden soldiers. The capacity of the two general hospitals, designed to accommodate 1,000 patients each, was steadily increased until it reached a figure three times that number.

The sick rate continued to outstrip even this notable expansion. This fact, combined with the shortage of gasoline, made it necessary at the beginning of March to limit evacuation to the general hospitals to two types of cases: first, those requiring medical or surgical treatment not available at the clearing stations; and, second, those in

---

[75] Ibid.; Cooper, Med Dept Activities, p. 55.
[76] Cooper, Med Dept Activities, pp. 57–61.
[77] Kennard, Observations on Bataan, p. 3.

[78] Ibid.
[79] Waterous, Statement of Experiences, pp. 83–84.

MEDICAL CARE ON BATAAN. *Filipino soldiers waiting for treatment outside an aid station, above; interior of hospital, below.*

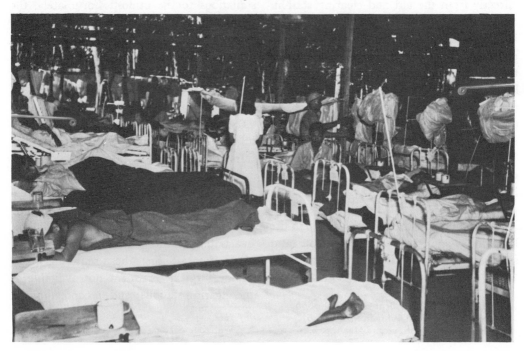

which the period of disability was expected to exceed twenty-one days.[80] To care for all other patients the clearing station of each medical battalion was converted into a hospital with 300 or more beds. Under ideal circumstances the clearing station was neither organized nor equipped to provide hospitalization. On Bataan, where conditions were far from ideal and where the Philippine Army medical units lacked much of the standard equipment normal in such elements, clearing stations were even less qualified to handle patients.

As the volume of patients increased, downward echelonment of hospitalization continued. Soon the collecting companies, designed to provide only emergency treatment to casualties, were converted into hospitals with 100 to 150 beds. Even with the addition of these units, hospital facilities had become so inadequate by the end of March that patients with minor ailments were treated in battalion and regimental aid stations. All medical installations on Bataan were bursting with patients and still they were not able to care for all the sick and wounded. The two general hospitals had about 7,000 patients; another 4,000 were being treated in a provisional hospital established by I Corps. Undetermined numbers were ill in division clearing and collecting companies. The 91st Clearing Company, 4,000 yards behind the front lines, had 900 beds; the 11th was handling 600 patients. And the number was growing daily. Everyone recognized that the hospitalization provided was "in direct conflict with the recognized principles of division medical service" and "a violation of all standard medical tactics," but, wrote the

surgeon, the main objective, the saving of lives and the relief of suffering, was achieved.[81]

The health of the command had a disastrous effect upon combat efficiency. This fact was noted first early in February and Wainwright had expressed his concern to MacArthur on the 26th of the month. The next month the situation grew more alarming. "The doctors say," wrote King's aide on 14 March, "that our combat efficiency is a little below 45 percent." [82] When Col. Harry A. Skerry inspected I Corps positions with General Casey early in March he found that in the sector held by a battalion of the 71st infantry the commander was so sick with dengue fever he could hardly accompany them. Of the 426 men in the battalion 126 were "clear off their feet." "From the standpoint of trained, well-fed troops . . .," wrote Skerry, "it was an utter nightmare." [83] In another unit, the 21st Division in II Corps, the men were so weak that many "were just able to fire a rifle out of the trench, and no more." [84]

These conditions were not confined to Philippine Army units; Americans and Philippine Scouts were equally debilitated by malnutrition and malaria. At a medical inspection of the 45th Infantry (PS), almost 20 percent of the command showed the physical effects of vitamin deficiency diseases, and over 50 percent complained of the symptoms of these diseases. Nutritional edema (swellings) and night blindness were the commonest symptoms. "Men were becoming so weak from starvation,"

---

[80] Memo, Surg Subsector D for Surgs 21st Div (PA) and 41st Div (PA), 6 Mar 42, copy in OCMH; Cooper, Med Dept Activities, p. 32.

[81] Cooper, Med Dept Activities, pp. 32–33. See also Luzon Force Rpt of Opns, Annex II, p. 1.
[82] Tisdelle, Diary, entry of 14 Mar 42.
[83] Skerry, Comments on Engineer Hist, No. 18.
[84] O'Day, 21st Div (PA), II, 39.

wrote the regimental surgeon, "that they could hardly carry the packs and in our last move I saw more Scouts fall out of the line of march than I had ever seen fall out any march before." [85]

The 31st Infantry, composed entirely of Americans, was as badly off as most other units. Though it had been in the front lines for only short periods during the campaign, and from 8 February to 3 April had been in a rest area to the rear, the regiment was hardly more effective than Philippine Army units which had been in the line since 8 December. The constant preoccupation of the American infantryman was food. "We were existing," wrote one of the officers, "on the little we received from quartermaster and what edible plants, roots, snails, snakes, wild chickens, bananas, wild pigs and anything else that we could find to eat." [86] Disease was taking a heavy toll and approximately 50 percent of the regiment was sick with malaria or dysentery.

By 3 April "what had once been an effective fighting unit was only a pitiful remains." [87] When the 31st Infantry, in Luzon Force reserve, was ordered into the line on 4 April, it was necessary to leave behind for evacuation to the hospital more than one third of the men. Some left sick beds to join their outfits. The efficiency of those who moved out was estimated at less than 50 percent. Along the line of march, many dropped out. "Hunger and disease," wrote the service company commander, "were greater enemies than the Japanese soldiers." [88]

---

[85] Rpt of 45th Inf (PS) Med Det in Cooper, Med Dept Activities, p. 44.
[86] Conrad, Opns of 31st Inf (US), p. 20.
[87] Ibid.
[88] Ibid., p. 21; Bess, Opns of Service Co, 31st Inf (US), 5 Jan 42–9 Apr 42, p. 40; Mead, Opns of 31st Inf (US), pp. 24–25.

Estimates of combat efficiency by division and corps commanders on Bataan bore out fully the tragic picture painted by junior officers. By the middle of March General Parker, II Corps commander, placed the combat efficiency of the troops in his corps at only 20 percent, adding that it was becoming less with the passing of each day. He attributed the deterioration of his men to the starvation diet of 1,000 calories daily, the rapid spread of malaria, the high incidence of dysentery, diarrhea, and beriberi, nerve fatigue, and the shortage of clothing and equipment. [89] The situation in I Corps was no better. Fully 75 percent of the men, wrote Wainwright, were unfit for action by 12 March, the date he relinquished command to General Jones. The reasons he gave were similar to those presented by Parker, with the addition of hookworm and the lack of shelter halves, blankets, and raincoats. [90]

Morale

The ability of the men on Bataan to fight could not be measured by physical standards alone. Where all men bore the signs of enforced privation and suffering, there was no question of separating the fit from the unfit. Only necessity and the will to fight could give meaning to the tactical dispositions assumed by the troops.

The Japanese knew this and made crude attempts to corrupt the spirit of resistance. Flying low over Bataan, their aircraft often dropped propaganda leaflets instead of bombs on the Americans and Filipinos below. These leaflets appealed to the basest emotions: race prejudice, jealousy, hate,

---

[89] SLF and II Corps Rpt of Opns, p. 48, Annex V, USAFFE-USFIP Rpt of Opns.
[90] NLF and I Corps Rpt of Opns, p. 28, Annex IV, USAFFE-USFIP Rpt of Opns.

avarice, and deceit. Some were designed to induce the desertion of the Filipinos; others pointed out that the pay of the Philippine Army troops would be worthless in the future. "Take my word you are exposing your life in danger without any remuneration," declared one handbill. "There is nothing so pointless." [91] The life of the Filipino under the Japanese occupation was painted in glowing colors. "I am enjoying life as a Filipino of the New Philippines," said a former Philippine soldier in one of the leaflets. "Throw away your arms and surrender yourself to the Japanese Army," proclaimed another handbill, "in order to save your lives and enrich your beautiful future and the welfare of your children." [92]

MacArthur's departure was also exploited by the Japanese in their effort to create dissatisfaction. Some leaflets exploited the theme of starvation, and one pictured Corregidor entirely surrounded by heaping plates of turkey, meat, fruit, cake, and bottles of whiskey and wine. Other illustrated leaflets dwelt on the theme of sex and crudely pictured the soldier's wife in the arms of a war profiteer.

So far as is known the effect of these propaganda sheets was negligible. Some men made a hobby of collecting them, and exchanged duplicates to fill out their collections. "Majors Poole, Crane, and Holmes got me some," exulted Col. Ray M. O'Day, "including the red and white ribbon streamers attached to the beer cans and addressed to General Wainwright." [93] This acquisition was particularly prized for it contained a demand for Wainwright's surrender.

Japanese radio propaganda was more effective than the leaflets. The Japanese-controlled Station KZRH in Manila broadcast a special program for American soldiers every night at 2145. The program was much like that presented by Tokyo Rose, to whom so many Ameircan soldiers listened at a later period of the war. The theme song of the program was "Ships That Never Come In," followed by popular recordings calculated to make the men homesick. "The damned Nips," wrote Major Tisdelle, "have got a new propaganda program that does not help our morale any. The men joke happily, but underneath they are disquieted." [94]

The Americans had their own radio station on Corregidor, "The Voice of Freedom," which broadcast three times a day. Records, evidently collected at Corregidor, were played during these programs, which also consisted of news commentaries and items of local interest. At least one officer had a low opinion of the program, describing its offerings as propaganda "so thick that it served no purpose except to disgust us and incite mistrust of all hopes." [95] Station KGEI in San Francisco also broadcast a "Freedom for the Philippines" program each night to which most of the men listened. The reaction to these programs was mixed.

During the early part of the campaign, most officers are agreed, morale was high despite the shortages of food and equipment. The victories of early February raised the spirit of the troops and confirmed them in the belief that they could hold out until reinforcements arrived. Aid had been promised time and again, and officers and men alike placed all their hopes for the future

---

[91] Rad, MacArthur to AGWAR, No. 387, 3 Feb 42, WPD Ready Ref File, Phil.
[92] Copies of these and other Japanese propaganda leaflets are on file in Mil Intel Library.
[93] O'Day, 21st Div (PA), II, 36.

[94] Tisdelle, Diary, entry of 16 Feb 42.
[95] Mallonée, Bataan Diary, II, 63.

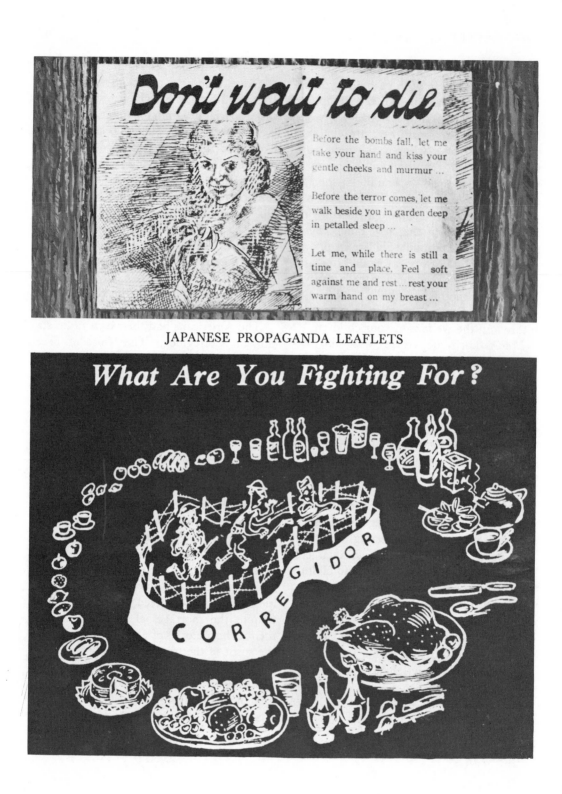

Don't wait to die

Before the bombs fall, let me take your hand and kiss your gentle cheeks and murmur ...

Before the terror comes, let me walk beside you in garden deep in petalled sleep ...

Let me, while there is still a time and place, Feel soft against me and rest ... rest your warm hand on my breast ...

JAPANESE PROPAGANDA LEAFLETS

What Are You Fighting For?

CORREGIDOR

on the fulfillment of this pledge. Without it there was nothing left but defeat and disaster.

While much of the faith in the timely arrival of reinforcements was based only on the desperate desire to believe it to be so, there was at least one tangible assurance to which men could point. On 15 January, a week after the troops had reached Bataan, General MacArthur had addressed a message to the entire command. Every unit commander was made personally responsible for reading and explaining the message, and all headquarters were directed to be sure that these instructions were carried out. MacArthur's message to the troops was a promise of aid and a call to valor. "Help is on the way from the United States," he had said. "Thousands of troops and hundreds of planes are being dispatched. The exact time of arrival of reinforcements is unknown as they will have to fight their way through. . . ." Declaring that no further retreat was possible, he asserted that "our supplies are ample" and that it was imperative to hold until aid arrived.[96] Though the message carefully stated that the date of arrival was not known, the hungry men, grasping eagerly at every straw, assumed that it would come soon. A soldier-poet expressed the mood of the men when he wrote:

. . . MacArthur's promise in every mind.
"The time is secret but I can say
That swift relief ships are on the way
Thousands of men and hundreds of planes—
Back in Manila before the rains!
With decorations and honors, too."
MacArthur said it, it must be true.[97]

[96] Ltr Order, USAFFE to All Unit Comdrs, 15 Jan 42, sub: Msg from Gen MacArthur, copy in OCMH.
[97] Lee, "Abucay Withdrawal," *Nothing But Praise,* p. 22.

Disillusionment came hard. The weeks went by, January gave way to February, and still no large reinforcements had come. Many men began to doubt that aid would arrive at all. Only a few men had definite knowledge of what was on the way and they confided in no one. When Colonel Mallonée jokingly asked Colonel Brezina about the relief expedition, Brezina's "eyes went poker-blank" and "his teeth bit his lips into a grim thin line."[98] Most regular officers had made their own estimate of the situation and had reached the conclusion that time was against them. They could see their men growing weaker every day, the hospitals fuller, and the supplies smaller. But they continued to hope for the relief expedition, the TNT (Terrible 'N' Terrific) force, which would arrive in storybook fashion before the end.

These hopes received a rude blow on Washington's Birthday, 22 February, in President Roosevelt's fireside chat on the progress of the war. Inviting his listeners to look at their maps, the President emphasized the global nature of the struggle, the vast distances to be spanned, the large areas to be held, and the desperate situation of the United Nations. As he spoke of the tremendous tasks facing the American people and the sacrifices that must be made, it became clear to his listeners on Bataan that he was placing the Philippines in their proper perspective "in the big picture of the war."[99] No prospect of the arrival of relief could be found in the President's message. One officer wrote in his diary that though "the President means to cheer us up," his talk "tends to weaken morale." "We are not interested in what the production will be in 1943–44 and 1945," he said.

[98] Mallonée, Bataan Diary, II, 55.
[99] *Ibid.,* 69.

"VOICE OF FREEDOM" *broadcasts to the men on Bataan.*

"All we want are two things, but we need them right now." [100]   Others took a more pessimistic view.   "Plain for all to see," wrote Colonel Mallonée, "was the handwriting on the wall, at the end of which the President had placed a large and emphatic period.   The President had—with regret— wiped us off the page and closed the book." [101]

Despite the explanations of the "Voice of Freedom," MacArthur's departure for Australia on 12 March struck another blow at morale.   A large part of the faith in the timely arrival of reinforcements had been based on the presence of General MacAr-

thur.   His prestige among the Filipinos can hardly be exaggerated.   Among American officers, to many of whom he was already a legend, his reputation placed him on a lofty eminence with the great captains of history. Mallonée undoubtedly expressed the feelings of many when he affirmed his belief that MacArthur "would reach down and pull the rabbit out of the hat." [102]   With MacArthur gone, those who refused to give up hope argued that if anybody could bring supplies to the Philippines it was MacArthur.   His presence in Australia, they declared, was the best guarantee that help was coming.   As proof they could repeat the assertions broadcast so often over the "Voice of Freedom," or cite MacArthur's

[100] Tisdelle, Diary, entry of 23 Feb 42.

[101] Mallonée, Bataan Diary, II, 69.   See also Samuel I. Rosenman, compiler, *The Public Papers and Addresses of Franklin D. Roosevelt, Humanity on the Defensive, 1942* (New York, 1950), pp. 105–16.

[102] Manonée, Bataan Diary, II, 67.   See also Alexander, Personal Recollections of Bataan, p. 104

first public statement on reaching Australia. At that time he had said that the relief of the Philippines was his primary purpose. "I came through and I shall return," he had pledged.[103]

There were others, however, including the old-timers of World War I, who reasoned that the best place from which to direct the organization of the relief expedition was Corregidor. MacArthur's departure, they asserted, was proof that the promised reinforcements would never arrive.[104]

When, by the end of March, no rabbits had been pulled out of the hat, most Americans realized that the end was near. There was nothing left but to wait for the inevitable defeat and prison camp, or death.

The Filipino could expect ultimately to be returned to his home. For the American there was no such bright prospect. Death or capture was his certain fate. Strangely enough, he did not become despondent or bitter. He knew the worst now and there was little he could do other than to make the enemy pay dearly for victory. Meanwhile he made the best of his bad fortune, joked grimly about his fate, and hid his feelings under a cloak of irony.[105] It was in this vein that Lt. Henry G. Lee of the Philippine Division wrote the poem, "Fighting On."

I see no gleam of victory alluring
No chance of splendid booty or of gain
If I endure—I must go on enduring
And my reward for bearing pain—is pain
Yet, though the thrill, the zest, the hope are
    gone
Something within me keeps me fighting on.[106]

---

[103] New York *Times,* March 21, 1942.

[104] This paragraph and those immediately preceding are based on a large number of interviews and informal conversations with survivors of the campaign. For a printed reaction to MacArthur's departure, see Miller, *Bataan Uncensored,* pp. 191–92.

---

[105] Mallonée, Bataan Diary, II, 69–70.

[106] Lee, *Nothing But Praise,* p. 33.

CHAPTER XXII

"Help is on the Way"

Since early January strenuous attempts had been made to get food and medical supplies to the men on Bataan and Corregidor. General MacArthur, and later General Wainwright, urged constantly and persistently, in the strongest terms, that the Japanese blockade must be broken, that greater efforts must be made and more drastic measures taken to relieve the Philippine garrison.

These requests were received in Washington with the greatest sympathy. Despite the fact that Allied strategy called for the defeat of Germany first, the bulk of the troops and supplies sent overseas during the early part of 1942 went to the Pacific. A blockade-running program was organized, first in Australia and the Netherlands Indies, and then in the United States. Surface vessels, combat aircraft, and even submarines were dispatched to the Philippines in the hope that some would get through with supplies for the weary and hungry men. No expense was too high, no effort too great to relieve the embattled garrison.

The total result of these activities was negligible. The Japanese hold on the Southwest Pacific and southeast Asia was too firm, their victories too rapid to allow the poorly prepared Allies time to organize the resources necessary to come to the aid of the Philippine garrison. The story of the attempt to break through the Japanese blockade, like the entire story of the campaign in the Philippines, is one of heroic efforts and final failure.

Running the Blockade

On 4 January, unaware that the War Plans Division of the General Staff had concluded only a day earlier that relief of the Philippines would require so large a force as to constitute "an entirely unjustified diversion," General MacArthur had suggested to the Chief of Staff that a plan for blockade-running be developed and put into effect immediately. "Some relief," he had added, "might be obtained on use of submarine transportation." [1] The suggestion to initiate blockade-running was not acted upon immediately, but the funds to organize such a program had already been allotted to two officers on their way to Australia.[2]

The proposal to send supplies by submarine did not secure such ready acceptance. Admiral Hart, when asked to send antiaircraft ammunition to MacArthur by submarine, replied that no underwater craft were available for such a mission.[3] MacAr-

[1] Rad, MacArthur to Marshall, No. 9, 4 Jan 42, AG 381 (11–27–41 Sec 1) Far East. See Chapter XIV above for a discussion of the WPD study of 3 January.

[2] Ltr, Moore, DCofS to Brett, 19 Dec 41, G–4 33861. The two officers were Col. Stephen J. Chamberlin and Lt. Col. Lester J. Whitlock, later MacArthur's G–3 and G–4.

[3] MacArthur's radio had been forwarded to the commander in Australia with instructions from Marshall to consider all means of getting supplies through to the Philippines. Rad, Marshall to Brett, No. 671, 5 Jan 42, WPD Ready Ref File, Phil. Admiral Ernest J. King also instructed Hart to assist in this effort, Rad, COMINCH to CINCAF,

thur's message to the Chief of Staff on this subject was a strong one. Hart's attitude, he declared for the second time in a month, was a defeatist one. "He accepts complete blockade which probably does not exist without effort to penetrate," he declared, and cited the case of two destroyers and a cargo vessel which had successfully made their way south from Manila Bay during the last ten days. "I urge," he wrote Marshall, "steps be taken to obtain a more aggressive and resourceful handling of naval forces in this area." [4]

Concrete plans to run supplies into the Philippines through the Japanese blockade began to take shape about the middle of January. The impetus was provided by MacArthur, who, on the 17th, after his failure to secure any strong support from Australia or the Netherlands Indies, recounted his difficulties in a long message to the Chief of Staff. [5] He reminded General Marshall that his men had been on half rations for some time and that "the food situation here is becoming serious." Measured in ship capacity his needs were not large and could easily be met by small or medium-sized vessels, which he recommended be dispatched to the Philippines along various routes. It seemed "incredible" to him that such an attempt had never been made. He had no doubt that if it were, "unquestionably" the ships would get through. Warning that the Filipinos would experi-

ence a "revulsion of feeling" if something was not done to send help quickly and that "hungry men are hard to handle," he asked that simultaneous efforts to send food be made from the United States and the Netherlands Indies. "I am professionally certain," he declared, "that his [the enemy's] so-called blockade can easily be pierced. The only thing that can make it really effective is our passive acceptance of it as a fact."

Actually, every effort was being made in Washington to send aid to the beleaguered garrison. But these efforts were not enough, nor were they being pushed, General Marshall believed, with the vigor and single-mindedness required to break the blockade. The command in Australia had no organization capable of quickly executing such a mission and no such sense of urgency as impelled MacArthur to insist that "the disastrous results" of the failure to provide aid "will be monumental." [6]

General Marshall himself undertook to impart this sense of urgency to his subordinates. To the commander in Australia he wrote that the situation in the Philippines was most serious and that "comprehensive efforts" to run the blockade must be organized. His directions were concise and clear

Use your funds without stint. Call for more if required. Colonel Chamberlin has a credit of ten million dollars of Chief of Staff's fund which can be spent in whatever manner latter deems advisable. I direct its use for this purpose. Arrange for advance payments, partial payments for unsuccessful efforts, and large bonus for actual delivery. Your judgement must get results. Organize groups of bold and resourceful men, dispatch them with funds by planes to islands in possession of our associates, there to buy food and charter vessels for service. Rewards for actual delivery

---

5 Jan 42, WPD Msg File. At the time all submarines but one, "which was lost about then," were to the north on other missions. Ltr, Hart to Ward, 19 Dec 51, OCMH.

[4] Rad, MacArthur to Marshall, No. 26, 9 Jan 42, WPD Ready Ref File, Phil. Admiral Hart points out that he never accepted "complete blockade" with regard to submarines. Ltr, Hart to Ward, 19 Dec 51, OCMH.

[5] Rad, MacArthur to Marshall No. 72, 17 Jan 42, AG 381 (11–27–41 Sec 1) Far East.

[6] *Ibid.*

Bataan or Corregidor must be fixed at level to insure utmost energy and daring on part of masters. At same time dispatch blockade runners from Australia with standard rations and small amounts of ammunition on each. Movement must be made on broad front over many routes. . . . Only indomitable determination and pertinacity will succeed and success must be ours. Risks will be great. Rewards must be proportional. Report initiation of plan.[7]

Similar instructions were sent to General Brett, General Wavell's deputy in the recently established ABDA Command. "The results of even partial success in this effort," Marshall told him, "would be incalculable, and it is my purpose to spare no effort or expense to achieve results."[8] That same day in Washington, Marshall selected General Hurley, former Secretary of War, to lend his "energetic support" to the scheme of blockade-running, and made available to MacArthur one million dollars, to be used as rewards to ship masters in the Islands.

Less than twenty-four hours after receiving MacArthur's message urging that the blockade be pierced, Marshall was able to inform the USAFFE commander that two officers from Washington with "practically unlimited funds" and with instructions to organize blockade-running "on a broad front" had already reached Australia; that he had one million dollars at his disposal to reward those who broke through the blockade; and that Hurley was leaving for Australia the next day.[9]

Under the impetus of Marshall's urgent instructions for a comprehensive program and the use of "bold and resourceful men,"

the headquarters in Australia prepared an ambitious schedule for the shipment to the Indies, and then the transshipment from there, of 3,000,000 rations—a sixty-day supply for 50,000 men—and a large quantity of ammunition.[10] Col. John A. Robenson, with six assistants and large funds, was sent from Darwin to Java with instructions to comb the Indies for food and small ships.

These plans apparently were not enough for General Marshall and he told General Brereton, then commanding in Australia, so in plain terms. Time did not permit the shipment of food to the Indies for transshipment, the Chief of Staff declared. Local resources in every port should be exploited by purchase, and agents with hard cash should be flown to every Dutch and British island in the area to collect food and ships. "Urgency of my instructions not fully appreciated," Marshall told Brereton, and closed with the injunction that "action and results are imperative."[11]

The difficulties which faced the men responsible for procuring supplies, ships, and crews were formidable. There were few vessels in Australia fast enough to run the blockade and large enough to carry sufficient cargo and fuel to make the round trip profitable. The assignment of a ship to such a mission was regarded by most as tantamount to its permanent loss. Finally, if a ship was chartered, it was exceedingly difficult to find the crew willing to embark on so perilous a voyage, no matter how high the reward. Altogether, about ten old coastal vessels of Philippine and Chinese registry were procured in Australia. In an effort to protect these vessels from hostile attack, they were

---

[7] Rad, Marshall to CG USAFIA, 17 Jan 42, AG 381 (11–27–41 Sec 1) Far East.

[8] Rad, Marshall to Brett, 17 Jan 42, WPD 4560-9.

[9] Rads, Marshall to MacArthur, No. 949, 17 Jan 42, OCS 18136-196; Marshall to Brett, 19 Jan 42, AG 381 (11–27–41 Sec 1) Far East.

[10] Maj Gen Julian F. Barnes, Rpt of Orgn of USAFIA, 7 Dec 41–30 Jun 42, AG Opns Rpt F–17.

[11] Rads, Brereton to TAG, and Marshall to Brereton, 19 Jan 42, both in AG 381 (11–27–41 Sec 1) Far East.

provided with guns, dummy stacks, neutral or Axis flags, and "all imaginable types of deceit." [12]

Colonel Robenson's difficulties in Java were fully as great as those encountered in Australia. Imbued with the importance of his mission, he was quickly disillusioned when he found that the British and the Dutch would not release ships for the hazardous run to the Philippines. Robenson had more success in securing rations and ammunition, but at the end of January still had no vessel on which to load the cargo. [13]

Despite these difficulties surprising progress was made in the plan to run the blockade. By 22 January, three days after his rebuke from Washington, Brereton reported to the Chief of Staff that the *Don Isidro*, a small Philippine freighter, had been chartered and was then being loaded with rations and ammunition at Brisbane. It would sail directly for Corregidor. The *Mormacsun*, with a larger capacity, was also loading at Brisbane. Since this vessel was under orders from Washington not to go farther north than the Netherlands Indies, it would sail to a Dutch port and there transfer its cargo to smaller vessels for the last leg of the journey. Additional rations and ammunition, Brereton told Marshall, were being assembled in Australia for shipment to the Indies. There they would be placed aboard small blockade-runners and sent to the Philippines. [14] He neglected to mention that he had had no success as yet in securing these small vessels.

Within two weeks the number of ships en route or scheduled to sail for the Philippines had grown to five. The *Don Isidro*, Maj. Gen. Julian F. Barnes reported from Australia, had already departed with 700 tons of rations. The *Coast Farmer*, an Army freighter with a speed of 10 knots, was loading at Brisbane and would sail immediately. The *Dona Nati*, with a capacity of over 6,000 tons, was also loading in Australia and was scheduled to depart within the week. Finally, the *Anhui*, a vessel of Chinese registry with a capacity of 2,500 tons, had been chartered and was then loading. It would follow the *Dona Nati*. The *Mormacsun*, Barnes told Marshall, was already loaded with 6,000 tons of balanced rations and ammunition, but was being held in port pending the completion of arrangements to charter two smaller vessels to carry its cargo northward from the Indies. [15]

General MacArthur was kept fully informed of the plans to break the Japanese blockade, but still felt that stronger measures were required. On 4 February, in a message to General Marshall, he called for a more aggressive strategy in the Far East and expressed the hope that his views would be presented "to the highest authority." [16] The message opened with the startling statement that Allied strategy, aimed at building up forces before the Japanese advance, was "a fatal mistake on the part of the Democratic Allies." He urged that the Japanese line of communications, "stretched over 2,000 miles of sea," be attacked instead. To counter the argument that naval forces for such attacks were not available, he pointed out that a great naval

---

[12] Ltr, CG USAFIA to CO Base 3, 20 Jan 42, Material on USAFIA Hist in AG Opns Rpt; ltr, CofS USAFIA to CO Base 1, 21 Jan 42, sub: Philippine Relief, AG, Effort to Supply Phil.

[13] Barnes, Rpt of Orgn of USAFIA, AG Opns Rpt F–17.

[14] Rad, Brereton to Marshall, No. 88, 22 Jan 42, AG 381 (11–27–41 Sec 1) Far East.

[15] Rad, Barnes to TAG, No. 154, 2 Feb 42, AG 381 (11–27–41 Sec 2A) Far East.

[16] Rad, MacArthur to Marshall, No. 201, 4 Feb 42, WDCSA 381 (2–17–42) Phil.

victory was not necessary; "the threat alone would go far toward the desired end." He predicted that the plan to build a base and acquire supremacy in the Southwest Pacific would fail and that the war would be indefinitely prolonged. The only way to defeat the enemy was to seek combat with him. "Counsels of timidity," he warned, "based upon theories of safety first will not win against such an aggressive and audacious adversary as Japan."

This was bold counsel indeed and was carefully considered in Washington from where the effort to send MacArthur the supplies he needed was being pushed with vigor and determination. General Marshall replied that he welcomed and appreciated MacArthur's views and "invariably" submitted them to the President.[17]

Summarizing the considerations which had determined Allied strategy, Marshall went on to explain that everyone recognized the advantages of an attack against Japan's line of communications. Two grim disasters had prevented the adoption of such a course. First, the Japanese had achieved flank security at the start of the war by seizing Wake and Guam and additional protection by their control of the Marshall and Gilbert Islands. At all these places they had strong air protection. Secondly, by their initial attack on Pearl Harbor, the Japanese had virtually eliminated the Battle Force of the Pacific Fleet. Much of the remaining naval strength of the Pacific Fleet was required to keep open the Allied line of communications to Australia and to assist in the establishment of bases in the South Pacific.

---

[17] Rad, Marshall to MacArthur, 8 Feb 42, WDCSA 381 (2–17–42) Phil.

But rather than do nothing at all, the Allies had decided to oppose Japanese expansion along the Malay Barrier simply because that was the only area in which they possessed the necessary bases from which to launch an attack. "The basis of all current effort," the Chief of Staff went on, "is to accumulate through every possible means sufficient strength to initiate operations along the lines you suggest. . . . In the meanwhile we are endeavoring to limit the hostile advance so as to deny him free access to land and sea areas that will immeasurably strengthen his war making powers or which will be valuable to us as jump off positions when we can start a general offensive."

Not only was MacArthur's efforts to secure a reorientation of Allied strategy in the Far East unsuccessful, but his doubts about the value of the help from Australia soon proved to be well founded. In spite of elaborate preparations and the expenditure of large funds, only three of the vessels which set out for the Philippines were successful in piercing the blockade. The *Don Isidro* and *Coast Farmer* left Australia on the same day, 4 February. The first went from Fremantle to Java to take on ammunition. There she was joined by the *Florence D.*, a Philippine freighter under U.S. naval control. To get the ship Colonel Robenson had had to offer the Filipino crew handsome bonuses ranging from more than $10,000 for the master to lesser amounts for other ranks, and life insurance in values of $500 to $5,000. On 14 February the *Don Isidro* and *Florence D.* set sail. Both vessels sailed eastward through the Timor Sea to Bathurst Island, then north. Five days after the start of the voyage they were discovered by Japanese planes and bombed. The first was left a disabled hulk and had to be beached; the *Florence D.* was sunk.[18]

The voyage of the *Coast Farmer* was more successful. She finally put in at a Mindanao port fifteen days after leaving Brisbane. The *Dona Nati* and the *Anhui* also made the trip successfully, arriving at Cebu in mid-March. These were the only vessels to reach the Philippines; they brought in more than 10,000 tons of rations, 4,000,000 rounds of small-arms ammunition, 8,000 rounds of 81-mm ammunition, and miscellaneous medical, signal, and engineer supplies.[19] The two Chinese ships of British registry chartered to carry the *Mormacsun* cargo left Fremantle in February, but the crews mutinied when dangerous waters were reached and brought the two vessels back to Darwin where they were unloaded. On 14 February the Dutch released four old freighters to Colonel Robenson for use on the Philippine run. By offering large bonuses and other financial inducements, he persuaded the Chinese crew of one of these vessels to make the voyage. It finally left on 26 February with a cargo of 720,000 rations, but was never heard from again. The others never left port.[20]

The unloading of the three ships that successfully completed the voyage to southern Philippine ports left their cargoes far from the battlefield. From Mindanao and Cebu the supplies still had to be transported northward through the inland seas to Manila Bay. For this leg of the journey fast interisland motor ships were used. The need for such a transport system had been recognized early in the campaign and General Sharp, commander of the Visayan-Mindanao Force, had requisitioned the best of the small boats. Altogether, about twenty-five boats, ranging in capacity from 300 to 1,000 tons, were chartered.[21]

The plan for running the blockade through the inland seas provided for the transfer of the cargo brought in from Australia and the Netherlands Indies to the smaller interisland craft. This would be done at night, at places rarely visited by the Japanese air and surface patrols. The small boats would then move northward in easy stages, traveling during the hours of darkness only. American officers would be placed aboard each vessel with orders to make certain that a real effort was made to run the blockade and to scuttle the ship rather than let it fall into enemy hands.[22]

The plan called also for the transportation to Corregidor of such food as could be procured locally—rice, sugar, fruits, coffee, and meat. In Manila Bay, for example, two 400-ton motor ships picked up the food collected by agents in southern Luzon and ran it across the bay to Corregidor. These two vessels were able to make several round trips, raising the total quantity of rice stocks by 1,600 tons.[23] But the bulk of the ships and supplies came from Cebu where the Army Transport Service and the Cebu Advance Depot were located. Originally estab-

---

[18] Barnes, Rpt of Orgn of USAFIA, AG Opns Rpt F-17; rad, TAG to CG USAFFE, 15 Feb 42, WPD 4560-21.

[19] Development of the U.S. Supply Base in Australia, a monograph prepared in 1949 by Maj. Richard M. Leighton and Mrs. Elizabeth Bingham, Control Div, ASF, copy in OCMH.

[20] *Ibid.;* rad, Brett to TAG, No. 1058, 25 Mar 42, WPD Msg File.

[21] V-MF Rpt of Opns, pp. 23, 35; QM Rpt of Opns, p. 39.

[22] V-MF Rpt of Opns, p. 36. The boats were first under the control of Sharp's headquarters, but on 8 February were placed under a branch of the Army Transport Service established in Cebu. Rad, USAFFE to Sharp, 8 Feb 42, Sharp Papers, OCMH.

[23] QM Rpt of Opns, pp. 39–40.

lished to issue supplies received from Luzon, the Cebu depot became the central collection point for supplies to be shipped to Bataan and Corregidor. Procurement offices were set up in the Visayas and in Mindanao and vast quantities of material were gathered. To these were added the food and equipment from Australia. By 10 April, when the Japanese occupied Cebu City, the depot had on hand a twelve-month food supply for the troops on Cebu and Panay and at least a six-month supply for the men on the other islands. In the hills and in scattered warehouses were another 12,000 tons of food, medicine, gasoline, and other supplies.[24]

Only a very small portion of the supplies gathered so painfully and hoarded so carefully in the south ever reached Manila Bay. The total could not have been more than a few thousand tons. The *Legaspi*, with a capacity of 1,000 tons, was the first of the interisland steamers to make the journey safely. On 22 January she brought a cargo of rice and other food from Panay to Corregidor, and in February completed another trip. On 1 March, while she was on her third trip, she was sunk by a Japanese gunboat off the north coast of Mindoro and her crew captured.

Late in February the *Princessa* made the run from Cebu to Corregidor with a cargo of 700 tons of food. At Mindanao the 2,500 tons of rations and 2,000 rounds of 81-mm. ammunition from the *Coast Farmer* were transferred to the *Elcano* and *Lepus*. The first got through to Manila Bay, but the *Lepus* was captured off Palawan on 28 February. The cargoes of the *Dona Nati*

and *Anhui* were loaded for transshipment at Cebu, but the ships failed to break through the tightening Japanese blockade. Ten of the interisland steamers were sunk by the enemy or scuttled by their crews to avoid capture, resulting in the loss of 7,000 tons of food, petroleum, and other miscellaneous supplies.[25]

In terms of supplies delivered to the battlefield, the blockade-running program from Australia and the Netherland Indies was a dismal failure. Of the 10,000 tons of rations which reached Mindanao and Cebu only about 1,000 tons—a four-day supply for the 100,000 soldiers and civilians on Bataan—reached Manila Bay. Even more distressing was the condition of the food when it finally reached the men. The containers in which the food was packed had broken open and the holds of the ships contained a miscellaneous pile of canned goods. All of it had to be sorted and repacked before it could be issued to the troops. Practically all the paper labels on the cans were destroyed so that they could not be identified without opening them. Flour and sugar sacks had broken open and the contents were spread loosely among the cans. Shovels had to be used to get these precious commodities back into new sacks. Onions and potatoes, piled on the decks during the voyage through tropical waters, were rotted and had to be destroyed almost before the eyes of the starving men. These "heart-breaking" conditions resulted in delays in unloading and, what was much worse, considerable loss of food to the weakened and hungry garrison.[26]

---

[24] Col John D. Cook, Cebu Depot QM Opns, pp. 1–5, App. A, QM Rpt of Opns; Col Melville S. Creusere, QM Supply, V-MF, V-MF Rpt of Opns, pp. 526–32.

[25] V-MF Rpt of Opns, p. 49; QM Rpt of Opns, pp. 59–60; Cook, Cebu Depot QM Opns, App. A, QM Rpt of Opns; Drake, Comments on Draft MS, Comment 14, OCMH.

[26] QM Rpt of Opns, pp. 69–70.

The Japanese invasion of the Netherlands Indies and the Allied naval defeats in the waters of the Dutch archipelago in late February and early March released Japanese naval and air forces for patrol of the seas just north of Australia. With that continent now under direct attack and in danger of invasion all plans to run the blockade from Australia came to an end. Ships and cargoes were desperately needed in Australia itself to meet the threat of hostile landings. This possibility had been foreseen earlier, and General Hurley, when he reached Java on 17 February, had told the Chief of Staff that the sea routes north of Australia were becoming increasingly hazardous. On his return to Melbourne a few days later he again made this point in a message to Marshall and referred to the "almost insuperable difficulties" in getting supplies to MacArthur.[27]

On 2 March Batavia in Java fell to the Japanese and the Dutch Government moved to the mountains. Clearly the end of resistance in the Netherlands Indies was in sight, and both Brett and Hurley agreed that it was no longer possible to continue the blockade-running program. This view, they told the Chief of Staff in a joint message, was shared by the officers directly responsible for running the blockade. In their opinion,

Routes to Philippines from Australia and vicinity are becoming increasingly hazardous and risking of ships and cargoes that cannot well be spared here appears no longer justified.

Routes to avoid the areas controlled by the enemy are as long as from Hawaii to Philippines.

Recommend therefore that Philippines be supplied from the United States via Hawaii through open sea areas in which the chance of reaching destination is much greater than through narrow channels between island and blockade areas of the southwest Pacific.[28]

Already the possibility of sending blockade-runners from the United States through Hawaii was under study in the War Department. This study had been requested by the President as a result of a strong message from MacArthur on 22 February.[29] The *Coast Farmer*, MacArthur had pointed out, had had no difficulty in penetrating the Japanese blockade, thus proving what he had been asserting all the time: that the blockade was ineffective. He suggested, therefore, that in view of the "thinness of the enemy's coverage" other routes including that across the central Pacific from Hawaii be utilized. The entire program to send him supplies, he declared bluntly, should be controlled from Washington rather than Australia where the commanders, "however able they may be, have neither the resources nor the means . . . to accomplish this mission." Nor did he believe it possible for commanders in Australia, "the actual zone of immediate or threatened conflict," to devote all their energies to the task of sending him supplies when their own problems seemed so urgent to them.

The size of the problem [he said] is greater than the means now being used to solve it. The prime requisite is the making available in the United States of the necessary ships and material, especially the former, and their continuous dispatch to destination. Nowhere is the situation more desperate and dangerous

[27] Rad, Hurley for Marshall, ABDACOM No. 2, 17 Jan 42, ABDACOM Msgs, SWPA Collection, OPD; memo, Hurley for Marshall, 21 Feb 42, OPD 381 PI, Sec 1, Case 21.

[28] Rad, Hurley and Brett for Marshall, No. 483, 4 Mar 42, AG 381 (11–27–41 Sec 3) Far East.
[29] Rad, MacArthur to Marshall, No. 344, 22 Feb 42, WPD Ready Ref File, Phil.

than here. . . . The quantities involved are not great but it is imperative that they be made instantly available in the United States and that the entire impulse and organization be reenergized and controlled directly by you. If it is left as a subsidiary effort it will never be accomplished.[30]

On the receipt of this message, the supply experts in the War Department began a quick survey of the problem. Maj. Gen. Brehon B. Somervell, then G–4, summed up their findings in a series of recommendations to the Chief of Staff on the 22d.[31] Declaring that direct supply of the Philippines from Honolulu was "practical and desirable," he recommended that three World War I destroyers, converted to cargo vessels with a capacity of 1,500 tons each, be assigned this mission. One of these could be sent immediately from New Orleans to Mindanao, and the others could follow in early March. He recommended also that three additional converted destroyers then in the Caribbean should be procured by the Army and placed on this run. Arrangements were quickly made to send supplies to New Orleans and to procure the additional vessels. Marshall then reported these arrangements to the President and notified MacArthur of the new efforts being made to send supplies across the Pacific directly to the Philippines.[32]

The schedule for shipments from the United States called for six sailings, the first vessel to leave New Orleans on 28 February, the last on 22 March. But numerous difficulties arose to upset the schedule. There

were delays in assembling the cargoes and in selecting the best routes for the ships to follow. The Navy had no gun crews to put on the ships and there was further delay till they could be secured. Finally, the first vessel, originally scheduled to leave on 28 February, sailed from New Orleans on 2 March. Two others followed during the month. Routed through the Panama Canal to Los Angeles and then to Honolulu, these ships were still in Hawaiian waters when the campaign in the Philippines ended. Three other converted destroyers left the west coast between 16 March and 11 April but before they were long at sea it was clear they could not reach the Philippines before the campaign ended and they were diverted to other areas.[33] Thus ended the effort to run supplies through the blockade by surface ships.

Submarines and aircraft as well as surface vessels were utilized in the desperate attempt to bring aid to the Philippine garrison. The use of submarines for this purpose, as has been noted, was opposed most strongly by Admiral Hart, commander of naval forces in Wavell's headquarters.[34] General Wavell supported this view and when he assumed command declared that with his present resources he could see no possibility of "affording General MacArthur support he appears to expect." [35] When, on 17 January, Marshall sent strong messages to Australia and Java calling for an all-out effort to break the Japanese blockade, Wavell had replied that the diversion of submarines to

[30] Ibid.

[31] Memo, Somervell for Marshall, 22 Feb 42, sub: Supply of U.S. Forces in Phil, OCS 18136-258.

[32] Memo, Marshall for Roosevelt, 24 Feb 42, WPD 4560-26; memo, Marshall for Roosevelt, 28 Feb 42, sub: Blockade-Runners via Hawaii, OCS 18136-268.

[33] Messages dealing with these vessels can be found in AG 384.3 GHQ SWPA, and in Hist Branch, Off of Chief of Trans, SWPA files, Phil Shipping.

[34] Rads, COMINCH to CINCAF, and Brett to Marshall, 9 Jan 42, both in WPD Msg File.

[35] Rad, Wavell to Marshall, ABDACOM No. 53, 15 Jan 42, WPD SWPA Collection.

transport duty would reduce the opposition he could bring to bear against the enemy.[36]

General Marshall granted the validity of Wavell's and Hart's objections and admitted they were correct in principle. But he also pointed out that Wavell had overlooked the moral effect of receiving even occasional small shipments. MacArthur, he reasoned, was containing a large number of Japanese, planes, and ships, and the longer he held out the more chance there was that the Japanese would be unable to put all their forces in the ABDA area. This consideration, he declared, justified the use of submarines to carry small quantities of critical items to Corregidor.[37] "As you know," he wrote Admiral King, "we are making strenuous efforts to organize blockade running on an extensive scale. . . . However, under present conditions, I think it is important that small shipments of supplies reach MacArthur by submarine or otherwise every ten days or two weeks." [38] King agreed with this view and Wavell's orders to send aid to MacArthur, by submarine if necessary, remained unchanged.

Altogether, ten submarines made the effort to reach the Philippines. One, loaded with ammunition, had been sent out by Hart on King's instructions. Another, with a cargo of 3-inch antiaircraft ammunition, had left Hawaii on 12 January. MacArthur reported the safe arrival of these two submarines in February, the last one reaching the Islands from Hawaii on 3 February.[39] During that month three more submarines made the voyage to the Philippines: *Swordfish* arrived on the 19th and evacuated President Quezon; *Sargo* brought one million rounds of .30-caliber ammunition to Mindanao; and *Permit,* sent to evacuate General MacArthur, took on instead torpedoes and naval personnel.

The next month only two submarines reached the Islands. *Seadragon,* en route to patrol off the Indochina coast, was ordered to Cebu to carry a load of rations to Corregidor. Though she picked up 34 tons of rations and almost 12,000 gallons of petroleum, she was able to unload only one fifth of her cargo before being ordered out. *Snapper,* assigned the same mission, succeeded in unloading 46 tons of food and 29,000 gallons of diesel oil before leaving.

The *Swordfish* made one more trip. Leaving Fremantle in Australia on 1 April with a cargo of 40 tons of food, she was diverted en route and after a short patrol returned to port and unloaded her cargo. *Searaven* left the same port a day after the *Swordfish* with 1,500 rounds of 3-inch antiaircraft ammunition, but was also diverted and failed to deliver any of the shells to Corregidor. The final trip was made at the beginning of May, when the *Spearfish,* on patrol off Lingayen Gulf, picked up twenty-five men and women, including twelve nurses, just before the surrender.[40] One other submarine from Hawaii attempted to reach Corregidor with a cargo

---

[36] Rad, Wavell to Combined CsofS, 24 Jan 42, WPD Ready Ref File, Australia. Marshall's message of the 17th is discussed on page 3, above.

[37] Memo, Marshall for King, 29 Jan 42, sub: Atchd Msg from Wavell . . . on use of Submarines, WPD 4560-9.

[38] *Ibid.*

[39] Combined CsofS, 1st Mtg, 23 Jan 42, ABC 381 Phil, OPD Reg Doc; rad, MacArthur to Marshall, No. 274, 13 Feb 42, WDCSA 381 (2-17-42) Phil.

[40] Rpt, COM TF 51 to COM SWPA, 15 May 42, sub: Submarine Relief Activities, Phil, Serial FF6-4, A16-3, copy in OCMH. This document lists all the submarines and their cargo.

of 100 tons of medical supplies but turned back when Bataan fell.

The total effort by the submarines added only 53 tons of food to MacArthur's stores—enough for only one meal for two thirds of the men on Bataan—3,500 rounds of 3-inch antiaircraft ammunition, 37 tons of .50-caliber and 1,000,000 rounds of .30-caliber ammunition, and about 30,000 gallons of diesel oil. In terms of results the effort seemed hardly worthwhile.

The amount of supplies brought into the Philippines by aircraft from Australia and the Netherlands Indies was more substantial but limited to items which weighed little and were small in size. Obviously rations, which were most desperately needed, could not be sent in sufficient quantity to make any difference to the garrison on Bataan and Corregidor. Altogether, there were ten air shipments, starting on 26 January and continuing through 3 May. The first consisted of two planes, an LB–30 and a B–24, which carried 10,000 morphine tablets, other medical supplies, and ammunition. MacArthur reported their safe arrival at Del Monte Airfield in Mindanao to the Chief of Staff early in February.[41] There was time for only one more shipment, including 50,000 quinine tablets, before the Japanese destroyed the hangar at Darwin, where the supplies destined for the Philippines were stored. As a result air transport operations were delayed until other supplies could be gathered at Batchelor Field near Darwin.[42]

During the month of March three shipments by air were made to Mindanao—on the 11th, 16th, and 26th. These flights were more notable perhaps for what the planes brought out than for what they took in. Of the four B–17's that left on the 11th, only one reached Mindanao with a cargo of 1,600 pounds of medical supplies, some signal equipment, and antiaircraft spare parts. The group of B–17's that made the flight on the 16th and 17th brought back to Australia General MacArthur, his family, and his staff. The final March flight took in 5,000 pounds of critical signal equipment and 1,160 pounds of medical supplies (including 1,000,000 quinine tablets). On the return journey the planes carried President Quezon, who had gone only as far as Panay by submarine, and his staff. The largest number of shipments was made in April, and a respectable quantity of medical, signal, and ordnance equipment reached Mindanao during that month. The pilot of the last flight, made on 3 May, found the airdrome occupied by the Japanese and hastily turned around.[43]

The total air effort from Australia resulted in the accumulation of a large quantity of critically needed supplies on Mindanao. Some reached Corregidor by air, in small aircraft which flew in at night to land on the navy strip on the tail of the island. But the bulk of the supplies could not be moved northward where they were desperately needed. Like the rations brought in by the blockade-runners, only a very small amount of the precious air cargo ever reached the battlefield.

By mid-March the opportunity to bring supplies to Bataan and Corregidor had been lost. During the first month and a half of the campaign such an effort might well have

[41] Rads, MacArthur to Marshall, Nos. 177 and 188, 1 and 2 Feb 42, AG 381 (11–27–41 Sec 2 A) Far East.
[42] Ltr, CINC SWPA to CG U.S. Army Air Services, 14 May 42, sub: Phil Relief Shipments, with incls, AG 384. 3M. The inclosures provide a detailed breakdown of each shipment by type of supply and quantity, the plane, and the name of the pilot. A consolidated report is included among the inclosures.

[43] *Ibid.*

been successful. But time was required to gather vessels and cargoes and to organize the men and resources. The Japanese did not give the Allies the time so badly needed. They advanced so rapidly in the Netherlands Indies that they closed the routes between Australia and the Philippines before the blockade-running program was well under way. The route northward from Mindanao and the Visayas to Manila Bay was blocked not long after. Thereafter, no matter how many tons reached the depot at Cebu or the airfield at Del Monte, they would be of little use to the men on Bataan.

While the effort to run the blockade may not have paid dividends in terms of tonnages delivered to the troops, it was nevertheless one that could be amply justified on military and political grounds. The effort had to be made, no matter what the cost. The American people demanded that much at least. Strategically, any measure that might upset the Japanese timetable and contain a large number of Japanese troops was worth trying. Nor could the moral effect on the troops in contact with the enemy be overlooked. No one could be sure in January and February that the blockade would prove unbreakable; politically, strategically, and morally it was necessary to make the attempt. The gallant stand of the Philippine garrison required it; MacArthur demanded it; and the American people supported it.

Last Efforts

Toward the end of March, with Wainwright's assumption of command, a final and frantic effort was made to get food, vitamin concentrates, and medicine. In the messages to Washington a new and desperate note of urgency became evident. For the first time

the War Department received concrete figures on the number of troops in the Philippines when Wainwright reported that he had 90,000 men on Bataan alone. This fact could hardly be believed in Washington and Marshall asked for specific figures, declaring that 90,000 "is greatly in excess of what we understood was there." [44] When Wainwright's reply arrived it proved even more startling than his first statement. On Bataan and Corregidor alone, the strength of the command, including naval elements and civilians subsisted by the Army, was 110,000.[45]

There was not the slightest possibility that sufficient food for even a fraction of this force could be sent, but Marshall told Wainwright not to hesitate to ask for any assistance that was practicable. "It is a matter of continuing concern to me," he assured the recently appointed USFIP commander, "as to what additional measures the War Department might take to strengthen and sustain your gallant defense. . . . Your recommendations always receive my immediate personal attention." [46] Similar assurances had already been given by the President.

Following a lengthy, eleven-page requisition to the War Department, which could not possibly have been filled even under more favorable circumstances, Wainwright reviewed for General Somervell the supplies received from outside sources since the start of the campaign and explained his present situation. "Our desperate needs at the mo-

---

[44] Rad, Marshall to Wainwright, No. 1280, 31 Mar 42, OPD 320.2 Phil (3–31–42).

[45] Memo, Actg CofS for President, 8 Apr 42, sub: Food Situation in Phil, CofS File, Bataan–Corregidor; rad, Wainwright to WD, 2 Apr 42, OPD 381 PI (3–1–42).

[46] Rad, Marshall to Wainwright, 26 Mar 42, Msgs to Gen Wainwright, OPD Exec O.

ment," he told the War Department G–4, "are subsistence and limited medical supplies, particularly quinine sulphate." [47]

The urgency of the request was emphasized in a separate message to the War Department in which he spoke of the high incidence of malaria and other diseases on Bataan and asked for a one-month supply of various drugs essential to the health of his command.[48] Two days later he bluntly warned the Chief of Staff that disaster was imminent unless supplies arrived soon. There was only enough food on Bataan, he stated, to last until 15 April "at one-third ration, poorly balanced and very deficient in vitamins." If, by that time, supplies did not reach him, "the troops there will be starved into submission." [49]

To this estimate, MacArthur, who received a copy of the message, took sharp exception. Without minimizing the critical conditions on Bataan he maintained that there had been enough food there before he left to last until 1 May. "It is of course possible," he told the Chief of Staff, "that with my departure the vigor of application of conservation may have been relaxed." [50] To Wainwright he expressed his confidence that the efforts then being made to break the blockade would bring in enough food to last for an indefinite period and categorically repudiated any idea of surrender. "I am utterly opposed," he asserted, "under any circumstances or conditions to the ultimate capitulation of this command. If food fails,"

he directed Wainwright, "you will prepare and execute an attack upon the enemy." [51]

But the chief problem, to reach Wainwright with supplies, still remained unsolved. From Washington General Marshall used all his authority to send Wainwright the things he so desperately needed. In messages to Australia and Hawaii he ordered that every means at hand be utilized to send aid; all supply agencies in the War Department were impressed with the urgency of the situation; and the Navy was asked to make submarines available. Lt. Gen. Delos C. Emmons, Hawaiian Department commander, was directed to send a vessel loaded with 3,600 tons of concentrated food to Manila Bay immediately. "Spare no effort to push this movement," the Chief of Staff ordered. "You are authorized to pay crew liberal bonus." [52] Within the week a vessel manned by a Navy crew and loaded with 1,000,000 rations, 340 tons of meat, 20 tons of cigarettes, 158 tons of milk, 200 tons of rice, and 548 tons of ammunition had left Honolulu. The journey would take twenty-two days, sixteen more than the Japanese were to allow the Bataan garrison.[53]

MacArthur was asked to intensify his efforts from Australia to relieve Wainwright and to send small boats capable of running the Japanese blockade between Mindanao and Corregidor. The need for quinine was so pressing, Marshall told MacArthur, that he was to send all he could collect by air immediately to Mindanao. Submarines

[47] Rad, Wainwright to Somervell, No. 600, 26 Mar 42, AG 381 (11–27–41 Sec 3) Far East.

[48] Rad, Wainwright to TAG, No. 605, 26 Mar 42, WPD Ready Ref File, Phil.

[49] Rad, Wainwright to Marshall, No. 625, 26 Mar 42, Msgs from Gen Wainwright, OPD Exec 0.

[50] Rad, MacArthur to Marshall, No. 56, 1 Apr 42, WPD Ready Ref File, Phil.

[51] Ibid.; rad, MacArthur to Wainwright, No. 68, 4 Apr 42, AG 384.1, GHQ SWPA.

[52] Rads, Marshall to Emmons, No. 2030, 29 Mar 42, Emmons to Marshall, No. 3088, 31 Mar 42, and Wainwright to Marshall, No. 632, 31 Mar 42, all in WPD 400 Phil (2–27–42).

[53] Rad, Marshall to MacArthur, No. 885, 4 Apr 42, WPD 400 Phil (2–27–42).

furnished by the Navy would carry other supplies. "Report date of initial shipment by plane, type, and quantity of items," the Chief of Staff directed.[54] In reply MacArthur asserted that he had already, at Wainwright's request, sent all the quinine and vitamin concentrates he had been able to gather on short notice. In addition he was planning to send another load by air soon and would station the plane in Mindanao to fly supplies northward.[55]

Marshall even sought to get Wainwright help from China. On 30 March he asked Lt. Gen. Joseph W. Stilwell to look into the possibilities of sending food to the Philippines by ship. Stilwell replied that there was no chance of getting blockade-runners, but that he would try to secure planes and food for such a venture. While he was still trying, Bataan fell.[56]

As each expedient failed to bring in supplies, more and more desperate and extreme measures were proposed in a vain attempt to break through the blockade. When Wainwright requested three submarines to transport supplies from Cebu, they were quickly made available although their transfer seriously limited naval operations. Two underwater craft on patrol west of the Philippines were ordered to Cebu to load supplies for Corregidor, and two others were readied at Fremantle for the trip north. The meager results of this mission have already been recounted.[57]

Wainwright proposed, on 27 March, still another scheme to break through the blockade. This proposal, first made to MacArthur, called for a surprise attack against Japanese naval forces in Visayan waters and in Subic Bay by medium or heavy bombers sent from Australia to Mindanao. Such an attack would have a fair chance, Wainwright thought, of temporarily disrupting the blockade so that some of the food tied up in Cebu could be brought in. As a last resort, he suggested that ten B-17's be stationed at Del Monte and, "by making a round trip each day, deliver a few days reduced ration for Bataan troops." Where these heavy bombers would land was never made clear.[58]

MacArthur agreed to send the bombers at some indefinite date in the future and Wainwright completed his arrangements. Within a few days all was in readiness. Two ships of 500 tons each, one loaded with food and the other with gasoline, were waiting at Cebu and Iloilo. Others were standing by and would be loaded and ready to sail when the first bombers attacked. During the voyage to Corregidor, the vessels would be covered by three P-40's then being assembled in Mindanao. Wainwright had convinced himself by this time that the air attacks would disrupt the blockade "for a considerable period of time," and that he would be able to move all the supplies on Cebu, an amount sufficient to subsist the

[54] Rad, Marshall to MacArthur, No. 91, 27 Mar 42, AG 381 (11–27–41 Sec 3) Far East.
[55] The file marked Messages from General MacArthur in Operations Division, Executive Office Files, contains a series of messages detailing MacArthur's efforts to send critically needed items to Wainwright.
[56] WPD 400 Phil (2–27–42), Cases 9 and 10.
[57] Rad, Wainwright to Marshall through COMINCH, 300940 Mar 42, Msgs to MacArthur, OPD Exec O. Other messages dealing with this matter can be found in the same file and in WPD Ready Ref File, Phil. Col. Stuart Wood, G–2, USFIP, prepared a staff study on the use of submarines to bring in supplies on 20 March 1942, a copy of which is in OCMH.
[58] Rad, Wainwright to MacArthur, No. 154, 27 Mar 42, AG 311.23 (4 Feb 42) GHQ SWPA. This scheme seems to have originated with Colonel Wood, G–2, USFIP, who, on 25 March, submitted a staff study proposing that heavy bombers be used to disrupt the blockade. A copy of this study is in OCMH.

Bataan garrison for one month, to Corregidor. All he needed to carry out this ambitious plan, he told MacArthur, was heavy bombers.[59] On the 4th MacArthur told him that the planes were being prepared and would "be available sometime the following week." [60]

Days passed but no planes came. At Cebu and Iloilo eight ships, fully loaded with rations and medicine, lay at anchor. They were still there when the Japanese occupied Cebu on the morning of 10 April. The bombers finally reached Mindanao the next day, too late to help the men on Bataan.[61]

Despite every effort it had proved impossible to relieve the men on Bataan. The beginning of April found them at their weakest—their fighting edge blunted and their capacity to resist at the lowest ebb. The effects of a three-month-long starvation diet, incessant air and artillery bombardment, and the ravages of disease could be seen in the gaunt bodies and sunken eyes of Americans and Filipinos alike. The loss of hope and the psychological impact of war are recorded only in the diaries and speech of those fortunate enough to survive. By 1 April, wrote General King's surgeon, the combat efficiency of the troops in Luzon Force "was rapidly approaching the zero point." [62]

---

[59] Rad, Wainwright to MacArthur, No. 154, 4 Apr 42, AG 384.1, GHQ SWPA.

[60] Rad, MacArthur to Wainwright, No. 25, 4 Apr 42, AG 384.1, GHQ SWPA.

[61] The ships, fortunately, had been scuttled before the Japanese arrived. Cook, Cebu Depot QM Opns, p. 3, App. A, QM Rpt of Opns; QM Rpt of Opns,

pp. 43, 50, 54; Craven and Cate, *The Army Air Forces in World War II*, I, 417–18.

[62] Luzon Force Rpt of Opns, p. 1.

CHAPTER XXIII

Preparations for Battle

During the lull which settled over the battlefield on Bataan after the middle of February, both sides completed their preparations for the coming offensive. Throughout March General Homma trained and organized the fresh troops which poured into the Philippines from all parts of the rapidly expanding empire, and made careful and elaborate plans for a fresh assault against the stubborn American-Filipino line. The defenders, dug in along the line occupied late in January, used the interlude in battle to train and to improve their positions. What they needed most to strengthen their capacity to resist was food and medicine, but none was forthcoming. At the end of March, when the combat efficiency of the defenders was lowest, the Japanese moved into position for what Homma fully intended would be the final attack.

The American Line

With the exception of a few scattered detachments hiding out in the mountains of Luzon, all of the troops of General King's Luzon Force were crowded into the southern tip of Bataan. In this area, less than 200 square miles, were I and II Corps, force reserve, the Service Command, two coast artillery (antiaircraft) regiments, the Provisional Tank Group, two battalions of 75-mm. guns (SPM), plus engineer and signal troops. So crowded was Bataan that enemy aircraft "could drop their pay loads at almost any point or place and hit something of military value."[1]

The total strength of the units in the Luzon Force was 79,500. Fully three quarters of that total were Philippine Army troops; the rest were Philippine Scouts (8,000) and Americans (12,500). In addition, Luzon Force employed approximately 6,000 civilians and fed another 20,000 Filipino refugees.[2] A detailed breakdown of the strength of the combat elements is revealing. Not one of the eight Philippine Army divisions had its authorized strength of 7,500. General Bluemel's 31st Division was numerically the strongest, with 6,400 men; the 71st, whose combat elements had been absorbed by General Stevens' 91st Divison, had only 2,500. The others—the 1st, 2d, 11th, 21st, 41st, and 51st—had less than 6,000 men each.[3]

The organization and deployment of the forces on Bataan at the end of March did not differ much from what they had been during the preceding two months. (Map 18) The front line still stretched across the peninsula, behind the Pilar–Bagac road, from Orion on the east to Bagac on the west, a distance of thirteen miles. The right half of the line was held by Parker's II Corps; the left, now commanded by General Jones, by I Corps. The corps boundary roughly bisected the southern portion of the peninsula, extending southward along the Pantin-

---

[1] Collier, Notebooks, III, 39.
[2] Luzon Force Rpt of Opns, G–1 Annex, p. 1.
[3] Ibid., table in G–1 Annex.

gan River across the heights of the Mariveles and thence to Mariveles Bay via the Panikian River.[4]

Parker's corps on the Manila Bay side of the peninsula consisted in mid-March of approximately 28,000 men. The eastern anchor of the line was still held by Col. John W. Irwin's 31st Infantry (PA), which was stretched along the coast from Limay northward to Orion. To its left was the provisional regiment composed of Air Corps troops and led by Col. Irvin E. Doane. The 31st Division (less most of two regiments) extended the line about a mile westward where the remnants of the 51st Division, organized as a combat team, tied in with it. The left anchor of II Corps was formed by the 21st and 41st Divisions (PA) deployed in front of Mt. Samat. Guarding the beaches from Limay southward to the corps boundary were the 2d Division (less the 1st and 2d Philippine Constabulary Regiments), a company of tanks, and a battery of SPM's. In corps reserve Parker had the 33d Infantry (PA), less its 1st Battalion, and two engineer battalions.

In the I Corps sector, from east to west, were the 2d Philippine Constabulary Regiment, the 11th, 1st, and 91st Divisions (PA), the last with the 71st and 72d Infantry attached. The 2d Constabulary held the important position on the right flank, tying in with II Corps in the Pantingan River valley, a potentially dangerous corridor leading deep to the rear of the Orion–Bagac line. On the I Corps left, the 91st Division was responsible not only for that portion of the line which included the West Road but for the coast as far south as the

Binuangan River. Defense of the beaches below this river was assigned to the 1st Constabulary, a battalion of the 88th Field Artillery (PS), and miscellaneous Air Corps units. Jones's reserve consisted of the 45th Infantry (PS) and the horseless 26th Cavalry. Total strength of the corps was 32,600 men.

Elements of the Philippine Division, which never saw action as a unit during the campaign, were retained by General King in Luzon Force reserve. Numbering over 5,000 men, this reserve force was composed of the American 31st Infantry, the 57th Infantry (PS), and the Provisional Tank Group. During the first days of April two engineer battalions were taken off construction work on the trails and road and brought into reserve as combat troops. One of these was the 14th Engineer Battalion (PS) of the Philippine Division; the other, the American 803d Engineer Battalion.

The inadequacy of communications and the large number of separate units on the line made it necessary to continue the sector organization established late in January. In II Corps these sectors were designated as before, alphabetically from A to E. Sectors A and B consisted of the two right elements of the line. In each the unit commander was also the sector commander. General Bluemel commanded Sector C, which included his 31st Division elements as well as the 51st Combat Team. Sector D coincided with the front held by the 21st and 41st Divisions and was commanded by General Lough who used his Philippine Division staff as the sector staff. The beach defenses were organized as Sector E under General Francisco, commander of the 2d Division.

The sector organization in I Corps differed from that of the corps to the right. Here only three sectors were established. On

---

[4] The description of the line is from Luzon Force Rpt of Opns, G–3 Annex, pp. 1–3; NLF and I Corps Rpt of Opns, pp. 22 ff; SLF and II Corps Rpt of Opns, pp. 37–46, 50.

the east of the line, from the corps boundary midway to the coast, was the Right Sector, commanded by General Brougher. Next to it was the Left Sector which included the 1st and 91st Divisions. General Stevens had assumed command of this sector when Jones took over command of the corps. Corresponding to Sector E in II Corps was the South Sector under General Pierce, responsible for defense of the beaches. Thus, Jones dealt with only three subordinate commanders for his entire force, and Parker with five.

The large number of artillery pieces concentrated in the small area held by Luzon Force represented the main support of the infantry. In I Corps there were 50 pieces, most of which were of 75-mm. caliber. There were no 105's, and of the 16 155-mm. pieces only 2 were howitzers. The artillery on Parker's side, where the danger was considered greatest, numbered twice as many pieces. Seventy-two of these were 75-mm. guns, 12 were 2.95-inch mountain guns, and the remainder were GPF's of 155-mm. caliber. In addition, 31 naval guns, ranging in size from one-pounders to 3-inchers, had been allotted the two corps for use in beach defense. Army artillery consisted of 27 75-mm. guns (SPM); two antiaircraft regiments, the 200th and 515th, in position to cover the airfields and rear installations, with one battery of 3-inch guns and two batteries of 37-mm. guns in support of the forward area; and one seacoast gun. Despite this imposing array of artillery, the effectiveness of its support was limited by the terrain, the absence of air observation, and the lack of 105-mm. howitzers, fire control, and communications equipment, as well as motor transportation.[5]

---

[5] Luzon Force Rpt of Opns, p. 7; Mallonée, Bataan Diary, II, 80.

Dominating the battlefield and offering excellent observation over a large portion of the front was Mt. Samat, on the left of II Corps. From the coastal plain on the east the ground rises gently at first, then more precipitately, to a height of almost 2,000 feet at the peak of Samat. The mountain and the surrounding country is covered with heavy, hardwood timber. Huge trees, six feet in diameter, rise to a height of 80 to 100 feet. Beneath, the foliage is dense, much of it covered with large thorns to impede the soldier and tear his clothing to shreds. Numerous streams and rivers drain the northern slopes of the Mariveles Mountains, cutting across the Orion–Bagac line and forming river valleys which provided pathways to the south. Heavy forests line the steep banks of the rivers and the undergrowth makes movement difficult even along the narrow trails. Only on the east coast, with its swamps and cane fields, is the ground flat and clear enough to offer fields of fire.

Movement throughout this forbidding area was limited to pack trails and the coastal road. In front and paralleling the line was the Pilar–Bagac road, to which the engineers had constructed a cutoff from KP 136 in front of the 51st Combat Team to Orion on the coast. From the Pilar–Bagac road a number of trails led south. In the II Corps sector, the main north-south trails were 2 and 4 on the east slopes of Mt. Samat and 6 and 29 on the west. Connecting 4 and 29 was Trail 429. In I Corps Trails 15 and 7 offered the enemy a choice of routes into the American position. Lateral communication behind the lines was provided by a series of east-west trails which the engineers had connected during January and February. In general, this road linked Trails 7 and 9 on the west with Trail 8 on the east and intersected the north-south trail system. But all movement, though free from observation, would be closely restricted by the nature of the roads.[6]

Radiating in all directions from the Mariveles Mountains are a large number of rivers and streams which trace their way, like the veins on the back of a man's hand, across the southern portion of Bataan. The Pantingan, which formed the corps boundary, flows north from the Mariveles Mountains to meet the Tiawir River near the Pilar–Bagac road. The Tiawir flows east, changes its name to Talisay, then continues on to Manila Bay. Parallel to the Pantingan and only a short distance to the east is the Catmon which also flows north from the Mariveles Mountains to join the Tiawir-Talisay River. Flowing northeast and east from Mt. Bataan and Mt. Limay to Manila Bay are numerous rivers, the largest of which are the San Vicente, Mamala, Alangan, and Lamao. These rivers derived their military importance from the fact that they lay across the axis of an enemy advance from the north. Only the southernmost of these rivers, however, the Lamao, which flows between steep, heavily wooded banks, presented a serious obstacle. The others, reduced to a trickle during the dry season, could only delay an enemy momentarily.

Since the middle of February, when the pocket fights had ended, there had been little action on Bataan. During this lull every effort had been made to improve the battle line and to train the Philippine Army soldier. Schools were established and a training program organized which utilized fully the knowledge of the enemy acquired through bitter experience during the preceding months. Success in jungle warfare,

it was now clear, depended upon the ability of the individual soldier to a larger degree than in any other type of warfare. One of the first lessons learned was that no soldier should carry more than the absolute minimum required in combat, an old lesson that had to be learned time and again. All the soldier needed was his primary weapon, ammunition, hand grenades, entrenching tools, which few had, and first-aid packet. Everything else should be left behind, for it would only impede his progress through the dense undergrowth and limit his efficiency when he finally met the enemy.

To prepare the soldier for combat, commanders were enjoined to impress upon him the necessity for keeping under cover at all times. This elementary precaution was especially necessary for the Philippine Army troops whose knowledge of military matters was often limited to close order drill and the elements of military courtesy. "We are gradually getting the Philippine Army personnel to lay flat on the ground instead of cowering under trees . . .," remarked one officer, "and we are suffering fewer casualties." [7] Americans and Filipinos alike were cautioned to be on the alert for the many tricks used by the Japanese soldier. One favorite Japanese ruse, the men were told, was to demoralize the enemy by creating the impression that he was being fired on by his own artillery. This effect the Japanese easily produced by timing their own artillery and mortar fire to that of the Americans. In particular, the men were warned against stopping to examine dead Japanese or abandoned equipment. Even at this early stage of the war the Japanese ruse of shamming death until the enemy was near enough for attack had already been observed. "The only safe

---

[6] Skerry, Comments on Engineer Hist, Nos. 10 and 15; SLF and II Corps Rpt of Opns, p. 37.

[7] Tisdelle, Diary, entry of 6 Feb 42.

solution," it was concluded, "is to consider each Japanese as potentially dangerous unless he has surrendered or is dead." [8]

The validity of the tactical doctrines summarized in the manuals and taught in the schools of the Army was proved sound on the battlefield of Bataan. Unit commanders were reminded to pay close heed to first principles. Thorough and careful reconnaissance, experience had shown, should precede the selection and establishment of a position. Stress was placed on the necessity for a clear understanding of responsibility for maintaining contact between adjacent units. At all times units would have to patrol vigorously to the front and flanks, in recognition of the Japanese skill in finding gaps in the line and unprotected flanks. In an effort to train the Filipino a school for scouting and patrolling was established. Instruction was provided by selected officers and men from the Philippine Division who went forward to the front-line units to conduct the school. [9]

"Constant and aggressive patrolling between strong points and centers of resistance" was recommended as the most effective method of combating infiltration. Strong points were to be made mutually supporting, with an all-around defense, and organized in checkerboard manner for a defense in depth. If a small enemy force should succeed in infiltrating to the rear, a USAFFE training memorandum advised, front-line units should remain in place and not be stampeded. The reserve would be used to drive out the Japanese while front-line units provided supporting fire. [10]

In attacking through the jungle the troops were taught to advance slowly. Japanese foxholes and machine gun nests, it was pointed out, would have to be reduced one by one, usually by individuals armed with hand grenades. These men would have to be supported by continuous fire from the squad or platoon. The necessity for halting the advance one to two hours before darkness was stressed in all training. At that time defensive perimeters would be established to prepare for the customary Japanese night attack. The period before nightfall, it was noted, was the best time to serve the one cooked meal of the day.

During the advance the infantry was advised it could not expect close support from the artillery. To provide this support an elaborate wire communications system extending to each assault company would be required, an obvious impossibility on Bataan where wire was in short supply. Battalion commanders were told that artillery units would be placed in direct support and that they could call for fire as needed. Unlike the artillery, mortars could be used with effect in close combat in the jungle when ammunition was available.

One of the most valuable lessons learned during the early days of the fighting was that the light tanks of the Provisional Tank Group could be extremely useful in jungle warfare. Many infantry commanders had expressed dissatisfaction with the support received from the tanks, while the tankers felt that their arm was not understood by the others. Part of the difficulty undoubtedly stemmed from the fact that the tanks were under the control of the group commander who was himself subordinate only to MacArthur's headquarters. Contributing to the misunderstanding was the relative newness of armor and the lack of apprecia-

[8] Tng Memo 5, USAFFE, 26 Feb 42, AG 353 (10 Jan 42) Phil Rcds.

[9] SLF and II Corps Rpt of Opns, p. 46; Bluemel, 31st Div (PA) Rpt of Opns, p. 17.

[10] Tng Memo 4, USAFFE, 12 Jan 42, AG 353 (10 Jan 42) Phil Rcds.

tion by infantry commanders of the potentialities and proper use of tanks.

USAFFE headquarters attempted to remedy this shortcoming. Tanks and infantry, it taught, should operate as a team, with the foot soldier following close behind the tank. This advice was based upon the observation that the Japanese usually remained in concealed positions until the tanks had passed and then opened up on the infantry at a moment when it was deprived of armored support. Experience had shown that, except under unusual circumstances, armor was most effective in attacks against limited objectives where it could be supported by infantry fire. Although a co-ordinated infantry-tank attack would of necessity be slow, the advantage gained by the tank's ability to destroy the enemy's prepared positions, it was believed, would more than compensate for the loss of speed. Under no circumstances, warned USAFFE in a training memorandum, were the tanks to be employed as pillboxes or left forward without infantry protection.

The Americans learned valuable lessons from the Japanese landings behind I Corps late in January. The best defense against these landings, it had been observed, was the occupation of all bays and beaches with "vigilant and aggressive" troops armed with machine guns.[11] Since there were not enough men to cover all possible landing sites, only the most likely could be covered in this manner. Mobile reserves could be used in the event of a landing at an unguarded beach. As the enemy approached close to shore he would be extremely vulnerable to automatic weapons fire. "Get the Japanese before he lands," advised USAFFE. "Ten minutes of accurate fire placed on the Japa-

nese just prior to and during the period of attempted landing may save three or four days necessary to hunt him in the brush and woods." [12]

While these lessons were of undoubted importance in the training of the troops during the lull in battle, of more immediate importance was the improvement of fortifications and the strengthening of the Orion–Bagac line. Staff officers from Corregidor as well as from headquarters on Bataan made frequent inspections of the front lines and pointed out deficiencies in the defenses. Among the faults noted were the failure to clear fields of fire, the improper placement and camouflage of foxholes, and the location of wire entanglements without regard for tactical dispositions. These faults were summarized by USAFFE late in February and instructions issued for strengthening the line. "Organization of positions must be continued beyond the foxhole stage," it directed; "reserve and support positions prepared; trenches dug; drainage arranged for; camouflage improved; clearing of fields of fire extended to the front to include all foliage and cover afforded the enemy within small arms range." [13] Commanders and their staffs were enjoined to supervise and check the positions established, suggest improvements, and correct errors. Particular attention was to be given to sanitation which, USAFFE noted, had been neglected by front-line units. "The health of the command," it warned, "may be seriously endangered by neglect of these measures." [14]

The improvement of the defenses along the main line of resistance and the beaches circling the southern tip of Bataan contin-

---

[11] Tng Memo 10, USAFFE, 1 Feb 42, AG 353 (10 Jan 42) Phil Rcds.

[12] Ibid.
[13] Tng Memo 14, USAFFE, 25 Feb 42, AG 353 (10 Jan 42) Phil Rcds.
[14] Ibid.

ued throughout March. Trained techni-
cians of the 14th Engineer Battalion (PS)
visited all units on the line and gave instruction and assistance in fortifications.[15]
Though limited by shortages of equipment
and defense materials, the men along the
front strung barbed wire and constructed
tank traps and obstacles. In I Corps the
engineers planted three large mine fields
along the most probable routes of hostile advance and laid about 1,400 improvised
box mines and thirty-five submarine depth
charges, secured from Corregidor. In the
11th Division (PA) sector, by the end of
March, the entire front was covered by a
wall or palisade of bamboo poles twelve
feet high. Though it had little value as protection against enemy attack, this wall did
provide concealment and bolster morale.[16]

While much work remained, the main
line of resistance and the beach defenses had
been considerably improved by the end of
the month. In the opinion of General Casey,
defensive positions on Bataan were well conceived and constructed, deriving their
strength from cleared fields of fire and "suit-
ably emplaced" automatic weapons with
"both grazing and enfilade fire." [17]

Anticipating the possibility that all combat troops would be needed to halt a break-
through, General King ordered all II Corps
service units to be ready to take over defense
of the beaches to release the 2d Division for
counterattack. Service unit commanders
were required to reconnoiter the trails leading to their assigned sectors to determine the
quickest route to the beach and a trial run

was made on 28 March under cover of darkness.[18] In I Corps General Jones ordered
the establishment of four switch positions
in the Pantingan River valley, on his right
flank, on the assumption that the main effort, as before, would be made between the
two corps.[19]

Luzon Force made its own preparations.
These included the pooling of buses and
trucks, gassed and ready for immediate
movement, in the reserve area. In this way
the 31st Infantry (US) and the 57th Infantry (PS), in force reserve, could be
moved quickly to any threatened portion of
the line. Fearful also of the "pitifully thin"
beach defenses, Luzon Force organized a
battery of 75-mm. guns (SPM) and a company of tanks into a mobile reserve and
ordered them "to reconnoiter roads and
avenues of approach." [20] By the end of
March the half-starved and poorly equipped
Americans and Filipinos had done all they
could to prepare for attack. The signs that
such an attack would soon come were clear;
"the handwriting was vivid on the wall." [21]

Japanese Preparations

During March General Homma completed his own plans and preparations. He
had every reason to believe that this time
his efforts would be crowned with success.
Since 8 February, when he had abandoned
his fruitless efforts to reduce Bataan,
Homma had received large reinforcements.
Like the Americans he had utilized the lull
in battle to reorganize his force and to train
and rest his weakened troops. They were
now ready, he thought, for the final effort
to bring the campaign to a quick close.

---

[15] SLF and II Corps Rpt of Opns, p. 46.

[16] Skerry, Comments on Engineer Hist, No. 19;
NLF and I Corps Rpt of Opns, p. 29; Note by Gen
Brougher on 11th Div Tng Memo, 4 Mar 42, copy
in OCMH.

[17] Memo, Chief Engineer, GHQ SWPA for CofS
GHQ, AG 307.24 (10–25–42E) GHQ SWPA.

[18] Luzon Force Rpt of Opns, p. 3.

[19] NLF and I Corps Rpt of Opns, p. 29.

[20] Collier, Notebooks, III, 60.

[21] Wainwright, General Wainwright's Story, p. 76.

At the end of February the Japanese had been in desperate straits. At that time their infantry strength on Bataan had been reduced to approximately 3,000 effectives. Both the *65th Brigade* and the *16th Division* had been so sadly depleted that the *14th Army* chief of staff described them as "a very weak force." [22] These heavy losses had been due only in part to battle casualties; disease and shortages of food and medicine had also taken their toll.

Even by Japanese standards the lot of the soldier on Bataan was not an enviable one. Certainly he was not well fed. During January *14th Army*'s supply of rice had run low and efforts to procure more from Tokyo and from local sources in the Philippines had proved unavailing. As a result the ration had been drastically reduced in mid-February. Instead of the 62 ounces normally issued the troops of Japan, the men on Bataan received only about 23 ounces, plus small amounts of vegetables, meat, and fish which were distributed from time to time. To this they added whatever they could buy, steal, or force from an unwilling civilian populace. [23]

Severe shortages of medical supplies and equipment had further limited the effectiveness of Japanese operations on Bataan. The *14th Army* had begun the campaign

with but one month's supply of quinine and in January its use as a prophylaxis for all but front-line troops had been discontinued. After 10 March even troops in combat were denied the drug which was thereafter reserved for those hospitalized with malaria. Those sick with diphtheria received no medication and the treatment of actual or potential tetanus, gangrene, and dysentery cases was limited by the very small amount of the drugs on hand. Between 1 January and 31 March approximately 13,000 Japanese soldiers were hospitalized as nonbattle casualties alone. Since the military hospitals could accommodate only 5,000 patients in the period when battle casualties were greatest, it was impossible to provide adequate medical treatment for the sick and wounded. [24]

The condition of his men, therefore, as well as the unexpectedly strong resistance from the American and Filipino troops, had forced Homma to discontinue offensive operations in February. *Imperial General Headquarters* in Tokyo, which had earlier taken from Homma the *48th Division* and most of his air force, now became concerned over the failure to bring the campaign to an end. [25] Elsewhere Japanese armies had met with spectacular success and *General Headquarters* felt that it could now spare the forces necessary to complete the conquest of the Philippines.

This decision was in no sense an indication that the Army high command was satisfied with the performance of *14th Army*. It was not and soon made its displeasure evident by shifts in Homma's staff. Inspecting officers from Tokyo visiting

---

[22] USA *vs.* Homma, p. 2457, testimony of Gen Wachi. See also *ibid.,* Homma's testimony on p. 3062, Nakajima's on p. 2575, and Defense Exhibit Y, a casualty chart prepared by the *14th Army* surgeon. *65th Brig* Opns Rpt, p. 34; *14th Army* Opns, I, 116, 231.

[23] USA *vs.* Homma, pp. 2536, 2876–79, 2848, 3122, testimony of Homma and of Col Shusuke Horiguchi, *14th Army* surgeon.
The normal Japanese field ration consisted of rice, fish, vegetables, soup, and pickled plums or radishes. Other items, such as meat, sweets, and fruits, were issued on special occasions. Handbook of Japanese Military Forces, TM–E 30–480, 15 Sept 44, pp. 177–79.

[24] USA *vs.* Homma, pp. 2831–50, testimony of Horiguchi. See also testimony on pp. 2680–83, 2792, 2799, and Defense Exhibit Y.

[25] Hist, *Army Sec, Imperial GHQ,* p. 42.

Manila had found many *14th Army* officers comfortably settled in the capital while the battle for Bataan was at its height. "If the tactical situation went well," General Homma later commented wryly, "that would have been all right for everybody." [26] Unfortunately for these officers the battle did not go well and on 23 February *General Headquarters* relieved General Maeda, Homma's chief of staff, as well as the operations and training officer and the supply officer of *14th Army* headquarters. Maeda's place was taken by Maj. Gen. Takaji Wachi who arrived in the Philippines about 1 March.[27]

During the latter part of February and throughout the month of March Japanese reinforcements poured into the Philippines. With the individual replacements received during this period both the badly hit *65th Brigade* and *16th Division* were strengthened and revitalized. In February General Nara received about sixty officer replacements and, the following month, 3,500 men to take the place of the troops he had lost during the January attack against II Corps. The *16th Division* received a similar number of men about the same time.[28]

The largest single addition to Homma's *14th Army* came when the *4th Division,* led by Lt. Gen. Kenzo Kitano, arrived from Shanghai. Kitano had learned "unofficially" that his division was to be transferred on 4 February but it was not until a week later

that he received orders to move out. By the 27th of the month the first convoy, comprising division and infantry group headquarters, one infantry regiment, plus artillery and service troops, had reached Lingayen Gulf. The remainder of the division followed in successive convoys and by 15 March almost the entire *4th Division* was on Luzon.

The arrival of the *4th Division* did not produce any great enthusiasm at *14th Army* headquarters—the division was poorly equipped and numbered only 11,000 men; its infantry battalions had three instead of four rifle companies; it lacked antitank guns and two of its four field hospitals.[29] In General Homma's opinion, Kitano's division was the "worst equipped" division in the entire Japanese Army, and, he later noted, had he been forced to rely on it alone to begin his offensive he would not have been "competent to attack." [30]

On 26 February, the day before Kitano's first group landed, a strong detachment from the *21st Division* arrived in the Philippines. This force, led by Maj. Gen. Kameichiro Nagano, *21st Infantry* group commander, and called the *Nagano Detachment,* numbered about 4,000 men and was composed of the group headquarters, the *62d Infantry,* a battalion of mountain artillery, and a company of engineers. Nagano had been en route from China to French Indochina with the rest of the *21st Division* when he had received the orders from

---

[26] USA *vs.* Homma, p. 3228, testimony of Homma.

[27] *Ibid.,* and Defense Exhibit A; *Southern Army Opns,* p. 19. General Maeda gives his own reasons for his relief in Interrog of Maeda, 10 May 47, Interrogations of Former Japanese Officers, Mil Hist Div, GHQ FEC, I.

[28] *14th Army* Opns, I, 123; *65th Brig* Opns Rpt, Mt. Samat, p. 34; ltr, Chief, Hist Div, SSUSA, to G–2, GHQ FEC, 9 Nov 48, 3d Ind, 16 Aug 49.

[29] USA *vs.* Homma, pp. 2841–42, testimony of Horiguchi; Interrog of Gen Kitano, 1 May 47, Interrogations of Former Japanese Officers, Mil Hist Div, GHQ FEC, I; *14th Army* Opns, I, 119; ltr, Chief, Hist Div, SSUSA, to G–2 GHQ FEC, 9 Nov 48, 3d Ind, 16 Aug 49.

[30] USA *vs.* Homma, p. 3063, testimony of Homma. Kitano had served under Homma in 1935–36 as a regimental commander when the latter commanded a brigade of the *4th Division.*

Southern Army that sent him to the Philippines.[31] Arriving too late to participate in the final offensive was the *10th Independent Garrison* which landed at Lingayen Gulf on 2 April. Intended as an occupation force, this organization consisted of five independent battalions of infantry but lacked supporting arms and services.[32]

Artillery reinforcements began to reach the Philippines in the middle of February and continued to arrive in increasing numbers until the first week in April. Included among these units were a balloon company and an artillery intelligence regiment. To control the large number of artillery units, Homma was also given the *1st Artillery Headquarters*, led by Lt. Gen. Kishio Kitajima, which was shipped from Hong Kong late in March.[33] *Imperial General Head-*

quarters also provided air reinforcements for the coming offensive by giving Homma two heavy bombardment regiments consisting of a total of sixty twin-engine bombers. The two regiments flew in from Malaya and landed at Clark Field on 16 March. Naval air units were also dispatched to Luzon to assist *14th Army* air elements which were reorganized into the *22d Air Brigade* under Maj. Gen. Kizo Mikami. By the beginning of April, therefore, Homma had a sizable air force to throw against the defenders of Bataan.[34]

While recently arrived and veteran units alike were put through a rigorous training program, *14th Army* staff officers made preparations for the coming offensive. The final plan, completed on 22 March, was based on the incorrect assumption that the defenders numbered 40,000 men and were deployed along three lines: the first along Mt. Samat, the second along Mt. Limay, and the final line near Mariveles at the tip of the peninsula.[35] (*Map 21*) To break through this defense in depth, *14th Army* proposed to make a co-ordinated infantry-

---

[31] Hist of Indo-China Opns, 1941–45, Japanese Studies in World War II, No. 24, pp. 12–13, OCMH; *Southern Army* Opns, pp. 4–5, 19.

[32] *14th Army* Opns, I, 119. The unit was led by Col. Torao Ikuta and is referred to in some sources as the *Ikuta Detachment*.

In addition to the strong reinforcements sent to Luzon, *Imperial General Headquarters* dispatched units to other portions of the Philippine Archipelago to hasten the occupation of the Visayas and Mindanao. Thus far only Mindoro, a portion of Mindanao, and a few small islands seized at the start of the war were in Japanese hands. On 10 March elements of the *5th* and *18th Divisions* from Malaya and Borneo were assigned the task of occupying the central and southern Philippines. In early April these units arrived in Lingayen Gulf, were augmented by *14th Army* supporting and service troops and organized into two detachments for operations in the south. See below, Ch. XXVIII.

[33] *14th Army* Opns, I, 119–20; USA *vs.* Homma, p. 2635, testimony of Kitajima. The artillery reinforcements consisted of the following units:

1st Arty Hq
1st Field Heavy Arty Regt (240-mm. howitzers)
2d Independent Heavy Arty Btry (240-mm. howitzers)
3d Independent Mountain Arty Regt (75-mm. mountain guns)
3d Mortar Bn
14th Independent Mortar Bn (300-mm. mortars)

2d Independent Mortar Bn (150-mm. mortars)
20th Independent Mountain Arty Bn (75-mm. mountain guns)
One Co, *21st Field Heavy Arty Bn* (150-mm. howitzers)
5th Arty Intel Regt
3d Tractor Unit
1st Balloon Co

[34] *14th Army* Opns, I, 156; *5th Air Gp* Opns, pp. 58, 70–71; ltr, Chief, Hist Div, SSUSA, to G–2 GHQ FEC, 9 Nov 48, 3d Ind, 16 Aug 49.

[35] USA *vs.* Homma, pp. 2457, 2576. At his trial General Homma explained that his intelligence officer had estimated enemy strength on Bataan as 25,000 men, but that he, Homma, believed this figure to be too low. He had told his intelligence officer so and had directed him to "go back and estimate again." The next estimate was 40,000. "So," explained Homma at his trial, "in my estimation, I told him it must be 60,000, but I have no data to contradict you, so I accept your estimation." *Ibid.*, pp. 3064–65.

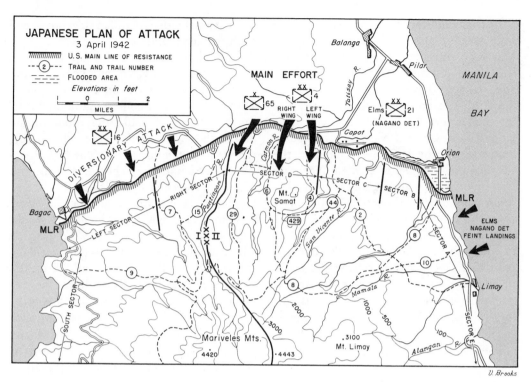

MAP 21

artillery-air assault along a narrow front, with Mt. Samat as the initial objective. From here the Japanese would push on to the Mt. Limay line, supported, if necessary, by an advance along the East Road. Once this line was gained, *14th Army* would bring the campaign to an end by seizing Mariveles. Preparations for the assault against Corregidor would begin immediately thereafter.[36]

[36] The description of the Japanese plan is based upon: *14th Army* Opns, I, 128–42, 146–56, II, 17–42; *5th Air Gp* Opns, pp. 54–63; Interrog of Kitano, 1 May 47, Interrogations of Former Japanese Officers, Mil Hist Div, GHQ FEC, I; Statements of Lt Col Hiromi Oishi, *4th Div* staff, 2 Oct 50, ATIS Doc 62639, and Col Motohiko Yoshida, CofS *4th Div,* 28 Jul 49, ATIS Doc 62642, both in Statements of Japanese Officials on World War II, GHQ FEC, Mil Intel Sec, III, 113, IV, 548.

797-257 O—66—28

In contrast to his expectations for a speedy victory in January, Homma, who had by this time acquired a healthy respect for his opponent, now believed that it would take about a month to complete the conquest of Bataan: one week to seize Mt. Samat, two weeks to crack the Limay line, and one more week to mop up. "I do not know," Homma wrote, "whether the enemy on Bataan will try to fight to the end at their first and second line, whether they will retreat back to Corregidor and fight, escape to Australia, the Visayas or Mindanao, or give up at the right time, but I still propose to prepare for the worst." [37]

[37] *14th Army* Opns, II, 16, Homma Notes, and I, 129; USA *vs.* Homma, p. 3065, testimony of Homma.

Instructions for the coming offensive were issued to all major commanders on 23 March at a meeting in San Fernando. General Kitano, commander of the *4th Division*, was told that his division would carry the burden of the main assault in front of Mt. Samat and that he would receive close support from General Nara's *65th Brigade*. Protection of the left (east) flank of the advance was assigned to General Nagano's *21st Division* detachment, and the *16th Division* commander, General Morioka, was given the mission of making a feint attack in front of I Corps. Beginning the next day, 24 March, General Mikami's *22d Air Brigade*, aided by naval aircraft, would begin an intensive air assault against the American line, and just before the ground assault opened General Kitajima's artillery would join in the attack to soften up the opposition.

There was no disagreement over the selection of 3 April as D Day. But zero hour was not fixed without a good deal of discussion. General Kitano and his *4th Division* staff urged that the ground assault begin at noon. To delay until later in the day, they argued, would needlessly expose the troops to enemy artillery fire before the attack. The *65th Brigade* commander, General Nara, with three months' experience on Bataan, felt that the Americans would take advantage of the daylight hours to mass their extremely effective artillery fire against the advancing infantry if the attack jumped off too early. He preferred to delay zero hour until dusk and move forward under cover of darkness. Since no agreement could be reached, Colonel Nakayama, *14th Army* operations officer, presented a compromise plan fixing the time of the infantry attack at 1500. A disagreement over the objectives of the first day's attack was also settled by compromise;

thereafter the detailed planning proceeded with few interruptions.

The plans finally drawn up for the 3 April offensive provided for a heavy air and artillery bombardment on the morning of D Day. After a five-hour preparation the assaulting infantry would move out to the attack, the *65th Brigade* on the right (west), the *4th Division* on the left. The first objective, Mt. Samat, was to be taken at the end of the first week of operations.

The Japanese would advance in three columns. The right (west) column would consist of General Nara's *65th Brigade* whose main force would march up the Pantingan River valley, along Trail 29, on the extreme left of the II Corps line. One element of the brigade was to remain west of the Pantingan River, in I Corps, to maintain contact with the *16th Division*. Nara's objective was control of the area west of Mt. Samat. When he had gained this objective, he was to halt his troops, reorganize, and prepare to seize the commanding heights of the Mariveles Mountains.

The *4th Division* was to advance in two columns. On the right, next to the *65th Brigade* and making the main effort, was Maj. Gen. Kureo Taniguchi's *Right Wing*, consisting of the *61st Infantry*, one battalion of the *8th Infantry*, the *7th Tank Regiment* (less two companies), and artillery and service units. Taniguchi, the infantry group commander of the *4th Division*, was to take his men across the Tiawir River and down along the Catmon River, in the center of Sector D, toward Mt. Samat. The *4th Division's Left Wing*, organized around the *8th Infantry* and led by Col. Haruji Morita, the regimental commander, was to form the easternmost column of the Japanese drive. It was to advance down Trail 4, against the

Philippine Army's 21st Division on the right of Sector D, directly toward the first objective, Mt. Samat.

Supporting the advance of the *4th Division* and the *65th Brigade* would be the *16th Division* and the *Nagano Detachment*, initially in Army reserve. The former, with attached artillery and tanks, was to protect the right (west) flank of the assault. On 31 March, three days before the main effort began, Morioka would begin a feint attack against I Corps, and thereafter maintain constant pressure against that corps to pin down General Jones's troops. By 8 April Morioka was to be ready to move the bulk of his division eastward to support the advance of the *4th Division*. An element of the *Nagano Detachment* was to protect the *4th Division*'s east flank and later the entire detachment was to divert the enemy and pin down his beach defense troops by feinting landings along the east coast of Bataan, between Orion and Limay.

By the end of the first week of operations, General Homma estimated, the *4th Division* would be approaching the Mamala River, and the *65th Brigade,* the foothills of the Mariveles. Along the river Homma expected to encounter the strong defenses of the Limay line, a line which existed only in Japanese estimates and plans. With the *16th Division* ready to move east to the support of the *4th Division* and with the *Nagano Detachment* poised to advance down the East Road, Homma hoped to be able to pierce the defenses of this line and defeat the American and Filipino force in two weeks. After that, operations would consist largely of mopping up. Homma's estimates in this case, unlike those he had made earlier in the campaign, were extremely conservative. General Kitano, who had not yet been in combat on Bataan, was far more sanguine

about the results of the initial attack. Once Mt. Samat had been taken and the II Corps front rolled back, he believed, only "a pursuit of the Americans" would be required.[38] For once the more optimistic of the Japanese estimates proved correct.

Prelude to Attack

During the second week of March the month-long lull which had followed the Japanese withdrawal from the Orion–Bagac line came to an end. American and Philippine patrols now began to meet opposition from a counterreconnaissance screen which Homma had thrown forward to mask preparations for the coming offensive. As the days passed Japanese patrols became more active, and troops along the outpost line reported skirmishes with the enemy who was already moving out to the line of departure. By the last week of March the Japanese had pushed forward their screen to within 1,000 yards of the American line.[39]

There were other equally obvious signs after the middle of March that the Japanese would soon renew the attack. Observers reported that they were moving supplies and troops into Bataan and building roads. Enemy aircraft, rarely seen in the month following the Japanese withdrawal, now began to appear in increasingly large numbers, attacking front-line troops, artillery positions, and supply areas to the rear.

---

[38] Interrog of Kitano, 1 May 47, Interrogations of Former Japanese Officer, Mil Hist Div, GHQ FEC, I.

[39] Collier, Notebooks, III, 52, 59; O'Day, 21st Div (PA), II, 35–36; *14th Army* Opns, I, 122–23; Luzon Force Rpt of Opns, G–2 Annex. A daily report on the enemy build-up is contained in the messages of General Beebe to MacArthur, and Wainwright to the War Department in G–3 USFIP Journal, 19 Mar–19 Apr 42, AG 461 (1 Apr 42) Phil Rcds.

The presence of many small boats and native craft at the mouth of the Pampanga River on the north shore of Manila Bay hinted at the possibility of amphibious attacks along the east coast of Bataan, similar to those made earlier against I Corps. Through the month the Japanese shelled the American positions intermittently with 75-mm. guns mounted on the largest of these boats. Though their marksmanship was poor, their fire increased apprehension of a landing behind the lines.[40]

Japanese artillery activities increased also. The Japanese guns which had been silent for several weeks began to sound again and an observation balloon floating over the high ground west of Abucay gave notice of the arrival of larger Japanese pieces than the Americans had yet encountered.[41]

To these portents of a new Japanese offensive General Homma added a direct warning of dire consequences if the Bataan defenders did not surrender. In a message to General Wainwright, copies of which were dropped over Bataan in beer cans, Homma praised the valiant stand made by the Americans and Filipinos but declared that he now had large enough forces and supplies "either to attack and put to rout your forces or to wait for the inevitable starvation of your troops. . . ." He urged Wainwright to be sensible and follow "the defenders of Hongkong, Singapore and the Netherlands East Indies in the acceptance of an honorable defeat." To do otherwise, he pointed out, would be disastrous. The message closed with the ominous warning that if Wainwright did not reply by noon of the 22d, Homma would consider himself "at liberty to take any action whatsoever."[42]

More specific information about Homma's intentions came on the night of 24 March when some Filipino troops found on the body of a Japanese officer a detailed order for a reconnaissance in force of the Mt. Samat area. The order specified that information was to be obtained about routes of advance for tanks, favorable points for river crossings, and American artillery positions around Mt. Samat. The document further revealed that, following the reconnaissance, some time after 26 March the Japanese would attack in the Mt. Samat region and even indicated "with considerable exactitude" the plan of the attack.[43]

By now the Japanese air and artillery bombardment had made life for the sick and hungry men on Bataan a living hell. Enemy planes, unopposed except for a few antiaircraft guns, were over the American lines at all hours of the day, bombing and strafing at will. "Every few minutes," wrote an American officer, "one plane would drop down, lift up the tree branches and lay one or two eggs. Every vehicle that tried to move, every wire-laying detail, infantry patrols, even individuals moving in the open were subject to these spot bombings."[44] Japanese artillery concentrated on front-line positions and on the Americans' larger

---

[40] Luzon Force Rpt of Opns, p. 2 and G–2 Annex; Collier, Notebooks, III, 52, 58–59; Mallonée, Bataan Diary, II, 79–80.

[41] Quintard, Diary, entries of 19 Mar–1 Apr 42; Luzon Force Rpt of Opns, p. 7; Collier, Notebooks, III, 59, 62.

[42] The text of the surrender message is in the exhibits of the trial of General Homma, Prosecution Exhibit 421.

[43] Luzon Force Rpt of Opns, G–2 Annex; SLF and II Corps Rpt of Opns, p. 47; Emerson, Opns of II Phil Corps, 10 Jan–8 Apr 42, pp. 21–22; Fortier, Notes on 41st Div (PA), p. 5; ltr, Fowler to author. 22 Mar 49, OCMH.

[44] Mallonée, Bataan Diary, II, 80.

SEEKING COVER IN A TRENCH NEAR LAMAO *during an air attack.*

guns, co-ordinating with the air forces in an effort to knock out the American artillery. Though the effort was unsuccessful, by destroying communications and shelling observation posts and battery positions, the Japanese lowered the efficiency of the artillery "to a considerable extent." [45]

While the matériel losses from the bombings were not very great, the effect of the air-artillery attack, which increased in severity daily, on the efficiency of the troops was pronounced. The men were under shelter a good part of the time and many began to show a marked reluctance to move far from cover. The alert might sound in the midst of a meal or while the men were at rest, and everyone would dash for shelter. Rank made no difference; the men headed

for the nearest foxhole and remained there until the attack was over. One Filipino officer, three times wounded and returned to duty each time, strangely enough usually found himself in sole possession of any foxhole he selected. The men estimated that his luck had run out and when he hopped into a foxhole they promptly jumped out and ran for another.[46] Work was constantly being interrupted by the bombardment, and officers inspecting the defenses spent fully half their time in a ditch. "These high bombers get my goat," wrote Colonel Quintard in his diary. "You never know when they are going to unload, and the waiting gets hard; when they do unload any

[45] Luzon Force Rpt of Opns, p. 7.

[46] Capt Andrew D. Shoemake, 41st FA (PA), p. 32, Chunn Notebooks. Shoemake was instructor of the 2d Battalion, 41st Field Artillery (PA).

place near, it sounds like an express train bearing down on you for a few seconds before they hit." [47]

On 28 March, *14th Army* issued final orders for the offensive, and all troops began to move forward to the line of departure. The *65th Brigade,* with elements on both sides of the Pantingan River, pushed in the outpost line of the 21st and 41st Divisions and took up a favorable position for the attack, To its east, the *4th Division* advanced from the assembly area to the front and by 2 April both wings of the division were posted along the north shore of the Tiawir-Talisay River. The *Nagano Detachment,* the easternmost unit of the Japanese advance, was already in position to carry out its mission. Far to the west, in front of I Corps, the *16th Division* had already tied

in with the *65th Brigade* and begun to make feint attacks against General Jones's line. [48]

By 2 April all preparations had been completed and the Japanese could announce publicly over the radio that they were ready to begin "an all out offensive in Bataan." [49] "Our four groups [the *4th* and *16th Divisions,* the *Nagano Detachment,* and the *65th Brigade*] have been brought into line and on a front of 25 kilometers ten flags are lined up," wrote General Homma on the eve of the attack. "Artillery is plentiful. There are also enough special guns, and supply arrangements have been completely prepared . . . . There is no reason why this attack should not succeed." [50]

---

[48] *14th Army* Opns, I, 143–44; Luzon Force Rpt of Opns, p. 2; SLF and II Corps Rpt of Opns, p. 49; Oster and Richards, 21st Inf (PA), p. 10, Chunn Notebooks.

[49] USAFFE-USFIP Rpt of Opns, p. 47.

[50] *14th Army* Opns, II, 17, Homma notes.

---

[47] Quintard, Diary, entry of 28 Mar 42.

CHAPTER XXIV

The Final Japanese Offensive

Friday, 3 April, was not only the day Homma had selected to open the offensive; it was also a religious and national holiday for the soldiers on both sides of the battle line. For the Christian defenders it was the Friday of Holy Week, and the more devout observed the anniversary of the Crucifixion with prayers and fasting. For the Japanese, the 3d of April marked the anniversary of the death of the legendary Emperor Jimmu, the first ruler to sit on the imperial throne. In Japan there would be religious ceremonies and feasting; on Bataan the soldiers of Hirohito, a direct descendant of the Emperor Jimmu, would celebrate the day in more warlike manner. If all went well, they might gain victory in time to make the emperor's birthday, 29 April, a day of special rejoicing.[1]

---

[1] Japanese sources used in the preparation of this chapter include: *14th Army* Opns, I, 147–50, 156–63, II, Maps 12 and 13; *5th Air Gp* Opns, pp. 72–74; USA *vs.* Homma, p. 2651, testimony of Kitajima; Statements of Col Oishi, 2 Oct 50, ATIS Doc 62639, and Col Yoshida, 28 Jul 49, ATIS Doc 62642, both in Statements of Japanese Officials on World War II, GHQ FEC, Mil Intel Sec, III, 113–15, IV, 548–51.

American sources of a general nature include: USAFFE-USFIP Rpt of Opns, pp. 57–59; Luzon Force Rpt of Opns, pp. 3–4; SLF and II Corps Rpt of Opns, pp. 50–56; Collier, Notebooks, III, 71–74; Quintard, Diary, entries of 3–6 Apr 42; Phil Div Rpt of Opns, pp. 24–27; Mallonée, Bataan Diary, II, 81, 90–91. References to the detailed accounts of operations are cited below.

Capture of Mt. Samat

On Good Friday the sun rose in a cloudless sky and gave promise of another hot, dry day so like those which had preceded it with endless monotony. From the top of Mt. Samat two American officers serving as artillery observers could plainly see the heavy Japanese guns, two to three miles behind the line, making ready to fire. Before their view was obscured they counted nineteen batteries of artillery and eight to ten mortar batteries. Observers to their east reported many more batteries of light artillery massed in close support of the infantry.[2] At 0900 this large array of guns, howitzers, and mortars, altogether almost 150 pieces, began to register on their targets.

The Japanese began firing for effect at 1000 and continued to fire with only one half-hour pause until 1500, in what was undoubtedly the most devastating barrage of the campaign, equal in intensity, many thought, to those of the first World War.[3] Simultaneously, the bombers of the *22d Air Brigade* came out in force to add the

---

[2] Mallonée, Bataan Diary, II, 81; Shoemake, 41st FA (PA), p. 32, Chunn Notebooks; interv, author with Maj Winston A. Jones, 41st FA (PA), 8 May 49. Shoemake and Jones were the two American observers.

[3] Mallonée, Bataan Diary, II, 81; Ellis, 23d Inf (PA), p. 14, Chunn Notebooks; ltr, Col Wetherby to author, 22 May 51, OCMH.

weight of their bombs to the constant stream of shells falling upon the defenders huddled in their foxholes. In the 150 sorties flown that day, General Mikami's air force dropped more than sixty tons of bombs. Smaller aircraft swooped low over the front lines, strafing troops and vehicles at will, while far above them observation planes guided the bombers toward those batteries brave enough to reply to the Japanese barrage. "It was agonizing," wrote the commander of an antiaircraft battery, "to watch the heavies sail serenely over us, 1,000 yards beyond our maximum range." [4]

The effect of the air-artillery bombardment was devastating. So violent and continuous were the explosions, so thunderous the din that it seemed as though "all hell" had broken loose.[5] Many of the defenses so carefully constructed during the weeks preceding the attack "were churned into a worthless and useless mess." [6] Telephone lines and artillery positions were knocked out. Fire spread rapidly when the cane fields and bamboo thickets were set ablaze and the smoke and dust lay so thick over the battlefield that observers atop Mt. Samat were unable to direct fire. By 1500 the artillery and aircraft had done their work. At that time the infantry and armor moved out to the attack.

Penetration

The air and artillery preparation which had begun at 1000 that morning had been concentrated against the comparatively narrow front on the extreme left of II Corps,

---

[4] Maj John McM. Gulick, Memoirs of Btry C, 91st CA (PS), p. 106, copy lent to author by Major Gulick, OCMH.
[5] Quintard, Diary, entry for 3 Apr 42.
[6] Collier, Notebooks, III, 71.

held by the troops of Sector D. It was in this sector, commanded by General Lough, that the American line was stretched thinnest, and it was in this sector that the Japanese first came.

Sector D extended from KP 136 on the Pilar–Bagac road westward for about 5,000 yards to the corps boundary along the Pantingan River. Bisecting the sector front was the Catmon River, which, with the Pantingan, offered a natural route of advance southward. (*Map 22*) In addition to these two river valleys, Sector D contained three excellent north-south trails, two of which connected with the main east-west trail system. The westernmost of these was Trail 29, between the Pantingan and the Catmon. About five miles in length, this trail ran from the Pilar–Bagac road along the western foothills of Mt. Samat to Trail 8, the main east-west line of communication in II Corps. Along the east bank of the Catmon was Trail 6, which also began at the Pilar–Bagac road and ran to Trail 8. East of Mt. Samat was the third of the north-south trails in Sector D, Trail 4. In addition to Trail 8, lateral communication in Sector D was provided by Trail 429. This trail ran due east from Trail 29 to Trail 6 which it joined until it cleared the western foothills of Mt. Samat. At that point it branched east again, skirting the southern edge of the mountain to meet Trail 4 near the boundary of Sectors D and C.

Sector D was held by two Philippine Army divisions. On the right (east), in front of Mt. Samat, was the 21st Division, led by Brig. Gen. Mateo Capinpin, and next to it, on the extreme left of the II Corps line, was General Lim's 41st. Both divisions had their three infantry regiments posted along the main line of resistance which generally paralleled the Pilar–Bagac road just south

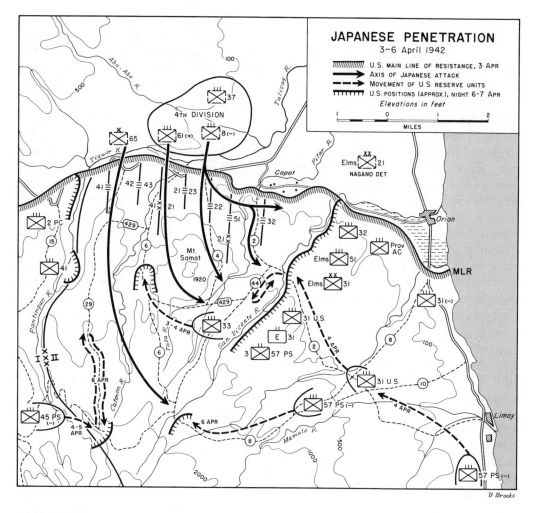

JAPANESE PENETRATION
3–6 April 1942

U.S. MAIN LINE OF RESISTANCE, 3 APR
AXIS OF JAPANESE ATTACK
MOVEMENT OF U.S. RESERVE UNITS
U.S. POSITIONS (APPROX.), NIGHT 6-7 APR
Elevations in feet

MILES

D Brooks

MAP 22

of the Tiawir-Talisay River. About 1,500 yards to the rear was the regimental reserve line. With their three regiments on the line and with the few remaining elements deployed elsewhere, both divisions would be hard pressed if the need for reserves should arise.

In the 21st Division area General Capinpin had placed two of his regiments, the 22d and 23d, east of the Catmon River,

with the former holding the division right flank and tying in with Sector C to the right. The 21st Infantry on the division left flank held both banks of the Catmon as well as Trail 6, which cut diagonally across the regimental area from the right front to the left rear. General Lim's regiments were posted in order, with the 43d on the right, tying in with the 21st Infantry, the 42d in the center, and the 41st holding down the division and sector flank along the Pantingan. Across the river, on the extreme right of the I Corps line, was the 2d Philippine Constabulary.

Against this front the Japanese had massed the entire force committed to the assault, the *65th Brigade* and the *4th Division* both heavily reinforced. With the exception of one battalion west of the Pantingan, all of General Nara's reinforced brigade was concentrated before the 42d Infantry where Trail 29 joined the Pilar–Bagac road. The *Right Wing* of the *4th Division*, led by General Taniguchi and consisting of tanks, the *61st Infantry*, a battalion of the *8th Infantry*, plus supporting and service elements, had taken up a position north of the Tiawir, opposite the center of Sector D, and was poised to strike down Route 6 and the Catmon River valley. The division's *Left Wing* (*8th Infantry*), which was not scheduled to attack until the 5th, was farther to the east and north, facing the two right regiments of the 21st Division.

At 1500, when the air and artillery bombardment shifted south, the *65th Brigade* and Taniguchi's *Right Wing* moved out to the assault. Nara's troops on the left (west) bank of the north-flowing Pantingan, supported by heavy mortar fire, pushed hard against the 2d Philippine Constabulary to reach the I Corps main line of resistance. Though it was unable to penetrate the I Corps line, this force, a reinforced battalion, presented a real threat to Jones's right flank and prevented him from coming to the aid of the adjacent units in Parker's corps. Nara's main effort, however, was made against II Corps. Here, the bulk of his brigade, led by tanks, pushed down against the center of the 41st Division and by late afternoon reached the 42d Infantry

main line of resistance, where, according to plans, it should have halted. The Japanese had expected to meet opposition there, but the line was not occupied, whereupon Nara ordered his men to continue southward along Trail 29. By nightfall the brigade had scored an advance of about 1,000 yards.

Taniguchi's force to the left (east), led by tanks of the *7th Tank Regiment*, crossed the Tiawir just north of the boundary between the 43d and 21st Infantry, in the center of Sector D. Two 37-mm. antitank guns had been emplaced here to oppose a crossing, but they had been put out of action by the heavy bombardment earlier in the day. Once across the river Taniguchi led his men against the main line of resistance. After desultory fire the Filipinos scattered and Taniguchi advanced without difficulty. Before halting for the night he had taken his men about 1,000 yards down Trail 6. The Japanese advance for the first day of the attack exceeded even their most optimistic estimates.[7]

The lack of opposition to the Japanese advance on the afternoon of 3 April was due entirely to the effects of the air and artillery bombardment earlier that day on the hungry and weakened troops of the 41st Division. It was upon this division that the weight of the shells and bombs had fallen and in its area that the damage had been greatest. Dazed and demoralized by the in-

[7] The account of action in the 41st Division sector is based on the American and Japanese sources cited at the beginning of the section and upon the following records of the 41st Division: Fortier, 41st Div (PA) Rpt of Opns, pp. 5–6, copy in OCMH; Fortier, Notes on 41st Div (PA), pp. 12–14, 91; Shoemake, 41st FA (PA), pp. 32–33, and Lt Max Kissel, Hist of 42d Inf (PA), 3–9 Apr 42, p. 29, both in Chunn Notebooks; Wetherby, Opns of 41st Inf (PA), 2–10 Apr 42, in Fortier, Notes on 41st Div (PA), pp. 164–69; ltr, Wetherby to author, 22 May 51, OCMH; interv, author with Maj Jones, 41st FA (PA), 8 May 49.

tensity of the five-hour-long artillery concentration and the ferocity of the strafing and bombing attacks, choked and blinded by the smoke and dust, literally burned out of their positions by the brush fires which sprang up everywhere along the front lines, the Filipinos had fled south in disorganized and unruly mobs. Nothing and no one could stop them. When one officer ordered some of his men back into the line, they "stared dumbly" at him and continued on their way to the rear.[8] Even before the Japanese tank-infantry attack had begun to roll, the 41st Division had ceased to exist as an effective military organization.

The units most affected by the bombardment and the assault were the 42d and 43d Infantry. The first, in the center of the division front where bamboo fires burned fiercely, had retreated in a disorderly fashion, some of the men following Trail 29 into the 41st Infantry area, and others drifting eastward to join the retreating 43d on the western slopes of Mt. Samat. Only the 41st Infantry on the extreme left of the line, which had escaped the full weight of the preliminary bombardment, had withdrawn in an orderly fashion. Augmented by a continuous stream of stragglers from the 42d, the regiment had fallen back to its regimental reserve line near the junction of Routes 29 and 429 and held firmly there all afternoon. Early in the evening, on the basis of misunderstood or garbled orders, the regiment began to move south toward Trail 8.

The 21st Division had also suffered heavily from the day's bombardment, but only its westernmost element, the left battalion of the two-battalion 21st Infantry, had broken. Posted in front of the Pilar–Bagac road, on the west bank of the Catmon River, this battalion stood in the path of Taniguchi's powerful *Right Wing,* and when the enemy tanks appeared the Filipinos, "shattered by incessant shelling and bombing, weak from dysentery, malaria, and malnutrition," fled to the rear.[9] The right battalion of the regiment, however, held firm. Hurriedly organizing the scattered elements of the left battalion, the regimental commander, Lt. Col. William A. Wappenstein, was able by nightfall to re-establish his line with a refused left flank along the east bank of the Catmon.

News of the rout of the 41st Division and the disintegration of the corps left flank reached General Parker, the corps commander, late in the afternoon of Good Friday. The danger was immediate and compelling and he quickly released the only unit he had in reserve, the 33d Infantry (PA), less the 1st Battalion, to General Lough, commander of Sector D. The regiment, led by Maj. Stanley Holmes, moved out at dusk, under orders to establish a defensive position across Trail 6 between Mt. Samat and the Catmon River by morning of the 4th.

Sector D headquarters, too, took prompt measures to stem the rout of the 41st Division and set up a line in front of the advancing Japanese. The 42d Infantry, hopelessly disorganized and scattered, it apparently wrote off as a total loss, but General Lough thought there was still a chance to salvage the shattered 43d and use it against the Japanese. On the evening of the 3d he sent Col. Malcolm V. Fortier, senior instructor of the 41st Division, northward to help reorganize the regiment and lead it back up the Catmon valley to a position west of the 33d Infantry. Later that night, the sector G–3, Col. Robert J. Hoffman, learning that the 41st Infantry had retreated to the junction

---

[8] Lt Henry Harris, Hist, 41st Engineer Bn (PA), p. 34, Chunn Notebooks.

[9] O'Day, 21st Div (PA), II, 5.

of Trails 29 and 8, sent the regiment back along Trail 29 with orders to occupy the regimental reserve line. Thus, by the morning of the 4th, if all went well, there would be three regiments, the 41st, 43d, and 33d, in position to oppose a Japanese advance south along the Pantingan and Catmon valleys.

Homma's original plan had been a cautious one, calling for a limited advance on 4 April to gain positions from which to launch the drive on Mt. Samat. But the unexpected success of the first day's action justified a bolder course and on the evening of the 3d he ordered the *4th Division* and the *65th Brigade* to disregard earlier orders and to continue their advance toward Mt. Samat next day. Their attack would be preceded by a co-ordinated air and artillery bombardment almost equal in intensity to that which had preceded the Good Friday attack.

When Homma's orders reached them, both commanders quickly revised their plans and prepared to attack the next morning. The *65th Brigade* on the west would continue its drive south up the Pantingan valley, on both sides of the river. The *4th Division's Right Wing* would advance along the line of the Catmon River, and the *7th Tank Regiment* east along the Pilar-Bagac road. Colonel Morita's *Left Wing*, which had not been in action on the first day of the offensive, would cross the Tiawir-Talisay River in front of the right half of Sector D, the area held by the 22d and 23d Infantry, during the morning. Once across the river it would pause to reorganize, then attack in force at about noon, at the same time that Taniguchi's infantry moved out to the assault.

American plans to place three infantry regiments in the path of the Japanese ad-vance were only partially successful. When Colonel Fortier reached the 43d and the remnants of the 42d Infantry on the western slopes of Mt. Samat on the night of the 3d, he found the men still bewildered and demoralized. American officers had sought vainly to calm them and restore some semblance of order, and Fortier was able to round up only several hundred men from the two regiments. After the men had been served hot coffee, they started advancing along the trail in the darkness toward their new position west of the Catmon River. There was no difficulty with the 41st Infantry. This regiment, which Colonel Hoffman had ordered forward on the night of 3–4 April, reached its former regimental reserve line between Trail 29 and the Pantingan River without incident by 0930 of the 4th.

Major Holmes's 33d Infantry, numbering about 600 men, had begun its march west along the section of Trail 429 which extended south of Mt. Samat early on the evening of the 3d.[10] The men, many of whom had just risen from sick beds, moved slowly in the darkness, passing large numbers of stragglers pouring back to the rear. "Few had arms of any kind. . . . Few even had packs . . .," wrote Capt. Robert M. Chapin, 3d Battalion commander. "I asked several what unit they were from but they just looked at me blankly and wandered on." [11] When the regiment turned north on Trail 6, the stream of stragglers ended and the advance was more rapid. At a zigzag about a mile north of the intersection Major

---

[10] In addition to the general sources cited, the account of the 33d Infantry (PA) is based upon: Maj Holmes, Hist, 33d Inf (PA), p. 27A, and Harris, 41st Engineer Bn (PA), p. 34, both in Chunn Notebooks; Chapin, Hist of 33d Inf (PA), 3–9 Apr 42, pp. 1–4, 9, OCMH.

[11] Chapin, Hist of 33d Inf (PA), p. 3.

Holmes found a platoon of the 41st Engineer Battalion busily constructing tank obstacles and decided to set up his line there, in position to block the Japanese advance in the Catmon valley. By dawn the regiment was deployed in depth across the trail with flank guards out to warn of an unexpected attack.

The Disintegration of Sector D

The Japanese resumed the offensive on the morning of 4 April with another heavy artillery preparation, co-ordinated with bombing and strafing attacks by the *22d Air Brigade*. The first salvos passed over the 33d Infantry astride Trail 6 to fall on the luckless men of the 42d and 43d Infantry about a mile to the south. Again they stampeded, heading back along Trail 6 "for all they were worth." Until they reached the junction of Trails 6 and 8, about 4,500 yards to the south, that evening, wrote Colonel Fortier, "we could do nothing to stop them." [12] Thus, even before the Japanese infantry had moved out, one third of the force expected to hold the Pantingan and Catmon valleys had given way.

The advance of the *65th Brigade* in the Pantingan valley met with little serious opposition. Only the 41st Infantry, now back on its original reserve line between Trail 29 and the Pantingan River, stood in its way. Shortly after 0930, after Japanese planes had strafed the trail to clear the way for the infantry advance, Nara's men hit the front and right of the 41st Infantry line. Unable to stand against the weight of the assault and in danger of being outflanked, the

Filipinos withdrew to a new line about 600 yards to the rear. Here they held until 1700 when the *65th Brigade* moved around their unprotected right flank, threatening to take them from the rear. For the second time that day the 41st withdrew, this time to a point about 1,000 yards farther south, where it established a semicircular position on the Pantingan River with the arc facing east, just short of Trail 29. Though its own position was more secure, the regiment could no longer block General Nara's route south along Trail 29.

The advance of the *4th Division* against the center and right elements of Sector D met with the same success that attended Nara's efforts that day. Arrayed against the center of the line was General Taniguchi's *Right Wing,* strongly supported by the armor of the *7th Tank Regiment.* This force opened its attack at about 0830 of the 4th with an armored thrust across the Tiawir River to the Pilar–Bagac road. Having gained the road, the tanks moved eastward to strike the refused left flank of the 21st Infantry. The main line of resistance in this area ran in front of the Pilar–Bagac road, with the result that the advancing armor turned the defender's line and penetrated to the rear of his positions.

The 21st Division, hurt badly by the morning's bombardment, was ill prepared to meet the attack. On the left the 21st Infantry fell back in disorder before the crushing attack of the Japanese tanks. The 23d on the right bent back its exposed flank, offering protection to the retreating men of the 21st. The entire attack lasted for only a short time and at its conclusion, even before his infantry had moved into action, Taniguchi was in control of both banks of the Catmon River and the area formerly occupied by the 43d and 21st Infantry.

---

[12] Fortier, 41st Div (PA) Rpt of Opns, p. 6. The Japanese that day flew 133 sorties and dropped a total of 87 tons of bombs on II Corps alone. *5th Air Gp Opns,* p. 73.

General Lough's troops now held only about one-third of the original main line of resistance in Sector D.[13]

That same morning the third column of the Japanese assaulting force, the *Left Wing* of the *4th Division,* composed of Colonel Morita's reinforced *8th Infantry* (less one battalion), entered the action for the first time. Jumping off from the north bank of the Tiawir-Talisay, opposite the 23d and 22d Infantry (the only two units in Sector D still on the main line of resistance), Morita's men crossed the river under cover of artillery and air support at about 0900, occupied the line of departure, and prepared to attack south later in the day. The 23d Infantry, already under pressure from the tank column to the west, and now threatened by a strong force on its front, began to fall back at about 1000. The 22d, on the division and sector right flank, followed suit soon after, thus completing the withdrawal of the last unit from the sector main line of resistance.

Though the Japanese had already scored important gains, neither of the *4th Division*'s two columns had yet begun the day's offensive. The advance of the *Right Wing*'s tanks along the Pilar–Bagac road and the *Left Wing*'s main force across the Tiawir had been designed to secure positions from which the infantry would jump off at noon. At 1100 General Taniguchi asked for an hour's grace, explaining that he needed more time to prepare after the rapid advance of the day before. This request was readily granted.

---

[13] This account of action in the 21st Division area is based upon the general sources cited in note 1 and upon the following records dealing with the 21st Division (PA): O'Day, 21st Div (PA), I, Part 2, 4–6, II, 40–42; Capt J. C. Ellis, 23d Inf (PA), p. 14, and Oster and Richards, 21st Inf (PA), p. 10, both in Chunn Notebooks.

Colonel Morita, too, was directed to hold up his attack for an hour so that both wings would move out simultaneously. These new instructions never reached Morita, however, for the American artillery had cut his telephone lines, and promptly at noon he began the attack. Japanese artillery, unaware of Morita's assault, laid down a barrage in the area into which the *Left Wing* was moving, firing "at both friendly and enemy units simultaneously ." [14] Fortunately for the Japanese cause, Morita's men suffered few casualties and a disaster was narrowly averted. Aside from this misadventure, the advance of the *Left Wing* was uneventful. The 22d and 23d Infantry had already abandoned the main line of resistance and Morita's *8th Infantry* continued south for about one mile before halting for the night.

At 1300 the *Right Wing* moved out, crossing the Catmon and pushing southeast through the area abandoned by the 21st Infantry earlier in the day. By nightfall it had reached the northern foothills of Mt. Samat.

Untouched by the Japanese attack of the 4th was the 33d Infantry at the zigzag on Trail 6, west of Mt. Samat. What artillery fire it received during the day was not directed at it specifically but was intended to neutralize the area on Taniguchi's right flank. The Japanese seemed to be unaware of the regiment's existence, and Holmes, though he sent out patrols to the north, east, and west, had little knowledge of the situation along the front. Aside from the few stragglers who came down the road and a battalion of the 41st Field Artillery some distance to his right rear, on the south slopes

---

[14] Statement of Col Oishi, 2 Oct 50, ATIS Doc 62639, Statements of Japanese Officials on World War II, GHQ FEC, Mil Intel Sec, III, 114.

of Mt. Samat near Trail 6, the regiment was alone.

At the end of the day's action, the Japanese were in possession of the entire main line of resistance in Sector D. The 41st Division had been routed and the 21st forced back to the reserve line in front of Mt. Samat, its left flank hanging in the air. The 65th Brigade had pushed south up the Pantingan valley, twice outflanked the 41st Infantry, and now stood ready to march unimpeded down Trail 29. The 4th Division had taken the 21st Division on its left flank, forced it off the main line of resistance, and then launched a co-ordinated flank and frontal assault to gain control of the Catmon valley. The Japanese were now one day ahead of schedule and in position to storm the heights of Mt. Samat, the first objective of the offensive begun on the morning of Good Friday.

Easter Sunday

Homma's original plan for the seizure of Mt. Samat had called for a regrouping of the 4th Division's two columns once the northern foothills of the mountain had been reached, shifting the strength of the division from the right to the left wing, then attacking in force along the east slopes down Trail 4. At the same time the 65th Brigade was to continue its drive west of Mt. Samat toward Mariveles, while the 16th Division and the Nagano Detachment prepared to join in the attack against the Limay line. The only change made in this plan as a result of the unexpected gains won on 3 and 4 April was to move the schedule ahead. Anticipating an earlier attack against the Limay line than originally planned, Homma, on the night of the 4th, ordered the 16th Division to move east "as soon as possible" and the

Nagano Detachment to prepare for an attack against Orion.[15]

The regrouping of the 4th Division for the attack against Mt. Samat was accomplished with little difficulty on the night of 4–5 April. General Taniguchi, taking his tanks and one battalion of the 61st Infantry, moved over to the Left Wing. Reorganized and strengthened, this wing became the main striking force of the 4th Division. Command of the Right Wing, reduced to less than one regiment, the 61st, plus attached troops, passed to Col. Gempachi Sato. Division artillery moved south of the Talisay to provide the necessary support for the infantry advance, and the 37th Infantry, in division reserve, took up a position behind the Left Wing. It was the Left Wing under Taniguchi which was to make the main effort down Trail 4 next morning. Sato's wing was to seize the heights of Mt. Samat then continue down the south side of the mountain to the line of the Tala River, the jumping-off point for the next attack.

At dawn, 5 April, the Japanese resumed their devastating air and artillery bombardment. It was Easter Sunday and many of the Americans and Filipinos were attending dawn services "in the fastness of the jungle" when the shells and bombs began to fall.[16] For them the day of the Resurrection was not the joyous occasion it had been in peacetime. The services, wrote one officer, had "a serious atmosphere for us," and chaplains, invoking divine guidance, did not fail to ask as well for "deliverance from the power of the enemy."[17]

---

[15] 14th Army Opns, I, 158.

[16] O'Day, 21st Div (PA), II, 4.

[17] Ibid.; INS Summary 101, 5 Apr 42, AG 000.75 (4–13–42) MB. The sermon cited was delivered by Chaplain J. K. Borneman, a Protestant.

The attack began at 1000 when both columns of the *4th Division* moved out. The strengthened *Left Wing*, making the main attack against the right flank of the 21st Division, soon ran into unexpectedly stubborn resistance. The Filipinos, supported by two battalions of the 41st Field Artillery on the south slope of Mt. Samat and by artillery from the adjoining sectors, put up so stiff a fight that one Japanese officer described it as "the fiercest combat in the second Bataan campaign." [18] Against this determined opposition, Taniguchi's men made little headway and by early afternoon were still pinned down on Trail 4, far short of their objective.

The *Right Wing* under Colonel Sato had meanwhile been pushing ahead unopposed on the exposed left flank of the 21st Division, up the northwest slopes of Mt. Samat. Near the summit it met a single platoon of the 21st Infantry which it easily routed and at 1250 secured possession of the mountain top. The position of the 41st Field Artillery, whose fire was so effectively pinning down General Taniguchi's *Left Wing* on Trail 4, was now untenable, and the artillerymen were forced to evacuate. Before they did, they destroyed their equipment and rolled their guns over the cliffs.

No longer pinned down by the artillery General Taniguchi promptly resumed the offensive. At 1400 he sent one of his battalions across the northeast slopes of the mountain in a flanking movement while increasing pressure on the defenders to his front. The disorganized but hard-fighting 21st Division troops, deprived of their artillery support, were in no condition to stand against the powerful *Left Wing* alone and

shortly before 1530 began to fall back. Only scattered elements along Trail 4 barred Taniguchi's way south and he and his men easily pushed toward the line of the Tala River, below Mt. Samat.

That same afternoon Sato's *Right Wing* made its way unopposed down the southern slopes of Mt. Samat. At 1630 advance elements of this force reached the command post of the 21st Division near the junction of Trails 4 and 429. Taken by surprise, officers and men of the headquarters took flight, the majority moving west along Trail 429 to set up a new command post a mile away, at the junction of that trail and Trail 6. General Capinpin, the division commander, was not among those who reached safety; he had become separated from his staff during the disorganized flight and been captured by the Japanese.

Hardly had the new command post been established when it had to be abandoned because of the appearance at 1700 of Japanese troops near the trail junction. These troops were a part of Sato's force which had come down the west side of Mt. Samat during the afternoon. After routing the 21st Division headquarters, the Japanese hit the remaining battalion of the 41st Field Artillery still in position west of Mt. Samat. The artillerymen fled to the rear, leaving their guns behind. "No Americans killed, wounded or decorated," wrote an officer of the battalion at the conclusion of the action.[19] That night Taniguchi and Sato joined forces at the old 21st Division command post near Trail Junction 4–429.

Between dawn of Good Friday and nightfall of Easter Sunday, in three days of infantry and tank assaults accompanied by the largest artillery and air bombardments

---

[18] Statement of Col Oishi, 2 Oct 50, ATIS Doc 62639, Statements of Japanese Officials on World War II, GHO FEC, Mil Intel Sec, III, 114.

[19] Shoemake, 41st FA (PA), p. 33, Chunn Notebooks.

of the campaign, the Japanese had gained the first objective in their final drive to end the siege of Bataan. They had broken through the American line, swept aside the troops of Sector D, virtually destroyed two Philippine Army divisions, and seized Mt. Samat. Homma's hopes, twice frustrated, of turning General Parker's flank and driving II Corps into Manila Bay, thus ending the campaign, were near realization. Only a successful counterattack, or an unexpectedly strong stand by a foe already reduced to near impotence by starvation and disease, could deprive him of the long-delayed victory.

6 April: The Day of Decision

The events of 6 April determined the fate of the Bataan garrison. On that day the weary American and Philippine troops made a desperate effort to drive back the enemy and regain the main line of resistance. At the same time the Japanese launched a fresh offensive to the south and east. The two forces met head on and by evening the issue had been decided.

Plans and Preparations

Since the Japanese penetration on the afternoon of Good Friday, the Americans had been laying plans for a counterattack while seeking vainly to halt the enemy advance. The means with which to launch such an attack were extremely limited. Corps reserve, consisting of less than one regiment, had been committed on the first day of the offensive without any visible effect on the enemy's operations. Most of the troops in Sector D had been routed and could not be relied upon for a counterattack. By the second day of the offensive

it had become evident that, if the Japanese were to be stopped and the main line of resistance regained, fresh troops would have to be thrown into the battle.

At the start of the attack Luzon Force had in reserve the American 31st Infantry, the Scouts of the 57th Infantry—both a part of the Philippine Division—the Provisional Tank Group, and two battalions of combat engineers. The third regiment of the Philippine Division, the 45th Infantry (PS), was in I Corps reserve. Only a few days before, General King, the Luzon Force commander, had ordered the 31st to Lamao, behind II·Corps, and the 45th Infantry to the junction of Trails 7 and 9, behind I Corps. The 57th remained farther south, in position to move to the support of either corps.

When news of the Japanese attack first reached General King on 3 April he ordered the 31st Infantry to move under cover of darkness to "a position of readiness" near the junction of Trails 10 and 2.[20] From there it could move north on Trail 2 or west on Trail 10 to almost any point along the front. At the same time King ordered the Provisional Tank Group (less two companies) to move to the direct support of Parker's imperiled corps. There was nothing more that General King could do that day. Parker had already released his reserve to the Sector D commander and every effort was being made to re-form the shattered 41st Division and to establish a line in front of the advancing Japanese.

When, on the morning of 4 April, the 21st Division fell back from the main line of resistance, General King took prompt measures to avert the threatened disaster in II Corps. He gave to Parker, who already had the support of the Provisional Tank Group, the American 31st Infantry, possibly the

[20] Luzon Force Rpt of Opns, p. 4.

most carefully hoarded unit of the Philippine campaign, and ordered the battle-tested 45th Infantry (PS), less the 1st Battalion, east across the Pantingan to the junction of Trails 29 and 8 in the II Corps area. The 57th Infantry King retained in force reserve, but ordered it to move forward that night to the bivouac area vacated by the 31st Infantry. The 14th Engineer Battalion (PS), part of the Philippine Division, and the Americans of the 803d Engineer Battalion (US) were ordered to discontinue all engineering activities and to assemble immediately in preparation for combat. Thus, at the end of the second day's attack, Luzon Force had given General Parker two regiments of the Philippine Division, placed the third in "a position of readiness" behind his line, and ordered the tanks to give him direct support.

With these forces the corps and sector commanders made their plans for a counterattack.[21] On the 4th, before the reinforcing units had reached their designated assembly areas, Parker released to General Lough the 31st Infantry, the 45th Infantry (less the 1st Battalion), and one company of tanks. With these troops, and those already in his sector, Lough was to launch a counterattack on the morning of the 6th to regain first the reserve line and finally the main line of resistance.

At 1600 of the 4th the 45th Infantry began its march east toward II Corps. By dawn the next morning it had crossed the Pantingan and reached Trail Junction 8–29. The 31st Infantry and Company C, 194th Tank Battalion, began their march north along Trail 2 toward the battle area at 2000 of the 4th. They found the road almost completely blocked by retreating Filipinos and took three hours to reach the San Vicente River, where, at an abandoned bivouac area, the 31st Infantry halted for the night. The tankers presumably camped near by and next day marched west to join the 45th Infantry.

Easter Sunday was a hectic day at Sector D headquarters. Between frantic phone calls to and from units in front of the advancing Japanese the staff prepared its plan for the counterattack. This plan, completed late on the afternoon of the 5th, provided for a co-ordinated drive, starting at 0600 on the 6th, north on the three trails in Sector D toward the reserve line. On the right, east of Mt. Samat, the 31st Infantry would attack north on Trail 4. The remnants of the 21st Division, the extent of whose disastrous rout that afternoon was still not fully known at Sector D headquarters, would advance up the slopes of Mt. Samat. The 33d Infantry, in position at the zigzag on Trail 6, was to advance along that trail, between the Catmon River and the western slopes of Mt. Samat. The remnants of the 42d and 43d Infantry, about four hundred men, were to push north from Trail Junction 6–8 along Trail 6 behind the 33d In-

[21] In addition to the sources cited below for specific or controversial points, this section is based upon the following: Ltr, Doyle to Ward, 8 Jan 52, OCMH; Diary, Col Brady, CO 31st Inf (PA), filed in a separate folder entitled Brady Papers, OCMH; Capt William E. W. Farrell, 31st Inf S–2, Notes for Regtl Hist, in Brady Papers, pp. 20–21, OCMH. Another version of the same source entitled Farrell Diary is filed in Bluemel, 31st Div (PA) Rpt of Opns, p. 70. Three studies prepared by students at The Infantry School were also used for 31st Infantry (US) operations: Conrad, Opns of 31st Inf (US), pp. 20–21, 24; Mead, Opns and Mvmts of 31st Inf (US), pp. 25–26; Bess, Opns of Service Co, 31st Inf (US), p. 29.

For armored operations, the following were used: Prov Tank Gp Rpt of Opns, p. 23; Miller, *Bataan Uncensored*, pp. 196–202.

Many of the sources for the counterattack disagree on times and places, and the author has often had to adopt a reconstruction at variance with the majority of the sources, but one which seemed most reasonable and was in accord with those facts which were not in dispute.

fantry. If they could not advance they were to hold Trail Junction 6–8, near which Sector D headquarters was located. Farther west, the Scouts of the 45th Infantry, supported by a company of tanks, would advance north on Trail 29 to the reserve line formerly held by the 41st Infantry. That regiment, which had crossed the Pantingan to the safety of I Corps area during the day, was directed in separate orders to recross the river that night and establish a line across Trail 29.[22]

For the counterattack General Lough would have the support of the troops in Sector C to his right. The 51st Combat Team, on that sector's left flank, would launch its own attack when the 31st Infantry reached its line. General Bluemel, the Sector C commander, also promised artillery support in addition to the scheduled 30-minute artillery barrage preceding the counterattack.[23] In sector reserve General Lough had the 57th Infantry (PS), recently released by Luzon Force. Elements of that regiment were already moving toward the San Vicente River, behind the 31st Infantry.

General Homma had no intention of waiting passively for an American counterattack. He had the initiative and had scored a victory which he intended to exploit fully. His plans for 6 April called for an attack against Sector C, which now formed the left flank of II Corps line, and a continuation of the drive southward toward the Limay River.

The main effort that day would be made by the *4th Division,* one portion of which would strike east to seize the Capot area in Sector C while the bulk of the division pushed southeast toward the Limay River. The right (west) flank of the Japanese advance would be guarded by the *65th Brigade* on Trail 29. Elements of the brigade had already moved overland toward Trail Junction 6–8, and Nara was directed to continue his efforts to seize that important road junction while protecting the *4th Division's* right flank. The division's east flank would be protected by the *Nagano Detachment.* Reinforced with a company of tanks, Nagano was to send one column forward to the Talisay River in position to join later in the attack against the Limay line, while the remainder of his detachment maintained pressure against the enemy line across the East Road. As before, *14th Army* artillery would fire a preliminary bombardment while the *22d Air Brigade* would strike at enemy artillery positions, vehicles, and troop concentrations.[24]

Under cover of darkness, Easter Sunday, both sides prepared for the next day's attack. The Japanese were confident and the odds were in their favor. For the Americans it was a gamble, but one that had to be taken. To it they had committed most of their reserves. If the counterattack failed they would be hard pressed to prevent the enemy from rolling up the rest of the line and driving the corps into Manila Bay.

All hopes for success rested on the comparatively fresh troops of the Philippine Division, two of whose regiments were in the line and one in reserve. Understrength, weakened by disease and starvation, these regiments were hardly a match for the Japa-

---

[22] For the movements and preparations of the 41st Div (PA) and 33d Inf (PA), see: Fortier, 41st Div (PA) Rpt of Opns, p. 6; Fortier, Notes on 41st Div (PA), pp. 14, 15, 170–71; ltr, Wetherby to author, 22 May 51, OCMH: Holmes, 33d Inf (PA), p. 27A, Chunn Notebooks; Chapin, Hist of 33d Inf (PA), p. 10.

[23] Bluemel, 31st Div (PA) Rpt of Opns, p. 21.

[24] *14th Army* Opns, I, 161–63.

nese. The 31st Infantry, when it moved out from its bivouac area at Lamao on 3 April, had to leave behind about one third of the men for evacuation to the hospital. Many who should have remained behind rose from their sick beds to join their comrades. Along the line of march, men fell out of rank, too exhausted to continue. The efficiency of those who reached the front line could not have been more than 50 percent.[25] It is not surprising, therefore, that General Wainwright, when he visited Bataan on the 5th, approved the plans for the morrow's counterattack "with misgivings as to the outcome." [26]

The American Counterattack

The mission of the 31st Infantry in the counterattack of the 6th was to advance north on Trail 4, east of Mt. Samat, to the reserve line of the 21st Division. The regiment, in position at the intersection of the San Vicente River and Trail 2 when it received its orders, was to move to Trail Junction 4–429, the designated jump-off point, sometime during the evening of the 5th and move out from there at 0600 the next morning.

Almost immediately this plan miscarried. Late on the afternoon of the 5th General Taniguchi's powerful *Left Wing*, advancing south on Trail 4, had routed the 21st Division elements along the trail and Colonel Sato's *Right Wing* had hit the division command post on Trail Junction 4–429. When informed of these events, sector headquarters changed the 31st Infantry's jump-off point to Trail Junction 44–429, about 1,300

yards east of the original starting position.[27] The regiment now would have to recapture Trail Junction 4–429 before it could even begin its counterattack along Trail 4.

On the evening of the 5th the regiment moved out from its bivouac near the San Vicente River toward its new assembly area, with the 1st Battalion in the lead. The battalion's mission was to secure Trail 44 from its starting point on Trail 2 to its junction with Trail 429, a distance of about 1,300 yards. The remaining battalions were to pass through the 1st, the 2d taking position west of the trail junction and the 3d to the south. As it passed through the 1st Battalion shortly after midnight, the 2d Battalion came under fire from the Japanese who had secured Trail Junction 4–429 and were advancing along Trail 429 toward the 31st Infantry's new assembly area. If unchecked they might seize Trail Junction 44–429 too, depriving the Americans of even this jump-off point. Lt. Col. Jasper E. Brady, Jr., now commander of the 31st Infantry, ordered his 2d Battalion to press forward quickly to occupy this last trail junction before the Japanese. The battalion accomplished its mission, but only with difficulty and after a fight lasting several hours.[28]

---

[27] Trail 44 extended from the intersection of Route 2 and the San Vicente River southward along the west bank of the river to Trail 8.

[28] In addition to the sources cited in the preceding section, this account is based upon: Amato and Murphy, 2d Bn, 45th Inf (PS), pp. 14–15, Croom, Hist, 3d Bn, 45th Inf (PS), pp. 15–16, and Anderson, 57th Inf (PS) Opns, p. 6, all three in Chunn Notebooks; Lt Col Joaquin Esperitu, Brief Hist of 22d Inf (PA), p. 8; ltr, C. A. McLaughlin to author, 14 Jun 49, OCMH; Col Young, CO 51st Combat Team, Opns of 51st Combat Team, in Bluemel, 31st Div (PA) Rpt of Opns, p. 23; Capt Robert A. Barker, Opns of Antitank Co, 31st Inf (PA), Brady Papers, pp. 13–14, OCMH; ltr, [CO 21st Inf] to TAG PA, 30 Dec 45, sub: Opns of 21st Inf (PA), copy in OCMH; Mallonée, Bataan Diary, II, 90.

---

[25] Mead, Opns and Mvmts of 31st Inf (US), pp. 25–26; Conrad, Opns of 31st Inf (US), pp. 20–21; Bess, Opns of Service Co, 31st Inf (US), p. 29.

[26] Wainwright, *General Wainwright's Story*, p. 78.

While this action was in progress, the main body of Taniguchi's *Left Wing* was attacking the remnants of the 21st Division on Trail 4. Encircled and isolated, the Filipinos sought desperately to break through the Japanese ring and make their way back to safety. Most were killed or captured, but some escaped. Of these a small number reached the American lines. The news they brought of the disintegration of the 21st Division and the strength of the Japanese on Trail 4 was disquieting. On the basis of these reports Colonel Brady concluded that his regiment of about 800 men, most of them in poor condition, was faced by a much stronger force than had been thought. Even if he could launch a successful counterattack he doubted that he could hold any gains made with the few men he had. He therefore halted his men until he had presented his conclusions to General Lough. Unable to reach Sector D headquarters by telephone, he sent Lt. Col. Peter D. Calyer, his operations officer, together with some of the 21st Division men, in a jeep to General Lough's command post to present these new facts and to get further instructions.[29]

Not long after Calyer had left, the main force of Taniguchi's *Left Wing* approached the 31st Infantry outposts on Trail 429. The situation was urgent and Brady again sought to reach sector headquarters by telephone. This time he was successful and soon had General Lough's G–3 on the line. Informed of the situation, the G–3 changed Brady's orders and assigned the 31st Infantry a defensive mission. Instead of attacking, the regiment was to hold Trail Junction 44–429 at all costs. A short time later Colonel

Calyer returned from sector headquarters with written confirmation of the new orders.

On receipt of these orders Brady pulled back the tired men, who had been trying all night to advance west along Trail 429 toward the original jump-off point, and issued new orders for the establishment of a defensive line facing west across the trail junction. The 1st Battalion would take up a position on the right (north) and the 2d on the left. Contact by patrol would be maintained with the 51st Combat Team to the north, on the refused left flank of Sector C. Regimental headquarters and the reserve 3d Battalion would take up a position about a mile to the east near the former bivouac area at the intersection of Trail 2 and the San Vicente River. By morning these moves had been completed and the men of the 31st Infantry settled down to hold the trail junction.

On the west, along the line of the Pantingan, the counterattack of 6 April got off to a good start. Shortly after midnight, 5 April, the 300 men of the 41st Infantry moved out from their position on the west bank of the Pantingan, climbed the 300-foot bluffs of the river and struck east toward Trail 29. Their aim was to establish a line across the trail, about 200 yards below Trail Junction 29–429, to which the Scouts of the 45th Infantry could advance the next morning. At about 0200 the 41st Infantry reached its former bivouac area, occupied by a small number of men from the *65th Brigade,* and succeeded in routing the surprised Japanese, bayoneting those who lay asleep. The regiment then pushed ahead and reached the trail by daybreak. There it was met and halted by a *65th Brigade* counterattack. The Japanese, whose strength finally reached that of a re-

[29] Brady, Diary, entry of 6 Apr 42, and Farrell, Notes for Regtl Hist, pp. 20–21, both in Brady Papers, OCMH.

inforced battalion, hit the Filipinos on three sides and by noon had forced them back to a defensive line along the river. Here the 41st Infantry held, hoping that the 45th Infantry, attacking north along Trail 29, would soon arrive.[30]

The counterattack of the 45th Infantry (less 1st Battalion) had begun at 0200 of the 6th. At that time the regiment, with the 3d Battalion in the lead, had moved out to the line of departure. From there, the Scouts had advanced cautiously along Trail 29 in the dark. Company C, 194th Tank Battalion, supporting the attack, did not catch up with the Scouts until daylight, after an all-night march over the mountains from the east. It was not until midmorning that the regiment made contact with the enemy when it pushed aside the *65th Brigade* outposts. Resistance thereafter was stronger and early in the afternoon the Scouts had to beat off a flanking attack. The tanks, held to the trail by the dense undergrowth on each side, could be of little assistance. At about 1500, after an advance of approximately 2,500 yards, the regiment came to a halt before a strong Japanese position astride the trail.

The 45th Infantry had been under heavy enemy mortar fire all day but, with a limited supply of shells, had refrained from returning fire. At this point the Scout commander, Colonel Doyle, decided to use half of the 3d Battalion's ten 81-mm. shells to open a hole in the Japanese line through which the tanks could thrust. The tank commander agreed to this plan and later in the afternoon the mortars opened fire. The few shots proved surprisingly effective. The Japanese

on the trail fell back so quickly that the Scouts pushed into the breach before the tanks could move up. It was fortunate that they did for the trail had been heavily mined and a tank advance might have proved disastrous.

Despite his success, Colonel Doyle was uneasy. Patrols sent out to establish contact with I Corps to the west and the 33d Infantry to the east had either failed to return or reported they had met only enemy units. It was now late afternoon and Colonel Doyle decided that it was too risky to continue the advance as long as his flanks were unprotected. He therefore halted his men and ordered them to dig in for the night. With his executive officer and the tank commander, he went back to his command post in the rear to report to General Lough and ask for instructions. When reached on the telephone, Lough confirmed Doyle's decision and ordered him to consolidate his gains that evening in preparation for a fresh attack the next morning. Several thousand yards to the north, in position along the high bluffs of the Pantingan, the men of the 41st Infantry were still waiting for the Scouts to reach them.

It was in the center, along the line of the Catmon River and Trail 6, that the counterattack of 6 April ended disastrously. There the plan called for an advance by the 33d Infantry, backed up by the remnants of the 42d and 43d Infantry. But the Japanese had begun moving into this area the day before, and on the 5th General Nara had sent the bulk of his brigade overland in two columns to seize Trail Junction 6–8. A portion of this force had struck the "hungry, spiritless" stragglers of the 42d and 43d as they were moving north on Trail 6 to join in the counterattack. At the first sign of the enemy, the men had broken and fled. All efforts to put

---

[30] Wetherby, Opns of 41st Inf (PA), in Fortier, Notes on 41st Div (PA), pp. 171–72; ltr, Wetherby to author, 22 May 51, OCMH. Japanese sources do not mention the action of the 41st Infantry (PA).

them back in place were fruitless; they simply disappeared into the jungle, leaving the vital Trail Junction 6–8 open to the advancing Japanese. The 33d Infantry, like the 41st, waited in vain for the counterattacking troops to reach it. During the afternoon the 33d, too, came under attack and its last communications to the rear were destroyed. Presumed lost, the regiment spent the night in fearful apprehension of an enemy attack the next morning.

Before the day was over it was already evident that the carefully planned counterattack was a failure. On the east the 31st Infantry had not even been able to reach the line of departure. The 21st Division, routed on the night of 5–6 April, made no effort to carry out its part of the plan to restore the line. In the center the 42d and 43d had again been routed and the 33d Infantry surrounded. Only on the west, along Trail 29, had the Americans met with any success that day. But the victory was a hollow one, for the 41st Infantry was still cut off and the Japanese were threatening a move which would isolate the 45th from the rest of the troops in Sector D.

The Japanese Attack

The Japanese attack on 6 April, which began simultaneously with the American counterattack, accomplished decisive results. This attack, made by the *4th Division* and *65th Brigade,* had a double objective: to seize the high ground in Sector C, near Capot, and to push forward to the line of the Limay River. The task of the *65th Brigade* was a subordinate one. It was to protect the right flank of the *4th Division* drive while seizing the high ground near Trail Junction 6–8.

Nara's advance on the 6th, though not a part of the main drive planned for that day, proved far more decisive than the Japanese had thought. His two columns advancing overland in a southeasterly direction from Trail 29 hit and routed the 42d and 43d Infantry with no difficulty. The Japanese kept going down Trail 6 and shortly after noon advance elements of the brigade reached and seized Trail Junction 6–8 where General Lough had his headquarters. By this move the Japanese bisected Sector D and cut General Lough off from his forces to the east.

Just east of the trail junction was a portion of the 57th Infantry (PS). This regiment, sector reserve for the counterattack, was in the process of moving up to the front line when its 1st Battalion met General Nara's forward elements around noon. The arrival of the 2d Battalion later in the day coincided with the arrival of additional troops from the *65th Brigade.* Any chance of regaining the trail junction was now gone; the Scouts were finding it difficult even to maintain their position east of the trail junction. The situation was extremely serious and at 1600 General Lough, who had moved his command post west to the vicinity of Trail Junction 8–29, ordered Colonel Doyle to withdraw his 45th Infantry along Trail 29 and establish contact with the 57th Infantry.

Colonel Doyle, whose men had made the only gains of the day, had only a short time before halted his men and ordered them to dig in for the night. He now had to move the tired Scouts out of their position, turn them around, and march them back to the point from which they had started at 0200 the night before. That prospect alone was discouraging enough but at the conclusion of the march they were expected to continue east along Trail 8, then fight their way through the roadblock at Trail Junction 6–8 to re-establish contact with the 57th Infantry. Until they did, General Lough and his forces west of the block would be separated from the rest of Sector D and from II Corps.

The attack of the *4th Division* against Sector C, the main Japanese effort of the 6th, was equally disastrous to the American cause. This sector, whose main line of resistance at the start of the Japanese offensive had extended for 4,500 yards eastward from Sector D, had by 6 April given way on the left. On the 4th, on orders from corps, General Bluemel had pulled back his outpost line to the Pilar–Bagac road and prepared for an attack against his left flank. This attack had not materialized, but when the 21st Division had fallen back before Taniguchi's *Left Wing* on the 5th, leaving the left flank of Sector C exposed, General Bluemel had requested permission to fall behind the San Vicente River. Plans for the counterattack had already been made and corps turned down Bluemel's request, ordering him instead to bring his left flank unit, the 51st Combat Team, back to the Pilar River, thus refusing his line sharply.

Bluemel's desire to fall back to the San Vicente River was an understandable one. That river formed a natural obstacle to the advance of an enemy moving, as the Japanese were, in a southeasterly direction. It cut diagonally across the rear of Sector C to the right of the sector main line of resistance, then turned east to Orion and the bay. Behind its banks a line could be formed which would protect the most vital portion of the corps main line of resistance covering the East Road, as well as Trails 8 and 2. If it should prove necessary to fall back, there

were other rivers, the Mamala, the Alangan, and the Lamao, which would provide natural defensive positions for a planned withdrawal.

The abortive counterattack by the 31st Infantry had begun in Sector C, at the intersection of the San Vicente River and Trail 2. By morning of the 6th that regiment had established a line facing north and west across Trail Junction 44–429, maintaining contact by patrol with the refused left flank of the 51st Combat Team to the north. It was in this area that the Japanese attack came.

When he received his orders on the night of the 5th to seize the area around Capot, General Kitano, the *4th Division* commander, was already convinced that his troops had scored a major success. He decided therefore to commit his reserve, the *37th Infantry* (less one battalion), to this new enterprise rather than weaken his main force on Trail 4. Convinced also, by the experience of the *65th Brigade* in its attacks against Sector C in late January and early February, that a frontal assault would be hazardous, he decided upon a flanking attack. Orders to Col. Jiro Koura, therefore, specified that the *37th Infantry,* reinforced with tanks, artillery, and engineers, would step off from the northeast foothills of Mt. Samat and strike the sharply refused left flank of Sector C in an effort to take the objective from the rear.

At 1030 of the 6th Colonel Koura's force, led by six or seven tanks of the *7th Tank Regiment,* jumped off. The tanks hit the main line of resistance from the north, just above Trail 2 where a portion of the Antitank Company of the 31st Infantry (US) was posted. Heavy fire from two 37-mm. guns halted the tank attack, but the guns, lacking armor-piercing shells, were unable to knock out the enemy tanks. But this was not the main Japanese effort. The bulk of Koura's infantry had struck from the west against the 51st Combat Team in place behind the Pilar River. Before the morning was over, they had overrun the 51st Engineers and forced the entire line back. Trail 2 now lay open to the advancing Japanese and the entire left of Sector C was imperiled.

The main force of the *4th Division,* meanwhile, had been increasing its pressure against the 31st Infantry (US) guarding Trail Junction 44–429 to the south. Here Taniguchi's men, advancing east along Trail 429, had been pushing strongly against the 2d Battalion on the left (south) in an effort to turn the American flank and get behind Sector C. By 1400 the pressure had become so great that Colonel Brady had to commit Companies L and K from his reserve battalion to the threatened flank. Enemy planes, which had been overhead all day, now intensified their attacks while the Japanese infantry pushed ever harder. Finally, at 1500, when he had lost all contact with the withdrawing 51st Combat Team to the north, Colonel Brady gave the order to withdraw.

The possibility of a withdrawal had been foreseen by sector headquarters. Brady's first orders had been to hold the trail junction at all costs. Around noon General Lough had modified these orders to allow Brady to withdraw if necessary to the San Vicente. At 1500, therefore, the regiment began to move to its new position behind the river, with the two reserve companies covering the withdrawal. The maneuver was a difficult one for the tired men, many of whom were too weak to carry their machine guns through the jungle and up the steep ravines. Companies L and K, using to good advantage their small supply of

81-mm. mortar shells, succeeded in disengaging the enemy and rejoined the regiment which by nightfall was in its new position. There was nothing now to prevent a juncture between Taniguchi's men and the *37th Infantry* advancing south on Trail 2.

By 1600 of the 6th it was evident that a line in front of the San Vicente could not be held and at that time General Parker directed a general withdrawal to the river. Bluemel, who had three times before requested permission to pull back to the San Vicente, was given command of the 31st Infantry and the 3d Battalion, 57th, and directed to establish his line along the river's east bank.

From the main line of resistance in Sector B, the new line would extend in a southwesterly direction through Sector C to link up with the 57th Infantry troops facing the Japanese on Trail Junction 6–8. On the north, to the left of Sector B, was the 32d Infantry (PA). Next to it, across Trail 2, were the remaining elements of the 51st Combat Team and some 31st Division (PA) troops. Below the trail was the American 31st Infantry with the 31st Engineer Battalion (PA) to its left. The 3d Battalion, 57th Infantry, under Major Johnson, which moved up to the San Vicente on the night of the 6th, took up a position on the left of the engineers, on the south flank.

Southwest of this line, east of Trail Junction 6–8, was the rest of the 57th Infantry. In the same order which established the San Vicente line, Parker placed all the Sector D troops east of Trail 6 under Col. Edmund J. Lilly, Jr., the 57th commander, and gave him the 201st and 202d Engineer Battalions (PA) from corps reserve. Lilly's mission was to recapture the trail junction and establish contact with the 45th Infantry to the west.

The two engineer battalions were to move up that night and take a position on the right of the 1st and 2d Battalions of the 57th, to tie in Lilly's force with the 3d Battalion of the regiment on the south flank of the San Vicente line. When this move was completed, the II Corps line would extend west from Orion along the Orion cutoff, then southwest behind the San Vicente River across Trail 2 to Trail 8 east of the trail junction.

When the action of the 6th was over the Americans and Filipinos found themselves in a desperate situation. The carefully prepared counterattack launched that morning had failed dismally and the enemy had quickly seized the initiative to score decisive gains. He had secured the vital Trail Junction 6–8 to cut off General Lough, with the 45th and 41st Infantry, from II Corps. All of the important north-south trails in Sector D—29, 6, and 4—as well as Trail 44 and a portion of Trail 2, were now in his hands. He had driven in the left half of the II Corps line, split the two corps, occupied Mt. Samat, and threatened to turn the unhinged II Corps flank and push on to the bay.

To forestall this move the Americans had established a sharply bent and shortened line behind the San Vicente River. The men on this line were already weakened and partially disorganized. Two entire divisions and a regiment had been lost. Another two regiments and a sector headquarters had been cut off. The remaining troops, in poor condition at the start, were hardly fit for combat. Most of the reserves had been committed, and additional forces would have to come largely from Jones's intact I Corps. The outlook was bleak.

For the men on Bataan there was only one bright spot in an otherwise gloomy picture. At the start of the offensive General Wainwright had ordered an increase in the rice ration, to be taken from the Corregidor reserves, and had sent to General King all but 5,000 cases of C rations of the supplies in the Bataan reserve held on the island. By the 5th the ration issue had been increased to 27 ounces, still far below the minimum required but double the daily issue since 22 March. The allotment of flour to American troops was increased from 1.44 to 2.88 ounces; the rice ration went up from 8.5 to 17 ounces and canned meat from 1.22 to 2.44 ounces. The Filipinos, instead of wheat, received an additional allowance of rice and canned fish.[31] An antiaircraft battery commander was surprised one morning when he received more rations than he expected. "There were," he noted, "a few cans of Abalone, which defied preparation; a little more salmon and tomatoes and some type C [rations], and wonder of wonders, some cigarettes." [32]

In an Army Day broadcast General Wainwright spoke bravely of those who were "privileged to be charged with the defense of this distant bastion." [33] But his official dispatches show a clear appreciation of the catastrophic events of the past twenty-four hours. To Washington he reported that the enemy had driven a wedge into the right center of his front, that the air and artillery

---

[31] QM Rpt of Opns, p. 51; Luzon Force Rpt of Opns, G–4 Annex, p. 3. It is entirely possible that many of the units did not receive the increase. Ltr, Doyle to Ward, 8 Jan 52, OCMH.

[32] Gulick, Memoirs of Btry C, 91st CA, p. 108, OMCH.

[33] INS Summary 102, 6 Apr 42, AG 000.75 (4–13–42) MB.

bombardment begun on the 3d had continued without letup, and that fresh enemy troops had been thrown into the battle and were gaining ground slowly.[34]

In his message to General MacArthur, Wainwright added the significant details which would enable the commander of USAFFE to form his own estimate. The enemy, Wainwright explained, had penetrated to Trail 8, 7,000 yards south of the main line of resistance, seized Mt. Samat, and routed three Philippine Army divisions.

To MacArthur these events signified imminent disaster. "It is apparent to me," he told the Chief of Staff, "that the enemy has driven a wedge between I and II Corps and is still advancing." [35] By the time this estimate reached Washington, disaster had already overtaken the luckless men on Bataan.

[34] Rad, Wainwright to AGWAR, 7 Apr 42, USFIP G-3 Journal, 19 Mar–19 Apr 42, AG 461 (1 Apr 42) Phil Rcds.

[35] Rads, MacArthur to Marshall, No. 116, 8 Apr 42, Msgs from Gen MacArthur, OPD Exec O; Wainwright to MacArthur, 7 Apr 42, USFIP G-3 Journal, 19 Mar–19 Apr 42, AG 461 (1 Apr 42) Phil Rcds.

CHAPTER XXV

The Disintegration of II Corps

The story of the last two days of the defense of Bataan is one of progressive disintegration and final collapse. Lines were formed and abandoned before they could be fully occupied. Communications broke down and higher headquarters often did not know the situation on the front lines. Orders were issued and revoked because they were impossible of execution. Stragglers poured to the rear in increasingly large numbers until they clogged all roads and disrupted all movement forward. Units disappeared into the jungle never to be heard from again. In two days an army evaporated into thin air. (*Map 23*)

7 April: Disintegration

Action on the 7th opened with an attempt to wrest from the Japanese control of Trail Junction 6–8. This was to be accomplished by simultaneous attacks against the junction from the east and west, along Trail 8. The attack from the east was to be made by a force led by Colonel Lilly and consisting of two battalions of the 57th Infantry, plus the 201st and 202d Engineer Battalions (PA) from corps reserve. The 45th Infantry and Company C, 194th Tank Battalion, were to drive east from Trail Junction 8–29 to meet Colonel Lilly. When contact was established between the two forces, the II Corps line would extend from the San Vicente River westward along Trail 8 to the Pantingan and tie in with I Corps, thus presenting a bent but unbroken line to the advancing Japanese.

The 45th Infantry's plan for the attack against the trail junction was a cautious one. Of the regiment's two battalions only one, the 2d, reinforced with a platoon of two tanks, was to attack. The 3d Battalion and the rest of the tank company would remain at Trail Junction 8–28, where General Lough had his command post, to prevent the Japanese on Trail 29 from cutting off the route of withdrawal. If the 2d Battalion's attack proved successful, the 3d Battalion would move forward later.[1]

General Nara's troops at the trail junction were well prepared for the 45th Infantry's attack. Just west of the junction they had established a strong defensive position, ideal for an ambush. South of the trail was a steep, thickly forested hill; to the north the ground dropped sharply to a deep, rocky ravine. The trail itself bent sharply at this point so that advancing troops, limited to the trail by the terrain on both sides, would have no warning of an attack.

At about 0100, 7 April, the reinforced 2d Battalion moved out in column of com-

---

[1] The account of the fight for the trail junction is based upon: Amato and Murphy, 2d Bn, 45th Inf (PS), pp. 15–16, and Croom, Hist, 3d Bn, 45th Inf (PS), pp. 16–17, both in Chunn Notebooks; Miller, *Bataan Uncensored*, pp. 202–05; Wetherby, Opns of 41st Inf (PA), in Fortier, Notes on 41st Div (PA), pp. 172–73; Lilly, 57th Inf (PS) Opns Rpt, p. 6, OCMH; Phil Div Rpt of Opns, pp. 27–28; Luzon Force Rpt of Opns, p. 4; *14th Army* Opns, I, 164, II, Map 12.

panies, with battalion and regimental headquarters bringing up the rear. In the van were the two tanks and a platoon of Company F. The Scouts and tankers, in almost continuous action since the night of the 5th, trudged along uncomplainingly in the darkness. An hour and a half after the first elements moved out, the point of the column reached the bend in the trail and marched unsuspectingly into the ambush. At almost the same moment that the Scouts sighted the roadblock, the Japanese opened fire and knocked out the lead tank. The second tank escaped with slight damage, but a jeep carrying six officers was destroyed, the driver and two riders killed, and three others wounded. Within a short time the infantry had formed a line and were laying down a heavy concentration of fire on the Japanese roadblock.

At the first burst of fire Colonel Doyle had gone forward to the head of the column to take command. The situation was confused and the units disorganized, but Doyle kept his men in action until the coming of daylight, when it became evident that there was no possibility of breaking through to the trail junction. At that time he ordered his troops to withdraw to the Pantingan River. Under cover of heavy machine gun fire, the battalion and the remaining tank turned around and began their weary march back along Trail 8, past their starting point, Trail Junction 8–29, and on to the Pantingan River. By about 1000 the withdrawal of the 2d Battalion was completed. The 3d Battalion and the remainder of the tanks, which had been under pressure from the Japanese advancing down Trail 29, had to fight their way out. Enemy infantrymen tried to cut off their retreat, but the tankers fought a successful delaying action and at

1800 the last of the 3d Battalion reached the river.

The inability of the 45th Infantry to break the Japanese hold on Trail Junction 6–8 ended all hopes of uniting the separated elements of Sector D and General King attached General Lough's headquarters, the 45th Infantry, and the remaining troops of Sector D still west of the trail junction to I Corps. These troops thereupon crossed the Pantingan and established a defensive line along its west bank. The 41st Infantry to the north was also ordered across the river that day and completed the maneuver without interference.

The scheduled attack of the 1st and 2d Battalions, 57th Infantry, was never made. The Japanese maintained steady pressure against these battalions whose left (west) flank was unprotected and before the day was far advanced had worked around that flank. At the same time another Japanese force, consisting of elements of Colonel Sato's *61st Infantry*, moved into the gap between the southern extremity of the San Vicente line and the 57th Infantry. This space was to have been filled by the 201st and 202d Engineer Battalions who were just moving in when the Japanese struck. The Filipinos promptly turned and fled into the jungle when they found themselves in the midst of the Japanese. With both flanks in danger of envelopment, the Scouts, at 1700, were forced to pull back to the east. The use of Trail 8 was now lost to the Americans.

The 33d Infantry (PA), the only unit remaining west of Mt. Samat, met a disastrous end on the 7th. Isolated by the tide of battle and presumed lost, the regiment had spent the night of 6–7 April preparing for an attack that was inevitable now that its position had been discovered by the enemy. At 0600, after an hour-long mortar preparation, the Japanese infantry began the assault. The Filipinos held up well at first but by mid-afternoon began to break. Once the reaction had set in, the regiment quickly became demoralized. The men, overwrought and jumpy after five days of intense mental strain and physical hardship, became panic stricken and fled into the jungle. Major Holmes, their commander, reluctantly issued orders for a withdrawal. The wounded remained in place with the medical officers to surrender. The rest of the men, singly and in small groups, slipped into the jungle to try to make their way back to safety. Few succeeded.[2]

While the *65th Brigade* and the *61st Infantry* were consolidating their hold on the area formerly occupied by Sector D, the *4th Division* and the *Nagano Detachment,* aided by artillery and air power, were reducing the recently established San Vicente River line. Signs of the disintegration of the units posted along the river were apparent almost as soon as the demoralized troops took their new positions. During the night of 6–7 April, even before the Japanese artillery had opened fire, large groups of soldiers began to move back to the rear. Some were stopped and put back into the line, but panic was spreading and the ominous signs of demoralization were too clear to be ignored.

At dawn the Japanese artillery opened up with a repetition of the terrific bombardment that had preceded every attack since the 3d, and Japanese aircraft appeared overhead. During the day the bombers flew 169 sorties and dropped approximately 100 tons

of explosives on II Corps installations alone. At least ten bombs fell on General Hospital No. 2 at Little Baguio which had been hit a week earlier. One ward was demolished, extensive damage caused to other buildings, and 73 men killed. Of the 117 injured, 16 died later. When the attack was over, the hospital area was covered with debris and fallen trees. The pharmacy was hit and most of the drugs destroyed. Kitchen utensils were strewn over the grounds and the hospital records blew about like confetti. Under the wreckage were the mangled bodies of patients, and "the air was rent by the awful screams of the newly wounded and the dying."[3]

The Japanese infantry and armor moved out on the heels of the artillery preparation, hitting the Filipino troops before they could recover from the effect of the shelling. First to cross the San Vicente was the *Nagano Detachment* which, at 0730, struck the 32d Infantry on the right of Sector C, then turned east along the Orion cutoff to strike the Provisional Air Corps Regiment in Sector B. Supported by tanks, Nagano's men advanced rapidly into the area held by the grounded airmen who, lacking antitank weapons to oppose the armored point of the attack, fell back without a fight. The 31st Infantry (PA) in Sector A—not to be confused with the American 31st Infantry on the left of the San Vicente line—withdrew in disorder after a heavy air and artillery attack, leaving to the Japanese the last remaining portion of II Corps' original main line of resistance.[4]

[2] Chapin, Hist of 33d Inf (PA), pp. 16–21, OCMH; Holmes, 33d Inf (PA), p. 27A, Chunn Notebooks.

[3] Juanita Redmond, *I Served on Bataan* (New York: J. B. Lippincott Company, 1943), p. 111. See also Cooper, Med Dept Activities, pp. 56–57. The Japanese later apologized for the bombing.
[4] *14th Army* Opns, I, 164–65, II, Maps 12 and 13; *5th Air Gp* Opns, pp. 74–75. The account of the loss of the San Vicente line is based upon:

Even before the Japanese ground forces attacked, the Sector C line had begun to crumble. The first unit to break under the impact of the air-artillery bombardment was the 51st Combat Team. It was followed soon by the 32d Infantry (PA) and other elements of General Bluemel's 31st Division which had fled at the appearance of Nagano's troops. Soon a disorganized mass of Filipino troops, many without arms, uniforms, or equipment, began to stream to the rear. When General Bluemel, rifle in hand, attempted to place some stragglers in the line, they bolted at the first sign of an enemy air-artillery attack. "It seemed," wrote Colonel Young, the 51st Combat Team commander, "that whenever a stand of any kind was made, low flying airplanes bombed or fired on the troops." [5]

The American and Scout units holding the left (south) half of the San Vicente line fared little better than the Philippine Army troops. They held firm under the heavy bombardment which began at 0700, but at about 1030, when Colonel Morita's *8th Infantry, 4th Division,* crossed the San Vicente, they, too, began to fall back. By noon Colonel Brady had ordered his 31st Infan-

try (US) to withdraw by battalions and to reassemble near the intersection of Trails 2 and 46, about 2,000 yards to the southeast.[6] Though the 3d Battalion, 57th Infantry, on the left of the line, had not yet come under attack, its position was now untenable and it began to withdraw. Its orders were to fall back to Trail 46 and to take up a position on the left of the 31st Infantry. By early afternoon the San Vicente line had evaporated.

The withdrawal of the 31st and 3d Battalion, 57th, was a difficult one. With the Japanese in control of Trail 44 and a portion of Trail 2, the men had to travel cross-country to reach their new position. Many were wounded and all were weak from lack of food and sleep. Units, already partially disorganized, became further disorganized so that it was almost impossible to maintain contact. Before long, the line of march became a line of stragglers in which "it was almost every man for himself." [7]

Late on the afternoon of the 6th General King had taken the 26th Cavalry (PA) from I Corps reserve and ordered it to Trail Junction 2–10. By morning of the 7th the horseless cavalrymen were in position at that trail junction, only a short distance in front of the Mamala River and about one mile behind Trail 46, the destination of the last two elements to evacuate the San Vicente line. During the morning, when the disintegration of that line had already become evident, General King released the cavalry regiment, together with the 803d Engineer Battalion (US) and the 14th

---

Bluemel, 31st Div (PA) Rpt of Opns, pp. 24–25; Young, 51st Combat Team, p. 3, in Bluemel, 31st Div (PA) Rpt of Opns; Bess, Opns of Service Co, 31st Inf (US), pp. 32–33; Mead, Opns and Mvmts of 31st Inf (PA), pp. 26–27; Mendelson, Opns of Prov Air Corps Regt, pp. 21–22; Blanning, CO 2d Sq, 26th Cav (PS), War Diary, p. 4, OCMH; Johnson, 57th Inf (PS) Diary, pp. 18–19; Maj Karol Bauer and Lt Gregory Williams, 31st Inf (PA), pp. 20–21, Lt Harold A. Morey, 32d Inf (PA), p. 23, and Lt Walter S. Strong, Hist, 31st Inf (US), p. 3, all three in Chunn Notebooks; Brady, Diary, p. 5, Brady Papers, OCMH; Farrell, Diary, in Bluemel, 31st Div (PA) Rpt of Opns, p. 71; Farrell, Notes for Regtl Hist, Brady Papers, pp. 21–22, OCMH.

[5] Young, 51st Combat Team, in Bluemel, 31st Div (PA) Rpt of Opns, p. 3.

[6] Trail 46 extended about five miles in a northeasterly direction from Trail Junction 8–44, across Trails 2 and 38, to join the East Road about a half mile south of Orion.

[7] Conrad, Opns of 31st Inf (PA), p. 25. See also Johnson, 57th Inf (PS) Diary, p. 18.

Engineer Battalion (PS), to the II Corps commander, who by now had decided to establish the next line at the Mamala River.[8] Parker thereupon directed the 26th Cavalry commander, Col. Lee C. Vance, to report to General Bluemel, who was now the only general officer on the front line.[9]

While the cavalrymen moved up to Trail Junction 2–46, Maj. William E. Chandler, the regimental S–2 and S–3, walked ahead to find General Bluemel whose exact whereabouts was unknown. About 1,000 yards north of the junction he met the general, who "cheered up a bit" on learning of the presence of the 26th Cavalry.[10] Bluemel and Chandler then traveled together to the cavalry command post where the general ordered the regiment to establish a holding position behind which he could form a line along the Mamala.

Colonel Vance quickly deployed his men in two lines. In front, on a hill at Trail Junction 2–46, was the 2d Squadron; the 1st held a delaying position some distance to the rear, just north of Trail Junction 2–10. During the afternoon elements of the 31st Infantry (US) and the 3d Battalion, 57th Infantry (PS), straggled through the cav-

alry line and were directed to an assembly area on the south bank of the Mamala River, at Trail 2. Not long after, the 2d Squadron of the 26th Cavalry, at Trail Junction 2–46, was hit by Colonel Morita's *8th Infantry* which was moving rapidly along Trail 2. Unable to rout the cavalrymen by a frontal assault, Morita sent his men around the flanks, forcing the Filipinos back through the 1st Squadron to Trail Junction 2–10. As soon as this maneuver was completed, the 1st Squadron began to fall back, past the trail junction, toward the Mamala River. At that moment the Japanese artillery opened up and "a storm of interdiction fire fell on the junction." [11] Simultaneously, planes of the *16th Light Bombardment Regiment* dive-bombed the men and vehicles on the trail. Losses, especially in the 1st Squadron, were heavy, and it was late afternoon before the decimated regiment crossed the Mamala River.

General Bluemel had spent the afternoon assembling his forces along the south bank of the river. In addition to the cavalry regiment he now had the remnants of 31st and 57th Infantry, and the 14th and 803d Engineer Battalions. None of his men had eaten since breakfast, and many of them had had their last meal on the morning of the 6th. He had few vehicles and almost no heavy weapons. The prospects of holding off a determined Japanese attack with these troops were not bright.

Around dusk, when he began to receive artillery fire and when Japanese troops were observed working their way forward, firing sporadically, General Bluemel decided "that the Mamala River line could not be held." [12] Actually, the Japanese had not yet crossed the river. Forward elements

---

[8] The Mamala River flows east from Mt. Limay, parallel to and south of Trail 10, across Trail 2, to empty into Manila Bay at Limay.

[9] The account of the effort to establish a line at the Mamala River is based upon: Luzon Force Rpt of Opns, p. 5; ltr, Parker to Ward, 16 Jan 52, OCMH; Chandler, "26th Cavalry (PS) Battles to Glory," Part 3, *Armored Cavalry Journal* (July–August 1947), pp. 20–21; Chandler, Outline Hist of 26th Cavalry (PS), p. 12; Blanning, War Diary, pp. 4–6; Bluemel, 31st Div (PA) Rpt of Opns, pp. 26–28; Collier, Notebooks, III, 75–77; Mallonée, Bataan Diary, II, 95–96; Farrell, Notes for Regtl Hist, Brady Papers, p. 21, OCMH; Farrell, Diary, in Bluemel, 31st Div (PA) Rpt of Opns, p. 71; SLF and II Corps Rpt of Opns, p. 57.

[10] Chandler, "26th Cavalry (PS) Battles to Glory," Part 3, *Armored Cavalry Journal* (July–August 1947), p. 20.

[11] *Ibid.*, p. 21.

[12] Bluemel, 31st Div (PA) Rpt of Opns, p. 28.

of the *4th Division* had reached the north bank, but the *Nagano Detachment* was still north of Trail 46. Since the high bluffs on the north bank "completely commanded" the line on the south shore, it is doubtful if the position would have been tenable in any event.[13] Hoping to gain twenty-four hours to rest and feed his men and prepare a stronger position, Bluemel ordered a withdrawal to the Alangan River, 4,000 yards to the south. The men were to break off all contact with the enemy, withdraw under cover of darkness, and be in position by dawn of 8 April. There he hoped to have time to prepare for a fresh Japanese attack. Corps headquarters approved this plan and at Bluemel's request ordered the retreating troops of Sectors A and B to fall in on Bluemel's right the next morning.

During the day both Wainwright and King had sought desperately to find some way to stem the Japanese advance. While Bluemel was striving to establish a line at the Mamala, General King had decided "to place everything possible" there.[14] Since all his reserves as well as the reserves of both corps had already been committed, he took a desperate chance that the Japanese would not attempt to land behind the lines and ordered Jones and Parker to withdraw the troops on beach defense—the 1st and 4th Philippine Constabulary Regiments—and throw them into the line then forming. To General Wainwright he sent word by his chief of staff, Brig. Gen. Arnold J. Funk, that the situation on Bataan was critical.

Wainwright's scheme for retrieving the situation was to launch an attack eastward from I Corps along the general line of Trail 8. He hoped in this way to tie in I Corps

with the troops along the Mamala River and again form an unbroken line across the peninsula. Unaware that the Mamala line was already being evacuated and that II Corps had so far deteriorated that even if the attack succeeded the I Corps troops would find no line to tie into, General Wainwright ordered the attack at 1600. The 11th Division (PA) would make the assault.[15]

On receipt of this order, General King sent his G–3, Col. James V. Collier, to I Corps headquarters to transmit the order orally. When General Jones received the order he expressed his belief that it was impossible of execution. In his opinion the men of the 11th Division were too weak to cross the Pantingan gorge even if unopposed; certainly they would be unable to drag any heavy equipment or artillery with them. Furthermore, Jones told Collier, at least eighteen hours would be required to get the division out of the line and in position to attack. After telephone conversations between Wainwright, King, and Jones, the USFIP commander decided to leave the execution of his order to General King's discretion.

The decision was now King's. On the basis of Jones's estimate, he withheld the order to attack. Instead, he directed Jones to pull back to the line of the Binuangan River, about five miles south of the main line of resistance, in four phases. This move would place I Corps' right flank, exposed by the withdrawal of II Corps, on the slopes of the Mariveles Mountains, and reduce substantially the lightly defended beach line.

---

[13] Mallonée, Bataan Diary, II, 92.
[14] Collier, Notebooks, III, 76.

[15] The account of this order is based upon the following conflicting sources: Luzon Force Rpt of Opns, p. 5; USAFFE-USFIP Rpt of Opns, p. 60; Collier, Notebooks, III, 77; intervs, author with Gen King, 12 Feb 47, Gen Jones, and Col Collier, 20 Nov 46, OCMH; Brougher, 11th Div (PA) Surrender, p. 1, copy in OCMH.

That night General Wainwright could report to Washington only a succession of retreats.

Continued heavy enemy pressure, constant bombing, strafing, and shelling of front line units [he wrote] forced all elements of the right half of our line in Bataan to fall back. A new defensive position is forming on the high ground south of the Alangan River. . . . The left half of our line, due to an exposed flank, withdrew on orders and is taking up a defense position south of the Binuangan River. Fighting is intense, casualties on both sides heavy.[16]

For the Japanese, the offensive which General Homma had expected to last a month was all but won by the night of the 7th. They had gained possession of the entire main line of resistance in II Corps, and forced the evacuation of the Mamala River line where they had supposed the Americans and Filipinos had their main defenses. "That," remarked General Homma, "was beyond our expectation." [17]

The cost had been light. The *4th Division*, the spearhead of the assault, had lost 150 men killed and 250 wounded during a rapid advance which had netted about 1,000 prisoners and a large number of small caliber weapons. Losses in the *65th Brigade*, which captured over 100 prisoners and considerable equipment, totaled 77 dead and 152 wounded. The *Nagano Detachment* had suffered no casualties.[18]

---

[16] Rad, Wainwright to AGWAR, 8 Apr 42, and notes of telephone conversation between G–3 USFIP, and CofS Luzon Force, made at 1745, 7 Apr 42, both in USFIP G–3 Journal, 19 Mar–19 Apr 42, AG 461 (1 Apr 42) Phil Rcds.

[17] USA *vs.* Homma, p. 3065, testimony of Homma.

[18] *14th Army* Opns, I, 165. Colonel Yoshida, *4th Division* chief of staff, confirmed these figures and stated that casualties for the *4th Division* on Bataan totaled 400 killed and wounded. Statement of Yoshida, ATIS Doc 62642, 28 Jul 49, Statements

With the Americans and Filipinos in full retreat, General Homma decided to push on "without delay" instead of pausing at the Mamala River as he had originally planned. His next objective, he decided, would be Cabcaben on the southeast tip of the peninsula, and at 2300 he issued orders for the next day's attack. The *4th Division* would strike for the Real River west of Cabcaben. The *65th Brigade* to its west would occupy Mt. Limay and the heights of Mariveles, and the *Nagano Detachment* would advance down the East Road on the left (east) of the division toward Cabcaben itself. The *16th Division*, then assembling near Balanga where Homma had his headquarters, was to advance behind Nagano's troops and prepare for the final thrust toward Mariveles. As before, the attacking units would have the support of *14th Army* artillery and the *22d Air Brigade*.[19] For the first time the artillery commander received orders to open fire on Corregidor when he got within range of the island fortress.

8 April: Chaos

Orders for the establishment of a line along the south bank of the Alangan River called for a withdrawal during the night of 7–8 April by the forces under General Bluemel and Col. John W. Irwin, and the occupation of the new position by dawn of the 8th. The units under Bluemel—the 31st Infantry (US), the 57th Infantry (PS), the 26th Cavalry (PS), the 803d Engineer Battalion (US), and the 14th Engineer Battalion (PS)—were to hold the left (west) of the line, from Trail 20 to the confluence of the Alangan and the Paalungan River,

---

of Japanese Officials on World War II, GHQ FEC, Mil Intel Sec, IV, 548.

[19] *14th Army* Opns, I, 166–67.

a distance of about 2,500 yards.[20] Colonel Irwin's force, consisting of the 31st Infantry (PA) and Constabulary troops taken from beach defense, was to hold the right portion of the line and block the East Road. Artillery support would be provided by the intact 21st Field Artillery (PA), a Provisional Field Artillery Brigade formed from three battalions of Scouts, a few fixed naval guns, and the three remaining 155-mm. guns of Col. Alexander S. Quintard's 301st Field Artillery (PA).[21]

The positions taken by the troops on the morning of the 8th did not conform to plan. In the confusion of the withdrawal, units crossed and took up positions some distance from those assigned. The American 31st and the Scout 57th Infantry, for example, had to exchange positions. The 803d Engineer Battalion did not occupy its position at all but continued south after it crossed the river. Only the 14th Engineers and the 26th Cavalry went into their assigned positions. The engineers took over the left of the line astride Trail 20, and the cavalrymen fell in on their right (east). From there eastward there were large gaps in the line. Between the cavalry regiment and the 31st

Infantry (US) was an open space of over 1,000 yards. To the right of the Americans was another gap, and the 57th Infantry, Bluemel's right flank unit, had both its flanks exposed. The unauthorized withdrawal of the 803d Engineers had made the establishment of contact between Bluemel and Irwin a physical impossibility.

All units on the line were so decimated as to make their designations meaningless. The 31st Infantry (US) had but 160 men; the 26th Cavalry, 300; the 57th Infantry, 500. Altogether Bluemel had 1,360 men in the three regiments and one battalion under his command. Irwin's force of two regiments numbered but 1,200 men. All the troops were half starved and exhausted. "We were all so tired," wrote one officer, "that the only way to stay awake was to remain standing. As soon as a man sat or laid down he would go to sleep." [22] After five days under intense air and artillery bombardment and successive defeats, it was doubtful if the men "cared very much what happened." [23]

Even before the Japanese infantry struck the Alangan line it was already crumbling under heavy and sustained air bombardment lasting most of the morning. Japanese observation planes had spotted the troops hastily organizing their positions and at about 1100 fighters and light bombers appeared over the Alangan. Flying low, they dropped incendiary bombs on the area held by the 31st Infantry (US) and the 57th Infantry, setting fire to the dry cogon grass and bamboo thickets. The infantrymen turned fire fighters to avoid being burned out of their positions.

Farther east Colonel Irwin's 31st Infantry (PA) along the East Road came under heavy air attack about the same time. The

[20] Trail 20 extended for about eight miles in an arc from Limay southward to Lamao. It crossed the Alangan, which is midway between the two villages, about two and a half miles from the coast. The Paalungan River joins the Alangan about one and a half miles east of Trail 2 and the two then flow east as one stream to empty into Manila Bay.
[21] The account of operations on 8 April is based upon: Luzon Force Rpt of Opns, p. 5; SLF and II Corps Rpt of Opns, p. 58; Bluemel, 31st Div (PA) Rpt of Opns, pp. 29–32; Quintard, Diary, entry of 7–8 April 42; Chandler, "26th Cavalry Battles to Glory," Part 3, Armored Cavalry Journal, (July–August 1947), pp. 21–22; Lilly, 57th Inf (PS) Opns Rpt, pp. 6–7; Brady, Diary, pp. 5–6, Brady Papers, OCMH; Farrell, Diary, in Bluemel, 31st Div (PA) Rpt of Opns, p. 71; Farrell, Notes for Regtl Hist, in Brady Papers, p. 22, OCMH; Mallonée, Bataan Diary, II, 99–103.

[22] Blanning, War Diary, p. 5.
[23] Quintard, Diary, entry of 7–8 Apr 42.

Filipinos, who were digging their foxholes when the planes came over, fled for cover and had to be rounded up after the planes had passed. When the bombers came back again, the men again threw down their entrenching tools and fled, and again they had to be brought back. With each successive attack, the number of men on the line, some of them forced into position at pistol point, became fewer. The Constabulary troops east of the 31st Infantry also fled, and by about 1500, before a single Japanese soldier had appeared, Colonel Irwin's portion of the line was entirely deserted.

Enemy planes did not limit their attacks that morning to the men along the Alangan River. They struck at artillery positions, supply points, troops, and vehicles. The most profitable targets were the trails, clogged with dazed and weakened men stumbling to the rear. A Japanese pilot could hardly miss on a strafing run over this uninterrupted line of disorganized troops, and the ditches along the trails were lined with the dead and wounded.[24]

The Japanese infantry reached the Alangan River at about 1400, when advance patrols appeared in front of the 57th Infantry. Before long the enemy infantrymen found the exposed right flank and began to filter to the rear of the Scouts. At about the same time other small groups of Japanese struck the 31st Infantry (US) to the west. The Americans, reduced to less than company strength, were forced to fall back at 1700, and the 57th, with both its flanks exposed, followed suit.

The main Japanese effort that afternoon was made against the 14th Engineer Battalion and the 26th Cavalry by a force consisting of the *8th Infantry* and the *7th Tank Regiment*. The tanks, advancing along Trail 20, reached the engineers shortly after 1600, but were stopped in their tracks at the block the Scouts had established. The tanks could not turn on the narrow trail, and the crewmen were kept inside by small-arms fire from the engineers. Without the help of infantry, the Japanese tanks became, in effect, pillboxes from which the tankers fired their small arms, machine guns, and 47-mm. guns without visible effect on the block. The engineers, though they had the tanks at their mercy, lacked the antitank guns to knock them out.

To the right (east) of the roadblock, the 26th Cavalry had come under attack from the *8th Infantry* whose advance elements had forced back the 31st and 57th. The Japanese worked their way around the hastily refused right flank of the cavalrymen, threatening to take them from the rear. By late afternoon it appeared doubtful if the 26th Cavalry, which was now under fire from the tanks at the block, would be able to maintain its position.[25]

About this time, General Bluemel, whose only communication with the front-line units was by runner, learned that the 31st and 57th Infantry were falling back. "To hold the Alangan River line," he concluded, "was now an impossibility."[26] Reluctantly he gave the order for the 14th Engineer Battalion and the 26th Cavalry to withdraw, and at 1830, as darkness settled over the battlefield, the men began to fall back again. That evening, the main force of the *4th Division* crossed the river and pushed on toward Cabcaben.

The advance of the *Nagano Detachment* along the East Road met with little re-

---

[24] Tisdelle, Diary, entry of 8 Apr 42; Mallonée, Bataan Diary, II, 100.

[25] Blanning, War Diary, p. 6; *14th Army* Opns, II, Map 12.

[26] Bluemel, 31st Div (PA) Rpt of Opns, p. 32.

sistance. By 1700 Nagano's troops were on the river line and ready to move on behind the rapidly retreating Philippine Army and Constabulary troops. Only the tanks and the remaining 75-mm. guns (SPM) stood in the way of the advancing Japanese. But the effectiveness of the armor and self-propelled 75's was severely limited by the absence of infantry support and their inability to move freely along the crowded trails. Though they made every effort to organize a holding position they, too, were forced to pull back.[27] The East Road, which the Japanese had carefully avoided since their disastrous assault early in January, now lay open.

The situation everywhere along the front was obscure. With troops jamming all roads and with communications so uncertain as to be nonexistent, even front-line commanders did not know where their units were at any given moment. Higher headquarters, forced to rely on runners and the armored group radio net for information, were even less informed than the unit commanders. It was not until 1800, for example, that General King learned that the Alangan line had been penetrated on the east. By that time the two Japanese columns—the *Nagano Detachment* and the *4th Division*—were already south of the river and pushing forward rapidly along the East Road and Trail 20.

To Luzon Force headquarters, the chief threat seemed to be developing along the East Road, which provided the enemy clear

passage to Mariveles. With the tanks and 75-mm. guns (SPM) in retreat and already nearing Cabcaben and with his last reserves committed, General King attempted to form a line with the only organized unit remaining, the Provisional Coast Artillery Brigade (AA).[28] At about 1900 he directed Col. Charles G. Sage, the brigade commander, to destroy all his antiaircraft weapons except those which could be used by infantry and to form his men along the high ground just north of Cabcaben. At the same time he released the 1st Philippine Constabulary, then in transit from I Corps, to II Corps and ordered it into position on the left of the brigade.[29]

While the artillerymen were attempting to establish a line at Cabcaben, Bluemel's scattered force was nearing the Lamao River. The retreat from the Alangan had been a difficult one. The men of the 31st Infantry (US) and the 57th Infantry had been forced to fall back through the jungle and by now were in the last stages of exhaustion. The 14th Engineer Battalion and the 26th Cavalry, which had withdrawn along Route 20, had found the march less trying, but had suffered other mishaps, and one element of the 26th Cavalry, covering the withdrawal, had been lost in the jungle and never again joined the regiment.

It was about 2130 when General Bluemel and the last of the covering force reached the Lamao. At that time he received telephone

---

[27] Material on the action of the tanks and SPM's during the last days of the campaign is scanty and vague. This account is based upon: Capt L. E. Johnson, 194th Tank Bn, S–3 Rpt, 14 Sep 43, in Diary of Lt Col E. B. Miller, CO 194th Tank Bn; Prov Tank Gp Rpt of Opns, p. 24; Bluemel, 31st Div (PA) Rpt of Opns, pp. 30–31. The Japanese aircraft were under orders to pay particular attention to vehicular movements. *5th Air Gp* Opns, pp. 74–75.

[28] The brigade had been formed on 7 April from Groupment A and consisted of the 200th Coast Artillery (AA) and the 515th Coast Artillery (AA), both composed of Americans. The former was a New Mexico National Guard unit and had provided the personnel for the latter when it was organized just after the start of war. Prov CA Brig (AA) Rpt of Opns, Annex IX, USAFFE-USFIP Rpt of Opns.

[29] Collier, Notebooks, III, 79–80; Luzon Force Rpt of Opns, p. 6; SLF and II Corps Rpt of Opns, p. 69.

orders from General Parker to form a line along the Lamao River and within the hour he had his men across the river and in an assembly area.[30] But the establishment of a line was not so easily accomplished. None of the officers knew the area and the moonless night made it difficult to find defensible positions along which to deploy the troops. After a discouraging reconnaissance in the darkness Bluemel, who by now was using the 26th Cavalry staff as his own, concluded that a line behind the Lamao "was not feasible." [31] Unable to reach either corps or Luzon Force headquarters, he finally turned for aid to General Wainwright, who could only advise him to use his own judgment.[32]

Even without precise information on Bluemel's situation it was already evident to General King that II Corps had disintegrated. Reports from officer patrols and from the tanks and the self-propelled 75's clearly reflected the chaotic state of the command. There was no chance that the 1st Philippine Constabulary would reach Colonel Sage before daylight, and little possibility that any of the retreating troops could be organized in time to be placed on the line Sage was trying to establish near Cabcaben. Nevertheless orders were issued directing the 26th Cavalry to fall in on the right of Provisional Coast Artillery Brigade. The cavalrymen evidently did not receive these orders and when the artillerymen, a half hour before midnight, occupied the last remaining line, they stood alone.[33]

At 2330, when his position was already hopeless, General King received fresh orders from Corregidor directing him to launch an offensive with I Corps northward toward Olongapo, the Japanese base at the head of Subic Bay. In issuing these orders Wainwright was merely carrying out his own orders from General MacArthur, who, on 4 April, had instructed him to "prepare and execute an attack upon the enemy along the following general lines," when the situation became desperate.

1. A feint by I Corps in the form of an "ostentatious" artillery preparation.
2. A "sudden surprise attack" by II Corps toward the Dinalupihan–Olongapo Road at the base of the peninsula, made with "full tank strength" and "maximum artillery concentration."
3. Seizure of Olongapo by simultaneous action of both corps, I Corps making a frontal attack and II Corps taking the enemy "in reverse" by an attack from the west, along the Dinalupihan–Olongapo Road.

"If successful," MacArthur explained, "the supplies seized at this base might well rectify the situation. This would permit operation in central Luzon where food supplies could be obtained and where Bataan and the northern approaches to Corregidor could be protected." Even if the attack did not succeed, many of the men would be able to escape from Bataan and continue to fight as guerrillas.[34]

Even before he issued the orders for an attack, Wainwright already knew it was impossible of execution. Earlier that day he had notified the War Department that the

[30] Bluemel, 31st Div (PA) Rpt of Opns, p. 32; Luzon Force Rpt of Opns, p. 6.
[31] Bluemel, 31st Div (PA) Rpt of Opns, p. 32.
[32] Ibid.; Wainwright, General Wainwright's Story, p. 81.
[33] Collier, Notebooks, IV, 2; Prov CA Brig (AA) Rpt of Opns, p. 8; Chandler, "26th Cavalry (PS) Battles to Glory," Part 3, Armored Cavalry Journal (July–August 1947), p. 22; Bluemel, 31st Div (PA) Rpt of Opns, p. 34. The G–3 Annex of the Luzon

Force Report of Operations states that the 26th Cavalry (PS) did go into the line as ordered, but other records do not confirm this view. Colonel Vance states that the orders were not received, and even if they had been could not have been executed. Ltr, Vance to Ward, 18 Dec 51, OCMH.
[34] Rad, MacArthur to Wainwright, No. 68, 4 Apr 42, AG 384.1, GHQ SWPA.

withdrawal of both corps had become necessary because of the weakness of the troops who had subsisted for so long on one-half to one-third rations. Even the best of his regiments, he said, "were capable of only a short advance before they were completely exhausted." [35]

In his message to MacArthur he had given clear warning that the end was near. The tactical situation, he explained, was fast deteriorating and the men were so weakened by hunger and disease that they had "no power of resistance" left. "It is with deep regret," he had written, "that I am forced to report that the troops on Bataan are fast folding up." [36] When he received no change in orders, he had no recourse but to direct General King to launch the attack toward Olongapo.

The attack order was received at Luzon Force headquarters during the height of confusion and chaos caused by the disintegration of II Corps. Except for a single issue of half rations, the food stocks on Bataan had been exhausted. Already the depot commanders were standing by for orders to destroy their equipment and the Chemical Warfare Service was dumping its chemicals into Manila Bay. At Mariveles the Navy had begun demolitions an hour before and the flames were already lighting up the sky. Nevertheless General King put in a call to the I Corps commander and explained that he had received orders to launch an attack immediately. General Jones replied that his corps was in the midst of a withdrawal to the Binuangan River, ordered the night before. Moreover, he declared, the physical

condition of his troops was such that an attack under any condition was impossible. General King accepted this estimate without question and with it the responsibility for refusing to transmit to Jones an order which he knew could not be executed. [37] Apparently he did not inform General Wainwright of this decision.

As the precious hours went by and no word reached Corregidor about the attack, General Wainwright had his chief of staff, General Beebe, telephone directly to General Jones to ask if he had received the order. When Jones replied that the order had not been transmitted, Beebe told him that he would probably receive instructions to attack shortly. General King soon learned of Beebe's call and at three o'clock in the morning, 9 April, he telephoned USFIP at Corregidor to inquire if I Corps had been removed from his command. Through his chief of staff who took the call, Wainwright assured the Luzon Force commander that he was still in command of all the forces on Bataan. There was no further discussion of the attack order, but Wainwright apparently still believed that an effort would be made to carry it out. [38] This telephone call at 0300 of the 9th was the last conversation Wainwright had with King. Already two emissaries had gone forward with a white flag to meet the Japanese commander.

[35] Rad, Wainwright to MacArthur, No. 197, 8 Apr 42, USFIP G–3 Journal, 19 Mar–19 Apr 42, AG 461 (1 Apr 42) Phil Rcds. This message is a paraphrase of the one sent to Washington.
[36] Rad, Wainwright to MacArthur, No. 199, 8 Apr 42, USFIP G–3 Journal, 19 Mar–19 Apr 42, AG 461 (1 Apr 42) Phil Rcds.
[37] Cooper, Med Dept Activities, p. 35; Luzon Force Rpt of Opns, p. 6; Collier, Notebooks, IV, 2; intervs, author with Gen King, 12 Feb 47, Gen Jones, and Col Collier, 20 Nov 46, OCMH; Brougher, 11th Div (PA) Surrender, p. 1; Alexander, Personal Recollections of Bataan, p. 122.
[38] Wainwright, General Wainwright's Story, pp. 81–82; USAFFE-USFIP Rpt of Opns, p. 61. Colonel Alexander, who was in King's command post that night, confirms this telephone conversation. King, he says, declared, "I want a definite answer as to whether or not General Jones will be left in my command regardless of what action I may take." Alexander, Personal Recollections of Bataan, pp. 123–24.

CHAPTER XXVI

Surrender

When, late in the evening of 8 April, General Wainwright ordered a counterattack by I Corps in the direction of Olongapo, General King had already reached the conclusion that he had no alternative but to surrender. By that time all chance of halting the Japanese advance, much less launching a successful counterattack, was gone. The last of his reserves as well as those of the two corps had been committed. On the left, I Corps was still intact but was in the process of withdrawal in an effort to tie in its right flank with the rapidly crumbling II Corps. General Parker's corps on the right had completely disintegrated and no longer existed as a fighting force. Efforts to hold at the Alangan River had failed and General Bluemel had reported soon after dark that his small force of 1,300 Scouts and Americans was in retreat. The Provisional Coast Artillery Brigade (AA) had been ordered to destroy its antiaircraft equipment and form as infantry along the high ground just south of the Cabcaben airfield, near the southern tip of the peninsula. On the night of 8 April this unit formed the only line between the enemy and the supply and service elements around Cabcaben and Mariveles. "II Corps as a tactical unit," wrote King's G–3, "no longer existed." [1]

The deterioration of the line in the II Corps sector gave the enemy free passage to the south where the hospitals with their 12,000 defenseless patients, already within reach of Japanese light artillery, were located. Philippine Army troops were in complete rout and units were melting away "lock, stock, and barrel." Headquarters had lost contact with the front-line troops and could no longer control the action except through runners or the armored vehicles of the SPM battalion. The roads were jammed with soldiers who had abandoned arms and equipment in their frantic haste to escape from the advancing Japanese infantry and armored columns and the strafing planes overhead. "Thousands poured out of the jungle," wrote one observer, "like small spring freshets pouring into creeks which in turn poured into a river." [2]

Even if General King had been able at the last moment to muster enough arms and men to oppose the Japanese advance it is extremely doubtful that he could have averted or even delayed the final disaster. The men on Bataan were already defeated and had been for almost a week. Disease and starvation rather than military conditions had created the situation in which General King now found himself. The men who threw away their arms and equipment and jammed the roads and trails leading south were beaten men. Three months of malnutrition, malaria, and intestinal infections had left them weak and disease-ridden, totally incapable of the sustained

---

[1] Collier, Diary, III, 80.

[2] *Ibid.*, IV, 2.

physical effort necessary for a successful defense.

General Wainwright was well aware of the disintegration of the Luzon Force. His messages to Marshall and MacArthur on the 8th gave a clear picture of impending doom. Late that night he had told MacArthur, "with deep regret," that the troops on Bataan were "fast folding up," and that the men were so weak from malnutrition "that they have no power of resistance." [3] MacArthur, in turn, had alerted Washington to the danger. "In view of my intimate knowledge of the situation there," he warned the Chief of Staff, "I regard the situation as extremely critical and feel you should anticipate the possibility of disaster there very shortly." [4] By the time this warning reached Washington silence had fallen on Bataan.

If the situation appeared critical to those on Corregidor and in Australia, how much blacker was the future to General King on whom rested the responsibility for the fate of the 78,000 men on Bataan. As early as the afternoon of 7 April, when the last of the Luzon Force and I Corps reserves had been committed without appreciably delaying the enemy, he had realized that his position was critical. It was then that he sent his chief of staff, General Funk, to Corregidor to inform Wainwright that the fall of Bataan was imminent and that he might have to surrender. Funk's face when he told Wainwright about the physical condition of the troops and the disintegration of the line, "was a map of the hopelessness of the Ba-

taan situation." [5] While he never actually stated during the course of his conversation with Wainwright that General King thought he might have to surrender, Funk left the USFIP commander with the impression that the visit was made "apparently with a view to obtaining my consent to capitulate." [6]

Though Wainwright shared King's feelings about the plight of the men on Bataan, his answer to Funk was of necessity based upon his own orders. On his desk was a message from MacArthur which prohibited surrender under any conditions. When Wainwright had written ten days earlier that if supplies did not reach him soon the troops on Bataan would be starved into submission, MacArthur had denied his authority to surrender and directed him "if food fail" to "prepare and execute an attack upon the enemy." [7] To the Chief of Staff he had written that he was "utterly opposed, under any circumstances or conditions to the ultimate capitulation of this command. . . . If it is to be destroyed it should be upon the actual field of battle taking full toll from the enemy." [8]

---

[3] Rad, Wainwright to MacArthur, No. 199, 8 Apr 42, USFIP G–3 Journal, AG 461 (1 Apr 42) Phil Rcds.

[4] Rad, MacArthur to Marshall, No. 116, 8 Apr 42, Msgs from Gen MacArthur, OPD Exec O. A note on this copy states that only one copy of the radio exists, in the Chief of Staff files.

[5] Wainwright, General Wainwright's Story, p. 79. See also Funk, Comments on Draft MS, p. 16, OCMH.

[6] Rad, Wainwright to MacArthur, No. 398, 4 May 42, AG 384.1, GHQ SWPA. This message was written almost a month after the surrender in answer to MacArthur's request for a complete explanation of King's action.

[7] Rad, MacArthur to Wainwright, No. 68, 4 Apr 42, AG 384.1, GHQ SWPA; Wainwright, General Wainwright's Story, p. 79.

[8] Rad, MacArthur to Marshall, No. 56, 1 Apr 42, AG 384.3, GHQ SWPA. In this message MacArthur had explained that he had "long ago" prepared a "comprehensive plan," and that he had not told Wainwright about it "as I feared it might tend to shake his morale and determination." He offered also to attempt to return to the Philippines "to rejoin this command temporarily and take charge of this movement." General Marshall's reply was noncom-

Wainwright was further limited in his reply to Funk by President Roosevelt's "no surrender" message of 9 February. This message, it will be recalled, had been given MacArthur at the time Quezon had made his proposal to neutralize the Philippines. On Wainwright's assumption of command a copy of the original text had been sent to him, with the statement that "the foregoing instructions from the President remain unchanged." [9] In his reply to the President, Wainwright had promised "to keep our flag flying in the Philippines as long as an American soldier or an ounce of food and a round of ammunition remains." [10]

Under direct orders from the President and MacArthur "to continue the fight as long as there remains any possibility of resistance," Wainwright, therefore, had no recourse but to tell General Funk on the 7th that Bataan must be held. In the presence of his chief of staff he gave Funk two direct orders for General King: first, that under no circumstances would the Luzon Force surrender; and second, that General King was to counterattack in an effort to regain the main line of resistance from Bagac to Orion. "I had no discussion with General King," Wainwright later explained to MacArthur, "which might in any way have led

him to believe, either that capitulation was contemplated, or that he had authority to send a flag of truce. On the contrary I had expressly forbidden such action. General King did not personally broach the subject of capitulation to me." [11] When Funk left Wainwright's office with the orders to attack there were tears in his eyes. Both he and Wainwright knew what the outcome would be. [12]

While Wainwright's orders are understandable in terms of his own instructions, they placed General King in an impossible position. He was now under orders to launch a counterattack which he knew could not be carried out. If he could hold his position he might avert the necessity of surrender but even this proved impossible, as the events of the 7th and 8th showed. The only alternative remaining to King if he followed Wainwright's orders was to accept the wholesale slaughter of his men without achieving any military advantage. Under the circumstances, it was almost inevitable that he would disobey his orders.

Wainwright evidently appreciated King's position, and even expected him to surrender. Some years later, after his return from prison camp, he wrote: "I had my orders from MacArthur not to surrender on Bataan, and therefore I could not authorize King to do it." But General King, he added, "was on the ground and confronted by a situation in which he had either to surrender or have his people killed piecemeal. This would most certainly have happened to him within two or three days." [13]

---

mittal. He stated that "we were interested to learn of your intentions in the event that efforts to supply the Philippines should prove inadequate," and agreed that any action was preferable to surrender. In answer to MacArthur's offer to lead the last desperate attack himself, Marshall wrote: "Should it become necessary for you to direct a last resort attack with the objectives you outline, we feel sure that Wainwright and his forces will give a good account of themselves." Rad, Marshall to MacArthur, No. 1087, 4 Apr 42, AG 384.3, GHQ SWPA.

[9] Rad, Marshall to Wainwright, No. 1234, 24 Mar 42, Msgs to Gen Wainwright, OPD Exec O.

[10] Rad, Wainwright to Marshall for the President, No. 598, 26 Mar 42, Msgs from Gen Wainwright, OPD Exec O.

[11] Rad, Wainwright to MacArthur, No. 398, 4 May 42, AG 384.1, GHQ SWPA.

[12] Wainwright, *General Wainwright's Story*, p. 79; Intel Rpt, Lt Comdr Denys W. Knoll, Intel Officer, 16th Naval Dist, to Director of Naval Intel, p. 12, Off of Naval Rcds.

[13] Wainwright, *General Wainwright's Story*, p. 83.

At just what point in the last hectic days of the battle of Bataan General King made his decision is not clear. He may already have decided to surrender on the 7th when he sent Funk to Corregidor, for even at that time it was evident that defeat was inevitable. The next day, sometime during the afternoon, King instructed his senior commanders to make preparations for the destruction of all weapons and equipment, except motor vehicles and gasoline, but to wait for further orders before starting the actual destruction. At the same time he told General Wainwright that if he expected to move any troops from Bataan to Corregidor, he would have to do it that night "as it would be too late thereafter." [14] When Colonels Constant Irwin and Carpenter came to Bataan to discuss the withdrawal of the 45th Infantry (PS) with the Luzon Force staff they "gained the impression" after a conversation with King that he felt the decision to surrender "might be forced upon" him. [15]

The inability of General Bluemel's force to hold the line at the Alangan River on the 8th must have been the deciding factor in General King's decision to surrender. He learned of Bluemel's predicament after dark when General Parker reported that the Alangan River position had been turned from the west and that all units were withdrawing. As a last desperate measure he ordered Colonel Sage's antiaircraft brigade to establish a line south of the Cabcaben airfield. By 2300 it was evident that it would be impossible to reinforce the last thin line, which was still forming, and that there was nothing to prevent the enemy from reaching the congested area to the south. It was at this time that General King held "a weighty, never to be forgotten conference" with his chief of staff and his operations officer. [16]

At this meeting General King reviewed the tactical situation very carefully with his two staff officers and considered all possible lines of action. Always the three men came back to the same problem: would the Japanese be able to reach the high ground north of Mariveles, from which they could dominate the southern tip of Bataan as well as Corregidor, as rapidly if the Luzon Force opposed them as they would if their advance was unopposed. The three men finally agreed that the Japanese would reach Mariveles by the evening of the next day, 9 April, no matter what course was followed. With no relief in sight and with no possible chance to delay the enemy, General King then decided to open negotiations with the Japanese for the conclusion of hostilities on Bataan. He made this decision entirely on his own responsibility and with the full

[14] Rad, Wainwright to MacArthur, No. 398, 4 May 42, AG 384.1, GHQ SWPA; interv, Lt J. C. Bateman with Maj Tisdelle, aide to Gen King, 22 Jan 46, copy in OCMH; Tisdelle, Diary, entry of 8 Apr 42.

[15] Rad, Wainwright to MacArthur, No. 398, 4 May 42, AG 384.1, GHQ SWPA. Colonel Irwin states that he made only one trip to Bataan during the last days before its surrender and that was on 7 April to request General King to release the 31st Infantry (US) for movement to Corregidor. At that time, he asserts, General King told him that it might be necessary to surrender. Wainwright, when informed of this, "was not surprised or interested." Irwin, Comments on Draft MS, p. 6, OCMH.

[16] Collier, Notebooks, IV, 2; Luzon Force Rpt of Opns, p. 6; intervs, author with Gen King, 12 Feb 47, and Col Collier, 20 Nov 46, OCMH. Colonel Alexander, who was in King's command post that night, states that as soon as General King finished his telephone conversation with Jones, presumably in connection with Wainwright's order to counterattack, he sent for General Parker and his chief of staff. Parker, therefore, may have been present at the conference. Alexander, Personal Recollections of Bataan, p. 122.

knowledge that he was acting contrary to orders.[17]

Having made his decision, General King called his staff to his tent at midnight to tell them what he had determined to do and why. At the outset he made it clear that he had not called the meeting to ask for the advice or opinion of his assistants. The "ignominious decision," he explained, was entirely his and he did not wish anyone else to be "saddled with any part of the responsibility." "I have not communicated with General Wainwright," he declared, "because I do not want him to be compelled to assume any part of the responsibility." Further resistance, he felt, would only be an unnecessary and useless waste of life. "Already our hospital, which is filled to capacity and directly in the line of hostile approach, is within range of enemy light artillery. We have no further means of organized resistance."[18]

---

[17] Intervs, author with Gen King, 12 Feb 47, Col Collier, 20 Nov 46, and Maj Tisdelle, OCMH. Times differ in all accounts and no participant presents exactly the same version as the others. Under tremendous emotional strain men's memories are not too reliable. King, for example, did not mention the meeting with Funk and Collier but spoke of a staff meeting; Collier did not mention what had happened at the meeting but fixed the time and circumstances. The account of this meeting, as well as of the negotiations for the surrender which follows, is based on these interviews and on numerous informal conversations, diaries, and scattered accounts. Differences in time and in substance have been adjusted on the basis of internal evidence.

[18] Collier, Notebooks, IV, 3–4. There is no copy of King's remarks in existence and the present version is taken from Collier's notes. The substance is corroborated by General King and other officers. Colonel Alexander states that when King made his decision to surrender he telephoned Corregidor and spoke to General Beebe, Wainwright not being available. "Tell General Wainwright," Alexander reports King as saying, "that I have decided to surrender Bataan. . . . This decision is solely my own, no member of my staff nor of my command has helped me to arrive at this decision. In my opinion,

Though the decision to surrender could not have surprised the staff, it "hit with an awful bang and a terrible wallop." Everyone had hoped for a happier ending to the grim tragedy of Bataan, and when General King walked out of the meeting "there was not a dry eye present."[19]

There was much to do in the next few hours to accomplish the orderly surrender of so large and disorganized a force: all units had to be notified of the decision and given precise instructions; selected individuals and units had to be sent to Corregidor; and everything of military value had to be destroyed. The first task was to establish contact with the Japanese and reach agreement on the terms of the surrender. Col. E. C. Williams and Maj. Marshall H. Hurt, Jr., both bachelors, volunteered to go forward under a white flag to request an interview for General King with the Japanese commander. Arrangements for their departure were quickly made. They would time their journey so as to arrive at the front lines at daylight, just as the destruction of equipment was being completed.

In the event the Japanese commander refused to meet General King, Williams was authorized to discuss surrender terms himself. These terms were outlined in a letter of instructions King prepared for Williams. The basic concession Williams was to seek from the Japanese was that Luzon Force headquarters be allowed to control the movement of its troops to prison camp. Williams was also instructed to mention spe-

---

if I do not surrender to the Japanese, Bataan will be known as the greatest slaughter in history." Alexander, Personal Recollections of Bataan, p. 123. This statement conflicts with the statements of the principals that the decision to surrender was not communicated to Wainwright.

[19] Collier, Notebooks, IV, 4.

cifically the following points if he discussed terms with the Japanese:

a. The large number of sick and wounded in the two General hospitals, particularly Hospital #1 which is dangerously close to the area wherein artillery projectiles may be expected to fall if hostilities continue.

b. The fact that our forces are somewhat disorganized and that it will be quite difficult to assemble them. This assembling and organizing of our own forces, necessary prior to their being delivered as prisoners of war, will necessarily take some time and can be accomplished by my own staff and under my direction.

c. The physical condition of the command due to long siege, during which they have been on short rations, which will make it very difficult to move them a great distance on foot.

d. . . .

e. Request consideration for the vast number of civilians present at this time in Bataan, most of whom have simply drifted in and whom we have to feed and care for. These people are in no way connected with the American or Filipino forces and their presence is simply incidental due to circumstances under which the Bataan phase of hostilities was precipitated.[20]

While Williams and Hurt were making preparations to leave, every effort was made to warn all unit commanders of the decision to surrender. There was no difficulty in alerting II Corps since Parker's command post was now adjacent to King's; General Jones was notified by telephone. The two corps commanders in turn informed the units under their control. Bluemel, whose troops had reached the Lamao River, was instructed by Parker to hold his line only until daylight. When he asked what would happen at that time he was told that "a car carrying a white flag would go through the lines on the east road . . . and that there must be no firing after the car passed." [21]

Bluemel told his regimental commanders and directed them to alert their own officers immediately. Not all units were informed so promptly, and it was only by a narrow margin that these units escaped disaster the next morning.

When Colonel Williams and Major Hurt finally started toward the front lines about 0330 of the 9th, the destruction of equipment was already under way.[22] Depot and warehouse commanders had been alerted about noon of the 8th to prepare for demolitions and about midnight the order to begin the destruction was given by Luzon Force headquarters. Some commanders anticipated the order and destruction of equipment began somewhat earlier than midnight. The Chemical Warfare depot began to dump chemicals into the bay during the afternoon and completed the task during the night.[23]

As though nature had conspired to add to the confusion, an earthquake of serious proportions shook the peninsula "like a leaf" at about 2130.[24] About an hour later the Navy started to destroy its installations at Mariveles. "Pursuant to orders from General Wainwright," Captain Hoeffel informed the Navy Department, "am destroying and sinking Dewey Drydock, Canopus, Napa, Bittern tonight." [25] Soon the rumble of explosions could be heard from Mariveles

[20] Memo, King for Williams, 8 Apr 42, sub: Instructions for Col E. C. Williams, copy in OCMH.
[21] Bluemel, 31st Div (PA) Rpt of Opns, p. 33.

[22] Extract from the Diary of Major Hurt, copy in OCMH. The section of the diary dealing with Hurt's experiences on 9 April has been published in Chunn, Of Rice and Men, pp. 5–9. Major Tisdelle states the two men started forward at 0200. USA vs. Homma, p. 2302, testimony of Tisdelle.
[23] Activities of the Chemical Warfare Service in the Philippines, Sec C, CWS Hist Sec, p. 57; Luzon Force Rpt of Opns, p. 7; USFIP G–4 Journal, 8–9 Apr 42, AG 461 (25 Dec 41) Phil Rcds.
[24] Collier, Notebooks, IV, 2.
[25] Rad, Com 16 to COMINCH, 8 Apr 42, 081430, Off of Naval Rcds.

while flames shot high above the town, lighting up the sky for miles around. The climax came when the *Canopus* blew up with a tremendous roar. "She seemed," wrote an observer, "to leap out of the water in a sheet of flame and then drop back down heavily like something with all the life gone out of it." [26]

The Navy's fireworks were but the prelude to the larger demolitions that were to follow when the Army's ammunition was destroyed. Though stored in the congested area adjacent to General Hospital No. 1, the engineer and quartermaster depots, and Luzon Force and II Corps headquarters, the TNT and ammunition had to be destroyed where they were. There was no time to move them to a safer place and hardly time to transfer the hospital patients away from the danger area. In the dumps were hundreds of thousands of rounds of small-arms ammunition and artillery shells of all calibers. Powder trains were laid to the separate piles of ammunition, and shells of larger caliber were set off by rifle fire.

Destruction began shortly after 2100 and at 0200 the first TNT warehouses went up with an explosion that fairly rocked the area. Then followed a most magnificent display of fireworks. Several million dollars worth of explosives and ammunition filled the sky "with bursting shells, colored lights, and sprays of rainbow colors. . . . Never did a 4th of July display equal it in noise, lights, colors or cost." [27] After the explosion shell fragments of all sizes fell like hail and men in the vicinity took refuge in their foxholes. The headquarters building at King's command post, a flimsy structure about 200 by

20 feet, was knocked over by the blast and the furniture was scattered in all directions. When morning came the men were surprised to note that all overhead cover was gone. "It is miraculous," wrote one officer, "that we came through this." [28]

In the confusion and disorganization of the last night of the battle, the evacuation of personnel to Corregidor proved difficult and sometimes impossible. The 45th Infantry (PS), which Wainwright had requested, never reached Mariveles where the barges waited. The regiment was in the I Corps area in the Pantingan valley when it received the orders to move, but it was unable to make the journey in time and was caught on Bataan. [29]

The nurses were more fortunate. Most of them did escape but only after harrowing experiences. Given thirty minutes to make ready for the journey, the nurses were cautioned to take with them only what they could carry. They boarded trucks in the darkness and made their way south at a snail's pace along the congested East Road. The group from General Hospital No. 2 was held up by the explosions from the ammunition dump which went up just as the convoy reached the road adjacent to the storage area. These nurses almost failed to get through. The barge left without them shortly before daylight and it was only through the "vim, vigor, and swearing" of General Funk that a motor boat was sent from Corregidor to carry them across the North Channel. They left the Mariveles dock after daylight and despite the bombs

---

[26] Gulick, Memoirs of Btry C, 91st CA (PS), p. 115.

[27] Collier, Notebooks, IV, 6.

[28] Tisdelle, Diary, entry of 8 Apr 42.

[29] NLF and I Corps Rpt of Opns, p. 30; intervs, author with Gen King, 12 Feb 47, and Col Collier, 20 Nov 46, OCMH; memo, QM USFIP to CofS USFIP, 8 Apr 42, sub: QM Plan, Evacuation of Bataan, AG 401 (2 Jan 42) Phil Rcds.

and bullets from a lone Japanese plane reached Corregidor in safety.[30]

Altogether about 2,000 persons, including 300 survivors of the 31st Infantry (US), Navy personnel, some Scouts from the 26th Cavalry, and Philippine Army troops, escaped from Bataan in small boats and barges that night. The remainder of General King's force of 78,000 was left behind to the tender mercy of the Japanese.[31]

Meanwhile, Colonel Williams and Major Hurt had gone forward to meet the Japanese commander. They began their journey in a reconnaissance car with motorcycle escort, but, unable to make progress against the heavy traffic moving away from the front lines, were soon forced to abandon the car. Williams climbed on the back of the motorcycle and continued forward, leaving Hurt to make his way as best he could on foot. "After talking to myself," wrote the major in his diary, "saying a few prayers, wondering what is in store for me in the future, bumming rides and a lot of walking" against the tide of "crouching, demoralized, beaten foot soldiers," he met Williams again on the East Road, two miles south of the front lines.[32] By this time the Colonel had acquired a jeep and driver and the two men started forward again. Except for the faraway explosions and "the chattering teeth of our driver," all was quiet.

Williams and Hurt reached the front line without further incident. There they found

Lt. Col. Joseph Ganahl with some tanks, two 75-mm. guns (SPM), and a few troops. At 0530 Ganahl and his men withdrew, leaving Williams, Hurt, and the driver alone. An hour later, as the sky was turning light, they drove forward into Japanese-held territory. Soon after about thirty "screaming" Japanese with "bayonets flashing" rushed at them.[33] Waving a bedsheet, their improvised white flag, both men descended from the jeep with raised hands. For the moment the entire mission was in jeopardy but fortunately a Japanese officer arrived and Williams was able to make him understand by signs and by waving his instructions in the officer's face that he wished to see the commanding officer. The Japanese got into his car, motioning for Williams and Hurt to follow. With a sigh of relief they drove on, past American prisoners with wrists tied behind them and Japanese soldiers making ready for the day's tasks. After a three-mile ride, their jeep was halted and the two Americans were taken to meet General Nagano whose detachment was moving down the East Road. An interpreter read Williams' letter of instructions, and, following a brief discussion, Nagano agreed to meet General King at the Experimental Farm Station near Lamao, close to the front lines.[34]

Hurt was sent back to get the general and Williams was kept at Japanese headquarters. Escorted to the front lines by Japanese tanks, Major Hurt made his way down the East Road, "past blown-up tanks, burning trucks, broken guns," and reached Luzon Force headquarters at 0900.[35] Within a few minutes General King was ready to go forward.

[30] Collier, Notebooks, IV, 7; Funk, Comments on Draft MS, p. 17, OCMH; Wainwright, General Wainwright's Story, p. 81; Redmond, I Served on Bataan, pp. 123–28.
[31] Wainwright, General Wainwright's Story, pp. 86–87.
[32] Hurt, Diary, in Chunn, Of Rice and Men, p. 6. The present account is based largely on this source. Colonel Williams did not prepare any notes of his experience and efforts to secure additional information from him have not been successful.

[33] Ibid., p. 7.
[34] Ibid., pp. 7–8; Collier, Notebooks, IV, 7–8.
[35] Hurt, Diary, in Chunn, Of Rice and Men, p. 8.

SURRENDER ON BATAAN

On Corregidor General Wainwright spent the night in ignorance of these events. At 0300 he spoke to King on the telephone but King did not mention his decision to surrender.[36] It was only three hours later, at 0600, that General Wainwright learned from his assistant operations officer, Lt. Col. Jesse T. Traywick, Jr., that General King had sent an officer to the Japanese to arrange terms for the cessation of hostilities. Shocked, he shouted to Traywick, "Go back and tell him not to do it." [37]

But it was too late. Williams and Hurt were already on their way to meet Nagano and General King could not be reached by telephone or radio.[38] Regretfully General Wainwright wrote to MacArthur:

---

[36] Wainwright, *General Wainwright's Story*, p. 81. General King's aide states that King spoke to General Beebe, not Wainwright, at this time. This is borne out by Wainwright, who explained in a message to General MacArthur that he could not hear well because of a poor connection and had given the phone to Beebe. Rad, Wainwright to MacArthur, No. 398, 4 May 42, AG 384.1, GHQ SWPA; interv, Bateman with Tisdelle, 22 Jan 46.

Colonel Alexander reports that after this telephone conversation King told his staff that Wainwright would not agree to the surrender of Bataan but that he would not interfere. King then went on to say, Colonel Alexander recollects, that if he survived he expected to be court-martialed, and he was certain that history would not deal kindly with a commander who would be remembered for having surrendered the largest force the United States had ever lost. Alexander, Personal Recollections of Bataan, p. 124.

[37] Wainwright, *General Wainwright's Story*, p. 82.

[38] In his message No. 398 of 4 May 1942 to MacArthur, cited above, Wainwright explained,

SURRENDER ON BATAAN

At 6 o'clock this morning General King . . . without my knowledge or approval sent a flag of truce to the Japanese commander. The minute I heard of it I disapproved of his action and directed that there would be no surrender. I was informed it was too late to make any change, that the action had already been taken. . . . Physical exhaustion and sickness due to a long period of insufficient food is the real cause of this terrible disaster. When I get word what terms have been arranged I will advise you.[39]

"We had direct communication with General King by telephone and radio up to the time of initiation of move to surrender." There is some disagreement over this point, and many of the officers claim that communications with Bataan were not interrupted until later in the day and that they talked with other officers on Bataan after 0600.

[39] Rad, Wainwright to MacArthur, No. 200, 9 Apr 42, AG 384.1, GHQ SWPA.

797–257 O–66—31

For General King, Wainwright had no criticism. "It has never been and is not my intention to reflect upon General King," he later told MacArthur, "as the decision which he was forced to make required unusual courage and strength of character."[40] Soon he would be forced to make the same decision.

It was about 0900 when King, in his last clean uniform, went forward to meet General Nagano. He felt, he said later, like General Lee who on the same day seventy-seven years earlier, just before his meeting with Grant at Appomatox, had remarked: "Then there is nothing left to do but to go

[40] Rad, Wainwright to MacArthur, No. 398, 4 May 42, AG 384.1, GHQ SWPA; Wainwright, *General Wainwright's Story*, p. 83.

and see General Grant, and I would rather die a thousand deaths." [41] With King when he left his command post were his two aides, Majors Wade Cothran and Tisdelle; his operations officer, Colonel Collier; and Major Hurt, who was to guide them to the meeting place. General Funk remained behind to supervise the completion .of the demolitions and the arrangements for the surrender of the Luzon Force.

The group left in two jeeps. In the first were Collier and Hurt; 150 yards to the rear in the second jeep were the general and his aides. Despite the white flags prominently displayed on both vehicles and wildly waved by Collier and Tisdelle, they were immediately bombed and strafed by low-flying Japanese aircraft. Fortunately the road was a winding one and offered ample protection on each side. The planes came in at very low altitude, sprayed the road with their machine guns or dropped a string of small bombs, made a wide circle, then banked and came in again for another try. "One smart boy," wrote Colonel Collier, "dropped out of formation and . . . cut loose with his machine guns just in front of a curve." [42] Only the whine of the ricocheting bullets warned the driver of the first jeep in time to avert disaster by jamming on his brakes and piling into the embankment. "The attack passed like a Texas whirlwind" and the men stopped with relief and "took

a full breath of good fresh air." [43] The attacks were almost continuous and at least once in every 200 yards the entire group was forced to jump hastily from the vehicles and seek cover in a ditch or behind a tree.

After more than an hour of this game of hare and hounds, when the general's uniform was as disheveled as those he had left behind, a Japanese reconnaissance plane appeared over the road and the pilot dipped his wings and waved in recognition. Apparently this was the signal to the attacking planes to keep away and the rest of the journey was uneventful. At the bridge over the Lamao River the group passed Japanese soldiers with fixed bayonets but were allowed to proceed without interference. Waiting for them was the Japanese soldier who had guided Major Hurt to the front lines earlier. He greeted them courteously and escorted them to a house near by in front of which General Nagano was seated with Colonel Williams. It was now 1100; the general and his party had spent two hours traveling a distance of about three miles. [44]

General Nagano, who spoke no English, opened the meeting by explaining through an interpreter that he was not authorized to make any arrangements himself but that he had notified General Homma an American officer was seeking a meeting to discuss terms for the cessation of hostilities. A representative from *14th Army* headquarters, he told King, would arrive very soon. A few minutes later a shiny Cadillac drew up at the building before which the envoys were waiting

---

[41] This remark is attributed to King by the authors of a manuscript history of the Philippine Campaign entitled Triumph in the Philippines and prepared by the Combat History Division, G–1, U.S. Army Forces, Western Pacific, page 203. General King did not repeat it in his conversations with the present author. The quotation can be found in Douglas S. Freeman, *R. E. Lee, a Biography* (New York and London, 1934–1935), IV, 120.

[42] Collier, Notebooks, IV, 10.

[43] *Ibid.*

[44] Collier, Notebooks, IV, 8–12; Hurt, Diary, in Chunn, *Of Rice and Men,* p. 8. This volume also contains an account by Major Tisdelle, pages 10–13, presumably written after the war. The present author has preferred to use Major Tisdelle's Diary, entry of 9 April 1942.

DISCUSSING SURRENDER TERMS *with Colonel Nakayama. Facing forward, left to right, Col. Everett C. Williams, Maj. Gen. Edward P. King, Jr., Maj. Wade Cothran, and Maj. Achille C. Tisdelle.*

and Colonel Nakayama, the *14th Army* senior operations officer, emerged, accompanied by an interpreter.[45] General King rose to greet him, but Nakayama ignored him and took a seat at the head of the table. King resumed his seat at the opposite end, erect with his hands forward in front of him. "I never saw him look more like a soldier," wrote his aide, "than in this hour of defeat." [46]

Nakayama had come to the meeting without any specific instructions about accepting a surrender or the terms under which a surrender would be acceptable. Apparently

there was no thought in Homma's mind of a negotiated settlement. He believed that the American envoy was a representative from General Wainwright and had sent Nakayama to represent him since he was unwilling to meet with any person of lesser rank.[47]

The discussion got off to a bad start when Colonel Nakayama, fixing his glance on General King, asked: "You are General Wainwright?" When King said he was not and identified himself, Nakayama asked where Wainwright was and why he had not

[45] Interv, Bateman with Tisdelle, 22 Jan 46; Col Nakayama, Negotiations with Gen King, 26 Aug 49, ATIS Doc 50246.

[46] Tisdelle, Diary, entry of 9 Apr 42.

[47] The account of the negotiations is based upon: Nakayama, Negotiations with King, 26 Aug 49, ATIS Doc 50246; USA *vs.* Homma, pp. 2305, 3143, testimony of Homma; Prosecution Exhibit 425, deposition of King; interv, author with Gen King, 12 Feb 47; Tisdelle, Diary, entry of 9 Apr 42.

come. The general replied that he did not speak for the commander of all forces in the Philippines but for his own command alone. He was then told that he would have to get Wainwright and that the Japanese could not accept any surrender without him. Again King declared that he represented only the forces on Bataan and that he could not get Wainwright. The Japanese were apparently insisting on a clarification of King's relation to Wainwright in order to avoid having to accept the piecemeal surrender of Wainwright's forces.

General King finally persuaded Nakayama to consider his terms. He explained that his forces were no longer fighting units and that he was seeking an arrangement to prevent further bloodshed. He asked for an armistice and requested that air bombardment be stopped at once. Nakayama rejected both the request for an immediate armistice and the cessation of air bombardment, explaining that the pilots had missions until noon and that the bombardment could not be halted until then. King then asked that his troops be permitted to march out of Bataan under their own officers and that the sick, wounded, and exhausted men be allowed to ride in the vehicles he had saved for this purpose. He promised to deliver his men at any time to any place designated by General Homma. Repeatedly he asked for assurance that the American and Filipino troops would be treated as prisoners of war under the provisions of the Geneva Convention.

To all these proposals Nakayama turned a deaf ear. The only basis on which he would consider negotiations for the cessation of hostilities, he asserted, was one which included the surrender of all forces in the Philippines. "It is absolutely impossible for me," he told King flatly, "to consider negotiations . . . in any limited area." [48] If the forces on Bataan wished to surrender they would have to do so by unit, "voluntarily and unconditionally." Apparently General King understood this to mean that Nakayama would accept his unconditional surrender. Realizing that his position was hopeless and that every minute delayed meant the death of more of his men, General King finally agreed at about 1230 to surrender unconditionally. Nakayama then asked for the general's saber, but King explained he had left it behind in Manila at the outbreak of war. After a brief flurry of excitement, Nakayama agreed to accept a pistol instead and the general laid it on the table. His fellow officers did the same, and the group passed into captivity.

No effort was made by either side to make the surrender a matter of record with a signed statement. General King believed then and later that though he had not secured agreement to any of the terms he had requested he had formally surrendered his entire force to Homma's representative. The Japanese view did not grant even that much. As Nakayama later explained: "The surrender . . . was accomplished by the voluntary and unconditional surrender of each individual or each unit. The negotiations for the cessation of hostilities failed." [49] King's surrender, therefore, was interpreted as the surrender of a single individual to the Japanese commander in the area, General Nagano, and not the surrender of an organized military force to the supreme enemy commander. He, Colonel Williams, and the two aides were kept in custody by the Japanese as a guarantee that there would be no further resistance. Though they were not

[48] Nakayama, Negotiations with King, 26 Aug 49, ATIS Doc 50246.
[49] *Ibid.*

so informed, they were, in fact, hostages and not prisoners of war.

Colonel Collier and Major Hurt, accompanied by a Japanese officer, were sent back to headquarters to pass on the news of the surrender to General Funk. On the way, they were to inform all troops along the road and along the adjoining trails to march to the East Road, stack arms, and await further instructions. Orders for the final disposition of the troops would come from Homma. Meanwhile, by agreement with Nagano, the Japanese forces along the east coast would advance only as far as the Cabcaben airfield.[50]

The battle for Bataan was ended; the fighting was over. The men who had survived the long ordeal could feel justly proud of their accomplishment. For three months they had held off the Japanese, only to be overwhelmed finally by disease and starvation. In a very real sense theirs had been "a true medical defeat," the inevitable outcome of a campaign of attrition, of "consumption without replenishment."[51] Each man had done his best and none need feel shame.

The events that followed General King's surrender present a confused and chaotic story of the disintegration and dissolution of a starved, diseased, and beaten army. This story reached its tragic climax with the horrors and atrocities of the 65-mile "death march" from Mariveles to San Fernando.[52] Denied food and water, robbed of their personal possessions and equipment, forced to march under the hot sun and halt in areas where even the most primitive sanitary facilities were lacking, clubbed, beaten, and bayoneted by their Japanese conquerors, General King's men made their way into captivity. Gallant foes and brave soldiers, the battling bastards had earned the right to be treated with consideration and decency, but their enemies had reserved for them even greater privations and deeper humiliation than any they had yet suffered on Bataan. How hard their lot was to be none knew but already many faced the future with heavy heart and "feelings of doubt, foreboding, and dark uncertainty."[53]

---

[50] Interv, author with Collier, 20 Nov 46, OCMH; Collier, Notebooks, IV, 12–13; Funk, Comments on Draft MS, p. 11, OCMH; USA vs. Homma, Prosecution Exhibit 425, testimony of King.

[51] Rpt, Surg LF to CG LF, 30 Jun 42, sub: Med Aspects of the Surrender, prepared in prison camp and lent to the author. A copy is on file in OCMH.

[52] The individual surrender of units and the death march are not treated in this volume since they did not affect the course of military operations on Bataan. The documents dealing with the march can be found among the prosecution exhibits and in the testimony of the trial of General Homma. The death march has been covered in an M. A. thesis prepared by the author's research assistant, Stanley L. Falk, at Georgetown University, entitled "The Bataan Death March."

[53] Collier, Notebooks, IV, 18.

PART FIVE

CORREGIDOR AND THE SOUTHERN ISLANDS

CHAPTER XXVII

The Siege of Corregidor

Though the fall of Bataan ended all organized opposition on Luzon, it did not give the Japanese the most valuable prize of all, Manila Bay. So long as Corregidor and its sister forts across the entrance to the bay remained in American hands, the use of the finest natural harbor in the Orient was denied them. And before General Homma could report to his already impatient superiors in Tokyo that he had accomplished his mission, he would also have to occupy Mindanao to the south as well as the more important islands in the Visayan group in the central Philippines.

The campaign for the Philippine Islands was not yet over. Though he had won the most decisive battle of that campaign, Homma still had to take Corregidor and the islands south of Luzon before the Japanese could integrate the archipelago into the Greater East Asia Co-Prosperity Sphere.

The Harbor Defenses of Manila Bay

Since the days of the Spaniards, Corregidor had been used as an outpost for the defense of Manila. (*Map 24*) By a system of semaphore signals from the island the Spaniards were able to receive warning of the approach of any hostile force in time to alert the forts in and around the capital. Later, they constructed minor fortifications on the island as an outer line of defense and as a screen for the larger guns emplaced along the Cavite shore south of Manila Bay,

and at Fort Santiago in Manila. By 1898, when Admiral Dewey sailed into Manila Bay, the Spaniards had on Corregidor three large cannons, each with a range of about one mile. Two of these faced Cavite; the other pointed north toward Bataan. In addition the Spaniards had twelve other coastal guns to defend the approaches to the capital city: on El Fraile and Caballo Islands, which, like Corregidor, lay across the entrance to the bay; along the southern tip of Bataan; and along the Cavite shore.

After the cession of the Philippines to the United States, a vast construction program designed to defend Manila by sealing off the entrance to Manila Bay was begun. During the years before the first World War, forts were built on Corregidor and the adjoining islands in the bay. By 1914 the task was completed. The Americans could now boast of an elaborate defense system in Manila Bay, so strong as to justify the name Gibraltar of the East. Reflecting the doctrine of the era in which they were built, the forts were designed to withstand attack from the sea by the heaviest surface vessels then known.[1]

The development of military aviation in

---

[1] The description of the fortifications in Manila Bay is based on the following sources: Harbor Defenses Rpt of Opns, pp. 1–16, Exhibits C, K, and M; American Fixed Coast Defenses in the Philippine Islands, Mil Rpts, No. 23, Nov 44, MID WD, p. 30; Lt Col Gwinn V. Porter, AA Defense of Corregidor, (paper prepared for Command and General Staff School, 1946–1947), pp. 1–10; ltr, Admiral Rockwell to Gen Ward, 18 Jan 52, OCMH.

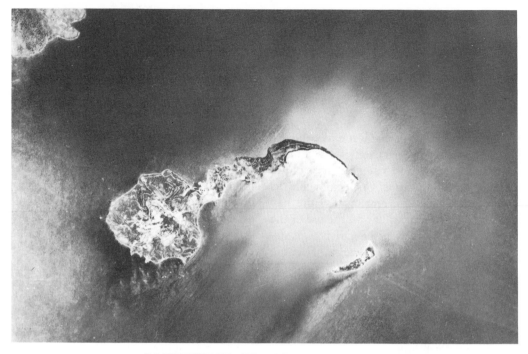

CORREGIDOR. *Tip of Bataan, upper left.*

the decade of the 1920's struck a sharp blow at the effectiveness of this carefully wrought and vastly expensive system of defenses. Nothing could be done to remedy the weakness of the forts, however, for by the Washington Naval Treaty of 1922 the construction of additional fortifications as well as the modernization of those already built was prohibited. Major construction after 1922, therefore, was limited to antiaircraft positions and to the tunnels dug into the solid rock of Malinta Hill on Corregidor, presumably as a storage area for supplies. When the Japanese attacked in December 1941, the defenses of Corregidor and the adjoining islands were little different from what they had been twenty-five years earlier.

Of the four fortified islands in Manila Bay, Corregidor, the site of Fort Mills, was the largest, measuring three and a half miles in length and one and a half miles at its widest point. With its bulbous head pointed toward the west and its tail stretching eastward, this tadpole-shaped island separated the bay entrance into a north and south channel. Corregidor had narrowly missed being two islands, for at the junction of the head and tail it narrowed to 600 yards and dropped to a height only slightly above sea level. This low area was known as Bottomside and contained two docks, the barrio of San Jose, shops, warehouses, a power plant, and cold-storage units. Directly to the east of Bottomside was Malinta Hill with its labyrinth of tunnels. Beyond, stretched the tail of the island, where a small airfield and a navy radio intercept station were located.

West of the narrow neck which connected the tail with the head of the tadpole was a small plateau known as Middleside. Here

MALINTA HILL, *looking south. Low area, center, is Bottomside.*

were located the hospital, quarters for commissioned and noncommissioned officers, a service club, and two schools for the children of the island. Beyond, lay the heavy head of the tadpole, rising 500 feet above the sea. Called Topside, this area contained the headquarters, barracks, and officers quarters, grouped around the traditional parade grounds. The ground was high almost to the beach line where it dropped precipitously to the water's edge. Cutting into the cliffs were two ravines, James and Cheney, which gave access from the beaches to the crowded area above. These ravines, together with Ramsey Ravine which led to Middleside, were the critical points in the defense of Corregidor against hostile landings.

Critical also to the defense of Corregidor and the ability of its garrison to hold out against a sustained attack was the safety of its power plant. Fresh water for the island had to be brought by barge from Mariveles or pumped from the twenty-one deep wells on the island. Perishable food could be kept in that tropical climate only by power-driven cold-storage plants. The large seacoast gun batteries, though equipped with emergency power sets, relied on the power plant, and ventilation for the vast underground tunnels depended on electrically operated blowers. Although there were sixty-five miles of roads and trails on the island, much of the heavy equipment was moved over an electric railroad with thirteen and a half miles of track which led to all important military installations. The garrison, therefore, was dependent in a very real sense on the island's power plant, and it was natural that those concerned with planning the defense should make every provision to

guard against its destruction by bombardment.

The most extensive construction on Corregidor was the tunnel system under Malinta Hill. Consisting of a main east-west
passage 1,400 feet long and 30 feet wide,
the tunnel had 25 laterals, each about 400
feet long, branching out at regular intervals from each side of the main passage.
The underground hospital was housed in a
separate system of tunnels north of the main
tunnel and had 12 laterals of its own. It
could be reached either through the main
tunnel or by a separate outside entrance on
the north side of Malinta Hill. Opposite the
hospital, under the south side of Malinta,
was the Navy tunnel system, connected to
the main tunnel by a partially completed
low passageway through the quartermaster
storage lateral. Reinforced with concrete
walls, floors, and overhead arches, blowers
to furnish fresh air, and a double-track electric car line along the east-west passage, the
Malinta Tunnel furnished bombproof shelter for the hospital, headquarters, and shops,
as well as a vast labyrinthine underground
storehouse.

The armament of Corregidor was formidable. Its seacoast defense alone consisted
of 23 batteries, many with their own names
and traditions. Altogether, Corregidor had
a total of 56 coastal guns and mortars, all
of World War I vintage, ranging in caliber
from 3 to 12 inches. (*Table 9*) The longest
range cannon were the two 12-inch guns of
Batteries Smith and Hearn, with a hori-
zontal range of 29,000 yards and all-around
traverse. In addition, there were six 12-inch
guns with a range of 17,000 yards, and ten
mortars of the same caliber. Nineteen of
Corregidor's guns were the 155-mm. GPF's,
capable of a range of 17,000 yards. The ten
3-inchers had the shortest range. The sup-

TABLE 9—ARMAMENT ON CORREGIDOR

Number of batteries	Caliber	Number of guns
	Seacoast Artillery	
2	12-inch mortars.......	10
5	12-inch guns..........	8
1	10-inch...............	2
1	8-inch................	2
2	6-inch................	5
8	155-mm. GPF.........	19
4	3-inch................	10
23	Total	56
	Antiaircraft Artillery (Including Southern Bataan)	
2	SL Sperry 60-inch[a] ...	10
7	3-inch	28
4	.50-caliber	48
13	Total..............	(guns) 76 (SL) 10

[a] Searchlight.
Source: Harbor Defenses Rpt of Opns, Annex C.

ply of seacoast ammunition was ample but
there was little of the type suitable for attacking land targets and no star shells to
provide illumination for night fire. North
and south of the island were extensive mine
fields planted by the Army and Navy.

Antiaircraft equipment consisted of 3-
inch guns with a vertical range of 27,000
and 32,000 feet (depending on the type of
ammunition used), .50-caliber machine
guns, and 60-inch Sperry searchlights. Defending Corregidor from air attack were 24
of these 3-inch guns, 48 machine guns and
5 searchlights. Another battery of 3-inchers
was emplaced on the southern tip of Bataan
to tie in with these on Corregidor. Ammunition for the antiaircraft weapons was less
plentiful than that for the seacoast guns, and
there was a critical shortage of mechanically
fuzed 3-inch high explosive shells.

MALINTA TUNNEL

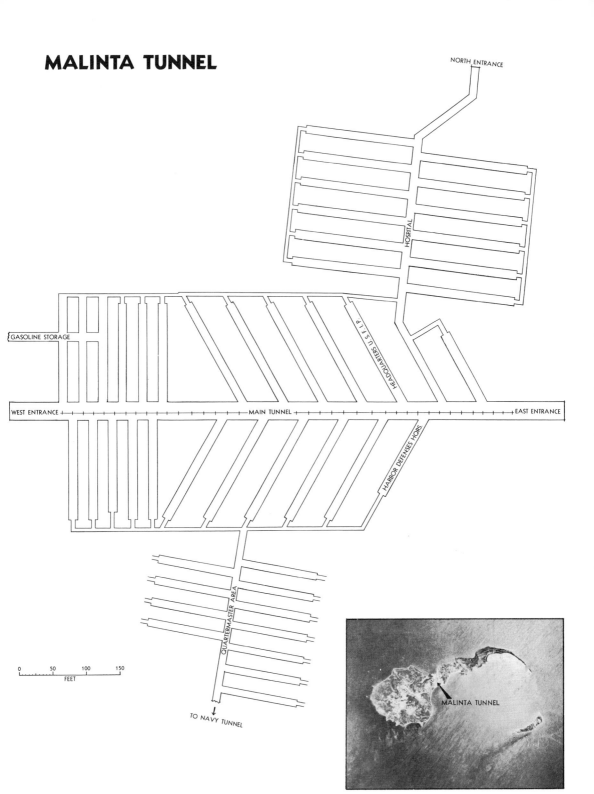

NORTH ENTRANCE

HOSPITAL

GASOLINE STORAGE

HEADQUARTERS U S F I P

WEST ENTRANCE ⊢————————— MAIN TUNNEL —————————⊣ EAST ENTRANCE

HARBOR DEFENSES HORS

QUARTERMASTER AREA

0   50   100   150
FEET

TO NAVY TUNNEL

MALINTA TUNNEL

Before the war, the Corregidor garrison consisted principally of headquarters, artillery, and service troops. The combined strength of the four fortified islands in Manila Bay at that time did not exceed 6,000 men, most of whom were stationed on Corregidor. After 8 December the population of these garrisons swelled rapidly. First came the survivors of the Cavite naval base, then the headquarters and service troops from Manila. MacArthur's headquarters was established on Corregidor on 25 December and with it came the 809th Military Police Company, two ordnance companies, an engineer company, and service detachments. When Olongapo was evacuated on 26 December, the 4th Marines were also transferred to Corregidor, swelling its population by over 1,000 men. Before the first blow hit that island, it was already crowded with the men of all services and a dizzying pyramid of headquarters.

The defenses of the three other islands in the entrance to Manila Bay were hardly less formidable, proportionately, than those of Corregidor. Caballo (Fort Hughes), just south of Corregidor, was the next largest in size. Only about one quarter of a square mile in area, this island rose abruptly from the bay to a height of 380 feet on its western side. The east coast, which was lower than the rest of the island, was vulnerable to amphibious attack and a marine detachment of about 100 men was sent there to augment the garrison. Later, 200 sailors from Corregidor were added to the marine detachment and Comdr. Francis J. Bridget, who had commanded the naval battalion in the Battle of the Points, assumed command of the beach defenses. His force was almost doubled when the crews of four gunboats, about 225 men, were sent to the island. By the end of

April the garrison of Fort Hughes numbered about 800 men of whom 93 were marines and 443 belonged to the Navy. The antiaircraft defenses of the island were tied in with those of Corregidor and consisted of four 3-inch guns. Seacoast artillery numbered thirteen pieces: two 14-inch guns, four 12-inch mortars, two 6-inch guns, three 155-mm. GPF's, and two 3-inchers. (*Table 10*)

TABLE 10—ARMAMENT ON FORTS HUGHES, DRUM, AND FRANK

Number of batteries	Caliber	Number of guns
Fort Hughes (Caballo)		
2	14-inch.............	2
1	12-inch mortar......	4
1	6-inch..............	2
2	155-mm. GPF.......	3
2	3-inch..............	(4 AA) 6
3	SL.................	3
11	Total.............	(guns) 17
		(SL) 3
Fort Drum (El Fraile)		
2	14-inch.............	4
2	6-inch..............	4
2	3-inch..............	(2 AA) 3
2	SL.................	2
8	Total.............	(guns) 11
		(SL) 2
Fort Frank (Carabao)		
2	14-inch............	2
1	12-inch mortar......	8
1	3-inch..............	(AA) 4
1	155-GPF...........	4
1	75-mm. (beach defense)	3
2	SL.................	2
8	Total.............	(guns) 21
		(SL) 2

Source: Harbor Defenses Rpt of Opns, Annex C; Brig Gen Samuel L. Howard, Rpt on 4th Marines, p. 18, USMC Hist Sec.

FORT DRUM. *El Fraile Island before the concrete battleship was constructed, above; and after, below.*

About four miles south of Fort Hughes lay Fort Drum, the most unusual of the harbor defenses. Cutting away the entire top of El Fraile Island down to the water line and using the island as a foundation, the engineers had built a reinforced concrete battleship, 350 feet long and 144 feet wide, with exterior walls of concrete and steel 25 to 36 feet thick. The top deck of this concrete battleship was 40 feet above the low-water mark and had 20-foot-thick walls. Equipped with four 14-inch guns in armored turrets facing seaward, a secondary battery of four casemated 6-inch guns, and antiaircraft defense, the fort with its 200-man garrison was considered, even in 1941, impregnable to attack.

The southernmost of the fortified islands was Carabao, only 500 yards from the shores of Cavite Province. Except at one point along its eastern shore, the island rises precipitously from the sea in cliffs more than 100 feet high. On this uninviting island the Americans had placed Fort Frank, which late in 1941 had a military garrison of about 400 men, mostly Philippine Scouts. Its armament consisted of two 14-inch guns, eight 12-inch mortars, four 155-mm. GPF's, as well as antiaircraft and beach defense weapons.

All four forts in Manila Bay, as well as Fort Wint in Subic Bay, had been formed before the war into an organization called the Harbor Defenses of Manila and Subic Bays which, in August 1941, became a part of the Philippine Coast Artillery Command. Both were commanded by Maj. Gen. George F. Moore who also commanded the Corregidor garrison. The 5,700 men assigned to the Harbor Defenses were organized into three seacoast and one antiaircraft artillery regiments, headquarters, and service troops. The three seacoast units included the American 59th and the Philippine Scout

91st and 92d. The 60th, the antiaircraft regiment, was composed of Americans. About 600 Philippine Army soldiers in training were organized into the 1st and 2d Coast Artillery Regiments (PA), but operated under the control of the two Scout regiments.[2]

General Moore commanded not only the seacoast and antiaircraft artillery but the beach defenses and inshore patrol as well. To exercise tactical control over all elements of his force, he had four major commands. Seaward defense he placed under Col. Paul D. Bunker who, in turn, commanded four groups, two of which covered North Channel and two South Channel. All antiaircraft units were under Col. Theodore M. Chase, commander of the 60th Coast Artillery. In addition to the normal mission of providing defense against air attack, Chase also maintained an air warning service for the fortified islands and for vessels in the bay. Though each fort commander was responsible for local defense, General Moore had an executive for beach defense who co-ordinated the plans for each of the islands. The inshore patrol remained a naval function, but under the principle of unity of command, Capt. Kenneth M. Hoeffel, USN, was under Moore's tactical control.

By the end of 1941 all that could be done in the limited time since funds had been made available in midyear to improve the defenses of Corregidor and the adjoining

---

[2] Harbor Defenses Rpt of Opns, Exhibit K. The strength of the major units was as follows:

Unit	Officer	Enlisted	Civilian
HD Hq Btry	30	255	290
59th CA	64	1,264	55
60th CA	72	1,896	65
91st CA	38	764	28
92d CA	37	458	20
1st CA	50	428	12
2d CA	2	74	3
Mine Planter	7	32	3

islands had been accomplished.[3] But the basic weakness of the harbor defenses— their vulnerability to attack from the air and from their landward flanks—was never corrected. They accomplished their mission, the denial of Manila Bay to the enemy, without firing a single round at a hostile warship; Japanese cruisers and destroyers blockading the bay stayed well out of range of Moore's heavy guns. But when Bataan fell the flank protection of Corregidor disappeared and the fortress was left exposed to destruction by air and artillery attacks and to landings by hostile forces.

The First Aerial and Artillery Attacks

First word of the Japanese attack against Pearl Harbor reached General Moore from the Navy radio intercept station on Corregidor at 0340, 8 December, about the same time that General Sutherland relayed the news to the commander in chief. The garrisons of the four fortified islands had been on the alert for eight days and all battle stations were manned. There was little Moore could do except notify his commanders and instruct the sea, antiaircraft, and beach defense commanders to double their precautions against a surprise dawn attack. At 0620 official notification that a state of war existed between the United States and Japan came from MacArthur's headquarters, and the Navy temporarily closed Manila Bay to outbound traffic. About four hours later the first air-raid alarm sounded over Corregidor.[4]

This first alarm and those that followed during the next three weeks proved groundless. The Japanese did not attack Corregidor on 8 December and had no plan to do so at the start of war. But they had no intention either of bypassing the island fortress. They fully appreciated its strategic significance and its importance in the scheme of defense, but their first task was to seize Manila and defeat MacArthur's army. The conquest of Corregidor would follow "as soon as possible." [5]

The Aerial Attacks

Hardly had news of the evacuation of Manila and the transfer of MacArthur's headquarters to Corregidor reached Homma on 28 December when he ordered the *5th Air Group* to begin operations against the island. Manila would soon be his and though MacArthur's army had not yet been defeated, Homma may have believed that he could soon move against Corregidor. Homma's plans, by agreement with the Navy, provided for a joint attack in which Lt. Gen. Hideyoshi Obata's *5th Air Group* (Army) would be supplemented by the planes of the *11th Air Fleet* (Navy). The

---

No. 12, 15 Nov 43, MID WD, pp. 37–52; Porter, AA Defense of Corregidor, pp. 10–17; Rockwell, Narrative of Naval Activities in Luzon Area, pp. 8–22, Off of Naval Rcds; Gen Marquat, USAFFE AA Officer, Rpt of Performance of U.S. CA in Manila-Bataan Campaign, copy in OCMH; Gulick, Memoirs of Btry C, 91st CA (PS); diaries of Col Bunker, Maj Tisdelle, and Capt Roland G. Ames (including letters to his wife), all in OCMH.

The basic Japanese sources are: *14th Army Opns*, I, pp. 13–14, 25, 96, 115, 124–36; *5th Air Gp* Opns, *passim;* Japanese Naval Opns in Phil Invasion, Japanese Studies in WW II, No. 13, pp. 17–18, OCMH.

[5] *14th Army* Opns, I, 25. Presumably this would be some time in January or early February since the defeat of MacArthur's army was to be accomplished forty-five days after the landing.

---

[3] For a detailed account of the measures taken during the last six months of 1941, see Harbor Defenses Rpt of Opns, pp. 10–16, and Exhibit E.

[4] The account which follows is based upon the following sources: Harbor Defenses Rpt of Opns, pp. 16–79, and Exhibits E through M; The Siege of Corregidor, Mil Rpts on the United Nations,

Army air force would strike first, at noon of 29 December, "with its whole strength." An hour later the Navy bombers were to take over. The bombardment would continue for two and a half hours, until 1430, and would, General Obata hoped, "destroy the center of the American Far East Command." [6]

Almost exactly on schedule, at 1154 of the 29th, the first flight of 18 twin-engine bombers of the *14th Heavy Bombardment Regiment,* covered by 19 fighters, approached Corregidor at a height of 15,000 feet and in regular V formation. The flight broke into smaller flights, of 9 and 3 planes, which passed lengthwise over the island, then back, dropping 225- and 550-pound bombs on the headquarters buildings and barracks. For the half hour they were over the target, the planes of the *14th Heavy Bombardment* dropped almost fifty bombs.

At 1230, 22 bombers of the *8th Light Bombardment Regiment,* accompanied by 18 dive bombers of the *16th Light Bombardment Regiment,* had their turn. The light bombers followed the same pattern as the first flight, dropping their sixty-six 225-pound bombs on installations and buildings on Bottomside and Topside. The dive bombers, loaded with 35-pounders, attacked from an altitude of 3,000 feet, though to the men on the ground the planes appeared to be at treetop level.

When the dive bombers left at 1300, the Navy bombers came in. Numbering about 60 planes, the naval formation continued the attack against the island and shipping in the bay for another hour. Altogether, the Americans estimated, the Japanese used about 81 mediums and 10 dive bombers and dropped about 60 tons of bombs during these two hours. None of the few remaining

American aircraft rose from the recently established fighter base on Bataan to dispute their supremacy of the air on this occasion or during any of the attacks that followed.

In this first attack the antiaircraft defenses at Fort Mills, Fort Hughes, and southern Bataan gave a good account of themselves, firing a total of 1,200 rounds of 3-inch ammunition. Score for the 3-inchers was thirteen medium bombers. It was with considerable satisfaction that Capt. Roland G. Ames, commander of Battery C (Chicago), 60th Coast Artillery (AA), wrote after the attack that his men "had performed wonderfully" in their first encounter with the enemy and had brought down at least three Japanese planes. [7]

The dive bombers, too, were met by strong and effective opposition. The .50-caliber machine guns of the antiaircraft command downed four of the planes in their first low-level strafing attack. Thereafter, according to American sources, the Japanese did not again attempt to dive-bomb targets on Corregidor until the end of April.

The men had paid little heed to the alarm when it first sounded, since none of the previous air warnings had been followed by attack. Some of those who had recently arrived on the island with the transfer of headquarters from Manila to Corregidor casually took up a better position to watch the large enemy formation. One officer in the concrete building on Topside which housed USAFFE headquarters mounted to the second floor for a clearer view of the proceedings. Hardly had he arrived there when he heard "an ominous, whirring whistle, which rapidly increased in crescendo." He made a wild jump for the stairway, later claiming

---

[6] *5th Air Gp* Opns Order A, No. 171, *5th Air Gp* Opns, p. 40.

[7] Ltr, Ames to his wife, 30 Dec 41, in Ames, Diary. Captain Ames copied in his diary the letters he wrote to his wife and which he sent out whenever he had the opportunity.

that "the whistle of my descent must have rivalled that of the falling bomb." [8] Others were equally surprised and displayed a tendency to head for the corners of the rooms where they fancied they were safer than elsewhere. Fortunately windows and entrances had been sandbagged and broken glass caused few casualties.

The first bombs hit the vacated station hospital and many of the wooden structures on Topside and Middleside. One bomb struck the post exchange, went through the roof and three concrete floors, buried itself in eight feet of earth, and left a crater about twenty feet in diameter. Fully half the barracks and headquarters buildings were demolished and only a part of the foundation of the officers' club remained after the bombing. Many of the structures were of corrugated iron, and the danger from flying bits of metal was often as great as that from the bombs. Bottomside, after the bombing, appeared to be "one huge mass of jagged and bent sheet iron." [9] Fire sprang up at many points so that to an observer on Bataan the island appeared to be enveloped "in clouds of dust and black smoke." [10] Altogether about 60 percent of all wooden buildings on Corregidor were destroyed during the first bombings. Headquarters, USAFFE, promptly moved into Malinta Tunnel the next day.

Fortunately, damage to military installations, the major target of the Japanese aircraft, was comparatively slight. Two of the gun batteries suffered minor damage which was repaired within twenty-four hours. Several of the small vessels docked at Bottomside and at anchor near the island were hit, and two Philippine Army planes at Kindley

Field on the tail of the tadpole were destroyed. Power, communication, and water lines were temporarily disrupted but little permanent damage was wrought. Casualties for the day were twenty killed and eighty wounded.

After the first bombings there was a marked change in the reaction of the men. Before the 29th, despite warning, they had crowded the doorways and windows to watch the planes and speculate about probable targets, safe in the knowledge that Corregidor would not be hit. "All of us," wrote Captain Ames, "were too careless of bombs and bullets at first." [11] But that attitude quickly changed. "Now," noted Colonel Bunker, commander of the Seaward Defenses, "they all stampede for the nearest cover and get as far under it as possible." [12] As a matter of fact, it soon became difficult to get some of the men out of their shelters, even when there were no planes overhead.

There was a marked change, too, in the attitude toward the weather after the first attack from the air. Bright moonlight, "by which we had wooed our sweethearts and wives," carried the threat of night attack. It gave away the position of vessels and made the large searchlights of the harbor defenses nearly useless. The beautiful sunrise and sunset of the tropics lost their attractiveness when enemy planes chose that time for attack. In the muted light of dawn and dusk it was difficult to pick out the attacking aircraft. Clouds, unless they were high and solid, were considered "a curse" by the antiaircraft gunners, and cloud formations through which enemy aircraft could drop for a bombing run were a "pet hate." The feared typhoons, on the other hand, were eagerly awaited. "We prayed for them

---

[8] Collier, Notebooks, II, 53.
[9] Tisdelle, Diary, entry of 29 Dec 41.
[10] Gulick, Memoirs of Btry C, 91st CA (PS), p. 40.

[11] Ames, Diary, entry of 29 Dec 41.
[12] Bunker, Diary, entry of 4 Jan 42.

. . .," wrote Captain Ames, "to break up and destroy Jap planes and ships." [13]

For the next eight days, until 6 January, the Japanese continued to bomb Corregidor intermittently, with less and less effect and at greater cost to themselves. There were no enemy aircraft over the island on the 30th, when President Quezon was inaugurated for the second time, or on the 31st. There is some indication of air action on the first day of the New Year, but it was on the 2d, the date Manila was occupied, that the Japanese came back in force.

The day was overcast, with a low ceiling of shifting clouds. Shortly after the noon hour the first enemy bombers burst through a hole in the low-hanging clouds, released their bombs, then flew up into the safety of the clouds. Altogether fifty-four enemy aircraft participated in the attack that day. They left behind, in Colonel Bunker's words, "a scene of destruction." On a tour of inspection, he saw huge sections of corrugated iron "scattered in painfully distorted shapes" all over the parade ground, and "gaping, square, empty openings" in the barracks.[14]

The bombardment of the 2d was the beginning of a five-day assault during which hardly a yard of the island did not feel the effects of the enemy bombs. Except for the attacks on the 2d and the 5th, the sole enemy target was Corregidor. On the 2d, Fort Drum, and on the 5th, Fort Frank came in for their share of the bombs but were never the primary targets.

The pattern of the daily Japanese attacks was usually the same. During the morning a lone photo reconnaissance plane, whose pilot the Americans referred to as familiarly as Photo Joe or The Lone Ranger, would circle Corregidor and the other fortified islands for a time and then return to base. About 1230 the bombers would come in, flying at an altitude well above 20,000 feet and at a speed of about 160 miles an hour, bomb the island for about two hours, then fly off. Until the last day, they approached the target from the same direction in a large V formation, then broke up into smaller formations for the run over the island. Only at the end did the Japanese abandon this regular formation and approach the target from different directions in scattered formations and at varying altitudes.

Total damages for the six days' bombing were extensive. On the 2d and 3d the buildings on Topside and Middleside were hit again and two of the island's precious water tanks destroyed. On the 4th the principal target was the wharves, shops, and warehouses on Bottomside. The next day a barge was bombed and set afire. It drifted into shore and set fire to a diesel oil dump near the power plant. On the 6th there was a tragic accident when thirty-four men took cover in an incomplete bomb shelter. A large bomb fell near the structure, which collapsed and killed thirty-one of the men. By the 7th practically all unprotected surface installations had disappeared or were in ruins. Bomb craters were uniformly scattered over the island and one could hardly walk more than twenty-five yards in any direction without stumbling into one.

The worst destruction was caused by fire. Barely adequate during peacetime, the Fort Mills fire department proved unable to cope with the conditions created by the hail of

[13] Ames, Diary, undated "Sidelights," following letter of 6 January 1942 to his wife.

[14] Bunker, Diary, entry of 3 Jan 42. Japanese records make no mention of the attacks after 29 December. Information about these attacks is derived entirely from the American sources cited.

GUN EMPLACEMENTS ON CORREGIDOR. *Coastal defense gun at Cheney Battery, above; below, 3-inch antiaircraft gun M3.*

bombs. Much material, such as lumber, hardware, mattresses, and medical and chemical warfare supplies, which had been stored on the surface in wooden buildings, was burned. Concrete structures suffered less from the bombings and from fire, and the supplies stored in them were salvaged.

After the first attack no effort was made to keep the electric railroad line on the island in operation. It had been hit in so many places and was so exposed that it was fruitless to attempt its repair. Almost daily the main telephone cables were cut by bombs. Crews worked at night to repair them, but the next day the lines would be cut again. The maintenance of communications was a never-ending task, and there was never time to bury the cables deep enough to place them out of reach of the bombs.

The armament of the island suffered comparatively slight damage. The coastal batteries with their magazines and power plants had been bombproofed before the war and escaped almost unscathed. The more exposed antiaircraft units suffered more from the bombings than the seacoast batteries, but such damage as was caused was repaired quickly, usually within twelve hours. There were some casualties among the gun crews, but they were not serious enough to interfere with operations. The largest number of casualties came to those who failed to take shelter or were careless. There is no record of the total casualties for the period from 29 December to 7 January, but at least 36 men were killed and another 140 wounded during the first, second, and last days of the attack alone.

The air attacks against Corregidor ended on 6 January, the day the Bataan campaign opened. They had proved costly to the Japanese and had produced no decisive military results. But even if they had and if Homma had wished to continue to bomb the island after 6 January, he would have been unable to do so. By that time the *5th Air Group* was preparing to move to Thailand, and Homma was left with only a small air force which he could ill spare for attacks against Corregidor. Except for sporadic raids by three or four planes and occasional dive bombing and strafing, the first aerial bombardment was over.

The Artillery Bombardment

Events thus far had not worked out as the Japanese had planned. The occupation of Manila had not given them the use of its fine harbor or the large military stores they had expected to find there. MacArthur had refused battle on the plains of Manila, and drawn his forces back into the Bataan peninsula intact. The occupation of Corregidor, which was next on the Japanese timetable, now had to be deferred for the lengthy and expensive campaign on Bataan. If the first air attacks against the island fortress had been intended as the prelude for a landing, they had been wasted.

To have attempted the investment of the Gibraltar of the East while the Bataan peninsula was in American hands would have been disastrous and foolhardy. The heights of the Mariveles Mountains dominated the small island only two miles offshore and were vital to its control. Even before the war the Japanese had recognized the intimate relationship between Bataan and Corregidor and in their prewar estimates had noted the flank protection Bataan offered to the island. "Mt. Mariveles in southern Bataan forms the left wall of the bay entrance," one Japanese estimate concluded, "and because it is covered with dense forests, use of siege guns and heavy equipment to attack this fortress is impossible." [15]

The southern shore of Manila Bay offered only partial protection to the islands lying at the bay entrance. Here the ground was less mountainous and overgrown than on Bataan, and in the vicinity of Ternate, opposite the tip of Bataan, there were few obstacles to military movement. Into this area could be brought heavy equipment and siege guns. Once emplaced, these guns could bring the southernmost of the islands, Forts Frank and Drum, under assault. It was from here that the next attack against the harbor defenses came.

Toward the end of January reports began to reach Corregidor of the movement of Japanese artillery into Cavite Province. By the 25th, according to observers on the mainland, the Japanese had emplaced their guns in defiladed positions near Ternate, only about six air miles from Fort Drum on El Fraile Island and eight miles from the neighboring Fort Frank on Carabao Island.

The reports were correct. A Japanese artillery unit called the *Kondo Detachment* was indeed moving into position along the southern shore of Manila Bay. Formed by *14th Army* on 24 January, this unit was under the command of Maj. Toshinori Kondo and consisted initially of four 105-mm. guns and two 150-mm. cannons. Kondo's orders were "to secretly deploy" near Ternate and "prepare for fire missions" against Corregidor, El Fraile, and Carabao Islands and against shipping in Manila Bay.[16] By the first week of February, despite interdiction fire from Fort Frank, Kondo had completed his preparations and was awaiting further orders.

He did not have long to wait. On 5 February, his orders arrived and next morning at 0800 the *Kondo Detachment* opened fire against the fortified islands. Fort Drum was the principal target that day and the Japanese guns hit it almost one hundred times during the three-hour attack. By accident or design, the choice of the early morning hours for the attack placed the sun behind the Japanese and made observation by the Americans difficult. They replied as best they could with their 14- and 6-inch guns, and Fort Frank assisted with its 12-inch mortars, but scored no hits. Thus began an artillery duel that was to continue intermittently for almost two months.

Until the middle of February the daily attacks followed much the same pattern. Major Kondo's 105's and 150's usually opened fire in the morning, to be answered by counterbattery fire from the large guns of the harbor defenses. Later the Japanese fired at odd intervals during the day. Forts Frank and Drum, closest to Ternate, received the heaviest weight of shells and the greatest damage but their guns were never put out of commission and their effectiveness never seriously impaired. Damage to Corregidor was limited to occasional hits on buildings and vehicles.

During the course of the bombardment the Japanese hit upon a scheme to strike a vital blow at Fort Frank without firing a single shot. Learning from the natives that the fort received its supply of fresh water from a dam near Calumpan on the Cavite shore, they dispatched a demolition squad to locate and destroy the pipeline. On 16 February, the Japanese found the line and pulled up the section just below the dam.

Fort Frank, fortunately, had its own distillation plant and Colonel Boudreau, who had assumed command of the fort after the

[15] *14th Army* Opns, I, 13–14.
[16] *Ibid.*, 96.

evacuation of Fort Wint in December, directed that it be placed in operation at once. But its use required valuable fuel and Boudreau was understandably reluctant to expend the gasoline he needed for his guns to distill sea water. On the 19th, therefore, he made an effort to repair the pipeline and sent a group of fifteen volunteers to the mainland for that purpose. Before the men could restore the line they were attacked by a Japanese patrol of about thirty men. In the fight that followed, the Americans and Filipinos, with the support of 75-mm. guns from Fort Frank, destroyed the entire patrol, suffering only one casualty.[17] The fifteen men then returned to Fort Frank safely but without having accomplished their mission. That night the Japanese retaliated by burning the barrio of Calumpan. It was not until 9 March that Colonel Boudreau was able to repair the broken water pipe.

The intensity of the Japanese attacks increased after the middle of February, when Major Kondo received two additional 150-mm. howitzers. With these reinforcements came instructions from Homma "to demoralize the enemy."[18] The daily bombardments thereafter became more severe and reached their height on 20 February. Starting at 0930 that morning the guns of the reinforced *Kondo Detachment* fired steadily at one-minute intervals until late afternoon. The only serious damage was to the power plant on Corregidor and to several observation posts at Fort Hughes. After that date the Japanese fire diminished until, by the beginning of March, it presented no real threat to the harbor defenses. "In general," wrote the commander of the Seaward Defenses, "the Japs are resorting to nuisance firing daily and usually from a single gun."[19]

The slackening of enemy fire at the end of February did not mean that the attack was over. On the basis of intelligence reports, General Moore concluded that the Japanese were merely "marking time waiting for reinforcements."[20] This view was confirmed when native informants reported that the Japanese were selecting new gun positions in the Pico de Loro hills southwest of Ternate and improving the trails leading into the interior. In an effort to hinder this move, General Moore ordered his seacoast batteries to place interdiction fire on roads and bridges in the vicinity of Ternate, but without observable effect. The Japanese continued to make their preparation for a fresh attack without serious interference from the coastal batteries in the bay.

The Japanese force which assembled in the Pico de Loro hills during the first two weeks of March was considerably stronger than the *Kondo Detachment*. To that unit had been added the *1st Heavy Artillery Regiment,* the *2d Independent Heavy Artillery Battery,* both equipped with 240-mm. howitzers, and the *3d Tractor Unit* with prime movers for the heavy guns. The *Kondo Detachment* had been dissolved and a new organization, the *Hayakawa Detachment,* formed. Col. Masayoshi Hayakawa, commander of the *1st Heavy Artillery,* led the reorganized force, and, according to the usual Japanese practice, gave it his name. By 15 March all preparations for the stepped-up artillery bombardment of the harbor defenses had been completed.

The attack opened at 0730 of the 15th with a volley from the 240-mm. howitzers

[17] Harbor Defenses Rpt of Opns, p. 37. The claims made by the volunteers were accepted by General Moore and have been used by the author in the absence of any evidence to the contrary.
[18] *14th Army* Opns, I, 115.

[19] Bunker, Diary, entry of 19 Feb 42.
[20] Harbor Defenses Rpt of Opns, p. 38.

and continued throughout the day. Although all four islands came under fire, Forts Frank and Drum bore the brunt of the bombardment. Approximately 500 shells fell on Fort Frank alone; another 100 on Fort Drum. Two of Frank's batteries, one of 155-mm. guns and the other of 3-inch antiaircraft guns, were almost entirely destroyed, and two other batteries were put out of commission temporarily. Fort Drum escaped more lightly. Its only damage came when a shell penetrated the armor of the 6-inch battery on the south side and burst inside the casemate, filling the concrete battleship with flames, smoke, and fumes. Fortunately, there were no casualties. Despite every effort during the day to neutralize the enemy fire, the bombardment continued until afternoon. "It hurt me like blazes," wrote Colonel Bunker on Corregidor, "to see my friends under fire and be so powerless to help them." [21]

The attack continued with unabated vigor the next day and with varying intensity for five days thereafter. As on the 15th, all four forts came under fire, but the weight of the attack was again directed against the two southernmost islands. The heaviest bombardments came on the 16th and 21st. On both days the concrete battleship fairly shook under the impact of the large shells. Every time one of them hit the casemate of the 6-inch guns a flash of fire was observed, and during the height of the attack there were fire alarms as often as every five minutes. Fortunately there was no general conflagration and no serious damage.

Fort Frank was not so fortunate. On the 16th a 240-mm. shell penetrated eighteen inches of concrete around one of its 12-inch batteries, passed under a six-foot concrete

wall and exploded below the powder room. The floor of the battery was shattered and sixty cans of mortar powder overturned, but, miraculously, none exploded. It was on the morning of the 21st that Fort Frank suffered its "greatest loss" of the war when a 240-mm. shell penetrated the 18-inch concrete roof of one of its tunnels and struck in the midst of a line of men waiting for yellow fever shots. Twenty-eight of the men were killed and another forty-six wounded. [22]

The damage wrought by the artillery attacks between 15 and 21 March was considerably greater than any inflicted by the 105's and 150's of the *Kondo Detachment*. Fort Frank, the larger target and the one closest to the enemy, was the most vulnerable of the forts and "got a fearful working-over." [23] All of its surface guns—four 3-inch antiaircraft and four 155-mm. GPF guns— were visible to the enemy and were badly damaged. The depressed 12-inch mortar battery and two 14-inch disappearing guns were also hit, but were quickly repaired and put back in action. Fort Drum, the concrete battleship, came under as severe a bombardment as Frank, but was better able to withstand the battering. Every square foot of the interior surface of the casemates was deeply dented and torn by fragmentation, and between eight and fifteen feet of its reinforced concrete deck was whittled away. But though its two antiaircraft guns were ruined beyond repair, the principal target of the Japanese, the 14-inch turret guns, were never put out of action.

So heavy were the attacks against Frank and Drum that the commanders of both forts, fearing a hostile landing, had doubled their beach defenses immediately. This pre-

---

[21] Bunker, Diary, entry of 15 Mar 42.

[22] Maj Joe C. East, March 21st Fort Frank Shelling, a 2-page typescript in OCMH.

[23] Bunker, Diary, entry of 15 Mar 42.

caution was a wise one, for the Japanese did actually plan to capture both Forts Frank and Drum, and had even designated the unit which was to make the assault. General Homma canceled this plan, however, in order to strengthen the force he was assembling late in March for the final attack against Bataan. The landing craft which had been collected for the attack, about forty-five bancas, were later destroyed by 75-mm. gunfire from Fort Frank.

Throughout the long-range artillery duel the effectiveness of American counterbattery fire was limited by the difficulty of locating the Japanese guns. There was no flash during daylight, and both Kondo and Hayakawa were careful to take every precaution to avoid giving away their position. They camouflaged their guns skillfully, moved them when necessary, and even sent up false smoke rings when their batteries were in action. The American and Filipino artillerymen tried to fix the enemy's position by the use of sound waves, but this method proved too delicate and complicated. Another method, admittedly less accurate but easier to use, was to compute the enemy's position by the line of falling duds. The results could rarely be checked, but the batteries of all four forts fired daily, hopeful that they might knock out some of the Japanese guns with a lucky hit.

For a time firing data was received from a small group of volunteers on the mainland led by Capt. Richard G. Ivey of the 60th Coast Artillery (AA). Ivey had established an observation post on high ground along the south coast of the bay and, until he was driven out on 15 February, served as a spotter, sending his information by walkie-talkie radio. Even this observed fire proved of doubtful effectiveness. During one bombardment, when Ivey's reports appeared inconsistent, the fire control center asked him how he knew there was a Japanese gun in the position. "He replied," wrote Colonel Bunker, "that he couldn't see it, but *judged by the sound* that it was there." [24] When fire was shifted to another target, the observer's instructions, which failed to distinguish between deflection and range, were just as confusing and the fire was discontinued.

Rarely was General Moore able to secure the services of the few remaining aircraft to fly reconnaissance. When he did the results were most gratifying. One such occasion came on 9 February, when Capt. Jesus A. Villamor, in an obsolete Philippine Army training plane equipped with a camera, set out to take photographs of the Ternate area. Protecting his slow and unarmed biplane were six P-40's. Villamor completed his mission, but on the way back the formation was attacked by six enemy fighters. While Villamor came in with his precious photographs, the P-40's engaged the enemy in a spectacular fight over Bataan. In the space of a few minutes the American pilots brought down four of the enemy fighters and fatally damaged the remaining two. Only one P-40 was lost. [25] Meanwhile the photographs taken by Villamor were printed and rushed to Corregidor where they were collated with reports from observers on the ground. The counterbattery fire that followed proved remarkably accurate and several direct hits were scored.

The difficulties of counterbattery fire were further increased when the Japanese moved their guns to the Pico de Loro hills

---

[24] *Ibid.*, entry of 15 Feb 42. The italics are Colonel Bunker's.

[25] Ind, *Bataan: The Judgment Seat*, pp. 288–92.

where they could be reached only by high trajectory fire. Few of the coastal guns in the harbor defenses, which had been designed for use against warships, had sufficient elevation to clear the high ground before the enemy positions. Their difficulty is illustrated by the experience of the men of Battery Hearn on 21 March, who, "in a desperate effort to silence the Japs," opened fire with their 12-inch guns. "We wound up," Colonel Bunker wrote, "with our guns elevated against the elevation stops—and that wasn't any too much." [26]

The only weapon in the armament of the harbor defenses with the high trajectory required to deliver effective counterbattery fire under these circumstances was the 12-inch mortar. There were twenty-two of these pieces on the four islands, but their usefulness against land targets was limited by the lack of sound ranging equipment and the shortage of ammunition with instantaneous fuzes. There was an ample supply of armor-piercing, fixed, delay fuze ammunition with a small bursting charge. This type was designed for use by coast artillery against warships but was of little use in the situation the Seaward Defenses then faced. These shells buried themselves deep in the earth before exploding and caused little damage to men and installations near by. The ideal ammunition against the targets presented by the Japanese guns on the Cavite shore was the personnel type with instantaneous point detonating fuze. There were about 1,000 such shells, of 12-inch caliber and weighing 670 pounds, but even this small amount could not be used freely, for it would be desperately needed when Bataan fell and the enemy placed his heavy guns on the slopes of the Mariveles Mountains.

A small quantity of additional instantaneous fuze ammunition was obtained as a result of experiments made by Colonel Bunker. He modified the fuze of the 1,070-pound shells used in the 12-inch guns by removing the .05-second delay pellet, thus detonating the shell more quickly. When he test-fired two such shells he got "beautiful results, up to my wildest hopes." The effect, he noted, was equal to that of a personnel shell, "both in dirt thrown up and in noise made." [27] But though the modified projectile exploded on impact, it had only a small bursting charge and a limited effect. Thus, despite every effort to secure effective counterbattery fire, the Americans were never able to prevent the Japanese from firing almost at will.

The artillery duel which had begun early in February came to an end on 22 March. Though the Americans reported artillery fire from the Cavite shore until early in April, it could not have come from the *Hayakawa Detachment*. That force had been disbanded on the 22d and its elements ordered to rejoin their parent units for the final attack against Bataan, then about to open. Whatever guns remained behind were of smaller caliber and were intended only to annoy the defenders.

Life Under Siege

Since the first air attacks at the end of December the garrisons of the four fortified islands had worked steadily to repair the damages and improve their positions. On Corregidor a tunnel, begun in 1921 but discontinued because of treaty agreements, was rapidly pushed to completion to serve as a command post for the Seaward Defenses. The island's defenses were further

---

[26] Bunker, Diary, entry of 21 Mar 42.

[27] *Ibid.*, entry of 5 Mar 42.

strengthened by the addition of an 8-inch gun with a range of 24,000 yards and a 360-degree traverse. This gun was brought over from Bataan and mounted on a prepared concrete base near Malinta. Though it was tested and ready for use by 4 March, no crew was available and the gun never fired a shot at the enemy. At Fort Hughes, one 155-mm. gun facing the sea was dismounted, moved through the tunnel, and emplaced on the opposite side of the island, pointing toward Bataan.

Vital installations were strengthened in various ways. Around the large well at the west end of Malinta Tunnel the engineers placed a circular parapet of sandbags, and over the gasoline storage area on Morrison Hill they placed two feet of heavily reinforced concrete, which they then camouflaged. Similar protection was given the Harbor Defenses telephone exchange at Topside. Near the entrance to Malinta Tunnel and in the port area at Bottomside, the engineers constructed tank obstacles consisting of square concrete posts reinforced with steel rails. About the same time, they placed roofs over the 75-mm. guns supporting the beach defense troops to give them protection against dive bombers.

Shortcomings in the design and location of various installations had become apparent by this time and these were corrected when the intensity of the enemy fire declined. Early plans had not taken into consideration the possibility of artillery fire from the Cavite shore and some of the tunnel entrances now faced the oncoming shells. After one attack Colonel Bunker checked his firing data and concluded that the main entrance to the Seaward Defenses command post "now points exactly along the Jap trajectory." [28] Where possible, other openings were constructed, but in most cases protection was provided by baffle walls.

With the technical advice of the engineers practically all the batteries began to build their own tunnels. Some dug tunnels where there was no apparent reason for one. "We have to be at our gun practically all the time," observed one battery commander, whose men were hard at work on a tunnel, "so we may not be able to spend too much time, if any at all, in a tunnel." [29] Even the troops on beach defense caught the fever and, with whatever materials they could beg or borrow, dug tunnels and constructed overhead protection. "It is safe to venture a guess," wrote the engineer cautiously, "that if all the tunnels constructed on Corregidor after hostilities commenced were connected end to end the resultant summation would not be less than two miles." [30]

Life on the four fortified islands in Manila Bay settled into a dreary routine. When the men were not building fortifications or going about their daily chores, they had little to do. Complaints were frequent and often dealt with the subject of food. The ration had been cut in half on 5 January, at the same time it had been cut on Bataan. The more enterprising of the men found ways of their own to increase the amount and vary the monotony of the ration, but the opportunities were fewer than on Bataan. Sunken or damaged barges washed close to shore offered a profitable field for exploitation during the early days of the campaign. One unit filled its trucks with a cargo of dried fruits salvaged from one such barge and stored it

---

[28] *Ibid.*, entry of 25 Mar 42.
[29] Ames, Diary, note to ltr of 24 Jan 42.
[30] Harbor Defenses Rpt of Opns, Exhibit E, p. 4.

away for future use. "Now," wrote Colonel Bunker, "if they'll only drink a lot of water, they'll be fixed fine." [31]

Some even managed to procure liquor in this way. One of the barges sent out from Manila just before the Japanese occupation had been loaded with whiskey from the Army and Navy Club. It was sunk in shallow water and many of the men spent their off-duty hours diving in the oil-coated waters in the hope of bringing up a bottle. Before the military police took over to relieve the lucky divers of their catch as they reached the shore, a large number of soldiers had laid in a stock of the precious commodity.[32] President Quezon's yacht is also said to have supplied at least one unit with a store of fine wine. When it was being unloaded one dark night, it is reported that an officer directed the dock hands to load two trucks simultaneously. When the job was finished, one of the trucks silently disappeared into the night with its valuable cargo, never to be seen again.[33]

Life everywhere on the islands went underground and the symbol of the new mole-like existence was Malinta Tunnel. "Everyone who doesn't need to be elsewhere," observed Captain Ames, "was in a tunnel—chiefly Malinta." [34] During the bombings it was always jammed with Americans and Filipinos who huddled back against the boxes of food and ammunition stacked along the sides to a height of six feet. Crowded into the tunnel were the highest headquarters in the Philippines, the lawful government of the Commonwealth, the 1,000-bed hospital, vast quantities of supplies, power plants, machinery, and other vital installations. One lateral alone was taken over by USAFFE. Here General MacArthur had a desk, before which were lined up his staff officers' desks. To the rear were the double-decker beds where the staff slept. Malinta also housed those dignitaries who had been evacuated from Manila. The civilians followed the routine of the military garrison, but an exception was made for the women, who were assigned special facilities in an area known as the "ladies' lateral." [35]

For the men outside, a trip through the tunnel was an interesting experience and never failed to rouse wonder. Milling about were Philippine and American government officials, officers of all services and all ranks, nurses in white starched uniforms, war correspondents, laborers, repair and construction crews, barbers, convalescents, and frightened soldiers in search of safety. "It is a revelation to walk through these tunnels," wrote Captain Ames to his wife. "At one time you are rubbing elbows with the daughter of some P.I. [Philippine] official, dodging a lady war correspondent, talking to a naval officer, being jostled by a plumber, . . . and having your shoes mopped by some Filipino janitor." [36]

Outside the tunnel the men encountered unusual and sometimes strange sights. President Quezon, ill with tuberculosis and confined to a wheel chair, spent as much time as he could outside the dust-laden tunnel, as did the U.S. High Commissioner Francis B. Sayre. On 30 December a small group wit-

---

[31] Bunker, Diary, entry of 9 Jan 42. Captain Ames also mentioned the shipment of dried fruit in his diary on 6 January.

[32] Ames, Diary, 6 Jan 42.

[33] This story was picked up from several participants and cannot be supported by direct references to sources or interviews.

[34] Ltr, Ames to his wife, 12 Jan 42, in Ames, Diary.

[35] Amea Willoughby, *I Was on Corregidor*, pp. 103–04, 134–40.

[36] Ltr, Ames to his wife, 12 Jan 42, in Ames, Diary.

USAFFE HEADQUARTERS IN MALINTA TUNNEL. *General MacArthur with General Sutherland, March 1942.*

nessed Quezon's second inauguration in an impressive ceremony at the mouth of the tunnel and listened to speeches by the President, the High Commissioner, and General MacArthur. Some saw, too, larger sums of money and more gold than they had ever imagined in their youthful dreams of pirate treasure chests. But values change in war and they watched without visible emotion the unloading of the gold, silver, and securities of the Philippine treasury on the Corregidor docks and their removal to a strong room deep in the tunnel.

Life on the islands had its seamier side. Not all men were brave and each garrison had its share of "tunnel rats," the taunt reserved for those who never left the safety of Malinta Tunnel. Such men were said to have "tunnelitis," a disease characterized by a furtive manner and the sallow complexion associated with those who live underground. For these men, those outside the tunnel had only contempt, tinged perhaps with envy. "We say of them," wrote one of those on the outside, "that they will lose tunnel-credit if they are seen outside the tunnel. And we josh them about the DTS medal (Distinguished Tunnel Service) . . . if they gather plenty of tunnel credits. As opposed to shell-shocked, we say of confirmed 'tunneleers' that they are shelter-shocked." [37]

Such unfair judgments were perhaps inevitable where some men were exposed to danger and others, by reason of their assignment, enjoyed the safety—and discomfort—of Malinta Tunnel. Nerves wore thin during the enforced intimacy of the prolonged

[37] *Ibid.*, 6 Feb 42. See also Hanson Baldwin, "The Fourth Marines at Corregidor," Part 2, *Marine Corps Gazette* (December 1946), pp. 27–28.

siege, and there were few opportunities for recreation. During their idle moments men discussed the most fantastic rumors, deplored the lack of support from the United States, and commented smugly about the invariably misinformed "brass hats in Malinta Tunnel." And always the men exercised the immemorial right of the soldier to "gripe." The days passed thus with monotonous and dreary regularity, filled with work, idle conversation, and speculation about the future.

The Second Aerial Bombardment

Early in January, it will be recalled, *Imperial General Headquarters* had transferred the bulk of the *5th Air Group* out of the Philippines, leaving General Homma with only a small air force whose major mission was to support ground operations on Bataan. A month later, after *14th Army* had been badly beaten in its efforts to gain a quick victory on the Orion–Bagac line, Homma had received large reinforcements, including Army and Navy air units. From Malaya had come two heavy bombardment regiments, the *60th* and *62d,* with a total of sixty twin-engine bombers. This single accretion alone tripled Homma's air strength. In addition, the Navy had sent two squadrons of Bettys (land-based, twin-engine bombers), one squadron of Zekes (fighters), and one squadron of carrier-based bombers to the Philippines, thus making available for the offensive of late March and early April a considerably augmented air force.[38]

Homma's plan for the final assault against the defenders of Bataan had provided for a heavy artillery and aerial preparation, starting on 24 March and continuing until victory was achieved. To the air forces he had assigned a threefold mission: to support the advance of ground units, bomb forward and rear installations, and cut the line of supply between Bataan and Corregidor. All aircraft were given targets on Bataan; but the *60th* and *62d Heavy Bombardment Regiments* and the Navy were directed to bomb Corregidor as well. Careful plans were made for the period from 24 to 28 March and an agreement was concluded between the Army and Navy which made possible a unified plan of air action and the joint bombardment of targets by the aircraft of both services. After the 28th the bulk of the heavy bombers were to concentrate on Bataan, but, "in order to demoralize the enemy and to boost the fighting spirit of our army," a small number of planes would continue to bomb Corregidor every few hours around the clock.[39]

The aerial attack opened on schedule simultaneously with the artillery preparation on Bataan, at dawn of the 24th, when the first of the Army's six bomber squadrons rose from Clark Field and headed toward Corregidor. At the same time two navy squadrons (twenty-four Bettys) stood by to take off from their base at Clark near Manila to join in the attack. At 0924 the air-raid alarm, the seventy-seventh of the campaign, sounded on Corregidor. One minute later, the first enemy flight of nine Army bombers came over the island to drop their 550- and 1,100-bombs. They were followed by the remaining Army squadrons which, in turn, gave way to the Navy's planes. The attack continued during the day and that night, when three more planes made a nuisance raid against the island. Alto-

[38] This account of Japanese air plans and operations is based upon *5th Gp Opns,* pp. 59–76; *14th Army Opns,* I, 129–36; Comments of Former Japanese Officers Regarding The Fall of the Philippines, p. 74, OCMH.

[39] *5th Air Gp Opns,* p. 60.

gether, forty-five of the sixty twin-engine bombers of the *60th* and *62d Heavy Bombardment Regiments* and the two squadrons of naval land-based bombers participated in the first day's attack to drop a total of seventy-one tons of bombs.

The next day the Japanese sent only three Army squadrons, twenty-seven planes, against Corregidor; the Navy, a similar number. This pattern continued until the 29th, the Navy planes alternating with the Army bombers. In addition small groups of planes came in over Corregidor every two or three hours "to carry out the psychological warfare and destroy the strong points, without failure." [40] The routine bombings continued steadily until 1 April, with at least one Army squadron attacking during the day and another at night. The Navy planes, which had no missions on Bataan, continued their bombardment of the island fortress in undiminished strength.

For the men on Corregidor it seemed as though they were living "in the center of a bull's-eye." [41] During the last week of March there were about sixty air-raid alarms lasting for a total of seventy-four hours. Bombings begun in the morning were usually resumed in the afternoon and again at night. Since the Japanese planes were now based on Clark Field or near Manila, they were able to remain over the target for longer periods than they had during the first bombardment in December. A graphic picture of the intensity of the bombardment can be gained from General Moore's summary of the first day's action.

24 March:
0707—Batteries Woodruff [Ft. Hughes, 14-inch guns], Marshall [Ft. Drum, 14-inch

guns], and Koehler [Ft. Frank, 12-inch mortars] opened fire on Cavite targets.
0924—Air Raid Alarm No. 77 sounded.
0925—Nine heavy bombers, a new type in the area, bombed Middleside and Morrison Hill.
0945—Twenty-seven heavy bombers came in over tail of Corregidor and bombed Middleside, closely followed by 17 heavies bombing Topside.
0950—Twenty-five planes followed by 9 more made another attack. Meanwhile, artillery shells from enemy batteries in Cavite were bursting on Corregidor.
Several fires were started, communication cable and water mains cut, and an ammunition dump of 75-mm. shells on Morrison Hill was set off. These shells were exploding for hours. Battery Wheeler [12-inch guns] had a direct bomb hit on the racer of No. 1 gun putting it out of action temporarily.
1110—All clear sounded.
1435—Air Raid Alarm No. 78. Nine heavy bombers approached Corregidor from the southeast. Bombs dropped on Kindley Field.
1438—Seven more planes from southeast with more bombs. Shelling from mainland also.
1529—All Clear.
1552—Air Raid Alarm No. 79. Nine heavy bombers hit Kindley Field again.
1620—All Clear.
1640—Air Raid Alarm No. 80. Mariveles and Cabcaben areas [Bataan] hit by 9 heavies.
1703—All Clear.
2053—Air Raid Alarm No. 81.
2115—First night air raid. Two medium bombers dropped incendiary bombs in Cheney Ravine, Corregidor. Later returned and bombed Bottomside. No damage reported.
2234—All Clear. [42]

The effect of so heavy a bombardment over the period of seven days might well have been disastrous had not the men profited from the earlier air attacks and built underground shelters. They had also learned how effectively sand could cushion

---

[40] *Ibid.,* p. 65.
[41] Tisdelle, Diary, entry of 3 Jan 42.

[42] Harbor Defenses Rpt of Opns, pp. 46–47.

the blow from a bomb and had made liberal use of sandbags. "It used to be hard to get the men to fill sandbags," wrote one officer. "Now it is hard to keep them from laying hands on all the sandbags available and filling them when those to whom they are allotted aren't looking." [43] The small number of casualties is ample evidence of the thoroughness with which the Corregidor garrison had dug in since the first attack on 29 December.

Installations of all kinds and critical supplies had also been placed under bombproof protection, and these suffered little damage during the bombardment. The few remaining surface installations, however, and supplies in open storage did not fare so well. On Bottomside, the theater, post exchange, and bakery were leveled to the ground and the Navy's radio station damaged. Wainwright's house, inherited from MacArthur, was destroyed on the first day of the attack. "I picked up the light walking stick which MacArthur had left for me," wrote Wainwright, "and walked down to Malinta Tunnel to live there the rest of my time on Corregidor." [44] Several ammunition dumps were hit, exploding the shells in storage, and a quantity of TNT blown up. But losses, on the whole, were small and were quickly repaired by crews which cleared the roads and cleaned out the debris left by exploding bombs.

The Japanese, too, seemed to have profited by their earlier experience and had "learned," Captain Ames observed, "to dodge AA fire." [45] They came in at higher altitudes than before, between 22,000 and 28,000 feet, in formations of nine planes or less. During daylight they made their bombing runs out of the sun, changing course and altitude immediately after the moment of release. Earlier the antiaircraft gun batteries had been able to get in about ten salvos before the Japanese flew out of range, usually bringing down the lead plane of the formation. When the enemy changed his tactics, the antiaircraft guns could get in fewer salvos and could no longer count on the lead plane maintaining the same course.

Under ideal conditions antiaircraft guns form a ring around the defended area, or a line in front of it, from where they can strike enemy aircraft before they reach the objective. On Corregidor it was not possible, for obvious reasons, "to follow the book." The antiaircraft guns could not engage the enemy until he was almost over the island. Moreover, by being located on the target, they became "part of what is being bombed," with the result that their efficiency and freedom of fire was limited most at the moment of greatest need. "Naturally our job is to fire on the bombers," wrote Captain Ames, ". . . and if possible prevent the bombing. Fire we do, but prevent the bombing we cannot." In a letter which never reached his wife he graphically explained the difficulty which beset all the antiaircraft men.

The bombers come over; we see them drop their bombs—all the while we are tracking them with our instruments—our guns point upward more and more steeply; the bombs continue downward on their way towards us. Then our indicators show that the bombers are "in range". We open fire. In about 15 seconds our guns are pointing as nearly straight up as they can, and hit the mechanical stop. We cease firing. The bombs whistle; we duck for a few seconds while the bombs burst, and pop up again to engage the next flight. When fighters come in one after another we stay up while the bombs hit all around us. . . .

Some of the bombers come in higher than we can shoot. In such cases we vainly wait for

[43] Ames, Diary, entry of 26 Mar 42, and ltr to his wife, 8 Jan 42.

[44] Wainwright, *General Wainwright's Story*, p. 74.

[45] Ames, Diary, entry of 24 Mar 42.

our indicators to show "in range", and take cover (duck behind our splinterproofs) just as the bombs begin to whistle.[46]

The most serious limitations on the effectiveness of the 3-inch guns arose from the shortage of mechanically fuzed ammunition, which could reach to a height of 30,000 feet. There was an adequate supply of ammunition with the powder train fuze, effective to a height of about 24,000 feet, but only enough of the longer range type for one of the ten antiaircraft batteries. On 3 February a submarine had brought in 2,750 more rounds of mechanically fuzed ammunition, and it became possible to supply an additional battery. Thus, when the enemy planes came in at an altitude of more than 24,000 feet, only two batteries could reach them. The remaining batteries of the antiaircraft command, equipped with powder train fuzes, could only watch idly while the Japanese leisurely dropped their bombs. Nonetheless, the contribution of these batteries, though negative, was a valuable one. By forcing the enemy to remain at extremely high altitude, they decreased his accuracy and diminished the effectiveness of the bombardment.

From the outset it had been necessary to conserve even the powder train fuzed shells, 30 percent of which were duds. This had been accomplished by limiting each gun to six rounds for any single target on any given course. The opening weeks of the war proved the most expensive in terms of rounds fired to planes destroyed, 500 rounds being required for each plane. This inaccurate fire was due to inexperience, the irregular functioning of powder train fuzes, and variation in the muzzle velocity. Between 8 December and 11 March the 3-inch gun batteries in the harbor defenses expended

over 6,000 rounds for a total of 52 aircraft knocked down, or about 120 rounds per plane. With increased experience of both fire control crews and gunners and improved fire discipline, this average was steadily bettered until, by the beginning of April, the expenditure rate went under 100 rounds per plane, an excellent score even under the most favorable conditions.

In February an effort was made to use the 12-inch mortars for antiaircraft fire in the hope that a salvo from these pieces, bursting in the midst of the enemy formation, would discourage mass bombing. The 670-pound shells were first fitted with the powder train fuze but the shell would not explode. Next, the 155-mm. shrapnel and the mechanical antiaircraft fuze were tried, but they failed also to detonate the charge. "If it can be made to work," thought Colonel Bunker, "it will sure jolt the Japs." [47] But the problem was never solved, and at the end of the campaign Ordnance still did not know whether the 12-inch shell would not explode because of the low rotational velocity or the size of booster charge in the fuze.

With the second aerial bombardment of Corregidor the Japanese for the first time resorted to night bombing. During this period they made twenty-three such attacks, delivered by small groups of bombers from an altitude of 24,000 to 27,000 feet. In almost every case the searchlight batteries illuminated the planes before they reached the bomb release line. Many of the pilots seemed to be confused by the lights and turned away to approach from another direction; others jettisoned their bombs or

---

[46] Ltr, Ames to his wife, 20 Jan 42, Ames, Diary.

[47] Bunker, Diary, entry of 20 Mar 42. This scheme and the efforts to put it into effect were neither supported nor indorsed by Colonel Chase, the antiaircraft commander, who regarded the entire project as, "to say the least, fantastic." Chase, Comments on Draft MS, pp. 23–24, OCMH.

abandoned the attack altogether. Those that got through were apparently too nervous and too anxious to get back to bomb with any accuracy. On the whole, the night attacks proved ineffective and after 6 April were discontinued.

By the beginning of April, the aerial bombardment was virtually over. Little additional damage had been received and comparatively few casualties had been suffered by the men who had had two months to prepare. All eyes were now turned to Bataan, upon which the Japanese had concentrated their entire air and artillery strength in preparation for the final assault. For the next ten days, while the fight for Bataan ran its grim course to a bloody and tragic end, the men on Corregidor and its sister fortresses were granted a brief respite. Their turn, they knew, would come soon.

CHAPTER XXVIII

The Southern Islands

As long as the decisive struggle for control of the Philippines was being fought on Luzon, the islands to the south were safe from invasion. At no time during the first four months of the war did General Homma have sufficient troops to conduct operations simultaneously in both areas. Having established a foothold on Mindanao, at Davao, late in December, he had been forced to limit operations in the south to air and naval reconnaissance. It was not until April, as the Bataan campaign was drawing to a close, that Homma had a large enough force to embark on the conquest of the southern islands. The opening gun of this campaign sounded on 10 April, one day after the Bataan campaign ended. (*Map 1*)

The Islands and Their Defense

Mindanao, the southernmost island in the Philippine Archipelago, has an area of more than 36,000 square miles and is second in size to Luzon. Its coast line is irregular and its bays afford shelter at many places for a hostile fleet. Much of the beach line is flat and two large river valleys offer easy routes of advance into the interior. The Zamboanga Peninsula jutting westward from the center of the island into the Sulu Sea is virtually indefensible and easily cut off at its narrow neck from the rest of Mindanao. Along the northeast coast is the Diuata Mountain range; in the wild and largely unexplored interior extinct volcanoes rise to formidable heights.[1]

Transportation and communications on Mindanao were greatly inferior to those on Luzon. There were no railroads on the island and only two highways. The longest of these, Route 1, followed a circuitous route from Digos on the east coast across the narrow waist of Mindanao to Cotabato then northward to the northeast tip of the island. The stretch of road between that point and Davao was still under construction in 1941. Route 3, named the Sayre Highway in honor of the Philippine High Commissioner, extended southward through central Mindanao for a distance of about 100 miles, linking the northern and southern arms of Route 1. The northern stretch of the road was well surfaced and usable in all weather, but the southern portion had a clay surface which, after a rain, "reminded one of the glutinous stuff found near the Black Hills in South Dakota."[2]

Additional means of transportation on Mindanao were provided by small vessels,

---

[1] The physical description of the islands south of Luzon is based upon Civil Affairs Handbook: Philippine Islands, Vols. I–XII, ASF Manual M 365-1 to 12.

[2] Col William H. Braddock, Rpt of Force Surgeon, Visayan-Mindanao Force, in V-MF Rpt of Opns, p. 550, Annex XI, USAFFE-USFIP Rpt of Opns. The Visayan-Mindanao Force Report contains, in addition to General Sharp's report, the reports of unit and sector commanders, listed as appendixes but numbered seriatim.

which moved freely along the coast and up the island's two large navigable rivers, the Agusan and Rio Grande de Mindanao. The first flows north through a wide and marshy valley on the inland side of the Diuata Mountains on the east coast to empty into the Mindanao Sea. The second, called simply the Mindanao River, flows south and west through central Mindanao, parallel to the Sayre Highway and Route 1, to empty into Moro Gulf at Cotabato.

Between Mindanao and Luzon lie the islands of the Visayan group, the most important of which are Cebu, Panay, Negros, Leyte, and Samar. Most of these islands consist of a central mountain area surrounded by coastal plains. Panay, split north and south by a comparatively large central plain between two mountain ranges, has the largest level area of the group. Cebu, the most mountainous, has the least.

The road net throughout the Visayas is generally the same: a primary coastal road all or part way around each island, with auxiliary roads linking important points in the interior to the ports along the coast. None of these roads, in 1941, had more than two lanes, and most were poorly surfaced and winding. On the most highly developed of the islands—Cebu, Negros, and Panay—there were short stretches of railroad. Coastal shipping supplemented the road and rail system in the islands and linked the islands of the Visayan group with each other and with Mindanao.

The defense of Mindanao and the Visayas—comprising a land area half again as large as Luzon—rested with the Visayan-Mindanao Force, commanded by Brig. Gen. William F. Sharp, who had his headquarters initially on Cebu. This force was composed almost entirely of Philippine

Army troops. Of the five divisions mobilized, in the south, only three, the 61st, 81st, and 101st, remained in the area. The other two divisions, the 71st and 91st, moved to Luzon, leaving behind their last mobilized regiments, the 73d and 93d. In addition, a large number of provisional units and some Constabulary units were formed on the outbreak of the war.

General Sharp's problems were similar to those faced by the commanders on Luzon. His untrained men lacked personal and organizational equipment of all types. There were not enough uniforms, blankets, or mosquito bars to go around, and though each man had a rifle—the Enfield '17—not all understood its use. Moreover, many of the rifles were defective and quickly broke down. Machine guns of .30- and .50-caliber were issued, but many of these were defective also and had to be discarded. Spare parts for all weapons were lacking and guns that ordinarily would have been easily repaired had to be abandoned. There were no antitank guns, grenades, gas masks, or steel helmets for issue, and the supply of ammunition was extremely limited.[3]

General Sharp's most serious shortage was in artillery weapons. At the start of the war he had not a single piece in his entire command and as a result organized the artillery components of his divisions as infantry. On 12 December he received from Manila eight old 2.95-inch mountain guns, three of which were lost two weeks later at

---

[3] The account of shortages in the Visayan-Mindanao Force is based on V-MF Rpt of Opns, pp. 16–26, 41–42, 47–48, 68–71; Gen Chynoweth, 61st Div (PA) and Visayan Force Rpt, pp. 1–7, OCMH; Col Hiram W. Tarkington, There Were Others, Chs. I–II. The last is a manuscript volume which Colonel Tarkington has made available to the author.

MAJ. GEN. WILLIAM F. SHARP AND HIS STAFF, 1942. *Back row, standing left to right: Maj. Paul D. Phillips (ADC) and Capt. W. F. O'Brien (ADC). Front row, sitting left to right: Lt. Col. W. S. Robinson (G-3), Lt. Col. Robert D. Johnston (G-4), Col. John W. Thompson (CofS), General Sharp (CG), Col. Archibald M. Mixson (DCofS), Lt. Col. Howard R. Perry, Jr. (G-1), Lt. Col. Charles I. Humber (G-2), and Maj. Max Weil (Hq Comdt and PM).*

Davao. The remaining five pieces constituted Sharp's entire artillery support throughout the campaign.

To alleviate the shortages in clothing, spare parts for weapons, and other equipment, factories, staffed and operated by Filipinos, were established. They were able to turn out such diverse items as shoes, hand grenades, underwear, and extractors for the Enfield. Unfortunately there was no way to manufacture small-arms ammunition or artillery pieces, and these remained critical items until the end.

General Sharp's mission, initially, was to defend the entire area south of Luzon. When organized resistance was no longer practicable, he was to split his force into small groups and conduct guerilla warfare from hidden bases in the interior of each island. Food, ammunition, fuel, and equipment, were to be moved inland, out of reach of the enemy, in preparation for such a contingency. Those supplies that could not be moved were to be destroyed.[4]

At the end of December, after he had made his decision to withdraw to Bataan, General MacArthur informed the Visayan-Mindanao Force commander that he could expect no further aid from Luzon and instructed him to transfer the bulk of his

---

[4] V-MF Rpt of Opns, pp. 26–28.

troops to Mindanao for the defense of that island and its important airfield at Del Monte.[5] The move to Mindanao began immediately and was completed early in January. With Sharp's headquarters and most of the troops on Mindanao, the Visayas assumed a secondary importance in the defense of the south. In the event of attack it would be virtually impossible to reinforce any of the islands in that group from Mindanao. Each of the six defended islands—Cebu, Panay, Negros, Leyte, Samar, and Bohol—was now dependent upon its own garrison and resources to meet a Japanese invasion.[6]

The organization of the Visayan-Mindanao Force established early in January lasted only about one month. On 4 February, in an effort to facilitate the delivery of supplies expected shortly from Australia, USAFFE assumed direct control of the garrisons on Panay and Mindoro, both a part of General Sharp's command. A month later, a week before MacArthur's departure for Australia, the remaining Visayan garrisons were separated from General Sharp's command which was then redesignated the Mindanao Force. The five garrisons in the Visayas were then organized into the Visayan Force and placed under Brig. Gen. Bradford G. Chynoweth, who had commanded on Panay. As coequal commanders, Sharp and Chynoweth reported directly to higher headquarters on Corregidor.[7] This separation of the Visayan-Mindanao Force clearly reflected MacArthur's desire to insure the most effective defense of Mindanao,

which he hoped to use as a base for his promised return to the Philippines.

Japanese planning for operations in the south did not begin until late in the campaign. The initial *14th Army* plan for the conquest of the Philippines contained only brief references to Mindanao and the Visayas, which were expected to fall quickly once Manila was taken. During the months that followed the first landing, Homma showed little interest in the islands south of Luzon. But even had he desired to move into that area, he would have been unable to do so. In February the campaign on Bataan had reached a stalemate. *Imperial General Headquarters,* informed of Homma's situation and worried over his slow progress, pressed for an early end to the Philippine campaign and finally, early in March, sent the needed reinforcements. With them came orders to begin operations in the south concurrently with those against Bataan and Corregidor.[8]

It was several weeks before the troops scheduled for use in the south reached the Philippines. The first contingent came from Borneo and arrived at Lingayen Gulf on 1 April. It consisted of *Headquarters, 35th Brigade,* and the *124th Infantry,* both from the *18th Division.* Led by Maj. Gen. Kiyotake Kawaguchi, the brigade commander, this force, with the addition of *14th Army* supporting and service troops, was organized into a separate detachment known as the *Kawaguchi Detachment.* Four days later elements of the *5th Division* from Malaya, consisting of the headquarters of Maj. Gen. Saburo Kawamura's *9th Infantry Brigade* and the *41st Infantry,* reached Lin-

---

[5] For MacArthur's views on the importance of Mindanao, see above, Chapter XIV.

[6] V-MF Rpt of Opns, pp. 62–63.

[7] *Ibid.,* pp. 6–7, 29–33, 44–45; ltr, Sutherland to Chynoweth, 3 Feb 42, sub: Instructions, AG 430 (25 Dec 41) Phil Rcds.

[8] Statement of Col Takushiro Hattori, in Statements of Japanese Officials on World War II, I, 316; *Southern Army* Hist, pp. 14, 17; Hist, *Army Sec, Imperial GHQ,* pp. 42–43.

gayen. With these troops, augmented by service and supporting troops, Homma formed the *Kawamura Detachment*. These two detachments, plus the *Miura Detachment* already at Davao, constituted the entire force assigned the conquest of the southern Philippines.[9]

The Visayas

The creation of the Visayan Force on 4 March had brought a change in commanders and a renewed vigor to the preparations for a prolonged defense of the islands in the Visayan group. In the force were about 20,000 men organized into five separate garrisons, each with its own commander. The largest of these was Col. Albert F. Christie's Panay Force which consisted of the 61st Division (PA), less the 61st and 62d Infantry, and the 61st Field Artillery which Sharp had taken to Mindanao. To replace these units, the island commander had organized the 64th and 65th Provisional Infantry Regiments. The addition of miscellaneous Constabulary troops brought the total of Christie's garrison to about 7,000 men.

Col. Irvine C. Scudder, commander of the troops on Cebu, where Visayan Force headquarters was located, had about 6,500 troops, including the 82d and 83d Infantry (PA), the Cebu Military Police Regiment, a Philippine Army Air Corps detachment, and miscellaneous units. On Negros were about 3,000 troops under the command of Col. Roger B. Hilsman, who had led the force opposing the Japanese landing at Davao. Leyte and Samar were held by a hastily improvised force of 2,500 men led by Col. Theodore M. Cornell, and Bohol by

about 1,000 men under Lt. Col. Arthur J. Grimes.[10]

General Homma's preoccupation with Bataan gave General Chynoweth, the Visayan Force commander, an additional month in which to make his preparations. Much had already been accomplished when he assumed command, and under his direction the defenses were rapidly brought to completion. On Cebu and Panay, where the defenses were most elaborate, the men had constructed tank obstacles, trenches, and gun emplacements, strung wire, and prepared demolitions. Airfield construction was pushed rapidly on all the islands. Panay alone had eight. Negros had an air and sea warning system and was able to alert the other garrisons of the approach of enemy planes and ships. Most of the work on these and other defenses was done by civilians, thus leaving the troops free to continue their training.[11]

Perhaps the most interesting feature of the preparations for the defense of the Visayas was the program known as Operation *Baus Au,* Visayan for "Get it Back." Initiated by General Chynoweth during his tenure as the commander of the Panay garrison and then adopted on Cebu, Operation *Baus Au* was the large-scale movement of goods, supplies, and weapons into the interior for use later in guerrilla warfare. Secret caches were established in remote and inaccessible places, and at mountain hideouts which could be reached only by steep, narrow trails barely passable for a man on foot.

---

[9] *14th Army* Opns, I, 214–15.

[10] V–MF Rpt of Opns, pp. 32–33, 79–81.

[11] Col Scudder, Rpt of Mil Activities in Cebu, 2 Dec 41–4 Mar 42, Col Cornell, Narrative of Events, Hq Samar–Leyte Sector, and Col Hilsman, Hist of the Negros Sector, all in V–MF Rpt of Opns, pp. 96, 397–98, 484, 490–92; Chynoweth, 61st Div (PA) and Visayan Force Rpt pp. 7, 11.

The 63d Infantry, which did most of the *cargador* work on Panay, adopted as its insignia a carabao sled loaded with a sack of rice and bearing the inscription *Baus Au.*[12]

The effect on the civilian population of Operation *Baus Au* and other measures for a prolonged defense in the interior was unfortunate. The Filipinos felt that they were being abandoned and their faith in the American protector was badly shaken. What they expected was a pitched battle at the beaches ending in the rout of the enemy. "They took great pride in their Army," noted Colonel Tarkington, "and having been indoctrinated for years with the idea of American invincibility, were all for falling on the enemy tooth and nail and hurling him back into the sea." [13]

Japanese knowledge of conditions in the Visayas was accurate and fairly complete. Though they did not know the exact disposition of the troops in the area, they knew which islands were defended and the approximate size of the defending force. Homma was confident that with the reinforcements from Malaya and Borneo he could seize the key islands in the group. His plan was to take Cebu with the *Kawaguchi Detachment* and Panay with the *Kawamura Detachment*. These two forces, in co-operation with the *Miura Detachment* at Davao, would then move on to take Mindanao. That island conquered, the remaining garrisons in the Philippines could be reduced at leisure if they did not surrender of their own accord.

No time was wasted in putting this plan into effect. On 5 April, four days after the *Kawaguchi Detachment* reached Lingayen

Gulf, it was aboard ship once more, headed for Cebu. With 4,852 trained and battle-tested troops, General *Kawaguchi* had little reason to fear the outcome.

The Cebu Landings

First word of the approach of the Japanese reached General Chynoweth on the afternoon of 9 April, during a meeting with his staff and unit commanders. Three Japanese cruisers and eleven transports, it was reported, were steaming for Cebu from the south. All troops were alerted and a close watch kept on the enemy flotilla. That night further news was received that the Japanese force had split in two, one, sailing along the west coast, the other along the east. By daylight the enemy vessels were plainly visible, with the larger of the convoys already close to the island's capital, Cebu City, midway up the east coast. Shortly after dawn the Japanese in this convoy landed at Cebu City; at about the same time the men in the other convoy came ashore in the vicinity of Toledo, on the opposite side of the island.[14]

Defending the capital, where Kawaguchi had landed the bulk of his troops, was the Cebu Military Police Regiment of about 1,100 men under the command of Lt. Col.

---

[12] Chynoweth, 61st Div (PA) and Visayan Force Rpt, pp. 7, 12–15; Tarkington, There Were Others, pp. 47–49.

[13] Tarkington, There Were Others, p. 48.

[14] The account of operations on Cebu is based upon: Chynoweth, 61st Div (PA) and Visayan Force Rpt, pp. 13, 16–24, 33; Tarkington, There Were Others, pp. 265–81; Scudder, Rpt of Mil Activities in Cebu, and Lt Col Howard J. Edmands, Rpt of Invasion of Cebu, last two in V-MF Rpt of Opns, pp. 401, 436–51.

The Japanese apparently made more than two landings but their exact number and location cannot be fixed with certainty. American sources list as many as seven landings along both coasts. The only available Japanese source simply states that the *Kawaguchi Detachment* landed "on the east coast of Cebu." *14th Army Opns*, I, 214.

PANAY

LEYTE

NEGROS

U

Toledo

B

CEBU CITY

Cantabaco

Naga   Talisay

E

C

BOHOL

0   25
        MILES

Howard J. Edmands. Edmands' mission, like that of other unit commanders on the island, was to hold only long enough to allow the demolition teams to complete their work, then fall back into the hills. "I had no idea of being able to stop the Japs," explained General Chynoweth, "but I thought we could spend two or three days in withdrawal." [15]

The fight for Cebu City lasted only one day. Faced by a foe superior in numbers and weapons, the defenders fell back slowly, fighting for the time needed to block the roads and destroy the bridges leading into the interior. By the afternoon the fight had reached the outskirts of the city and at 1700 the Japanese broke off the action. Under cover of darkness Edmands pulled his men back to previously selected positions about ten miles inland, along a ridge which commanded the approaches from Cebu City to the central mountain area. Though the Japanese were in undisputed control of the capital at the end of the day, Edmands had achieved his purpose. He had gained the time needed by the demolition teams, and his regiment was still intact and withdrawing in good order.

The Japanese enjoyed equal success that day on the west side of the island, in the neighborhood of Toledo. Western terminus of the cross-island highway, that town was an important military objective. But, on the assumption that the narrow channel along the west would discourage an enemy from landing there, only a small force, the 3d Battalion, 82d Infantry (PA), had been placed in that area. The Philippine Army battalion opposed the enemy landing vigorously but without success and finally fell back along the cross-island highway toward

the town of Cantabaco, leaving the Japanese in possession of Toledo.

At Cantabaco, midway across the island, the highway split in two. One branch turned northeast to pass close to Camp X, where General Chynoweth had his headquarters, then southeast to Talisay. The southern branch led into Naga. At both places there was a defending force of Filipinos whose route of withdrawal depended upon the security of Cantabaco. Should the Japanese pursuing the 3d Battalion, 82d Infantry, gain control of that town, the defenders would be cut off.

General Chynoweth appreciated fully the importance of Cantabaco to the defense of Cebu. Even before the Japanese landings, in anticipation of difficulty there, he had brought Colonel Grimes and his 3d Battalion, 83d Infantry, from Bohol to support the defenses of western Cebu. Now, on the afternoon of the 10th, he ordered Grimes to cover Cantabaco, and as an added precaution sent a messenger with orders to his reserve battalion in the north to move down to the threatened area. Grimes, "eager to get into the fray . . . started out with a gleam in his eye," and Chynoweth, confident that he had things reasonably well in hand, settled down for a good night's sleep. [16]

He got little rest that night. Time and again he was awakened by anxious staff officers who reported that the enemy was approaching from the direction of Cantabaco. Despite these reports Chynoweth remained confident. He had received no message from Grimes, and he felt sure that if the enemy had broken through at Cantabaco, Grimes would have sent word. Moreover, there had been no explosions to indicate that the demolition teams along the road were doing their work. He had in-

---

[15] Chynoweth, 61st Div (PA) and Visayan Force Rpt, p. 17.

[16] *Ibid.*

spected these demolitions himself and felt sure that if the enemy had passed Cantabaco, the charges would have been set off. But at 0330, when the sounds of battle became louder, Chynoweth's confidence began to wane. The enemy was undoubtedly nearing Camp X. A half hour later all doubts vanished when large groups of Filipinos, the outposts of Camp X, appeared in camp. They seemed hypnotized, fired in the air, and refused to obey commands in their haste to flee. After a brief conference with his staff, Chynoweth decided to pull back to an alternate command post on a ridge a half mile to the north and await developments there.

The collapse of the Cantabaco position had been the result of an unfortunate and unforeseen combination of events. The demolition teams in which Chynoweth had placed so much faith had waited too long and when the enemy appeared, led by tanks or armored cars, they had fled. Like his commander, Colonel Grimes believed that the enemy would be halted by blown bridges and obstacles along the road. Not hearing the sound of explosions, he, too, concluded that the Japanese were still at a safe distance. In his confidence he drove forward to familiarize himself with the terrain and was captured by an enemy patrol. Deprived of their commander, his men "stayed quite well hidden." [17] So well were they hidden that even the Japanese were unaware of their presence.

The reserve battalion had never even started south. The messengers sent to that battalion failed to return, and if the battalion commander did receive Chynoweth's order to move to Cantabaco, he never complied with it. Instead, the battalion moved

farther north, well out of reach of the enemy.

Opposed only by the retreating 3d Battalion, 82d Infantry, which was quickly dispersed, the Japanese had advanced swiftly from Toledo through Cantabaco and then along the Talisay and Naga roads. It was the Japanese force along the Talisay road that had scattered the Camp X outposts and forced upon Chynoweth the realization that his plans for the defenses of Cantabaco had miscarried.

With the enemy in possession of the cross-island highway, the fight for Cebu was over. Nothing more could be accomplished in central Cebu and on the night of the 12th, Chynoweth, with about 200 men, started north to his retreat in the mountains. From there he hoped to organize the few units still remaining on the island into an efficient guerrilla force. The Japanese did not claim the complete subjugation of the island until 19 April, but Wainwright had already conceded the loss of Cebu three days earlier when he ordered General Sharp to re-establish the Visayan-Mindanao Force and take command of the remaining garrisons in the Visayas. [18]

The Seizure of Panay

When General Chynoweth, the first commander of the Panay garrison, assumed command of the Visayan Force and moved to Cebu in mid-March, he had named as successor Colonel Christie, his chief of staff. Under Christie's leadership work on the island's defenses continued and by mid-

---

[17] Ibid., p. 23.

[18] Rads, Wainwright to Sharp, Sharp to Wainwright, No. A-43, and Wainwright to Christie, all dated 16 Apr 42, USFIP G-3 Journal, 19 Mar-19 Apr 42, AG 461 (1 Apr 42) Phil Rcds.

April preparations for the expected Japanese attack had been virtually completed.[19]

As on Cebu the plan of defense provided only for delaying action to allow the demolition teams to complete their work. The 61st Division (PA) and other troops on the islands, altogether 7,000 men, were to fall back to previously selected positions until they reached the mountains to the north. From there, well provided with the food and supplies gathered as a result of Operation *Baus Au,* Christie would wage guerrilla warfare against the enemy until such time as reinforcements arrived.

The enemy landing came at dawn, 16 April, and was made by the *Kawamura Detachment* of 4,160 men. The bulk of General Kawamura's troops came ashore at Iloilo, at the southeast corner of Panay, and a smaller force landed at Capiz to the north. Two days later a third landing was made at San Jose, along the southwest coast.[20] None of the landings was opposed. By 20 April General Kawamura had occupied the strategic points of the island, and so far as he was concerned the campaign was over.

For Colonel Christie, safe in his well-stocked mountain retreat, the campaign had just begun. Wild game was plentiful; he had ample fresh water, 500 head of cattle, 15,000 bags of rice, hundreds of cases of canned goods, and an adequate supply of fuel. Machine shops had been constructed in the mountains, and when his supply of rice gave out there was a mill to thresh more. Almost immediately he began to send his men out on hit-and-run raids. These so aroused the Japanese that they organized a punitive expedition at San Jose to capture Christie and destroy his headquarters. A Filipino agent sent warning of the Japanese plans and an ambush was prepared by a company of men armed only with bows and arrows, spears and bolos. Hidden along the sides of the pass leading to Christie's hideout, the Filipinos with their primitive weapons took the Japanese completely by surprise, killed many, and sent the rest posthaste back to San Jose. But the successes of guerrilla warfare could not disguise the fact that, with the principal towns and road net in their hands, the Japanese controlled the island.

By the seizure of Cebu and Panay, the Japanese had secured a firm grip on the most important islands in the Visayas. The forces still holding out on Negros, Samar, Leyte, and Bohol were considerably smaller than those already defeated and driven back into the hills, and the Japanese were confident that these islands could be occupied at will. By 20 April the campaign for the Visayas was, for all practical purposes, at an end, and General Homma was free to send the *Kawaguchi* and *Kawamura Detachments* against Mindanao.

Mindanao

The Japanese force that landed at Davao on 20 December had been a small one. It had consisted of two groups, one of which, the *Sakaguchi Detachment,* left soon after for Jolo Island and the Netherlands Indies. The other group, led by Lt. Col. Toshio Miura and consisting of the *1st Battalion,*

---

[19] The account of operations on Panay is based on Tarkington, There Were Others, pp. 297–306. The Visayan-Mindanao Force Report of Operations contains no report of activities on Panay after Chynoweth's departure, and none was prepared by Colonel Christie. Interv, author with Christie, 6 May 47. The only Japanese account is in *14th Army* Opns, I, 215.

[20] Rads, Wainwright to AGWAR, 16 Apr 42, and Del Monte, no sig, to Ft Mills, 20 Apr 42, both in USFIP G–3 Journal, 19 Mar–19 Apr 42, AG 461 (1 Apr 42) Phil Rcds.

33d Infantry, plus miscellaneous troops, had remained on Mindanao.[21] Time and again Colonel Miura had attempted to extend his control into the interior but without success. Indeed, had he not had air and artillery support and had his men not been equipped with automatic weapons, it is doubtful if he could have remained on the island.

Since General Sharp's arrival on Mindanao early in January much had been done to prepare the island's defenses. With the additional troops transferred from the Visayas, Sharp had organized the island into five defensive sectors: the Zamboanga Sector; the Lanao Sector, in the northwest; the Cagayan Sector, in the north-central portion of the island; the Agusan Sector, in the east; and the Cotabato-Davao Sector in the central and south portion of the island. The last was the largest of the sectors and was divided into three subsectors: Digos, Cotabato, and Carmen Ferry. To each sector was assigned a force of appropriate size whose commander reported directly to Mindanao Force headquarters at Del Monte, ten miles inland from the northern terminus of the Sayre Highway and adjacent to the Del Monte Airfield. (*Map 25*)

Despite occasional flurries along the Digos and Agusan fronts and, in March, some action in Zamboanga, which the Japanese occupied early that month, the troops on Mindanao continued their training.[22]

Individual and unit training continued at a steady pace and was supplemented by special instruction at a school in infantry tactics in central Mindanao. The school was staffed by Philippine Scouts of the 43d Infantry.[23]

The greatest drawback to the training program was the shortage of ammunition. The supply was so limited that its expenditure on the firing range was prohibited. Instead, the men spent long hours in simulated fire, with doubtful results. "A few rounds fired by the soldier," observed Colonel Tarkington, "would have demonstrated to him the capability of his weapon, acquainted him with its recoil, and paid dividends in steadier marksmanship." [24] Most of the men who fought on Mindanao never fired a live round before they went into battle.

While General Sharp sought to strengthen the defenses of Mindanao, the Japanese completed their plans for the seizure of the island. The plan finally adopted provided for a co-ordinated attack from three directions by separate forces toward a common center, followed by a quick mop-up of the troops in the outlying portions of the island. One of these forces, the *Miura Detachment,* was already on the island, on garrison duty at Davao and Digos, a short distance to the south. It was to be relieved by a battalion of the *10th Independent Garrison* and then strike out from Digos toward the Sayre Highway. Its route of advance would be northwest along Route 1, which intersected

---

[21] The landing at Davao is described above, in Chapter VI.

[22] The landing at Zamboanga was made by about 220 Japanese of the *32d Naval Base Force* on 2 March 1942 after a brief fight with Lt. Col. Albert T. Wilson's troops of the Zamboanga Sector. On 6 March Sharp ordered Wilson to withdraw to the mountains and conduct guerrilla operations. The Japanese, having secured the town of Zamboanga and established a seaplane base there, made no

effort to expand their control. Wilson, The Defense of Zamboanga, in V-MF Rpt of Opns, pp. 484–86; Japanese Landing at Zamboanga, ATIS Doc 62680, 20 Jul 51, Mil Hist Div, GHQ FEC, pp. 1–5.

[23] Inactive for many years, the 43d Infantry (PS) was reactivated with two companies, C and E, at the start of the war with Scouts from the 45th Infantry (PS) on duty at Zamboanga.

[24] Tarkington, There Were Others, p. 345.

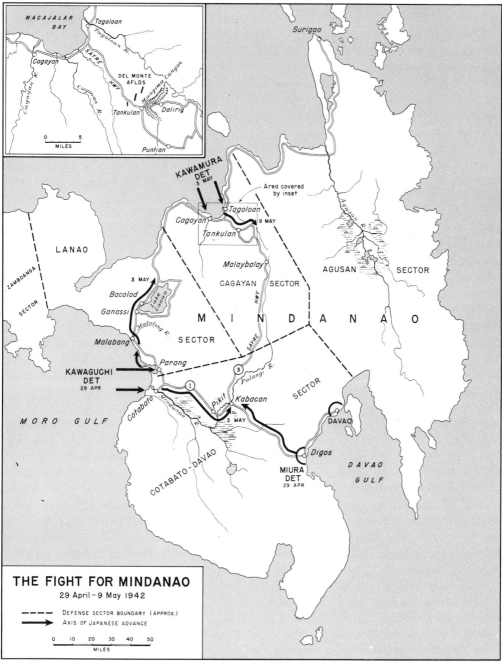

MACAJALAR
BAY

Tagoloan

Tagoloan R.

Cagayan

SAYRE HWY

DEL MONTE
AFLDS

Cagayan R.

Cugman R.

Mangima Canyon

Tankulan

Dalirig

Puntian

0 ————— 5
MILES

Surigao

KAWAMURA
DET
3 MAY

Area covered
by inset

Tagoloan

Cagayan   9 MAY

Tankulan

Agusan R.

LANAO

ZAMBOANGA SECTOR

Malaybalay

CAGAYAN   SECTOR

AGUSAN   SECTOR

3 MAY

Bacolod

Ganassi

Lake Lanao

M I N D A N A O

Matalıng R.

Malabang

SECTOR

SAYRE HWY

Parang

③

KAWAGUCHI
DET
29 APR

①

Pikit

Pulangi R.

Kabacan

SECTOR

DAVAO

Cotabato

Mindanao R.

3 MAY

MORO   GULF

COTABATO-DAVAO

Digos

MIURA
DET
29 APR

DAVAO
GULF

THE FIGHT FOR MINDANAO

29 April – 9 May 1942

- - - - -   DEFENSE SECTOR BOUNDARY (APPROX.)

━━━▶   AXIS OF JAPANESE ADVANCE

0   10   20   30   40   50
MILES

R. Johnstone

MAP 25

the Sayre Highway about midway across the island.

The other two forces committed to the Mindanao operation, the *Kawaguchi* and *Kawamura Detachments,* would have to make amphibious assaults. Each would be relieved of responsibility for the security of the island it had occupied, embark in the waiting transports, and sail under naval escort by divergent routes to its designated target. General Kawaguchi was to take his men ashore at Cotabato midway along the west coast, at the mouth of the Mindanao River. From Cotabato, which was joined to Route 1 by a five-mile stretch of highway, he would send part of his force east toward the Sayre Highway to meet Colonel Miura's troops marching west. The rest of the detachment was to land at Parang, about twelve miles north of Cotabato, and push north along Route 1, past Lake Lanao, then east along the island's north shore to join with the *Kawamura Detachment.*

Kawamura was to come ashore in northern Mindanao at the head of Macajalar Bay, the starting point of the Sayre Highway. While a small portion of his force struck out to the west to meet Kawaguchi's men, the bulk of the detachment would march south through central Mindanao, along the Sayre Highway. Ultimately, elements of the three detachments—one marching east, another west, and the third south—would join along the Digos–Cotabato stretch of Route 1 across the narrow waist of the island.[25]

Late in April three battalions of the *10th Independent Garrison* took over garrison duty on Mindanao, Cebu, and Panay. Colonel Miura immediately moved south from Davao to Digos to prepare for his advance along Route 1, while Kawamura and Ka-

waguchi began to embark their troops for the coming invasion. First to sail was the *Kawaguchi Detachment* which left Cebu on 26 April in six transports escorted by two destroyers. Kawamura's departure from Panay came five days later and brought him to Macajalar Bay as Kawaguchi's troops were fighting their way northward to greet him. Wainwright's order to Sharp on 30 April, to hold all or as much of Mindanao as possible with the forces he had, found that commander already engaged with the enemy on two fronts.[26]

The Cotabato–Davao Sector

Early on the morning of 29 April, the emperor's birthday, the *Kawaguchi Detachment* began to land at Cotabato and Parang, midway up the west coast of Mindanao.[27] The seizure of both towns was vital to Kawaguchi's plan. From Cotabato he could advance inland to the Sayre Highway by way of Route 1 or in small boats by way of the Mindanao River. From Parang he could send his men north toward Lake Lanao and the north coast of the island, or southeast to join the rest of the detachment heading toward the Sayre Highway.

Defending Cotabato and the surrounding area were troops of the 101st Division (PA)—101st Infantry (less 1st and 3d Battalions), the 2d Battalion, 104th Infantry, and a battalion of the 101st Field Artillery, organized and equipped as infantry—strengthened by Constabulary troops and

---

[25] *14th Army* Opns, I, 214–15.

[26] Rads, Sharp to Wainwright, No. F–317, 27 Apr 42, No. F–144, 28 Apr 42, and Wainwright to Sharp, 30 Apr 42, and USFIP Combined G–2 and G–3 Rpts, 36–38, 26–28 Apr 42, all in USFIP G–3 Journal, 20 Apr–3 May 42, AG 461 (1 Apr 42) Phil Rcds; *14th Army* Opns, I, 215.

[27] Rad, Del Monte, no sig, to CG USFIP (20X), 30 Apr 42, USFIP G–3 Journal, AG 461 (1 Apr 42) Phil Rcds; *14th Army* Opns, I, 215.

service units. This entire force was under Lt. Col. Russell J. Nelson, the Cotabato subsector commander. Half of his men he had placed in and around the town; the rest were posted farther inland covering Route 1 and the Mindanao River.

The men of the *Kawaguchi Detachment* encountered little resistance getting ashore at Cotabato, where the demolition teams had already completed their work. Their advance through the town, however, proved more difficult. There they were opposed by the 2d Battalion, 104th Infantry, which put up a stubborn resistance until enemy aircraft, presumably from Zamboanga, entered the fight. The battalion then pulled back to a previously prepared position on the outskirts of Cotabato where it prepared for an extended stand.[28] Events beyond its control made this impossible.

Earlier in the day a portion of the Japanese force which had landed near Parang began to push southeast toward the junction of Route 1 and the Cotabato road. At about 1530 these Japanese made contact with the 3d Batalion, 102d Infantry, which was defending the north flank of the Cotabato force. In the engagement that followed, the Filipinos held firm for more than three hours, but finally, at 1900, broke contact and withdrew along Route 1, leaving the road to Cotabato open. The position of

---

[28] The account of operations in the Cotabato-Davao area is based upon the following reports in the Visayan-Mindanao Force Report of Operations: Brig Gen Joseph P. Vachon, Cotabato-Davao Force Summary of Events, 29 Apr–10 May 42, pp. 301–15; Col Nelson, Rpt of Events and Opns, pp. 318–28; Lt Col Reed Graves, Opns Rpt Digos Sector, 28 Apr–10 May 42, pp. 343–45; Col Ben-Hur Chastaine, Rpt of Opns in Samar-Leyte and Agusan Sectors, pp. 163–67; Lt Col John H. McGee, Diary of 101st Inf (PA), 30 Apr–11 May 42, pp. 331–34. The author also used the basic report itself, pp. 51–54, and Tarkington, There Were Others, pp. 314–419.

the 2d Battalion, 104th Infantry, which had resisted the Japanese advance through the town earlier in the day, was now untenable. In danger of being cut off and taken from the rear, the battalion reluctantly abandoned its position on the outskirts of Cotabato and pulled back through the road junction to Route 1.

The next day, 30 April, General Kawaguchi began his advance eastward toward the Sayre Highway and a meeting with Colonel Miura's troops. Most of his troops moved overland by way of Route 1, but Kawaguchi did not neglect the water route offered by the Mindanao River. Three hundred of his men in armored barges took this route, which paralleled Route 1 and from which the water-borne troops could easily reach that road by trail. Both advances were supported by aircraft.

There was little action during the day. Colonel Nelson, the sector commander, received reports on the progress of the two Japanese columns but was most concerned about the troops sailing up the river. There was nothing to prevent this force from disembarking along the river bank and moving up one or more of the numerous trails to Route 1 to establish a roadblock behind Nelson's retreating men. Before the day was over, Nelson was receiving reports of just such movements, as well as the presence of Japanese troops in Pikit, where the Mindanao River crossed Route 1 at a point only about eight miles from the Sayre Highway.

The report that Japanese troops were in Pikit was even more disquieting to Colonel Nelson than the reports of hostile landings along the banks of the Mindanao River. If true, his force was already cut off. He decided therefore to move his men away from the road and onto the trails leading north. By doing so he left himself free to accomplish his principal mission, which was to protect the routes north of Route 1. The decision made, he ordered the destruction of roads and bridges and placed small covering forces along the main trails to cover his withdrawal. There was nothing to prevent Kawaguchi now from consolidating his control of the entire stretch of Route 1 from Cotabato to Pikit.

Kawaguchi's rapid advance eastward toward the Sayre Highway, which intersected Route 1 at Kabacan, eight miles east of Pikit, placed him in an excellent position to cut off the escape route of the troops in the Digos subsector. These troops, who were retreating westward along Route 1 before the *Miura Detachment,* would have to pass through Kabacan before they could make their way north along the Sayre Highway. If Kawaguchi could reach Kabacan ahead of the Filipinos, he might not only cut them off but take them from the rear. Indeed, the Japanese appear to have anticipated this possibility and Colonel Miura's orders were to keep the Digos force engaged long enough to allow Kawaguchi to reach Kabacan.[29]

The Digos force had been under pressure since the middle of April. Led by Lt. Col. Reed Graves, this force consisted of the 101st Field Artillery (PA), less one battalion, and the 2d Battalion, 102d Infantry (PA). By the 28th of the month, after a particularly heavy attack, it was clear to Colonel Graves that the Japanese on his front were about to make a major effort. The next morning, simultaneously with the landing of the *Kawaguchi Detachment* at Cotabato, Colonel Miura began his advance westward to-

[29] This reconstruction of the Japanese plan is based upon a statement made by Colonel Miura to General Vachon after the surrender. Vachon, Cotabato-Davao Force, Summary of Events, in V-MF Rpt of Opns, p. 315.

ward the Sayre Highway, supported by low-flying aircraft from Davao. Graves's troops opposed the Japanese advance stubbornly, and effectively broke up the initial assault with mortar fire.

Action during the next two days was indecisive, and consisted largely of air attacks and patrol actions. On 2 May, Colonel Miura again launched a full-scale attack. This time he opened with a four-hour artillery and mortar preparation supplemented by the strafing attacks of seven dive bombers. When the infantry moved out at 1300 it had the support of three tanks. Again the Japanese were halted and the fight ended at 1700 with a victory for the Filipinos.

Graves's brave stand proved a fruitless gesture, for two hours later, at 1900 of the 2d, he was ordered to withdraw immediately toward the Sayre Highway. The order came from the commander of the Cotabato–Davao Sector, Brig. Gen. Joseph P. Vachon, who had sent a small force to Kabacan to delay the Japanese approaching from the west. The Digos force would have to make good its escape while there was still time. Further resistance, no matter how successful, would only increase the peril to Colonel Graves and his men. That night they began to evacuate the position they had held so stubbornly since 28 April. Next day, with the 2d Battalion, 102d Infantry, acting as rear guard, the Digos force began to march toward Kabacan and the Sayre Highway.

Kabacan now became the focal point of the fight in the Cotabato–Davao Sector. General Vachon was determined to hold the southern terminus of the Sayre Highway as long as possible and placed all the troops he could muster there. In addition to the force he had already sent to delay Kawaguchi's march eastward from Pikit, he directed Colonel Graves and the troops of the Carmen Ferry subsector to hold the Sayre Highway. The *Kawaguchi Detachment* successfully fought its way to Kabacan, but arrived too late to close the trap on the Digos force. All Kawaguchi's efforts to clear the Sayre Highway and make his way northward failed. Vachon's troops held firm until the end of the campaign a week later.

Those of General Kawaguchi's men who came ashore at Parang on the morning of 29 April met an entirely different reception from that which greeted the men landing at Cotabato. Here they were met at the beaches by the regulars of the 2d Infantry, 1st Division (PA).[30] Under the leadership of Col. Calixto Duque, the Filipinos had established strong defensive positions on the beach and when the first hostile landing parties made their appearance at 0400 of the 29th they ran into heavy and effective fire from machine guns.

For more than six hours, until 1100, the 2d Infantry held its ground. Finally, in danger of being outflanked by a Japanese force that had landed a short distance to the south, the regiment fell back to a previously prepared position about two miles inland.[31] After sending a small detachment southward to establish contact with the force landing at Cotabato, Kawaguchi's men moved into the town. By late afternoon they had established contact with the southern

force and were in firm possession of Parang. Their next objective was the coastal town of Malabang, twenty-two miles to the northwest.

Guarding Malabang was the 61st Infantry (PA), led by Col. Eugene H. Mitchell. Alerted by the landings to the south, Mitchell had ordered his demolition teams to stand by and sent his men into their previously prepared positions along the west bank of the Mataling River, just above the town. In Malabang, guarding the trail which led northwest out of the town past the right flank of the Mataling line, was the 3d Battalion's Company K. To the rear were two 2.95-inch mountain guns, manned by men of the 81st Field Artillery (PA).

Rather than march his men along the twenty-two mile stretch of Route 1 which separated Parang and Malabang, General Kawaguchi apparently decided to utilize the transports which had brought them to Mindanao. Leaving a small detachment to guard the town, he sent his troops back to the ships late on the night of the 29th and set sail for Malabang. At about 0300 of the 30th, at a point a few miles south of the objective, the Japanese began to land.[32] A half hour later Company K, 61st Infantry, reported that enemy light tanks had passed its position.

Action along the Mataling line opened at dawn. Within a few hours, after suffering heavy casualties, the Filipinos were forced to give way on the left. In danger of having his flank turned, Colonel Mitchell reinforced the left but was unable to regain the ground lost. Finally, at 1400, he ordered the right battalion to attack in the hope that he could

---

[30] The 1st Division (PA) was a part of the regular establishment of the Philippine Army. Division headquarters and the other two regiments, the 1st and 3d, fought on Luzon. The 2d Infantry was stationed in the south before the war. Its strength was 880 men, but approximately 300 of these were sick with malaria when the Japanese attacked.

[31] This account of operations in the Lanao Sector is based upon: Tarkington, There Were Others, pp. 333–40; Col Eugene H. Mitchell, Hist of 61st Inf (PA), and Brig Gen Guy O. Fort, Hist of 81st Division (PA), last two in V-MF Rpt of Opns, pp. 185–93, 272–85.

[32] Japanese sources state that a landing was made at 0300 at a point south of Malabang. *14th Army Opns*, I, 215. The author has made the most reasonable reconstruction possible with the few facts available.

thus relieve the pressure on the left. The attack, though it gained some ground, failed in its objective, for the Japanese had brought more troops as well as artillery into position before the Mataling line.

The diversionary attack having failed, Colonel Mitchell decided to place his entire force in the threatened area. To do this he had to abandon the right portion of the line and call in his reserve. It was a gamble but his only alternative was to give up the Mataling line entirely. Orders for the attack went out late on the afternoon of the 30th, just before the Japanese attacked again. Advance elements of the reserve battalion arrived in time to participate in the fight that followed, but the right battalion never received its orders, and at 2000 Colonel Mitchell was forced to abandon the Mataling line.

The route of withdrawal was along Route 1. With one company as rear guard, the right and reserve battalions withdrew in an orderly fashion to a new position four miles to the north. The left battalion, unable to use Route 1, withdrew by a circuitous route along a back trail and did not join the rest of the regiment until the next afternoon. Save for patrol and rear guard action there was no fighting that night.

The Japanese attacked Colonel Mitchell's new position at 0730 the next day, 1 May. Again they struck at the flank of the Filipino line and at 1030 Mitchell was forced to order a second withdrawal. This time he fell back five miles. In the confusion one company was cut off, but Colonel Mitchell was compensated for this loss by the addition of two companies of the 1st Battalion of the 84th Provisional Infantry Regiment, which joined him when he reached his new position. Later in the day the 120 survivors of the battalion which had withdrawn from

the Mataling line along a back trail straggled into camp, and with this force Colonel Mitchell began to prepare for the next attack. His orders from the sector commander, Brig. Gen. Guy O. Fort, were to hold his position at all cost.

The Japanese, who had lost contact with the retreating Filipinos during the morning, reached the new line at about 1300. While their infantry prepared for the attack, they kept the Filipinos pinned down with artillery, mortar, and machine gun fire. At dusk, the volume of Japanese fire increased and, shortly after, the infantry moved out in a full-scale attack. Within a short time they had overrun Colonel Mitchell's defenses and were threatening his command post. By 2300, when the Japanese called off the attack, the defending force had practically disappeared.

Rounding up all the men he could find, altogether about thirty, Mitchell made his way to the rear. At about 0230 he encountered a detachment of sixty men from the 81st Division (PA) on the road and began to establish a holding position. The men had just set to work when they were struck by a Japanese motorized column which scattered the tired and dispirited men. Colonel Mitchell's luck had run out. Twice he had escaped the Japanese, but this time he was captured. With the rout of the 61st Infantry and the capture of its commander, the Japanese gained control of all of Route 1 as far north as Lake Lanao.

Only one regiment of the Lanao force, Lt. Col. Robert H. Vesey's 73d Infantry (PA), was still intact. With two battalions in the vicinity of Lake Lanao and the third on beach defense to the north, this regiment stood directly in the path of Kawaguchi's advance. At the first news that the enemy was approaching, Colonel Vesey set out for

Ganassi at the southwest corner of the lake to meet him. Here a secondary road branched off to circle the east shore while Route 1 continued northward along the west side of the lake. By holding this town, Vesey believed, he could prevent the Japanese from gaining access to either road. A preliminary skirmish at Ganassi on the morning of 2 May convinced him that the town was not defensible and that afternoon he withdrew to Bacolod on the west shore of Lake Lanao to make his stand. The Japanese promptly sent a small force along the east road, but it presented no immediate threat to the defenders at Bacolod.

The line finally established at Bacolod by Colonel Vesey extended from Lake Lanao across Route 1 and was held by the two battalions of the 73d Infantry reinforced with stragglers from the 61st Infantry. Along the front was a narrow stream which flowed under a bridge across Route 1 to empty into the lake. As an added precaution, the bridge was destroyed as soon as the troops were in position. Additional protection was afforded the troops on the far side of the stream, opposite the demolished bridge, by a 2.95-inch mountain gun.

The Japanese who had reached Ganassi early on the morning of 2 May had halted to await the arrival of the rest of the force which moved up during the day. Early the next morning the entire force, with light tanks in the lead, advanced north along Route 1. By 0800 the tanks had reached the destroyed bridge in front of the 73d Infantry line and halted. One tank sought to cross the shallow stream but was hit by a shell from the 2.95-inch mountain gun and knocked out. The others made no further effort to cross. With Route 1 blocked, the rest of the Japanese column came to an abrupt halt and the troops poured out of the trucks. Before they could deploy and take cover, they were hit by withering fire from the far side of the stream, "which made up in its concentration at point-blank range what it lacked in accuracy." [33] The toll on the Japanese side was heavy.

Despite this first setback the men of the *Kawaguchi Detachment* continued to press forward. Soon they had the support of artillery and a single plane, which alternately attacked and observed the 73d Infantry position. Unable to make any headway by frontal assault, the Japanese sought to turn the enemy's flanks. Their efforts proved successful before the morning was out and shortly after noon Colonel Vesey gave the order to withdraw.

The record of the 73d Infantry for the rest of that day, 3 May, is one of successive withdrawals. Each time Colonel Vesey put his two battalions into position, the Japanese broke through. So closely did the enemy motorized column pursue the Filipinos that they scarcely had time to organize their defenses. By midnight Vesey had taken his men back in the hills north of Lake Lanao, where he paused to reorganize his scattered forces. The Japanese made no effort to follow. The victory was theirs and the road along the north shore lay open.

Between 29 April and 3 May, General Kawaguchi with a force of 4,852 men and some assistance from the *Miura Detachment* had gained control of southern and western Mindanao. Only in the north, in the Cagayan Sector, were the Filipinos still strong enough to offer organized resistance. But already on the morning of 3 May, the third of the forces General Homma had as-

---

[33] Tarkington, There Were Others, p. 338.

signed to the Mindanao operation, the *Kawamura Detachment,* had begun to land along the shore of Macajalar Bay.

The Cagayan Sector

In the critical Cagayan Sector, which included the northern terminus of the Sayre Highway and the vital Del Monte Airfield, General Sharp had the Mindanao Force reserve, none of which had yet been committed, and the 102d Division (PA). This division, formed from existing and provisional units after the outbreak of war, consisted of the 61st and 81st Field Artillery, organized and equipped as infantry, and the 103d Infantry. Col. William P. Morse, the division and sector commander, believing that an attack in his sector would most likely come from the sea and have for its objective the seizure of the Sayre Highway, had posted his troops along Macajalar Bay, between the Tagoloan and Cagayan Rivers. Holding the four miles of coast line from the Tagoloan west to the Sayre Highway was Lt. Col. John P. Woodbridge's 81st Field Artillery and a 65-man detachment from the 30th Bomb Squadron (US). The stretch of coast line from the highway to the Cugman River, equal in length to that held by Colonel Woodbridge, was defended by the 61st Field Artillery under Col. Hiram W. Tarkington. On the left (west), extending the line to the Cagayan River, was Maj. Joseph R. Webb's 103d Infantry.[34]

First warning of the approach of the enemy reached General Sharp's headquarters on the afternoon of 2 May when a reconnaissance plane sighted the convoy carrying the *Kawamura Detachment* north of Macajalar Bay. The troops on beach defense were immediately alerted, and that night, after the convoy had entered the bay, the demolition plan was put into effect. Shortly after, about 0100 of the 3d, the Japanese troops began coming ashore at both extremities of the line, at Cagayan and at the mouth of the Tagoloan River. Supported by fire from two destroyers offshore, the Japanese by dawn had secured a firm hold of the beach line between the Tagoloan and the Sayre Highway.

Those of Kawamura's men who came ashore in the vicinity of Cagayan met a warm reception. Unable to prevent the enemy from landing, Major Webb attacked the beachhead with two companies. So successful was the attack that only the withdrawal of the 61st Field Artillery on his right prevented him, Webb believed, from driving the enemy back into the sea. With his right flank exposed, Webb was forced to break off the engagement and pull his men back.

Meanwhile General Sharp had sent additional troops to hold the Sayre Highway. Up until now he had refused to commit his reserve. But with half of Mindanao in enemy hands and with the Japanese landing more troops within a dozen miles of his headquarters, he decided that the time had come to throw all available troops into the fight. Closest to the scene of action was a detach-

---

[34] The account of operations in the Cagayan Sector is based upon: V-MF Rpt of Opns, pp. 54–61; Col Morse, Rcd of Action and Events, in V-MF Rpt of Opns, pp. 349–54; Tarkington, There Were Others, Ch. XV. Detailed accounts of the action of specific units in V-MF Rpt of Opns are as follows: Maj Paul D. Phillips, Hist of 2.95 Gun Det, pp. 176–84; Woodbridge, Narrative Activities of 81st FA, 3–10 May 42, pp. 229–34; Tarkington, Narrative of Action of 61st FA, 3–10 May 42, pp. 235–

42; Lt Col Allen Thayer, 62d Inf (PA), pp. 248–51; Maj John C. Goldtrap, Narrative of Events 93d Inf, pp. 252–66; Webb, Mindanao Campaign of 103d Inf, pp. 287–94; Maj Allen L. Peck, initialed memo dealing with opns of Cos C and E, 43d Inf (PS), 29 Apr–9 May 42, pp. 381–87.

ment under Maj. Paul D. Phillips, armed with three 2.95-inch guns, all that remained of the artillery in the Mindanao Force. Farther to the rear were the 62d and 93d Infantry (PA). Sharp ordered all three units to move up to the line. Pending the arrival of the two regiments, Phillips' detachment was to take up a position behind a deep crater on the Sayre Highway and block any Japanese attempt to advance south. When it was joined later in the day by the 62d and 93d Infantry Sharp would have a strong line, supported by artillery, in the path of the Japanese.

Major Phillips' detachment had hardly set up its guns when, at 0730, it came under fire from the Japanese advancing along the Sayre Highway. In the initial attack the detachment was forced back about 700 yards. Fortunately, the Japanese failed to press their advantage and Phillips was able to organize another holding position at his new location. He was joined here early in the afternoon by advance elements of the 93d Infantry; the rest of that regiment when it reached the area prepared a second position a short distance to the south. The 62d Infantry, whose assembly area was farther south on the Sayre Highway, failed to join the other two units that day.

To General Sharp "events seemed to be moving satisfactorily." [35] Although the enemy controlled the beaches and the northern terminus of the Sayre Highway, his own troops had disengaged without loss and were in position along a secondary line of defense. Already part of his reserves were blocking the highway and other troops were moving up to their support. So optimistic was the general that he set his staff to work on a plan to counterattack north along the highway next morning.

_____
[35] V-MF Rpt of Opns, p. 56.

The optimism at force headquarters was quickly dissipated when reports of Japanese progress during the day began to come in. The enemy, it was learned, had pushed back the 61st and 81st Field Artillery. The 103d Infantry had resisted more stoutly but was also falling back and in danger of being outflanked. General Sharp's hopes for a counterattack were dealt the final blow when, at 1600, Colonel Morse ordered a general withdrawal to defensive positions astride the Sayre Highway, about six miles south of the beach. The move was to be made that night under cover of darkness.

Before this plan could be put into effect it was changed by General Sharp, who, after a conference with Morse, Woodbridge, and Webb, decided to establish his next line even farther south than the line already selected. The position selected paralleled the Mangima Canyon, a formidable natural barrier east of the town of Tankulan, and the Mangima River. At Tankulan the Sayre Highway splits, one branch continuing south then east, the other east then south. Before the two join, eight air miles east of Tankulan, they form a rough circle bisected from north to south by the Mangima Canyon and River. East of the junction of the canyon and the upper road lies the town of Dalirig; to the south the river cuts across the lower road before Puntian. Possession of these two towns would enable the defenders to block all movement down the Sayre Highway to central Mindanao.

At 2300, 3 May, General Sharp issued orders for the withdrawal to the Mangima line. The right (north) half of the line, the Dalirig Sector, was to be held by the 102d Division which had been reorganized and now consisted of the 62d Infantry, the 81st Field Artillery, the 2.95-inch gun detachment, and the two Philippine Scout companies of the 43d Infantry from force reserve. The Puntian Sector would be held by the 61st Field Artillery and the 93d Infantry. Colonel Morse would command the troops in Dalirig; Col. William F. Dalton, those before Puntian. The 103d Infantry, cut off by the Japanese advance was made a separate force and assigned the mission of defending the Cagayan River valley.

The withdrawal was completed on the morning of 4 May when all units reached their designated positions. The remainder of that day as well as the next, during which time the Japanese limited themselves to aerial reconnaissance and bombardment, was spent in organizing the line. In the Dalirig Sector, Lt. Col. Allen Thayer's 62d Infantry, closely supported by the 2.95-inch gun detachment, occupied the main line of resistance along the east wall of Mangima Canyon. Companies C and E, 43d Infantry (PS), Colonel Morse's reserve, were stationed in Dalirig, and in a draw 500 yards behind the town were the 200 men of the 81st Field Artillery, which had had a strength of 1,000 when the Japanese landed. Colonel Dalton, with two regiments, used the lull in battle similarly to dig in before Puntian.

On the morning of 6 May the Japanese resumed the attack. Their approach toward Tankulan was reported by patrols of the 62d Infantry which for the past two days had moved freely in and around the town. During the morning advance elements of the *Kawamura Detachment* passed through Tankulan and began to advance along the upper road toward Dalirig. Late that afternoon the Japanese moved into Tankulan in force and began to register their artillery on Dalirig.

There was little action the next day. Jap-

anese artillery, well out of range of Major Phillips' 2.95-inch guns, dropped their shells accurately into the 62d Infantry line while their aircraft bombed and strafed gun positions and troops. The left battalion suffered most from the bombardment and Colonel Thayer finally had to send in his reserve battalion to bolster the line.

The artillery and air attacks continued until the evening of the 8th when, at 1900, General Kawamura sent his infantry into action. In the darkness many of the Japanese were able to infiltrate the Filipino line where they created considerable confusion. During the height of the confusion two platoons mysteriously received orders to withdraw and promptly pulled out of the line. Their march to the rear came as a complete surprise to company, battalion, and regimental headquarters, none of which had issued the order. The two platoons were quickly halted, but before they could return to the front they were attacked by a small force of Japanese infiltrators. Other 62d Infantry troops joined the fight but in the darkness it was impossible to distinguish between friend and foe. It was only after the personal intervention of Colonel Thayer that the Filipinos, whose fire was doing more to panic the men on the line than the efforts of the enemy, were persuaded to cease fire.

The action continued through the night of 8–9 May. The 62d Infantry held on as long as possible but by morning the tired and disorganized Filipinos had been pushed off the main line of resistance and were falling back on Dalirig. Already the 2.95-inch gun detachment had pulled out, leaving only the two Scout companies of the 43d Infantry to face the enemy.

In the Puntian Sector the Japanese were content to keep Colonel Dalton's troops in place by artillery fire. Until the night of 8–9

May, Dalton had been able to maintain contact with the 62d Infantry on his right (north) but during the confusion which marked the fighting that night he lost contact. In an effort to relieve the pressure on Thayer's regiment he launched his own attack the next morning. Though the attack was successful it failed to achieve its purpose, for the disorganized 62d Infantry was already in full retreat.

Undeterred by Colonel Dalton's gains in front of Puntian, General Kawamura continued to press his advantage in the north. At about 1130 of the 9th, as the 62d Infantry began to withdraw through Dalirig, his men entered the town from three sides and struck the retreating Filipinos. Already disorganized, the troops of the 62d Infantry scattered in all directions. The two Scout companies in the town, under the leadership of Maj. Allen L. Peck, made a brave stand but finally withdrew just before their positions were encircled.

The escape route of the fleeing troops lay over flat, open country, devoid of cover. Pursued by small-arms and artillery fire and strafed by low-flying aircraft, the retreating units lost all semblance of organization. Each man sought whatever protection he could find, discarding his equipment when it impeded his progress. What had begun as a withdrawal ended in a complete rout, and by the end of the day the Dalirig force had virtually ceased to exist. Except for 150 survivors of the 2.95-inch gun detachment in position five miles east of Dalirig, the upper branch of the Sayre Highway lay open to the invaders.

Along the southern branch of the highway Colonel Dalton and his two regiments still held firm at Puntian. But already Kawamura was sending additional troops to this sector and increasing the pressure against the Puntian force. Whether Dalton would be able to hold was doubtful, but even if he did his position was untenable. The enemy could sweep around his north flank from the direction of Dalirig or take him from the rear by continuing along the upper road to its junction with the lower road, then turning back toward Puntian. There was no way out.

Whatever consolation General Sharp derived from the fact that the Puntian force was still intact was tempered by the bitter realization that the Mangima line had been breached and the bulk of his force destroyed. "North front in full retreat," he radioed General MacArthur. "Enemy comes through right flank. Nothing further can be done. May sign off any time now." [36] Except for the resistance of scattered units, the Japanese campaign in Mindanao was over.

---

[36] Rad, Sharp to MacArthur, 9 May 42, GHQ SWPA G–3 Journal, P.I. Opns Rpts.

CHAPTER XXIX

Japanese Plans and American Defenses

While the Japanese were extending their control over Mindanao and the islands of the Visayas they were making final preparations to take Corregidor and bring to an end the long campaign in the Philippines. With the southern tip of Bataan in their possession they could now emplace artillery on the heights of the Mariveles Mountains and along the shore near Cabcaben, only two miles across the channel from Corregidor. Once the antiaircraft batteries had been knocked out by the artillery, their aircraft would be able to fly low over the island and drop their bombs with greater accuracy than had been possible before. Such an aerial-artillery bombardment, the Japanese be-

HEAVY CLOUDS OVER CORREGIDOR. *"With the southern tip of Bataan in their possession they could now emplace artillery on the heights of the Mariveles Mountains and along the shore near Cabcaben, only two miles across the channel from Corregidor."* Arrows indicate planned Japanese landings.

lieved, would result in the destruction of the formidable defenses of the Gibraltar of the East and prepare the way for a landing.

The most optimistic American estimates, once Bataan had fallen, did not give Corregidor much chance of holding out long against a determined Japanese effort to take the island. There was only enough food to last the Americans and Filipinos from six to eight weeks at most. At the end of that time, even if the Japanese did not attack, the garrison would have to surrender. Despite General Wainwright's brave pledge "to hold my present position with God's help until a major diversion releases the pressure on us here," it was clear that Corregidor was doomed.[1] "The life of this fortress," predicted MacArthur after the fall of Bataan, "is definitely limited and its destruction certain unless sea communication can be restored." If this could not be accomplished, he told the Chief of Staff, "you must be prepared for the fall of the harbor defenses." [2]

The Japanese Plan

General MacArthur's view was fully shared by General Homma. With the surrender of Bataan he was free to begin the final phase of his four-month-long campaign to defeat the combined American and Philippine army. That such an offensive would have to be made was evident almost immediately. The Americans and Filipinos on Corregidor showed no disposition to surrender with the Bataan garrison; indeed, they continued to resist with grim tenacity. "Though almost all enemy resistance on Ba-

taan peninsula collapsed by April 9th," the Japanese reported regretfully, "the enemy in the Corregidor Fortress did not abandon its will to fight. Therefore the Army decided to attack. . . ." [3]

Preliminary Plans and Preparations

Plans for the assault against Corregidor began to take shape on 9 April, but it was not until the end of the month that these plans assumed final form. Troops, landing boats, and equipment had to be assembled. Provision had to be made for the administration of the area already occupied and for the mop-up of isolated centers of resistance. The men who had fought on Bataan had to be rested, re-equipped, and trained for amphibious operations. But General Homma did not intend to waste any time. While these necessary measures were being taken, the air and artillery attacks against Corregidor would be intensified, and its defenses knocked out to prepare the way for the landing to come.[4]

The first major question to be decided was the selection of the unit to make the assault. Before 9 April it had been generally understood by the *14th Army* staff and by some of the senior commanders on Bataan that, if operations against Corregidor proved necessary, the *Nagano Detachment* would make the attack. "Lt. Gen. Homma, though informally, often declared this," wrote Col. Motohiko Yoshida, *4th Division* chief of staff, "even before the commencement of

---

[1] Rad, Wainwright to MacArthur, No. 218, 13 Apr 42, AG 384.1, GHQ SWPA.

[2] Rad, MacArthur to Marshall, No. 228, 13 Apr 42, AG 384.3, GHQ SWPA.

[3] *14th Army* Opns, I, 174.

[4] This description of Japanese plans and preparations is based upon: *14th Army* Opns, I, 173–210; II, Annexes 7–12; *5th Air Gp* Opns, pp. 78–84; USA *vs.* Homma, pp. 3089–94, 3178–79, testimony of Homma, p. 2635–63, testimony of Gen Kitajima, Arty Officer, *14th Army*.

the attack on Bataan." [5] It was with considerable surprise, therefore, that the *4th Division* staff learned unofficially from Col. Motoo Nakayama, Homma's senior operations officer, on 9 April, that their division had been chosen instead. That day *14th Army* orders directed the *4th Division* to advance toward Mariveles and, after routing the enemy to its front, "make preparations to land on Corregidor Island." [6] This was the first time, asserted Yoshida, that the division staff "began to deliberate on the matter." [7]

While the *4th Division* staff was deliberating "on the matter," *14th Army,* in a series of orders issued between 9 and 13 April, outlined the basic plan and defined for its major elements their role in the forthcoming campaign. The *4th Division* was officially designated as the assault unit and was reinforced with the *7th Tank Regiment* and additional artillery taken from the *16th Division.* It was ordered to assemble its main force in the area north of Cabcaben and there make preparations for the coming attack while taking all precautions to insure secrecy and provide defense against artillery, fire from Corregidor. The division was to send patrols to Cabcaben and along the coast to the south to reconnoiter "the enemy situation and topography," and to train for landing operations, removal of beach obstacles, and climbing cliffs such as would be found at the target. [8]

To the *16th Division* Homma assigned the mission of executing a feint attack against El Fraile and Carabao Islands from the Cavite shore. Before leaving for southern Luzon, General Morioka was to turn over to the *4th Division* one attached battalion of mountain artillery; to Army artillery one attached battery of 150-mm. howitzers and the *22d Field Artillery Regiment,* less elements; and to Army one regiment to guard the west coast of Bataan. The *65th Brigade* and the *Nagano Detachment* were ordered to north and central Luzon for garrison duty; they would have no part in the operations against Corregidor.

The air force and the Army artillery were given a major role in the preliminary stages of the projected campaign. The *22d Air Brigade* was to suspend large-scale bombing operations for a two-week period in order to repair its planes and make ready for the intensive bombardment which would precede the landings. Army air operations during these weeks would consist of daily reconnaissance missions over Corregidor and the adjoining islands and harassing raids to "demoralize enemy troop on Corregidor Island and shell warships and ships in the area." [9] Navy land-based, twin-engine bombers would continue to bomb Corregidor during this period.

General Kitajima's *14th Army* artillery had perhaps the most important task, after the infantry, in the reduction of Corregidor. It was to neutralize the enemy's guns, destroy the installations on the island, sink vessels in the bay, and "simultaneously cooperate in the landing operations." [10] The first objectives were to be the antiaircraft

[5] Statement of Col Yoshida, 28 Jul 49, ATIS Doc 62642, Statements of Japanese Officials on World War II, GHQ FEC, Mil Intel Sec, IV, 551.
[6] *14th Army* Opns, I, 170.
[7] Statement of Yoshida, 28 Jul 49, ATIS Doc 62642, Statements of Japanese Officials on World War II, GHQ FEC, Mil Intel Sec, IV, 551.
[8] Statement of Lt Col Hiromi Oishi, *4th Div* Staff, 2 Oct 50, ATIS Doc 62639, *ibid.,* III, 115.

[9] *14th Army* Opns, I, 174.
[10] *Ibid.,* 170.

guns, short-range batteries, and the "flank defenses" at each end of the island. Kitajima was to bring all his guns to southern Bataan, to the vicinity of Cabcaben and the high ground just north of Mariveles, with the greatest secrecy. There the guns were to be dispersed and placed under the ample concealment provided by the jungle for protection against counterbattery fire. Provision would also be made, *14th Army* directed, for diversionary fire to deceive the enemy as to the time and place of landing. To support the *16th Division* in its feint attack against El Fraile and Carabao, one battery of heavy guns located near Ternate was ordered to cooperate with the division and shell these islands to heighten the impression of an attack from the Cavite shore.

Kitajima received strong reinforcements for the operation. Between 9 and 13 April *14th Army* assigned to him additional batteries of 150- and 105-mm. howitzers, most of the *22d Field Artillery Regiment*, and, somewhat later, the *4th Division's* artillery regiment. When the full-scale bombardment of Corregidor began, Kitajima had under his command eighteen batteries, a balloon company, an artillery intelligence regiment, and a company of prime movers.[11] The eighteen batteries consisted of 116 field pieces, ranging in size from 75-mm. guns to 240-mm. howitzers. In detail, this armament included:[12]

240-mm. howitzers	10
150-mm. guns	10
howitzers	36
105-mm. guns	16
howitzers	12
75-mm. guns	32
Total	116

In drawing up final plans for the assault, General Homma encountered two serious problems, neither of which had apparently been anticipated. The first of these was to bring into Manila Bay the landing craft required to transport the *4th Division* to Corregidor and to protect the invasion force during the shore-to-shore movement. The bulk of *14th Army's* craft was located in Lingayen Gulf or at Olongapo on the Subic Bay (west) side of Bataan. "I had to bring down the landing boats from Lingayen," Homma later explained, "but it could not be done by land, so they must come by sea." [13] To get them into Manila Bay would require a hazardous journey through the North Channel under the guns of Corregidor and within striking distance of the PT boats. During daylight boats in the channel could be plainly seen from Corregidor; at night, if there were many boats, the noise of their engines would be sure to be heard.

While *14th Army* was studying the problem of assembling its landing craft in Manila Bay, the Navy undertook to send two of its small boats through the North Channel between Corregidor and Mariveles in broad daylight. They got as far as Mariveles when the guns on Corregidor opened fire. Badly damaged, they fled to safer waters. The Navy's effort, which Homma called "very indiscreet," alerted the Americans to the Japanese plan and forced the Japanese to

---

[11] *Ibid.*, 178. A balloon company consisted of about 150 men, 25 vehicles, and 1 observation balloon. The artillery intelligence regiment was a sound and flash unit, consisting of a headquarters group, a survey unit, a plotting unit with nine plotting stations and a sound detector unit with six listening posts. The regiment was commanded by a lieutenant colonel and had about 675 men. Handbook of Japanese Military Forces, TM-E-30-480, 15 Sep 44, p. 47.

[12] USA *vs.* Homma, p. 2651, testimony of Kitajima.

[13] *Ibid.*, p. 3089, testimony of Homma.

be very cautious about bringing the Army's landing boats through the channel.[14]

On 14 April the Army conducted its own test to determine whether small boats could enter Manila Bay through North Channel. The trial run was made at night with about a half-dozen vessels and was accompanied by air and artillery attacks to drown out the noise of the engines and divert the attention of the Corregidor garrison. The test proved successful and Homma decided to bring the bulk of the small craft at Lingayen, Nasugbu, and Olongapo into Manila Bay and thence to Cavite to be outfitted and trained. The next day he ordered the *21st Independent Engineer Regiment,* based at Manila and Olongapo, to supervise the transfer of the landing boats into the bay. The *4th Division,* Army artillery, and the *22d Air Brigade* were to cover the movement.

Starting on the night of the 15th, the small boats began to enter Manila Bay. During the next week about forty landing barges came in by sea and twenty more of a smaller type were transported overland from Olongapo to Orani on the Manila Bay side of Bataan. Armored boats, gunboats, and fishing boats also slipped through the channel and made their way to Cavite. But the operation was a slow one since only a small number of boats could get through each night, and it was not until early May that all the craft needed had been assembled.

The second major problem that faced the planners—and for a time placed the entire operation in jeopardy—was the outbreak of malaria in the *4th Division.* The shortage of medical supplies and food had plagued General Homma throughout the campaign, and even before the 3 April attack he had had 15,500 men in the hospitals. After the fall

of Bataan, when the troops entered the low, malaria-infested river valleys in the southern part of the peninsula, the sick rate rose sharply. Of the 30,600 patients in Japanese hospitals during the month of April, 28,000 were malaria victims.[15] The *4th Division* was hardest hit, and when, about the middle of April, one of its regiments reported for training in amphibious operations it numbered only 250 men. At one time the strength of the division dropped to one third of normal. General Homma importuned his superiors for quinine and additional hospital facilities and finally received 300,000 quinine tablets by air at the end of the month. With this supply the malaria epidemic was brought under control just in time to meet the scheduled date for the assault.

The Plan

By 17 April the preliminary phase of the planning had been completed, ten days later the plan itself was ready, and on 28 April *14th Army* published the field order for the attack. It was not until 2 May that the date for the assault was finally released to the troops.

The delay in releasing the date of the attack was due in part to security. But even if Homma had wished, he could not have fixed the time much earlier. First, there had been difficulty in assembling the landing craft, and then had come the outbreak of malaria in the *4th Division.* Despite pressure from *Imperial General Headquarters* in Tokyo and despite his own desire for an early end to the campaign, Homma had been forced to defer the attack several times. On 9 April he had been optimistic and boasted to Colonel Collier, the only Ameri-

---

[14] *Ibid.,* p. 3090, testimony of Homma.

[15] *Ibid.,* pp. 2845–47, testimony of Col Shusuke Horiguchi, Med Officer, *14th Army.*

can officer to whom he spoke after the surrender, that he would have Corregidor "within a week." [16] He soon revised this estimate and set his sights first on 25 and then 27 April. But it was not until the malaria epidemic had been checked and the required number of landing craft assembled in Manila Bay that Homma could fix with confidence the date for the start of operations. That time did not come until the beginning of May and it was then that *14th Army* designated 5 May as the X Day of the plans published earlier.[17]

In planning for the assault against Corregidor, the Japanese had the advantage of a precise and detailed knowledge of the target, gained possibly from prisoners of war. They knew the designation and strength of the four artillery regiments in the harbor defense, the position and armament of all but two of the major seacoast batteries, as well as the location of most of the smaller guns and of all important installations. They had considerable information on the island's water supply, communications system, road and rail nets, power plants, storage areas, and barracks. Their maps were almost as detailed as those used by the Americans.

Information on the infantry defenses of the island was not as detailed and accurate as that on the artillery. In their estimates

the Japanese assumed the existence of an infantry defense in depth. In front of the beach obstacles they believed they would encounter the first line, protected on the flanks by light artillery. The main line they placed behind the obstacles, with a third line, heavily protected with artillery and machine guns "to the rear." This last line, the Japanese noted, would be defended "at all cost." [18]

Though their intelligence about Corregidor was amazingly full and correct, the Japanese had little information about Malinta Tunnel. They knew of its existence, and during the campaign acquired much vague information about it. The more they heard about it, the more obsessed they became with the entire subject of tunnels. Before the Bataan campaign was over, many Japanese seem to have become convinced that the Americans had constructed a tunnel from Corregidor to Bataan. They questioned officers captured on Bataan in an effort to find the secret entrance on the Bataan side and refused to believe their captives, who insistently denied the existence of such a tunnel. It was with reluctance that they abandoned the notion of a secret tunnel.[19]

The plan finally evolved for the landings called for a closely co-ordinated artillery-air preparation, followed by "a sudden blow" consisting of two separate amphibious infantry-tank assaults made on successive nights at opposite ends of the island by the *4th Division*. Both forces would drive inland until they joined at a point just west of the

---

[16] Collier, Notebooks, IV, 20. Collier, who had gone forward with a Japanese officer on 9 April to carry the news of the surrender to General Funk, had been taken to *14th Army* headquarters later and there met General Homma.

[17] USA *vs.* Homma, pp. 2465–67, 3081–82, testimony of Homma; interv, Col Walter E. Buchly with Homma, Manila, Mar 46; Drake, Comments on Draft MS, Comment 17, OCMH; Statement of Maj Kiyoshi Onuma, *4th Div* Staff, 8 Aug 49, ATIS Doc 62640, Statements of Japanese Officials on World War II, GHQ FEC, Mil Intel Sec, III, 157. "I remember," said Onuma, "that it took until about 1 or 2 May to bring landing craft to Manila Bay."

[18] *14th Army* Opns, II, 72.

[19] Prov Tank Gp Rpt of Opns, p. 26; interv, Col Buchly with Homma, Manila, Mar 46. General Drake states that even after they took Corregidor, the Japanese were seeking the entrance on the Corregidor side of the tunnel. Drake, Comments on Draft MS, Comment 18, OCMH.

narrow neck of the tadpole. If all went well, Corregidor would be in Japanese hands on the second day of the attack, after which the *4th Division* would occupy Caballo. El Fraile and Carabao Islands would be seized next, if necessary by elements of the *16th Division* from Cavite.

The tactical scheme had not been settled without debate. The *14th Army* planners had first contemplated only one landing on Corregidor, on the head of the tadpole, and had relayed this decision to the *4th Division* staff. Reconnaissance by the division soon disclosed that the area selected faced the precipitous cliffs which dropped from Topside to the water's edge. A landing here would be difficult and dangerous, and the division staff argued that the initial landing should be made by a small force along the tail of the island where the ground was low and flat. Once a foothold was secured, then the main force could land on the head. Though two landings would create difficulties, the division staff felt that these would be offset by the early seizure of a beachhead and the support the main force would have from the initial landing party. The army planners finally agreed to this solution, and it became a part of the final plan.[20]

For the operation *14th Army* attached to Kitano's *4th Division* two sea operation units, each consisting of an independent engineer regiment with attached elements. The *1st Sea Operation Unit (23d Independent Engineer Regiment)* was to transport the assault force and to assist in the landing. It numbered about 110 small boats of various types, equipped with heavy machine guns. The *2d Sea Operation Unit,*

whose mission was to protect the amphibious force during the shore-to-shore movement and during the landing, was composed of most of the *21st Independent Engineer Regiment,* elements of the *3d Sea Operation Unit,* almost two battalions of light artillery, an antitank company and an antiaircraft artillery section. It was organized into eleven gunboat units, each consisting of two to four gunboats or fishing boats equipped with machine guns, automatic guns, and light artillery.

While the *4th Division* and its attached elements were preparing for the assault, the artillery would continue the bombardment begun on 10 April. Except for counterbattery fire and "inevitable operations," artillery action during the month of April was to be kept at a minimum in order to conserve ammunition. Thereafter, until the landings, all the guns in *14th Army* artillery would be brought to bear against Corregidor. The seacoast batteries still in operation on Corregidor would be "annihilated," antiaircraft guns and searchlights knocked out, and defensive installations, short-range cannons, and beach obstacles in the landing areas demolished.

Throughout the entire period of preparation the fire of the artillery was to be coordinated with air operations. During April only one squadron of Army bombers and some Navy land-based bombers would attack Corregidor, concentrating on key objectives such as antiaircraft and artillery positions. Other aircraft would fly reconnaissance missions over Manila Bay and the fortified islands during this period to secure information about the enemy and to gather target data for the artillery. After 29 April the rest of the *22d Air Brigade* would join in the attack against the island and enemy

[20] Statement of Oishi, 2 Oct 50, ATIS Doc 62639, Statements of Japanese Officials on World War II, GHQ FEC, Mil Intel Sec, III, 115.

shipping, giving special attention to targets on the north shore, from Cavalry to Morrison Points.

In the belief that the Corregidor garrison might surrender during the course of the operation, *14th Army* issued detailed instructions "for the reception of truce-flag bearers." No unit was to receive the bearer of a flag of truce unless he represented the commander of the American and Filipino forces. If that officer "has already escaped," then the bearer must represent the senior commander on Corregidor. The appearance of an emissary carrying a white flag was to be reported immediately to *14th Army,* which would conduct the negotiation for surrender. All units were cautioned that the arrival of an emissary from the American commander with a flag of truce would not in itself mean the termination of hostilities. "Until a definite order is issued," *14th Army* declared, "the attack will be continued." [21]

14th Army also took every precaution to conceal its intentions from the Americans on Corregidor. All units were enjoined time and again to observe the greatest secrecy, and the *4th Division* and Army artillery were ordered to "strictly avoid the main road" on Bataan during the hours of daylight. To prevent leaks through the Filipino population, *14th Army* forbade communication between civilians and military personnel and in those areas where the assault troops were most active moved the inhabitants out altogether.

For a time *14th Army* attempted to create the impression that the attack on Corregidor had been abandoned. The *16th Division* was ordered to suspend its open preparations for the feint landing, but "to continue secretly to prepare for the attack." Artillery operations were limited to occasional shelling, and propaganda issued by the Army headquarters avoided mention of an attack and stressed the point that the problem of Corregidor would be solved in time by "nothing more than blockade." Meanwhile, the Japanese "pretended to devote" themselves to military administration and mopping-up operations. To strengthen this impression, Homma made a grand entry into Manila to celebrate the emperor's birthday on 29 April "as gayly and grandly as possible." After the ceremonies he left the capital announcing that he was going to Mindanao to assume command of operations there. In reality he and his staff returned to *14th Army* headquarters at Balanga where final preparations for the invasion of Corregidor were being made.[22]

The American Defenses

When Bataan fell the men on Corregidor knew that their days were numbered. With the Japanese artillery literally aiming down their throats, they could have no illusions about the future. But there was no noticeable decline of morale once it was made clear that the island would not be surrendered without a fight. One battery commander called his men together and talked with them realistically about their situation and their prospects. "The men all swore," wrote a staff sergeant, "that the enemy would have to come and take Morrison Hill [the battery location] if they wanted it." [23] This feeling seems to have been general throughout the command and was expressed by Wainwright when he wrote to

[21] *14th Army* Opns, I, 198.

797–257 O–66—35

[22] *Ibid.,* 195.
[23] Hopkins, Personal and Official Notes of Btry C, 60th CA (AA), entry of 9 Apr 42. copy in OCMH.

President Roosevelt, "Our flag still flies on this beleaguered island fortress." "I meant to see," he added later, "that it kept flying."[24] All that he or anyone else could do was to prepare for the inevitable attack with the determination to make it as costly as possible to the enemy.

Beach Defense

Until the evacuation of Manila at the end of December, local defense of the island had been provided by a small number of artillerymen, who performed this task in addition to their other duties. Such an arrangement had not permitted an effective defense or left time for the construction of strongly fortified positions. This deficiency had been recognized but it was not until Admiral Hart made the 4th Marine Regiment available on 24 December that steps were taken to correct the weaknesses of Corregidor's defenses.[25]

By chance, Col. Samuel L. Howard, commander of the 4th Marines, was in Manila when Hart turned the regiment over to the Army "for tactical employment." He reported immediately to General MacArthur and then to General Sutherland who gave him his orders. They were brief and to the point: "Proceed to Corregidor and take over the beach defenses of that island."[26]

---

[24] Wainwright, *General Wainwright's Story*, p. 85.
[25] This account of the beach defenses of Corregidor is based upon: Howard, 4th Marines Rpt of Opns, pp. 10–19, USMC Hist Sec; Baldwin, "The Fourth Marines at Corregidor," Part 1, *Marine Corps Gazette* (November 1946), pp. 13–18, Part 2 (December 1946), p. 30; Maj Harold E. Dalness, Opns of the Prov Bn, 4th Marines (paper prepared for the Advanced Officers Course, 1949–50, The Infantry School), pp. 4–7; Beach Defense Arty Tabulation, Exhibit G of Harbor Defenses Rpt of Opns.
[26] Howard, 4th Marines Rpt of Opns, p. 10, USMC Hist Sec.

Howard thereupon returned to his regiment at Olongapo to prepare for the move. Within a week the entire regiment had reached Corregidor and on 29 December Colonel Howard was designated commanding officer of the beach defenses.

The 4th Marine Regiment, which had arrived from Shanghai only a month earlier, had been considerably reinforced since the start of the war. The 766 marines who had escaped from China had been organized into a two-battalion regiment in which each battalion consisted of only one machine gun company and two rifle companies. The companies, moreover, had only two of their platoons. When war came, the regiment had absorbed the Marine detachment of the Olongapo naval station and had organized a third platoon in the rifle companies as well as two additional companies from other Marine detachments in the Islands. On reaching Corregidor the regiment gained enough men to form a 3d Battalion by absorbing the marines who had formerly been stationed at Cavite. The strength of the regiment (less detachments) now totaled 66 officers and 1,365 enlisted men, substantially the same strength it had at the end of the campaign. It carried with it when it moved to Corregidor a 6-month supply of rations for 2,000 men, more than ten units of fire for all weapons, a two-year supply of clothing, and sufficient medicine and equipment for a 100-bed hospital.

The arrival of the marines filled a serious gap in Corregidor's defenses. There had never been enough men on the island to man the large seacoast guns, the antiaircraft defenses, and the beaches as well. Before the war barbed wire had stretched along those beaches which offered possible landing sites, and pillboxes had been erected deep in the ravines leading to Topside and

TABLE 11—STRENGTH, HARBOR AND BEACH DEFENSES, ABOUT 15 APRIL 1942 [a]

	Army			Marines	Navy		Civilian		Total
	U.S.	P.S.	P.A.		U.S.	Phil.	U.S.	Other [b]	
Fort Mills..................	4,492	1,028	1,742	1,514	1,715	400	315	1,987	13,193
Fort Hughes................	276	0	0	93	443	0	27	40	879
Fort Drum..................	189	0	0	10	0	0	0	6	205
Fort Frank.................	55	270	76	0	0	0	1	49	451
Total................	5,012	1,298	1,818	1,617	2,158	400	343	2,082	14,728

[a] This tabulation is probably not entirely correct, but it represents a summary of the best data available.
[b] Mostly Filipinos, but including Chinese and perhaps others.
Source: Harbor Defenses Rpt of Opns, Exhibit K, p. 13.

Middleside.[27] But, as Colonel Howard observed in his initial reconnaissance, much remained to be done to guard against an enemy landing.

When Howard assumed command of Corregidor's beach defense the island was already organized into three sectors, and he deployed his regiment accordingly. In the East Sector, which stretched from the tip of the tail to the narrow neck and included Malinta Tunnel, he placed his 1st Battalion. The 3d Battalion took over responsibility for the area to the west, the Middle Sector, which included most of the barracks and installations on Topside and Middleside. The western end of the island was designated the West Sector and its defense assigned to the 2d Battalion. In reserve Howard kept the headquarters and service company.

As soon as the marines reached their assigned positions at the end of December they began to improve existing defenses and to prepare new ones. Some work had already been done in the West and Middle Sectors,

[27] Lt. Comdr. T. C. Parker, "The Epic of Corregidor-Bataan," U.S. Naval Institute Proceedings, LXIX, No. 1 (January 1943), 12.

but, except for a final defense line on the east side of Malinta Hill, there were no defenses east of Malinta Tunnel. The marines turned to with vigor and in the next three months laid miles of barbed wire—twenty-one miles of wire were laid in the East Sector alone—planted land mines, dug tank traps, trenches, and tunnels, cleared fields of fire, built gun emplacements, set up interior and switch positions, and established final defense lines in each sector.

As more men reached the island they were assigned to Colonel Howard's beach defenses and by the middle of April, after the influx from Bataan, he had under his command about 4,000 men of whom only 1,352 were marines. (Table 11) The rest came from the Navy which contributed 895 men, the Philippine Army (929) men, and the U.S. Army. This group constituted a heterogeneous force of doubtful strength. It included Filipino messboys, ground crews of the Philippine Army Air Force, survivors of the submarine tender Canopus, and Scout artillerymen. Few of these men had had any infantry training. Those who had come from Bataan had to be completely outfitted

MARINE SERGEANT TEACHING FILIPINOS *the operation of a machine gun.*

and equipped and were in such "deplor- able" physical condition as to be "unfit for combat duty." [28]

With the ragged and weakened refugees from Bataan Colonel Howard fleshed out the Marine force in each sector. The East Sector, which had consisted of less than 400 men from the 1st Battalion, 4th Marines, was brought up to a strength of 1,115. Strength of the Middle Sector where the 500 men of the 3d Battalion were stationed, was brought up to the same total by the addition of Army and Navy personnel. The 2d Battalion in the West Sector was rein- forced with almost 600 men, for a total of 915. No provision was made to shift any of the troops to a threatened area, so that if a landing came at one point it would

have to be met by the troops in that sector.

The reserve, which had formerly con- sisted of the Headquarters and Service Company (300 men), was considerably strengthened by the addition of a provisional 4th Battalion in the Marine regiment. This battalion, organized on 10 April with let- tered companies Q, R, S, and T, was com- posed largely of Navy enlisted men with a sprinkling of soldiers from Bataan. The commander was a Marine major and the officers were drawn from both services. Most of the 500 sailors in the battalion had special skills, years of service and high rat- ings, but none knew even the fundamentals of infantry fighting. They were mature and serious, however, and learned quickly. Training facilities were limited and equip- ment meager but the incentive was great. The men spent their days training; their

---

[28] Howard, 4th Marines Rpt of Opns, p. 16, USMC Hist. Sec.

nights attending lectures. "The chips were down," wrote one of their officers, "and there was no horseplay." [29]

In addition to the 4,000 men assigned to beach defense, Colonel Howard could count on the use of practically all troops on the island in the event of an emergency. A plan was prepared and approved which provided for the formation of two reduced battalions manned by personnel from the seacoast defenses, and for the utilization of quartermaster, engineer, military police, and "all other available personnel" when the "beach defense situation" became serious. [30] Even civilians were assigned to defense sectors.

Artillery support for the men on beach defense was provided by one 155-mm., twenty-three 75-mm., and two naval guns of 3-inch caliber. For use against night landings Howard had eleven searchlights, six of which were placed in the East Sector, guarding Malinta Tunnel and the approaches from Bataan. To that sector he also assigned ten of the 75-mm. guns, some of them old British models. The men in the Middle Sector, which included the docks and the installations on Topside and Middleside, had the support of the single 155-mm. gun, seven of the 75's, one 3-incher, and three searchlights. The West Sector was less heavily defended than the others and had only four 75's and one naval gun.

Seacoast and antiaircraft defenses on Corregidor were still intact. Though the enemy air attacks during the past three months had destroyed most of the wooden buildings and left deep scars everywhere on the island, they had not wrought serious damage to the coastal batteries or to the 3-inch antiaircraft guns. Ordnance magazines with four feet of reinforced concrete had withstood even direct hits; lighter concrete structures had been damaged but rarely demolished. "After the fall of Bataan," wrote one officer, "we had more artillery in operation than we had had at the start of the war." [31] Forts Drum and Frank, which had been subjected to frequent artillery bombardment by the Japanese along the Cavite shore, had not fared as well. Corregidor, too, would soon feel the destructive effects of massed artillery fire which in one day could inflict more damage than three months of air attacks.

The Condition of the Troops

The condition of the troops was not yet desperate. Morale was still high and most men thought they could give a good account of themselves if the Japanese should attempt to take the island by assault. Some even believed they had an excellent chance to beat off an attack. "The marines can't see how the Japs can take Corregidor," wrote an artilleryman. "I hardly can either!" [32] The men talked about the possibility of reinforcement, about food, liquor, and women— "the things that soldiers have always talked about—but never," wrote a marine, "about the hopelessness of our position. Never once did I hear anybody despair." [33]

The health of the command was generally good. The casualties from the bombings had not been severe and the effects of a limited diet were not yet apparent. Mild respiratory

[29] Dalness, Opns of Prov Bn, 4th Marines, p. 7.
[30] Howard, 4th Marines Rpt of Opns, p. 16, USMC Hist Sec.

[31] The Siege of Corregidor, Mil Rpts on UN, No. 12, 15 Nov 43, p. 50, MID WD.
[32] Hopkins, Personal and Official Notes of Btry C, 60th CA (AA), entry of 19 Mar 42, p. 185. The diary notation was probably made by the battery commander, Captain Ames.
[33] Quoted in Baldwin, "The Fourth Marines at Corregidor," Part 2, *Marine Corps Gazette* (December 1946), p. 33.

LIFE IN MALINTA TUNNEL

diseases caused by confinement in the damp, dust-laden tunnel were the most frequent reasons for hospitalization. Diarrhea and food poisoning were fairly common, but dysentery and malaria, the twin scourges of Bataan, were rare on Corregidor. Hospital facilities in the tunnel, though not ideal, were far superior to those on Bataan and there was an ample supply of drugs for the small number of patients.[34]

Malinta Tunnel was still the focus of all activity on Corregidor and became after 9 April even more crowded and hectic than before. A newcomer from Bataan, Capt. John McM. Gulick, described it as "a gigantic beehive" over which neon lights "cast their bluish glow." Along its sides the crates were piled higher than ever and the double and triple deck bunks were more numerous; overhead was a maze of wires, pipes, and ducts. The number of men in the tunnel had increased and a steady stream, which Captain Gulick described as "dense crowds," moved up and down the main axis and into the many laterals on various errands. The dust was thicker than ever, the odors more pronounced and disagreeable, the vermin more numerous, and the hum of the auxiliary diesel power plants and ventilators more penetrating. Everywhere were "cryptic initial signs" describing the activity of each cluster of desks. The ambulance siren sounded more often now but a hush still fell over the tunnel when a jeep carrying a wounded man drove through.[35]

---

[34] Cooper, Med Dept Activities, p. 83.

[35] Gulick, Memoirs of Btry C, 91st CA (PS), p. 122, copy in OCMH.

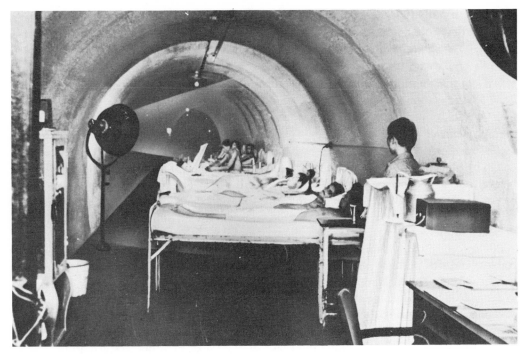

LIFE IN MALINTA TUNNEL

The power plant on the island had been hit occasionally during the aerial bombardment but the Japanese had not made any systematic effort to destroy the plant itself or the power lines that led to the cold-storage plant and the water pumps that kept the reservoir filled. There had been some damage, and the danger of a complete breakdown in the power system was a source of constant concern. But there was still enough fuel for the portable diesel engines in the tunnel to last at least until the end of June.[36]

Corregidor's water supply, because it was dependent upon the power plant, was perhaps the most vulnerable point of Corregidor's defense. Even before the surrender of Bataan there had been frequent periods when water was not available because of power failures or damage to the pumps. When the water lines were damaged, water was distributed at various points on the island and each unit sent its own trucks for the day's supply. The water was carried in 12-inch powder cans, two by five and a half feet, ideal for storage but heavy when full and difficult to handle. The water crews normally made the trip at night over the crater-filled roads to the distribution points. There they might have to wait for hours to draw their supply. "It was a ticklish job." [37]

By the beginning of April the supply of water had become a real problem. On the

[36] The Siege of Corregidor, Mil Rpts on UN, No. 12, 15 Nov 43, pp. 43, 50, MID WD.

[37] Lt Col Earl L. Barr, Hist of Btry M, 60th CA (AA), p. 8, copy in OCMH. See also Gulick Memoirs of Btry C, 91st CA (PS), p. 155.

2d of the month Colonel Bunker noted in his diary that "our water situation is getting critical," [38] and on the 3d, in anticipation of the fall of Bataan, all units were directed to lay in a reserve supply. At that time there was in the reservoirs a total of 3,000,000 gallons, but that would not last long if the pumps or power plant failed.[39]

The men on Corregidor ate two meals a day. The morning meal, prepared the night before and served before daylight, usually consisted of toast and coffee, when there was coffee, and occasionally a piece of bacon or sausage. Supper was served after dark, about 2000, and consisted of salmon, canned vegetables, and rice pudding. Sometimes there was fresh beef or stew. Most units were able to serve half a sandwich and a cup of hot beverage or soup during the noon hour, but many men kept pieces of bread in their pocket to gnaw on during the long interval between meals.[40]

The ration, though adequate to maintain health, did not provide sufficient bulk to satisfy the appetite. Men no longer had the "comfortably full" feeling provided by the peacetime ration, and missed certain foods such as sugar, canned milk, coffee, and canned or dried fruits, which were by now extremely scarce.[41] Rice had become an increasingly important part of the ration and, though it was not favored by the Americans, it did provide bulk in the diet. Fortunately there were always enough other foods on hand to add flavor and variety to the rice dishes. But the American soldiers never became fond of rice and complained frequently. "This rice diet fills you up *temporarily*," wrote Colonel Bunker, "but it doesn't stick to your ribs." [42]

The air attacks during the preceding three months had disrupted the normal distribution of rations from time to time and occasionally a bomb had hit a kitchen, with tragic loss for the men who had to miss a meal or lose a particularly prized item on the menu. One battery lost its fruit jello in this way. "The fruit in the dessert," mourned the battery commander, "represented the saving of canned fruit for a couple of weeks and it was the pride of the mess sergeant." [43] The cold-storage plant was damaged during the air attack of 28 March and the next day all units received unexpectedly large issues of fresh meat and then none at all until the refrigerators were repaired. Finally, about 3 April, in expectation of heavier air and artillery attacks, all units received additional allowances of food, to be stored in their kitchens.[44] But even during the heaviest bombardments there was no loss of food, which was safely stored under guard in Malinta Tunnel and in the cold-storage plant.

As on Bataan, there was a strong feeling among the troops on beach defense and at gun positions that those close to the source of supply in the tunnel enjoyed better meals than they. This belief was probably unfounded but it was true that until the end of March naval personnel received foods which were not available to Army troops. The Navy, though it had cut the ration and limited its men to two meals a day, maintained its own separate food stores and issued a larger and more varied ration than that provided by the Army. Long after cof-

[38] Bunker, Diary, entry of 2 Apr 42.
[39] The Siege of Corregidor, Mil Rpts on UN, No. 12, 15 Nov 43, pp. 42, 45, MID WD.
[40] Baldwin, "The Fourth Marines at Corregidor," Part 2, *Marine Corps Gazette* (December 1946), p. 32; Barr, Hist of Btry M, 60th CA (AA), p. 4.
[41] Barr, Btry M, 60th CA (AA), p. 4.

[42] Bunker, Diary, entry of 28 Apr 42.
[43] Barr, Btry M, 60th CA (AA), p. 6.
[44] The Siege of Corregidor, Mil Rpts on UN, No. 12, 15 Nov 43, p. 43, MID WD.

fee, sugar, jam, and canned fruit had disappeared from the Army menu they were still available in the Navy messes. When General Wainwright arrived on Corregidor to assume command on 21 March he ordered the Navy to place its stores in the common pool, and thereafter the sailors received the same ration as the soldiers.[45]

Despite the shortages there was never any real danger of starvation on Corregidor. The quantity of food on hand when Bataan fell was sufficient to last about ten weeks more. This food had been forehandedly laid aside early in the campaign in the expectation that if and when Bataan was lost the Philippine Division would make its final stand on Corregidor. To provide for this contingency MacArthur, on 24 January, had ordered General Moore, the Harbor Defenses commander, to maintain a reserve large enough to feed 20,000 men—twice the

number then on the island—on half rations until 30 June. Before he left for Australia, he cautioned Moore not to permit "any encroachments" against this reserve.[46]

When Wainwright came to Corregidor on 21 March to assume command of USFIP he found that food was more plentiful and the men better fed than on Bataan. With the plight of the emaciated troops there still fresh in his mind, he requested permission from MacArthur to reduce the carefully hoarded reserves by an amount equal to a month's half rations for the planned garrison of 20,000 men. Approval was granted at the beginning of April and Wainwright was able to send additional food to Bataan during the last days of the battle. It was "little more than a crumb," he wrote later, but it reduced Corregidor reserves "to a point where I figured . . . that our 11,000 defenders would consume it all by June 20, 1942, on less than half rations." [47] It was to be more than enough.

---

[45] Knoll, Intel Rpt, 16th Naval Dist, 12 Mar–3 May 42, p. 10; Drake, Comments on Draft MS, Comment 22, OCMH; ltr, Rockwell to Ward, 18 Jan 52, OCMH. Admiral Rockwell states that to the best of his recollection Army and Navy food had been pooled long before the end of the campaign, but he does not give the date.

[46] Harbor Defenses Rpt of Opns, p. 42; Col Chester H. Elmes, QM Opns, Fort Mills, pp. 2–3, App. F of QM Rpt of Opns.

[47] Wainwright, General Wainwright's Story, p. 72; Harbor Defenses Rpt of Opns, p. 50.

CHAPTER XXX

The Last Twenty-Seven Days

Hardly had the Bataan garrison surrendered than those Japanese batteries that had reached Cabcaben opened fire on Corregidor to begin the final twenty-seven-day siege of the island. The intermittent air attacks of the preceding three months paled into insignificance beside the massed artillery from Bataan. "One day's shelling," remarked one officer, "did more damage than all the bombing put together." [1] Areas that had been heavily wooded were entirely denuded. In some places not "a stick, not a leaf" was left. Trees, "once so dense . . . that they shut out the sun," were shot away or burned, leaving only charred stumps.[2] Deep craters, empty shell cases, and huge fragments of concrete pockmarked the landscape. The beach defenses were demolished, the huge seacoast guns silenced, and the antiaircraft batteries reduced to impotence during these twenty-seven days. At the end of the bombardment the island was literally a shambles, a "moving picture version of No Man's Land in World War I." [3]

The Preliminary Bombardment

On 9 April the first Japanese artillery, a 75-mm. gun battery, reached Cabcaben. In plain sight of the Americans on Corregidor, the battery opened fire, marking what Colonel Bunker, commander of the Seaward Defenses, called "a crucial point in our operations—a milestone." [4] This first attack was promptly answered by the 155-mm. guns of Battery Kysor located on the north shore of Corregidor. Thereafter, on orders from General Wainwright who feared American shells would fall on the hospitals, civilian camps, and friendly troops in southern Bataan, the Corregidor batteries were prohibited from firing on the peninsula. This order remained in effect until 12 April when counterbattery fire against located enemy targets was authorized.[5]

Japanese aircraft, lacking targets on Bataan, also turned their attention to Corregidor on the 9th. At about the same time that the 75-mm. guns opened up from Cabcaben, high-flying bombers made their first attack on the island since the end of March. Between 1630 and 2030, the *22d Air Brigade* sent 44 light and 35 heavy bombers plus 20 Navy twin-engine bombers against Corregidor, with results which the Japanese described as "very successful and effective." [6] Actually this bombardment was no more effective than earlier bombings, but one lucky hit landed among the

---

[1] The Siege of Corregidor, Mil Rpts on UN, No. 12, 15 Nov 43, p. 50, MID WD.

[2] Quoted in Baldwin, "The Fourth Marines at Corregidor," Part 2, *Marine Corps Gazette* (December 1946), p. 35.

[3] The Siege of Corregidor, Mil Rpts on UN, No. 12, 15 Nov 43, p. 50, MID WD.

[4] Bunker, Diary, entry of 9 Apr 42; *14th Army Opns*, I, 169.

[5] Harbor Defenses Rpt of Opns, pp. 52–53, 55; Wainwright, *General Wainwright's Story*, pp. 92–93.

[6] *14th Army Opns*, I, 178.

cables controlling the mine field in the bay. Until the cables were repaired "practically the whole mine field [was] out." [7] Fortunately the Japanese were not aware of the damage they had wrought.

During the days that followed the Japanese brought up their heavier guns in preparation for the more intense bombardment to follow. General Kitajima, *14th Army* artillery officer, took every precaution to insure the most effective use of the eighteen batteries under his command. He divided the target area into three zones, corresponding roughly to the beach defense sectors, and assigned a specific zone to each battery. Careful tests were made to insure the accuracy of each piece and all targets were inclosed by bracket fire. The balloon company moved from Abucay to the heights of Mariveles where it could observe fire on Corregidor. At the first sight of the balloon the Americans christened it Peeping Tom. The intelligence regiment was also brought south and by the 13th had set up its flash and sound equipment. For the Japanese artillery the conditions were almost ideal.[8]

By 12 April many of the Japanese batteries were in position and at 0600 that day the bombardment of Corregidor began in earnest. Most of the fire came from 75-mm. and 105-mm. guns; the 150-mm. guns did not get into action on a large scale until a few days later. On the 12th, also, the batteries on Cavite opened fire on Corregidor, while Japanese aircraft made nine separate attacks against the island. Counterbattery fire, the prohibition against which had been partially lifted that day, only brought down an answering barrage from the enemy. It

was, wrote Colonel Bunker, "a rough day all day." [9]

During the next week, when the 150-mm. howitzers joined the attack, the tempo of the Japanese bombardment increased steadily. For the first time the armament of the island received heavy damage. The first guns to be put out of action were the seacoast guns on the north shore facing Bataan and visible to the Japanese. By the 14th three 155-mm. gun batteries, each with two guns, and one 3-inch battery of four guns had been destroyed. The vulnerable directors and height finders on Topside were badly damaged, too, but the operators were able to keep at least one in operation at all times.

The Japanese did not neglect the searchlights. Whenever one showed its light, they quickly "shot hell out of it." [10] Apparently they had their guns registered on the fixed seacoast searchlights. To test this theory Colonel Bunker ordered one light to be turned on for fifteen seconds, scarcely enough time for the enemy to register, load, and fire. After that time a man turned off the light and ran. He was scarcely twenty yards away when Japanese shells fell on the searchlight. "Which proved," noted Colonel Bunker, "that the Japs had their guns

---

[7] Bunker, Diary, entry of 9 Apr 42.
[8] *14th Army* Opns, II, App. VIII, pp. 37–45.

[9] Bunker, Diary, entry of 12 Apr 42. In addition to the sources cited below, this section is based upon: Harbor Defenses Rpt of Opns, pp. 53–72; The Siege of Corregidor, Mil Rpts on UN, No. 12, 15 Nov 43, pp. 43–50, MID WD; Baldwin, "The Fourth Marines at Corregidor," Part 2, *Marine Corps Gazette* (December 1946), pp. 32–35; Wainwright, *General Wainwright's Story*, pp. 86–114; Col Chase, AA Defense Comd Rpt of Opns, pp. 16–17, Exhibit F, Harbor Defenses Rpt of Opns; intervs, author with Col Stephen M. Mellnik, Gen Drake, Col Chase and Lt Col John McM. Gulick, at various times.
[10] Bunker, Diary, entry of 14 Apr 42.

loaded, laid, and men at the lanyards with orders to shoot instantly when the light showed." [11]

Casualties during the first days of the bombardment were low. At the first sign of an air attack or artillery bombardment those men whose batteries were not in action would take shelter in one of the numerous tunnels that had been and were still being built. But only the thick reinforced concrete shelters could provide protection against a direct hit. On the 15th seventy Filipinos died a terrible death when they took shelter in excavations behind their battery on Morrison Hill. So intense was the enemy fire that the overhanging cliffs collapsed and sealed the entrances to the shelters, burying the Filipinos alive.

There were moments of heroism as well as tragedy. On the 16th, four men of Battery B, 60th Coast Artillery (AA)—Capt. Arthur E. Huff and three volunteers—earned Silver Stars when they left shelter during an intense bombardment to raise the American flag. A shell fragment had struck the 100-foot flagpole on the Topside parade ground and severed the halyard. "Slowly, terribly, the flag began to descend," but before it reached the ground the four men gathered it into their arms. Quickly repairing the broken halyard, they raised the flag and ran back to shelter.[12]

The intensity of the air and artillery attacks increased during the latter part of April. After the 18th the 240-mm. howitzers which had been moved from Cavite added their weight to the bombardment. With

high-angle fire and heavy charges they were able to hit targets which the flat trajectory weapons had been unable to reach, and to blast the heavily reinforced concrete protecting the large-caliber coastal guns. On the 24th they put Battery Crockett, with two 12-inch guns, out of commission, demolished the protective barricades, ruined the shot hoists, and started fires which fortunately were brought under control before they reached the powder room. The next evening, a 240-mm. shell exploded outside the west entrance of Malinta Tunnel where a large group of men had gathered for a breath of fresh air and a smoke before turning in. "There was a panic-stricken rush for the gate, but the concussion had closed it and it could not be opened from the outside." Then another shell landed. "We worked all that night," wrote a nurse, "and I wish I could forget those endless, harrowing hours." [13] At least thirteen were killed outright; more died later, and the number of wounded was estimated as high as fifty.

The shelling never really stopped. With over one hundred pieces ranging in size from 75-mm. guns to the giant 240-mm. howitzers, the Japanese were able to fire almost steadily. They destroyed gun emplacements, shelters, beach defenses, buildings—almost everything on the surface—at a rate that made repair or replacement impossible. First they concentrated on the north shore batteries and, when most of these were destroyed or neutralized, adjusted fire on the batteries on the opposite shore. They fired at regular periods, starting just before dawn and continuing until about noon. There was a lull during the early afternoon—Colonel Bunker called it a Japanese siesta—after which the fire would begin again about

---

[11] *Ibid.*

[12] Wainwright, *General Wainwright's Story*, pp. 90–91. Wainwright's account is incorrect as to the date and men involved. He does give credit later to these men for a somewhat similar occurrence on 3 May. *Ibid.*, pp. 109–10. An account of the 16 April incident is included in Chase, Comments on Draft MS, pp. 33–34, OCMH.

[13] Redmond, *I Served on Bataan*, pp. 144–45.

BATTERY CROCKETT

1500 to continue with varying intensity almost until midnight. Usually by 1000 most telephone communications had been knocked out. Crews repaired the lines during the night but the next morning they would be cut again.

Air attacks usually accompanied the shelling from Bataan and followed the same schedule. Between 9 April and the end of the month there were 108 air alarms, totaling almost eighty hours. Practically all of the attacks were directed against Corregidor. At first the planes came in at high altitude, over 20,000 feet and beyond the range of all but two of the antiaircraft batteries. But as the days passed and damage to equipment and installations mounted, the Japanese pilots became bolder. They came in at lower altitudes and bombed more accurately. It became more and more difficult for the defenders to keep their guns and height finders serviceable. During some periods there was but one height finder in operation and the altitude of attacking planes had to be sent by telephone to all antiaircraft batteries.

The air and artillery attacks of April reached their height on the 29th of the month, Emperor Hirohito's birthday. The day began with an air alarm, the 260th of the campaign, at 0730, when two flights of bombers came over Fort Hughes and three dive bombers hit the South Dock on Corregidor and the Malinta Tunnel entrances. At the same time Peeping Tom, the observation balloon, rose over Cabcaben and the Japanese batteries on Bataan opened up on Bottomside targets. About a half hour later six more planes dropped their loads on Malinta Hill and the artillery loosed concentrated fire against both portals of the tunnel and on the North Dock. While an observation plane hovered overhead, the Japanese artillery shifted fire to Topside at 0820. After a brief lull Japanese aircraft came over the island again, and the artillery registered hits on targets on Middleside. At 1000 Japanese shells reached two ammunition dumps which blew up with a tremendous explosion.

The attacks continued without letup through the afternoon, and by evening large sections of Corregidor lay shrouded under a dense cloud of smoke or dust. Grass fires were burning everywhere and ammunition from the two dumps was still exploding. Installations on Malinta Hill were a shambles. Observation stations had been destroyed; the power plant for the large seacoast searchlight was burned out; and three of the 75-mm. beach defense guns, as well as a 1.1-inch quadruple mount, were demolished. That night two Navy PBY's brought in some medicine and 740 mechanical fuzes from Australia, an empty gesture for a garrison which was reeling under the effects of the heaviest bombardment of the war.

Brave efforts were made to deliver counterbattery and antiaircraft fire. About 18 April the 155-mm. gun batteries were taken out of their exposed positions, organized into one-gun mobile units, and placed in defiladed positions. Called "roving guns," each was equipped with a prime mover. After firing from one location until the enemy discovered their presence and had time to mass his own fire, the roving guns would move out. They were, in General Moore's opinion, "our main dependence for counterbattery fire . . .," and were supplemented after 20 April by "roving lights"—two

searchlights which moved from one position to another.[14]

Forts Frank and Drum also fired counterbattery. Both had 14-inch guns which could be used against Bataan but the two at Fort Frank were of the open, disappearing-carriage type, easily blanketed by fire from Cavite, and could fire only sporadically. The 14-inch guns at Fort Drum were of the turret type and fired steadily. They were still firing at 5-minute intervals at the time of the surrender, when every other gun on the fortified islands had been silenced.

The most effective counterbattery fire was delivered by Corregidor's Batteries Geary and Way, both with 12-inch mortars.[15] The former consisted of two pits, each with four pieces. Battery Way, with only one pit of three mortars, had been out of service for several years, and it was not until Battery E of the 60th Coast Artillery (AA) from Bataan became available that these mortars were reconditioned for use. On 28 April the weapons were test-fired and reported ready for action.

Both 12-inch mortar batteries had an ample supply of the standard armor-piercing shells with the .05-second delay fuze. But these shells could do little damage to the Japanese artillery. For that, the instantaneous fuze 670-pound personnel shell was required, and there were only 400 rounds on Corregidor. Ordnance could modify the delay fuze of the armor-piercing shell so that it would explode on impact, but the process was a slow one. All the men that could be spared were put on the job, but the output for a single day never exceeded twenty-five shells.

[14] Harbor Defenses Rpt of Opns, p. 58.
[15] Bunker, Diary, passim.

BATTERY WAY, *12-inch mortar pit. (Photograph taken in 1945.)*

With their excellent observation posts and air reconnaissance, the Japanese soon had all the fixed installations pinpointed and could loose accurate and adjusted concentrations of fire on them at the first sign of activity. Most of their attention, however, was given to Batteries Geary and Way which, with their high-angle fire and 670-pound personnel shells, represented the greatest threat. Battery Way was soon reduced to two guns, and on 2 May Japanese 240-mm. shells penetrated Geary's magazine, which blew up with an explosion that rocked the island and hurled the 10-ton barrels of the 12-inch mortars about like match sticks. One was found 150 yards from its mount, on the island's cratered golf course. Another was blown through three feet of reinforced concrete into an adjoining powder magazine.

A reinforced concrete slab weighing about six tons flew a thousand yards, cut through a tree trunk about four feet in diameter, and came to rest in a ravine. Estimates of the casualties varied from eight to twenty-seven men killed, with many more injured. Four men were buried under the debris. There was no difference of opinion on the damage. The eight guns were ruined, the shells destroyed, and the entire battery reduced to rubble.[16]

Health and Food

No one on Corregidor was free from the constant bombardment except those in the

---

[16] Gulick, Memoirs of Btry C, 91st CA (PS), p. 181; Statement of Lt Murray Glussman, USNR, in Hayes, Rpt on Med Tactics, Off of Naval Rcds.

tunnels under Malinta Hill, and the garrison could not, as General Wainwright observed, fight back from there.[17] By now life in Malinta Tunnel had become almost intolerable. Dust, dirt, great black flies, and vermin were everywhere, and over everything hung the odor of the hospital and men's bodies. During an air attack, when the large blowers were shut off, the air, offensive at best, became foul and the heat almost unbearable. Sometimes the lights failed and the gloom of the tunnel flickered into darkness. Under such conditions, "sun snatching" became a necessity. Between raids men would crowd the entrances to breathe deeply the gasoline fumes and dust which passed for fresh air.

Crowded into enforced intimacy, on short rations, and under constant strain, men grew tense and irritable. Many lost their temper over minor incidents; conflicts long hidden rose to the surface. Values changed and men's virtues and defects were magnified. The mood of life in the tunnel impressed itself indelibly on Mrs. Maude R. Williams, a hospital assistant who had come over from Bataan. With eloquence and deep feeling she recorded these impressions in her diary.

Under the deepening shadow of death life on Corregidor took on a faster, more intense tempo. The smallest and most simple pleasures became sought after and treasured as they became increasingly rare and dangerous—an uninterrupted cigarette, a cold shower, a stolen biscuit, a good night's sleep in the open air.

There was a heightened feeling that life was to be lived from day to day, without illusions of an ultimate victory. Many sought forgetfulness in gambling. There was no other way to spend the accumulated pay that bulged in their pockets and they rattled the dice or played endless bridge, rummy and poker.

Jam sessions attracted great crowds which gathered in the dark and hummed softly or tapped feet to the nostalgic swing of the organ, a haunting guitar, or a low moaning trombone. Sometimes a nurse and her boy friend of the evening would melt into a dance. . . . The eyes of the onlookers would grow soft and thoughtful, while other couples would steal out into the perilous night. . . .

Still others sought the consolations of religion and the symbols of another world, a better world of sweet and eternal peace. The Catholics gathered at dawn in the officers mess of Malinto Tunnel where one of the tables was converted into a simple altar, and kneeling on the bare cement under the high white washed vault they listened devoutly and a little desperately to the same hushed phrases that had been whispered in the Catacombs.[18]

Life outside the tunnel was less uncomfortable but more precarious. Those on beach defense or in gun positions could, if they wished, sleep in the fresh air and escape the dust occasionally. They were less crowded and had more freedom of movement. But the strain on them was great, too. When the shells came over or the bombs dropped they took cover and hoped for the best. All movement on the island became hazardous and uncertain. The roads, which at one time had been effectively camouflaged by trees, "were now bare and clearly visible shelves along the steep side of the island." [19] At any moment artillery fire might fall on men and vehicles. Captain Gulick, commander of Battery C, 91st Coast Artillery, was caught in such a barrage with his Filipino driver.

---

[17] Wainwright, *General Wainwright's Story*, p. 92.

[18] Leon M. Guerrero, "The Last Days of Corregidor," *The Philippine Review* (May 1943).
[19] Hopkins, Personal and Official Notes of Btry C, 60th CA (AA), entry of 2 May 42, Gen Info, copy in OCMH.

To my terror [he wrote] it began to move toward us. There was a high rocky hill to my right and another to my left. Neither afforded any shelter whatsoever. We began to run hoping to get around the side of the hill. The barrage walked after us at about a pace equal to our own. We rounded the hill and saw in front of us the ruins of the Ordnance warehouses blown up by bombs in December. The ground was heap after heap of concrete chunks and exploded 75 shells and casings. Suddenly the barrage behind us lifted and came down about 400 yds in front of us slightly to our left. We ran to the right. The curtain of fire lifted again and came down on our right moving towards us. Terror and desperation seized us. We were panting, sweating, and scared. It seemed as if the Jap artillery was playing cat and mouse with us. . . .

We ran down the old trolley tracks with barrages or concentrations behind and on both sides of us. Suddenly again up ahead shells began to land. . . . We reached a drainage ditch and threw ourselves in it. Dead leaves had cloaked its depth so that we sank down about 3 feet. It was hot, dirty, and almost smothering. But we were so exhausted by terror and by running that we could only lie there panting and perspiring.[20]

As the days passed, life on Corregidor became more uncomfortable. Kitchens were hit and meals had to be cooked and distributed in the dark. The concentration of a group of men was sure to bring down artillery fire from Bataan. Meals became haphazard; men ate when and where they could. By the beginning of May the enemy attacks had become so frequent that the proper preparation of meals was impossible; feeding the troops, "a catch-as-catch can proposition." "It became martyrdom," wrote a naval officer, "to expose one's self for messing."[21]

At the start of the bombardment, on 14 April, Colonel Constant Irwin, General Wainwright's operations officer, had urged an increase in the ration. The shelling and bombing, he had pointed out, would probably become more severe during the next few weeks, and men on half rations could not be expected to stand the strain without a marked decrease in their combat efficiency. By the time the Japanese were ready to take the island by assault, Irwin believed, the defenders would be too weak to fend off an attack. He recommended, therefore, that the food reserves set aside at the start of the campaign be used to supplement the half ration and keep the men strong, "physically and mentally."[22]

Before making a decision on Irwin's recommendation, General Wainwright ordered his chief of staff to make a study of the total amount of food on hand, including the stock of the Navy and the Marine unit. The result showed that there was only enough food to carry the garrison through the month of June on half rations. If the issue was doubled, the supply would be exhausted within a month. Wainwright could not gamble on a landing before that time. Even if he did and if he successfully fought off an enemy attempt to take the island, he would have to surrender ultimately for lack of food. For these reasons he vetoed Colonel Irwin's proposal and ordered the half ration continued "until more food is in sight."[23]

The garrison, therefore, continued to subsist on half rations or less while the meals, because of the bombardment and the destruction of kitchens, became less appetizing and nourishing than ever. "For supper," one

---

[20] Gulick, Memoirs of Btry C, 91st CA (PS), pp. 137–39.

[21] Statement of Lt Comdr Ernest Marion, in Hayes, Rpt on Med Tactics, Off of Naval Rcds.

[22] Carrier note, G–3 to CofS USFIP, 14 Apr 42, no sub, AG 430.2 Phil Rcds.

[23] Ibid., with attached pencil notes initialed W [Wainwright] and LB [Lewis Beebe].

Marine wrote, "we had a sort of stew which consisted mainly of rice and a couple of pieces of bread, and maybe a little jam." [24] Col. Carlos Romulo, newscaster for Corregidor's "Voice of Freedom," noted that "sometimes we had a soggy slice [of bread] with our breakfast and sometimes we did not." He could tell in this way whether the bakery had been hit during the last raid. A piece of cheese he had acquired as a gift before Quezon's departure "moved between my fingers," when he decided to eat it almost two months later. "So unfastidious can hunger make one," he observed, "I ate the cheese after removing its small inhabitants." [25]

By now the private caches of food and whiskey were gone. Only those few who had hoarded their supplies still had any left. What they had, they saved for special occasions. When Captain Gulick reached Corregidor after the fall of Bataan, he visited an old friend and was received "with open arms" and a bottle of "President Quezon's champagne." "We swilled the warm champagne in the sunlight," he reminisced, "ate peanut butter sandwiches, and swapped stories. . . . Truly war has its moments greater than those of peace." [26] Some of those who had no whiskey used the methods of manufacture adopted later in the war by troops stationed on dry Pacific Islands. Cleaning up a battery position, Captain Gulick was surprised to find that one of the swabbing tubs "was being illegally employed to hold a mash of dried raisins and

prunes." [27] The result, his men could have told him, was a satisfying and intoxicating beverage variously called raisinjack and jungle juice.

By the end of April the first signs of malnutrition had made their appearance. Beriberi and scurvy were observed at about this time and the symptoms of avitaminosis were noted by unit commanders whose men showed a decrease in combat efficiency. In one antiaircraft battery Vitamin A deficiency had already affected the vision of the gun crews. "The BC [battery commander] got cod liver oil and boric acid solution from the hospital," wrote one of the men, "to try to combat this." [28]

With the increased intensity of the Japanese bombardment at the end of April came a sharp increase in the number of casualties. "Every day it seemed that the line of stretchers grew longer. The narrow hospital corridors were crammed with the wounded, the sick, and the dying; the convalescents were hurried out to make room for fresh casualties." The hospital staff, overworked and under an intolerable strain, became short-tempered. Nurses snapped at one another, at the male attendants, and at the patients. "And every day when the red light in front of the Harbor Defense headquarters went out and the air raid was over, the grimy unwashed bodies would come in on their stained stretchers, carried on a wave of silence and spreading fear."

With the influx of patients the hospital expanded into three more laterals until by 25 April it had a capacity of 1,000 beds. Double and triple deck bunks were used for patients and hospital attendants alike. Linen

---

[24] Quoted in Baldwin, "The Fourth Marines at Corregidor," Part 2, *Marine Corps Gazette* (December 1946), p. 32.

[25] Romulo, *I Saw the Fall of the Philippines*, pp. 245, 246.

[26] Gulick, Memoirs of Btry C, 91st CA (PS), p. 131.

[27] *Ibid.*, p. 142.

[28] Hopkins, Personal and Official Notes of Btry C, 60th CA (AA), entry of 27 Apr 42, Gen Info.

was scarce and its use avoided, since "to go outside to hang out the laundry is a needless risk of life." Space, as everywhere in the tunnel, was at a premium; water was scarce and the power system uncertain. During a bombardment the concussion could be felt even in the hospital laterals deep in the tunnel. Bottles, dishes, and loose objects rattled on the shelves and tables; the lights flickered and sometimes failed. "My hands tremble," wrote an aide on duty in the operating room. "when I'm giving anesthetics." [29]

Some units had their own medical facilities, and some, like the 4th Marines, had a comparatively well-equipped hospital with a complete medical staff. One unit recently arrived from Bataan soon acquired a dispensary, a medical officer, and a hospital of sorts. Such facilities were acquired by various means and, when requisitions failed to bring the needed supplies, sometimes "an old friend and drinking companion" could be found in the tunnel hospital.

None of these units was able to treat serious injuries or ailments; only the Malinta Hospital could provide treatment for such cases. And it was, in the view of some, reluctant to do so unless the patient was brought in—not an easy task during the bombardment. "Our malaria cases had increased," wrote Captain Gulick, whose battery had come from Bataan, ". . . yet the hospital refused to send an ambulance." When informed that the men had a temperature of 104 degrees, Gulick wrote wrathfully, the hospital authorities suggested that "the men walk to the tunnel." [30]

The task of bringing the sick and wounded to the Malinta Hospital had always been a difficult one. Now it became hazardous as well. There had been only two ambulances at the start of the campaign, and one of these had been quickly destroyed. The other, "in some mysterious way," had escaped destruction and was still in operation.[31] Its services had to be supplemented by the vehicles of those units whose men required hospitalization, a fact which the men did not always appreciate.

The effects of the continuous bombardment could be seen not only in the mounting toll of wounded but in the haggard faces of the men. Shelling robbed men of sleep; short rations, of needed vitamins and energy. "The strain," wrote an officer, "is beginning to tell. The men looked and acted weary." [32] For the first time cases of battle fatigue were reported to the hospital. Some men, such as the one whose friend's "shell-torn head flew past his face," went out of their minds.[33] But the number of mental cases reported was surprisingly small. The Corregidor surgeon noted only "six to eight" throughout the campaign. He could not account for the low rate of psychotic and neurotic disorders but offered the theory that it was due to the fact that there was no rear area to send the men for rest, no letup in the bombardment. "Here the war was always with us," he explained, "and once the adjustment was made, there were no new adjustments to be made." [34]

---

[29] Quotes in this and the preceding paragraphs are from Guerrero, "The Last Days of Corregidor," *The Philippine Review* (May 1943). See also Redmond, *I Served on Bataan*, p. 149.

[30] Gulick, Memoirs of Btry C, 91st CA (PS), pp. 145, 153–54.

[31] Cooper, Med Dept Activities, p. 11, Annex XIV, USAFFE–USFIP Rpt of Opns.

[32] Barr, Btry M, 60th CA (AA), p. 17, copy in OCMH.

[33] Redmond, *I Served on Bataan*, p. 142.

[34] Cooper, Med Dept Activities, pp. 18, 84. In this connection see the report by Sitter, Psychiatric Reactions Observed on Corregidor and Bataan and in Japanese Captivity, copy in OCMH.

Perhaps the most alarming consequence of the Japanese bombardment was the damage to the power plant which operated the water pumps and searchlights, raised and lowered the big guns, and supplied Malinta Tunnel with fresh air and light. The main power plant at Bottomside had been damaged repeatedly but never so seriously that it could not be repaired. The large seacoast batteries had their own emergency generators but their use required fuel "and the Staff," as Colonel Bunker observed, "won't give us enough gas for that." [35] There was a reserve dynamo in the tunnel and another smaller engine for emergency use in the hospital, but even these sometimes would fail and more than once surgery was performed by flashlight. By the end of April the main power plant was operating at only a fraction of its capacity and General Moore estimated that Corregidor would be without power in another month.

The supply of water, already critical, became the most important single problem for the men on Corregidor. It was the dry season and there had been no rain for months. The level of the reservoirs on the islands dropped rapidly and there was no way to replenish the supply. Enemy shells were constantly striking the pumps, puncturing the water pipes, or damaging the power plant. So frequently did this occur that it was possible to pump water into the reservoirs only one day during the month of April. The rest of the time either the pumps or the power plant were out of commission.

So serious had the shortage of water become by the end of the month that the daily allowance for personal use had been reduced to one canteen. For men who had to do heavy physical work in the open on a sun-baked tropical island where the temperature soared up to 100 degrees during midday and where the dust from explosions lay heavy, the lack of water was not only a major inconvenience but a serious threat to health.

Men used their slim ration of water with the greatest care, took "handerchief baths" and devised ingenious methods to make a canteen last through the day. "Many a night," wrote Captain Gulick, "I washed myself with a cup of water and by standing in a basin saved the water to use over again on, first, my underwear, and then my socks. Order of laundering was very important. The dirtiest item always came last. . . ." [36] Showers became a rare luxury and men spoke of them with as much longing as they did of steaks smothered in mushrooms, French fried potatoes, crisp salads, and ice cream.

The Preassault Bombardment

At the beginning of May, Japanese artillery and aircraft opened the final phase of the bombardment, the phase in which, Homma's orders read, they would "overwhelmingly crush" the island's defenses and "exterminate" its defenders, "especially the ones concealed in wooded areas." [37] By that time all forces were ready and began to move into position for the assault. As soon as the remaining guns, searchlights, and pillboxes had been destroyed and the beach obstacles blasted out of the way, the troops of the *4th Division* would embark for Corregidor.

The Americans received their first hint of the Japanese landing plan on 1 May when artillery fire from Bataan was con-

---

[35] Bunker, Diary, entry of 12 Apr 42.

[36] Gulick, Memoirs of Btry C, 91st CA (PS), p. 156.

[37] *14th Army Opns*, II, 53.

centrated on the narrow tail of the island and on the area around James Ravine, which provided a pathway from the beach to Topside. The intensity of the attack was hardly justified by the installations remaining in either area. Observers could only conclude that the enemy was concentrating his fire in preparation for the landing.[38]

The attack on 1 May was discouraging to those who believed that the bombardment of 29 April represented the enemy's maximum effort. The first shells began dropping before dawn and continued until midnight. At 1515 the 274th air alarm of the war was sounded and eight bombers dropped their loads before the entrances to Malinta Tunnel. "Much mess equipment, motor transportation and communications destroyed," General Moore noted in his report.[39] A half hour later, then twice more before dark, air alarms sounded and bombs dropped on the island. That night, when Lt. Col. Earl L. Barr, executive officer of the 60th Coast Artillery (AA), returned to Malinta Tunnel from a visit to the antiaircraft battery at Kindley Field, he encountered a "morgue-like gloom."[40]

The next day was even worse. The artillery from Bataan opened up at 0730, then the planes came in. It was not until three hours later that the all clear sounded. The respite lasted only thirty minutes, after which the Japanese guns opened fire again. Until 1945, except for two lulls of one and two hours' duration, the attacks were continuous. During a five-hour period of the day, 3,600 shells of 240-mm. caliber, in addition to shells of other sizes, fell in the vicinity of Batteries Geary and Crockett on

Topside. The rate of fire of the 240-mm. howitzers alone was twelve shells per minute. "Moore and I," wrote General Wainwright, "delving further into the mathematics of the fury, estimated . . . that the Japs had hit the rock with 1,800,000 pounds of shells," in addition to the bombs dropped by Japanese aircraft during thirteen air raids.[41] It was the heaviest concentration of fire yet experienced on Corregidor.

As on the day before, the attacks of the 2d were directed at the north shore in those areas where the landing would be made. It was on this day that the Battery Geary magazine was hit and the entire battery destroyed with a "shock like that of an earthquake."[42] The entire shore line facing Bataan was heavily worked over and Bottomside, "except for the Power Plant and Cold Storage Plant which had an almost charmed life," was thoroughly saturated with shells of all calibers. "It was a nasty place to cross . . .," wrote one man. "One felt positively in the spotlight for artillery batteries on Bataan as he walked from the Power Plant to the tunnel."[43]

Malinta Hill and the area to the east received a heavy shellacking also on the 2d. At the end of the day the whole tail of the island was covered by a cloud of dust and small fires were burning everywhere, "in the shell-scarred tree trunks and stumps," and in the woods. Fanned by a brisk west wind, the fires spread rapidly and were brought under control only after all the men in the area had turned fire fighters.[44]

[41] Wainwright, General Wainwright's Story, pp. 110–12. Wainwright states that this weight of shells fell on 4 May, not the 2d, but he attributes his figures to General Moore who places the attacks on the 2d. Harbor Defenses Rpt of Opns, p. 65.
[42] Hopkins, Personal and Official Notes of Btry C, 60th CA (AA), entry of 2 May 42, Gen Info.
[43] Ibid.
[44] Barr, Btry M, 60th CA (AA), p. 15.

[38] The Siege of Corregidor, Mil Rpts on UN, No. 12, 15 Nov 43, p. 46, MID WD.
[39] Harbor Defenses Rpt of Opns, p. 64.
[40] Barr, Btry M, 60th CA (AA), p. 15.

JAPANESE BOMBERS OVER CORREGIDOR

Sunday, 3 May, was a repetition of the day before. There were five air-raid alarms during the day, with the planes again concentrating on James Ravine and Kindley Field. The enemy aircraft over the field met no fire from the antiaircraft batteries, whose guns and height finders had already been damaged or destroyed. Artillery fire during the day was so heavy that the dust blinded the spotters observing counterbattery fire. "Situation here is fast becoming desperate," Wainwright reported to General Mac-Arthur at the end of the day's action. "With artillery that outranges anything we have except two guns, he [the enemy] keeps up a terrific bombardment as well as aerial bombing." [45]

That night an American submarine on patrol in the South China Sea stopped out-side the mine channel for an hour before returning to Australia for torpedoes. It took out 25 passengers, all that could be crowded into its tight interior. Among the passengers were Colonel Constant Irwin, who carried a complete roster of all Army, Navy, and Marine personnel still alive; Col. Royal G. Jenks, a finance officer, with financial accounts; Col. Milton A. Hill, the inspector general, 3 other Army and 6 Navy officers, and about 13 nurses. Included in the cargo sent from Corregidor were several bags of mail, the last to go out of the Philippines, and "many USAFFE and USFIP records and orders." [46]

---

[45] Rad, Wainwright to MacArthur, No. 392, 3 May 42, AG 384.1, GHQ SWPA.

[46] Harbor Defenses Rpt of Opns, pp. 67–68. All or part of these records ultimately reached The Adjutant General and are on file in the Historical Records Section, Departmental Records Branch, AGO. They were used in the preparation of this volume and are cited by their appropriate AG number, followed by the symbol Phil Rcds. Other

The intensity of the air and artillery bombardment reached a new peak on 4 May, despite Wainwright's belief that "the tempo of the Jap shelling" could not "possibly be increased." [47] Japanese fire from Bataan that day was the heaviest of the campaign and totaled 16,000 shells of all calibers in a period of 24 hours. So intense was the bombardment, so continuous the "drum-fire of bursting shells," that it resembled machine gun fire in its staccato regularity.[48] As before, the chief targets were the beach defenses along the north shore at James Ravine and between North and Cavalry Points. Observation planes overhead adjusted artillery fire while bombers, in six separate attacks, concentrated on the east end of the island and on the few remaining vessels of the inshore patrol.

During the day observers on Topside had sighted fifteen landing barges off the southeast coast of Bataan, moving north. The observers thought the enemy vessels were trying to get out of range of American counterbattery fire; more probably they were headed toward Lamao to pick up the assault troops. There was little doubt by now that a Japanese landing would soon come.

The ability of the Corregidor garrison to withstand a Japanese assault after the continuous shelling of the past three weeks was doubtful. There had been six hundred casualties since 9 April and those who had escaped injury were in poor physical condition. Most of the coastal guns and searchlights had been destroyed and the beach defenses had suffered extensive damage. The sandbagged machine gun positions had been so battered that they presented "a topsy-turvy appearance." [49] "Considering the present level of morale," Wainwright informed General Marshall on the 4th in response to a request for his frank opinion, "I estimate that we have something less than an even chance to beat off an assault." [50]

But the Japanese were not yet ready for the assault. They needed one more day to complete the destruction of Corregidor's defenses and on the morning of the 5th opened up with everything they had. While the batteries on Cavite laid down a barrage on the southern shore of the island, the Bataan batteries gave the north shore the most terrific pounding of the war. "There was a steady roar from Bataan," wrote Captain Gulick, "and a mightier volume on Corregidor. A continuous pall of dust and debris hung over everything. There was a feeling of doom mingled with wonder. . . ." [51]

---

records had been sent to Australia by air, directed to General Sutherland. So far as is known this latter group of records has never reached the files of The Adjutant General. Rad, Wainwright to MacArthur, No. 261, 13 Apr 42, AG 370.05 GHQ SWPA. A partial list of the contents of this shipment, which included the general staff journals and supporting documents, is contained in ltr, Irwin to TAG, 12 Apr 42, sub: Transmittal of Docs, USFIP G–3 Journal.

[47] Wainwright, *General Wainwright's Story,* p. 110.

[48] Harbor Defenses Rpt of Opns, p. 69. The number of shells is estimated in The Siege of Corregidor, Mil Rpts on UN, No. 12, 15 Nov 43, p. 46, MID WD.

[49] The Siege of Corregidor, Mil Rpts on UN, No. 12, 15 Nov 43, p. 50, MID WD. In a message to General MacArthur on the 3d, Wainwright summarized his losses to date. He had left at that time four 12-inch guns; one 12-inch mortar; sixteen 155-mm. guns, only nine of which bore on Bataan; and seven 3-inch guns, of which four bore on Bataan. "Serious losses in AA fire control equipment and searchlights," he went on, "renders AA ineffective, except one battery. Great toll has been taken of machine guns both ground and AA, as well as automatic weapons of all types." Rad, Wainwright to MacArthur, No. 392, 3 May 42, AG 384.1, GHQ SWPA.

[50] The message is reproduced in full in Wainwright, *General Wainwright's Story,* pp. 112–13.

[51] Gulick, Memoirs of Btry C, 91st CA(PS), p. 184.

From Corregidor there was little answering fire. Only three 155-mm. guns remained in operation; practically all the other seacoast artillery, the famous batteries of Corregidor—the 12-inch mortars and rifles, the 6-, 8-, and 10-inch disappearing guns—were silent. The 14-inch guns of Forts Drum and Frank were still able to fire, but targets on Bataan were at extreme range and, except for the guns on Fort Drum, their fire was sporadic.

The bombardment of the 5th destroyed the little that was left to stop a Japanese assault. Those beach defense guns along the north shore which had given away their positions were knocked out, searchlights were put out of action, land mines detonated, barbed wire entanglements torn up, and machine gun emplacements caved in. By the end of the day, wrote General Moore, the beach defenses on the north side of the island "were practically non-existent." [52]

All wire communication was gone by late afternoon. Telephone lines were torn up by the exploding shells and all efforts to repair them were unavailing. One battery commander repaired the line to his battalion headquarters, but "three minutes after the job was done the line was out again." "This time," he wrote despairingly, "we couldn't even locate the broken ends." [53] "Command," observed General Moore, "could be exercised and intelligence obtained only by use of foot messengers," a means of communication, he added, which was "uncertain under the heavy and continuous artillery and air action." [54]

When the bombardment let up momentarily late in the afternoon the dust lay so heavy over the island that the men on Topside could hardly make out the features of Bottomside below them. Beyond that they could not see. Even the topography of the island had changed. Where there had been thick woods and dense vegetation only charred stumps remained. The rocky ground had been pulverized into a fine dust and the road along the shore had been literally blown into the bay. Portions of the cliff had fallen in and debris covered the entire island. The Corregidor of peacetime, with its broad lawns and luxuriant vegetation, impressive parade ground, spacious barracks, pleasant shaded clubs and bungalows, its large warehouses and concrete repair shops, was gone. The island lay "scorched, gaunt, and leafless, covered with the chocolate dust of countless explosions and pitted with shellholes." [55]

Men were living on nerve alone, and morale was dropping rapidly. All hope of reinforcement had long since disappeared. There was only enough water to last four more days at most and no prospect that the pipes and pumps could be repaired. In any event the power plant would not last more than a few weeks. There was a limit to human endurance and that limit, General Wainwright told the President, "has long since been passed." [56]

So intense a bombardment in so concentrated an area could only mean that the Japanese had completed their preparations for the assault. "It took no mental giant," wrote Wainwright, "to figure out, by May 5, 1942, that the enemy was ready to come against Corregidor." [57] He already knew

---

[52] Harbor Defenses Rpt of Opns, p. 71.
[53] Gulick, Memoirs of Btry C, 91st CA (PS), p. 187.
[54] Harbor Defenses Rpt of Opns, p. 72.

[55] Guerrero, "The Last Days of Corregidor."
[56] The full text of the message, sent on 6 May 1942, is in Wainwright, *General Wainwright's Story*, pp. 122–23.
[57] *Ibid.*, p. 114.

from agents in Manila that the Japanese *4th Division* had completed landing maneuvers and that thousands of bamboo ladders, to be used presumably to scale the cliffs of Corregidor, had been built. The moon would be full that night.

At 2100, just after a particularly intense concentration on the eastern end of the island the sound locators of the antiaircraft command picked up the noise of the motors of a large number of landing barges in the vicinity of Limay. The information was relayed to H Station, General Moore's command post in Malinta Tunnel, which alerted all units and ordered beach defense troops to their stations. About an hour later barges were observed approaching the tail of the island and at 2230 the order went out to "prepare for probable landing attack." [58] The full moon, "veiled by streaks of heavy black clouds," was just rising when, shortly before midnight, the Japanese artillery fire suddenly ceased and "its bass roar was replaced by the treble chattering of many small arms." [59] A few minutes later a runner from the beach defense command post arrived at H Station with the news that the Japanese had landed at North Point.

---

[58] Harbor Defenses Rpt of Opns, p. 71.

[59] Gulick, Memoirs of Btry C, 91st CA (PS), p. 188.

CHAPTER XXXI

The Fall of Corregidor

For almost a month the Japanese had been preparing for this moment. Every precaution had been taken to insure the success of the assault and so bring to an end the six-month-long campaign to take the Philippines. Yet General Homma watched the troops embark for the shores of Corregidor with trepidation. Of the three critical moments of the campaign, he told the military commission at his trial, "this was the third."[1]

The troops in the assault craft that approached the north shore of Corregidor on the night of 5 May were from General Kitano's *4th Division*. Homma's plan, it will be recalled, had provided for two landings, to be made on successive nights at opposite ends of the island, and Kitano had accordingly organized his reinforced division into two forces: a left (east) wing and a right (west) wing. The first, which was landing on Corregidor on the night of the 5th, consisted of the *61st Infantry*, reinforced with tanks from the *7th Tank Regiment*, and artillery and service elements. It was led by Col. Gempachi Sato, commander of the *61st*. The right wing, under the *4th Division* infantry group commander, Maj. Gen. Kureo Taniguchi, was the stronger of the two forces and was composed of the *37th Infantry*, one battalion of the *8th In-*

fantry, an element of the *7th Tank Regiment*, several artillery units, and service elements. It was to land the following night on the beach below Topside, near James Ravine.[2] (*Map 24*)

14th Army had completed its preparations for the coming assault during the latter part of April. Ammunition, heavy equipment, and landing boats had been brought to the assembly area, working parties organized to handle the supplies, and combat troops put through the final stages of training. When the landing boats of the *1st Sea Operation Unit* had been assembled and equipped, the *4th Division* began amphibious training along the east coast of Bataan, north of Limay, and the *16th Division* did the same in the Cavite area. Rehearsals had been held and equipment tested at the end of the month to put everything in order for the final test.

The Japanese fully expected the fight to be a hard one. The troops making the landing had been carefully trained in landing operations and close-in fighting. Special attention had been given to methods of removing beach obstacles and reducing strongly fortified positions, and provision was made for the use of smoke screens. Enough rations,

---

[1] USA *vs.* Homma, p. 3095, testimony of Homma. The other two critical moments came during the Lingayen landing and after the abortive effort in late January and early February to break through the Orion–Bagac line on Bataan.

[2] This account of Japanese plans and preparations is based upon: *14th Army* Opns, I, 173–207, II, Annexes 7–12; *5th Air Gp* Opns, pp. 78–84; USA *vs.* Homma, pp. 3089–94, testimony of Homma; Statement of Col Yoshida, 9 Feb 50, ATIS Doc 62644, Statements of Japanese Officials on World War II, GHQ FEC, Mil Intel Sec, IV, 553–57.

fuel, and ammunition to last one week had been issued to the troops. In anticipation of a water shortage, extra canteens had been distributed and provision made for an additional supply of fresh water at the target.

On 27 April—at a conference attended by representatives of the *4th Division, 14th Army* artillery, the *22d Air Brigade,* and the Navy—liaison and co-operation between the assault units, the artillery, and the air forces had been arranged. Two days later the air force had begun the final phase of its operations and for a week concentrated on targets along the north shore of Corregidor and on enemy shipping in the bay. On 5 May Maj. Gen. Kizo Mikami, commanding the *22d Air Brigade,* had had reconnaissance and bombardment aircraft over Corregidor constantly to report on the movement of troops on the island and to soften up the enemy defenses.

The artillery had begun its preparatory fire on 1 May and by the evening of the 5th had laid waste the entire north shore of Corregidor. That night, after the first troops had embarked at Lamao, the artillery concentrated first on the remaining mobile guns and searchlights on the island and then on the stretch of beach between Infantry and Cavalry Points. Just before the landing, the artillery had shifted its fire westward, to Malinta Hill. To assist in artillery fire that night and next day, General Kitajima had placed a liaison group of sixty men in the assault boats. They would go ashore with the first waves and establish artillery observation posts on Malinta Hill as soon as it was taken.

By the time the artillery and air forces had opened the final phase of the bombardment, the *4th Division* had won its fight against malaria and was ready to move into the assembly area. On 4 May, X minus 1,

Colonel Sato had assembled his left wing units in the Lamao River valley, near Cabcaben, and the next day marched them to Lamao where, at dusk, they began to embark for Corregidor. The run to the island was made in darkness, the troops expecting to land about 2300, an hour before moonrise. Earlier that day, after Sato moved out, General Taniguchi's right wing assembled near Cabcaben in preparation for their assault the next night, 6 May.

Colonel Sato's plan was to land the first waves at high tide near Cavalry Point, on the north shore of the narrow tip of the island. Later waves were to come in shortly after and land to the right (west), between Cavalry and Infantry Points. As soon as the beachhead was secure, the troops in the first wave, about a battalion in size, would drive south toward Kindley Field. The rest of Sato's force would push west toward Malinta Hill which was to be occupied by daybreak, 6 May. (*Map 26*)

On the night of 6 May, General Taniguchi's right wing would embark at Lamao and head for the north shore of Corregidor, between Battery and Morrison Points. If all went well the men would land a half hour before midnight and move inland, presumably through James Ravine. One portion of the force was to strike across the island to the south shore; the rest eastward toward Malinta Hill. Meanwhile, Colonel Sato's men were to resume their advance westward from Malinta Hill to join the right wing. When the two groups met, they would combine, under Taniguchi's command, to mop up any remaining enemy resistance. By X plus 2, 7 May, if all went well, the battle for Corregidor would be over.

The plan miscarried almost immediately. At the time the men embarked, the tide on

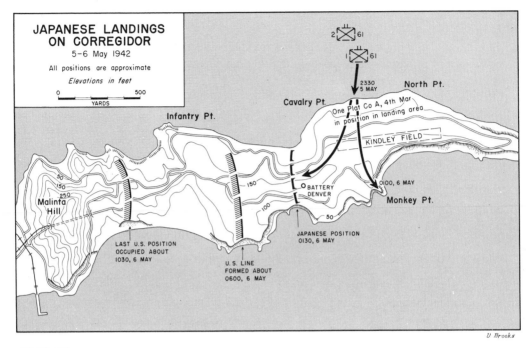

MAP 26

the Bataan shore was flowing west, out of Manila Bay. The Japanese took it for granted that the current off Corregidor would be flowing west also. Contrary to expectation, the current at the target flowed in the opposite direction and the landing force "was naturally swept away." [3] Instead of arriving off Corregidor between Infantry and Cavalry Points, the selected landing site, it approached the island at a point about 1,000 yards to the east, near North Point.

Most of the officers who had planned the landing had not "dreamed that there would be any slip-ups." They thought the peculiar shape of the island would forestall any errors. But, as one Japanese officer later wrote, "the island lost its odd shape as it was approached and it did not serve as a particular landmark." [4]

Most of the 4th Division staff attributed their difficulty in part to the 1st Sea Operation Unit. They felt that the boats were handled inefficiently and that the commander did not have the unit under control during the embarkation and the journey to the target. Because the men of the 1st Sea Operation Unit had had experience in shore-to-shore operations in the Singapore campaign, and were "high-spirited," 4th Division officers felt they had "made light" of the Corregidor assault and failed to train adequately. "The unit later discovered," wrote Colonel Yoshida, "that it had paid dearly for this lack." [5]

[3] Statement of Yoshida, 9 Feb 50, ATIS Doc 62644, Statements of Japanese Officials on World War II, GHQ FEC, Mil Intel Sec, IV, 554.

[4] Ibid.

[5] Ibid. See also Statement of Col Oishi, 2 Oct 50, ATIS Doc 62639, ibid., III, 116.

Not only did the Japanese come in east of the designated beaches, but they became separated during the approach and landed at different times and at some distance from each other. The landing plan had provided that the two battalions of the *61st Infantry* land abreast, with the *1st Battalion* on the right (west). Off Cabcaben, in the assembly area, Colonel Sato, who was with the *1st Battalion,* discovered that the *2d Battalion,* which should have been on his left, had "strayed" and was now on his right flank. Charitably attributing this error "to the mental strain" and the "distractions" of the commander of the landing craft, Sato ordered the *1st Battalion* to go ahead. The *2d Battalion* was to follow and to change course so that it would reach the beach in its proper place on the left of the formation. It was never able to do so or to catch up with the *1st Battalion.*

Colonel Sato might have corrected the formation by sending the *1st Battalion* westward so that it would once again become the right element. Actually such a course would have compensated partially for the eastward drift of the entire flotilla, but he had no way of knowing this. What he feared most was his own artillery fire. The landing plan provided for the bombardment on the right (west) of the landing beaches "to cover its right flank," and if the landing craft veered too far to the right, they would come under friendly fire. It was for this reason, explained one officer, that "the unit kept on drifting to the left without even knowing the exact location of the landing point." [6]

This confusion during the approach, plus the failure to make proper allowance for current and tide, brought the Japanese to the wrong beaches and in the wrong order. The *2d Battalion,* which had "strayed" to the right, never recovered from its initial error and came in late. The *1st Battalion* arrived somewhat east of the place designated for the *2d Battalion,* which found itself coming in toward a strange shore near the tail of the island and far from the area upon which the artillery had laid down its preparatory fire. Mutual support of the two battalions, which had been provided for in this plan, was impossible. "Thus," explained Colonel Yoshida, "the Division was forced to start fighting under disadvantageous conditions. . . . A long, desperate struggle and heavy sacrifices were required to break the situation." [7]

The Americans and Filipinos on shore, unaware of the confusion in the Japanese ranks and still reeling under the effects of the bombardment, met the enemy with every weapon they could muster. One 2-gun 75-mm. battery near the tail of the island, just east of North Point, had never disclosed its position and it opened fire, together with some 37-mm. guns, at a range of about 300 yards, on the incoming landing craft. The few remaining searchlights were turned on but were quickly shot out by artillery fire from Bataan. But there was enough light for the guns on shore from the tracers which "like a 4th of July display danced and sparkled pinkly from Kindley Field to Monkey Point." [8] At point-blank range they struck the surprised and confused Japanese, sank a number of the boats, and caused many casualties. "Beach defense officers at

[6] Statement of Yoshida, *ibid.,* IV, 554, 555. See also USA *vs.* Homma, pp. 3091–92, testimony of Homma.

[7] Statement of Yoshida, IV, 553.
[8] Gulick, Memoirs of Btry C, 91st CA (PS), p. 188, copy in OCMH. See also Harbor Defenses Rpt of Opns, p. 73.

SEARCHLIGHT ON CORREGIDOR

seemed as though "a hundred guns rained red-hot steel on them." Eyewitnesses at Cabcaben described the scene as "a spectacle that confounded the imagination, surpassing in grim horror anything we had ever seen before." [10]

The Japanese, who had believed they could come ashore "without shedding blood," lost heavily during the landing. Although the *1st Battalion* reached the beach on schedule under supporting fire from *14th Army* artillery, it was hard hit. Estimates of its casualties varied from 50 to 75 percent.[11] Casualties in the battalion which came in late exceeded those of the first landing, one Japanese officer placing the number of drowned alone in his own unit at 50 percent. Total casualties for both landings were estimated at several hundred, and one Japanese officer claimed that only 800 men of the 2,000 who made the attempt reached the shore.[12]

Though the Japanese attempted no further landing that night the Americans believed that they had and that it had been frustrated. At about 0440, as dawn was breaking, small boats believed to be landing barges were seen approaching the Bottomside area of Corregidor. All remaining guns were directed to fire on these craft and on Cabcaben where other boats could be seen. Battery Stockade, with two 155-mm. fixed

the scene," wrote an observer, "reported that the slaughter of the Japanese in their barges was sickening." [9]

By this time the moon had risen and the clouds had drifted away. Thus, when the *2d Battalion* of Colonel Sato's *61st Infantry* approached the shore shortly before midnight, it was clearly visible to the men on the beach. There was now enough light for artillery fire, and the Americans opened up with everything they had. The remaining 12-inch mortar of Battery Way went into action with a boom, followed by the shriek of the rotating bands. From nearby Fort Hughes came fire from the mortars of Battery Craighill while the remaining smaller guns at both forts, the 3-inchers and the 75's, dropped their shells on the landing barges nearing the shore. To the Japanese in the small boats it

[9] The Siege of Corregidor, Mil Rpts on UN, No. 12, 15 Nov 43, p. 48, MID WD.

[10] Kazumaro Uno, *Corregidor: Isle of Delusion* (Press Bureau, *Imperial Japanese Army, GHQ, China,* September 1942), p. 19. This is a wartime propaganda book written in English by a press correspondent who was an eyewitness to the landing and interviewed participants.
[11] *Ibid.,* p. 17. Uno states that "less than 30 percent of the men reached the shore." Colonel Yoshida states that losses in this wave were slight, but does not indicate their extent. Statement of Yoshida, p. 556.
[12] Harbor Defenses Rpt of Opns, p. 73; The Siege of Corregidor, Mil Rpts on UN, No. 12, 15 Nov 43, p. 49, MID WD.

guns and two more roving batteries, hit the approaching formation with damaging effect. Fort Drum opened fire at a range of 20,000 yards and dropped over 100 rounds on the vessels. Ordered to shift fire to the North Channel, the commander at Drum replied that he could not see any targets because of the dense cloud of smoke and dust over Corregidor. "Just fire in the smoke, anywhere between you and Cabcaben," he was told, "and you can't miss them." [13]

Though the Americans were mistaken in their belief that they had driven off a third assault, they had succeeded in sinking and damaging many more of the enemy's fleet of small boats. Between half and two thirds of the landing craft leaving Bataan that night had been put out of action. When Homma received the report of "the disastrous state" of his troops and the loss in landing craft he was thrown into an "agony of mind." [14]

The situation was not as bad as Homma believed. Troops of the *1st Battalion, 61st Infantry,* had come ashore near North Point at about 2310, and, after a brief fight with the men of Company A, 4th Marines, stationed along the north shore from Malinta Hill to the east tip of the island, had established a beachhead on the island. One portion of the battalion advanced south across the tail to the south shore and by 0100 had reached Monkey Point and cut off those troops on the eastern tip. The rest of the battalion had turned west and advanced along the axis of the island toward Malinta Hill, the main objective of the landing. By 0130 this force had taken the position formerly occupied by Battery Denver on a ridge in

the narrow neck between Infantry and Cavalry Points. There the Japanese established a north-south line across the island. [15] Already the tanks and artillery were coming ashore.

Thus far, the fighting had been confused and un-co-ordinated. The 1st Battalion, 4th Marines, holding the East Sector and a shore line about 10,000 yards long, had only one company on the north shore, with one platoon posted in the area where the Japanese landed. Opposition at the beaches, therefore, had been slight and the Japanese had been able to advance swiftly. It was only when he heard voices "not American" that a marine on Denver Hill realized the enemy had reached that point. "The place," he wrote, "seemed to have Japs all over it." [16] Not until 0200, when the situation had clarified, was it discovered that only two platoons stood between the enemy and Malinta Tunnel. At that time the first elements of the reserve, two companies, were committed.

Meanwhile General Moore had stripped his seacoast batteries to provide additional troops for the beach defenses. At the first news of the landing, men from the 59th Coast Artillery (Batteries Cheney, Wheeler, and Crockett) were made available to Colonel Howard. Later other coast and antiaircraft artillerymen were released from their assignments and formed as infantry troops.

---

[13] Fort Drum Annex, p. 10, Exhibit M, Harbor Defenses Rpt of Opns.

[14] USA *vs.* Homma, pp. 3093–94, testimony of Homma.

[15] The action on the island is reconstructed from: Baldwin, "The Fourth Marines at Corregidor," Part 3, *Marine Corps Gazette* (January 1947), pp. 23–29; Howard, 4th Marines Rpt of Opns, pp. 19–21, USMC Hist Sec; Harbor Defenses Rpt of Opns, pp. 72–75; Dalness, Opns of the Prov Bn, 4th Marines, pp. 10–18; Statement of Yoshida, pp. 555–56.

[16] Quoted in Baldwin, "The Fourth Marines at Corregidor," Part 3, *Marine Corps Gazette* (January 1947), p. 24.

Placing these men in position east of Malinta Hill proved a most difficult task. They had to move from their battery positions, across Bottomside which was under intermittent but intense enemy artillery fire, into Malinta Tunnel via the west entrance, through the tunnel, then out by way of the east entrance. By this time the Japanese were concentrating artillery fire on this entrance, the only avenue of approach to the thin line in front of the Japanese. One enemy barrage caught Battery C of the 59th Coast Artillery on its way across Bottomside, killing one officer and wounding a number of men.

Between 0200 and 0400 the Japanese made no advances but threw back three counterattacks against their Denver Battery line. While their artillery continued to pound away at Malinta Hill and the area to the west, pinning the Americans and Filipinos to the ground, the men of the *2d Battalion, 61st Infantry,* joined their comrades in the *1st Battalion.* With these reinforcements, Colonel Sato was able to increase the pressure on the Marine line in front of him.

At 0430 Colonel Howard decided to send in the last of his reserves. The danger of a break-through was too serious to delay any longer. With the 2d and 3d Battalions, 4th Marines, held in place in the Middle and West Sectors by the threat of additional landings, he had only the untrained men of the 4th Provisional Battalion and the artillerymen. These he sent into the line with orders to counterattack and regain control of the east end of the island.

It was an impossible assignment. The 4th Provisional Battalion, led by Maj. Francis Williams, USMC, was not a battalion at all. Many of its officers and most of its men were neither qualified nor trained as infantrymen; it was not organized as a battalion of infantry and did not have the equipment and weapons normal in an infantry battalion. It was, one of the officers remarked, simply "a group of 500 sailors with 500 rifles—nothing more." [17]

The 4th Provisional Battalion had moved into Malinta Tunnel earlier that morning and had been waiting at the east entrance for several hours when it received orders to counterattack. During that time the men had suffered acute discomfort from the heat and dust and from the concussion of shells falling just outside the entrance. They had witnessed also a steady stream of wounded marines brought into the tunnel past their position, a sight that "did little to boost the morale of the men about to move into the battle area." [18]

At 0430 Major Williams moved his battalion out in a column of companies. Before the last company cleared the tunnel, the company at the head of the column had already suffered casualties from artillery fire. All along the avenue of approach the battalion ran into interdiction fire and it had gone only 500 yards before it was dispersed by a heavy concentration. With much difficulty the column was formed again and managed to move forward to within 200 yards of the front. There Major Williams formed a skirmish line, and the battalion completed its journey in this formation.

The sector assigned the provisional battalion comprised the left (north) portion of the thinly held line facing the Japanese dug in on both sides of Denver Hill. The right side of the line was taken over by the Headquarters and Service Company, 4th

---

[17] Dalness, Opns of the Prov Bn, 4th Marines, p. 20.
[18] *Ibid.,* p. 13.

Marines, plus miscellaneous Army and Navy troops. In reserve were sixty men of the 59th Coast Artillery led by Capt. Herman H. Hauck.

Preparations for the counterattack were completed by 0600 and fifteen minutes later the men moved out. The Japanese, surprised by this "obstinate and bold counterattack," [19] fell back, and the Americans made gains along both flanks. In the center, where the Japanese had emplaced a heavy machine gun in one of Denver Battery's gun pits, the counterattack stalled. Other means failing, Lt. Bethel B. Otter, USN, commander of Company T, 4th Provisional Battalion, and five volunteers set out "with the strong determination to get the gun that dealt so much misery to Company T and the rest of the Battalion." [20] Armed with hand grenades the six men crawled to within thirty yards of the gun pit, then hurled the grenades. Their aim was accurate and the machine gun was put out of action, but other Japanese troops moved in and opened fire on the Americans, killing Otter and four of the men.

On the north end of the line, the advancing men of Company Q discovered two assault boats, loaded with Japanese troops, hung up on the rocks. A small group of men was sent down to the beach to pick off the helpless enemy. It took thirty minutes and the expenditure of several thousand rounds of ammunition for the untrained sailors to complete the job.

To the Japanese the situation on Corregidor seemed desperate. They were still some distance from Malinta Hill, which was to have been occupied by dawn. Without

control of this hill, the landing of the 4th Division's right wing, scheduled for 2330 of the 6th, would be a risky undertaking. The problem was discussed at 4th Division headquarters early that morning and some members of the staff argued strongly for a one-day postponement of the attack scheduled for that night. The proposal was seriously considered but final decision deferred, pending the outcome of the day's action. Nothing more was done than to urge "the left flank unit to keep on attacking." [21]

The Japanese were worried, too, about their supply of ammunition, which was dangerously low. The amount originally allotted for the assault was adequate but the small boats which were to have brought ammunition ashore after the landings were in such haste to get out of range of American fire that they "threw the ammunition into the nearby waters and returned to Bataan." By 1100, it was estimated, the Japanese on shore would have been out of ammunition. "When I recall all this," wrote Colonel Yoshida, "I cannot but break into a cold sweat." [22]

Back at 14th Army headquarters on Bataan, General Homma spent a sleepless night waiting for the news that Malinta Hill had been taken. Repeatedly he sent his aide to 4th Division headquarters to ask about the progress of operations on Corregidor and "every time I was disappointed." Even division headquarters had no clear picture of the situation "because the lines of the hostile troops got mixed up." With the 2,000 men he believed had been put ashore facing a force estimated at 14,000 men, there was a real danger, Homma felt, that his troops might be driven back into the sea. "I had plenty of troops on this side of the

[19] Statement of Oishi, 2 Oct 50, ATIS Doc 62639, Statements of Japanese Officials on World War II, GHQ FEC, Mil Intel Sec, III, 116.
[20] Dalness, Opns of the Prov Bn, 4th Marines, p. 16.

[21] Statement of Oishi, III, 116.
[22] Statement of Yoshida, IV, 556.

sea," he explained later. "[But] I could not send reinforcements with the 21 boats which were left." The news that the Americans were counterattacking, therefore, threw him into a panic. "My God," he exclaimed, "I have failed miserably on the assault." [23]

Homma need not have been so concerned. Actually, the assault had not failed and the counterattackers had already run into serious trouble. Small detachments of Japanese had infiltrated the left of the American line and were firing at the rear of the advancing troops. The Japanese had also set up their light artillery and were now using it with devastating effect against the American troops on the line. Finally, at 0800 Colonel Howard had decided to commit the last of his reserves, Captain Hauck and the sixty men of the 59th Coast Artillery. By this time the counterattack, though netting the Americans about 300 yards in some sectors, had bogged down for lack of supporting weapons and reinforcements.

The final blow came shortly before 1000 when the Japanese sent the three tanks they had brought ashore into action. The tanks advanced to the ridge line and, according to Colonel Yoshida, "annihilated the powerful enemy in the vicinity." "This action," he went on to explain, "not only made it possible for the two battalions to establish liaison with each other but also caused the enemy commander to . . . report this fact to the United States." [24] Though this sweeping claim for the tanks is not borne out by the facts, it is true that the first appearance of armor on the front panicked the troops and caused some to bolt to the rear. It took the combined efforts of commissioned and noncommissioned officers to calm the troops and prevent a rout. [25] "The effect of the tanks," concluded the Japanese, "was more than had been anticipated." [26]

By 1000 the situation of the Americans was critical. The troops on the front line were pinned down securely. Attempts to move forward were discouraged by the enemy's heavy machine guns and light artillery; movement to the rear only brought the men under fire from the heavier guns on Bataan and strafing aircraft. The tanks were in action and there were no weapons with which to stop them. Casualties had been heavy and the wounded men were still in the line. There were no litter bearers, and if there had been, the injured could not have been evacuated. The walking wounded were allowed to go to the rear, but most of those who availed themselves of this opportunity became "litter or Graves Registration cases." [27] Already between 600 and 800 men had been killed and about 1,000 more wounded. To continue the fight when there was no hope of being able to hold out longer than a few more hours would be a needless sacrifice of lives.

Perhaps the deciding factor in the decision to lay down arms was the fear of what might happen that night. It was apparent from the artillery fire on James and Cheney Ravines, where only two companies were posted, that a landing would soon be made there. All reserves had been committed and practically all guns had been destroyed. Even if the Japanese did not make another landing it was virtually certain that the enemy on the east end of the island would reach the tunnel, with its 1,000 wounded men, in a few

---

[23] USA *vs.* Homma, pp. 3093–94, testimony of Homma.

[24] Statement of Yoshida, IV, 555.

[25] Dalness, Opns of 4th Prov Bn, 4th Marines, p. 17.

[26] Statement of Yoshida, IV, 555.

[27] Dalness, Opns of the Prov Bn, 4th Marines, p. 17.

hours. The result would be wholesale slaughter.[28]

On the basis of this estimate of the situation, General Wainwright at 1000 decided to surrender, to sacrifice one day of freedom in exchange for several thousand lives. Like General King, who had surrendered Bataan four weeks earlier, Wainwright had made his estimate and concluded there was nothing to be gained by further resistance.

Having made his decision, Wainwright ordered Beebe to broadcast a surrender message to General Homma. General Moore was to put into effect the previously prepared plan for the destruction of all arms larger than .45-caliber, to be accomplished by noon. At that time the American flag on Corregidor would be lowered and burned and the white flag hoisted. These arrangements made, Wainwright announced his decision to President Roosevelt and General MacArthur.

With broken heart and head bowed in sadness but not in shame [he told the President], I report . . . that today I must arrange terms for the surrender of the fortified islands of Manila Bay. . . . Please say to the nation that my troops and I have accomplished all that is humanly possible and that we have upheld the best traditions of the United States and its Army. . . . With profound regret and with continued pride in my gallant troops, I go to meet the Japanese commander.[29]

---

[28] Wainwright, *General Wainwright's Story*, pp. 185–86.

[29] Rad, Wainwright to Roosevelt, 6 May 42. A copy of this message as well as the one to General MacArthur is reproduced in Wainwright, *General Wainwright's Story*, pp. 122–23.

CHAPTER XXXII

The End of Resistance

General Wainwright's decision on the morning of 6 May to surrender to the enemy was the beginning of a strange series of events. Considerable difficulty was encountered in arranging a meeting with General Homma and the conference that followed took an entirely unexpected turn. It was not until midnight of the 6th, fourteen hours after the men on Corregidor had destroyed their weapons, that the Japanese agreed to a cessation of hostilities.

The surrender of scattered detachments hiding out in the mountains of north Luzon and of General Sharp's Visayan-Mindanao Force presented even greater difficulties. There the last of the troops did not lay down their arms until almost a month later. Only then did the Japanese admit that organized resistance in the Philippines had ended and accord to their captives the status of prisoners of war.

General Wainwright's Orders

Unlike General King, who had been forced to violate his instructions and keep from his superior any knowledge of his decision to surrender the Luzon Force, Wainwright was able to make his decision unhindered by restrictions from higher headquarters. He had not always had this freedom of action. Until 9 April he had been bound, as had General MacArthur before him, by President Roosevelt's order

"to fight as long as there remains any possibility of resistance."[1] On that day, the day of General King's surrender, the President modified this order and gave General Wainwright full authority to act on his own judgment.

The decision to change Wainwright's instructions had been initiated in Washington just before the surrender of Bataan. Alerted by reports from MacArthur and Wainwright, Maj. Gen. Joseph T. McNarney, acting in Marshall's absence, had informed the President on 8 April (Washington time) that the situation on Bataan was extremely serious and the collapse of its defense imminent. Reminding President Roosevelt of his instructions to MacArthur, "issued at a time when it appeared necessary to make very clear . . . the nature of the defense expected," McNarney suggested that the President might wish now to modify these instructions. "It is possible," he wrote, "that in the literal execution of these orders General Wainwright may be tempted to carry them through to an illogical extreme. I think there should be no doubt that his resolution and sense of duty will preclude any untoward or precipitous action, but on the other hand, it is possible that greater lati-

---

[1] Rads, Roosevelt to MacArthur, No. 1029, 9 Feb 42, CofS Phil Situation File; Marshall to Wainwright, No. 1234, 24 Mar 42, Msgs to Gen Wainwright, OPD Exec O. See Chapter XX, above, for the relevant portions of the text of the President's message to MacArthur.

tude in the final decision should be allowed him." [2]

President Roosevelt accepted McNarney's suggestion readily, and that same day, 8 April—the 9th, Philippine time—approved the text of a message for Wainwright modifying his earlier instructions. Explaining that he was changing his orders "because of the state to which your forces have been reduced by circumstances over which you have had no control," the President told Wainwright that he was free to make "any decision affecting the future of the Bataan garrison." "I . . . have every confidence," the President wrote, "that whatever decision you may sooner or later be forced to make will be dictated only by the best interests of your country and your magnificent troops." [3]

Roosevelt's message to Wainwright was not sent directly to Corregidor but went instead to General MacArthur in Australia with instructions that it be forwarded to Corregidor if he, MacArthur, concurred "both as to substance and timing." [4] The message reached MacArthur at about the same time as Wainwright's dispatch carrying the news that Bataan had surrendered. Since, in his view, "the action taken on Bataan anticipated the authority conveyed in the message," he saw no need to change

Wainwright's instructions. [5] In effect, this was a "non-concurrence" of the President's message to Wainwright, which remained on his desk.

But the progress of events had already invalidated MacArthur's decision. The President, on hearing news of the surrender of Bataan and before receiving MacArthur's reply, apparently decided that Wainwright needed assurance of support immediately and he sent him the text of his message, including the instructions given MacArthur, from whom, he explained, no reply had yet been received. "Whatever decision you have made," Roosevelt told Wainwright, "has been dictated by the best interests of your troops and of the country." He then went on to express the hope that Wainwright would be able to hold Corregidor, but assured him "of complete freedom of action" and "full confidence" in any decision he might be forced to make. [6]

General Wainwright received the message on 10 April and sent an immediate acknowledgment expressing his understanding of the change in instructions as well as "heartfelt gratitude" for the President's confidence in his judgment. At the same time, he informed MacArthur of the President's message to him and of his reply. [7]

Wainwright waited in vain for a response from MacArthur. Although his new orders

[2] Memo, Actg CofS for the President, 8 Apr 42, sub: Bataan Situation, CofS Bataan-Corregidor File. Washington time is thirteen hours earlier than Manila time.

[3] Rad, Marshall to MacArthur, No. 1158, 8 Apr 42, AG 384.1, GHQ SWPA. Reproduced in Wainwright, *General Wainwright's Story*, pp. 83–84.

[4] The published version of the message in *General Wainwright's Story*, pages 83–84, does not contain the instructions to MacArthur. Apparently Wainwright received a copy of the message at the same time as MacArthur, but whether it was an information copy addressed to him or was picked up unofficially by the radio operator is not known.

[5] Rad, MacArthur to Marshall, No. 83, 9 Apr 42, Msgs from Gen MacArthur, OPD Exec O.

[6] Rad, Roosevelt to Wainwright, No. 1329, 9 Apr 42, CofS Supersecret File, Bataan-Corregidor. MacArthur was informed of the President's action at the same time. Rad, McNarney to MacArthur, No. 1173, 8 Apr 42, AG 384.1, GHQ SWPA.

[7] Rads, Wainwright to Roosevelt, No. 749, 10 Apr 42, OPD 381 P.I., Sec 1, Case 41; Wainwright to MacArthur, No. 204, 10 Apr 42, AG 384.1 GHQ SWPA.

had come directly from the President, he
was aware that initially they had been sent
to his immediate superior for approval.
That approval had never been given, and
Wainwright was understandably anxious to
have it. On 13 April, therefore, he raised
the subject again in a message to MacArthur. The President, he reminded MacArthur, had stated in his original dispatch that
it was to be forwarded if he, MacArthur,
concurred. Since he had not yet heard from
MacArthur on the subject, Wainwright
wrote, he could not avoid the conclusion
that MacArthur did not approve of the new
orders. The President, Wainwright asserted,
"appears to leave to my discretion the decision which I must ultimately make. . . . If
I am not correct in this assumption I hope
you will so advise me." [8]

General MacArthur's reply left no doubt
that he considered Wainwright free now to
make his own decisions. He explained why
he had not transmitted the original dispatch,
and then went on to say that the President's
later message "came direct to you . . . and
now gives you complete authority to use
your own judgment." [9] MacArthur's reply
put an end to the correspondence on Wainwright's instructions. The final decision was
his, and three weeks later, when he decided
to surrender, he did so entirely on his own
responsibility.

The Surrender of Corregidor

At 1030 on the morning of 6 May General Beebe stepped up to the microphone of
the "Voice of Freedom" and in tired but
clear tones read a message addressed to Gen-

eral Homma "or the present commander in
chief of the Imperial Japanese Forces on
Luzon." The message was from General
Wainwright and it contained his offer to
surrender.[10]

At about the same time that Beebe was
reading Wainwright's message to Homma,
the radio operator was flashing a message
in code to General Sharp on Mindanao.
This message represented Wainwright's last
desperate effort to salvage what he could
from defeat. In it he released to General
Sharp's command all forces in the Philippines, except those on the four fortified
islands in Manila Bay, and instructed Sharp
to report to General MacArthur immediately for orders. "I believe," he told Sharp,
"you will understand the motive behind this
order." [11]

Wainwright's motive was clear; it was
simply an effort to surrender as few men as
possible. By relinquishing command of all
troops except those in the Harbor Defenses,
Wainwright hoped to persuade General
Homma to accept the view that since the
troops in the south were not under his control he could not properly be held responsible for their surrender. Had he known of
General King's failure to persuade the Japanese to accept the surrender of the Luzon
Force, Wainwright might well have hesi-
tated before risking the success of the surrender negotiations by so transparent a ruse.

The message Beebe read that morning,
therefore, offered the surrender only of the
four islands in Manila Bay, "together with
all military and naval personnel and all

[8] Rad, Wainwright to MacArthur, No. 218, 13
Apr 42, AG 384.1, GHQ SWPA.
[9] Rad, MacArthur to Wainwright, 14 Apr 42, AG
241, GHQ SWPA.

[10] The message is printed in its entirety in Wainwright, General Wainwright's Story, p. 121.
[11] Rad, Wainwright to Sharp, 6 May 42, Sharp
Papers. The Sharp Papers consist of two envelopes
of messages and miscellaneous records belonging to
the general and turned over to the author by Mrs.
Sharp on Sharp's death. They are on file in OCMH.

existing stores and equipment," by noon of the 6th. At that time the white flag would be run up over Corregidor and its garrison as well as those of the other islands would cease fire, unless the Japanese attempted a landing in force. The message also covered in detail arrangements for a meeting between Wainwright and the Japanese commander. At noon, "if all of your firing and aerial bombardment has ceased," Beebe told the Japanese, Wainwright would send two staff officers by boat to Cabcaben to meet Homma's representative. This Japanese officer should be empowered to name the time and place of meeting of the two commanders. When these details had been settled and the American officer had returned to Corregidor, Wainwright would proceed to the designated point and there make the formal surrender to General Homma.[12]

When General Beebe completed the reading of the surrender message, it was broadcast in Japanese. No reply was received and the Japanese gave no indication that they had heard either broadcast. Shells from Bataan continued to fall on Corregidor and the Japanese troops on the island, who had been instructed to disregard a flag of truce and to attack until directed otherwise by *14th Army* headquarters, continued their advance toward the east entrance of Malin-

ta Tunnel. At 1100 and again at 1145 the message was rebroadcast, in English and Japanese, but still there was no reply. Promptly at noon, the white flag was hoisted over the highest point of the island and the troops on the four islands ceased fire.[13]

During the morning all arms larger than .45-caliber had been destroyed. The marines, misreading the order, had begun to smash their small arms as well, and others had followed suit until an officer had halted the destruction. All classified papers and maps had been torn or burned and lay in shreds and ashes on the floor of the tunnel. The codes and radio equipment had been smashed beyond recognition and the treasury of the Commonwealth Government reduced to trash. It took Col. John R. Vance, the finance officer, and his assistants several hours to cut up with scissors more than two million pesos. By noon, when the destruction was completed, Malinta Tunnel presented a scene of "unbelievable disorder, congestion, and confusion." [14]

The men in the tunnel had reached the end of their physical and mental resources. They were dirty, hungry, and completely exhausted. Some reacted violently to the order to destroy their arms and swore with bitter vehemence, but most were too tired to have any feelings at all. The quartermaster lateral had been thrown open and each man took what he wanted and went off to a quiet corner to eat his last meal before the Japanese moved in. Some lay

[12] Wainwright, *General Wainwright's Story*, p. 121. The account of the surrender is based upon the following sources: Wainwright, *General Wainwright's Story*, pp. 119–40; USA *vs.* Homma, Prosecution Exhibits 418 and 419 for Depositions of Gens Wainwright and Moore, pp. 2364–2409 for testimony of Lt Col John R. Pugh, pp. 3082–88, 3094–95, 3173–86, 3214–20 for testimony of Homma, pp. 2468–73 for testimony of Gen Wachi, p. 2590 for testimony of Nakajima; Questionnaire Dealing with Phil Opns, 5 Aug 49, ATIS Doc 49692; Statement of Col Motoo Nakayama, 26 Aug 49, ATIS Doc 50246; Leon M. Guerrero, "The Fall of Corregidor," *Philippine Review* (July 1943).

[13] Other flags were raised at the entrances to Malinta Tunnel. USA *vs.* Homma, Prosecution Exhibit 418, Deposition of Gen Moore. In international law, the white flag indicates only a desire to communicate with the enemy; it does not require the enemy to cease fire. FM 27–10, Rules of Land Warfare, p. 62.

[14] Col William C. Braly, *The Hard Way Home* (Washington, 1947), p. 5. See also Wainwright, *General Wainwright's Story*, p. 120.

down and went to sleep; others stared vacantly into space. "Such a sad, sad day . . .," wrote Mrs. Williams. "I can't tell you just how terrible this is." [15]

When the Japanese failed to reply to the noon broadcast or to honor the flag of truce, Wainwright was faced with the terrible threat of the total destruction of his now defenseless force. He made one last effort at 1230 to reach the Japanese commander by radio, but the result was the same as before. There was only one method left by which he could establish contact with General Homma—to send an officer forward under a white flag to the enemy lines to make arrangements with the local enemy commander. For this difficult and dangerous assignment Wainwright selected a Marine officer, Capt. Golland L. Clark, Jr. With a flag bearer, a musician, and an interpreter, Captain Clark set out shortly before 1300, during a lull in the battle. As the group passed through the American lines, the music sounded out and the flag bearer waved his white standard, a sheet tied to a pole. The Japanese allowed them to march through no man's land without interference, and in due time Captain Clark was taken to a colonel he believed to be the troop commander on Corregidor. To him he explained that General Wainwright was seeking a truce and wished to discuss the terms of surrender with General Homma. The Japanese officer, after consulting his superiors on Bataan, told Captain Clark that if Wainwright would come to his headquarters he would make arrangements to send him to Bataan. [16]

Within an hour after his departure Clark was back in Malinta Tunnel with the Japanese message. Immediately, General Wainwright, accompanied by General Moore and his aides, with Clark acting as guide, went forward toward the enemy lines. It was now 1400. [17] The party rode in a sedan as far as Denver Hill, then ascended the ridge on foot. Near the summit they were met by an English-speaking Japanese lieutenant and a colonel, who, Wainwright correctly guessed, was a staff officer.

What the Americans did not know was that the Japanese colonel was Nakayama, General Homma's senior operations officer and the man who had accepted General King's surrender. Homma had sent him to Corregidor the night before with orders to bring General Wainwright to him only if the American was ready to surrender all his troops. [18] It is not surprising therefore that when Wainwright explained that he wished to surrender only the four islands in Manila Bay, Nakayama replied with "an angry torrent of Japanese," the gist of which was that any surrender would have to include all forces in the Philippines. "In that case," replied Wainwright, "I will deal only with General Homma and with no one of less rank." [19] Nakayama thereupon agreed to take him to Bataan.

Nakayama's ready agreement to Wainwright's request for a conference with Gen-

---

[15] Williams, The Last Days of Corregidor, Supp., p. 2.

[16] Baldwin, 'The Fourth Marines at Corregidor," Part 4, Marine Corps Gazette (February 1942), p. 43; Wainwright, General Wainwright's Story, p. 124.

[17] There is little agreement on time in the sources. The discrepancies cannot be settled by personal interviews, since the participants, under the stress of the moment, had no clear conception of when things happened. The author has reconciled as far as possible the time given by the Americans with that of the Japanese to account for the known sequence of events.

[18] USA vs. Homma, pp. 3173–79, testimony of Homma, and p. 2529, testimony of Wachi.

[19] Wainwright, General Wainwright's Story, p. 125.

eral Homma was based on fresh instructions from *14th Army* headquarters. The news that a white flag had been raised over Corregidor had reached Homma about 1230. Apparently he had not heard the Beebe broadcasts, and this was the first intimation he had of Wainwright's desire to surrender.[20] Not long after, Nakayama, who was probably the officer Captain Clark talked with, had reported that Wainwright wished to see General Homma to arrange for the surrender of his force. At that time he was instructed to bring the American commander to Bataan.[21] When he met Wainwright shortly after 1400, therefore, the question of whether Homma would talk to the American had already been settled. Nakayama's only task was to make arrangements for the journey.

At the outset, Nakayama agreed to follow the arrangements made by the Americans. The boat set aside to take Wainwright to Bataan was docked on the south side of the island, and Lt. Col. John R. Pugh, the general's senior aide, went back to bring the boat around to the north dock. Wainwright also sent General Moore back to the tunnel "to look after things in his absence," and with him went his aide and Captain Clark. With his remaining aide, Maj. Thomas Dooley, Wainwright set out with Nakayama and the interpreter along the road to the north dock to meet Colonel Pugh. They had not gone far when they came under fire from Japanese artillery. Nakayama refused to go any further and insisted that they turn back. Wainwright had no choice but to agree and Nakayama led the group to Cavalry Point where Japanese troops were still debarking and sent out a call to Bataan for a boat. An

armored barge finally arrived and, after some difficulty in embarking, the group reached Cabcaben at about 1600.

On the dock when Wainwright stepped out was Maj. William Lawrence, his administrative assistant. He had made the journey to Bataan with General Beebe, Colonel Pugh, and Sgt. Hubert Carroll, Wainwright's orderly, in the boat originally selected for the trip. The others had gone forward to find Wainwright, but Lawrence had remained behind with the boat and now accompanied the general and Dooley to the meeting place, a house about three quarters of a mile to the north. There they were joined by Beebe, Pugh, and Carroll.[22]

For almost a half hour the six Americans waited tensely on the open porch of the house, facing Manila Bay, a short distance away. It was a windy day and from the beach rose a dense cloud of sand and dust. The only Japanese who approached was an orderly who brought cold water, which they accepted gratefully. Finally a group of photographers arrived and the Americans were ordered to line up on the lawn to have their pictures taken. They were still there at 1700 when General Homma drove up in a Cadillac, saluted with a vague flourish of the hand, and strode up to the porch. Behind him were his principal staff officers, correspondents, and more photographers. The Americans followed silently.

The contrast between the two rival commanders on the porch was striking. Unlike most Japanese, General Homma was a large man, about five feet ten inches in height, barrel-chested and heavy-set, weighing close to two hundred pounds. His manner was assured and his bearing erect. His regulation olive drab uniform, with white shirt open

---

[20] USA *vs.* Homma, pp. 3173, 3176–77, testimony of Homma, and p. 2468, testimony of Wachi.
[21] Statement of Nakayama, 26 Aug 49, ATIS Doc 50246.

[22] USA *vs.* Homma, Prosecution Exhibits 418 and 419, Depositions of Moore and Wainwright.

THE MEETING OF WAINWRIGHT AND HOMMA

at the collar, was fresh and crisp. Pinned to his chest were several rows of brightly colored decorations and ribbons, and at his side hung a sword. General Wainwright, who had earned the nickname "Skinny" long before he had undergone the privations of Bataan and Corregidor, was over six feet tall, but weighed only about 160 pounds. He was "thin as a crane," observed one of the Japanese correspondents, and "made a pathetic figure against the massive form of General Homma." [23] His uniform, the best he had, consisted of khaki shirt and trousers; he wore no decorations and carried only a bamboo cane to support a trick knee. In his eyes and in the deep lines etched in his face could be read the story of the withdrawal from Lingayen Gulf, the long, drawn-out

[23] The source of this quotation is unknown. It appears in a Japanese propaganda book and was copied by a colleague who neglected to note the title and has since forgotten the location.

siege of Bataan, and the terrific bombardment of Corregidor.

On the porch was a long table around which chairs had been placed. Homma took a seat in the center, facing the open side, and motioned his officers to sit down. General Wachi, *14th Army* chief of staff, took the seat on Homma's right, Nakayama the one on his left; the others filling in the spaces beyond. To the rear, between Homma and Nakayama, stood the interpreter. On the American side of the table were five officers, with Wainwright in the center, opposite Homma. To his left were General Beebe and Major Dooley; to his right Colonel Pugh and Major Lawrence. Behind the Japanese were their war correspondents, photographers, and newsreel camera men.

The meeting opened as soon as everyone was seated, without any exchange of courtesies. Wainwright made the first move by reaching into his pocket for his formal signed surrender note which he tendered to the Japanese commander.[24] Although General Homma could read and speak English, he did not look at the paper but turned it over to his interpreter to be read aloud in Japanese for the benefit of the other Japanese officers present. After it was read, Homma stated through the interpreter that the surrender would not be accepted unless it included all American and Philippine troops in the Islands. To this Wainwright replied that he commanded only the harbor defense troops. "Tell him," he said to the interpreter, "that the troops in the Visayan Islands and on Mindanao are no longer under my command. They are commanded by General Sharp, who in turn is under General MacArthur's high command."[25]

Homma refused to believe Wainwright's explanation. Repeatedly, he pointed out, the American radio had named Wainwright as commander of all troops in the Philippines. He had even seen, he said, the general order announcing Wainwright's assumption of command. Wainwright stubbornly insisted that the Visayan-Mindanao Force was no longer under his control. Shrewdly, Homma asked when he had released Sharp from his command. "Several days ago," Wainwright answered, adding that even if he did command the troops in the south he had no way of communicating with them. Homma brushed this argument aside easily. "Send a

staff officer to Sharp," he replied. "I will furnish a plane."[26]

The argument over command continued several minutes more but Wainwright would not budge from his position, asserting repeatedly that he did not have the authority to surrender the Visayan-Mindanao Force. Finally Homma rose, looked down at Wainwright, and said, "At the time of General King's surrender in Bataan I did not see him. Neither have I any reason to see you if you are only the commander of a unit . . . I wish only to negotiate with my equal. . . ."[27] He seemed ready to leave.

Wainwright was in no position to bargain. Uppermost in his mind was the thought that the troops on Corregidor were disarmed and helpless. If Homma refused now to accept his surrender, these men faced certain death. After a hurried conference with Beebe and Pugh, he agreed to surrender the entire Philippine garrison.[28] General Homma now refused to accept the surrender. "You have denied your authority . . .," he told Wainwright, "I advise you to return to Corregidor and think the matter over. If you see fit to surrender, then surrender to the commanding officer of the division on Corregidor. He in turn will bring you to me in Manila."[29] With these words Homma left the meeting.

---

[24] General Homma denied at his trial, and he was supported by his chief of staff, that the document was handed to him or read. USA vs. Homma, p. 3181. Wainwright's version is in *General Wainwright's Story*, pages 130–32, and in USA vs. Homma, Prosecution Exhibit 419, Deposition of General Wainwright.

[25] Wainwright, *General Wainwright's Story*, p. 131.

[26] *Ibid.*

[27] Uno, *Corregidor: Isle of Delusion*, p. 25. Uno was present at the meeting. His account does not agree with Wainwright's at this point, but it is supported by Lt. Col. Yoshio Nakajima, an operations officer on the *14th Army* staff. USA vs. Homma, p. 2590, testimony of Nakayima.

[28] Uno, *Corregidor: Isle of Delusion*, p. 25. Neither Wainwright nor Homma agree on this point. The author has accepted Uno's version because he was a bilingual observer and was not under the same strain as the participants. His account is not unsympathetic to the American cause.

[29] *Ibid.*, pp. 25–26.

After General Homma's departure, Wainwright offered his unconditional surrender to Colonel Nakayama, who had remained behind to take the Americans back to Corregidor. He agreed also to send one of his officers to Mindanao in a Japanese plane to persuade Sharp to surrender. "But in the back of my mind," he explained later, "was the strong hope that some way would still be found to avert the surrender of all forces." [30]

Colonel Nakayama refused to accept Wainwright's proposal and told him he would have to wait until he reached Corregidor. Homma's instructions, he explained, authorized only the commander of the Japanese forces on Corregidor to accept the surrender.[31] He then took the Americans back to Cabcaben by car and thence by boat to Corregidor, where they arrived late in the evening of 6 May.

The trip across the channel had been a long and stormy one, but not long enough for Wainwright to find a way out of his dilemma. MacArthur, he knew, expected Sharp's force to continue the fight as guerrillas and to keep alive resistance on Mindanao. He had done his best to achieve this aim, and Sharp was now free to conduct guerrilla operations. "But each time I thought of continued organized resistance on Mindanao," Wainwright recalled, "I thought, too, of the perilous position of close to 11,000 men and the wounded and nurses and civilians on Corregidor." [32] The lives of these men and women might well be the price of Sharp's freedom.

The dilemma in which Wainwright found himself might perhaps have been avoided had the organization which MacArthur established for the Philippines before his departure from Corregidor been retained. At that time, it will be remembered, he had established four forces: the Visayan Force, the Mindanao Force, the Luzon Force, and the Harbor Defenses. It was his intention then to exercise command over these forces from his headquarters in Australia through his deputy, General Beebe, on Corregidor. The War Department had changed this arrangement, and placed Wainwright in command of all forces in the Philippines.

At the time this decision was made, the reasons for overruling MacArthur and establishing the directing headquarters for operations in the Philippines on Corregidor had seemed compelling in Washington.[33] But if there had been no such headquarters, the Japanese would have had no alternative but to accept the surrender of each force when it was defeated on the field of battle. It is difficult to imagine on what basis they could have insisted that General MacArthur in Australia surrender all four forces in the Philippines. Nor was there any means, short of a direct threat of reprisals, by which they could force MacArthur to consider such a proposal. Even if they had followed the same procedure as on Bataan, where General King was told that he had not surrendered but had been captured, the effect would have been the same as the separate surrender of all four forces.

Wainwright could not consistently maintain his right to surrender only a portion of his force on the pretext that the remainder was no longer under his command. His presence on Corregidor and his well-recog-

---

[30] Wainwright, *General Wainwright's Story*, p. 133.

[31] Uno, *Corregidor: Isle of Delusion*, p. 26. Uno acted as interpreter on this occasion.

[32] Wainwright, *General Wainwright's Story*, p. 133.

[33] See above, Chapter XX, for a discussion of this decision.

nized position as commander of all forces in the Philippines made him especially vulnerable to pressure from the Japanese. Perhaps it was to avoid just such a situation that MacArthur established the organization he did, and in this desire may lie the true meaning of his cryptic explanations at the time to General Marshall that he had made these arrangements because of "the special problems involved," and the "intangibles of the situation in the Philippines." [84]

In the time between General Wainwright's departure from Corregidor and his return late that night, much had happened on the island. The Japanese had filtered around Malinta Hill, cutting it off from the rest of the island, and entered the tunnel by way of the east entrance. By about 1600 they had cleared out all Americans and Filipinos, except the hospital patients and staff officers, and were in complete possession of the tunnel. [85] Later that night, in accordance with their original plan, the Japanese had landed additional troops on the island.

The task of clearing the tunnel had not been an easy one. In the absence of Moore and Wainwright, General Drake, the USFIP quartermaster, had sent his assistant, Lt. Col. Theodore Kalakuka, who spoke Russian, to contact the commander of the approaching enemy force at about 1400. Ten minutes later Kalakuka had returned with a Japanese major and a Russian-speaking lieutenant. The major's response to Drake's request for an arrangement to avoid the useless slaughter of the already defeated Americans and Filipinos was a demand that the tunnel be cleared in ten minutes, an obvious impossibility. After some bickering, during which the principals' words had to be translated first into Russian and then English or Japanese, it was agreed that the men could remain in the tunnel but that a lane would be cleared down the center.

When the two Japanese officers left, Drake ordered the men against the walls and into the laterals, leaving as wide an open space as possible along the main tunnel. A short time later, the Japanese returned with about twenty men, equipped with flame throwers, demolition charges, and rifles. After a quick inspection, the two officers went through to the west entrance to stop the firing there. Other Japanese troops then entered and at bayonet point marched the docile Americans and Filipinos out of the tunnel. [86]

There was little Wainwright could do on his return to Corregidor late on the night of the 6th but surrender under the terms dictated by the Japanese. He could see the enemy's campfires all over the island and as he approached the tunnel he saw that it was already in enemy hands. There was no point in further delay and without waiting to complete the journey he asked Nakayama to take him to the local Japanese commander. His guides led him around Malinta Hill to the barrio of San Jose, and there, in the ruined market place, he met his opponent, Colonel Sato, commander of the *61st Infantry.*

---

[84] Rad, MacArthur to Marshall, No. 3, 21 Mar 42, WDCSA 320 (3-21-42) Phil.

[85] Brig. Gen. Charles C. Drake, "I Surrendered Corregidor," *Collier's,* January 8, 1949, p. 12; interv, author with Drake, 11 Mar 48. Drake's account is contradicted at some points by other senior officers. Ltr, Moore to author, 19 May 49, OCMH.

[86] Drake, "I Surrendered Corregidor," *Collier's,* January 8, 1949, p. 12; interv, author with Drake, 11 Mar 48. A longer manuscript version of General Drake's article, prepared at the request of the author, is in OCMH.

There was no discussion of terms. The surrender was unconditional and the document drawn up by the two men contained all the provisions Homma had insisted upon. Wainwright agreed to surrender all forces in the Philippines, including those in the Visayas and on Mindanao, within four days. All local commanders were to assemble their troops in designated areas and then report to the nearest Japanese commander. Nothing was to be destroyed and heavy arms and equipment were to be kept intact. "Japanese Army and Navy," read the closing paragraphs, "will not cease their operations until they recognize faithfulness in executing the above-mentioned orders. If and when such faithfulness is recognized, the commander in chief of Japanese forces in the Philippines will order 'cease fire' after taking all circumstances into consideration." [37]

It was midnight by the time the job was finished and the surrender document signed. Wainwright was then taken, under guard and through groups of captured Americans and Filipinos, to Malinta Tunnel, which by now was full of Japanese troops. After a brief conversation with General Moore, to whom he explained the reasons for his decision, he went to the small whitewashed room he had inherited from General MacArthur. With him was his aide and outside a Japanese sentry. Exhausted and humiliated, he threw himself down on his narrow cot. He had not slept and had hardly eaten since the terrible Japanese bombardment of the 5th. But sleep would not come easily. Though he had done all that he could, the forced surrender lay heavily on his mind. No man could be expected to endure more than he and his men had. This the President had

told him in the message received only a few hours before he had gone forward to surrender. Now, in the bitterest moment of his life, he could turn to the consolation of that message from his Commander in Chief:

In spite of all the handicaps of complete isolation, lack of food and ammunition you have given the world a shining example of patriotic fortitude and self-sacrifice.

The American people ask no finer example of tenacity, resourcefulness, and steadfast courage. The calm determination of your personal leadership in a desperate situation sets a standard of duty for our soldiers throughout the world. [38]

Promptly on the morning of 7 May Homma's intelligence officer, Lt. Col. Hikaru Haba, called on General Wainwright to discuss measures required to fulfill the terms of the surrender agreement. The most important step toward carrying out these terms was for Wainwright to reassume command of the Visayan-Mindanao Force and order General Sharp to surrender. Since he could not be sure that a direct order would accomplish this purpose, Wainwright decided to send Col. Jesse T. Traywick, his operations officer, to Mindanao with a letter explaining what had happened. In it he directed General Sharp to surrender the troops under his command and to pass on to General MacArthur the text of the letter and any other instructions given him by Colonel Traywick. "However, let me re-emphasize," he warned, "that there must be on your part no thought of disregarding these instructions. Failure to fully and honestly carry them out can have only the most disastrous results." [39]

The Japanese had still one more humiliation in store for General Wainwright. When

---

[37] The surrender document is printed in its entirety in Wainwright, *General Wainwright's Story*, p. 135–36.

[38] Quoted in full, *ibid.*, p. 118.
[39] This letter is published in its entirety, *ibid.*, p. 140.

GENERAL WAINWRIGHT BROADCASTING *surrender instructions over* Station KZRH, 7 May 1942.

the letter was completed, Colonel Haba announced that the general would go to Manila that afternoon to broadcast the surrender instructions. General Wainwright objected strenuously, but finally gave in when he realized that it would give Sharp an additional twenty-four hours to make his preparations and to inform General MacArthur of the situation.[40]   At 1700, when Haba called for him, he was ready. Accompanied by five of his staff officers he left for Manila, arriving, after many delays, shortly before

midnight. He was then taken directly to Radio Station KZRH where, in a voice husky with suppressed emotion, he broadcast the terms of the surrender to General Sharp, Col. John P. Horan, and Col. Guillermo Nakar, the last of whom commanded small detachments in northern Luzon.[41] The next morning, 8 May, Colonel Traywick, accompanied by Haba, left by plane

[40] *Ibid.,* p. 140.

[41] The text of this broadcast can be found in Visayan-Mindanao Force Report of Operations, pages 87–91. It was received in San Francisco by commercial radio and relayed to the War Department.

for Mindanao. Col. Nicoll F. Galbraith, Wainwright's supply officer, carried the same message for Horan, and Kalakuka went in search of Nakar.

Colonel Galbraith achieved a limited success in his mission. Horan had heard Wainwright's broadcast and had immediately sent one of his officers to confer with the Japanese commander in the area. This officer returned with the information that Colonel Galbraith was in Bontoc with surrender orders. On the 14th Horan surrendered personally and ordered his troops to assemble in preparation for surrender. But the men came in slowly, and Galbraith, with another American and a few Japanese officers, went into the mountains to try to round them up. Only a small portion of the troops surrendered. The rest remained in hiding, to become later the nucleus of one of the guerrilla forces in northern Luzon.[42]

Colonel Kalakuka's mission was even less successful in securing the surrender of Nakar's force, whose actual commander was Lt. Col. Everett L. Warner. General Wainwright had addressed his message to Nakar, the executive officer, rather than to Warner whose whereabout he did not know. The command arrangement in this group was extremely confused and apparently there was jealousy between the two men. Thus, when Kalakuka appeared on the scene he heard conflicting stories. Nakar refused to surrender, but Warner, with a small group of American officers, followed General Wainwright's orders. The bulk of the force remained in the mountains, and those who evaded the Japanese were organized into the 14th Infantry (PA) under Colonel Nakar,

which continued in existence as a guerrilla force.[43]

Meanwhile the Japanese had been having difficulty in other areas. On Palawan and in southern Luzon small detachments still persisted in offering resistance. The Japanese came to General Wainwright on 12 May and asked him why these forces had not surrendered, and why Colonels Horan and Nakar had not been heard from. He and his men, he was told, could not be considered prisoners of war until all opposition had ceased.[44] Nothing further could be done about the forces in northern Luzon, but to end the resistance in southern Luzon General Wainwright sent Colonel Pugh and two Filipino officers to Legaspi. They succeeded in halting hostilities there, and the Constabulary on Palawan surrendered without further difficulty.[45]

Surrender in the South

The story of the surrender of the Visayan-Mindanao Force is an even stranger one than that which preceded it. In the south few of the commanders were so hard pressed as to be incapable of further resistance and none had any desire to surrender. The Japanese had landed on only three islands. On two of these, Cebu and Panay, the local commanders had pulled back to well-stocked

---

[42] Ltr, Horan to Wainwright, 24 Jun 42, copy in OCMH.

[43] Hist of the Guerrilla Resistance Movement in P.I., Mil Intel Sec, GHQ SWPA, Ch. VI; Affidavit of Capt Warren A. Minton, copy in Chunn Notebooks. Colonel Nakar was captured on 29 September 1942. Colonel Kalakuka died of malaria on 30 October, while he was still working with the Japanese to secure the surrender of the guerrillas. Drake, Comments on Draft MS, Comment 28, OCMH.

[44] USAFFE-USFIP Rpt of Opns, pp. 91–92.

[45] Ibid.; General Wainwright's Story, p. 147.

and comparatively safe retreats in the mountains, from where they hoped to wage guerrilla warfare for an indefinite period. Any effort to drive them from these strongholds would involve the Japanese in a long and expensive campaign. On Mindanao, where the Japanese had committed larger forces and scored more important gains than elsewhere in the south, General Sharp's troops had been defeated, but elements of his force were still intact and capable of continuing organized resistance. Plans for their withdrawal to the more remote portions of the island, out of reach of the enemy, had already been made and the sector commanders were ready to put these plans into execution on orders from General Sharp.

On the morning of 6 May General Sharp received two messages. The first was the one in which Wainwright relinquished command of the Visayan-Mindanao Force and directed Sharp to report to MacArthur for orders. The second was from General MacArthur who, on learning of the surrender of Corregidor and without knowledge of Wainwright's instructions to Sharp, immediately ordered the commander of the Visayan-Mindanao Force to "communicate all matters direct to me." [46] With this dispatch MacArthur assumed command of the Visayan-Mindanao Force.

The first intimation Sharp had of Wainwright's intention to reassume command came from the latter's radio broadcast on midnight of the 7th. He immediately repeated the gist of the broadcast, which directed him in unmistakable terms to surrender, to MacArthur and asked for further instructions. The reply from Melbourne came promptly: "Orders emanating from General Wainwright have no validity. If possible separate your force into small elements and initiate guerrilla operations. You, of course, have full authority to make any decision that immediate emergency may demand." [47] At the same time, MacArthur informed the Chief of Staff of Wainwright's broadcast and of his own orders to Sharp. "I believe Wainwright has temporarily become unbalanced," he concluded, "and his condition renders him susceptible of enemy use." [48]

When General MacArthur made this judgment he was probably unaware of the circumstances which had dictated Wainwright's course of action during and after the surrender of Corregidor. He could not have realized that it was the fear of what would happen to the 11,000 men on Corregidor which had forced Wainwright to accept Homma's terms. Wainwright believed, as did many of the American officers on his staff, that the Japanese would kill their prisoners in cold blood if the commanders in the south did not surrender. [49]

There is no direct evidence that the Japanese actually made such a threat. In 1946, during the course of the Homma trial, Colonel Pugh stated that he had no personal knowledge that a threat had been made. But he added that General Wainwright certainly believed his men would be killed

---

[46] Rads, MacArthur to Sharp, No. 167, 6 May 42, and Sharp to MacArthur, 0415/Z/7, 7 May 42, both in AG 384.1, GHQ SWPA.

[47] Rad, MacArthur to Sharp, No. 676, 9 May 42, AG 384.1, GHQ SWPA.
[48] Rad, MacArthur to Marshall, No. 677, 9 May AG 384.1, GHQ SWPA.
[49] The Japanese were not a signatory to the Geneva Convention, but in February 1942, through the Swiss Government, they had agreed to adhere to the provisions relating to prisoners of war, reserving the right to make changes when necessary.

if Sharp did not surrender.[50] On the same occasion Wainwright testified that the Japanese told him they did not regard the Americans as prisoners of war but as hostages, "held to insure the success of the negotiations with forces in the south. . . ." "My principal concern," he said then, "was for fear that they would do what they said they would do; that is, slaughter all those people in the fortified islands unless the troops all over the Archipelago surrendered."[51]

Added to the threat, real or imagined, of what might happen to these men, practically all of whom were concentrated in a small area on the beach at Corregidor, was the threat reported to have been made to the men on Corregidor. For every day that the surrender was delayed, they were told, ten American officers would be executed. Wainwright admits he did not know of this threat at the time, and if made it was certainly never carried out.[52]

General Sharp's position on 8 May was not an enviable one. First Wainwright had released him and now sought to reassert his control. He had reported to MacArthur and from him had received complete authority to act on his own judgment. His legal right to ignore Wainwright's reassump-

tion of command and order to surrender was undeniable. But from the Manila broadcast he had received some intimation of the possible consequences of such a course. He decided, therefore, to await the promised arrival of Wainwright's emissary, Colonel Traywick, before making his decision. In the meantime, in accordance with MacArthur's instructions, he released from his control the island commanders in his force and directed them to prepare for guerrilla operations.

Colonel Traywick and Colonel Haba reached Mindanao by plane on the 9th and arranged a meeting with Sharp for the following day. At daybreak of the 10th hostilities were suspended temporarily, and during the afternoon Colonel Traywick, with Haba and several other Japanese officers, met General Sharp at his headquarters at Malaybalay on the Sayre Highway.[53] Traywick delivered Wainwright's letter and told Sharp the circumstances which had led to its preparation. He made clear that if the Visayan-Mindanao Force was not surrendered, the Japanese would probably reject the terms already agreed upon and would open fire on the prisoners on Corregidor. It was this threat that forced General Sharp to capitulate.[54]

General Sharp's decision to surrender placed him in exactly the same position

---

[50] USA vs. Homma, p. 2386, testimony of Pugh. General Drake states that he never heard such a threat made and never had the impression that the Japanese would kill their prisoners if Sharp did not surrender. "There was no cause to give me such an impression," he states. "Also, I never heard it voiced by anyone." Drake, Comments on Draft MS, Comment 28, OCMH.

[51] USA vs. Homma, Prosecution Exhibit 419, Deposition of Wainwright. Homma denied this in his testimony, and Wachi stated that the Americans were treated as captives rather than as prisoners of war until an order came from Imperial General Headquarters in August 1942. Ibid., pp. 2529, 3189.

[52] USAFFE-USFIP Rpt of Opns, p. 92; Wainwright, General Wainwright's Story, pp. 145–48.

[53] V-MF Rpt of Opns, pp. 61, 92; Tarkington, There Were Others, pp. 390–96.

[54] Interv, author with Col Robert D. Johnston, G-4 V-MF, 15 Apr 47, OCMH. Although Colonel Johnston was not present at the meeting between Sharp and Traywick, he was told about it many times by Sharp, while in prison camp. General Sharp, now deceased, never expressed officially the view that the threat was the reason for his decision to surrender. General Wainwright, in a letter to the author, stated that Sharp's position was hopeless and that he would have had to surrender very shortly in any case. Ltr, Wainwright to author, 14 Jan 49, OCMH.

Wainwright had been in on 7 May. He now had to reassume command of the officers he had released for guerrilla operations the day before. This he did on 10 May in a clear text message—he had destroyed his codes—rescinding his earlier instructions and directing his subordinate commanders to cease all operations at once, stack arms, and raise the white flag. One of his staff officers, he told them, would soon arrive with written orders and with detailed instructions. These orders, he concluded, were "imperative and must be carried out in order to save further bloodshed." [55] Later that night, at 1915, he announced his decision to General MacArthur. "I have seen Wainwright's staff officer," he explained, "and have withdrawn my order releasing commanders on other islands and directed complete surrender. Dire necessity alone has prompted this action." [56]

It was with great relief that General Wainwright heard from Colonel Traywick when that officer returned to Manila on 11 May that General Sharp had decided to place his forces again under Wainwright's command and to accept the order to surrender. This decision, he believed, averted a massacre and saved the Corregidor garrison.[57]

Wainwright's relief was premature. General Sharp's surrender orders proved far more difficult to enforce than had been anticipated. His troops were scattered among many islands; most of them were untrained Filipinos; and those who were safe in their mountain hide-outs showed no disposition

to give up their freedom. Communication between the islands was poor and it would be some time before the last troops laid down their arms. Until then the fate of the Corregidor garrison hung in the balance.

The detailed instructions to each commander were sent by courier on the 11th. In each case the commander was directed to assemble his men at a designated point and at a certain time. General Chynoweth, for example, was to bring his men to the northern outskirts of Cebu City; Christie to Iloilo City, and Colonel Cornell, commander of the Leyte-Samar Force, to Tacloban and Catbalogan. Land mines and other explosives that might cause injury or damage to the Japanese were to be removed within twenty-four hours, and those that could not be removed were to be plainly marked. All commanders were warned against the destruction of military or civilian property and urged to accord the Japanese "courteous and prompt obedience." [58]

The surrender on Mindanao was generally without incident, although here, as elsewhere, a large number of troops preferred to leave their units rather than become prisoners. Colonel Chastaine, unable to get his regiment to the appointed place in time, requested, and presumably secured, permission to arrive at a later date. Others may have had similar difficulties.[59] The most striking commentary on the enforced surrender came from General Fort, commander of the 81st Division (PA), who wrote to General Sharp: "Many of my officers encouraged me to disobey orders and continue—and strange to relate, Filipino and

[55] Rad, Sharp to Chynoweth, Hilsman, Cornell, Chastaine, Blancas, 10 May 42, Sharp Papers, OCMH.
[56] Rad, Sharp to MacArthur, No. 1, 10 May 42, Sharp Papers.
[57] Wainwright, *General Wainwright's Story,* p. 145.

[58] V-MF Rpt of Opns, pp. 99–103. Copy of the document of surrender is in Sharp Papers. Rad, Sharp to Chynoweth, Hilsman, Christie, Cornell, Blancas, 11 May 42, Sharp Papers.
[59] Rad, Chastaine to Sharp, No. 1, 13 May 42, Sharp Papers.

Moro officers—which I'll admit was a temptation as my own small force was undefeated and was growing stronger with the reorganization which I had undertaken. . . . I had difficulty in holding some of them true to discipline." [60]

The surrender of Chynoweth's troops on Cebu was not accomplished as easily as the surrender of those on Mindanao. Chynoweth had heard Wainwright's surrender broadcast on 6 May and received General Sharp's clear text message to surrender four days later. Reasoning that this order was either an enemy ruse or that it had been given at bayonet point, he decided to ignore it and instructed his communications officer not to acknowledge this or any further messages.[61] He next received a letter from the commander of the Japanese forces on Cebu urging immediate surrender to save lives. Chynoweth acknowledged receipt of the letter but made no move to surrender his force.

During the next two days the two commanders exchanged polite notes without reaching agreement. The correspondence came to an end when General Chynoweth asserted that he did not consider the order to surrender, "legally binding" since it had been given under duress. "We do not feel," he wrote, "that we can honorably surrender." [62] Copies of the correspondence were sent to the various units on Cebu, and the men were told that they could surrender individually if they wished to do so. Only two Filipinos and two Americans took advantage of this opportunity. General Chyno-

weth then made plans to move to Panay to join forces with Colonel Christie.[63]

On 13 May, while he was making preparations to leave the island, Chynoweth received a written message from Colonel Hilsman, commander on Negros. The message stated that a courier from General Sharp was on his way to Cebu to explain the situation to him and to negotiate the surrender. "That," wrote Chynoweth, "knocked us into a tail-spin." [64] Knowing that Sharp was in communication with General MacArthur, he believed that the order to surrender had been made with MacArthur's consent. But in the hope that MacArthur might intervene at the last moment and order him to continue the fight he instructed one of his men to "freeze on the radio."

Chynoweth could no longer put off the difficult decision. He did not wish nor did his situation require him to surrender. But both Generals Wainwright and Sharp had directed him to do so. "If MacArthur," he hoped desperately, "would only tell us now to hang on." [65] The only word received was that MacArthur had announced that he no longer had communications with the Philippines. That night Chynoweth sent word to the Japanese that he was awaiting a staff officer from General Sharp's headquarters and that no action would be taken until his arrival. He next notified the units under his command to assemble at a central point, prepared to surrender.

On 15 May General Sharp's courier arrived in Cebu. He gave Chynoweth the written terms of surrender, Sharp's order

---

[60] Ltr, Fort to Sharp, no date, V-MF Rpt of Opns, pp. 285–86. General Fort was later executed by the Japanese.

[61] The account of the surrender on Cebu is based upon Chynoweth, 61st Div (PA) and Visayan Force Rpt, pp. 33–37, OCMH.

[62] *Ibid.*, p. 34.

[63] Ltr, Chynoweth to author, 19 Feb 49, OCMH.

[64] Chynoweth, 61st Div (PA) and Visayan Force Rpt, p. 35, OCMH.

[65] *Ibid.*, p. 36. Up until February 1949 General Chynoweth believed that Sharp's instructions to surrender had MacArthur's support.

directing surrender, and a letter from Wainwright stating that "on no account were any commanders to make any attempts to evade the terms of surrender." The courier also told Chynoweth that the Japanese had concentrated the Americans on Corregidor under their guns and would kill them "if the surrender were not faithfully executed." [66] Chynoweth thereupon decided to surrender and immediately notified the Japanese commander of his decision. The next day he assembled the organized elements of his force and marched down out of the hills.

Of all the island commanders none was better prepared for guerrilla operations than the Panay commander, Colonel Christie. His forces were comparatively well trained and organized, his supplies ample, and his position secure. The Japanese had control of the road network on the island but showed little disposition to embark on operations in the interior. Already Christie had had some success in hit-and-run raids, and the one attempt at retaliation had ended in disaster for the Japanese. He had every reason to believe, therefore, that he could hold out indefinitely.[67]

Sharp's clear text message of 10 May directing him to surrender came as a shock to Colonel Christie. He acknowledged receipt of the order promptly, but expressed his opposition to it in very strong terms and questioned General Sharp's authority to issue such an order. He did not see "even one small reason" why he should surrender his force, because "some other unit has gone to hell or some Corregidor shell-shocked terms" had been made. "To satisfy me," he wrote, "I must have MacArthur's okay;

otherwise it may be treason." He closed his message with an appeal to General Sharp to give him a free hand in dealing with the enemy on Panay.[68]

General Sharp refused to accept Christie's answer and directed him to hoist the white flag and cease all operations at once. "Your failure to comply," he warned, "will produce disastrous results." Neither Wainwright's nor his surrender, he explained, had yet been accepted, and unless all the island commanders capitulated the Japanese would resume offensive operations. MacArthur, he told Christie, had been informed of his actions, and an officer, Colonel Thayer, was leaving by plane for Panay with written instructions and a personal message. He concluded his message with instructions for an immediate reply "indicating your compliance and actions." [69]

Colonel Christie persisted in refusing to accept Sharp's order, arguing, first, that it was unnecessary, second, that it would have an adverse effect on the civil population, and third, that he doubted the authority of either General Wainwright or General Sharp to order his surrender. He felt that to comply with Sharp's directions would "tend toward treason," and questioned whether the surrender of one island meant the automatic surrender of others. "I strongly urge you," he told General Sharp, "to have the approval of the War Department through MacArthur," adding that he intended to consult his immediate commander, General Chynoweth. He closed his message with a plea. "In this delicate situation please do not issue me any peremptory orders that will embarrass or get us into mutual conflict.

---

[66] *Ibid.,* p. 37.
[67] Interv, author with Col Christie, 6 May 47, OCMH.

[68] Rad, Christie to Sharp, No. 1, 10 May 42, Sharp Papers.
[69] Rad, Sharp to Christie, 11 May 42, Sharp Papers.

Rather do I want a free hand in carrying out my mission uninfluenced by any hysteria inherent in local action. No army surrenders portions still free, intact, and having a good chance of helping the general mission. Make me independent. Do not put me on the sacrifice block." [70]

General Sharp did not answer this message. His courier, Colonel Thayer, had already left for Panay to explain the situation to Colonel Christie. With him, Thayer carried a copy of Wainwright's letter to Sharp as well as one from Sharp himself. The last was moderate in tone and reflected a sympathetic understanding of the predicament in which Christie found himself. "Be it understood," Sharp wrote, "that I have the highest regard for your courageous and resolute stand. . . . However, developments of the war make such action utterly impractical *regardless* of the capabilities of your forces. If any other course were open to me I would most assuredly have taken it." Again he explained that neither Wainwright nor he were prisoners of war, but both had pledged the surrender of their forces. Christie was expected to do the same. That was the only course of action to take "in the name of humanity." [71]

Before Thayer's arrival with the letter, Christie sent Sharp another message asking what General MacArthur had said in response to Sharp's surrender message. As a matter of fact, MacArthur had not replied to this message at all. By this time Sharp had lost all patience with Christie. His reply was a curt order to surrender as directed. "No further comments from you are desired,"

he told Christie. "Acknowledge this message and state actions taken at once." [72]

Colonel Thayer finally reached Panay on 18 May. He explained to Christie that acceptance of Wainwright's surrender of Corregidor was conditional on the surrender of all forces in the Philippines, and that Christie's refusal to comply with orders was jeopardizing the success of the negotiations and the lives of the 11,000 men on Corregidor. The question Christie had to answer, therefore, was the same one the other island commanders had to answer: Was the holding of Panay, or any other island, important enough to justify the death of the Corregidor prisoners? He decided that it was not, and made arrangements to surrender. [73]

Before he assembled his men, Christie made one more effort to satisfy himself on the legality of his course. To each of his fellow commanders he sent a message explaining what he was doing and why, and asked each what action he had taken. Chynoweth had already surrendered, but Colonel Hilsman, who was having troubles of his own on Negros, wrote that "we must surrender or be classed as deserters by our own country and as outlaws by international law." [74] That night Colonel Christie informed General Sharp that he had talked with Thayer and had decided "to comply faithfully with your orders for the surrender of my division." [75] Two days later he

[70] Rad, Christie to Sharp, 12 May 42, Sharp Papers.

[71] Ltr, Sharp to Christie, 12 May 42, V-MF Rpt of Opns, pp. 108–09. Italics are General Sharp's.

[72] Rads, Christie to Sharp and Sharp to Christie, 18 May 42, Sharp Papers.

[73] Interv, author with Christie, 6 May 47, OCMH.

[74] Rad, Hilsman to Christie, 19 May 42. See also rad, Christie to CO, Negros, Samar, Leyte, Bohol, 19 May 42, Sharp Papers.

[75] Rad, Christie to Sharp, 19 May 42, Sharp Papers.

marched his troops to the Japanese lines. By that time approximately 90 percent of his men had vanished into the hills or gone back to their homes.[76]

On Leyte and Samar, where there were no Japanese, Colonel Cornell also refused to accept General Sharp's message of 10 May directing the surrender, on the ground that it had been sent in clear text. He continued with his plans to break up his force of about 2,500 men to carry on guerrilla operations. About 20 May General Sharp's courier arrived with written instructions for the surrender, and Colonel Cornell issued orders to his troops to comply. The Japanese arrived in Tacloban on 24 May and the surrender was effected two days later. Only 11 American officers, 40 Philippine officers, and 20 Philippine enlisted men surrendered; the rest disappeared into the hills.[77]

On Negros, where Colonel Hilsman commanded, trouble of a different sort developed. The Japanese had not landed on that island, and the troops were scattered. Under the leadership of Col. Carter R. McLennan, formerly commander on the island and now executive officer, Negros had been divided into five sectors and a battalion assigned to each. Food and ammunition had been distributed equally among the five sectors, and the battalion commanders had been released from regimental control to enable them to operate independently as guerrillas. When Hilsman received Sharp's radio instructing him to surrender, he informed the battalion commanders and civil authorities, but took no active steps, deciding to wait until he had received written instructions. On 18

May, Sharp's courier, Lt. Col. Charles I. Humber, Jr., arrived on Negros with these instructions. Immediately, the sector commanders were called into conference by Hilsman and told that if all troops in the Philippines did not surrender within a specified time, a certain number of the men captured on Corregidor would be executed each day that the surrender was delayed.[78]

Although Sharp's instructions required the commanding officer to go to Iloilo to arrange for the surrender, Colonel Hilsman accepted Colonel McLennan's offer to go in his stead. Accompanied by Humber, McLennan left on the morning of 20 May and reached Iloilo that night. He was received aboard a Japanese freighter, loaded with troops and ready to sail, by Col. Kumataro Ota, and the next day returned to Negros with the Japanese. The Japanese ran into scattered fire when they landed, but had no difficulty occupying the western coast.[79]

Meanwhile, Colonel Hilsman had made every effort to assemble his troops in a central area, but the sector commanders, with the support of civil authorities, refused to comply. The situation became more serious when civilians, as well as some of the troops, began to loot Japanese and Chinese commercial establishments. News of these events soon reached Mindanao, and General Sharp became alarmed. Pointedly, he reminded Hilsman that as local military commander he "must control all civilians and insure that no incidents of violence or bloodshed occur." [80]

---

[76] Interv, author with Christie, 6 May 47; rpt of interv with Maj Cledonia Ancheta, CO 2d Bn, 64th Inf (PA), OCMH.

[77] Cornell, Narrative of Events, Hq, Samar-Leyte Sector, V-MF Rpt of Opns, pp. 498–500.

[78] Rpt of Col McLennan, prepared at request of author, 19 Apr 49, in OCMH; interv, author with McLennan, 9 Feb 49, OCMH; Hilsman, Hist of Negros Sector, V-MF Rpt of Opns, pp. 487–88.

[79] McLennan Rpt, OCMH.

[80] Rad, Sharp to Hilsman, 16 May 42, Sharp Papers; interv, author with McLennan, 9 Feb 49, OCMH.

Despite his best efforts, Hilsman was unable to restore order or compel the Filipino troops to accept the surrender. Sharp's courier, Colonel Humber, finally had to ask that Brig. Gen. Manuel A. Roxas, Quezon's deputy in the Philippines, be sent to Negros to prevent an uprising "due to feeling and sentiment among civilian population . . . and the fear of Filipino troops and officers of being placed in concentration camps." [81] In his reply General Sharp did his best to allay the fear of the Filipinos. He pointed out that the Japanese on Mindanao had been "most lenient" in their treatment of civilians, and had asked civilian officials to remain at their posts. "Treatment of military forces," he added, "had been strictly in accordance with the Geneva Convention as indicated in our rules of land warfare." [82] To this Hilsman replied that he was doing everything in his power to follow the instructions he was receiving from General Sharp and from the Japanese. [83]

General Wainwright, too, was greatly concerned over the situation in Negros. There were approximately 200 Japanese internees on the island and the fear that they might be harmed by the rebellious troops was Wainwright's chief worry. "It was a fantastically ticklish situation," he recalled later, "with the lives of countless Americans and Filipinos hanging by the thread of the mutineers' unpredictability." [84] Momentarily he expected the Japanese to turn their guns on the Corregidor prisoners.

The date set for the surrender came and passed with no sign that the Filipinos would obey orders. Twice Hilsman persuaded Colonel Ota to grant an extension of time. When the second extension expired on 3 June, the Japanese agreed to accept Hilsman's surrender with the troops he had by then persuaded to come down out of the hills, about 95 percent of one battalion and 30 percent of two others. Two battalions never surrendered at all. [85]

During the next week the troops on outlying islands submitted to the Japanese, and by 9 June all forces in the Philippines, with the exception of certain small detachments in isolated areas, had surrendered. On that day General Wainwright was notified that all organized resistance had ended. "Your high command," the Japanese told him then, "ceases and you are now a prisoner of war." [86] The six-month-long struggle for control of the Philippine Archipelago was over. The victory which Homma had hoped to win by the middle of February was finally his on 9 June, four months later. Each day's delay had meant a loss of face for the Japanese, and General Homma paid the price. The campaign was hardly over when *Imperial General Headquarters* relieved him of command and brought him back to Tokyo, where he spent the rest of the war on the sidelines, as a reserve officer.

With the conquest of the Philippines, the Japanese gained the best harbor in the Orient, excellent bases from which to stage and supply their garrisons to the south and east, as well as a large population to contribute to the Greater East Asia Co-Prosperity

---

[81] Rad, Humber to Sharp, No. 2, 19 May 42, Sharp Papers.

[82] Rad, Sharp to Hilsman, 19 May 42, Sharp Papers.

[83] Rad, Hilsman to Sharp, 20 May 42, Sharp Papers.

[84] Wainwright, *General Wainwright's Story,* p. 148.

[85] Hilsman, Hist of Negros Sector, V-MF Rpt of Opns, pp. 487–88; rpt of interv with Lt Col E. R. Montilla, ACofS, G–3, Negros, OCMH; interv, author with McLennan, 9 Feb 49, OCMH.

[86] USAFFE-USFIP Rpt of Opns, p. 92.

AMERICAN GENERALS IN CAPTIVITY, *July 1942. Seated, left to right: Generals Moore, King, and Wainwright; two Japanese officers; Generals Parker and Jones. Standing, left to right: Japanese messenger; Generals Lough, Funk, Weaver, Brougher, Beebe, Bluemel, Drake, McBride, and Pierce; Colonel Hoffman (interpreter); and two Japanese soldiers.*

Sphere. They had driven the United States from its stronghold in the Far East, destroyed a combined American and Philippine Army of 140,000 men, and forced the Far East Air Force and the Asiatic Fleet back to the line of the Malay Barrier. In their possession, the Philippine Islands, extending 1,150 miles southward along the South China Sea from Formosa to Borneo and the Moluccas, constituted a formidable barrier to an Allied thrust from the east to cut the line of communication between Japan and the wealth of the Indies.

Though the Japanese had won an important victory, the American and Filipino troops had not given their lives and their freedom in vain. For six months they had kept alive resistance in the Philippines, ex-

acting heavy casualties from the enemy and immobilizing his forces. Not until *Imperial General Headquarters*, which had relegated the Philippines to a secondary place in the Japanese plan of conquest, had committed more men and planes than it had ever intended to the struggle was the campaign brought to an end. During the six months required to accomplish this task, the American and Filipino troops had retained their tenacious hold on Manila Bay and denied its use to the enemy. This was their mission, and it had been accomplished. But the Pacific Fleet, which was to have fought its way through to them by that time, never arrived. The fate of the Philippine garrison had been decided on the opening day of the war, at Pearl Harbor.

In the context of global war, the Philippines did not in 1942 possess great strategic significance. The Japanese tide had already swept around the Islands and over southeast Asia and the Indies, through the Bismarck Archipelago and the Solomons to Guadalcanal, and eastward across the Pacific as far as the Gilbert Islands. At the beginning of June the Japanese stood ready to move on Port Moresby, Midway, and the Aleutians, and to sever the line of communication between Australia and the United States. Everywhere, they had achieved phenomenal success, sweeping all resistance before them. Only in the Philippines had they been halted, and in this successful, though hopeless, resistance lay the real importance of the campaign. It demonstrated that the Japanese were not invincible, that they could be stopped by determined men, ably led, even when the odds were heavily in their favor. For an Allied world surfeited on gloom, defeat, and despair, the epic of Bataan and Corregidor was a symbol of hope and a beacon of success for the future. It was in this vein that President Roosevelt wrote to General Wainwright on the eve of his surrender:

"In every camp and on every naval vessel, soldiers, sailors, and Marines are inspired by the gallant struggle of their comrades in the Philippines. The workmen in our shipyards and munitions plants redouble their efforts because of your example. You and your devoted followers have become the living symbols of our war aims and the guarantee of victory." [87]

---

[87] Quoted in full in Wainwright, *General Wainwright's Story*, p. 118.

The Sources

Few military disasters of modern times are as sparsely documented or inadequately recorded in the official records as the defeat of America's forces in the Philippines in the first six months of World War II. Cut off from the United States almost immediately and encircled by a tightening blockade, the Philippine garrison soon became the only island of resistance in the rising tide of Japanese victory. Its sole remaining means of communication with the outside world was by radio. Occasionally an airplane or submarine reached Manila Bay with vitally needed supplies, carrying back on the outward voyage to Australia and Hawaii small and selected cargoes. Space was at a premium and there was room only for the nurses, correspondents, officials and their families, selected officers and enlisted men, and precious commodities such as the gold of the Philippine Commonwealth. Under the circumstances, records did not enjoy a high priority, and only a small number of official documents survived the campaign. Unofficial records and Japanese documents are far more numerous, and, with published works, constitute the main sources on which this volume is based.

Official Records

Among senior commanders in the Philippines there was a strong desire to justify their conduct of the campaign to their countrymen. This, they realized, could be done only if the record was preserved, and on at least three occasions during the course of the battle precious air and submarine space was set aside so that the most important records might be sent back to the United States. The first of these occasions was in February 1942 when General MacArthur sent out by submarine, in the custody of Francis B. Sayre, the High Commissioner, a footlocker filled with personal and official papers. This footlocker reached the United States safely and was stored in a bank in Washington for the duration of the war. It was then returned, by officer courier, to General Mac-Arthur and has remained in his possession since. Though its contents are not known, there is reason to believe that the footlocker contains material of value on the early part of the campaign.

The second shipment of records came in April 1942 when General Wainwright took advantage of the presence of two small aircraft on Corregidor to send to General Sharp on Mindanao fifteen packages of records, of undetermined bulk, to be delivered "in person to General Sutherland for forwarding to the Adjutant General, Washington, D. C."* Included in this shipment were General Wainwright's diaries and the general staff journals, with supporting documents. Only the five packages of G–3 records were inventoried and these consisted of ten journal files covering the period from 28 November to 10 April and twenty supporting documents including G–3 periodic reports, general and field orders, training memoranda, and the journals or reports of all the major commands in the Philippines.

---

*Ltr, Wainwright to Sharp, 12 Apr 42, Sub: Transmittal of USFIP Docs; rad, Wainwright to CG USAFFE, No. 261, 13 Apr 42, AG 370.05, GHQ SWPA; ltr, Irwin to TAG, 12 Apr 42, Sub: Transmittal of Docs.

The evidence that these records were received in Melbourne and placed in a vault in General Sutherland's office is indisputable. Their disposition thereafter is not known. The seven packages of G–4 records may have reached Washington, for there exist in the files of The Adjutant General, eight feet (one file cabinet) of records sent from Corregidor. These records, which deal largely with supply matters, have been used extensively in the preparation of this volume and were especially valuable in the study of shortages in food and medicine. When used, they were physically located in the Departmental Records Branch, AGO (Accession No. A51–75), and designated USAFFE-USFIP Records.* They have been cited throughout this volume by title and AG number, followed by the abbreviation Phil Rcds.

Assuming that the USAFFE-USFIP Records are a part of those sent from Corregidor in April 1942, the disposition of the remainder of the fifteen packages—the G–2 and G–3 journals, General Wainwright's diaries, and supporting papers (altogether eight packages)—remains a mystery. A careful search of the files of The Adjutant General in Washington and of GHQ, Far East Command (FEC) in Tokyo, successor to the 1942 headquarters in Australia, has failed to produce them, and the principals, Generals Wainwright and Sutherland, assert they have no knowledge of their whereabouts.

The third shipment of records from Corregidor was by submarine on 3 May, just before the fall of the harbor defenses. There is no description of these records other than the statement that they included "records and orders," but many, if not most of them, were probably finance and personnel records. Their final disposition is unknown, but it is entirely possible that the eight feet of USAFFE-USFIP records described above came from this shipment rather than the earlier one which went to General Sutherland in Australia. If that is so, then all fifteen packages of the second shipment have been lost.

Though there was little prospect that their records would survive, most of the units in the Philippines did their best nevertheless to maintain proper records in accordance with existing army practice. The quality of these records apparently varied considerably, depending on the unit's proximity to the enemy and on the interest and ability of commanders and clerks. Higher headquarters, which usually had the necessary personnel and equipment, kept the most complete records. Those of combat units, however, were sketchy. These units, composed largely of Filipinos, hastily mobilized and inadequately trained, had little opportunity to keep records. Some, even if they had wished to do so, could not have complied with regulations. They lacked clerical personnel and, in some instances, had first sergeants who could neither read nor write. To these difficulties was soon added another, the shortage of paper. The men had not been on Bataan long when paper became so scarce that orders had to be issued on the reverse side of prewar mimeographed regulations and administrative memoranda.

On Corregidor and the adjoining islands of the harbor defenses more careful records were kept. The units there were composed

---

*A detailed compilation of these records has been made by Dennis W. Ladd, entitled Inventory of Certain Records of United States Army Forces in the Far East and United States Army Forces in the Philippines, July 1941–May 1942, Finding Aid No. 31, DRB AGO.

of regulars—Americans and Philippine Scouts—trained and disciplined and accustomed to maintain records. Though subjected to air and artillery bombardment, they were in fixed positions and had ample opportunity to continue to keep accurate administrative and operational records. These, like the records on Bataan, were destroyed when the order was given to surrender.

With the capitulation of Corregidor and of the islands to the south, all communication with the Philippines came to an end. The entire garrison, an army of 140,000 men, passed into captivity and, except for the handful who escaped, no word of their fate reached the United States. Though most of the Filipinos were ultimately released from prison camp, there was no way by which they could communicate with the Allies except through the clandestine intelligence organization kept alive by funds and equipment from Australia. Nominally free, the former Filipino troops of MacArthur's and Wainwright's army were as effectively prisoners of the Japanese as if they had remained in prison camp.

It was only at the end of the war, with the return of the thin, emaciated American prisoners from Japanese camps in the Philippines, Japan, and Manchuria, that the War Department received an official report of the campaign. During their years in prison camp, higher commanders and their staff officers, on orders from General Wainwright and under the eyes of the Japanese, had begun the preparation of an operations report in anticipation of the day when they could present their own account of the disaster that had befallen American arms. These preliminary reports, written from memory, were ultimately collated into a single report by General Wainwright and a group of his former staff officers at Fort Sam Houston in 1946.

Entitled Report of Operations of USAFFE and USFIP in the Philippine Islands, 1941–1942, Wainwright's report covers the period of prewar preparations as well as the entire period of the campaign. It includes, therefore, the activities not only of his own command, USFIP, from 21 March to 6 May, but also those of MacArthur's earlier command, USAFFE, which was transferred with the general to Australia in March 1942. Since neither General MacArthur nor any members of his staff had assisted Wainwright in the preparation of his report, that report cannot be considered an authoritative statement of decisions made by USAFFE or of the operations conducted by that headquarters. But in the absence of a report from General MacArthur, it is the only account by a senior American commander, and the author has been obliged to rely upon it, despite its shortcomings on the level of command and decision. One copy is located in the Departmental Records Branch, AGO, and another is on file in the Office of the Chief of Military History. All references in this volume are to the latter.

The report is an ambitious and large work, with little form. Actually, it is a collection of separate reports, each organized and prepared differently, and attached to the basic report as an annex. There are eighteen such annexes, eight of which deal with the operations of major tactical commands, four with the activities of certain special staff sections, and six with miscellaneous matters, such as citations, lists of

units, and the organization of various headquarters.* Unfortunately, it contains the
report of only one of the divisions, the
Philippine Division, which fought on Luzon, and none of any unit smaller than a
division. Missing also are the reports of the
ordnance and artillery officers, and of
many of the service and administrative
headquarters.

---

*ANNEX I: USAFFE Staff
ANNEX II: Plan of Induction of Philippine
Army; Arrival of Units from the United States
ANNEX III: Headquarters Philippine Depart-
ment Staff
ANNEX IV: Report of Operations of North Luzon Force and I Philippine Corps in the Defense
of Luzon and Bataan, 8 December 1941–9 April
1942
ANNEX V: Report of Operations of South Lu-
zon Force, Bataan Defense Force and II Philip-
pine Corps in the Defense of South Luzon and Ba-
taan from 8 December 1941–9 April 1942
ANNEX VI: Report of Operations of Luzon
Force, 12 March 1942 to 9 April 1942
ANNEX VII: USFIP Staff
ANNEX VIII: Report of Philippine Coast Artillery Command and the Harbor Defenses of Manila and Subic Bays, 14 February 1941–6 May 1942
ANNEX IX: Report of Operations of Provisional
Coast Artillery Brigade in the Philippine Campaign
ANNEX X: Report of Operations of the Pro-
visional Tank Group, 1941–1942
ANNEX XI: Historical Report, Visayan-Min-
danao Force, Defense of the Philippines, 1 Septem-
ber 1941–10 May 1942
ANNEX XII: Report of Operations of the
Philippine Division
ANNEX XIII: Report of Operations Quarter-
master Corps, United States Army in the Philip-
pine Campaign, 1941–1942
ANNEX XIV: Medical Department Activities
in the Philippines, 1941–6 May 1942, and Includ-
ing Medical Activities in Japanese Prisoner of War
Camps
ANNEX XV: Report of Operations, Finance
Officer, USFIP, 8 December 1941–6 May 1942
ANNEX XVI: United States Forces Stationed
in the Philippines, 7 December 1941
ANNEX XVII: Report of Operations, Signal
Corps, United States Army, 8 December 1941–6
May 1942
ANNEX XVIII: Citations

Despite its deficiencies and its uneven nature Wainwright's report contains much of
value. Some of the annexes are ambitious
reports in their own right with numerous
appendixes of their own. Annex XI, Maj.
Gen. William F. Sharp's report on the
Visayan-Mindanao Force, for example, contains thirty-seven appendixes and fills more
than seven hundred pages. Comparable reports are those by Maj. Gen. George F.
Moore, commander of the Harbor Defenses
of Manila and Subic Bays, Brig. Gen.
Charles C. Drake, the quartermaster; and
Col. Wibb E. Cooper, medical officer on
MacArthur's and later Wainwright's staff.
Unfortunately, not all the annexes are as
adequate, the most deficient being those of
the tactical commands. The report of the
Luzon Force, for example, which covers the
critical period of the fighting on Bataan between 12 March and 9 April, is only eight
pages long, and the supporting reports of the
general staff fill only ten more pages.

Official records on the prewar period, and
on the place of the Philippines in the strategy of the war are far more plentiful than
those dealing with the campaign itself. Most
of these are in the custody of The Adjutant
General, filed at this writing in the Departmental Records Branch. The most useful
for this volume were those numbered: 320.2
(7–28–41), which deals with the organization and reinforcement of USAFFE; 381
(11–27–41) Far East, which consists of
seven separate bulky folders and contains
most of the messages sent to the Philippines;
and 400 (8–12–41), which contains material on the supplies sent to the Islands.

The organizational records of GHQ,
Southwest Pacific Area (SWPA), Mac-
Arthur's headquarters during the war, also
contain some material of value, especially
those files numbered 370.05, 384.1, and

384.3, Philippine Islands. When used they were physically located in the Kansas City Records Center, AGO. Wherever cited in the text, these files have been indicated by the symbol GHQ SWPA.

Most of the strategy and policy papers relating to the Philippines were filed originally in the War Plans Division (WPD), or its wartime successor, the Operations Division (OPD, now G–3) of the General Staff. These files when used were located in the Operations Division, but, with certain exceptions, have now been transferred to the Departmental Records Branch, AGO. Their integrity has been maintained, however, and they still bear the original WPD and OPD file numbers, which have been used throughout this volume. Included in this collection is the WPD Message File, the WPD Ready Reference File (Philippines), and the OPD 381 Philippine Islands File, all of which were particularly useful. The Chief of Staff files were handled in the same manner and are now also located in the Departmental Records Branch, AGO. Those files prepared before March 1942 are identified by the symbol OCS preceding the number; thereafter, by the symbol WDCSA. Most valuable for this volume are those designated OCS 18136, WDCSA 370.05 (3–17–42) Philippines, and WDCSA 381 (3–17–42) Philippines.

Though most of the WPD and OPD records of the 1941–1942 period have been turned over to The Adjutant General, G–3 still retains possession of certain files dealing with strategy and policy. Those used in the preparation of this volume are the former executive office files and the highly confidential strategy papers of the Registered Documents Collection of the Operations Division. The former contains about a half-dozen folders relating to the Philippine campaign, the most useful of which are the messages between General Marshall and Generals MacArthur and Wainwright. Materials from these files are identified in the notes by the abbreviations OPD Exec O and OPD Reg Docs.

Many relevant documents are included in the forty volumes produced as a result of the hearings of the Joint Committee (79th Congress) which investigated the attack on Pearl Harbor. Eleven of the volumes consist of hearings, eighteen of exhibits presented during the course of the hearings, and one of the majority and minority reports of the committee.

For air operations the author has relied largely on secondary accounts, but where necessary has extended his research into the files. In the case of the attack on Clark Field, the author has gone beyond the official Air Forces account, and has used all available files as well as interview material. Particularly valuable were the author's interviews with Lt. Gen. Richard K. Sutherland, the notes on which are filed in the Office of the Chief of Military History.

The Office of Naval Records also contains some material of value for this campaign. The reports of Admiral Thomas H. Hart and Rear Adm. Francis W. Rockwell, the former as commander of the Asiatic Fleet and the latter as 16th Naval District commander, were especially useful. Rockwell's report, which covers the period from 1 December 1941 to 19 March 1942, contains a number of supplementary reports as well as a portion of the War Diary of the 16th Naval District.

The operations of the 4th Marines are covered briefly in the postwar report of its commander, Col. Samuel L. Howard, filed in the Historical Division, USMC. Its regimental records, like those of Army units, were destroyed when Corregidor surrendered, and the story of the 4th Marines must be reconstructed from memoirs and interviews. Fortunately, this task had been accomplished in part for the author by Hanson W. Baldwin in a four-part article entitled "The Fourth Marines at Corregidor," published in the *Marine Corps Gazette* (November 1946–February 1947).

Unofficial Records

The inadequacy of the records dealing with operations, and the absence of journals, message files, map overlays, and after action reports from units lower than corps, would have made it impossible to write a detailed account of the Philippine campaign had it not been possible to supplement the official files with a wide variety of unofficial records. During the period in which this volume was in preparation, a total of approximately six feet of records of this type has been accumulated. These are filed in the Office of the Chief of Military History, and are so located when first cited in the footnotes.

Perhaps the least satisfying aspect of the USAFFE-USFIP Report of Operations was the absence of supporting reports by division and regimental commanders. Except for the report of the Philippine Division and the elements of the Visayan-Mindanao Force, Wainwright's report and accompanying annexes describe the campaign from the viewpoint of corps headquarters or higher. To have relied on it for combat operations, therefore, would have been most unsatisfactory and every effort was made to secure material on the operations of units smaller than corps. Fortunately, many American officers who commanded such units felt as strongly as their

superiors the compulsion to leave a record of their experiences. During their years in prison these men had discussed and compared their operations endlessly with their fellow prisoners and jotted down in cheap Japanese notebooks or on scraps of paper all they could remember and had learned. So scarce was writing material that the men covered every inch of space in the notebooks and wrote in characters so small as to be scarcely legible. These notebooks, hidden most ingeniously from the Japanese guards and brought back after the war, form the basis for the most important single collection of records dealing with combat operations of American and Filipino units in the Philippine campaign.

To secure this material the author embarked on an ambitious letter-writing program, made trips to various parts of the country, and induced many officers to support his requests by letters of their own. It was obviously impossible to reach every officer who had served as a unit commander or staff officer during the campaign, and no effort was made to do so. But letters were written to every division and regimental commander, the senior American instructors in Philippine Army units, and the most important staff officers. Only in exceptional cases were letters sent to battalion and company commanders.

The response to this campaign for material entirely justified the time and effort spent. Only in rare cases did officers refuse categorically to make their notebooks, diaries, and personal papers available. Some who had no records in their possession even volunteered to prepare reports for the author, offers which were gratefully accepted. As this material reached the author it was reproduced, usually by photostat and with the permission of the donor, a copy retained in the files of the Office of the Chief of Military History, and the original returned to the owner. Where the owner had carbon copies there was no necessity for reproduction. In rare instances, the originals were presented to the author as representative of the Office of the Chief of Military History. One such gift came from the widow of General Sharp who turned her husband's papers over to the author on that officer's death from a heart attack in 1947.*

The nature of this collection almost defies description. Included in it are letters written over a three-year period in prison camp but never sent, diaries, notes, poems, unit histories, reports, memoranda, accounts of single incidents or battles, memoirs, and preliminary narratives intended as the basis for a later, larger work which the writer hoped would be published. They vary widely in size and quality. Some are only one page long and others are ambitious works numbering several hundred pages. Some are written in the dullest prose imaginable; others have real literary merit. Some are accurate and detailed; others replete with loose generalizations. Common to all is the note of bitterness at what they believed to be their abandonment by their government and the desire to justify themselves to the future.

Among the records thus secured were accounts, written in prison camp, of the operations of most of the divisions and a large number of the regiments that fought on Luzon. Brig. Gen. Kearie L. Berry lent the author his account of the operations of 3d Infantry, 1st Regular Division (PA), which is actually a history of that division. From Col. Ray M. O'Day, senior instructor of the

21st Division (PA), came a history of that division in two thin typescript volumes. Brig. Gen. Clifford Bluemel's report on the operations of the 31st Division (PA), with its supporting documents, proved extremely useful, as did Col. Malcolm V. Fortier's notebook and notes on the 41st Division (PA). Maj. Gen. Albert M. Jones, who commanded in turn the 51st Division (PA), the South Luzon Force, and I Corps, has perhaps left a more complete record of his experience than any other commander, and his accounts, supported by those of his chief of staff, Col. Stuart C. MacDonald, form one of the basic sources for a history of the campaign. Completing the roster of division histories for operations on Luzon is Col. Clyde A. Selleck's Notes on the 71st Division (PA) which covers the activities of that division as long as it remained under his command. The operations of the divisions south of Luzon are described in the Visayan-Mindanao Force Report, which includes among its appendixes accounts by each of the division and sector commanders. Brig. Gen. Bradford G. Chynoweth prepared a separate account of the 61st Division (PA), at this author's request, and it has been used in preference to other reports.

It has not been possible to obtain accounts from three of the division commanders. Missing from the records, therefore, are the histories of the 2d Division (PC), composed of Constabulary troops, and two Philippine Army divisions, the 11th and 91st. Of these, the absence of a report from Brig. Gen. Luther Stevens on the 91st Division is the most serious, for it was that division which failed to hold at Cabanatuan, thereby permitting the Japanese to break through and imperil the withdrawal to Bataan. The lack of reports from the other two commanders is not as serious, and is compen-

*Mrs. Sharp later gave additional papers to The Adjutant General's Office. These are located in Departmental Records Branch, Accession No. A51-229, RG 499.

sated for, in the case of Brig. Gen. William E. Brougher's 11th Division, by regimental reports as well as excellent accounts of the division's most important engagement on Bataan, the Pocket Fights.

Supporting these unofficial division histories, as well as the official history of the Philippine Division, are unofficial accounts of the operations of many of the regiments and battalions. Perhaps the best are those of the 31st (US), 45th (PS), and 57th Infantry (PS), Philippine Division. In the case of the 45th—which figured largely in the Abucay fight, the Battle of the Points, the Pocket Fights, and the counterattack of 6 April—there is an account for each of the battalions. The operations of the 11th Infantry, 11th Division, are well covered in three separate reports, two of which were written by Col. Glen R. Townsend, the regimental commander. Operations of its sister regiments, however, are only sketchily covered in brief accounts. Reports from the regiments of other divisions are similar to those already noted, the weakest usually being just those where the division report itself is inadequate. There are accounts also of the operations of nondivisional units, such as the 26th Cavalry (PS), including a separate report by the commander of the 2d Squadron; the 192d and 194th Tank Battalions (US); and the 86th, 88th, and 301st Field Artillery. Unfortunately, the commander of the Provisional Air Corps Regiment, which for more than two months held a sector of the second line on Bataan, never prepared a report but the operations of other Air Corps units serving as infantry—the 17th, 21st, and 34th Pursuit Squadrons, which fought in the Battle of the Points—are briefly covered in separate accounts.

The most valuable single collection of small unit histories—including some of those already mentioned—are those which were gathered in prison camp by Capt. Calvin E. Chunn, 45th Infantry (PS). Resolved to write a history of the campaign if he survived the ordeal, Chunn began to collect material shortly after he reached Cabanatuan. He spoke with officers from almost every unit and secured from them information for an account of their operations. This information, together with other material, such as maps, diaries, statistics, orders, affidavits, he transcribed into his notebooks. Before he was transferred by the Japanese from Cabanatuan to a camp in Japan, he buried his voluminous notes in the prison compound at Cabanatuan where they were found after the war. Copies of the material in the notebooks were made and the originals returned to Captain Chunn, who by this time had reached the United States. One set of the copies was obtained by the author of this volume and is on file in the Office of the Chief of Military History. When used in this volume it is identified as Chunn Notebooks; the individual accounts are credited to the officer who supplied Captain Chunn with the information contained in the notebooks. Chunn, since separated from the service, is, at this writing, still at work on his history of the Philippine campaign.

The diaries, memoirs, and notebooks prepared in prison camp were often as useful in the preparation of this volume as the unofficial unit histories. Col. James V. Collier's four notebooks, which were written as a letter to his sons and cover the entire period of the campaign, were of particular value, since the writer was successively Assistant G–3 of USAFFE and G–3 of Luzon Force. The Bataan Diary (two volumes) of Col. Richard C. Mallonée, senior instructor of the 21st Field Artillery (PA), is a thoughtful and accurate account which deals with many more matters than one would expect from an officer who saw the war from a regimental headquarters. Though called a diary, it is actually a sustained narrative. Col. Paul D. Bunker's 190-page diary, closely written on sheets measuring 12 by 16 inches, is a true diary and consists of daily entries. Colonel Bunker was commander of the Seaward Defenses of Corregidor and his diary was especially valuable for those chapters dealing with operations there. Unfortunately, it contains no entries for the critical period between 29 April and 17 May 1942, when the Japanese landed and took the island.

The diary of Maj. William J. Priestley is unlike either Mallonée's or Bunker's. It is a compilation of the activities of various units, written by Priestley in prison camp on the basis of information supplied by other officers. Organized in a haphazard manner, it contains all sorts of miscellaneous information difficult to obtain elsewhere. Other diaries useful for a study of the campaign are those of Col. Alexander Quintard, commander of the 301st Field Artillery; Lt. Col. Arthur L. Shreve, artillery officer of the South Luzon Force; Maj. Achille C. Tisdelle, General King's aide; Maj. John McM. Gulick, commander of Battery C, 91st Coast Artillery (PS)—a work of genuine literary merit; and Capt. Roland G. Ames, commander of Battery Chicago, 60th Coast Artillery (AA).

After the reconquest of the Philippines and the release of the prisoners of war, a section was formed in MacArthur's headquarters for the processing of the survivors. This section, called the Recovered Personnel Section, G–1, soon began to receive finance, personnel, hospital, and prison records, as well as diaries and notebooks, prepared in

the same way as those mentioned above, all of which had been carefully wrapped and buried on Bataan, Corregidor, and the prison grounds to keep them out of Japanese hands. Before these records were sent to Washington or, in those cases where the papers were of no official value, returned to their owners or heirs, they were carefully screened for any information of value they might contain about the enemy. The entire collection was then microfilmed and deposited in the Records Administration Center, AGO. The author, however, has avoided references to the microfilm file and has used the originals, or photostat and typed copies, which, together with an 80-page index to the entire collection, is available in the Office of the Chief of Military History.

Despite the large amount of material thus collected, there was still little information on the operations of small units, of company and battalion size. In some cases the action of these units had been decisive and an accurate account was essential. This gap was filled largely with no effort on the author's part. On their return from prison camp, many of the survivors had been assigned as students at various schools of the Army—at The Infantry School, The Armored Force School, and at the Command and General Staff College. Required to write a term paper before completion of the course, most of these officers had naturally found a subject in the only campaign of World War II they had knowledge of. Since most of them had served as company and battalion commanders, it was natural also that they should write about the operations of small units.

To date about twenty such papers have been prepared. More than half of this number deal with elements of the Philippine Division, which was officered by Americans. The rest cover operations of elements of the 1st, 11th, 41st, and 91st Divisions, and miscellaneous units. Among this group is the only report of the Provisional Air Corps Regiment, prepared by Lt. Sheldon H. Mendelson while he was a student at The Infantry School, as well as an account entitled The First U.S. Tank Action in World War II, prepared by Lt. Col. Thomas Dooley, General Wainwright's aide, during his assignment to The Armored Force School. All of these papers were borrowed from those schools where they were prepared and returned there after they were used. Their location is indicated in the footnotes.

Though the unofficial unit histories, diaries, notebooks, and term papers made possible for the first time a reasonable reconstruction of the Philippine campaign, there were still many gaps which needed to be filled before a complete and authentic account could be written. Only the officers who had participated in the actions for which the accounts were incomplete or nonexistent, or who had been present when an important decision was made, could provide the missing information. This information the author secured in two ways, by letter and by interview. The letter-writing method was used when information of an operational nature was required, or when the distance was too great to permit personal conversation. Interviews were conducted with those officers who were readily available, or where the information needed could not easily be put in writing. The response to both methods was very gratifying and yielded an important body of records dealing with the campaign.

The correspondence file is of especial value, and the author has relied on it more heavily than on the interview. Those asked to supply information in writing usually produced more complete and accurate answers than those who gave their information orally. Often they drew sketches to illustrate their answers, and drew upon personal papers of whose existence the author had been unaware. Many officers asked to answer one or two questions wrote lengthy accounts of actions which had been imperfectly described in existing reports, thus creating an additional important source. Moreover, the signed letters constituted an important addition to the written record of the campaign.

Altogether the author has collected three thick folders of such material representing the replies of over one hundred officers, which are on file in the Office of the Chief of Military History. To these must be added the comments of those officers who read this volume, in whole or in part, while it was still in manuscript. These comments and additional information were carefully considered and are cited in the notes where applicable.

Unlike the correspondence carried on by the author, the interviews did not add greatly to the written record, although they were of great value during the preparation of the volume. To have made them a part of the record would have required the author to take copious notes during the interview, write up a report of the meeting, and then submit it to the officer interviewed for comment and signature. Without this last step, the notes would represent only the author's recollection and interpretation of the conversation. Such a procedure was not considered practical, although the author in many cases made his own notes of the interview to remind him of the more important points. It was felt that the presence of a secretary or the taking of notes would inhibit the conversation and destroy the chief value of the interview—the free expression of opinion. They were conducted therefore on a most informal basis, in home and office, in hotel lobby and restaurant, and, when the officers could be reached, by telephone or by walking along the lengthy passages of the Pentagon—almost daily during the preparation of the volume. The information thus secured was incorporated directly into the text and credited in the footnotes.

Japanese Records

The enemy records for the Philippine campaign fall into three major categories. The first and most important of these is composed of a group of histories or reports, part of a collection written by Japanese Army and Navy officers at the direction of G–2, Far East Command (FEC). These officers, working as civilians in the *1st* and *2d Demobilization Bureaus,* the former *Army* and *Navy Sections* of *Imperial General Headquarters,* prepared a large number of reports collectively titled Japanese Studies in World War II. The total number already completed and translated is well over one hundred and more are in preparation. Though the series contains large gaps and the individual studies vary widely in quality, it constitutes the most important single Japanese source on Japanese operations in the Pacific and in Asia during World War II.

Of this large collection, the author used three reports extensively. On the whole, these are more accurate and complete than those for later operations. The Japanese won this campaign and their records therefore were more complete. They did not have to rely, as they did for histories of later operations, on memory. Indeed, there is reason to believe that one of the six studies used was

797-257 O–66—40

written during the war by *14th Army* officers in the Philippines.

For this volume the most valuable Japanese source was the two-volume history entitled *14th Army* Operations. In a sense, all other Japanese documents are supplementary to it. It is detailed, reasonably accurate, and as complete as the after action reports of most units of comparable size. The first volume consists of the basic report, in narrative form, of *14th Army*'s operations on a day to day basis and includes the text or paraphrase of many important orders. In the second volume are the supporting documents: maps, intelligence reports, terrain studies, plans, as well as some brief but informative notes written by General Homma shortly before the opening of the final offensive on Bataan.

Neither the air nor naval accounts of Japanese operations in the Philippines are on the same scale as the *14th Army* history. The air force report, entitled *5th Air Group* Operations, contains a brief history of that headquarters as well as the history of its successor commands. It is extremely detailed in operational matters, providing in many instances the number and weight of bombs dropped on a single target, but somewhat vague in matters of decision and command. The naval history, Naval Operations in the Invasion of the Philippines, is the briefest and least satisfying of the reports on the Philippines, and contains hardly more than a brief account of naval surface and air activities in the opening days of the war.

Two other histories in the Japanese Studies in World War II, those of the *Army Section, Imperial General Headquarters* and of *Southern Army,* contain material of value on the Philippine campaign. Translated copies of these, as well as of the other histories, are on file in the Office of the

Chief of Military History, together with copies of the Japanese originals which were checked in every important case.

The second major category of Japanese source material for the campaign is the collection of the Allied Translator and Interpreter Section (ATIS) of General MacArthur's headquarters. During the war this section screened all enemy documents taken on the field of battle, translating and publishing those of immediate value. At the conclusion of hostilities, ATIS turned its attention to records of a historical nature and interrogated a large number of Japanese officers about their part in the war. These, like the wartime translations, were published in the ATIS series and distributed to interested agencies and commands. A complete set of these publications is on file in the Office of the Chief of Military History, as well as in the Military Intelligence Library, Department of the Army.

Those ATIS documents most useful in the preparation of this volume were the after action reports of the *65th Brigade* and *16th Division*. For the brigade there are two reports, one for the period 9–27 January 1942, when it fought in the Mt. Natib area, and another for the period 26 January–29 February 1942, covering operations in the vicinity of Mt. Samat (ATIS Enemy Publications 151 and 289). Together they provide a complete account of the brigade's operations during the first part of the siege of Bataan, as well as casualty figures, operations orders, maps, and similar material.

The report of the *16th Division* (ATIS Enemy Publication 355) covers the period 24 December 1941 to 3 January 1942 and was issued two days after the conclusion of the operations it describes—the Japanese landings at Lamon Bay and the advance through south Luzon to Manila. Unfortu-

nately, it lacks supporting documents and maps and is therefore of limited value.

Other ATIS documents of value are the postwar interrogations, statements of Japanese officers, and the answers to questionnaires sent to key officers by the author. Many of the interrogations were made specifically for historical purposes, either at the request of the G–2 Historical Section of MacArthur's headquarters in Tokyo or of the Office of the Chief of Military History. These, together with the statements secured from Japanese officers in response to specific queries, are available in the Office of the Chief of Military History and form an important supplement to the Japanese accounts already described.

Except for General Homma, who was executed in Manila in April 1946, almost every Japanese officer who had held an important post during the Philippine campaign has contributed to this volume. The Army headquarters was represented by Lt. Gen. Masami Maeda, Homma's first chief of staff; Col. Motoo Nakayama, senior operations officer; Lt. Col. Yoshio Nakajima, intelligence, then later, operations officer; Lt. Col. Monjiro Akiyama, air officer; and other lesser figures.

On the division level, information about the *48th Division* was secured from Col. Moriji Kawagoe, division chief of staff, and Maj. Makoto Nakahara, operations officer. Lt. Gen. Susumu Morioka was questioned about the activities of his *16th Division*, while Lt. Gen. Kenzo Kitano supplied information about his own division, the *4th*. Both interrogations were supplemented by statements from staff officers of the two divisions. Among these the most useful, perhaps, were those of Col. Motohiko Yoshida, *4th Division* chief of staff, and Lt. Col. Hiromi Oishi, operations officer. Interrogation of *65th Brigade* officers was inadequate, but this deficiency was no handicap to the historian who had the two excellent after action reports of that brigade.

The third major Japanese source consists of the transcript and exhibits of the trial of General Homma by an American military tribunal held at Manila in January and February of 1946. The thirty volumes of testimony and more than four hundred exhibits constitute a storehouse of information on the campaign—on plans, operations, the condition of Japanese troops, the "death march," the occupation of Manila, and the American surrender. Its chief value, however, lies in the fact that Homma's testimony constitutes a statement by the enemy commander of his conduct of the campaign, together with an explanation of the factors which influenced his most important decisions. In this respect, the enemy sources are more rewarding than the American. The records of the trial when used were in the custody of The Judge Advocate General but have recently been transferred to the Departmental Records Branch, AGO. Citations of the testimony at the trial and to interviews and statements retain the rank of the officers at the time of the action described in the text. In almost all cases, however, these officers had been demobilized and had no military status.

In addition to these three categories of Japanese material, the author has used a number of other enemy sources in the preparation of this volume. These include the numerous postwar interrogations and reports of the United States Strategic Bombing Survey (USSBS), which conducted a detailed study of many facets of the Japanese war effort. The published work of the survey consists of a summary report, two volumes of naval interrogations, and a large

number of volumes on the Japanese war effort. There are also many unpublished interrogations in the USSBS files, copies of which are available in the Office of the Chief of Military History.

In The National Archives of the United States is a large collection of untranslated Japanese military and naval documents obtained at the end of the war and returned to this country. These consist mainly of war diaries, usually of small units, and in some cases of collections of orders. The systematic use of these records would have required the services of a staff of translators for several years, a project which was neither practical nor profitable. Little use was made of this collection, therefore, except to scan it for the most relevant and useful documents.

Maps

To the difficulties of securing material on the tactical level must be added the lack of the type of maps and overlays required by the military historian. At the start of the war there were only four militarily significant maps of the Philippines in existence. Two of these were U.S. Coast and Geodetic Survey maps: one for the entire archipelago at the scale of 1:600,000; and the other, a topographic map consisting of seventeen sheets and covering the major islands, scaled at 1:200,000. The other two maps had been prepared by the Army engineers. The first of these was a topographic map and was based on a military survey made between 1911 and 1914. It covered only a portion of Luzon and was scaled at 1:63,360. The other, also a topographic map, was based on a more recent survey made in 1934 and 1935. Scaled at 1:31,680, it covered an even more restricted area than the 1:63,360, being limited to certain sectors of Luzon considered most critical for defense. There were enough copies of the first three of these maps for ordinary needs, but the last was available only in blueprint and in limited quantities.

The disadvantages of so inadequate a map coverage were perhaps not as serious as might be supposed. Many of the troops were fighting on their home islands in country they knew well. The Americans and Scouts had been over the ground many times before and had maneuvered on Bataan as late as January 1941. Those Filipinos who came from islands other than Luzon found the terrain little different from their own. Maps in the quantities needed by American forces in the Pacific later in the war were therefore not required in this campaign.

Facilities for map reproduction in the Philippines were excellent. The plants of the U.S. Coast and Geodetic Survey and of the Commonwealth Bureau of Public Works were both available to the military and operated until the evacuation of Manila, though the first was bombed on 23 December. Part of the equipment was then moved, with much difficulty, to Corregidor where the printing of maps on a limited basis was continued several months longer.

Facilities for the making of maps were not nearly as satisfactory. There was no headquarters base map plant, such as existed later in the war, in the Philippines at that time, no aerial photography, and only a few small mapping detachments in the field. Men trained to make maps were scarce, and in those days the making of maps was a long and arduous task. Little had been done during the years of peace to remedy these deficiencies. Like other military activities, map making had been severely curtailed for reasons of economy. It was fortunate indeed that the few areas mapped were those where most of the action took place and where

most Americans had maneuvered time and again.

During the first part of the campaign, the withdrawal to Bataan, the two maps most in demand were the 1:200,000 U.S. Coast and Geodetic Survey, and a road map of the island. The engineers had little difficulty meeting this demand, but when the troops moved back into the Bataan peninsula, having lost most of the maps distributed earlier, there were few up-to-date, large-scale maps available for distribution. By utilizing every field expedient the engineers were able to reproduce enough copies of the 1:63,360 and 1:31,680 maps, both of which, fortunately, included the peninsula, for general distribution to the troops. But both maps were hopelessly out of date and had to be supplemented by schematic sketches and overlays which were not based on any actual survey. As new road and trail information became available the sketches were revised and corrected prints in limited editions circulated to the units most directly concerned.

Like the records, the maps in the hands of the troops were destroyed just before the surrender. Those that were not, were appropriated by the Japanese as souvenirs and have since been lost without a trace. A few reached Australia, probably among the possessions taken out by Brig. Gen. Hugh J. Casey, the engineer officer of USAFFE, when he left with General MacArthur. But so scarce are these maps that General Wainwright could find only one—the 1:63,360 trail map of Bataan corrected in prison camp by an engineer officer—to include in his report. The rest of the maps in the report are of a later period.

The author has sought in vain for copies of the maps used by the troops in the Philippines, and for accompanying overlays, to secure exact information on troop dispositions, the location of gun emplacements, fields of fire, wire entanglements, demolitions, and the like. If the maps have survived, their owners treasure them too highly to allow their use by others. The author has found copies of the 1:63,360 and 1:31,680 engineer maps, but these lacked the information needed. Moreover, the latest maps of Bataan found are dated February 1942 and do not show the trails built between that time and the end of the campaign. Two of the engineer sketches showing the location of gun emplacements, demolitions, and similar installations, have been found, but these lack exact terrain information and troop dispositions.

To secure the information required in a tactical account the author has utilized every source open to him. Officers interviewed were asked to place their units on a map and to make whatever corrections or additions they could. With the numerous letters requesting material went maps and an added request to supplement and correct the information shown. Sketches drawn by others and data from later maps were also used. All this information was collated, but the result was not entirely satisfactory. Terrain descriptions varied; trails were differently numbered or named; the same name or number was applied to different trails; rivers were named and located differently on various maps and by different officers; boundaries between units could not be exactly fixed; and even the front lines described in the various accounts could not be reconciled. No final resolution of these and other discrepancies is possible since the original map and overlays have been lost.

The Japanese had difficulties of their own with maps, and for the invasion probably used a road map of the Philippines and hydrographic charts of their own. This lack was filled soon after the occupation of Manila when they captured a detailed U.S. Coast and Geodetic Survey photostat map of Bataan. This they lithographed and printed, then distributed to their own troops. A copy of this map, with Japanese troop dispositions and place names marked on it, was introduced as evidence in the trial of General Homma. It proved invaluable for fixing enemy positions and following enemy movements; without it the account of Japanese operations would have been less exact in many places.

Published Works

The number of books and articles dealing with the Philippine campaign and its aftermath is especially large, but of limited use. The dramatic defense by the Philippine garrison captured the imagination of the American public immediately, and articles began to appear early in 1942 as officers, public officials, and correspondents made their way by submarine and aircraft through the Japanese blockade. Throughout the year articles on the Philippines continued to appear in service journals and elsewhere, but in steadily diminishing numbers as American forces embarked on new ventures in North Africa, in the Solomons, and in New Guinea. Thereafter until the end of war, a period when those who could have written authoritatively about the Philippine campaign were in prison camp, there were few published works on the Philippines. To this early period belong such works as Lt. Col. William E. Dyess, *The Dyess Story* (New York, 1944); John Hersey, *Men on Bataan* (New York, 1942); Lt. Col. Allison Ind, *Bataan, The Judgment Seat* (New York, 1944); and Carlos P. Romulo, *I Saw the Fall of the Philippines* (New York, 1942).

The release of the prisoners, first those in the Philippines and then, after the surrender of Japan, those in Formosa, Japan, and Manchuria, was the prelude to a second large outpouring of books and articles about the campaign and about life in a Japanese prison camp. Like the first group, few of these are of real value for the student of military operations. The most significant is *General Wainwright's Story*, written with the aid of Robert Considine and published in 1946. Though it left much to be desired as a definitive account, *General Wainwright's Story* very possibly forestalled the publication by other commanders and staff officers of their own version of the campaign. Reluctant to engage in public controversy or disagree with their chief, they remained silent. Only Col. Ernest B. Miller, a National Guard officer and formerly commander of a tank battalion, has chosen to express his opposition to General Wainwright's views publicly in a volume entitled *Bataan Uncensored* (Long Prairie, Minn., 1949).

Other postwar volumes and articles by survivors deal mostly with prison camp, or with the isolated actions and operations of specific units. In the latter category are Lt. Col. William E. Chandler's three-part history of the 26th Cavalry (PS) in the *Armored Cavalry Journal* (March–August 1947); Lt. William F. Hogaboom's account of the action of the marines on Bataan in the *Marine Corps Gazette* (April 1946); Lt. Col. Harold K. Johnson's "Defense Along the Abucay Line" in the February 1949 issue of *Military Review;* Col. William C. Braly, "Corregidor—A Name, A Symbol, A Tradition," *Coast Artillery Journal*, LXXX, No. 4 (July–August 1947), pp. 2–9, 36–44, which is based on the official report of the commander of Har-

bor Defenses of Manila and Subic Bays; the story of the naval battalion in the Battle of the Points, written by William F. Prickett and published in the *Marine Corps Gazette* (July 1950); and Lt. Col. Bruce Palmer, Jr., "Covering the Withdrawal into Bataan," in the July 1950 issue of the *Infantry School Quarterly*.

At about the time these books and articles were published, the memoirs and histories of the war began to appear. Many of the former, written by men who had occupied high political and military posts during the war, touched briefly on the Philippines and cast additional light on obscure points. The most useful of these are: Manuel L. Quezon, *The Good Fight* (New York, 1946); Lt. Gen. Lewis H. Brereton, *The Brereton Diaries* (New York, 1946); Dwight D. Eisenhower, *Crusade in Europe* (New York, 1948); and Henry L. Stimson and McGeorge Bundy, *On Active Service in Peace and War* (New York, 1948).

Histories of the period first appeared in print in 1948, and, like the memoirs, were still coming out at the time this volume was completed. Most of these were and still are being prepared under the sponsorship of the armed forces, each of which maintains its own historical program. The Army's program, under which this volume was prepared, contains several volumes which deal with this period. Three of these, Mark Skinner Watson's *Chief of Staff: Prewar Plans and Preparations*, Ray S. Cline's *Washington Command Post: The Operations Division*, and Maurice Matloff's and Edwin M. Snell's *Strategic Planning for Coalition Warfare, 1941–1942*, have already been published in this series. Others which were used in manuscript and which are scheduled for early publication are Richard M. Leighton and Robert W. Coakley, The Logistics of Global Warfare, 1941–1943, and Rudolph A. Winnacker, The Secretaries.

In the Air Forces series, nominally part of UNITED STATES ARMY IN WORLD WAR II but prepared separately and published by the University of Chicago Press, the first volume, *Plans and Early Operations: January 1939 to August 1942* (Chicago, 1948), edited by Wesley F. Craven and James L. Cate, was especially useful. Though not a part of the official history, Walter D. Edmonds' *They Fought With What They Had* (Boston, 1951) belongs, in a sense, to this category since the author, a well-known novelist, secured much of his material during the war on a special mission for the Air Forces.   The 14-volume history of naval operations, written by Samuel Eliot Morison and published by Little, Brown & Company, includes eight volumes on the Pacific. The first of these (Volume III of the series), *The Rising Sun in the Pacific,* covers the first four months of the war and includes naval operations in the Philippine campaign.

In addition to these service histories, each of which presents a segment of the same war from a different point of view, there are other histories which provide valuable material and fresh points of view. These include J. F. C. Fuller, *The Second World War, 1939–45* (London, 1948); Robert E. Sherwood, *Roosevelt and Hopkins: An Intimate History* (New York, 1948); Hanson W. Baldwin, *The Great Mistakes of the War*

(New York, 1950); and Herbert Feis, *The Road to Pearl Harbor* (Princeton, 1950).

It is impossible to write about the Philippine campaign without dealing with the controversial figure of General MacArthur. Even before his relief from the Far East command in April 1951 he had already become the subject of numerous books and articles, few of which were objective in tone. His relief was the signal for a fresh flurry of books and articles dealing with his career, and some of these reviewed his conduct of the Philippine campaign. Like the earlier works, almost all of these were by stanch champions or violent critics. None contained any significant new material on the campaign. At the time this volume was completed at least two more books about MacArthur were scheduled for early publication and there was every indication that others would appear in the near future.

In this connection, one final note must be added. The manuscript and published sources here described represent the best material available at the time of writing. Undoubtedly additional material will appear. Some of the missing records may turn up in private collections or be found in some obscure corner of The Adjutant General's files. Still to be heard from are General MacArthur and his principal staff officers, most of whom are now retired; General King; and the men who commanded corps and some of the divisions on Bataan. Only then, when the full story of these men is known, will it be possible to fill in the gaps and round out the tactical detail of this volume.

Basic Military Map Symbols*

Symbols within a rectangle indicate a military unit, within a
triangle an observation post, and within a circle a supply point.

Military Units—Identification

Antiaircraft Artillery	◭
Armored Command	⬭
Army Air Forces	∞
Artillery, except Antiaircraft and Coast Artillery	•
Cavalry, Horse	⧄
Cavalry, Mechanized	⬰
Chemical Warfare Service	G
Coast Artillery	⬦
Engineers	E
Infantry	⊠
Medical Corps	⊞
Ordnance Department	⚬
Quartermaster Corps	Q
Signal Corps	S
Tank Destroyer	TD
Transportation Corps	⊕
Veterinary Corps	▽

Airborne units are designated by combining a gull wing symbol
with the arm or service symbol:

Airborne Artillery	•
Airborne Infantry	⊠

*For complete listing of symbols see FM 21–30, from which these are taken.

Size Symbols

The following symbols placed either in boundary lines or above the rectangle, triangle, or circle inclosing the identifying arm or service symbol indicate the size of military organization:

Squad . . . . •

Section . . . . ••

Platoon . . . . •••

Company, troop, battery, Air Force flight . . . . |

Battalion, cavalry squadron, or Air Force squadron . . . . . . | |

Regiment or group; combat team (with abbreviation CT following identifying numeral) . . . . | | |

Brigade, Combat Command of Armored Division, or Air Force Wing . X

Division or Command of an Air Force XX

Corps or Air Force XXX

Army XXXX

Group of Armies XXXXX

EXAMPLES

The letter or number to the left of the symbol indicates the unit designation; that to the right, the designation of the parent unit to which it belongs. Letters or numbers above or below boundary lines designate the units separated by the lines:

Company A, 137th Infantry . . . . A ⊠ 137

8th Field Artillery Battalion . . . . ⊡ 8

Combat Command A, 1st Armored Division . . . . A ▭ 1

Observation Post, 23d Infantry . . . . ⧍ 23

Command Post, 5th Infantry Division . . . . ⊠ 5

Boundary between 137th and 138th Infantry . . . . . . —137— | | | —138—

Weapons

Machine gun . . . . •→

Gun . . . . ●

Gun battery . . . . ⊔⊔⊔

Howitzer or Mortar . . . . ●

Tank . . . . ◇

Self-propelled gun . . . . ▭●

UNITED STATES ARMY IN WORLD WAR II

The multivolume series, UNITED STATES ARMY IN WORLD WAR II, consists of a number of subseries which are tentatively planned as follows: The War Department, The Army Air Forces, The Army Ground Forces, The Army Service Forces, The European Theater of Operations, The War in the Mediterranean, The War in the Pacific, The Middle East Theater, The China–Burma–India Theater, The Defense of the Western Hemisphere, Civil Affairs, Pictorial Record, The Technical Services, and Special Studies.

The following volumes have been published or are in press:*

The Army Ground Forces
> *The Organization of Ground Combat Troops*
> *The Procurement and Training of Ground Combat Troops*

The War in the Pacific
> *Okinawa: The Last Battle*
> *Guadalcanal: The First Offensive*
> *The Approach to the Philippines*
> *The Fall of the Philippines*

The European Theater of Operations
> *The Lorraine Campaign*
> *Cross-Channel Attack*
> *Logistical Support of the Armies (Volume I)*

The War Department
> *Chief of Staff: Prewar Plans and Preparations*
> *Washington Command Post: The Operations Division*
> *Strategic Planning for Coalition Warfare: 1941–1942*

The Technical Services
> *Transportation Corps: Responsibilities, Organization, and Operations*
> *The Quartermaster Corps: Organization, Supply, and Services, Volume I*

Pictorial Record
> *The War Against Germany and Italy: Mediterranean and Adjacent Areas*
> *The War Against Germany: Europe and Adjacent Areas*
> *The War Against Japan*

The Middle East Theater
> *The Persian Corridor and Aid to Russia*

The China–Burma–India Theater
> *Stilwell's Mission to China*

(Special Study)
> *Three Battles: Arnaville, Altuzzo, and Schmidt*

---

*Volumes on the Army Air Forces, published by the University of Chicago Press, are not included.

INDEX

ABDA Theater of Operations: 242, 356, 392, 399
Abe, Maj. Gen. Koichi: 183, 236
Abo-Abo River: 277, 287, 289, 289n
Abucay: 252, 263, 293, 316, 352, 418. *See also* Abucay–Mauban line.
Abucay Hacienda: 266, 266n, 274, 277, 286, 287, 288, 289, 290, 293
Abucay Line. *See* Abucay–Mauban line.
Abucay–Mauban line: 247–48, 266–78, 278–85, 285–290, 291, 294, 296, 304, 305, 312, 325, 326, 328, 329, 337, 345, 348, 351–52, 379.
Agno River: 107, 128, 133, 137–38, 144, 163, 169, 170–77, 178, 182, 186, 187, 195
Agno River line. *See* Agno River.
Agoo: 127, 128, 129, 132, 134, 136
Aguilar: 166, 169, 170
Agusan River: 596
Agusan Sector: 606, 607
Air force strength
    American: 23–24, 38n, 42–43, 49n, 95–96
    Japanese: 59
    Philippine Army: 26
Air Forces: 37–45. *See also* Far East Air Force; Philippine Army Air Force.
Air Forces units
    Commands
        V Bomber: 42
        V Interceptor: 42–43, 81, 85, 87, 94, 153, 156, 308
    Groups
        4th Composite: 23, 23n, 24, 50, 62
        5th Air Base: 50
        7th Bombardment: 38, 48, 97, 146n
        19th Bombardment (H): 38, 42, 50, 156, 239
        20th Air Base: 23, 24, 50
        24th Bombardment: 156
        27th Bombardment (L): 38–39, 42, 48, 50, 72, 115, 145, 156
    Squadrons
        2d Observation: 50
        3d Pursuit: 42, 84, 85, 87, 299, 302
        14th Bombardment: 38, 42
        17th Pursuit: 42, 84–87, 299
        19th Air Base: 23
        20th Pursuit: 42, 84–87, 117, 299
        21st Pursuit: 87, 107, 299, 305, 308, 310, 311
        27th Matériel: 23
        28th Bombardment: 42
        28th Matériel: 23
        30th Bombardment: 38, 42
        34th Pursuit: 43, 84, 87, 107, 299, 303, 308
        48th Matériel: 50
        93d Bombardment: 38, 42

Air Forces units—Continued
    Detachments
        Tow Target: 24, 50
        Weather: 24, 50
Air operations
    American: 62, 80–84, 89, 92, 105, 106–07, 113, 129, 142n, 151n, 403–04, 488
    Japanese: 57, 59–60, 78–90, 92–97, 103, 108, 136–37, 272, 288, 294, 312, 334, 418, 421–22, 424–25, 427, 427n, 433, 444, 446, 449–50, 464, 479–84, 493–97, 518, 526–27, 536, 539, 547–49
Air photo and reconnaissance
    American: 82–83, 83n, 92, 96, 106, 488
    Japanese: 59, 228, 262–63, 451n, 526
Air transport operations: 400
Aircraft carriers
    Allied: 46, 78
    Japanese: 60, 60n, 78, 112–13
Aircraft losses
    American: 88, 88n, 95–96, 488
    Japanese: 88n, 480, 488
Aircraft reinforcements
    American: 37–45, 146n
    Japanese: 414, 493
Aircraft tender: 91
Aircraft types
    fighters: 38, 39, 42, 43, 48, 85–88, 88n, 92, 95–96, 106, 142n, 146n, 318, 322, 488
    heavy bombers: 31, 38, 38n, 39, 42–43, 48, 64, 80–81, 81n, 82–86, 88–90, 92, 92n, 97, 97n, 105, 106, 111, 113, 155–56, 358, 360, 400, 403–04
    light bombers: 42, 115, 145–46, 146n, 147, 400
    naval: 46, 48, 91, 92, 94, 129, 156, 540
Airfields
    Batchelor Field: 97, 113, 129, 156, 400
    Clark Field: 23, 38, 43, 44, 48, 58, 59, 79–90, 92, 92n, 96, 97, 100, 105, 107, 117, 118, 208, 213, 255, 263, 414, 493, 494
    Del Carmen Field: 94
    Del Monte: 43, 70, 88, 92n, 96, 97, 111, 238, 239, 360, 400, 401, 403, 501, 508, 516
    Hickam Field: 38, 78
    Iba Field: 96
    Kindley Field: 481, 494, 547, 548, 553, 555
    Naguilian: 128, 132
    Nichols: 23, 43, 58, 84, 92, 94, 96, 107, 117, 234
    Wheeler Field: 78
Akin, Brig. Gen. Spencer B.: 359n
Akiyama, Lt. Col. Monjiro: 58n, 208
Alangan River: 408, 438, 447, 448, 449–50, 449n, 451, 454, 457
Alangan River line. *See* Alangan River
Alexander, Lt. Col. Irvin: 179, 257, 303–04

U.S. GOVERNMENT PRINTING OFFICE : 1966 O—797-257